Random House Webster's
LARGE PRINT CROSSWORD PUZZLE DICTIONARY

Random House Webster's
LARGE PRINT
CROSSWORD
PUZZLE
DICTIONARY

Stephen P. Elliott, Editor

Random House Reference

New York Toronto London Sydney Auckland

Foreword

I am delighted Random House adds to its roster of publications a crossword puzzle dictionary in large type for readers who need or prefer larger than regular size print. In undertaking this project, the editors have exerted every effort to conform to criteria set by the National Association for Visually Handicapped (NAVH).

As the pioneer in large print, NAVH encourages and oversees publication of government and corporate forms and informational materials, in addition to offering consultation to publishers of large print books. When requirements are met, NAVH grants its prestigious "Seal of Approval."

The extremely readable *Random House Webster's Crossword Puzzle Dictionary* conforms to NAVH's strict standards and will, I am certain, be warmly welcomed by all who use and enjoy large print.

Dr. Lorraine H. Marchi
Founder/ CEO,
NAVH

Preface

Although various word games and puzzles have existed almost since the beginnings of language, the modern crossword puzzle is a 20th-century innovation. The first newspaper crossword appeared on December 21, 1913, in the New York World, and this new type of word puzzle quickly captured the public's fancy. Within a decade, crossword puzzles were featured in most American newspapers, and they soon became the rage in England as well. Since the 1920s, crossword puzzles have been a standard feature of daily newspapers and have proved enormously popular when collected in book form.

Now found in almost every language and in variations ranging from theme puzzles to diagramless puzzles, crosswords are available for almost any age and vocabulary level. Those who solve crossword puzzles invariably relish the challenge of completing a puzzle, of "getting it right." When faced with a clue they cannot answer, they resist "cheating"—looking at the puzzle's solution. One way out of this difficulty is to consult a reference work—just as the puzzle's creator may have done in finding words or crafting clues. Yet neither a dictionary nor an encyclopedia nor an almanac contains the necessary information in a useful, quick-reference format. A standard dictionary might give a few synonyms for a word, an encyclopedia would give information about countries or historical figures, and an almanac usually has information about sports figures or the Academy Awards, but only a crossword puzzle dictionary combines in one handy volume the information that might be found in all three. Equally important, it does so without extraneous information and with the convenience of an arrangement by the number of letters in each word, and it includes the many words that are common in crossword puzzles but too obscure to be in other references.

Random House Webster's Large Print Crossword Puzzle Dictionary, drawing on the Random House Webster's line of dictionaries and thesauri, with research into a host of other topics, answers the need of crossword puzzlers for one single-purpose reference work. In addition to general vocabulary and synonyms, there are entries covering history; the natural and physical sciences, literature; music, painting, and other arts; religion; mythology; sports; popular culture; and current affairs, among others. Longer items provide easy-to-find detailed information on the continents and countries of the world, states of the United States, U.S. presidents, the months of the year, and other items of special interest. This large print edition has special emphasis placed on the pop cultural questions that are now such an important part of puzzledom—sports teams, TV characters, even authors and works of literature.

While *Random House Webster's Large Print Crossword Puzzle Dictionary*'s primary purpose is to meet the needs of the growing numbers of people who find crosswords both relaxing and challenging, even a cursory glance will demonstrate the book's usefulness as a reference for trivia buffs. From who won the first Academy Award for best actress (Gaynor) to the colleges of the Ivy League, it's all here.

How to Use This Book

The main entries in *Random House Webster's Large Print Crossword Puzzle Dictionary* are words or phrases likely to appear as crossword puzzle clues. Each entry consists of a clue word or phrase and a list of answer words, arranged first by the number of letters in each word and then alphabetically. For example, if the main entry—banal—is the clue for a five-letter answer, the answer "trite"—will be found alphabetically listed under the five-letter answer words. For phrases, such as contracted form, the answer could be "digest," "summary," or "synopsis." Entries may also contain indented subheads and secondary subheads. If, for instance, the clue is a phrase, like cotton fabric, the word cotton will be found as a main entry in the dictionary, and fabric will be found as a subhead under it, with such possible answer words as "terry," "poplin," and "gingham." In some cases, the answer can be found in more than one place. For example, if the clue is third U.S. president, the answer could be found by looking under the main entry Jefferson, or by looking under the main entry President of the United States.

There are also cross references for alternate spellings and very closely related items. Many terms that do not have explicit cross references may still have valuable additional answers at related entries. The reader is encouraged to look up synonyms even when there is no explicit cross reference. To take one example, the clue canine has a short entry in this book, but dog has a much longer list that could be examined as well. The main entries, subheads, secondary subheads, and numbers all appear in boldface type; the answer words are in regular roman type. Most punctuation and accent marks have been omitted, since they are not used in puzzle answers; occasionally, apostrophes and other marks have been included in answers to make them more readable.

 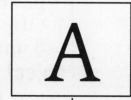 

aardvark
  also: 7 ant bear **8** anteater
  native to: 6 Africa
  food: 4 ants **8** termites
  name means: 8 earth hog, earth pig

Aaron
  brother: 5 Moses
  sister: 6 Miriam
  successor: 7 Eleazar
  deathplace: 3 Hor

Aaron, Henry (Hank)
  sport: 8 baseball
  position: 8 outfield
  record: 8 homeruns

abandon 4 dash, drop, elan, jilt, junk, quit, stop **5** ardor, cease, forgo, gusto, leave, let go, scrap, verve, waive **6** desert, give up, spirit **7** discard, forfeit, forsake, freedom **8** abdicate, evacuate, run out on

abase *see* **7 degrade**

abashed 3 shy **5** cowed, fazed **7** ashamed, bashful, daunted, humbled **8** confused

abate 3 ebb **4** cool, dull, ease, fade, slow, wane **5** allay, quell, quiet, slack **6** dampen, go down, lessen, recede, reduce, soften, weaken **7** assuage, curtail, dwindle, fall off, lighten, mollify, relieve, subside **8** decrease, diminish, fade away, mitigate, moderate, palliate, slack off, slow down, taper off

abbey 6 chapel, church, friary **7** convent **8** cloister, seminary

abbreviate *see* **8 truncate**

abdicate 4 cede, quit **5** forgo, waive, yield **6** abjure, give up, resign **7** abandon **8** renounce

abdomen 3 gut, pot **5** belly, tummy **6** paunch, venter **7** stomach **8** pot belly

abduct 5 seize, steal **6** kidnap **7** bear off **8** carry off, take away

Abednego
　companion: **6** Daniel
　friend: **8** Meschach,
　　Shadrach

Abel
　father: **4** Adam
　mother: **3** Eve
　brother: **4** Cain, Seth
　killer: **4** Cain

aberration **5** lapse, quirk **6**
lunacy, oddity **7** anomaly,
madness **8** delusion,
insanity, mutation

abet **3** aid **4** back, goad,
help, spur, urge **5** egg on
6 assist, incite, lead on,
second, uphold, urge on **7**
support, sustain **8**
advocate, join with

abeyance **5** delay, on ice,
pause **6** hiatus, recess **7**
latency **8** deferral,
dormancy, inaction

abhor **4** hate, shun **5** scorn
6 detest, eschew, loathe **7**
despise, disdain, dislike **8**
execrate, recoil at

abide **3** sit **4** bear, last, live,
stay, stop **5** brook, dwell,
stand, tarry, visit **6**
accept, endure, linger,
remain, reside, suffer **7**
sojourn, stomach **8** stand
for, submit to, tolerate

ability **4** bent **5** flair, knack,
power, skill **6** acumen,
talent **7** faculty, knowhow
8 aptitude

abject **3** low **4** base, mean,
vile **6** sordid **7** ignoble **8**
complete, cringing,
hopeless, horrible, terrible,
thorough, wretched

abjure **6** desert, give up,
recant, reject **7** abandon,
disavow **8** renounce

ablaze **5** afire, eager, fiery **6**
aflame, fervid, on fire,
red-hot **7** blazing,
burning, excited, fervent,
flaming, glowing, ignited,
zealous **8** feverish,
hopped-up

able **3** apt, fit **4** good **5**
adept **6** adroit, expert,
fitted **7** capable, equal to,
learned **8** adequate,
skillful, talented

able-bodied **5** beefy, hardy,
husky, lusty, thewy **6**
brawny, hearty, robust,
rugged, strong, sturdy **8**
athletic, muscular,
powerful, stalwart

ablution **4** bath, wash **7**
bathing, washing **8**
cleaning, lavation

abnegate **5** forgo, waive

6 abjure, eschew, give up, refuse **7** abstain **8** renounce

abnormal 3 odd **4** rare **5** queer, weird **7** bizarre, curious, deviant, strange, unusual **8** aberrant, atypical, deformed, freakish, uncommon

abode 3 pad **4** home, nest **5** house **7** address, habitat, lodging **8** domicile, dwelling

abolish 3 end **5** annul, erase, quash **6** cancel, repeal, revoke **7** nullify, rescind, squelch, vitiate, wipe out **8** abrogate, set aside

abominable 4 base, evil, foul, vile **5** awful, lousy **6** cursed, horrid, odious **7** heinous **8** accursed, horrible, terrible, wretched

aboriginal 5 first, prime **6** native **7** ancient, endemic, primary **8** earliest, original, primeval

abort 3 end **4** fail, halt, stop **7** call off **8** miscarry

abound 4 gush, teem **5** swarm **6** thrive **7** run wild **8** be filled, be rich in, flourish, overflow

about 2 in, of, on **4** in re, near **5** circa **6** abroad, almost, around, circum, nearly **7** close to

about-face 5 shift **6** switch **7** reverse **8** reversal

above 4 atop, over **5** aloft, north, supra **6** before, beyond, dorsal, excess, heaven, higher **7** earlier **8** in heaven, overhead, superior, upstairs

abracadabra 5 charm, magic, spell **6** voodoo **7** sorcery **8** exorcism

abrade 3 rub **4** file, fray **5** chafe, erode, grate, scour, scuff **6** scrape **7** scratch

Abraham
  former name: 5 Abram
  son: 5 Isaac **6** Midian **7** Ishmael
  nephew: 3 Lot
  sacrificed Isaac at: 6 Moriah

Abraham's bosom 6 heaven

abrasive 5 harsh, nasty, rough, sharp **6** biting, coarse **7** caustic, chafing, grating, rasping **8** annoying

abreast 6 in rank **7** aligned **8** arm in arm

abridge *see* **8 truncate**

abroad 3 out **4** rife **5** astir, forth **7** at large **8** overseas

abrogate *see* **6 repeal**

abrupt 4 curt, rude **5** blunt, brisk, crisp, gruff, hasty, quick, rapid, sharp, short, swift **6** sudden **7** brusque, uncivil **8** impolite

Absalom
  father: 5 David
  brother: 7 Solomon **8** Adonijah
  half-brother: 5 Amnon
  defeated at: 6 Gilead
  killed by: 4 Joab

abscond 3 fly **4** flee, skip **5** split **6** escape, run off, vanish **7** make off, run away, take off **8** steal off

absent 3 cut, out **4** away, AWOL, gone **5** blank, empty, vague **6** dreamy, musing, truant, vacant **7** faraway, missing, out of it, removed

absentee 6 no show, truant

absent-minded 5 blank, vague **6** dreamy

absolute 4 full, pure, real, sure **5** sheer, total, utter **7** certain, genuine, perfect, supreme **8** complete, decisive, definite, outright, positive, reliable, thorough

absolution 5 mercy **6** pardon **7** amnesty, release

absolve *see* **6 acquit**

absorb 3 fix, get **5** grasp, rivet, sop up **6** arrest, digest, engage, enwrap, ingest, occupy, soak up, suck up, take up **7** consume, drink in, engross, immerse

abstain 5 avoid, forgo **6** desist, eschew, refuse, resist **7** decline, refrain

abstemious 3 dry **5** sober **7** ascetic, austere, sparing, spartan **8** teetotal

abstinence 8 chastity, sobriety

abstract 4 take **5** brief **6** arcane, digest, precis, remote, remove, resume, subtle **7** abridge, extract, general, isolate, obscure, outline, summary, take out **8** abstruse, compress, condense, esoteric, profound, separate, synopsis, withdraw

abstruse 4 deep **6** arcane, remote, subtle **7** complex, obscure **8** abstract, esoteric, puzzling

absurd 4 wild **5** crazy, funny, kooky **6** screwy, stupid **7** asinine, comical, foolish, idiotic **8** farcical

Abu Dhabi
  capital of: 3 UAE

abundant 4 rich, rife **5** ample **6** enough, galore, lavish, plenty **7** copious, profuse, replete, teeming **8** brimming, prolific

abuse 4 harm, hurt **6** berate, carp at, defame, deride, injure, injury, malign, misuse, rail at, revile, tirade, vilify **7** assault, bawl out, beating, cruelty, cursing, harming, slander, torment, upbraid **8** belittle, denounce, ill-treat, mistreat, ridicule, scolding, sneering, torments

abut 4 join, meet **5** touch **6** adjoin, border

abutment 4 prop, stay **5** brace, union **7** contact, meeting, support **8** buttress, junction, shoulder, touching

abysmal 4 deep, vast **7** endless, immense

8 complete, enormous, profound, thorough, unending

abyss 4 gulf, void **5** depth, gorge, gully, nadir **7** fissure **8** crevasse

acacia 9 gum arabic
  also called: 5 thorn **6** mimosa, wattle

academic 4 moot **6** remote, school **7** bookish, erudite, general, learned, scholar **8** abstract, educated, pedantic, studious

Academy Awards
  also called: 5 Oscar
  first actor: 8 Jannings
  first actress: 6 Gaynor
  first director: 7 Borzage **9** Milestone
  notable actors: 4 Cage, Foxx, Hurt, Muni, Peck, Penn, Rush **5** Brody, Crowe, Finch, Fonda, Gable, Hanks, Irons, March, Niven, Scott, Tracy, Wayne **6** Bogart, Brando, Cagney, Carney, Cooper, Crosby, De Niro, Duvall, Ferrer, Heston, Holden, Lemmon, Marvin, Newman, Pacino, Schell, Spacey, Voight

7 Abraham, Benigni, Brynner, Coleman, Douglas, Hackman, Hoffman, Hopkins, Milland, Olivier, Poitier, Steiger **8** Borgnine, Crawford, Day-Lewis, Dreyfuss, Guinness, Harrison, Kingsley, Laughton

notable actresses: 4 Cher, Hunt, Neal, Page **5** Bates, Berry, Booth, Davis, Field, Fonda, Hayes, Kelly, Lange, Leigh, Loren, Smith, Swank, Tandy, Taylor, Wyman, Young **6** Foster, Garson, Hunter, Keaton, Kidman, Matlin, Rainer, Rogers, Spacek, Streep, Theron **7** Andrews, Bergman, Burstyn, Colbert, Dunaway, Hayward, Hepburn, Jackson, Magnani, Paltrow, Roberts, Shearer **8** Bancroft, Christie, Crawford, Fletcher, Fontaine, Holliday, MacLaine, Minnelli, Pickford, Sarandon, Signoret, Thompson, Woodward

notable directors: 3 Lee **4** Ford, Hill, Lean, Mann, Reed, Wise **5** Allen, Capra, Cukor, Demme, Fosse, Kazan, Stone, Wyler **6** Beatty, Benton, Brooks, Cimino, Curtiz, Forman, Gibson, Howard, Huston, Mendes, Wilder **7** Cameron, Coppola, Costner, Fleming, Jackson, McCarey, Nichols, Pollack, Redford, Robbins, Stevens **8** Eastwood, Friedkin, Levinson, Minnelli, Polanski, Zemeckis **9** Minghella, Spielberg, Zinnemann

notable pictures: 4 Gigi **5** Crash, Marty, Rocky **6** Ben-Hur, Gandhi, Hamlet, Oliver!, Patton **7** Amadeus, Chicago, Platoon, Rain Man, Rebecca, Titanic **8** Cimarron, The Sting, Tom Jones

accede *see* **6 assent**

accelerate 4 rush, spur **5** hurry, impel **6** hasten, step up **7** advance, augment, further, promote, quicken, speed up **8** expedite

accent 4 hint, tone **5** drawl, touch, twang **6** detail, stress **7** feature **8** emphasis, ornament, tonality, trimming

accept 3 buy **4** avow, bear **5** admit **6** assume **7** agree to, fall for, swallow **8** accede to, assent to

access 3 way **4** door, gate, path, road **5** entry **6** avenue, course, entree **7** gateway

accessible 5 handy, on tap, ready **6** at hand, nearby, on hand **8** possible

accessory 4 plus **6** accent, cohort, detail **7** adjunct, partner **8** addition

accident 4 fate, luck **5** crash, fluke, wreck **6** chance, mishap **7** smashup

acclaim *see* **6 praise**

acclimate 5 adapt, enure, inure **6** adjust, orient **8** accustom

accolade 5 award, honor, prize **6** praise, trophy **7** acclaim, tribute **8** applause, citation

accommodate 3 aid, fit **4** help, hold **5** adapt, board, house, lodge, put up **6** adjust, assist, billet, modify, oblige, supply **7** bed down, conform, contain, furnish, provide, quarter, shelter

accompany 5 guard, usher **6** attend, back up, convoy, escort, follow **7** conduct, support **8** chaperon

accomplice *see* **6 cohort**

accomplish *see* **7 achieve**

accomplishment 4 deed, feat, gest, gift **5** skill, geste **6** talent **7** success, triumph, victory

accord 4 cede, give, jibe **5** agree, allow, award, grant, match, tally **6** bestow, render, square, tender, unison **7** concede, entente, harmony, rapport **8** be in tune

accordingly 2 so **4** ergo, then, thus **5** hence **6** thence, whence **8** suitably

accost 3 nab **4** hail, halt, stop **6** call to, salute, waylay **7** solicit **8** approach, confront

account 3 IRA, use **4** deem, hold, note, rank,

rate, sake, tale **5** basis, books, cause, count, gauge, honor, judge, merit, score, story, think, value, weigh, worth **6** esteem, reckon, record, regard, report, repute, view as **7** clarify, explain, grounds, justify, version **8** appraise, estimate

accountable 6 guilty, liable **7** at fault, to blame **8** beholden, culpable

accountant 3 CPA **7** actuary, auditor

accounting 5 cause **6** answer, motive, reason **7** warrant

accoutrements 4 gear **7** apparel **8** supplies **9** equipment, trappings **11** accessories, furnishings **13** paraphernalia

Accra, Akkra capital of: 5 Ghana

accredited 8 ascribed, assigned, endorsed, licensed

accretion 4 rise **6** growth **7** accrual **8** addition, increase

accrue 4 grow **5** add up, amass **6** pile up **7** build up, collect **8** increase **10** accumulate

accurate 4 true **5** exact, right **7** careful, correct, perfect, precise **8** faithful, truthful, unerring

accursed 4 base, foul, vile **6** cussed, horrid, odious **7** hellish **8** damnable, horrible, infamous

accuse 4 cite **5** blame **6** charge, indict **7** arraign, upbraid **8** reproach

accustomed 3 set **5** fixed, prone, trite, usual **6** cliche, common, inured, normal, used to, wonted **7** general, given to, regular, routine **8** everyday, expected, familiar, habitual

ace 2 A-1 **3** top, one **4** A-one, star, tops **5** crack, pilot, super **6** expert, master, tip-top, victor, winner **7** one-spot **8** champion, top-notch, top-rated,

acerbity 7 acidity, sarcasm **8** acridity, acrimony, sourness, tartness

ache 4 hurt, pain, pang, want **5** crave, mourn, smart, throb, yearn **6** be sore, desire, grieve, hanker, hunger, lament, sorrow, suffer, twinge **7** agonize, long for **8** soreness

Acheron
river in: 5 Hades
ferryman: 6 Charon
carries: 4 dead

achieve 2 do **3** get, win **4** earn, gain **5** reach **6** attain, effect, finish, obtain **7** acquire, fulfill, procure, realize **8** arrive at, carry out, complete

Achilles
mentioned in: 5 Iliad
teacher: 6 Chiron
war: 6 Trojan
vulnerability: 4 heel
killed: 6 Hector
killed by: 5 Paris

acid 4 sour, tart **5** acrid, harsh, nasty, sharp **6** biting, bitter, ironic **7** acerbic, caustic, crabbed, cutting, pungent **8** scalding, scathing, stinging, vinegary

acknowledge 3 own **5** admit, allow, grant, yield **6** accede, accept, answer, assent, concur **7** concede, confess, own up to, reply to **8** call upon, thank for

acme *see* **6 summit**

acolyte 3 fan **6** helper, novice **7** admirer, devotee, groupie **8** adherent, altar boy, follower

acquaint 4 meet, tell **6** advise, inform, notify, reveal **7** apprise **8** disclose

acquiesce 5 admit, agree, allow, bow to, grant, yield **6** accede, assent, comply, concur, give in, submit **7** concede, conform, consent

acquire 3 get, win **4** earn, gain **6** attain, obtain, pick up, secure **7** achieve, capture, procure, realize

acquisition 4 gain **5** prize **8** property, purchase

acquisitive 6 greedy **7** selfish **8** covetous

acquit 3 act **5** clear **6** behave, excuse, exempt, let off, pardon **7** absolve, comport, conduct, deliver, release, relieve, set free **8** liberate, reprieve

acre
one-fourth: 4 rood
one-half: 3 erf **5** erven
two-thirds: 5 cover

ten: 6 decare **7** furlong
one hundred twenty: 4
hide

acrid *see* **4 acid**

acrimony 5 anger, scorn, spite **6** animus, malice, rancor, spleen **7** ill will **8** asperity, derision

acrophobia
fear of: 7 heights

acrostic 6 cipher, puzzle **7** acronym

act 2 do **3** bit, gig, law **4** bill, deed, do it, fake, feat, move, play, pose, show, skit, step, work **5** edict, enact, feign, front, order, put-on **6** action, affect, behave, decree, stance **7** execute, go about, mandate, measure, operate, perform, portray, routine **8** function, pretense, simulate

Actaeon
form: 6 hunter
changed into: 4 stag
transformed by: 5 Diana
killed by: 6 hounds

action 3 act **4** deed, feat, move, step, suit, work **5** force, power **6** battle, combat, effect, effort, motion **8** activity,

endeavor, exertion, progress

activate 4 stir **5** drive, impel, start **6** prompt, propel, turn on **7** actuate **8** energize, mobilize, motivate, vitalize

active 4 busy, spry **5** agile, alert, alive, peppy, quick **6** acting, at work, frisky, lively, nimble **7** engaged, on the go, working **8** animated, occupied, vigorous

activist 4 doer **6** zealot **7** apostle **8** advocate, exponent

act of war 4 raid **6** attack, strike **7** assault, offense **8** invasion

actor 3 ham **4** doer, star **6** player, walk on **7** starlet, trouper **8** thespian
type: 4 hero **5** cameo **7** feature, leading

actual *see* **8 tangible**

actuality 4 fact, life **5** being, truth **6** effect, living, verity **7** reality

actually 5 truly **6** indeed, in fact, really, verily
Latin: 7 ex facto

actuate 4 move, stir

5 drive, impel, rouse **6** arouse, incite, induce, prompt **7** animate, inspire, trigger **8** activate, motivate

acumen 6 wisdom **7** insight **8** keenness, sagacity

acute 4 keen **5** sharp **6** clever, peaked, severe **7** intense **8** critical, piercing

adage *see* **5 maxim**

adagio 4 slow

Adam
  wife: 3 Eve
  son: 4 Abel, Cain, Seth
  home: 4 Eden
  grandson: 4 Enas **5** Enoch

adamant 3 set **4** firm **5** fixed, rigid, tough **7** uptight **8** obdurate, resolute, stubborn

Adams, John
  presidential rank: 6 second
  party: 10 Federalist
  state represented: 2 MA
  defeated: 9 Jefferson
  vice president: 9 Jefferson
  notable events of lifetime/ term: 9 XYZ Affair
  wife: 7 Abigail (Smith)
  children: 10 John Quincy

Adams, John Quincy
  presidential rank: 5 sixth
  party: 4 Whig **10** Federalist
  state represented: 2 MA
  defeated: 4 Clay **7** Jackson **8** Crawford
  vice president: 7 Calhoun
  political career: 5 House **6** Senate
    secretary of: 5 state
    minister to: 6 Russia **7** Britain, Prussia **8** Portugal
  father: 4 John
  mother: 7 Abigail (Smith)

adapt 3 fit **4** suit **5** alter, frame, shape **6** adjust, change, modify, rework **7** conform, convert, fashion, make fit, remodel, reshape

add 4 join **5** affix, sum up, total **6** append, attach, join on, reckon, tack on **7** combine, compute, count up, enlarge, include **8** figure up, increase

addendum 7 codicil **8** addition

addict 3 fan, nut **4** buff, head, hook, user **5** freak, hound **6** junkie, votary **7** acolyte, devotee, druggie, habitue **8** adherent

addiction 5 craze, mania, quirk 6 fetish, hangup 8 fixation

Addis Ababa
capital of: 8 Ethiopia

addle 5 mix up 6 muddle 7 confuse, nonplus, stupefy 8 befuddle

address 4 talk 5 greet, orate 6 salute, speech, talk to 7 lecture, oration, speak to, write to 8 dwelling, locality, location

adept 3 apt 4 able, good 6 adroit, expert, gifted, master 7 skilled 8 skillful

adequate 3 fit 4 so-so 5 ample 6 enough 7 fitting 8 passable, suitable

adhere 3 fix 4 glue, hold, keep 5 cling, paste, stick 6 be true, cement, cleave, fasten, glue on, keep to 7 abide by, be loyal, stand by 8 maintain

adhesive 4 glue 5 epoxy, paste 6 cement, gummed, mortar, solder, sticky 8 adherent, clinging

adieu 4 by-by, ciao, ta-ta 5 adios, aloha 6 bye-bye, goodby, so long 7 a demain, cheerio, goodbye,

good day 8 a bientot, au revoir, farewell, godspeed, toodle-oo

adjacent 6 beside, next to 8 abutting, touching

adjoining 6 joined 7 joining 8 next-door, touching

adjourn 3 end 4 move 5 close 6 put off, recess 7 dismiss, suspend 8 break off, dissolve, postpone, withdraw

adjudicate 4 rule 5 judge 6 settle 7 adjudge

adjure *see* 7 **beseech**

adjust 3 fix, set 4 move 5 adapt, alter, order 6 change, modify 7 conform 8 accustom, regulate

adjutant 3 ADC 4 aide

ad-lib 6 make up

administer 3 run 4 boss, give 5 apply 6 direct, govern, manage, tender 7 oversee 8 dispense

administration 5 brass 8 officers

administrative head 3 CEO 7 manager 8 chairman, director

admire 5 prize, value 6 esteem, praise 7 respect

admirer 3 fan 5 swain 6 suitor, votary 7 acolyte, devotee, groupie 8 disciple, follower

admission 3 fee 5 entry 6 access, entree, tariff, ticket 8 entrance

admit 3 let 5 allow, grant, let in, own up 6 induct, permit 7 concede, confess, profess, welcome 8 let enter

admixture 4 mess, olio 5 blend 6 jumble, medley 7 amalgam, melange, mixture 8 mishmash

admonish *see* 5 **scold**

ado 4 fuss, stir, to-do 5 furor 6 bother, bustle, flurry, fracas, furore, hubbub, pother, racket, tumult, uproar 7 flutter, trouble, turmoil

adobe 3 mud 4 clay, silt, tile 5 brick, marly 6 earthy 7 clayish

adolescent 3 lad 4 lass, teen 5 minor, youth 6 callow, lassie 7 babyish, girlish, puerile 8 childish, juvenile, teenager, young man, youthful

Adonis
    favorite of: 9 Aphrodite
    killed by: 4 boar

adopt 3 use 4 take 6 accept, affect, assume, choose, employ, follow, take up 7 approve, embrace, espouse, utilize

adorable *see* 4 **cute**

adore 4 like, love 5 exalt, fancy, prize 6 admire, dote on, revere 7 cherish, glorify, idolize, worship 8 hold dear, venerate

adorn 5 array 6 bedeck 7 bejewel, deck out, furbish 8 decorate, ornament

adrift 4 lost 5 at sea 6 afloat 8 confused, drifting, unmoored, unstable

adroit *see* 6 **clever**

adulation 7 fawning 8 flattery

adult 3 big, man 5 elder, of age, woman 6 granny, mature, parent, senior, x-rated 7 grownup 8 seasoned

adulterate 3 cut 4 thin 5 water 6 dilute

adultery 3 sin

adulthood 8 maturity, ripeness

adumbrate 3 dim 6 darken, sketch 7 obscure, outline 8 intimate

advance 3 pre 4 gain, lend, loan, pass, step 5 add to, offer, prior 6 assign, binder, growth, move up, pay now, propel, send up 7 bring up, forward, further, improve, in front, lay down, press on 8 increase, overture, progress

advanced 7 extreme, far gone, radical

advantage 3 aid 4 boon, edge, help 5 asset, clout 6 profit 7 benefit, comfort, service, success, support

advent 5 onset, start 6 coming 7 arrival

adventure 5 geste, quest 7 emprise, venture 8 escapade

adventurer 4 hero 7 heroine, upstart 8 romantic, vagabond

Adventures of Sherlock Holmes
  author: 5 Doyle
  character: 6 Holmes, Hudson, Watson 8 Moriarty

adventurous 4 bold 5 brave, risky 6 daring 7 valiant 8 intrepid, perilous

adversary 3 foe 5 enemy, rival 8 opponent

adversity *see* 8 **hardship**

advertise 4 show, tout 5 vaunt 6 reveal 7 display 8 proclaim

advertisement 4 spot 5 blurb, flier, pitch, promo 6 notice, poster, want ad 7 leaflet, placard, trailer 8 circular, handbill

advice 4 news, view, word 6 report 7 account, counsel, message, opinion, tidings 8 guidance

advise 4 tell, urge, warn 6 enjoin, exhort, inform, notify, report 7 apprise, caution, counsel, suggest 8 admonish

advise against 5 deter 8 dissuade

adviser, advisor 4 aide 5 coach, guide, tutor 6 egeria, mentor, nestor 7 monitor, teacher 8 Dear Abby, director

advocate 4 back, urge 5 favor 6 advise, backer, lawyer, patron 7 advance, apostle, counsel, endorse, espouse, further, pleader, promote, propose, push for, support **8** argue for, attorney, believer, champion, defender, press for, promoter, upholder

Aegir
  origin: 5 Norse
  form: 5 giant
  god of: 3 sea

aegis 4 wing **5** favor, guard **7** backing, shelter, support **8** advocacy, auspices, guaranty

aelurophobia
  fear of: 4 cats

Aeneas
  hero of: 4 Troy
  mother: 5 Venus
  ancestor of: 6 Romans

Aeneid
  author: 6 Virgil

Aeolus
  other name: 5 Eolis
  ruler of: 5 winds
  founder of: 8 Aeolians

aerial 3 air **4** airy **5** by air, lofty **6** dreamy, flying, unreal **7** antenna, elusive, soaring, tenuous **8** airborne, ethereal

aeronautics 6 flight, flying **8** aviation

aerophobia
  fear of: 6 flying

Aeschylus
  author of: 8 Oresteia

Aesculapius
  origin: 5 Roman
  god of: 7 healing **8** medicine

Aesir
  also: 4 Asar
  origin: 5 Norse
  leader: 4 Odin **5** Othin
  home: 6 Asgard

aesthetic *see* **8 Esthetic**

Afars and the Issas *see* **8 Djibouti**

affable *see* **6 genial**

affair 5 amour, event, party **6** effort, matter **7** concern, episode, liaison, pursuit, romance, shindig **8** activity, business, function, incident, interest, intrigue, occasion

affect 4 fake, move **5** adopt, alter, fancy, feign, put on, touch **6** assume, change, modify **7** embrace, concern, imitate, impress **8** interest, relate to

affectation 4 airs, sham **5** put-on **6** facade **8** false air, pretense

affection 4 love **6** liking, malady, warmth **7** ailment, disease, illness **8** disorder, fondness

affiance 6 engage, pledge **7** betroth

affidavit 4 oath **8** document

affiliate 3 arm **4** ally, join, part **5** merge, unite **6** branch **7** chapter, connect, consort **8** division

affinity *see* **8 penchant**

affirm 4 aver, avow, hold **5** claim **6** allege, assert, ratify, uphold **7** confirm, contend, declare, endorse, profess, support, sustain **8** maintain, proclaim, validate

affix 3 fix, tag **4** glue, seal **5** add on, paste, put on, set to, stick **6** attach, fasten, tack on

afflict 5 beset **6** plague **7** oppress, torment **8** distress

affluent 4 rich **6** loaded **7** moneyed, wealthy, well-off **8** well-to-do

afford 4 bear, give, lend,

risk **5** grant, offer, yield **6** chance, impart, manage, supply **7** command, furnish, provide, support

affray 4 fray **5** brawl, melee **6** fracas **7** contest, scuffle **8** conflict

affright *see* **4 fear**

affront 4 slur **5** abuse, wrong **6** injury, insult, offend, slight **7** offense, outrage, provoke, put-down **8** ignominy, rudeness

afghan 5 shawl, throw **7** blanket **8** covering, coverlet

Afghanistan
capital/largest city: 5 Kabul
parliament: 10 Loya-Jirgah
radical group: 7 Taliban
leader: 4 amir, emir
mountain: 9 Hindu Kush
highest point: 9 Istoro Nal
river: 4 Oxus **5** Kabul **8** Amu Darya
sea: 5 Darya
physical feature:
   pass: 6 Khyber
religion: 5 Islam
feature:

game: 8 buz-kashi
hat: 7 karakul

aficionado 3 fan, nut **5** freak, pupil **7** devotee, pursuer, student **8** disciple

afloat 5 at sea **6** adrift, wafted **7** sailing, wafting **8** drifting, floating

afraid 5 sorry **6** scared **7** alarmed, anxious, chicken, fearful, panicky, unhappy **8** cowardly, timorous

Africa
country: 4 Chad, Mali, Togo **5** Benin, Congo, Egypt, Gabon, Ghana, Kenya, Libya, Niger, Sudan, Zaire **6** Angola, Gambia, Guinea, Malawi, Rwanda, Uganda, Zambia **7** Algeria, Burundi, Comoros, Eritrea, Lesotho, Liberia, Morocco, Namibia, Nigeria, Reunion, Senegal, Somalia, Tunisia **8** Botswana, Cameroon, Djibouti, Ethiopia, Tanzania, Zimbabwe **9** Cape Verde, The Gambia, Mauritius, Swaziland
desert: 5 Namib **6** Sahara

8 Kalahari
island: 5 Bioko, Pemba **6** Canary **7** Comoros, Madeira, Mayotte, Reunion **8** St Helena, Zanzibar **9** Ascension, Cape Verde, Mauritius
river: 4 Juba, Nile **5** Congo, Niger **6** Ubangi **7** Zambezi
lake: 4 Chad **6** Albert, Edward, Kariba, Malawi **8** Victoria
falls: 8 Victoria
mountain: 5 Atlas **9** Ruwenzori
homeland: 5 Venda **6** Ciskei **8** Transkei
game reserve: 6 Kruger **9** Serengeti

African Queen, The
director: 6 Huston
cast: 6 Bogart, Morley **7** Hepburn
setting: 5 Congo

after 4 next, post **5** later **6** behind

aftereffect 6 result

aftermath 6 payoff, result, sequel, upshot **7** outcome **8** follow-up, offshoot

after the fact 4 late **5** tardy **7** belated, delayed, too late

afterword 4 coda **8** addendum, epilogue

again 3 bis **4** also, anew, more **6** encore **7** besides **8** moreover, once more
Latin: 6 de novo

against 7 opposed **8** conflict, contrary, opposite

Agamemnon
  king of: 7 Mycenae
  leader of: 6 Greeks
  fought in: 9 Trojan War
  father: 6 Atreus
  brother: 8 Menelaus
  daughter: 7 Electra **9** Iphigenia
  son: 7 Orestes

agape 4 agog **6** amazed, gaping **8** wide open

agate
  species: 6 quartz
  type: 3 eye **4** moss, onyx, ring
  source: 4 Ider **6** Brazil **7** Uruguay

age 3 eon, era **4** date **5** epoch, phase, ripen **6** mature, mellow, period, season **7** develop, make old **8** life span, lifetime

ageless 7 classic, eternal **8** enduring, timeless

agenda 6 docket **7** program **8** schedule

agent 4 doer **5** cause, envoy, force, means, mover, power **6** deputy **7** vehicle **8** advocate, emissary, executor

agglomeration 4 heap, mass, pile **5** bunch, clump **7** cluster

aggrandize 5 bloat, exalt, widen **6** beef up, expand, extend, puff up **7** amplify, broaden, build up, distend, enhance, enlarge, inflate, magnify, stretch **8** escalate, increase

aggravate 3 vex **4** rile **5** anger, annoy **6** nettle, worsen **7** inflame **8** heighten, increase, irritate

aggregation 3 mob **4** army, band, bevy, crew, gang, host, mass, pack **5** crowd, horde, swarm **6** throng **7** cluster

aggressive 4 bold **5** harsh, pushy **7** dynamic, hostile, intense, vicious, warlike, warring, zealous **8** forceful, militant

aggrieved *see* **6 grieve**

aghast 6 amazed **7** shocked, stunned **8** appalled

agile *see* **6 nimble**

agitate 3 jar, mix **4** beat, goad, rock, stir **5** alarm, churn, shake, upset **6** excite, incite, foment, stir up, work up **7** disturb, provoke, shake up, trouble **8** disquiet

aglow 4 warm **5** fiery **6** ablaze, red-hot **7** blazing, glowing, radiant, shining

agnostic 5 pagan **7** atheist, doubter, heathen, heretic, infidel, skeptic

ago 4 gone, over, past **5** since **6** gone by **7** earlier **8** backward

agony *see* **7 anguish**

agoraphobia
    fear of: 6 spaces

agrarian 5 rural **7** farming **8** pastoral

agree 4 jibe **5** admit, allow, chime, grant, match, tally **6** accede, accept, accord, assent, concur, settle, square **7** concede, conform, consent, support **8** coincide, side with

agreement 4 deal, pact **6** accord **7** bargain, compact, concert, concord, harmony, promise **8** affinity, alliance, contract, covenant

agriculture 7 farming, tillage **8** agronomy

aground 5 stuck **6** ashore **7** beached **8** grounded, stranded

ague 5 chill, fever **7** malaria, shivers

Ahab
    wife: 7 Jezebel

ahead of time 5 early **6** before, in time, sooner **7** betimes, earlier

aid 4 abet, alms, dole, help **5** serve **6** assist, foster, relief **7** advance, charity, further, promote, subsidy, support, sustain **8** donation, minister

Aida
    opera by: 5 Verdi

aide 5 gofer **6** deputy, helper **7** abettor, acolyte **8** adherent, adjutant, follower, retainer, sidekick

aide-de-camp 3 ADC **4** aide **6** helper **8** adjutant

ail 4 pain **5** annoy, be ill, upset, worry **6** be sick, bother, sicken **7** afflict, make ill, trouble **8** be infirm, be unwell, distress

ailment 6 malady **7** disease, illness **8** disorder, sickness, weakness

ailurophobia
  fear of: 4 cats

aim 3 end, try **4** beam, goal, mean, plan, seek, want, wish **5** essay, focus, level, point, sight, slant **6** design, desire, direct, intend, intent, object, strive, target **7** attempt, purpose **8** ambition

Ainu
  native of: 5 Japan

air, airs 3 lay, sky **4** aura, look, mood, puff, song, tell, tone, tune, vent, waft, wind **5** blast, carol, ditty, draft, ozone, style, swank, utter, voice, whiff **6** aerate, breath, breeze, expose, manner, reveal **7** display, divulge, exhibit, hauteur **8** ambience, disclose, pretense, proclaim

airborne 5 aloft **6** aerial, Eolian **8** in flight

air current 4 puff, wind

5 blast, draft, whiff **6** breeze, zephyr

airfield 7 air base, airport, jet base **8** airstrip

airplane 3 jet **4** bird **5** crate, plane **7** airship, prop-jet **8** aircraft **9** aeroplane
  part: 3 fin **4** flap, nose, tail, wing **5** cabin, cargo, pylon **6** rudder **7** aileron, cockpit, turbine **8** elevator, fuel tank, fuselage, throttle, turbofan, turbojet

airport 5 field **7** air base, jet base **8** airdrome, airfield, airstrip **9** aerodrome **11** flying field **12** landing field, landing strip

airship 5 blimp **7** balloon

airy 5 light, merry, sunny, windy **6** breezy, cheery, drafty, dreamy, jaunty, lively **8** cheerful, ethereal

aisle 3 way **4** lane, path, walk **5** alley **6** avenue **7** passage, walkway **8** cloister, corridor

ajar 4 open **5** agape **6** gaping **8** unclosed

Ajax
  rescued body of:

8 Achilles
violated shrine of: 6
Athena
akin *see* **5 alike**
Alabama
abbreviation: 2 AL **3** Ala
capital: 10 Montgomery
largest city: 10
Birmingham
others: 5 Selma **6** Mobile
river: 3 Pea **5** Coosa **6**
Mobile **7** Alabama
alacrity 4 zeal **5** speed **6**
fervor **7** agility, avidity
alarm 4 fear **5** alert, panic,
scare **6** appall, dismay,
fright, terror, war cry **7**
agitate, disturb, terrify,
unnerve, warning **8**
affright, distress, frighten
alas
expresses: 4 pity **5** grief
6 sorrow **7** concern, woe
is me
Alaska
abbreviation: 2 AK **4**
Alas
capital: 6 Juneau
largest city: 9 Anchorage
tribe: 5 Aleut, Haida,
Inuit **6** Eskimo **7**
Ingalik, Tlingit
island: 5 Aleut **6** Kodiak,
Unimak **7** Diomede

8 Aleutian, Pribilof
mountain: 5 Coast **6**
Alaska, Brooks, Denali **8**
Aleutian, McKinley,
Wrangell
highest point: 6 Denali **8**
McKinley
physical feature:
bay: 7 Glacier, Prudhoe
peninsula: 5 Kenai **6**
Alaska, Seward
sea: 6 Arctic **8**
Beaufort
strait: 6 Bering
river: 5 Yukon **6** Copper
sled race: 8 Iditarod
Albania
capital/largest city: 6
Tirana, Tirane
lake: 5 Ohrid **6** Prespa **7**
Ochrida, Scutari,
Shkoder
highest point: 5 Korab
sea: 6 Ionian **8** Adriatic
physical feature:
peninsula: 6 Balkan
strait: 7 Otranto
king: 3 Zog
religion: 5 Islam
Alberta
abbreviation: 4 Alta
capital/largest city: 8
Edmonton
others: 7 Calgary

lake: 5 Banff
rivers: 3 Bow **4** Milk

album 2 CD, LP **4** book **6** record **8** register

alchemy 5 magic **7** sorcery **8** wizardry

alcohol 3 ale **4** beer, wine **5** drink **6** liquor **7** whiskey

alcoholic 3 sot **4** lush, soak **5** drunk, rummy, souse, toper **6** barfly, boozer **7** guzzler, imbiber, tippler **8** drunkard

alcove 3 bay **4** nook **5** niche **6** corner, recess **7** cubicle, opening

ale 4 beer, brew **5** stout

alehouse 3 pub **6** saloon, tavern **7** taproom

alert 4 warn, wary **5** alarm, aware, quick, siren **6** active, inform, lively, nimble, notify, signal **7** careful, heedful, on guard, warning **8** forewarn, vigilant, watchful

Aleutians
islands: 3 Fox, Rat **4** Attu, Near **5** Kiska
state: 6 Alaska
people: 6 Aleuts

Alexander the Great
battle: 5 Issus
birthplace: 5 Pella
conquered: 6 Darius, Persia
father: 6 Philip
wife: 6 Roxana

alga, algae 6 fungus **8** pond scum
contains: 4 agar **5** algin
type: 3 red **5** brown, green **9** blue-green
forms: 4 kelp **5** dulse **7** diatoms, seaweed **8** plankton, rockweed

Alger, Horatio
genre: 9 dime novel

Algeria
capital/largest city: 7 Algiers
others: 4 Oran
mountain: 5 Atlas
highest point: 5 Tahat
physical feature:
desert: 6 Sahara
wind: 7 sirocco
people: 4 Arab **6** Berber, Tuareg
religion: 5 Islam
feature:
French settler: 5 colon **8** pied noir
kingdom: 6 Numida
native quarter: 6 casbah, kasbah
food: 8 couscous

Algiers
   capital of: 7 Algeria
   center of city: 6 Casbah
Algonquian, Algonkian
   tribe: 3 Fox, Sac **4** Cree,
   Innu, Sauk **5** Miami **6**
   Abnaki, Atsina, Micmac,
   Ojibwa, Ottawa, Pequot
   7 Arapaho, Mahican,
   Mohegan, Mohican,
   Ojibway, Shawnee **8**
   Algonkin, Cheyenne,
   Chippawa, Delaware,
   Haaninin, Iliniwek,
   Illinois, Kickapoo,
   Menomini, Merrimac,
   Powhatan, Puyallop **9**
   Algonquin, Blackfoot
Ali, Muhammad
   formerly: 4 Clay **7** Cassius
   sport: 6 boxing
alibi 3 out **6** excuse **7**
   pretext
Alice's Adventures in
Wonderland
   author: 7 Carroll,
   Dodgson
alien 6 exotic, remote,
   unlike **7** distant, foreign,
   opposed, strange **8**
   contrary, newcomer,
   outsider, stranger
alienate 7 divorce

8 estrange, separate, turn
   away
alight 4 land **6** get off **7**
   descend, get down **8** come
   down, dismount
align 4 ally, even, join, side
   6 even up, line up
alike 4 akin, even, same **5**
   equal **6** evenly **7** equally,
   kindred, uniform **8** of a
   piece, parallel
alive 4 spry **5** alert, aware,
   eager, quick, vital **6**
   active, extant, lively,
   living, viable **7** animate, in
   force, not dead **8**
   animated, possible,
   spirited, vigorous
alkaline 3 lye **5** salty **7**
   antacid
all 4 each, full, very **5** any
   of, every, fully, total,
   utter, whole **6** each of,
   entire, to a man, utmost,
   wholly **7** highest, perfect,
   totally, utterly **8** any one
   of, complete, entirely,
   everyone
allay *see* **4 calm**
all but 6 almost, nearly **7**
   close to **8** not quite
all-consuming 3 hot **5** fiery
   6 ardent, fervid, raging,

red-hot **7** burning, fanatic, fervent, frantic, glowing, intense, zealous **8** frenzied

allege 3 say **4** aver, avow **5** claim, state **6** accuse, assert, impugn, impute **7** contend, declare, profess **8** maintain

allegiance 6 fealty, homage **7** loyalty **8** devotion, fidelity

allegory 5 fable **7** parable

allegro
   music: 4 fast

all-embracing 5 broad **6** all-out **7** general, overall **8** complete, sweeping, thorough

Allen, Woody
   wife: 6 Lasser, Previn, Soon-Yi

alleviate *see* **4 calm**

alley 4 lane **5** byway **7** passage, pathway

alliance 4 pact **5** union **6** league, treaty **7** compact, company

allied 4 akin, like **5** alike, joint **6** united **7** cognate, kindred, related, similar

all in 4 beat **5** spent, tired, weary **6** bushed, done in, pooped **7** drained,

wearied, worn out **8** dog tired, fatigued, tired out

all-inclusive 5 broad **6** all-out, entire **7** general, overall **8** absolute, complete, sweeping, thorough

allocate 5 allot, allow **6** assign, budget **7** earmark **8** set aside

allot 4 dole, mete **5** allow, grant **6** assign **7** appoint, consign, dole out, earmark, give out, mete out, provide **8** allocate, dispense, divide up

all-out 5 broad, total **7** maximum **8** complete, sweeping, thorough

all over 4 done **5** ended, kaput **8** finished

allow 3 let **4** give **5** allot, grant **6** assign, permit **7** agree to, approve, concede, provide **8** allocate, sanction

allowance 5 grant **6** bounty, income, ration **7** annuity, payment, pension, stipend, subsidy **8** discount

alloy *see* **7 amalgam**

all right 2 OK **3** yes **4** fair,

hale, safe, sure, well **6**
hearty **7** healthy **8**
properly, unharmed
Spanish: 5 bueno

allspice
also called: 7 pimento

all told 5 in sum, total **6** in
toto **7** totally **8** as a
whole

allude 4 hint **5** refer **7**
mention, speak of, suggest
8 intimate

allure 4 bait, lure **5** charm,
tempt **6** entice, lead on,
seduce **7** beguile, enchant,
glamour

allusion 4 hint **7** mention

ally 5 unite **6** league **7**
combine, partner **8**
confrere

almighty 7 supreme **8**
absolute, infinite

almond
candy: 8 marzipan

almost 5 about **6** all but,
nearly **7** close to **8** not
quite, well-nigh

alms 3 aid **4** dole, gift **5**
mercy **6** relief **7** charity,
handout, largess, present,
subsidy, tribute **8**
donation, gratuity,
offering, pittance

aloe 4 balm
full name: 8: aloe vera
in: 6 lotion **7** shampoo

aloft 2 up **5** above, way up
6 high up, on high **7**
skyward **8** in the air, in
the sky, overhead

Aloha State
nickname of: 6 Hawaii

alone 4 only, sole **6** lonely,
single, singly, solely,
unique **7** forlorn **8**
deserted, forsaken,
isolated, lonesome,
peerless, singular, solitary

along 2 on **4** over **6** beside,
during, onward **7** abreast,
forward, through

aloof 3 icy **4** cold, cool **5**
above, apart **6** chilly,
formal, remote **7** distant,
haughty, high-hat **8**
detached, reserved

aloud 7 audibly

alpine 5 alpen, lofty **6**
aerial **8** elevated,
snow-clad, towering

already 5 early, so far **6**
before **8** formerly,
hitherto, until now

already seen
French: 6 deja vu

also 3 and, too **4** more,

plus **5** extra **6** as well **7** besides **8** moreover

altar 5 bomos **6** hestia, scribis **7** eschara **8** credence

alter 4 vary **5** amend **6** change, modify, recast, revise **7** convert, remodel

altercation 3 row **4** spat, tiff **5** brawl, broil, fight, melee, scene **6** affray, fracas, rumpus, scrape **7** discord, dispute, quarrel, scuffle **8** argument

alter ego 4 twin **5** match **6** double

alternate 3 sub **4** vary **5** alter, proxy **6** backup, change, deputy, rotate, second **7** another, standby, stand-in

although 3 but, yet **4** even **5** still **7** however

altitude 4 apex **6** height, vertex, zenith **8** eminence, tallness

altogether 5 fully, in all, in sum, quite **6** in toto, wholly **7** all told, totally, utterly **8** all in all, as a whole, entirely

altruistic 8 generous

alumnus, alumna 4 grad **8** graduate

always 7 forever **8** evermore

amalgam 5 alloy, blend, combo, union **6** fusion, league, merger **7** joining, mixture **8** alliance, compound, mishmash

amass 6 gather, pile up **7** acquire, collect, compile, round up **8** assemble

amateur 4 tyro **6** novice, non-pro **7** dabbler **8** beginner, hobbyist, inexpert, neophyte

amatory *see* **7 amorous**

amaze 3 awe **4** daze, stun **5** shock **7** astound, stupefy **8** astonish, surprise

Amazon
occupation: 7 warrior
sex: 6 female
queen: 9 Hippolyta
river: 6 Brazil

ambassador 5 agent, envoy **6** consul, deputy, legate, nuncio **7** attache, courier **8** diplomat, emissary

amber
formed from: 5 resin
color: 6 yellow

ambiance 3 air **4** aura,

mood, tone **5** tenor **6** spirit, flavor, milieu, temper **7** climate, setting

ambiguous 5 vague **7** cryptic, unclear **8** doubtful, puzzling

ambition 3 aim **4** goal, hope, plan, push, zeal **5** dream, drive **6** design, desire, intent **7** longing, purpose **8** striving

ambivalent 5 mixed **7** warring **8** clashing, confused, opposing, wavering

amble 6 ramble, stroll **7** meander, saunter

ambrosial 5 balmy **8** fragrant, luscious, perfumed

ambulatory 6 mobile, moving **7** walking

ambush 4 trap **5** blind, cover **6** attack, entrap, lay for, waylay **7** assault **8** hideaway, surprise

ameliorate *see* **6 remedy**

amen 5 truly **6** it is so, so be it, verily **8** hear hear

Amen
  also: 4 Amon **5** Ammon
  origin: 8 Egyptian
  king of: 4 gods

  represented by: 3 ram **5** goose

amenable 4 open **7** cordial, willing **8** obliging, yielding

amends 7 apology, defense, payment, redress **8** requital

amenity, amenities 8 civility, mildness, niceties

America, North
  country: 4 Cuba **5** Haiti **6** Belize, Canada, Mexico, Panama **7** Bahamas, Jamaica **8** Honduras **9** Costa Rica, Guatemala, Nicaragua **12** United States **17** Dominican Republic
  island: 5 Banks **6** Baffin, Kodiak **7** Bahamas, Bermuda **8** Victoria **9** Ellesmere, Greenland, Vancouver
  mountain: 5 Rocky, White **6** Alaska, Brooks, **7** Cascade, Olympic **8** Catskill, Wrangell
  highest point: 6 Denali **8** McKinley
  river: 3 Red **4** Ohio **5** Snake, Yukon **6** Copper, Fraser, Hudson, Nelson **8** Arkansas, Colorado, Columbia, Delaware,

Missouri
lake: 4 Erie **5** Huron **6**
Louise **7** Ontario **8**
Manitoba, Michigan,
Superior, Winnipeg **9**
Champlain, Great Bear,
Great Salt
ocean/sea/bay: 6 Arctic,
Bering, Hudson **7**
Chukchi, Pacific **8**
Atlantic, Beaufort **9**
Caribbean **10**
Chesapeake, St Lawrence

America, South
country: 4 Peru **5** Chile **6**
Brazil, Guyana **7** Bolivia,
Ecuador, Uruguay **8**
Colombia, Paraguay,
Suriname **9** Argentina,
Venezuela
city: 3 Rio (de Janeiro) **4**
Lima **5** Quinto **6**
Bogota, Recife **7**
Caracus **8** Salvador,
Santiago, Sao Paulo
island: 6 Chiloe, Chonos,
Marajo **9** Galapagos
lake: 5 Mirim, Patos,
Poopo **6** Viedma **8**
Titicaca **9** Maracaibo
mountain: 5 Andes
highest point: 9
Aconcagua
river: 6 Amazon, Parana
7 Orinoco, Uruguay

8 Araguaia, Paraguay,
Parnaiba
American Indian *see under*
Native Americans
amethyst
species: 6 quartz
color: 6 purple
month: 8 February
ami, amie 6 friend
amiable *see* **6 genial**
amigo, amiga 6 friend
amiss *see* **4 awry**
amity 6 accord **7** concord,
harmony **8** good will,
sympathy
ammunition 4 ammo, arms
5 shell **6** bullet, rocket **7**
missile, torpedo
ammunition dump 7 arsenal
8 magazine
amnesia 4 daze **5** fugue **6**
stupor **7** agnosia **8**
blackout
amnesty 6 pardon **8**
immunity, reprieve
amoeba, ameba 4 dyad,
germ, mold **5** spore, virus
6 fungus **7** ciliate, microbe
8 bacteria, reovirus
reproduction by: 7 fission
Amon *see* **4 Amen**
among 2 at **3** mid **4** amid,

with **6** amidst **7** amongst, between, betwixt

amorous 4 fond **6** ardent, doting, loving, tender **8** enamored, lovesick

amorphous 5 vague **8** formless, unshapen

amount 3 sum **4** bulk, mass **5** total **6** extent, volume **7** measure **8** quantity

amour 6 affair **7** liaison, romance **8** intrigue

amphibian 8 seaplane
  kind: 4 frog, newt, toad
  young: 6 larvae **7** tadpole **8** polliwog

amphitheater 4 bowl **5** arena **7** gallery, stadium **8** coliseum

amphora 3 jar, jug, urn **4** vase

ample 3 big **4** huge, vast, wide **5** broad, large, roomy **6** enough, plenty **7** copious, immense, liberal, profuse **8** abundant, adequate, extended, generous, spacious

amplitude 4 bulk, mass, size **5** range, reach, scope, sweep, width **6** extent, volume **7** bigness, breadth, compass, expanse

8 fullness, plethora, richness, vastness

amputate 5 sever **6** cut off, excise, lop off, remove

Amsterdam
  capital of: 7 Holland

amuck 4 amok, nuts **6** wildly **7** berserk, bonkers **8** crackers, insanely

amulet 5 charm **6** fetish **8** talisman

amuse 5 cheer, humor **6** absorb, divert, occupy, please **7** beguile, engross, enliven, gladden **8** interest

anagram 4 code **6** cipher

analects 8 extracts

analgesic 4 drug **6** opiate **7** anodyne **8** narcotic

analogous 4 akin, like **7** similar **8** parallel

analogy 6 simile **8** likeness, metaphor

analysis 4 test **5** assay, brief, study **6** digest, precis, review, search **7** breakup, inquiry, outline, summary, therapy **8** abstract, judgment, synopsis, thinking

analyst 5 judge **6** shrink,

tester 8 examiner, observer

analyze 5 assay, judge, study **7** examine **8** appraise, diagnose, evaluate, question

anarchy 5 chaos **6** utopia, mutiny **8** disorder **9** rebellion

anathema 3 ban **5** curse, taboo **7** censure

Anatolia *see* **7 Armenia**

Anatolian
  spoken in: 9 Asia Minor
  spoken by: 8 Hittites

anatomy 4 body **8** analysis

ancestor 8 begetter, forebear

ancestry 4 line, race **5** house, stock **6** family, origin **7** descent, lineage **8** heredity, pedigree

anchor 3 fix **4** hook, moor **5** affix, basis **6** fasten, secure **7** bulwark, defense, mooring, support **8** mainstay, security

anchorage 3 key **4** bund, dock, pier, port, quay, slip **5** berth, haven, jetty, wharf **6** harbor, marina **7** dockage, mooring, seaport

ancient 3 old **4** aged

5 early, hoary, Greek, olden, passe, Roman **6** age-old, bygone, old hat, remote **7** antique, archaic, classic, very old **8** long past, obsolete, primeval

ancillary 5 minor **7** adjunct **8** inferior

and 3 too **4** also, more, plus **8** as well as

Andersen, Hans Christian
  known for: 10 fairy tales

Andes
  highest point: 9 Aconcagua
  country: 4 Peru **5** Chile **6** Panama **7** Bolivia, Ecuador **8** Colombia **9** Argentina, Venezuela
  animal: 5 llama **6** alpaca, condor, huemul

Andorra
  capital/largest city: 14 Andorra-la-Vella
  mountain: 8 Pyrenees
  people: 7 Catalan **8** Andosian

and others 3 etc **4** et al **6** et alii **7** and so on **8** et cetera

Andrew 7 apostle
  brother: 5 Peter, Simon

Androcles
   origin: 5 Roman
   position: 5 slave
androgenous 8 bisexual
androphobia
   fear of: 3 men
and so on 3 etc **8** et cetera
anecdote 4 tale, yarn **5**
   story **6** sketch
anemic, anaemic 3 wan **4**
   dull, pale, weak **5** quiet **6**
   feeble, pallid **7** subdued **9**
   colorless **11** thin-blooded
   13 characterless
anemone 4 lily **5** plant **6**
   flower
anesthetic, anaesthetic 4
   drug **5** ether, local **6**
   caudal, opiate, spinal **7**
   general **8** narcotic,
   procaine
anesthetize 4 dope, drug,
   numb **6** deaden, sedate
anew 5 again, newly **6**
   afresh **8** once more
   Latin: 6 de novo
angel 3 gem **4** doll **5** jewel,
   power, saint **6** cherub,
   patron, seraph, throne,
   virtue **7** sponsor **8**
   cherabim, seraphim
Angel, fallen 5 Satan **6**
   Azazel **7** Lucifer

angelic 4 good, pure **5**
   ideal **6** divine, lovely **7**
   saintly **8** cherubic,
   ethereal, heavenly,
   innocent, seraphic
anger 3 ire, vex **4** bile, fury,
   gall, rage, rile **5** annoy,
   chafe, pique, wrath **6**
   choler, dander, enmity,
   enrage, hatred, madden,
   nettle, rankle, ruffle,
   spleen, temper **7** incense,
   inflame, outrage, provoke,
   umbrage **8** acrimony,
   embitter, irritate, vexation
angle 4 bend, cusp, edge,
   side, turn **5** focus, slant **6**
   aspect, corner **7** outlook **8**
   position
   kind: 5 acute, right **6**
      obtuse **8** straight
   point: 6 vertex
   measure: 7 degrees
Angola
   capital/largest city: 6
      Luanda
   highest point: 4 Moco
   river: 5 Congo, Zaire **7**
      Zambezi
   physical feature:
      basin: 8 Okavango
   people: 5 Bantu, Kongo **6**
      Ovambo **7** Bakongo

angst 5 dread **6** unease **7** anxiety

anguish 3 woe **4** pain **5** agony, grief **6** misery, sorrow **7** anxiety, despair, torment **8** distress

angular 4 bent, bony, lank, lean **5** gaunt, lanky, spare **6** jagged **7** crooked, scrawny **8** rawboned

animadversion 4 flak **7** nagging, quibble

animal 3 pet **5** beast, brute **6** mammal **8** creature, nonhuman, organism

Animal Farm
  author: 6 (George) Orwell

animate 4 fire, goad, move, stir, urge, warm **5** alive, impel, liven, set on **6** arouse, excite, fire up, incite, moving, prompt, spur on, vivify, work up **7** actuate, enliven, inspire, provoke, quicken **8** activate, energize, vitalize

animosity, animus 4 hate **5** anger **6** enmity, hatred, malice, rancor, strife **7** dislike, ill will **8** acrimony

anise
  flavor: 8 licorice

Anna Karenina
  author: 7 Tolstoy

annals 7 history, minutes, records **8** archives

Annam *see* **7 Vietnam**

anneal 6 harden, temper **7** toughen

annex 3 add **4** grab, join **5** affix, merge, seize **6** adjoin, append, attach, tack on **7** acquire, connect, subjoin

annihilate *see* **7 destroy**

anniversary 4 fete **7** holiday, name day **8** birthday, feast day

annotate 5 gloss **6** remark **7** comment, explain, expound **8** construe, footnote **9** elucidate, explicate, interpret **10** commentate

announce 5 augur, state **6** herald, reveal, signal **7** betoken, declare, divulge, give out, portend, presage, publish, signify, trumpet **8** disclose, foretell, proclaim

annoy *see* **8 irritate**

annual 4 weed **5** plant **6** flower, serial **7** gazette, journal, reports **8** bulletin, magazine, periodic

annuity 6 income **7** pension, stipend

annul *see* **7 nullify**

anodyne 4 balm **6** solace **7** comfort

anoint 3 oil **5** crown **6** ordain **8** put oil on

anomalous 3 odd **7** bizarre, strange **8** abnormal, atypical, peculiar

anon 4 soon, then **5** again, later **7** by and by, shortly **8** tomorrow

anonymous 7 unnamed **8** nameless, unsigned

another 4 else, more **5** extra, other **7** further, renewed

anser 5 goose **6** stupid **7** foolish **8** anserine

answer 3 say **4** fill, meet, suit **5** reply, serve, solve, write **6** be like, rejoin, retort **7** conform, fulfill, react to, resolve, respond **8** be enough, response, solution

ant
　　caste: 4 male **5** queen **6** worker **7** soldier
　　group of: 6 colony

antagonism 5 spite **6** animus, enmity, hatred, rancor, strife **7** discord, dislike, rivalry **8** aversion, clashing, conflict, friction

Antarctica
　　explorers: 4 Byrd, Ross **5** Crean, Scott **6** Wilkes **8** Amundsen **10** Shackleton
　　island: 4 Ross **5** Peter, Scott **6** Biscoe, Hearst **7** Ballery **8** Adelaide, Elephant
　　river: 4 Onyx
　　natural resource/mineral: 4 coal
　　bird: 4 skua **6** fulmar, petrel **7** penguin
　　sea: 4 Ross **5** Davis **6** Scotia **7** Weddell **8** Amundsen

ante 3 bet, pot **5** stake, wager

anteater 5 sloth **7** echidna **8** aardvark **9** armadillo

antecede 7 precede, predate **8** go before, preexist

antediluvian 7 antique, archaic **8** obsolete

antelope 8 ruminant
　　family: 7 Bovidae
　　kind: 3 doe, gnu **4** buck, deer, fawn, kudu, oryx, roan **5** bongo, eland, moose, sable **6** dik-dik,

duiker, impala **7** gazelle, gemsbok **8** steinbok

antenna 6 aerial, feeler

anterior 5 front, prior **7** forward, in front **8** previous

anthem 4 hymn, song **5** carol, ditty, music, paean, psalm **6** ballad, sacred **7** cantata **8** doxology

anthology 6 choice, digest **7** garland **8** analects, chapbook, extracts, treasury

Anthony, Susan B.
  leader in: 8 suffrage
  appears on: 6 (silver) dollar

anthropology
  term: 4 myth **6** custom, ritual **7** culture, kinship **8** artifact

antibiotic 4 drug **5** venom **6** poison **8** curative

antic, antics 5 larks, sport **6** pranks, tricks

anticipate 5 await **6** expect **7** count on, foresee, long for, look for, predict **8** envision, forecast, foretell

anticlimax 7 letdown **8** comedown

antidote 4 cure **6** remedy

Antigone
  author: 7 Anouilh **9** Sophocles
  character: 6 Ismene **8** Tiresias
    father: 7 Oedipus
    mother: 7 Jocasta
    brother: 8 Eteocles **9** Polynices
    sister: 6 Ismene
    uncle: 5 Creon
    cousin/lover: 6 Haemon

Antigua and Barbuda
  capital/largest city: 7 St John's
  island: 4 Long **5** Guana **7** Antigua, Barbuda, Redonda
  harbor: 7 English

anti-intellectual 5 yahoo **7** lowbrow

antipathy 6 enmity, rancor **7** disgust, dislike, ill will **8** aversion, distaste, loathing

antiphony 6 chorus **7** refrain **8** response

antipode 8 contrary, opposite

antiquated 5 dated, passe **7** antique, archaic **8** obsolete, outdated

antique 3 old **5** curio, relic **6** rarity **7** bibelot, trinket

antiseptic 6 iodine **7** aseptic, sterile **8** germ-free

antisocial 7 asocial, hostile **8** menacing, retiring, unsocial

antithesis 7 inverse, reverse **8** antipode, contrary, converse, opposite

antitoxin 5 serum **8** antidote

antler 4 horn, knob, rack **5** spike **6** shovel **8** deerhorn, troching
  part: 3 bay **4** brow **5** crown, royal

ant lion
  also: 8 lacewing **9** doodlebug

Antony, Mark
  other triumvirs: 7 Lepidus **8** Octavian (Caesar Augustus)
  lover: 9 Cleopatra
  cousin: 6 (Julius) Caesar
  wife: 7 Octavia
  battle: 6 Actium **8** Philippi

antonym 8 opposite

Anubis
  origin: 8 Egyptian
  god of: 5 tombs
  represented by head of: 6 jackal

anvil 5 block, incus

anxious 4 avid, keen **5** eager, tense **6** ardent, intent, uneasy **7** alarmed, earnest, fearful, fervent, fretful, uptight, worried **8** troubled

any 3 all, one **4** each, lone, sole, some **5** every **6** anyone, single, unique **7** anybody **8** anything, singular, solitary

anyway 6 anyhow **8** sloppily

A-1 *see* **3** ace

apace 4 fast **7** flat-out, hastily, quickly, rapidly, swiftly **8** speedily

Apache
  band: 9 Jacarilla, Mescalero
  leader: 7 Cochise **8** Geronimo

apart 4 afar **5** alone, aside **6** cut off **7** asunder, distant **8** by itself, divorced, isolated, separate

apartment 3 pad **4** flat **5** rooms, suite

apathy 8 coolness, lethargy, numbness

ape 4 copy, echo, mock

5 mimic **6** follow, mirror, monkey, parody, parrot **7** emulate, imitate, primate **8** travesty

kind: 5 chimp **6** gibbon **7** gorilla, siamang **9** orangutan

famous: 8 Godzilla, King Kong

aperture 3 gap **4** hole, rent, rift, slit, slot **5** chink, cleft, space **6** breach **7** fissure, opening, orifice

apex *see* **6 summit**

aphasic 4 dumb, mute

aphorism 3 saw **5** adage, axiom, maxim **6** dictum, old saw, saying, slogan, truism **7** epigram, proverb **8** apothegm

aphrodisiac 4 sexy **6** carnal, erotic, turn-on **7** fleshly, philter, raunchy **8** prurient

Aphrodite
  origin: 5 Greek
  goddess of: 4 love **6** beauty
  husband: 10 Hephaestus
  lover: 4 Ares
  corresponds to: 5 Venus

apiary 4 hive **7** beehive

apiece 4 each

aplomb 5 poise **7** balance **8** calmness, coolness

apocalyptic 4 dire **7** ominous **8** oracular

apocryphal 7 dubious **8** disputed, doubtful, mythical, spurious

apogee *see* **6 summit**

Apollo
  origin: 5 Greek, Roman
  god of: 5 light, music **6** beauty, poetry **7** healing **8** prophecy
  father: 4 Zeus
  mother: 4 Leto
  twin sister: 7 Artemis
  sons: 3 Ion **5** Iamus **8** Laodocus

apologetic 5 sorry **8** contrite, penitent

apology 6 excuse **7** defense

apostasy 7 atheism, perfidy **8** unbelief

apostate 6 bolter **7** heretic, seceder, traitor **8** defector, recusant, renegade, turncoat

apostle 5 envoy **6** zealot **7** pioneer, witness **8** activist, advocate, disciple, emissary, preacher

Apostles 4 John, Jude, Levi, Paul **5** Jacob, James,

Judas, Peter, Simon **6** Andrew, Philip, Thomas **7** Matthew **8** Barnabas, Matthais **9** Nathanael, Thaddaeus **11** Bartholomew

apothegm 3 saw **5** adage, axiom, maxim, motto **6** dictum, slogan **7** epigram, proverb **8** aphorism

apotheosis 7 epitome, essence

appall 4 stun **5** abash, alarm, repel, shock **6** dismay, offend, revolt, sicken **7** disgust, horrify, outrage, terrify, unnerve **8** frighten, nauseate

apparatus 4 gear **5** gismo, setup, tools **6** device, gadget, outfit, system, tackle **7** machine **8** material, utensils

apparel *see* **7 clothes**

apparent 4 open **5** clear, overt, plain **6** likely, marked, patent **7** blatant, evident, obvious, seeming, visible **8** clear-cut, distinct, manifest

apparition 5 ghost, shade, spook **6** spirit, wraith **7** phantom, specter **8** phantasm, presence, revenant

appeal *see* **5 plead**

appear 4 look, seem, show **5** arise **6** crop up, emerge, loom up, show up, turn up **7** be clear, be plain, come out, perform, surface **8** be patent **9** be evident, be obvious

appearance 4 look **5** guise, image **6** advent, aspect, coming **7** arrival, pretext **8** pretense

appease *see* **7 placate**

appellation 3 tag **4** name **5** title **6** handle **7** epithet, moniker **8** cognomen

append 3 add **4** join **5** affix **6** attach, hang on, tack on **7** subjoin, suspend

appendage 3 arm, leg **4** limb, tail **6** branch, feeler, member **7** adjunct **8** addition, offshoot, tentacle

appendix 7 codicil **8** addendum, addition

appertain 7 apply to, concern, refer to **8** bear upon, be part of, belong to, inhere in, relate to

appetite 4 zest **5** gusto **6** desire, hunger, liking, relish, thirst **7** craving, passion, stomach **8** penchant, yearning

appetizer 6 canape, dainty, savory, tidbit **8** aperitif, cocktail, delicacy **9** antipasto

appetizing 6 savory **8** alluring, enticing, inviting, tempting

applaud 4 clap, hail, laud **5** extol **6** praise **7** acclaim, commend **8** eulogize

apple 5 Malus
beverage: 5 cider **8** Calvados

Apple of discord
thrown by: 4 Eris
awarded to: 9 Aphrodite
awarded by: 5 Paris

applesauce 3 rot **4** bull, bunk **5** hokum, hooey **6** bunkum **7** baloney, hogwash, spinach **8** tommyrot

appliance 4 gear **6** device **7** fixture, machine

applicable 3 apt, fit **6** useful **7** apropos, fitting, germane **8** relevant, suitable

application 4 balm, form, suit, wash **5** claim, salve **6** appeal, lotion **7** request **8** dressing, entreaty, ointment, petition

apply 3 fit, use **4** suit **5** adapt, lay on, put on, refer **6** devote, direct, employ, relate **7** address, pertain, request, utilize **8** dedicate, exercise, petition, practice, spread on

appoint 3 fix, set **4** name **5** equip **6** assign, choose, engage, fit out, select, settle, supply **7** arrange, furnish, provide **8** decide on, delegate, nominate

apportion 5 allot, share **6** divide, ration **7** consign, deal out, dole out, prorate **8** allocate, disperse

apposite 3 apt **7** apropos, fitting, germane **8** material, relevant, suitable

appraise 5 assay, judge, value **6** assess, review, size up **7** examine, inspect **8** evaluate

appreciable 7 evident, obvious **8** clear-cut, definite

appreciate 4 like **5** prize, savor, value **6** admire, esteem, relish **7** cherish, enhance, improve, inflate, respect **8** treasure

apprehend 3 bag, nab, see **4** know **5** catch, grasp, seize, sense **6** arrest, collar **7** capture, discern, realize **8** perceive

apprehensive *see* **7 anxious**

apprentice 4 tyro **5** pupil **6** novice **7** learner, student **8** beginner, neophyte

apprise 4 tell **6** advise, inform, notify **8** disclose

approach 3 way **4** come, near, road **5** begin, equal, match **6** access, avenue, be like, method, system **7** advance, compare, passage, solicit **8** attitude, come near, resemble

approbation 6 praise **7** acclaim, support **8** applause, approval, sanction

appropriate 3 apt **4** take **5** allot, seize **6** assign, proper, seemly **7** apropos, correct, earmark, fitting, germane **8** allocate, relevant, suitable

approve 4 like, pass **5** allow **6** accept, affirm, defend, esteem, permit, praise,

ratify, second, uphold **7** condone, confirm, endorse, respect, sustain **8** accede to, advocate, assent to, concur in, sanction

approximate 5 guess, rough **6** reckon **7** inexact, verge on **8** estimate, relative

appurtenance 4 wing **5** annex, extra **7** adjunct **8** addendum, addition

April
  event: 5 taxes
  flower: 5 daisy **8** sweet pea
  French: 5 Avril
  gem: 7 diamond
  holiday: 6 Easter
  place in year:
    Gregorian: 6 fourth
    Roman: 6 second
  Spanish: 5 Abril
  zodiac signs: 5 Aries **6** Taurus

a priori 6 theory **7** opinion

apron 3 bib **5** smock **8** covering

apropos 3 apt **6** seemly **7** correct, fitting, germane, related **8** relevant, suitable

apt 5 prone **6** bright, clever, gifted, liable, likely, proper, seemly **7** apropos, fitting, germane, given to

8 inclined, relevant, suitable

aptitude 4 bent, gift, turn **5** flair, knack, skill **6** genius, talent **7** ability, faculty **8** capacity, facility, penchant, tendency

aqua 4 blue **5** water **6** bluish

Aquarius
symbol: 6 (water) bearer **7** (water) carrier
planet: 6 Saturn, Uranus
rules: 5 hopes **7** friends
born: 7 January **8** February

aquatic 6 marine **7** abyssal, fluvial, neritic, oceanic, pelagic **8** littoral

aqua vitae 7 alcohol

aqueduct 4 duct, race **7** channel, conduit

aqueous 4 damp **5** moist **6** liquid, serous, watery **7** hydrous **8** waterish

Arab
clothing: 3 fez **4** veil
country: 3 UAE **4** Iraq, Oman **5** Egypt, Libya, Qatar, Sudan, Syria, Yemen **6** Jordan, Kuwait **7** Algeria, Bahrain, Lebanon, Morocco,

Tunisia **11** Saudi Arabia
Holy City: 5 Mecca **6** Medina
holy war: 5 jihad
language: 6 Arabic
people: 7 Semitic
religion: 5 Islam

Arabia
country: 3 UAE **4** Oman **5** Qatar, Yemen **6** Kuwait **7** Bahrain **11** Saudi Arabia
Holy City: 5 Mecca **6** Medina
language: 6 Arabic
religion: 5 Islam

arable 6 fecund **7** fertile **8** farmable, fruitful, plowable, tillable

arachnid
class: 4 mite, tick **6** spider **8** scorpion
pairs of legs: 4 four

arachnophobia
fear of: 7 spiders

Arapaho
related to: 8 Cheyenne
ceremony: 8 sun dance

arbiter 5 judge **6** pundit, umpire **7** referee

arbitrary 6 chance, random **7** summary, willful **8** absolute, despotic, fanciful, personal

arbitrate 5 judge **6** decide, settle, umpire **7** adjudge, mediate, referee

arbor 5 bower, folly, kiosk **6** gazebo, grotto **7** pergola **8** pavilion

arc 3 bow **4** arch **5** curve **8** crescent, half-moon

arcade 6 loggia, piazza **7** archway, gallery, skywalk **8** cloister, overpass

arcane 6 mystic, occult **7** obscure **8** abstruse, esoteric, hermetic, mystical

arch 3 arc, bow, sly **4** bend, dome, main, span, wily **5** chief, curve, major, saucy, vault **7** cunning, primary, roguish **8** bow shape

archaic 5 passe **6** bygone **7** ancient, antique **8** obsolete

archangel 5 Satan, Uriel **7** Gabriel, Michael, Raphael

arched 4 bent **5** bowed **6** curved

archenemy 3 foe **7** archfoe, bugbear, nemesis, scourge **8** opponent

archeology
   term: 3 dig **6** midden
   ages: 4 Iron **6** Bronze

archer 6 bowman

8 spearman
   famous: 4 Tell (William) **5** Cupid, Robin (Hood)

archetype 5 model **7** classic **8** exemplar, original

architect 6 author, shaper **7** creator, deviser, founder, planner **8** designer, engineer

archives 6 annals, museum, papers **7** library, records

arctic 3 icy **5** gelid, polar **6** bitter, frigid, frozen **7** glacial, ice-cold **8** freezing

ardent 4 keen **5** eager, fiery, lusty **6** fierce **7** earnest, fervent, intense, zealous **8** spirited, vehement

ardor 4 love, zeal **5** gusto, verve, vigor **6** fervor, spirit **7** feeling, passion, rapture **8** devotion

arduous 4 hard **5** heavy, tough **6** severe, tiring, trying **7** onerous **8** toilsome, vigorous

area 4 turf, zone **5** arena, field, range, realm, scope, space, tract **6** domain, extent, region, sphere **7** expanse, portion, section, stretch, terrain **8** district, locality, precinct, province

arena 4 area, bowl, ring **5** field, lists, realm, scene, stage **6** circus, domain, sector, sphere **7** stadium, theater **8** coliseum, platform, province

Ares
   origin: 5 Greek
   god of: 3 war
   father: 4 Zeus
   mother: 4 Hera
   sister: 4 Hebe

argent 5 white **6** silver **7** shining, silvery

Argentina
   name means: 7 silver
   capital/largest city: 11 Buenos Aires
   mountain: 5 Andes
   highest point: 9 Aconcagua
   river: 5 Negro, Plata **6** Parana, Salado **7** Uruguay **8** Colorado, Paraguay
   physical feature:
      falls: 6 Grande, Iguazu **7** Iguassu
      lowland: 5 chaco
      plains: 6 pampas
   feature:
      cowboy: 6 gaucho **7** vaquero
      dance: 5 samba, tango, zamba **6** cuando, gaucho
      ranch: 8 estancia
      weapon: 4 bola
   food:
      dish: 7 criollo **8** empanada

Argonauts
   leader: 5 Jason
   ship: 4 Argo
   sailed to: 7 Colchis

argot 4 cant **5** idiom, lingo, slang **6** jargon, patois

argue *see* **7 quarrel**

argument 3 row **4** case, gist, plot, spat, tiff **5** clash, fight, story **6** debate, reason **7** dispute, outline, quarrel, summary **8** abstract, contents, squabble, synopsis

aria 3 air **4** solo, song, tune **6** melody, number **7** arietta, excerpt, section

Ariadne
   father: 5 Minos
   mother: 8 Pasiphae
   husband: 8 Dionysus
   gave thread to: 7 Theseus

arid 3 dry **4** dull **5** vapid **6** barren, dreary, jejune **7** dried-up, parched, tedious **8** lifeless, pedantic

Aries
symbol: **3** ram
planet: **4** Mars
rules: **11** personality
born: **5** April, March

arise **4** dawn, go up, rise, wake **5** awake, begin, climb, ensue, get up, mount, occur, set in, start **6** appear, ascend, crop up, emerge, result, wake up

arista **3** awn **7** bristle

aristocrat **4** duke, earl, lady, lord, peer **5** noble **7** Brahmin, duchess, grandee, marquis **8** countess, nobleman

aristocratic **5** noble, regal, royal **6** lordly, titled **7** courtly, genteel, refined **8** highborn, highbred

Arizona
abbreviation: **2** AZ **4** Ariz
capital/largest city: **7** Phoenix
explorer: **8** Coronado
feature:
  dam: **6** Hoover **8** Coolidge **9** Roosevelt
  tribe: **4** Hopi, Pima **6** Apache, Navaho, Navajo
  lake: **4** Mead **6** Havasu, Mohave, Powell **9** Roosevelt
  mountain: **5** White **6** Lemmon
  physical feature:
    canyon: **5** Grand
    desert: **6** Sonora **7** Painted
    forest: **9** Petrified
  river: **4** Gila, Salt, Zuni **8** Colorado

ark **3** box **4** ship **5** barge, chest **8** flatboat

Ark
built by: **4** Noah
landing place: **6** Ararat
groups: **5** pairs

Arkansas
abbreviation: **2** AR **3** Ark
capital/largest city: **10** Little Rock
mountain: **4** Blue **5** Ozark, Ouachita
river: **3** Red **5** Black, White **6** Saline **7** Buffalo **8** Arkansas, Ouachita **11** Mississippi

arm, arms **4** guns **5** brace, crest, equip, prime **6** branch, outfit, sector **7** forearm, fortify, prepare, protect, section, weapons **8** armament, blazonry, division, firearms, insignia, materiel, offshoot, ordnance, weaponry

armada **4** navy **5** fleet **8** flotilla, squadron

armadillo
   order: **8** Edentata
   body: **5** armor **6** plates
   habit: **9** nocturnal

Armageddon **8** doomsday
   author: **4** Uris

armament **4** arms, guns **7** weapons **8** ordnance

Armenia
   capital/largest city: **6** Erivan **7** Yerevan
   lake: **3** Van **4** Sevan
   mountain: **6** Ararat
   highest peak: **7** Aragats
   river: **6** Araxes, Tigris **9** Euphrates
   apostle: **7** Gregory

Armenian
   spoken in: **6** Russia, Turkey **7** Armenia

armistice **5** peace, truce

armlet **6** bangle **8** bracelet, ornament

arm of the sea **5** bight, firth, fjord (fiord), inlet **6** strait **7** channel, estuary, narrows

armoire **8** cupboard, wardrobe

armor **4** mail **5** chain **6** shield **7** bulwark

armory, arms depot **7** arsenal

army **3** mob **4** band, bevy, crew, gang, host, mass, pack **5** crowd, force, horde, swarm **6** legion, throng, troops **7** legions, militia **8** military, soldiers

aroma **4** odor **5** savor, scent, smell **7** bouquet, perfume **9** fragrance

aromatic **5** spicy **7** odorous, piquant, pungent, scented

around **4** near **5** about, circa

Around the World in Eighty Days
   author: **5** (Jules) Verne

arouse *see* **4** spur

arpeggio **5** chord, scale **8** flourish

arraign **6** accuse, charge, impute, indict **7** censure **8** denounce

arrange **4** file, plan, plot, pose, rank, sort **5** adapt, array, fix up, group, order, range, score **6** assort, design, devise, lay out, line up, map out, set out, settle **7** agree to, marshal, prepare, provide

8 classify, contrive, organize, schedule

arrant 4 rank **5** utter **7** extreme **8** flagrant, outright, thorough

array 4 deck, garb, pose, rank, robe, show **5** adorn, align, dress, group, order, place, range **6** attire, bedeck, clothe, deploy, finery, outfit, parade, set out, supply **7** apparel, arrange, marshal, raiment **8** clothing, garments, organize

arrest 3 end, fix, nab **4** bust, halt, hold, slow, stay, stop **5** block, catch, check, delay, pinch, rivet, roust, seize, stall **6** absorb, collar, detain, engage, occupy **7** attract, capture, engross, inhibit

arrive 4 come, near **5** get to, occur, reach **6** appear, befall, happen, show up, turn up **7** succeed **8** approach, make good

arrivederci 7 goodbye **8** farewell

arrogance *see* **7 conceit**

arrogate 5 adopt, claim, seize, usurp **6** assume **7** preempt **8** take over

arrow 3 bow **4** bolt, dart, nock **5** shaft **7** pointer

arroyo 4 wadi **5** gorge, gully **6** ravine, trench

arsenal 6 armory **7** weapons **8** magazine

art, arts 5 craft, knack, skill **6** genius **7** finesse, mastery, methods **8** artistry, facility, strategy
 goddess of: 6 Athena, Athene, Pallas, Saitis **7** Minerva

Artemis
 origin: 5 Greek
 form: 8 huntress
 habitat: 4 moon
 twin brother: 6 Apollo

artery 3 way **4** path, road, vein **5** aorta **6** street **7** channel, highway

artful *see* **6 clever**

Arthur
 began: 10 Round Table
 buried: 6 Avalon
 father: 5 Uther
 half-sister: 6 Morgan (le Fay)
 home: 7 Camelot
 island: 6 Avalon
 sword: 9 Excalibur
 wife: 9 Guinevere
 wizard: 6 Merlin

Arthur, Chester Alan
   presidential rank: 11
      twenty-first
   party: 10 Republican
   state represented: 2 NY
   succeeded upon death of:
      8 Garfield

article 4 item, part, term **5**
   count, essay, paper, piece,
   point, story, theme, thing
   6 clause, detail, matter,
   object, review, sketch **7**
   portion, product, proviso,
   write-up **8** division

articulate 4 join **5** hinge,
   state, utter, voice **6**
   convey, facile, fluent,
   hook up **7** connect,
   enounce, express **8**
   eloquent, organize

artifact 4 tool **7** manmade

artifice 4 hoax, ruse, trap,
   wile **5** blind, dodge, feint,
   guile, trick **6** deceit,
   device, tactic **7** cunning,
   slyness **8** foxiness,
   intrigue, scheming,
   trickery, wiliness

artificial *see* **4 fake**

artillery 6 cannon **7** big
   guns **8** ordnance

artisan 6 master

artist 6 expert, master **8**
   virtuoso

artless 4 naif, open, pure,
   true **5** crude, naive, plain
   6 candid, honest, humble,
   simple **7** natural, sincere **8**
   innocent, trusting

arty 6 dainty **7** foppish **8**
   affected, high-brow,
   overnice, precious

Aryan
   origin: 4 Asia **5** India
   family of languages: 5
      Hindi **7** Bengali, Panjabi
      9 Sinhalese

as 4 that, when **5** while **7**
   because, equally

as a group 7 en masse, in a
   body **8** as a whole,
   together

as a result 2 so **5** due to **7**
   because

as a whole 6 in toto **8** all
   in all

ascendancy, ascendance 4
   edge, rule, sway **5** power,
   reign **7** command, control,
   mastery **8** whip hand

ascent 4 rise **5** climb,
   grade, slope **6** rising **7**
   advance, incline, scaling,
   upgrade **8** mounting,
   progress

ascertain 5 learn **6** detect, verify **7** certify, find out, unearth **8** discover

ascetic 3 nun **4** monk, yogi **5** fakir, stern **6** essene, hermit, strict **7** austere, dervish, eremite, recluse, Spartan **8** celibate, cenobite, rigorous, solitary

Asclepius
  origin: 5 Greek
  god of: 7 healing **8** medicine
  father: 6 Apollo

ascribe 6 assign, credit, impute, relate **7** trace to **8** accredit, charge to

asea 4 lost **6** addled, adrift **7** puzzled **8** confused

Asgard
  home of: 4 Asar **5** Aesir
  origin: 5 Norse
  location of: 8 Valhalla

ash 4 dust **6** cinder **7** residue

ashamed 3 shy **7** abashed, bashful, prudish

ashen, ashy 3 wan **4** gray, pale **5** livid, pasty **6** anemic, leaden, pallid **8** blanched

ashore 6 on land **7** aground

Asia
  country: 4 Iran, Iraq, Laos, Oman **5** Burma, China, India, Japan, Macao, Nepal, Qatar, Syria, Tibet, Yemen **6** Bhutan, Brunei, Cyprus, Israel, Jordan, Russia, Sikkim, Taiwan, Turkey **7** Armenia, Bahrain, Georgia, Kashmir, Lebanon, Myanmar, Vietnam **8** Cambodia, Hong Kong, Malaysia, Maldives, Mongolia, Pakistan, Sri Lanka, Thailand **9** East Timor, Indonesia, Kirghizia, Singapore
  desert: 4 Gobi **6** Syrian **7** Arabian, Karakum **8** Kyzylkum
  island: 4 Java, Sulu **5** Ceram, Kuril, Japan, Sumba, Timor **6** Borneo, Flores, Taiwan **7** Celebes, Hainan, Sumatra **8** Moluccas, Sri Lanka, Tanimbar
  river: 2 Ob **3** Amu, Syr **4** Amur **5** Indus **6** Ganges, Mekong, Tigris **7** Hwang Ho, Yangtze, Yenisei **9** Euphrates, Irrawaddy
  lake: 6 Baikal **7** Aral Sea

mountain: 5 Altai, Urals **6** Pamirs, Taurus **8** Caucasus, Tien Shan **9** Himalayas, Hindu Kush, Karakoram

highest point: 7 Everest

lowest point: 7 Dead Sea

largest city: 6 Bombay, Mumbai

aside 4 away **5** apart **6** aslant, beside **7** whisper

asinine 5 silly **6** absurd, insane, stupid **7** foolish, idiotic, moronic, witless

ask 3 beg, bid, sue **4** call, pump, quiz, seek, urge **5** apply, claim, grill, plead, press, query **6** appeal, charge, demand, invite **7** beseech, entreat, implore, inquire, request, solicit **8** petition, question

askew 4 awry **6** aslant **7** crooked **8** cockeyed, lopsided, sleeping

asleep 6 dozing **7** napping

aspect 3 air **4** look, side **5** angle, facet, point **7** feature

aspersion 4 slur **5** abuse, smear **7** calumny, censure, obloquy, railing, slander **8** reproach, reviling

asphyxiate 5 choke **6** stifle **7** smother

aspire 4 seek **5** aim at, covet, crave **6** desire, pursue **7** hope for, long for, pine for, wish for **8** yearn for

ass 3 oaf **4** dolt, fool, jerk **5** booby, burro, dunce, idiot, moron, ninny **6** donkey, dum-dum, nitwit **7** half-wit, jackass **8** bonehead, imbecile, lunkhead, numskull

assailant 6 mugger **8** assailer, attacker, molester

assassinate 4 kill, slay **6** murder, rub out **7** bump off

assault *see* **6 attack**

assay 3 try **4** rate, test **5** essay, prove **6** assess **7** analyze, attempt **8** appraise, endeavor, estimate, evaluate

assemble 4 join, meet **5** amass, flock, rally **6** gather, heap up, muster, pile up, summon **7** collect, compile, connect, convene, convoke, marshal, round up

assent 5 agree, allow, grant,

yield **6** accept, accord, comply, concur, permit **7** approve, concede, consent, defer to **8** sanction

assert 4 aver, avow **5** argue, claim, state, swear **6** accent, affirm, avouch, insist, stress, uphold **7** contend, declare, profess **8** advocate, maintain, propound, set forth

assess 3 tax **4** levy **5** judge, value **6** charge **8** appraise, consider, estimate, evaluate, look over

assets 4 cash **5** goods, means, money **6** wealth **7** capital, effects **8** property, reserves

asseverate 4 aver, avow **5** state, swear **6** affirm, assert, attest, avouch, insist **7** certify, contend, declare, protect **8** maintain, proclaim

assiduous 6 dogged **7** earnest **8** constant, diligent, sedulous, tireless

assign 3 fix, set **4** give, name **5** allot, grant **6** charge, choose, invest **7** appoint, consign, entrust, mete out, specify

8 allocate, delegate, dispense, set apart

assignation 4 date **5** tryst **7** meeting

assignment 3 job **4** duty, post, task **5** chore **6** lesson **8** exercise, homework

assimilate 6 absorb, digest, imbibe, ingest, take in

assist *see* **4 abet**

assistance 3 aid **4** alms, help **6** relief **7** charity, service, stipend, subsidy, support

assistant 3 aid **4** aide, ally **5** aider **6** helper **7** partner **8** adjutant, co-worker, sidekick

associate 3 mix, pal, tie **4** ally, bind, chum, club, join, link, mate, pair, peer, yoke **5** buddy, crony, merge, unite **6** allied, couple, fellow, friend, hobnob, league, mingle, relate **7** combine, comrade, connect, consort, hang out, partner, related **8** confrere, co-worker, identify, intimate, sidekick

association 3 tie **4** body, bond, club, meld **5** blend, group, union **6** clique, league **7** combine, company, linkage, mixture, society **8** alliance, mingling, relation

assortment 5 array, stock, store **6** medley, motley **7** melange, mixture, variety **8** grouping, quantity

assuage *see* **8 mitigate**

assume 4 take **5** fancy, guess, infer, judge, seize, think, usurp **6** accept, deduce, gather, take on, take up **7** believe, imagine, presume, suppose, surmise, suspect **8** arrogate, shoulder, take over, theorize

assumed *see* **4 fake**

assumed name 5 alias **7** pen name

assuming 4 bold **5** nervy, pushy **6** brazen, cheeky **7** forward, haughty **8** arrogant, insolent

assurance 3 vow **4** oath **5** poise **6** binder, pledge **7** promise **8** averment, boldness, coolness, sureness, warranty

assured 4 sure **5** fixed

6 poised, secure **7** certain, settled **8** positive

Astaire, Fred
partner: 6 (Ginger) Rogers

astern 3 aft **5** abaft **6** behind

asteroid 6 debris

astir 2 up **5** afoot, awake **6** active, roused **8** in motion, out of bed

astonish *see* **5 amaze**

astound *see* **5 amaze**

astral 6 starry **9** celestial

astray 3 off **5** amiss **6** afield

astringent 4 acid, keen, sour, tart **5** brisk, sharp, stern, tonic **6** biting, severe **7** acerbic, bracing, puckery, styptic **8** curative, incisive, piercing, stabbing, vinegary

astrology 6 Zodiac
belief in: 8 siderism
term: 4 sign **5** house, trine **6** alnath, apheta, aspect **7** almuten, anareta, mansion, mundane, sextile **8** alkahest, nativity, quartile, synastry

astronomy
  term: 5 comet, orbit **6** apogee, meteor, nebula, parsec, quasar **7** azimuth, eclipse, equinox, perigee, transit **8** aphelion, asteroid, ecliptic, meridian, solstice

astute 3 sly **4** able, foxy, keen, wily **5** acute, sharp, smart **6** adroit, artful, bright, clever, crafty, shrewd, subtle **7** cunning, knowing, politic

Asuncion
  capital of: 8 Paraguay

asunder 4 rent **5** apart **8** in pieces, to shreds

asylum 4 home **5** haven **6** harbor, refuge **7** retreat, shelter **8** madhouse, preserve

at a distance 4 afar, away **5** above, aloof, apart **6** far off

at any rate 6 anyhow, anyway

at cross purposes 7 counter, opposed **8** contrary, converse, inimical, opposite **9** disparate

at ease 4 calm, cool **6** at rest, serene **7** content, relaxed, unmoved **8** composed

at fault 6 guilty **8** culpable

at hand 4 near, nigh **5** close, handy, on tap, ready **6** nearby **7** close by **8** imminent

atheism 8 apostasy, unbelief

Athena
  origin: 5 Greek
  goddess of: 4 arts **6** wisdom **7** warfare **9** fertility
  father: 4 Zeus
  mother: 5 Metis
  sprang from head of: 4 Zeus
  symbol: 3 owl
  corresponds to: 7 Minerva

Athens
  capital of: 6 Greece
  hill: 9 Acropolis
  marketplace: 5 Agora
  port: 7 Piraeus
  event: 8 Olympics

athlete 4 jock **8** champion

athletic 5 burly, hardy, husky, manly **6** brawny, robust, strong, virile **8** muscular, stalwart, vigorous

athletics **5** games **6** sports **8** exercise

at home **6** at ease, inside, shut in **7** indoors **8** confined
French: **4** chez

athwart **6** across **7** astride **8** sideways, sidewise

Atlanta
baseball team: **6** Braves
basketball team: **5** Hawks
football team: **7** Falcons
hockey team: **9** Thrashers

at large **5** astir, loose **6** abroad **8** as a whole, at length

Atlas
form: **5** Titan
supported: **3** sky

Atlas Shrugged
author: **7** Ayn Rand

at leisure **4** idle **7** off duty **8** inactive

atmosphere **3** air **4** aura, feel, mood, tone **5** color **6** spirit **7** feeling

at odds **6** unlike **8** contrary

atoll **6** island
made of: **5** coral
pool: **6** lagoon
famous: **6** Bikini **8** Eniwetok

atom **3** bit, dot, jot **4** iota,

mite, mote, whit **5** crumb, grain, scrap, shred, speck, trace **6** morsel **7** smidgen **8** fragment, particle

atomic **6** cobalt **7** fission, neutron, nuclear, uranium **8** hydrogen

atom part **6** proton **7** neutron **8** electron

atone **6** pay for, redeem, repent, shrive **7** expiate

at one's disposal **5** handy **6** at hand, on hand

at rest **5** quiet, still **6** asleep, at ease, serene **7** at peace, content **8** in repose

Atreus
wife: **6** Aerope
son: **8** Menelaus **9** Agamemnon

atrium **4** hall **6** cavity **7** auricle **8** entrance

atrocious *see* **8 horrible**

atrophy **7** decline **8** decaying, drying up

attach **3** fix **4** join **5** affix, allot, annex **6** append, couple, secure **7** connect, destine, earmark **8** allocate, be fond of, fasten to, make fast

attache **4** aide **5** envoy **6** consul **8** adjutant, diplomat, emissary, minister

attack 3 fit **4** damn, go at **5** abuse, blame, fault, fly at, onset, spasm, spell **6** assail, charge, impugn, strike, stroke, tackle **7** assault, censure, lunge at, offense, seizure **8** denounce, fall upon, invasion, paroxysm

attacker 6 mugger **7** accuser **8** assailer, opponent

attain 3 win **4** earn, gain, reap **5** reach **6** effect, obtain, secure **7** achieve, acquire, procure, realize

attempt 3 aim, try **4** seek **5** essay **6** attack, effort, hazard, strive, tackle, work at **7** assault, venture **8** endeavor

attend 4 go to, heed, mark, mind, note **5** serve, usher, visit **6** convoy, escort, follow, show up, squire, tend to **7** care for, conduct, observe, oversee, service **8** appear at, consider, frequent, harken to, listen to, wait upon **French: 4** oyez

attendance 4 gate **5** crowd,

house **8** audience, presence

attention 4 care, heed, mind, note, suit **5** court **6** homage, notice, regard, wooing **7** concern, respect, service, thought **8** civility, courtesy, devotion

attentive 5 alert, awake **6** intent, polite **7** devoted, heedful, mindful, zealous **8** diligent, obliging

attenuate 6 dilute, impair, lessen, reduce, weaken **7** draw out, spin out **8** decrease, diminish, enervate, enfeeble

attest *see* **6 affirm**

attic 4 loft **6** garret **7** mansard **8** cockloft

attire *see* **7 clothes**

attitude 3 air **4** pose **6** manner, stance **7** outlook, posture **8** demeanor, position

attorney 4 beak **6** lawyer **7** counsel **8** advocate

attract 4 draw, lure, pull **5** cause, charm, evoke **6** allure, beckon, entice, induce **7** bewitch, enchant **8** interest

attractive 4 chic, fair, foxy,

sexy **6** lovely, pretty **7** elegant, likable, sightly, winning **8** alluring, becoming, charming, engaging, enticing, fetching, handsome, inviting, pleasant, pleasing, tasteful, tempting

attribute 4 gift **5** facet, grace, lay to, trait **6** aspect, assign, credit, impute, talent, virtue **7** ability, ascribe, blame on, feature, quality, trace to

attrition 4 loss **7** erosion **8** abrasion, decrease, friction, grinding, scraping

attune 5 adapt **6** adjust, tailor **8** accustom

at work 4 busy **5** in use **6** active **7** engaged, working **8** occupied

atypical 7 unusual **8** abnormal, contrary, uncommon

auberge 3 inn **6** tavern

auburn 5 henna, tawny **6** russet **8** cinnamon, nut-brown

auction 3 sale **7** bidding **8** offering

audacious 4 bold, pert, rash, rude, wild **5** bossy, brave, fresh, gutsy, risky, saucy **6** brazen, cheeky, daring, plucky **7** defiant, forward **8** assuming, heedless, impudent, insolent, intrepid, reckless, stalwart, unafraid

audible 5 clear, heard **8** distinct

audience 4 talk **5** house **6** market, parley, public **7** hearing, meeting **8** assembly, audition

audit 5 check **6** go over, review, verify **7** balance, examine, inspect

audition 6 tryout **7** hearing

auditorium 4 hall **5** arena **7** theater **8** auditory, coliseum

auger 4 bore **5** drill **6** pierce

aught 3 all, zip **4** love, nada, null, zero **6** naught **7** a cipher, nothing **8** goose egg

augment 5 add to, boost, raise, swell **6** deepen, expand, extend **7** amplify, build up, enlarge, inflate, magnify **8** flesh out

augur *see* **7 prophet**

august 5 grand, lofty,

noble, regal **6** solemn, superb **7** eminent, exalted, stately, supreme **8** glorious, imposing, majestic

August
characteristic: 7 dog days
flower: 5 poppy
French: 4 Aout
gem: 7 peridot **8** sardonyx
place in year:
  Roman: 5 sixth
  Gregorian: 6 eighth
zodiac sign: 3 Leo **5** Virgo

au naturel 4 nude **8** uncooked

au pair 4 maid **5** nanny

aura 3 air **4** feel, mood **5** aroma **7** essence, feeling, quality **8** ambience

au revoir 7 goodbye **8** farewell

auspice 4 omen, sign **6** augury **7** portent, warning

auspicious 4 good **5** happy, lucky **6** benign, timely **7** hopeful

austere 5 rigid, spare, stark, stern **6** chaste, severe, simple, strict **7** ascetic, Spartan **8** rigorous

Australia
capital: 8 Canberra
largest city: 6 Sydney
island: 5 Cocos, Timor **7** Keeling, Norfolk **8** Flinders, Tasmania, Thursday **9** Admiralty
lake: 4 Eyre
mountain: 4 Blue **5** Snowy
highest point: 9 Kosciusko
river: 5 Snowy, Tamar **6** Murray **7** Darling, Derwent
sea: 5 Coral, Timor **6** Indian, Tasman **7** Pacific
physical features:
  bay: 5 Bight, Shark **6** Botany
  peninsula: 4 Eyre
  strait: 4 Bass
place: 7 outback **9** billabong
feature:
  animal: 5 dingo **7** wallaby **8** anteater, kangaroo, platypus **9** koala bear
  bird: 3 emu
  weapon: 9 boomerang

Austria
capital/largest city: 4 Wien **6** Vienna
lake: 8 Bodensee, Traunsee **9** Constance

mountain: **4** Alps **6** Tirols, Tyrols **9** Dolomites

river: **3** Inn **6** Danube

physical feature:
  mountain pass: **7** Brenner
  wind: **6** Foehen
  woods: **6** Vienna

resort: **5** Baden **9** Innsbruck

features: **8** yodelers
  clothing: **5** loden
  dance: **5** waltz
  festival: **8** Salzburg

authentic *see* **7 genuine**

author **4** poet **5** maker **6** father, framer, writer **7** creator, founder, planner **8** essayist, inventor, novelist, producer

authoritarian **5** harsh **6** severe, strict, tyrant **7** austere, fascist **8** autocrat, dogmatic, martinet

authoritative **5** sound, valid **6** lordly, ruling **7** factual, learned **8** arrogant, decisive, dogmatic, imposing, official, reliable

authorities **6** expert, police, pundit **7** scholar

authority **4** rule, sway **5** clout, force, might, power **6** esteem, weight **7** command, control, respect **8** dominion, prestige, strength

authorize **5** allow **6** enable, invest, permit **7** approve, certify, charter, confirm, empower, entitle, license, warrant **8** accredit, sanction, vouch for

autocracy **7** czarism, tyranny **8** autarchy, monarchy

autocrat **5** ruler **6** despot, tyrant **7** monarch **8** dictator, overlord

autograph **4** mark, sign **5** x-mark

automatic **6** reflex **7** natural, routine **8** electric, habitual, inherent

automaton **4** pawn, tool **5** golem, patsy, robot **6** puppet, stooge **7** android, cat's-paw, fall guy, machine

autonomy **7** freedom **8** home rule, self-rule

Autry, Gene
  horse: **8** Champion

autumn **4** fall

auxiliary **6** backup, helper **7** partner, reserve

avail **3** aid, use **4** help

5 serve **6** assist, profit **7** benefit, purpose, service, success, utilize

available 4 free, open **5** handy, on tap **6** at hand, on hand

avalanche 4 heap, mass, pile **5** flood **6** deluge **7** barrage, cascade, torrent

Avalon
   island of: 8 Paradise
   burial place for: 6 Arthur, heroes

avant-garde 7 leaders **8** pioneers, vanguard

avarice 5 greed **6** penury **8** rapacity, venality

Ave Maria 8 Hail Mary

avenge 5 repay **6** injure, punish **7** revenge

avenue *see* **5 route**

aver 4 avow **5** state, swear **6** affirm, assert, avouch, insist, verify **7** certify, contend, declare, profess, protest **8** proclaim

average 3 par **4** fair, mean, norm, so-so **5** ratio, usual **6** common, medial, median, medium, normal, not bad **7** the rule, typical **8** mediocre, midpoint, moderate, ordinary, passable, standard, standing, the usual

aversion 6 hatred, horror **7** disgust, dislike **8** distaste, loathing

avert 4 turn **5** avoid, deter, shift **7** beat off, deflect, fend off, keep off, prevent, ward off **8** preclude, stave off, turn away

aviator, aviatrix 4 bird **5** flyer, pilot **6** airman, fly-boy **7** birdman

avid 4 keen **5** eager, rabid **6** ardent, greedy, hungry **7** devoted, fanatic, intense, zealous **8** covetous, desirous, grasping

avocado 5 green
   used to make: 9 guacamole

avocation 5 hobby **7** pastime **8** sideline

avoid *see* **5 dodge**

avouch 5 argue, swear **6** affirm **7** declare **8** advocate, maintain

avow 3 own **4** aver **5** admit, state, swear **6** affirm, assert, reveal **7** confess, declare, profess

8 announce, disclose, proclaim

await 6 attend, expect **7** look for

awake 5 alert, aware, spark **6** arouse, awaken, bestir, excite, incite **7** alive to, heedful, inspire, mindful, provoke **8** open-eyed, vigilant, watchful

awaken 3 fan **4** fire **6** arouse, excite, kindle, revive, stir up

award 4 give **5** allot, allow, grant, honor, medal, prize **6** accord, assign, bestow, decree, trophy **7** appoint, concede, laurels, tribute **8** citation, confer on

aware 6 with it **7** alert to, alive to, awake to, mindful **8** apprised, informed, sentient

away 3 far **4** gone **6** absent, at once, way off **8** distance

awe 3 cow **4** fear **5** abash, alarm, amaze, dread, panic, shock **6** dismay, fright, horror, terror, wonder **7** perturb, quaking, respect, terrify **8** astonish, disquiet, frighten

awe-inspiring 5 giant, grand, great, noble **6** august, mighty **7** eminent, exalted, mammoth, sublime, supreme, titanic **8** colossal, enormous, gigantic, glorious, imposing, majestic, wondrous

awesome 6 solemn **7** amazing, fearful **8** alarming, dreadful, fearsome, majestic, wondrous

awestruck 6 humble **8** overcome

awful *see* **8 dreadful**

awkward 5 inept **6** clumsy, touchy, trying **7** unhandy **8** bungling, delicate, unwieldy
French: 6 gauche

awl 4 nail **6** gimlet

awning 4 hood **6** canopy **7** marquee **8** covering, sunshade

awry 5 amiss, askew, wrong **6** astray, uneven **7** crooked, twisted **8** unevenly

axe, ax 3 can **4** chop, fire, oust, sack **5** let go, split **6** bounce, cut out, remove

7 cut down, dismiss **8** get rid of, tomahawk

type: 4 pick **6** poleax **7** hatchet **8** tomahawk

axiom 3 law **5** basic **7** precept

axiomatic 5 banal, given **6** cliche **7** assumed **8** accepted, manifest

axis 4 stem **5** pivot, shaft **7** compact, entente, spindle **8** alliance

axle 3 bar, pin **5** shaft, wheel **7** spindle **8** crossbar

ayah 4 maid **5** nurse

aye 3 yea, yes

Azerbaijan
 capital/largest city: 4 Baku
 mountain: 8 Caucasus
 sea: 7 Caspian
 language: 6 Turkic
 religion: 6 Muslim

Aztec (Nahua, Mexica)
 location: 6 Mexico **9** Guatemala
 leader: 9 Montezuma
 conquerer: 6 Cortes, Cortez

azure 4 blue **5** lapis **6** cobalt **7** sky blue **8** cerulean

Baal 3 god **5** deity

Babbitt
   author: 5 Lewis

babble 3 coo, din, gab, hum
   4 blab, talk **5** prate **6**
   burble, clamor, drivel,
   gabble, gibber, gurgle,
   hubbub, jabber, murmur
   7 blabber, blather, chatter,
   prattle, twaddle **8**
   chitchat, rattle on

babe 3 tot **4** baby **5** child **6**
   infant

babe in the woods 8
   innocent

babel, Babel 3 din **6**
   bedlam, clamor, hubbub,
   tumult, uproar **7** turmoil

baboon 6 monkey
   characteristic: 4 mane,
      pads **6** muzzle
   location: 6 Africa
   most sacred: 6 Anobis

babushka 4 baba, veil **5**
   scarf, stole **8** kerchief

baby 3 wee **4** babe, tiny **5**
   humor, small, spoil, young

6 bantam, coddle, coward,
infant, little, minute,
pamper, petite **7** indulge,
neonate **8** sniveler

baby carriage 4 cart, pram
6 cradle

Babylonian god 3 Bel **6**
Marduk

Babylonian Mythology
   chief of gods: 6 Marduk
      8 Merodach
   demon: 6 Namtar
   goddess of love/war/
      fertility: 6 Ananna,
      Inanna, Ishtar **7** Astarte,
      Mylitta
   god of dead: 6 Nergal
   god of fire: 5 Ishum
   god of heaven: 2 An **3**
      Anu
   god of moon: 3 Sin
   god of sun: 3 Utu **7**
      Shamash
   god of wisdom: 4 Enki
   hero: 5 Ninib **7** Ninurta
   king: 9 Gilgamesh
   king of gods: 5 Enlil
   mother of gods: 5 Nammu

queen of heaven: 6 Ishtar
world of dead: 3 Kur
Baby Snooks 5 (Fanny) Brice
bacchanal 4 orgy **5** feast, revel, spree **6** frolic **7** carouse, debauch, revelry, wassail **8** carnival, carousal, festival
Bacchus
  also: 5 Evius **8** Dionysus
  god of: 4 wine **5** drama **9** fertility
  father: 4 Zeus
  mother: 6 Semele
  son: 6 Phlias **7** Narcaus, Priapus **8** Oenopion
bachelor 6 single
bacillus 3 bug **4** germ **7** microbe **8** pathogen
back 3 aid, ebb **4** abet, gone, help, hind, late, past, rear, tail **5** after, guard, minor, rural, spine, tardy **6** affirm, assist, attest, behind, dorsal, recede, recoil, remote, retire, return, revert, succor, tergal, uphold, verify **7** bolster, confirm, earlier, endorse, finance, overdue, promote, protect, reverse, sponsor, support, sustain, warrant

8 advocate, hindmost, sanction, validate, vouch for
back away from 7 back off, retreat **8** withdraw
backbiting 5 abuse, catty **6** gossip, malice **7** abusive, calumny, gossipy, hurtful, obloquy, slander **8** libeling, reviling
backbone 4 grit, guts, sand **5** basis, chine, nerve, pluck, spine, spunk **6** dorsum, mettle, spirit **7** bravery, courage, resolve **8** firmness, mainstay, strength, tenacity
back-country 4 farm **5** rural **6** rustic **7** farming
back down 7 back off **8** move away, withdraw
backdrop 4 flat **7** curtain, scenery
backer 4 ally **5** angel **6** patron **7** sponsor **8** investor, promoter
backfire 4 flop, miss **5** crash **6** fizzle, go awry **8** backlash, lay an egg, miscarry, ricochet
background 3 set **4** past, rear **5** flats **6** milieu **7** context, history, rearing,

setting **8** backdrop, breeding, distance, heritage, training

backhanded 7 awkward **8** reversed

backlog *see* **6 excess**

back matter 5 index **8** addendum, appendix

back off 7 retreat **8** back down, pull back, withdraw

backside 3 can **4** buns, butt, duff, prat, rear, rump, seat, tail **5** fanny **6** behind, bottom, settee, setter, sitter **7** keister, rear end **8** buttocks, derriere

back talk 3 jaw, lip **4** gall, guff, rude, sass **5** cheek **8** pertness, rudeness

backup 6 second **7** reserve, standby, stand-in

back up 4 abet **6** assist, uphold

backward, backwards 3 shy **4** dull, slow **5** dense, tardy, timid, wrong **6** behind **7** impeded, laggard, reverse **8** receding

backwater 3 ebb **5** slack **7** retreat, reverse **8** stagnant, withdraw

backwoods 5 rural, wilds **6** rustic, simple, sticks

7 boonies, country **8** woodland

bacon 3 pig **4** pork **6** gammon **8** porkslab
measure: 6 rasher

bacterium 3 bug **4** germ **5** virus **7** microbe **8** bacillus, pathogen

bad 3 ill, sad, sin **4** base, dire, evil, foul, glum, grim, mean, poor, rank, sick, sour, vile **5** acrid, acute, angry, awful, cross, false, fetid, grave, harsh, lousy, moldy, nasty, risky, sorry, unfit, wrong **6** ailing, bitter, faulty, gloomy, guilty, rotten, sinful, turned, unwell, wicked **7** corrupt, decayed, harmful, hurtful, lacking, naughty, noxious, painful, spoiled, tainted, unsound **8** grievous, inferior, menacing, polluted, villainy

bad faith 7 perfidy, treason **8** betrayal

badge 4 mark, seal, sign, star **5** brand, stamp **6** device, emblem, ensign, shield, symbol **7** earmark **8** hallmark, insignia

badger 3 nag, vex **4** bait,

goad **5** annoy, beset, bully, chafe, harry, hound, tease **6** coerce, harass, hector, nettle, pester, plague **7** provoke, torment, trouble **8** irritate
group of: **4** cete

badinage *see* **8 repartee**

bad judgment **5** folly

bad luck **6** mishap **7** ill wind **8** bad break

bad mark **4** blot **7** demerit

badmouthing **5** barbs **7** dissing, insults, slander

bad turn **4** harm, hurt **5** wrong **6** injury **7** ill turn **8** disfavor

baffle *see* **7 confuse**

bag **3** get, sag **4** hunt, kill, sack, take, trap **5** bulge, catch, droop, pouch, purse, shoot, snare **6** bundle, entrap, obtain, packet **7** acquire, capture, collect, ensnare **8** paper bag, protrude, suitcase

bagatelle **6** trifle **7** nothing, trinket

baggage **4** bags, gear **5** grips **6** trunks **7** bundles, effects, luggage, valises **8** movables, packages

Baghdad
capital of: **4** Iraq
founder: **8** (Caliph) al-Mansur
river: **6** Tigris

bagnio **4** bath, stew **5** house **6** bordel, prison **7** brothel **8** bordello, cathouse

Bahamas
capital/largest city: **6** Nassau
others: **8** Freeport
island: **3** Cat **4** Long **5** Berry, Exuma **6** Andros, Bimini, Caicos, Rum Cay **7** Crooked, Harbour, Watling **9** Eleuthera
sea: **8** Atlantic **9** Caribbean
physical feature:
  strait: **7** Florida
feature:
  native: **5** conch

Bahrain
capital/largest city: **6** Manama
island: **5** Hawar, Jidda **6** Sitrah **7** Bahrain
physical feature:
  gulf: **7** Bahrain, Persian
religion: **5** Islam

bail **3** dip **4** bond, lade **5** ladle, scoop, spoon

bailiff 6 deputy **8** marshall, overseer

bailiwick *see* **6 domain**

bait 3 vex **4** lure, ride, worm **5** annoy, bribe, harry, hound, tease, worry **6** allure, badger, come-on, harass, heckle, hector, magnet, needle **7** provoke

bake 3 fry **4** boil, burn, cook, sear, stew **5** grill, roast, saute, toast **6** braise, pan-fry, scorch, simmer **7** parboil, swelter

Baker, Norma Jean
 real name of: 6 Monroe

Balaam
 killed by: 6 Israel
 rebuked by: 3 ass

balance, balances 3 pay **4** mean, rest **5** poise, ratio, scale, sum up, tally, total, weigh **6** aplomb, equate, offset, scales, square, steady, weight **7** compare, compute, harmony, remnant, residue **8** equality, leftover, level off, parallel, presence, symmetry

Balanchine, George
 choreographer of: 4 Agon **6** Jewels **8** Episodes, Ivesiana, Serenade

balcony 4 deck **5** boxes, foyer, loges **6** loggia **7** portico, terrace, veranda

bald 4 bare, flat, open **5** blunt, naked, plain, stark, utter **6** barren, smooth **7** obvious **8** glabrous, hairless

balderdash *see* **8 nonsense**

bale 4 case, load, pack **6** bundle, packet, parcel **7** package

balefire 6 beacon

baleful 3 icy **4** cold, dire, evil **6** deadly, malign **7** ominous **8** sinister, spiteful, venomous

Bali
 province of: 9 Indonesia
 capital: 8 Denpasar
 highest peak: 6 Agoeng
 tree: 8 waringin

Balius
 horse of: 8 Achilles

balk *see* **6 resist**

Balkan
 ancient people: 4 Slav **5** Greek, Roman **8** Illyrian, Thracian
 mountain: 6 Balkan, Massif **7** Diwaric, Rhodope
 river: 6 Danube, Morava,

Vardar

sea boundary: 5 Black **6** Aegean, Ionian **8** Adriatic

state: 6 Bosnia, Greece, Serbia, Turkey **7** Albania, Croatia, Romania **8** Bulgaria, Slovenia **9** Macedonia

balky 6 mulish, ornery, unruly **7** restive, wayward, willful **8** contrary, perverse, stubborn

ball 3 hop, orb **4** prom, shot **5** dance, globe **6** pellet, soiree, sphere **7** bullets, globule **8** spheroid

Ball, Lucille

husband: 9 Desi Arnaz

children: 4 Desi **5** Lucie

roles: 9 Here's Lucy, I Love Lucy

ballad 3 lay **4** song **5** carol, ditty **6** chanty **8** folk song

ballast 6 weight **7** balance, control

ballet 4 Agon **5** Manon, Rodeo **6** Apollo, Parade **7** Giselle, Orpheus **8** Coppelia, Episodes, Ivesiana, Les Noces, Serenade, Swan Lake, The Doves

ballet company: 5 Kirov, Royal **7** Bolshoi, Joffrey

fast movement: 7 allegro

impresario: 7 Rambert **8** de Valois **9** Diaghilev

kick: 9 battement

position/step: 4 jete, plie, tour **5** saute **6** releve **7** en avant, fouette, on point, pas seul, turnout **8** batterie, cabriole, en dedans, en dehors, glissade

skirt: 4 tutu

slow movement: 6 adagio

term: 4 coda **5** barre **6** ballon

balloon 4 grow **5** belly, bloat **6** billow, blow up, dilate, expand **7** distend, enlarge, fill out, inflate **8** increase

ballot 4 poll, vote **5** slate **6** ticket, voting **7** polling

ballyhoo 4 hype, puff, push, tout **6** herald, hoopla **7** buildup, promote, puffery, trumpet **8** proclaim

balm 5 cream, salve **6** balsam, lotion **7** anodyne, comfort, unguent **8** curative, ointment, sedative

baloney 3 rot **4** bull, bunk **5** hokum, hooey, stuff

6 bunkum, hot air, humbug **7** hogwash, sausage, spinach **8** nonsense

balsam 3 fir **4** balm **5** cream, salve **7** unguent **8** ointment **9** Impatiens
  varieties: 2 He **3** Fir, She **4** Rose, Wild **6** Garden **8** Zanzibar

Baltic
  canal: 4 Kiel
  port: 4 Kiel, Riga **6** Danzig, Gdansk **7** Tallinn

Baltimore
  baseball team: 7 Orioles
  football team: 5 Stars **6** Ravens

balustrade 7 railing **8** baluster, banister, handrail

Bamako
  capital of: 4 Mali

Bambi
  author: 6 Salten
  character: 3 Ena **6** Faline, Flower **7** Thumper
  film made by: 6 Disney

bamboo 4 Sasa **7** Bambusa
  varieties: 4 Moso **5** Arrow, Black, Dwarf, Giant, Hardy, Hedge, Henon, Meyer, Pygmy, Simon, Stake **6** Buddha, Common, Forage, Oldham, Sacred, Sickle, Square, Tonkin **7** Allgold, Beechey, Mexican **8** Calcutta, Feathery, Heavenly, Narihira

bamboozle *see* **7 deceive**

ban *see* **6 forbid**

banal *see* **6 jejune**

banana 4 Musa
  varieties: 3 Fe'i **4** Fehi, Koae **5** Dwarf **6** Edible **7** Chinese
  similar to: 8 plantain

band 3 set **4** belt, body, club, crew, gang, hoop, join, pack, ring, sash **5** bunch, crowd, group, junta, party, strap, strip, swath, thong, troop, unite **6** caucus, circle, clique, gather, girdle

bandage 4 bind **5** dress **7** binding, plaster **8** compress, dressing

bandanna, bandana 5 scarf **8** kerchief

bandeau 3 bra **4** band **6** fillet **7** circlet **9** brassiere

bandit *see* **5 thief**

bandleader 6 master **7** maestro **8** director

famous: 4 Welk **6** Dorsey, Miller **8** Lombardo

bandy 4 swap **5** trade **6** barter **7** shuffle **8** exchange

bane 3 woe **4** ruin **5** curse, toxin, venom **6** blight, burden, canker, plague, poison **7** scourge, torment, tragedy **8** calamity, disaster, downfall, nuisance

bang 3 box, hit, pop, rap, tap **4** beat, blow, boom, clap, cuff, slam **5** burst, clout, crash, thump, whack **6** charge, report, wallop **7** delight **8** good time

Bangkok
    also: 9 Krung Thep
    capital of: 8 Thailand
    river: 10 Chao Phraya

Bangladesh
    capital/largest city: 5 Dacca
    river: 5 Padna **6** Ganges
    physical feature:
        bay: 6 Bengal
    religion: 5 Hindu, Islam

banish *see* **4 oust**

Banjo Eyes
    nickname of: 6 (Eddie) Cantor

bank 3 bar, row, tip **4** dike, dune, edge, file, flat, fund, heap, hill, keep, line, mass, pile, rank, reef, rise, save, side, tier, tilt **5** amass, array, brink, chain, knoll, mound, ridge, shelf, shoal, shore **6** barrow, line up, margin, string, supply **7** reserve, savings

bankrupt 5 broke **6** busted **8** depleted, in the red, wiped out

Banks, Ernie
    nickname: 5 Mr Cub
    sport: 8 baseball
    noted for: 7 hitting
    team: 4 (Chicago) Cubs

banner 4 flag **6** burgee, colors, ensign, record **7** leading, notable, pendant, pennant, winning **8** standard, streamer

banquet 4 dine **5** feast, revel **6** dinner, repast

Banquo
    character in: 7 Macbeth

bantam 3 hen, wee **4** cock, fowl, tiny **5** dwarf, pygmy, runt, small, teeny, weeny **6** little, midget, minute, petite **7** chicken, dwarfed, rooster, stunted

banter *see* **8 repartee**

Bantu
  means: 9 the people
  dwelling: 6 Africa
  tribe: 5 Xosas, Zulus **6**
    Swazis **7** Basutos,
    Kalanga

baptize 3 dub **4** name **8**
  christen

bar 3 ban, pub, rib, rod **4**
  band, bank, beam, belt,
  bolt, cake, curb, flat, line,
  lock, oust, pale, pole, rail,
  reef, snag, spar, spit, stay,
  stop **5** block, catch, court,
  debar, eject, evict, exile,
  expel, forum, ingot,
  jimmy, lever, limit, shelf,
  shoal, sprit, stake, taboo
  6 enjoin, fasten, forbid,
  lounge, paling, saloon,
  secure, streak, tavern **7**
  barrier, exclude, measure,
  prevent, taproom **8**
  alehouse, obstacle,
  obstruct, restrain, restrict,
  tribunal

Bara, Theda
  nickname: 7 The Vamp

Barabbas 6 robber **8**
  murderer

barb 3 cut, dig, nib **4** cusp,
  jibe, snag, spur, tine **5**
  point, prong, spike

6 insult **7** affront, barbule,
  bristle, prickle, putdown

Barbados
  capital/largest city: 10
    Bridgetown
  highest point: 7 Hillaby
  feature:
    sea crab: 7 shagger

barbarian *see* **6 savage**

barber 3 cut **4** trim **5** dress,
  shave, style **6** Figaro **7**
  arrange, stylist, tonsure

barbette 5 mound **7**
  bastion, rampart **8**
  platform

barbiturate 8 euphoria,
  hypnotic, sedative

bard 4 poet **6** rhymer,
  writer **8** epic poet,
  minstrel, poetizer

Bardot, Brigitte
  husband: 5 Vadim
  born: 5 Paris **6** France

bare 4 bald, mere, nude,
  open, show, thin, void,
  worn **5** basic, blank,
  empty, naked, offer, plain,
  scant, stark, strip **6**
  expose, meager, reveal,
  simple, unveil, vacant **7**
  exposed, uncover,
  undrape, undress **8**
  disrobed, marginal

barefaced *see* **6 brazen**

barely 4 just **6** almost, hardly **7** faintly, scantly **8** meagerly, only just, scarcely, slightly

barfly 3 sot **4** lush, soak **5** drunk, rummy, souse **7** tippler **8** drunkard

bargain 4 deal, pact **5** steal **6** accord, barter, dicker, haggle, higgle, pledge, treaty **7** promise **8** contract, covenant

barge 4 bust, scow, ship **6** launch, vessel **7** freight, intrude

bark 3 bay, cry, rub, yap, yip **4** flay, hide, howl, hull, husk, peel, rind, roar, skin, woof, yell, yelp **5** crust, scale, shout, strip **6** abrade, arf-arf, bellow, bow-wow, casing, cry out, holler, scrape **7** howling **8** covering, periderm

barn 4 mews **6** corral, stable

Barnabas
   companion: 4 Paul

baroque 6 florid, ornate

barracks 3 BOQ **4** base, camp **7** lodging **8** garrison

barrage *see* **7 torrent**

barrel 3 keg, tub, tun, vat **4** butt, cask, drum, tube **8** hogshead
   abbreviation: 3 bar, bbl

barren 3 dry **4** arid, dull **5** stale, waste **6** farrow, futile **7** austere, prosaic, sterile, useless **8** depleted, desolate, infecund

barricade 5 block, fence **7** barrier, bulwark, rampart **8** blockade, obstacle, obstruct

Barrie, Sir James M
   author of: 8 Peter Pan

barrier 3 bar **4** moat, wall **5** ditch, fence, hedge **6** hurdle, trench **7** rampart **8** blockade, handicap, obstacle

barring 3 but **4** save **6** except, saving **7** besides

barrister 6 lawyer **7** counsel **8** advocate, attorney

Barrow, Joe Louis
   real name of: 8 Joe Louis

Barrymore Family
   members: 4 Drew, John **5** Diana, Ethel **6** Lionel **8** John Drew

barter 4 swap **5** trade **8** exchange **11** interchange

base 3 bad, bed, key, low **4** camp, core, foul, mean,

post, root, vile **5** basis, dirty, gross, heart, petty, place, stand **6** abject, ground, locate, sordid, source, vulgar, wicked **7** alloyed, essence, install, model on, station, support **8** backbone, inferior, pedestal, rudiment, shameful, spurious

baseball
  term: 3 bag, ERA, fan, RBI, run **4** balk, base, bunt, bush **5** choke, curve, error, fungo, liner, pop-up, slide **6** assist, batter, cellar, double, dugout, duster, inning, on deck, relief (pitcher), rookie, single, slider, triple, umpire, windup **7** blooper, bullpen, catcher, cleanup, fly ball, home run, infield, pickoff, pitcher, rhubarb, rundown, shutout, slugger **8** bean ball, changeup, grounder, keystone, no hitter, outfield, pitchout, southpaw, spitball
  Hall of Fame:
    first elected: 4 Cobb (Ty), Ruth (Babe) **6** Wagner (Honus)

7 Johnson (Walter) **9** Mathewson (Christy)

bash 4 blow **5** blast, clout, crack, knock, party, whack **7** clopper **8** wingding

bashful *see* **3 shy**

basil
  also called: 6 tulasi
  symbol of: 4 hate, love

basilica 6 church

basin 3 pan, tub, vat **4** bowl, dale, dell, font, glen, sink **5** gulch, gully, stoup **6** crater, hollow, lavabo, ravine, tureen, valley **7** dishpan, washtub **8** lavatory, sinkhole, washbowl

bask 5 revel, savor **6** relish, wallow **7** delight **8** sunbathe

basketball
  term: 3 key **4** dunk, hoop, pick, post, trap, zone **5** court, guard, lay-up, pivot, point, press, steal **6** assist, basket, center **7** dribble, forward, palming, rebound, referee **8** charging, hook shot, jump shot, sixth man, turnover
  organizations: 3 NBA

4 NCAA, WNBA

Hall of Fame:
   first members: 5 Allen (Phog; Forrest Clare), Hyatt (Charles), Mikan (George), Olsen (Harold), Stagg (Amos Alonzo), Tower (Oswald) **6** Gulick (Luther), Hickox (Edward), Morgan (Ralph) **7** Carlson (Henry), Celtics (Original), Kennedy (Matthew) **8** Luisetti (Hank), Meanwell (Walter E), Naismith (James), Schommer (John)

bass 3 low **4** alto **5** basso **7** harmony **8** baritone, bass clef

bass
   types: 3 sea **4** rock **5** black **6** calico **7** striped, sunfish

bastard 6 impure **8** inferior, spurious

baste 3 sew **4** drip **5** roast **6** cudgel, flavor, stitch, thrash **7** moisten

bastinado 4 beat, blow, cane, drub **5** whale **7** beating **8** drubbing

bastion 4 fort **5** tower **6** pillar **7** bulwark, citadel, rampart **8** barbette, fortress

bat 3 hit, rod **4** cane, clip, club, cuff, mace, slug, sock **5** billy, knock, smack, stick, whack **6** cudgel, mallet, strike, thwack, wallop **7** clobber **8** bludgeon

batch 3 lot **5** bunch, crowd, group, stock **6** amount, number **8** quantity

bath 3 dip, tub **4** wash **5** sauna **6** douche, shower **7** washing **8** ablution, lavement
   type: 3 hip, mud **4** sitz **5** steam **6** shower, sponge **7** Turkish

bathos 4 corn, mush **5** slush **8** schmaltz

bathroom 2 WC **3** can, loo **4** head, john **5** biffy **6** toilet **7** commode, latrine **8** facility, lavatory, restroom, washroom

Bathsheba
   husband: 5 David, Uriah
   son: 7 Solomon

Batman
   character: 5 Joker, O'Hara (Chief), Robin

(Dick Grayson) **6** Alfred
7 Batgirl (Barbara
Gordon), Penguin,
Riddler **8** Catwoman
city: 6 Gotham

baton 3 bat, rod **4** club,
mace, wand **5** billy, crook,
staff, stick **6** cudgel, fasces
7 crosier, scepter, war club
8 bludgeon, caduceus

battery 3 set **4** army, band,
pack, team **5** block, cadre,
force, group, suite, troop
6 caning, cannon, convoy,
legion, lineup, outfit,
series **7** beating, brigade,
company, hitting **8**
armament, cannonry,
clubbing, drubbing,
flogging, ordnance,
squadron

battle 3 war **4** bout, duel,
feud, fray, meet **5** argue,
brawl, clash, fight, siege **6**
action, affray, combat,
debate, engage, tussle **7**
contend, contest, crusade,
dispute, quarrel, warfare **8**
campaign, conflict,
skirmish, struggle

battleship 4 Iowa **5** Maine
6 Oregon **7** carrier,
warship **8** Missouri
first: 7 Gloire

largest: 6 Yamato
German: 8 Graf Spee

batty *see* **5 crazy**

bauble 3 toy **4** bead **6**
geegaw, trifle **7** trinket **8**
gimcrack, ornament

bawdy *see* **6 vulgar**

bawl *see* **4 wail**

bawl out *see* **5 scold**

bay 3 cry, yap **4** bank,
bark, cove, gulf, howl,
nook, road, yelp **5** basin,
bayou, bight, fiord, firth,
inlet, niche, sound **6**
alcove, bellow, clamor,
lagoon, recess, strait **7**
howling, narrows,
yapping, yelping

bay (at bay) 7 trapped **8**
cornered

bay leaf
from tree: 6 (bay) laurel
transformation of: 6
Daphne
tree sacred to: 6
Apollo
symbol of: 7 victory
(laurel wreath)

bayou 4 slew **5** creek, inlet,
marsh, river, swamp **6**
outlet, slough, stream

Bay Psalm Book
author: 5 (John) Eliot

bazaar 4 fair, mart **6** market **8** carnival, exchange

beach 5 coast, shore **6** strand **8** littoral, seashore

beached 7 aground **8** grounded, stranded

beacon 4 beam **5** light **6** pharos, signal **7** seamark **8** bale-fire, landmark

bead 3 dot **4** blob, drop, pill **5** speck **6** bubble, pellet **7** droplet, globule **8** particle, spherule

beak 3 neb, tip **4** bill, nose, pike, prow **5** lorum, snout, spout **7** rostrum, snozzle **8** hooknose

beaker 3 cup **5** glass **6** vessel

beam 3 ray **4** emit, glow, prop, spar, stud **5** brace, glare, gleam, glint, joist, shine, width **6** girder, rafter, streak, stream, timber **7** breadth, expanse, glimmer, glitter, radiate, trestle **8** transmit

bean 9 Phaseolus
　bean curd: 4 tofu

be a party to 3 aid **4** abet **7** support

bear *see* **7 support**

bear
　combining form: 4 arct, ursi **5** arcto
　constellation: 4 ursa **9** ursa major, ursa minor
　family: 7 Ursidae
　kind: 3 sun **5** black, brown, koala, malay, panda, polar, sloth **6** kodiak, wombat **7** grizzly
　male: 4 boar
　young: 3 cub
　famous: 6 Smokey

beard 4 dare, defy, face, trap **5** brave **6** corner **7** stubble **8** bristles, confront, whiskers

bear down 4 push **5** press

bearer 5 Atlas **6** holder, porter **7** carrier **8** conveyer, producer

bear fruit 4 bear **6** mature **7** develop, prosper

bearings 3 way **6** course **8** position

bearish *see* **7 grouchy**

bear off 5 seize, steal **6** abduct, convey, kidnap

bear witness 4 back **6** attest **7** confirm, testify

beast 3 cad, cur, pig, rat **4** ogre **5** brute, swine

6 mammal, savage **8** creature

beat 3 bat, hit, mix, rap, tap, way **4** area, bang, best, blow, cane, club, drub, flap, flog, flop, lick, maul, path, rout, slap, time, whip, zone **5** clout, count, crush, flail, knock, meter, outdo, pound, punch, whack **6** accent, batter, course, defeat, domain, hammer, master, pummel, rhythm, strike, stroke, wallop **7** cadence, circuit, clobber, conquer, pulsate, surpass, trounce, vibrate **8** overcome, vanquish

beat around the bush 5 dodge, evade, hedge, stall

beatific 4 rapt **6** divine, serene **7** angelic, exalted, saintly, sublime **8** blissful, ecstatic, glorious, heavenly

Beatles 5 (Ringo) Starr **6** (John) Lennon **8** (George) Harrison **9** (Paul) McCartney

be at odds 6 differ **7** dispute, diverge **8** conflict, disagree

beat up 3 mug **4** lick, maul, whip **6** batter, pummel **7** assault, clobber

beat-up 4 shot **6** shabby **7** worn-out **8** battered

beau, beaux *see* **6 suitor**

beau monde 5 elite **6** gentry **7** society

beautiful 4 fair, fine **5** bonny, great **6** comely, lovely, pretty, seemly, worthy **7** radiant **8** alluring, gorgeous, handsome

beauty 4 boon, doll **5** asset, beaut, belle, grace, Venus **6** eyeful, looker **7** benefit, feature, goddess, stunner **8** radiance, splendor
goddess of: 6 Graces **9** Aphrodite, Charities
god of: 6 Apollo, Balder, Baldur **7** Angus Og, Phoebus, Pythias

beaver
young: 3 kit

be blessed with 3 own **4** have **5** enjoy **7** possess

because 2 so **3** for **4** that, then, thus **5** cause, hence, since **6** whence **7** whereas **8** inasmuch

Bechuanaland
now called: 8 Botswana

beck 3 bid 4 call 7 bidding, summons

beckon 4 call, coax, draw, lure, pull 6 allure, entice, invite, motion, signal, summon, wave at, wave on 7 attract, gesture

become 3 get 4 grow, suit, turn 6 go with 7 enhance, flatter, get to be

become one 3 wed 4 fuse 5 blend, marry, merge, unite 7 combine 8 coalesce

becoming 3 apt, fit 4 meet 6 pretty, proper, seemly, worthy 7 fitting 8 suitable

bed 3 cot, hay 4 band, bank, base, belt, bunk, crib, lode, plot, sack, seam, zone 5 berth, floor, layer, patch 6 bottom, cradle, pallet 7 deposit, stratum 8 bedstead

bedazzle 4 daze 6 dazzle 7 astound, confuse, enchant, fluster, nonplus 8 befuddle, bewilder, confound, dumfound

bed chamber 7 bedroom, boudoir

bed down 5 sleep 7 lie down, sack out

bedeck 4 deck, trim

5 adorn, array 7 garnish 8 decorate, ornament

bedevil 3 dog 5 annoy, hound, worry 6 badger, harass, pester, plague

bedizen 5 adorn, array 6 bedeck 7 bejewel, costume

bedlam 5 chaos 6 tumult, uproar 7 turmoil 8 madhouse

Bedouin, Beduin
  also: 4 Absi, Arab 5 nomad 7 bedawee
  Arabic: 6 badawi
  religion: 5 Islam

bedraggled *see* 7 **unkempt**

bedridden 7 invalid 8 disabled, immobile

bedroom 7 boudoir, chamber

bee
  caste: 5 drone, queen 6 worker
  group of: 5 grist, swarm
  variety: 5 mason, miner 6 alkali, cuckoo 8 burrower, honeybee 9 bumblebee, carpenter, plasterer

beech 5 Fagus

beef 4 heft, kick, meat 5 brawn, gripe, steer

6 cattle, grouch, grouse **7** grumble **8** complain

beehive 4 hive **6** apiary

beer 3 ale, keg, mum **4** bier, bock, brew, dark, faro, flip, gail, grog, gyle, hops, kvas, malt, mild, quas, scud, suds **5** chang, chica, draft, grout, kvass, lager, light, quass, scuds, stout, weiss **6** bitter, chicha, double, gatter, porter, spruce, stingo, swanky, swipes, wallop, zythum **7** bottled, cerveza, pangasi, pharaoh, Pilsner, tankard, taplash, tapwort **8** bock beer, cervisia, near beer, pilsener
   cup: 3 mug **4** toby **5** glass, stein **6** flagon, seidel **7** tankard **8** schooner
   ingredient: 4 hops, malt **5** yeast **6** barley
   maker: 6 brewer **8** brewster, maltster
   quantity of: 3 keg **4** case **7** six-pack
   small beer: 4 tiff **5** grout
   Tibetan beer: 5 chang

befall 5 ensue, occur **6** betide, chance, follow, happen

befitting 3 apt, fit **5** right **6** decent, proper, seemly **8** becoming, relevant, suitable

before *see* **5 prior**

before Christ
   abbreviation: 2 BC
   alternative: 3 BCE
   Latin: 2 AC

befoul *see* **5 sully**

befriend 4 help **6** assist, defend, succor, uphold **7** comfort, embrace, help out, protect, stand by, stick by, support, sustain, welcome **8** side with

befuddle *see* **7 confuse**

beg *see* **7 beseech**

beget 3 get **4** sire **5** breed, cause, spawn **6** effect, father, lead to **7** produce **8** engender, generate, occasion, result in

begin *see* **8 commence**

beginner 4 babe, tyro **6** author, father, novice, rookie **7** creator, founder, learner, starter, student **8** freshman, neophyte

begone 3 out **4** away, scat, shoo **5** be off, leave, scram **6** beat it, depart, get out, go away **7** get lost, vamoose

beg pardon 6 excuse

begrime *see* **4 soil**

begrudge 4 envy **5** covet **6** grudge, resent

beguile *see* **5 charm**

behalf 3 aid, for **4** part, side **5** favor **7** benefit, by proxy, defense, in aid of, support **8** interest

behavior 4 acts **5** deeds **6** action, habits, manner **7** actions, bearing, conduct, control **8** activity, attitude, demeanor, practice

behest 4 fiat **5** edict, order, say-so **6** charge, decree, ruling **7** bidding, command, dictate, mandate

behind 4 rump, seat, slow **5** abaft, after, fanny **8** buttocks, in back of

behind closed doors 7 sub rosa **8** in secret, secretly

behind the times 5 passe **7** archaic

behold *see* **7 witness**

behoove 4 suit **5** be apt,

befit 6 become, be wise **7** benefit **8** be proper

beige 3 tan **4** ecru, fawn **6** greige **8** brownish

Beijing
  also: 7 Peking
  capital of: 5 China
  square: 9 T'ien-an Men
  walled city: 5 Inner, Outer, Tatar

be in a class with 5 equal, match **6** be up to **7** compare **8** approach

being 4 core, life, soul **5** human **6** living, mortal, nature, person, psyche, spirit **7** essence, persona, reality **8** creature, existing

be in tune 4 jibe **5** agree, match, tally **6** accord, square **7** conform

Beirut, Beyrouth
  capital of: 7 Lebanon
  Phoenician name: 7 Berytus

Bel 3 god **5** deity

belabor 6 rehash, repeat **7** dwell on

Belarus
  other name: 10 Belorussia **11** Byelorussia, White Russia
  capital/largest city:

5 Minsk
river: 5 Dvina **7** Dnieper
physical feature: 6 Pripet
(Marshes)

belated *see* **4 late**

belch 4 burp, emit, gush,
spew, vent **5** eject, eruct,
erupt, expel, issue, spout,
spurt, vomit **7** cough up,
issuing **8** eruption

beleaguer *see* **3 vex**

belfry 4 dome **5** spire **7**
steeple

Belgium
capital/largest city: 8
Brussels **9** Bruxelles
mountain: 8 Ardennes
river: 3 Lys **5** Meuse **7**
Schelde
sea: 5 North
physical feature:
forest: 8 Ardennes
place:
battleground: 5 Bulge **8**
Waterloo
headquarters of: 2 EU **4**
NATO
food:
cheese: 9 Limburger

Belgrade, Beograd
capital of: 6 Serbia **10**
Yugoslavia
river: 4 Sava **6** Danube

belie 4 defy, deny, mask

5 cloak **6** betray, negate,
refute **7** conceal, falsify,
gainsay **8** disguise,
disprove

beliefs 5 canon, creed,
dogma, faith, tenet **6**
ethics, gospel, morals **8**
doctrine, morality

believe 4 hold **5** guess,
infer, judge, think, trust **6**
assume, credit, deduce,
rely on **7** count on, fall
for, imagine, presume,
suppose, surmise, suspect,
swallow, swear by **8** be
sure of, consider, depend
on, maintain, theorize

be like 5 equal, match **8**
approach, resemble

belittle 5 knock, scorn **6**
deride, malign **7** disdain,
put down, run down,
sneer at

Belize
capital: 8 Belmopan
mountain range: 4 Maya
highest point: 8 Victoria
physical feature:
gulf: 8 Honduras
peninsula: 7 Yucatan
swamp: 8 mangrove

bell 4 gong, peal **5** chime **6**
tocsin **7** ringing **8** carillon
16 tintinnabulation

bell buoy 5 float **6** signal

belle 4 star **5** queen **6** beauty **7** charmer

belligerent *see* **7 hostile**

bellow 4 bawl, roar, yell **5** shout, whoop **6** holler

bell tower 5 spire **6** belfry **7** steeple **9** campanile

bellwether 4 lead **5** doyen, guide, pilot **6** leader **8** director, shepherd

belly 3 abs, gut, yen **4** guts **5** taste, tummy **6** bowels, depths, desire, hunger, liking, paunch, vitals **7** abdomen, insides, midriff, stomach **8** appetite, interior, recesses

bellyache *see* **8 complain**

belong 6 go with **7** concern **8** attach to, be part of

beloved 4 beau, dear, love, wife **5** loved, lover **6** adored, fiance, spouse, steady **7** admired, darling, dearest, fiancee, husband, revered **8** endeared, loved one, precious

below 4 less **5** lower, under **6** in hell **7** beneath, on earth, short of **8** inferior

belt 4 area, band, land, sash, zone **5** cinch, layer, strip **6** circle, girdle, region, stripe **7** country **8** district, encircle

bemoan *see* **5 mourn**

bemused 5 dazed, fuzzy **7** muddled, stunned **8** confused

bench 3 pew **4** banc, seat **5** board, court, stool, table **6** settee **7** counter, take out, trestle

benchmark 4 norm **5** gauge, guide, model **7** example, measure **8** paradigm, standard

bend 3 arc, bow **4** flex, hook, lean, loop, mold, sway, turn, warp, wind **5** crook, curve, defer, force, shape, stoop, twist, yield **6** accede, attend, buckle, coerce, compel, crouch, give in, relent, submit **7** bow down, contort, control, succumb

beneath 5 below, lower, under

Benedict 5 groom **8** newlywed

Benedict XVI, Pope real name: 9 (Joseph) Ratzinger

benedictine
    type: 6 brandy, cognac **7** liqueur

benediction 6 prayer **7** benison **8** blessing

benefaction 4 alms, gift **5** grant **7** charity **8** bestowal, donation, offering

beneficent 6 benign, kindly **7** liberal **8** generous, salutary

benefit 3 aid, use **4** gain, good, help **5** asset, avail, serve, value, worth **6** assist, behalf, better, profit **7** advance, be aided, service **8** be helped, be served, blessing, interest

benevolence 7 charity **8** good will, kindness

Ben-Hur
    author: 7 (Lew) Wallace
    director: 5 (William) Wyler
    cast: 4 (Stephen) Boyd **6** (Charlton) Heston **7** (Jack) Hawkins **8** (Hugh) Griffith
    setting: 9 Palestine

benighted 4 dumb **5** crude, unhip **8** backward, ignorant, untaught

benign 4 good, kind, mild, nice, soft **5** balmy, lucky **6** genial, gentle, humane, kindly, tender **7** affable **8** gracious, harmless, pleasant, salutary

Benin
    capital: 9 Porto-Novo
    largest city: 7 Cotonou
    river: 4 Mono **5** Niger
    physical feature:
        gulf: 6 Guinea

Benny, Jack
    real name: 8 (Benjamin) Kubelsky

benumb 4 daze, dull **5** blunt **6** deaden **7** stupefy

be off 2 go **5** leave, scram **6** beat it, begone, cut out, depart, go away, set out **8** set forth, withdraw

be of use 3 aid **4** help **5** serve **6** assist **7** benefit

be on a par with 5 equal **6** be up to **7** compare

Beowulf
    great hall: 6 Heorot
    monster: 7 Grendel
    tribe: 5 Danes, Geats **8** Frisians

bequeath 4 will **5** endow, leave **6** impart **7** consign **8** hand down

bequest **6** legacy **8** bestowal

berate *see* **5 scold**

Berber
  spoken in: **6** (North) Africa, Sahara

bereave **3** rob **5** strip **6** divest **7** deprive

berg **4** floe **7** glacier, iceberg, icefloe

Berlin
  capital of: **7** Germany
  river: **5** Spree

Bermuda
  capital/largest city: **8** Hamilton
  others: **8** St George
  island: **4** Boaz **5** Coney **7** Bermuda, Ireland, Watford **8** Somerset, St Davids **9** St Georges
  sea: **8** Atlantic
  physical feature:
    harbor: **6** Castle
    hill: **5** Gibbs
  feature:
    dancers: **6** Gombey

Bermuda Triangle
  site of disappearing: **5** ships **6** planes

Bern, Berne
  capital of: **11** Switzerland

Bernhardt, Sarah
  nickname: **11** Divine

Sarah

born: **5** Paris **6** France

berry **3** egg **4** seed **5** fruit, grain, grape **6** dollar, kernel, tomato, banana **7** currant **8** allspice, bayberry, mulberry

berserk *see* **5 crazy**

berth **3** bed, job **4** bunk, dock, pier, post, quay, slip, spot **5** haven, niche, place, wharf **6** billet, employ, office **8** position

beryl
  color: **5** green **6** yellow

beseech **3** beg **4** pray **6** adjure **7** entreat, implore

beset **3** dog, set **4** bead, deck, stud **5** annoy, array, hem in, hound, worry **6** assail, badger, harass, pester, plague **7** bedevil, besiege, set upon **8** surround

beside **2** by **4** near **5** saved **6** except, nearby, unless **7** abreast, barring, without **8** let alone

beside oneself **4** wild **6** elated, joyful, joyous, raging **7** berserk, exalted, frantic, furious, ranting **8**

agitated, blissful, distrait, ecstatic, frenetic, frenzied

besides 3 but 4 also, save 6 as well, except, saving 7 barring 8 moreover

besiege 3 dog 5 annoy, beset, hound 6 assail, badger, harass, pester, plague 7 assault, bedevil 9 beleaguer 10 lay siege to

besmirch *see* 5 **sully**

besotted 5 drunk 6 sodden, soused, wasted, zapped, zonked 7 smashed

bespangle 3 dot 4 gild, star, stud 5 adorn, jewel 6 bedeck 7 dress up, festoon, garnish 8 decorate, ornament

best 3 top 4 most, pick 5 cream, elite 6 choice, finest, nicest, utmost 7 hardest, largest 8 foremost, greatest, superior, topnotch

bestial 5 cruel 6 brutal, savage 7 beastly 8 barbaric, depraved, inhumane, ruthless

bestir 4 goad, spur, stir, urge 5 rouse, speed 6 arouse, excite, hasten 7 quicken 8 activate

bestow *see* 6 **impart**

bet *see* 5 **wager**

bete noir 5 bogey 6 plague 7 bugaboo, bugbear 8 anathema, bogeyman

betoken 4 show 5 augur 6 attest, denote 7 portend, presage, signify 8 foretell

betray 4 dupe, fink, jilt, show, tell 5 rat on, trick 6 expose, reveal, squeal, tell on, unmask 7 abandon, deceive, divulge, lay bare, let down, let slip, sell out, two-time, uncover, violate 8 blurt out, disclose, give away

Betrayer 5 Judas (Iscariot)

betroth 6 commit, engage, pledge 7 espouse, promise 8 affiance, contract

better 3 top 4 more 5 finer, outdo, raise 6 bigger, enrich, exceed, fitter, larger, longer, refine, uplift 7 advance, elevate, enhance, farther, forward, further, greater, improve, mending, promote, surpass, upgrade 8 heighten, improved, increase, outstrip, stronger, superior

better than average see **3** ace

between 4 amid **5** among, entre **6** amidst, atwixt, shared **7** betwixt, joining

beverage 3 ade, ale, cup, nog, pop, tea **4** beer, brew, cafe, dram, grog, milk, soda, soup, wine **5** broth, caffe, cider, cocoa, draft, drink, juice, julep, lager, latte, leban, punch, toddy, water **6** bishop, coffee, cordial, eggnog, liquid, liquor, potion **7** limeade, seltzer, spirits, wassail **8** aperitif, cocktail, espresso, expresso, highball, lemonade, libation, potation

Beverly Hillbillies, The
character: 3 Jed **6** Granny, Jethro, Milton **8** Ellie May
family: 8 Clampett

bevy 4 band, body, herd, host, pack **5** brood, covey, crowd, drove, flock, group, horde, party, shoal, swarm **6** clutch, flight, gaggle, school, throng **7** company, coterie

beware 4 mind **7** look out **8** take care, take heed

bewilder see **7 confuse**

bewitch see **5 charm**

bey, beg 4 lord **6** prince **8** governor

beyond 2 by **4** over, past **5** above, later, ultra **6** abroad, except, yonder **7** farther, further, outside, passing **8** superior

beyond question 4 sure **6** surely **7** certain, decided, settled

Bhutan
capital/largest city: 6 Thimbu **7** Thimphu
feature:
dragon people: 7 Drukpas

bias 4 bent, sway **5** angle, slant **7** bigotry, feeling, leaning **8** tendency

bibelot 5 curio **7** trinket **8** ornament

bible 5 guide **6** manual **8** handbook

Bible 6 Gospel **7** the Book **8** good book, Holy Writ
first five books called: 3 Law **5** Torah **10** Pentateuch

Bible scholar 7 biblist **9** biblicist

Bible version 5 Douay

7 Vulgate **8** Peshitta **9** Gutenberg, Jerusalem, King James

Biblical animal 7 unicorn

Biblical measure 3 cab, cor **4** epah, omet, reed, seah **5** cubit, epheh, homer **6** shekel

Biblical personage 9 patriarch

Biblical plant 4 Rose (of Sharon) **6** hyssop

bicker *see* **7 quarrel**

bicycle 4 bike, ride **5** cycle, moped

bid 3 ask, say, try **4** call, tell, wish **5** greet, offer, order **6** beckon, charge, demand, direct, effort, enjoin, tender **7** attempt, proffer, propose, request **8** call upon, offering, proposal

bide 4 stay, wait **5** abide, dwell, stand, tarry **6** endure, linger, remain, suffer **8** tolerate

bifurcate 4 fork **5** split **6** branch, divide **7** diverge **8** separate

big 3 top **4** head, high, huge, just, kind, main, vast **5** adult, ample, bulky, chief, great, grown, heavy, husky, large, major, noble, prime, vital **6** heroic, humane, mature **7** eminent, grown-up, haughty, hulking, immense, leading, liberal, mammoth, massive, notable, pompous, sizable, weighty **8** boastful, bragging, colossal, enormous, gigantic

Big Apple nickname of: 7 New York

Bigfoot 4 Yeti **9** Sasquatch

big guns 4 VIPs **5** brass **6** cannon **7** bigwigs, top dogs **8** big shots, ordnance **9** artillery **14** heavy artillery, high muck-a-mucks **15** important people

bighearted 6 lavish **7** liberal **8** generous, handsome, princely, prodigal

bight 3 bay **4** bend, cave, road

bigotry 4 bias **6** racism

big shot 3 VIP **4** name **5** mogul, nabob, wheel **6** big gun, bigwig, fat cat, tycoon **7** big deal, magnate, notable **8** somebody

bigwig 3 VIP **7** big shot, notable

bikini 8 two-piece
   top: 3 bra
   bottom 5 thong
   topless: 8 monokini
   type: 6 string

Bikini 5 atoll

bile 4 gall, rage **5** anger, venom, wrath **6** choler, spleen

bilious 4 sick **5** angry, cross, huffy, nasty, testy **6** crabby, cranky, grumpy, queasy, sickly, touchy **7** grouchy, peevish **8** bile-like, greenish, nauseous, petulant, snappish

bilk *see* **7 deceive**

bill 3 act, fee, law **4** card, chit, list **5** tally **6** agenda, charge, decree, docket, poster, roster, ticket **7** account, charges, invoice, program, statute **8** banknote, proposal, register

billfold 6 wallet

billow 4 roll, wave **5** belly, cloud, crest, surge, swell **6** puff up **7** balloon, breaker

bin 3 box **4** cart, crib, silo **5** crate, frame, hatch **6** barrel, basket, bunker, hamper, holder, trough, vessel

binate 4 dual **6** double **7** coupled, two fold

bind 3 rim, tie **4** edge, gird, glue, join, lash, rope, trim, wrap **5** affix, chafe, cover, strap, tie up, truss **6** attach, compel, fasten, fringe, oblige, secure, swathe **7** bandage, confine, require **8** encumber, obligate

binder 4 glue, roux **5** paste **6** cement **8** notebook

binge 3 jag **4** bust, orgy, tear, toot **5** blast, drunk, fling, revel, spree **6** bender **7** carouse

biography 3 bio **4** life, vita **6** memoir **7** account, history

biology
   branch: 6 botany **7** zoology

birch 6 Betula
   varieties: 3 Low, Red **4** Fire, Gray **5** Black, Canoe, Dwarf, Paper, River, Swamp, Sweet, Water, White **6** Cherry,

Yellow **7** Monarch **8** Mahogany, Old-field

bird

anatomy: 3 bec, neb, nib **4** beak, bill, cere, crop, lora, lore, mala, nape, rump, tail, tuft, wing **5** alula, crest, crown, flank, larum, lorum, pilea, rosta **6** breast, gullet, pecten, pileum, pinion, syrinx, tarsus **7** ambiens, crissum, gizzard, rostrum **8** gigerium, pectines, scapular

aquatic/water: 3 auk, cob, ern, mew **4** cobb, coot, duck, erne, gony, gull, ibis, loon, rail, shag, skua, sora, swan, teal, tern **5** booby, cahow, crane, diver, goose, grebe, heron, murre, ousel, rotch, snipe, solan, stilt, stork **6** avocet, curlew, cygnet, dipper, fulmar, gannet, godwit, hagdon, jabiru, jacana, osprey, petrel, plover, puffin, rotche, scoter, wigeon **7** anhinga, bidcock, bittern, bustard, dovekey, dovekie, finfoot, mallard, moorhen, pelican, penguin, seriema, skimmer, widgeon **8** alcatras, baldpate, dabchick, flamingo, murrelet, umbrette

bird cage/home: 4 cote, mews, nest **5** roost **6** aviary, volary, volery **7** rookery

bird of ill-omen: 5 raven

bird of peace: 4 dove

bird of prey: 3 owl **4** gled, hawk, kite **5** buteo, eagle, glead, glede, harpy, saker **6** condor, elanet, elenet, falcon, musket, osprey, raptor **7** buzzard, goshawk, harrier, kestrel, stooper, vulture **8** caracara

bird of wonder/rebirth: 7 phoenix

carrion-eater: 4 aura **5** urubu **6** condor **7** buzzard, vulture

class: 4 Aves

combining form: 3 avi **4** orni **5** ornis **6** ornith **7** ornitho **8** ornithes

crow family: 3 daw, jay, kae **4** crow, rook **5** crake, raven **6** chough, corbie, magpie **7** corvine, jackdaw

duck family: 4 clee, coot,

lory, smew, teal, wood **5** eider, goose **6** scoter **7** gadwall, mallard, Muscovy, pintail, pochard **8** baldpate, redshank, shoveler

extinct: 3 auk, jib, moa **4** dodo, jibi, mamo **5** didus **8** Diatryma

flightless: 3 emu, ihi, moa **4** dodo, gorb, kagu, kiwi, rhea, weka **5** nandu **6** callow, kakapo, moorup, ratite, takahe **7** apteryx, horling, ostrich, peacock, penguin, roatelo **8** notornis

game: 4 duck, guan, rail, sora, teal **5** brant, goose, quail, snipe **6** chukar, colima, grouse, pigeon, plover, turkey **7** bustard, chicken, flapper, gadwall, mallard, pintail, prairie, widgeon **8** baldpate, bobwhite, moorfowl, pheasant, shoveler, tragopan, wildfowl, woodcock

group of birds: 3 nye **4** bank, bevy, cast, nide, sord **5** aerie, brood, covey, drove, flock, plump **6** covert, flight, gaggle, litter, spring

largest: 7 ostrich

legendary: 3 roc **6** simurg **7** phoenix, simurgh

loss of feathers: 7 molting

nocturnal: 3 owl **5** cahow, owlet, potoo **7** bullbat, dorhawk **8** guacharo, nightjar

pet: 4 myna **5** mynah **6** canary, parrot, pigeon **8** cockatoo, lovebird, parakeet

plumage: 8 ptilosis

poultry: 3 hen **4** duck **5** goose **6** pigeon, turkey **7** chicken, rooster **8** pheasant

talking: 4 myna **5** mynah **6** parrot

wingless: 4 kiwi, weka **7** apteryx

young: 4 eyas, gull **5** chick, piper, poult, squab **6** gorlin, pullus **7** flapper, nestler **8** birdikin, nestling

birth 5 blood, start, stock **6** family, origin, source, strain **7** bearing, descent, genesis, lineage **8** ancestry, breeding, delivery

Birth of a Nation, The
    director: 8 (D W) Griffith

birthstones
January: **6** garnet
February: **8** amethyst
March: **6** jasper
April: **7** diamond **8** sapphire
May: **5** agate **7** emerald
June: **5** pearl **7** emerald **9** moonstone
July: **4** onyx, ruby **8** star ruby
August: **7** peridot **8** sardonyx **9** carnelian
September: **8** sapphire
October: **4** opal **5** beryl
November: **5** topaz
December: **4** ruby **6** zircon **9** turquoise

biscuit **3** bun **4** cake, roll **5** cooky, scone, wafer **6** bisque, cookie, muffin, parking, simnel **7** cracker, dogbone **8** hardtack, zwieback

bisect **5** cross, split **8** cut in two

bishop **4** abba, pope **5** punch **6** cleric, despot, priest **7** pontiff, prelate, primate **8** overseer
of Rome: **4** pope
district: **7** diocese
headdress: **5** miter, mitre

bison **4** urus **6** wild ox, wisent **7** aurochs, buffalo

bistro **3** bar **4** cafe **6** tavern **7** cabaret

bit **3** dab **4** chip, drop, iota, mite, snip, whit **5** crumb, grain, pinch, scrap, shred, speck, spell, trace **6** dollop, moment, morsel, paring, trifle **7** droplet, granule, shaving, smidgen **8** fragment, particle
type: **5** auger, drill **6** gimlet, wimble **7** bradawl

bitch **3** nag **5** botch, brood, cheat, fault, shrew, spoil, witch, whine **6** kvetch, virago **7** blunder, bungle, grouse **8** complain, harridan

bite **3** bit, dab, dig, nip **4** gnaw, grip, snip **5** champ, crumb, gnash, prick, scrap, shred, smart, speck, sting, taste **6** morsel, nibble, pierce **8** mouthful, stinging

bit player **5** extra **6** walk on

bitter **4** acid, mean, sour, tart **5** acrid, angry, cruel, harsh, sharp **6** biting, morose, severe, sullen **7** acerbic, caustic, crabbed, painful **8** grievous, piercing, scornful, smarting, spiteful, stinging, wretched

bivalve 4 clam **5** pinna **6** cockle, mussel, mollusk, scallop **8** mollusca

bivouac 4 camp **5** tents

bizarre *see* **5 weird**

blabber 3 gab, gas, yak **4** blab, bull **5** prate **6** babble, drivel, gabble, gibber, gossip, jabber **7** blather, chatter, palaver, prattle, twaddle **8** blah-blah, chitchat

black, Black 3 bad, dim, jet **4** dark, evil, grim, inky **5** angry, ebony, murky, Negro, raven, sable **6** dismal, gloomy, somber, sullen, wicked **7** colored, furious, hostile, stygian, sunless, swarthy **8** moonless

blackball 3 ban, bar, cut **4** snub **5** debar **6** banish, outlaw, reject **7** boycott, exclude, keep out, shut out **8** pass over, turndown

blackberry 5 Rubus
　variety: 4 Sand **5** Swamp **7** Cut-leaf, Pacific, Running, Sow-teat

blackbird 3 ani **4** crow, rook **5** raven, slave **6** thrush **7** cowbird, grackle, redwing **8** song bird

blacken *see* **5 libel**

blackhearted 4 base, vile **6** sinful, wicked **7** ignoble

blacklist 3 ban, bar **4** shun **5** debar **6** reject **7** exclude, lock out, shut out **8** preclude

black magic 7 sorcery

blackmail 5 force **6** coerce, extort, payoff **7** squeeze, tribute **8** threaten

Black Prince 6 Edward (Prince of Wales)
　battles: 5 Crecy **8** Poitiers

bladder 3 bag, sac **4** cyst **5** pouch **7** blister, pustule, saccule, utricle

blade 4 epee, leaf **5** frond, knife, razor, saber, sword **6** cutter, needle, switch **7** scalpel

blah 4 bosh, dull, flat, guff, so-so **5** bland, ho-hum, hooey, vapid **6** boring, bunkum, dreary, hot air, humbug **7** blather, eyewash, humdrum, nothing, tedious, twaddle

8 claptrap, lifeless, listless, nonsense

blame **4** onus **5** fault, guilt **6** accuse, burden, rebuke **7** censure, condemn, reprove **8** reproach

blanch **4** fade **6** bleach, whiten **7** lighten

bland **4** blah, calm, dull, even, flat, mild **5** balmy, quiet, vapid **6** benign, smooth **7** calming, humdrum, nothing, prosaic, tedious **8** moderate, peaceful, soothing, tiresome, tranquil

blandish *see* **6 cajole**

blank **3** gap **4** dull, idle, void **5** clean, clear, empty, inane, plain, space **6** futile, hollow, unused, vacant, vacuum, wasted **7** useless, vacancy, vacuous **8** unmarked

blanket **4** coat, film **5** cloak, cover, quilt, throw **6** afghan, carpet, mantle, veneer **7** coating, overlay **8** covering, coverlet

blare **4** honk, peal, roar **5** blast **6** bellow, scream **7** resound, trumpet

blarney **4** fibs, line **5** pitch, spiel **6** hot air **7** coaxing, fawning, snow job, stories **8** cajolery, flattery

blasphemous **7** godless, impious, profane, ungodly

blasphemy **7** cursing, impiety **8** swearing

blast **4** bomb, boom, bore, gale, gust, honk, peal, roar, rush, toot **5** blare, bleat, burst, level, shell, surge **6** bellow, blow up, report **7** explode, torpedo **8** eruption

blasting material **3** TNT **8** dynamite

blatant *see* **7 obvious**

blather **4** stir **7** chatter, prattle **8** nonsense

blaze **3** ray **4** beam, burn, fire, glow, rush **5** blast, burst, flame, flare, flash, glare, gleam, shine **6** flames **7** glisten, glitter, shimmer, torrent **8** eruption, outbreak, outburst, radiance

blazer **4** coat **6** jacket

blazon **5** blare, boast **7** trumpet **8** proclaim

bleach **4** fade **6** blanch, whiten **7** lighten, wash out

bleak 3 icy, raw **4** bare, cold, grim **5** chill **6** barren, biting, bitter, dismal, dreary, frosty, gloomy, somber, wintry **7** nipping **8** desolate

Bleak House author: 7 (Charles) Dickens

bleat 3 baa, cry, maa **5** whine **7** whimper

bleb 6 bubble **7** blister

bleed 3 run, tap **4** leak, soak **5** drain, valve **6** fleece, suffer **7** diffuse, extract

blemish 3 mar, zit **4** blot, blur, flaw, mark, spot **5** spoil, stain, sully, taint **6** blotch, defect, smirch, smudge **7** tarnish

blend 3 mix **4** fuse **5** merge, unite **6** fusion, go well, merger, mingle **7** amalgam, combine, mixture **8** coalesce, compound

bless 4 give **5** endow, favor, grace, guard, honor **6** anoint, bestow, hallow, oblige, ordain **7** baptize, benefit, protect, support **8** dedicate, sanctify

blight 3 pox, rot **4** harm, kill, ruin, rust **5** blast, crush, curse, decay, smash, spoil, wreck **6** cancer, canker, dry rot, fungus, injure, mildew, plague, thwart, wither **7** cripple, destroy, scourge, shrivel **8** demolish

blind 4 dull, ruse **5** cover, dodge, front, shade **6** hidden, insane, obtuse, screen **7** obscure, pretext, unaware **8** disguise, heedless, ignorant, mindless, unseeing

blink 4 wink **5** flash, shine, waver **6** falter, flinch, squint **7** flicker, glimmer, shimmer, sparkle, twinkle

blintz, blintze 4 blin **5** crepe **6** blints **7** pancake

blip 3 dot, tap **4** spot **5** bleep, image **6** censor **7** replace

bliss 3 joy **4** glee **6** heaven, luxury **7** delight, ecstasy, rapture **8** gladness, paradise

blithe 3 gay **4** airy, glad **5** blind, happy, jolly, merry, sunny **6** casual, cheery, jaunty, jovial, joyous, lively **7** gleeful, radiant

8 carefree, careless, cheerful, debonair, exaltant, heedless, mirthful, uncaring

blizzard 4 blow, gale **5** blast **6** flurry, squall **7** tempest **8** snowfall

bloat *see* **5 swell**

blob 3 dab **4** daub, drop, glob, mass **7** globule, splotch

bloc 4 body, ring, wing **5** cabal, group, union **6** clique **7** combine, faction **8** alliance

block 3 bar, jam **4** cube, form, halt, mold **5** brick, check, choke, shape **6** hinder, impede, re-form, square, stop up, thwart **7** barrier, prevent, reshape **8** blockade, blockage, obstacle, obstruct

blockhead *see* **5 idiot**

blond, blonde 4 fair, gold, pale **5** light **6** flaxen, golden, yellow **8** light tan

Blondie
  creator: 5 (Chic) Young
  character:
    family: 8 Bumstead
    husband: 7 Dagwood
    children: 4 Baby

    (Dumpling) **6** Cookie **9** Alexander
  dog: 5 Daisy

blood 4 gore **5** birth, stock **6** family, source, spirit, temper **7** descent, lineage, passion **8** ancestry, heritage, vitality

bloodline 6 family **8** ancestry, pedigree

bloodshed 4 gore **6** murder, pogrom **7** carnage, killing, slaying **8** butchery, massacre

bloodstone
  month: 5 March

blood system
  part: 5 blood, liver **6** spleen

bloodthirsty *see* **6 savage**

blood vessel 4 vein **5** aorta **6** artery **7** carotid
  prefix: 5 angio

bloom *see* **7 blossom**

bloomers 8 knickers, trousers

blooper *see* **7 mistake**

blossom 4 grow **5** bloom **6** flower, thrive **7** burgeon, develop **8** flourish, progress

blot, blotch 3 dry **4** flaw,

mark, spot **5** smear, stain, taint **6** absorb, blotch, remove, soak up, stigma, take up **7** bad mark, blemish, splotch **8** besmirch

blouse 4 coat **5** drape, tunic, shirt, smock **6** camise, billow **7** blouson **8** casaquin

blow 3 box, hit, jab, pop **4** bang, bash, belt, cuff, gale, gust, honk, jolt, play, puff, sock, toot, wind **5** blast, burst, clout, crack, knock, punch, shock, smack, sound, storm, thump, upset, whack **6** exhale, rebuff, squall, wallop **7** breathe, explode, tempest, tragedy, whistle **8** calamity, disaster, expel air, reversal

blowhard 6 gascon **7** boaster, bragger, egotist **8** braggart

blubber 3 cry, fat, sob **4** bawl, flab, wail, weep **6** boohoo

bludgeon 3 bat, hit **4** club **5** billy, clout, stick **6** cudgel **7** clobber

blue 3 low, sad **4** aqua, down, navy **5** azure **6** bluish, cobalt, gloomy, indigo, morose **7** doleful **8** cerulean, dejected, downcast, sapphire

blue-blooded 5 noble, regal, royal **6** titled **7** courtly **8** highbred, wellborn

bluegrass 3 Poa

blue-pencil 3 cut **4** edit, trim **6** censor, cut out, delete, digest, reduce **7** abridge, shorten **8** condense, pare down

blueprint 4 plan **5** chart **6** design, scheme **7** diagram

blues 5 dumps **8** doldrums

bluff *see* **4 hoax**

blunder *see* **7 mistake**

blunt 4 curt, dull, numb, open **5** frank, rough, thick **6** abrupt, benumb, candid, deaden, dulled, soften, weaken **7** brusque, lighten, stupefy **8** edgeless, explicit, mitigate, moderate, tactless

blur 3 dim, fog, run **4** blot, haze, veil **5** bedim, befog, cloud, smear **6** blotch, darken, smudge, spread **7** becloud, obscure, splotch

blurb 2 ad **4** rave, spot **5** brief

blurt out

blurt out **4** blab, sing **7** confess, divulge, let slip **8** give away

blush **5** color, flush **6** redden **7** grow red, turn red **8** rosy tint

bluster **4** brag, crow, rant **5** bluff, boast, bully, gloat, noise, storm **7** bombast, bravado, crowing, swagger

boar
group of: **7** sounder

board **3** bed **4** deal, feed, food, slat **5** enter, get on, house, lodge, meals, panel, plank, put up **6** batten, billet, embark, go onto **7** council, quarter **8** tribunal

board game **4** Clue, Life, ludo **5** chess **7** Othello **8** checkers, cribbage, dominoes, draughts, fanorona, Monopoly, Scrabble
Indian: **7** pachisi **8** parchesi, shatranj
Japanese: **2** Go **3** I-go **5** Shogi
Chinese: **6** Ma-jong, wei-ch'i **7** Mah-jong, Ma-jongg **8** Mah-jongg

boast *see* **4 brag**

boat **4** ship **5** craft **6** vessel

bob **3** cut, hop, nod **4** clip, crop, dock, duck, leap, trim **5** dance, shear **6** bounce **7** shorten

bobcat **3** cat **4** lynx **7** wildcat

bode **4** omen **5** augur **6** herald **7** point to, portend, predict, presage, signify **8** forecast, foretell, precurse

bodice **3** top **5** stays, waist **6** bolero, corset, girdle **7** corsage **8** camisole

body **3** mob **4** bloc, bulk, form, mass **5** being, build, force, frame, group, shape, stiff, thing, torso, trunk **6** corpse, corpus, figure, league, person, throng **7** cadaver, carcass, combine, council, faction, remains, society **8** assembly, cohesion, congress, main part, physique

Boer, Boor **6** farmer **9** Afrikaner
ancestry: **5** Dutch

bog **3** fen **4** mire, sink **5** marsh, swamp **6** morass **7** be stuck **8** quagmire, wetlands

Bogart, Humphrey
   nickname: 5 Bogie
   wife: 6 (Lauren) Bacall

bogey
   term in: 4 golf

boggle 3 shy **4** balk, muff **5**
   botch, demure, hover,
   waver **6** bungle, shrink,
   wobble **7** blunder, stumble
   8 flounder, frighten,
   hesitate, hold back

Bogota
   capital of: 8 Colombia

bogus *see* **4 fake**

Boheme, La
   opera by: 7 Puccini

bohemian, Bohemian 6
   hippie **7** beatnik

boil 4 brew, burn, foam,
   fume, rage, rant, rave,
   sore, stew, toss **5** chafe,
   churn, froth, storm **6**
   bubble, fester, quiver,
   seethe, simmer, well up

boisterous 4 loud, wild **5**
   noisy, rowdy **6** unruly

bold 3 hot **4** loud, rude **5**
   brash, brave, fiery, fresh,
   saucy, vivid **6** brazen,
   cheeky, daring, flashy,
   heroic **7** forward **8**
   fearless, intrepid, unafraid,
   valorous

Bolivia
   capital:
      administrative: 5 La
         Paz
      legal: 5 Sucre
   largest city: 5 La Paz
   lake: 5 Poopo **8** Titicaca
   mountain: 5 Andes
   highest point: 8
      Ancohuma
   feature:
      animal: 5 llama **6**
         alpaca, vicuna
      boat: 5 balsa

bolster *see* **6 uphold**

bolt 3 bar, fly, peg, pin,
   rod, run **4** dart, dash, flee,
   gulp, jump, leap, lock,
   roll, rush, tear, wolf **5**
   bound, brand, catch,
   dowel, flash, hurry, latch,
   rivet, scoot, shaft, speed **6**
   fasten, gobble, hasten,
   hurtle, length, secure,
   spring, sprint, stroke

bomb 3 dud, egg **4** bust,
   fail, flop, mine **5** lemon **7**
   bombard, grenade, failure,
   washout

bombard *see* **5 hound**

bombast 3 pad **4** puff, rant
   6 cotton **7** bluster, fustian,
   palaver **8** boasting,

flummery, rhapsody, tall talk, verbiage

bona fide 4 real, true **5** legal **6** actual, honest, lawful **7** genuine, sincere

bonanza 8 gold mine, windfall

Bonanza
  family: 10 Cartwright
  cast: 6 (Lorne) Greene, (Michael) Landon **7** (Dan) Blocker, (Pernell) Roberts
  ranch: 9 Ponderosa

bonbon 5 candy, sweet **7** fondant

bond, bonds 3 tie **4** cord, knot, link, rope **5** irons, scrip, union **6** chains, pledge **7** compact, fetters, promise **8** affinity, bindings, manacles, security, shackles

Bond, James
  actor: 5 (Daniel) Craig, (Roger) Moore **6** (Timothy) Dalton **7** (Pierce) Brosnan, (Sean) Connery, (George) Lazenby, (Peter) Sellers
  author: 7 (Ian) Fleming
  employer: 3 MI-6
  foe: 7 Blofeld, SPECTRE

bone
  comprise: 8 skeleton
  contain: 6 marrow
  fitted together by: 5 joint
  held by: 8 ligament
  pulled by: 6 muscle
  specific: 3 rib **4** ulna **5** femur, skull, tibia **6** carpal, fibula, pelvis, radius, sacrum, tarsal **7** humerus, patella, scapula, sternum **8** clavicle, vertebra

bone chilling 3 icy **4** cold **5** harsh, sharp **6** arctic, biting, bitter, frigid **7** cutting, glacial

bonehead *see* **5** idiot

boneyard 4 dump **7** ossuary **8** Boot Hill, cemetery, junkyard

bonjour 5 hello **7** good day

bon mot 4 quip **7** epigram **9** witticism

Bonn
  former capital of: 7 (West) Germany

bonne amie 5 lover **6** friend

bonnet 3 cap, hat **4** cowl, hood, sail **5** cover, toque **7** chapeau **8** headgear

Bonnie and Clyde
  director: 4 (Arthur) Penn

cast: 6 (Warren) Beatty **7** (Faye) Dunaway, (Gene) Hackman, (Michael) Pollard

bonny *see* **6 comely**

bonus 4 gift **5** prize **6** bounty, reward **7** benefit, premium **8** dividend, gratuity

bon vivant 7 epicure, gourmet **8** gourmand, sybarite

bony 4 lean **5** gaunt, lanky, spare **6** skinny **7** angular

boo 3 pan **4** hiss **5** taunt **6** deride, heckle, revile **7** catcall **8** ridicule

boo-boo 4 goof, slip **5** boner, error **6** slip-up **7** blunder, mistake

boobtube 2 TV **3** box **5** telly **8** idiot box

boohoo 3 cry, sob **4** bawl, weep **7** blubber

book 4 bill, file, list, note, opus, post, tome **5** album, enter, index, slate **6** accuse, charge, engage, enroll, indict, insert, line up, record, tablet, volume **7** catalog, procure, program, put down, reserve **8** mark down, notebook, register, schedule, treatise

bookish *see* **8 academic**

booklet 5 folio **7** leaflet, program **8** brochure, circular, pamphlet

boom 3 bar **4** bang, beam, gain, grow, push, roar, spar **5** blast, shaft, spurt **6** growth, thrive **7** advance, prosper, thunder, upsurge **8** flourish, increase

boomerang 5 kalie, kiley, kylie, wango **6** atlatl, recoil **7** rebound, womerah, woomera **8** backfire, ricochet, trombush

boon 3 fun, gay **4** gift **5** favor, jolly, merry **6** kindly **7** benefit, bequest **8** blessing, donation, offering, pleasant

boondocks 4 bush, veld **6** Podunk, sticks **7** country, outback **8** frontier

boor 3 oaf **4** hick, lout, rube **5** brute, churl, yokel **6** rustic **7** bumpkin, hayseed, peasant

boost 4 hike, laud, lift, plug, push, rise **5** heave,

hoist, pitch, raise **6**
expand, foster, growth,
pickup, praise, upturn,
urge on **7** acclaim,
advance, develop, elevate,
further, support, sustain,
upsurge, upswing **8**
addition, increase

booth 3 pen **4** coop, nook,
tent **5** hutch, stall, stand,
table **7** counter **9**
cubbyhole, enclosure **11**
compartment

bootleg 5 hooch **7** illegal,
illicit **8** unlawful

bootlick 4 fawn **5** toady **6**
cringe, grovel **7** flatter,
truckle

bootmaker 7 cobbler

booty 4 gain, loot **5** prize **6**
boodle, spoils **7** pillage,
plunder, takings **8**
pickings, winnings

booze 4 bout, soak **5** drink,
hooch, spree **6** guzzle,
liquor, tipple **7** alcohol,
spirits, swizzle **8** cocktail
type: 3 gin, rum, rye **4**
beer, wine **5** vodka **6**
scotch **7** bourbon,
whiskey

boozer 3 sot **4** lush **5**
drunk, souse, toper **7**
tippler **8** drunkard

bordello, bordel 4 stew **5**
house **6** bagnio **7** brothel
8 cathouse

border 3 hem, rim **4** abut,
bind, brim, curb, edge,
join, line, pale, trim **5**
brink, flank, frame, limit,
skirt, touch, verge **6**
adjoin, fringe, margin **8**
be next to, boundary,
frontier, outskirt

bore 4 drag, drip, sink, tire
5 drill, drive, weary **6**
burrow, pierce, tunnel **7**
caliber, exhaust, fatigue,
wear out **8** gouge out

boredom 5 ennui **6** tedium
8 doldrums, dullness,
monotony

**Boris Godunov
author: 7** Pushkin

born 6 innate **7** natural

borne 6 afloat, braved **7**
carried, endured

**Borneo
other name: 10**
Kalimantan
**division of island:
independent: 6** Brunei
Malaysian state: 5
Sabah **7** Sarawak
part of Indonesia: 10
Kalimantan

boron
  compound: 5 borax

borough 4 burg, town **5** borgo, shire **6** county, parish **7** village **8** district, precinct, province, township

borrow 3 get, use **4** copy, take **5** filch, steal, usurp **6** obtain, pilfer, pirate **7** acquire

bosky 5 bushy, drunk, shaded, tipsy, treed **6** wooded

Bosnia and Herzegovina
  capital/largest city: 8 Sarajevo
  river: 4 Sava **5** Bosna, Drina
  sea: 8 Adriatic
  religion: 5 Islam **8** Orthodox

bosom 4 bust, core, dear, soul **5** chest, close, heart, midst **6** breast, center, spirit **7** beloved, nucleus

bosom buddy 4 chum **5** crony **6** cohort **7** best pal, comrade **8** alter ego, intimate, sidekick

boss 4 head, push **5** chief, order **6** leader, master **7** command, foreman, manager **8** employer

Boston
  airport: 5 Logan
  baseball team: 6 Red Sox
  basketball team: 7 Celtics
  dish: 10 baked beans
  hockey team: 6 Bruins
  project: 6 Big Dig
  river: 7 Charles

botch *see* **6 fumble**

bother *see* **8 irritate**

Botswana
  capital/largest city: 8 Gaborone
  river: 7 Limpopo **8** Okovango
  physical feature:
    desert: 8 Kalahari
    swamp: 8 Okovango

bottle 3 jar **4** vial **5** flask, phial **6** carafe, flagon, vessel **7** canteen

bottleneck *see* **4 clog**

bottom 3 can **4** base, core, foot, gist, root, rump, seat, sole **5** basis, belly, cause, fanny, heart, lower **6** depths, ground, lowest, origin, source **7** deepest, essence **8** backside, buttocks, pedestal

boudoir 7 bedroom

bough 4 limb **6** branch

boulder, bowlder 3 nob **4**

crag, knob, rock **5** block, stone **6** gibber **8** megalith

boulevard 6 avenue **7** parkway

bounce 3 bob, hop, pep **4** bump, life **5** bound, thump, verve, vigor **6** energy, jounce, spirit **7** rebound **8** dynamism, ricochet, vivacity

bound 3 bob, orb, rim **4** area, edge, jump, leap, line, mark, pale, romp, sure, tied **5** dance, fated, hedge, limit, orbit, range, realm, vault **6** border, bounce, prance, spring, tied up **7** certain, confine, flounce, going to, in bonds, limited, obliged, secured, trussed

boundary 3 rim **4** edge, line, pale **6** border, margin **8** frontier, landmark

bounty 3 aid **4** gift, help **5** bonus, favor, grant **6** giving, reward **7** charity, present **8** bestowal, donation, gratuity

bouquet 4 odor **5** aroma, scent, spray **7** essence, garland, nosegay, perfume

bourbon
variety of: 7 whiskey

origin: 7 America
ingredient: 4 corn

bourgeois 6 square **7** Babbitt, burgher **8** commoner, ordinary

bout 4 fray, term, tilt, turn **5** brush, clash, cycle, fight, match, set-to, siege, spell, spree **6** affair, battle, course, period, series **7** contest, go-round, scuffle, session, tourney **8** conflict, interval, skirmish, struggle

boutonniere 4 posy **7** nosegay

bow 3 arc **4** bend, knot, prow, stem **5** agree, curve, defer, front, stoop, yield **6** archer, comply, curtsy, give in, kowtow, relent, salaam, submit, weapon **7** concede, succumb, crescent

Bow, Clara
nickname: 6 It Girl

bowdlerize 6 censor

bowels 3 gut, pit **4** core, guts, womb **5** abyss, belly, bosom, heart, midst **6** depths, hollow, vitals **7** innards, insides, stomach, viscera **8** entrails, recesses

bowl 4 boat **5** arena, basin

6 cavity, hollow, tureen, valley, vessel **7** helping, portion, stadium

bowling
  variation: 7 ten pins **8** duckpins, fivepins **10** candlepins

box 3 bat, hit, rap **4** belt, cuff, slap, spar **5** booth, caddy, chest, crate, fight, punch, stall, whack **6** buffet, carton, coffer, strike, thwack **8** thumping

boxer 3 Ali (Muhammad) **4** Baer (Max), Ross (Barney) **5** Lewis (Lennox), Louis (Joe), Moore (Archie), Tyson (Mike) **6** Holmes (Larry), Tunney (Gene) **7** Corbett (James), Dempsey (Jack), Foreman (George), Frazier (Joe), Johnson (Jack), Leonard (Benny), Leonard (Sugar Ray) **8** Marciano (Rocky), Robinson (Sugar Ray), Sullivan (John) **9** Holyfield (Evander)

boy 3 lad **5** youth **8** man child
  French: 6 garcon

boycott 5 spurn **6** reject **7** exclude **8** spurning

boyfriend *see* **6 suitor**

Boy Wonder
  nickname of: 5 Robin **6** Mel Ott

brace 3 duo **4** pair, prop, stay **5** shore, strut, truss **6** couple, hold up, prop up, steady **7** bolster, bracket, fortify, prepare, support

bracelet 6 armlet, bangle

bracket 4 prop, rank, stay **5** brace, class, group, range, shore, strut, truss **6** prop up, status **7** shore up, support **8** category, classify, division, grouping

brackish 4 salt **5** briny, salty **6** saline

bract 4 leaf

Brady Bunch, The
  character: 3 Jan **4** Greg, Mike **5** Alice, Bobby, Carol, Cindy, Peter **6** Marcia

brag 4 crow **5** boast, vaunt **7** big talk, crowing

braid 4 knit, lace **5** plait, ravel, twine, twist, weave **7** entwine, wreathe

brain
  part: 7 medulla **8** cerebrum

brainchild 8 creation

brainless *see* **6 stupid**

brainy 5 smart **6** bright, clever

brainy group 5 Mensa

brake 4 curb, drag, halt, rein, slow, stay, stop **5** check **6** arrest **7** control

bramble 4 bush, vine **5** rough, shrub **7** thicket

branch 3 arm, leg **4** fork, limb, part, wing **5** bough, prong, spray **6** agency, bureau, divide, feeder, member, office, ramify **7** chapter, diverge, section, segment **8** division

brand 4 blot, kind, make, mark, sear, sign, slur, sort, spot, type **5** class, grade, label, smear, stain, stamp, taint **6** burn in, emblem, smirch, stigma **7** blemish, quality, variety **8** besmirch, disgrace

brandish 4 wave **5** shake, swing, wield **6** flaunt, waggle **7** display, exhibit, show off **8** flourish

brand new 4 mint **5** fresh, young **6** unused

brandy 6 cognac, grappa, kahlua, kirsch, metaxa **8** Armagnac, Calvados, Tia Maria

brash *see* **6 brazen**

Brasilia
capital of: 6 Brazil

brass 4 gall, sand, VIPs **5** cheek, nerve **8** audacity, boldness, chutzpah, officers, temerity

brass instrument 4 tuba **5** bugle **6** cornet **7** trumpet **8** trombone

brass tacks 4 crux, meat **7** details

brat 3 imp **4** chit **5** whelp **6** hoyden, rascal

Brauhaus 6 tavern **7** brewery

bravado *see* **7 bombast**

brave *see* **7 valiant**

brave deed 4 feat, gest **5** geste **7** exploit

Brave New World
author: 6 (Aldous) Huxley

brawl *see* **6 battle**

brawny 5 burly, husky **6** mighty, robust, strong **8** muscular, powerful

brazen 4 bold, open **5** brash, saucy **6** brassy, cheeky **7** forward

8 arrogant, immodest, impudent, insolent

Brazil
 capital: 8 Brasilia
 largest city: 8 Sao Paolo
 others: 3 Rio (de Janeiro)
 highest point: 7 Neblina
 river: 5 Negro **6** Amazon, Iguacu, Parana
 physical feature:
  waterfall: 6 Guaira, Iguacu **7** Iguassu
  beach: 7 Ipanema **10** Copacabana
 feature:
  dance: 5 samba **9** bossa nova
  fish: 7 piranha
  slum: 6 favela
 food:
  dried salted beef: 7 charque
  tea: 4 mate

Brazzaville
 capital of: 5 Congo

breach 3 gap **4** gash, hole, rent, rift, slit **5** break, chink, cleft, crack, split **7** crevice, failure, fissure, neglect, opening, rupture **8** defiance, trespass

bread 3 rye **4** food, pita **5** bucks, dough, money, wheat, white **6** staple

bread and butter 3 job **6** career, living **7** calling **8** business, vocation

breadbasket 3 gut **5** belly, tummy **6** paunch **7** abdomen, labonza, midriff, Midwest, stomach

breadth 4 area, size, span **5** range, reach, scope, width **6** extent, spread **7** compass, expanse, measure, stretch **8** latitude, wideness

break 3 cap, end, fly, gap, off, run, top **4** beat, bust, chip, dash, defy, flee, gash, halt, hole, rend, rent, rest, rift, rive, ruin, snap, stop, tame, tear, tell **5** crack, erupt, lapse, pause, sever **6** appear, better, breach, divide, escape, hiatus, lessen, recess, reveal, soften, subdue **7** control, cushion, destroy, disobey, fissure, opening, pull off, respite, run away, rupture, shatter, suspend **8** fracture, fragment, interval, separate

breakdown 6 mishap **7** crackup, decline, failure

8 analysis, collapse, disorder, division

breaker **4** cask, wave **6** comber **7** crusher

breakfront **5** hutch **7** cabinet **8** bookcase, cupboard

break-in **5** theft **7** robbery **8** burglary, stealing

breakneck **4** rash **5** risky **8** reckless, very fast

break of day **4** dawn **5** sunup **7** dawning, sunrise **8** daybreak

break the habit **4** kick, quit, stop **6** eschew, give up **8** renounce, withdraw

breakthrough **7** advance

breakup **5** split **7** crackup

breast **4** bust, core **5** bosom, chest, heart

breastwork **7** bastion, rampart **8** barbette

breath **4** wind **6** spirit

breathe **4** gasp, huff, pant, puff **5** utter **6** exhale, impart, inhale, murmur **7** respire, whisper

breathtaking **7** amazing, awesome **8** exciting

breech **4** rump, seat

6 behind **8** buttocks, haunches, hind part

breeches **5** pants **8** trousers

breed **4** bear, grow, kind, race, sire, sort, type **5** beget, cause, order, raise, spawn, stock **6** family, foster, strain **7** develop, nurture, produce, species, variety **8** generate, multiply

breeze **4** flit, pass, sail, snap, waft **5** coast, float, glide, sweep **6** zephyr

brew **3** ale **4** beer, boil, cook, form, make, plan, plot, soak, suds **5** begin, drink, hatch, ripen, start, steep, stout **6** cook up, devise, foment, gather, porter, scheme, seethe **7** arrange, brewski, concoct, ferment, mixture, prepare, produce, think up **8** beverage, contrive, initiate

bribe **3** sop **5** graft **6** buy off, grease, pay off, payola, suborn

bric-a-brac **7** baubles, gewgaws **8** bibelots, trinkets

bridal **7** nuptial, wedding **8** marriage

bridge 3 tie **4** band, bind, bond, link, span **5** cross, unify, union **7** catwalk, connect, liaison, viaduct **8** alliance, overpass, traverse

bridge
  derived from: 5 whist
  type: 7 auction **8** contract
  action: 3 bid **4** pass
  term: 4 slam **5** trump **6** double, renege, tenace

Bridgetown
  capital of: 8 Barbados

bridle *see* **6 muzzle**

brief 4 case **5** hasty, pithy, quick, short, swift, terse **6** advise, inform, precis, resume **7** capsule, compact, concise, defense, limited, prepare, summary **8** abstract, fill in on, fleeting, succinct

brier, briar 4 Rosa **5** Rubus, thorn **6** Smilax **7** bramble

brigade 4 crew, team, unit **5** corps, force, group, squad **6** legion, outfit **7** company

brigand *see* **5 thief**

bright 3 gay **4** glad, good, keen, rosy, sage, warm, wise **5** acute, alert, aware, grand, great, happy, jolly, merry, quick, sharp, smart, sunny, vivid **6** astute, blithe, brainy, clever, gifted, lively, shrewd **7** beaming, blazing, capable, glowing, hopeful, radiant, shining **8** cheerful, luminous, lustrous

brilliance, brilliancy *see* **7 radiant**

brim 3 fill, lip, rim **5** brink, flood, ledge, verge **6** border, fill up, margin, well up **8** overflow

brimless hat 3 cap **5** beret **6** beanie

bring 4 bear, make, take, tote **5** begin, carry, cause, fetch, force, start **6** convey, effect, induce **7** deliver, produce, usher in **8** generate, initiate, result in

bring down a peg 5 abase **6** humble **7** mortify

bring into line 5 adapt **6** adjust **7** conform, shape up

bring to light 6 expose, reveal, unveil **7** clarify, divulge, explain, uncover **8** disclose

bring to one's senses 3 jar **5** alarm, alert, shock

bring to terms 6 settle **7** mediate

brink 3 rim **4** bank, brim, edge **5** point, shore, skirt, verge **6** border, margin

briny 4 salt **5** salty **6** saline

brisk 4 busy, spry **5** alert, fresh, peppy, quick, swift **6** active, breezy, lively, snappy **7** bracing, chipper, dynamic, rousing **8** animated, bustling, spirited, stirring, vigorous

bristles 5 barbs, setae **6** quills **7** stubble **8** prickles, whiskers

British 6 Breton, Briton **7** English **8** Brittany

British Columbia
    abbreviation: 2 BC
    bordered by: 5 Idaho, Yukon **6** Alaska **7** Alberta, Montana
    Indian: 5 Haida **6** Nootka, Salish **8** Kwakiutl
    mountain: 5 Coast, Rocky **7** Cascade **8** Columbia
    river: 6 Fraser

British Guiana *see* **6 Guyana**

British Honduras *see* **6 Belize**

British Mythology
    god of rebirth/afterlife: 4 Gwyn
    chief of gods: 5 Woden
    island of paradise: 6 Avalon

Briton 4 Celt **6** Celtic **7** British

Brittany
    coast: 5 Armor
    country: 6 France
    inhabitant: 5 Celts **6** French, Romans
    language: 6 Breton

brittle 7 crumbly, fragile, friable

broach *see* **7 mention**

broad 4 full, open, wide **5** ample, clear, large, plain, rangy, roomy, thick **7** general, immense, obvious, sizable **8** extended, spacious, sweeping

broadcast 4 beam, show, talk **5** cable, radio, relay **7** program, send out **8** televise, transmit

broad-minded 7 liberal **8** amenable, catholic, flexible, tolerant, unbiased

Brobdingnagian 4 huge

5 giant **7** immense, mammoth **8** colossal, enormous, gigantic

broccoli
   variety: 6 Turnip **7** Italian

brochure 5 flier **6** folder **7** booklet, leaflet **8** circular, handbill, pamphlet

broil 3 fry **4** bake, burn, cook, sear **5** parch, roast, toast **6** scorch **7** blister

broke *see* **8 bankrupt**

broken 4 torn **5** rough, split, tamed **6** ruined, uneven **7** crushed, damaged **8** bankrupt, in pieces, ruptured

broken-down 6 beat-up, ruined **7** rickety, worn-out **8** battered, decrepit

broken-hearted 3 sad **6** gloomy, woeful **7** crushed, doleful, forlorn, unhappy **8** dejected, downcast, mournful

bromide 6 cliche **8** banality

Bronte
   sisters: 4 Anne **5** Emily **9** Charlotte

bronze 3 tan **5** metal **8** brownish, chestnut

brooch 3 pin **5** clasp

brood 4 chew, fret, mope, mull, sulk **5** cover, dwell, hatch, spawn, worry, young **6** chicks, family, litter **7** agonize, sit upon **8** children, incubate

brook 3 run **4** bear, rill, take **5** abide, allow, creek, stand **6** accept, endure, stream, suffer **7** rivulet, stomach **8** tolerate

broom 4 bush **5** besom, brush, whisk **7** sweeper

broth 5 stock **8** bouillon, consomme

brothel *see* **8 bordello**

brother 3 pal **4** chum, monk, peer **5** buddy, friar **6** cleric **7** comrade, kinsman, partner, sibling **8** confrere, landsman, monastic, relative, relation

brought 6 caused **7** carried, fetched, sold for **8** conveyed

brow *see* **4 brim**

browbeat *see* **6 harass**

brown 3 bay, dun, fry, tan **4** buff, cook, drab, fawn, puce, roan, rust **5** beige, camel, cocoa, hazel, khaki, saute, tawny, toast, umber **6** auburn, bronze, brunet, coffee, copper, ginger, russet, sorrel, walnut **8** brunette, chestnut, cinnamon, mahogany

Brown Bomber
  nickname of: 5 (Joe) Louis

brownie 3 elf **4** cake, puck **5** fairy, pixie **6** sprite

browse 3 eat **4** feed, scan, skim, surf **5** graze **6** nibble, peruse, survey **8** look over

bruise 3 mar **4** hurt, mark **5** abuse, wound **6** damage, injure, injury, offend **7** blacken, blemish **8** discolor

bruit 3 din **5** noise, rumor **6** clamor, hubbub, racket, report, uproar **7** clangor

Brunei
  capital/largest city: 17 Bandar Seri Begawan
  head of state: 6 sultan
  island: 6 Borneo **8** Sipitang
  religion: 5 Islam **6** Taoism **8** Buddhism **9** Christian
  feature: 3 oil

brunet, brunette 4 dark **5** black

Brunhild
  origin: 5 Norse **8** Germanic
  Scandinavian: 8 Brynhild
  husband: 6 Gunvar **7** Gunther
  won by: 6 Sigurd **9** Siegfried

brunt 5 force **6** impact, stress, thrust **8** violence

brush 4 bush, dust, fern, wash **5** clean, copse, flick, graze, groom, paint, run-in, scrub, sedge, set-to, shine, sweep, touch, whisk **6** battle, bushes, caress, duster, forest, fracas, polish, shrubs, stroke **7** bracken, cleanse, dusting, grazing, meeting, scuffle, thicket, varnish **8** skirmish, woodland
  type: 4 hair, nail, shoe, wash **5** paint, scrub, tooth **7** clothes

brush aside 6 slight **7** neglect **8** pass over

brush-off 3 cut **4** snub **5** brush **6** rebuff, slight **7** put-down, squelch

brusque *see* **5** gruff

Brussels
  capital of: 7 Belgium

headquarters of: **2** EU **3** EEC **4** NATO

brutal *see* **6 savage**

Brynhild *see* **8 Brunhild**

bubble, bubbles 4 bleb, boil, fizz, foam **5** froth **6** burble, fizzle, gurgle, seethe **7** air ball, blister, droplet, globule, sparkle

buccaneer 6 pirate **7** corsair

Buchanan, James
nickname: **7** Old Buck
presidential rank: **9** fifteenth
party: **8** Democrat
state represented: **2** PA
defeated: **7** Fremont **8** Fillmore
vice president: **12** Breckinridge
notable events of lifetime/
term: **11** Pony Express
raid by: **9** John Brown
Supreme Court case: **9** Dred Scott

Bucharest
capital of: **7** Romania, Rumania

buck 3 man **4** beau, deer, dude, kick, male **5** dandy **6** dollar, oppose **7** coxcomb **8** cavalier

bucket 3 can, hod, tub **4** cask, pail **5** scoop **6** vessel **7** pailful, pitcher, scuttle

Buckeye State
nickname of: **4** Ohio

buckle 3 sag **4** bend, clip, curl, hasp, hook, warp **5** bulge, catch, clasp **6** cave in, couple, fasten, secure **7** crumple **8** collapse

bucolic *see* **7 idyllic**

bud 4 open **5** shoot **6** flower, sprout **7** blossom, burgeon, develop

Budapest
area: **4** Buda, Pest **5** Obuda
capital of: **7** Hungary
river: **6** Danube

Buddha
also called: **5** Butsu
founded: **8** Buddhism
message: **6** dharma
tree: **2** bo **5** bodhi

Buddhism
action: **5** karma
doctrine: **6** duhkha **7** nirvana
founded by: **6** Buddha
rebirth: **7** samsara
religious community: **6** sangha

buddy *see* **4 chum**

budge 4 move, push, roll, stir, sway **5** shift, slide **6** change **8** convince, dislodge, persuade

budget 4 cost, plan **5** funds, means **6** moneys, ration **8** allocate

bueno 4 good

Buenos Aires
   capital of: 9 Argentina

buff 3 bug, fan, nut, rub, tan **4** swab **5** freak, hound, maven, sandy, straw **6** polish, smooth **7** devotee, leather

buffalo 5 bison **6** puzzle **7** mystify
   kind: 5 Water **7** African

buffet 3 box, hit, jab, rap **4** bang, beat, bump, cuff, meal, push, slap **5** baste, knock, pound, shove, thump **6** pummel, strike, supper, thrash, thwack, wallop **7** cabinet, counter **8** credenza

buffoon *see* **5 clown**

bug 3 nag **4** flaw, germ **5** annoy, fault, virus **6** badger, bother, defect, insect, pester **7** wiretap **8** listen in

buggy 4 cart **5** wagon **7** vehicle **8** carriage

bugle 4 horn **10** instrument

Bugs Bunny
   character: 4 Bugs **9** Elmer Fudd
   voice of: 8 Mel Blanc

build 4 body, form, make, mold, open **5** begin, brace, erect, forge, found, put up, raise, renew, set up, shape, start, steel **6** create, extend, figure **7** augment, develop, enhance, enlarge, fashion **8** increase, physique

building 7 edifice

building front 6 facade **8** frontage

Bujumbura
   capital of: 7 Burundi

bulb 3 bud **4** corm, seed **5** plant, tuber **8** swelling

Bulgaria
   capital/largest city: 5 Sofia
   mountain: 6 Balkan
   highest point: 6 Musala **8** Musallah
   river: 6 Danube
   sea: 5 Black
   religion: 5 Islam **8** Orthodox

bulge 3 bag, sag **4** bump, lump **5** curve, swell **6** excess **7** distend, project **8** protrude

bulk 4 body, mass, most, size **6** extent, volume, weight **8** enormity, hugeness, main part, majority, quantity

bull 2 ox **4** male
male of the: 3 elk **4** seal **5** moose, whale **6** bovine **8** elephant
constellation of: 6 Taurus

bulldoze 3 cow **4** bump, fell, push, rage, raze **5** abash, bully, drive, force, level, press, shove **6** coerce, hector, jostle, propel, subdue, thrust **7** flatten

bullet 4 ball, lead, shot, slug **7** missile **8** buckshot

bulletin 4 note **6** report **7** account, message, release **8** dispatch

bullfighting 6 torero **7** matador, picador **8** toreador

bullock 2 ox **4** beef, bull **5** steer

bull session 3 rap **4** talk

7 gabfest, palaver **8** dialogue

bull's-eye 5 black **6** center **7** exactly **8** on target

bully 3 cow **4** good **5** annoy, swell, tough **6** coerce, despot, harass, hurrah, hurray **7** coercer, ruffian **8** browbeat, bulldoze, domineer, frighten

bulrush 5 plant, sedge **7** cattail, papyrus

bulwark 5 guard **7** barrier, parapet, rampart, support, defense **8** mainstay

bum 3 beg **4** grub, hobo **5** cadge, idler, mooch, tramp **6** borrow, loafer, sponge **7** drifter, vagrant

bumble 6 bungle **7** blunder, stagger, stumble **8** flounder

bump 3 hit, jar, rap **4** bang, blow, butt, hump, jolt, knob, knot, lump, node, poke, slam, slap, sock **5** clash, crash, knock, punch, smack, smash, thump **6** bounce, impact, jostle, wallop **7** collide, run into **8** swelling

bumpkin 3 oaf **4** boor, lout

5 churl, yokel **8** ship beam

bump off *see* **6 murder**

bumptious *see* **6 brazen**

bun 4 coil, knot, roll

bunch 3 lot, mob **4** band, bevy, gang, heap, herd, host, knot, mass, pack, pile, team **5** array, batch, clump, crowd, group **6** amount, bundle, gather, huddle, number, string **7** cluster, collect **8** assemble, quantity

bundle 3 lot **4** bale, bind, heap, mass, pack, pile, wrap **5** batch, bunch, group, truss **6** amount, packet, parcel **7** package

bungalow 5 cabin, house, lodge **7** cottage

bungle 3 mar **4** flub, goof, miff, ruin **5** botch, spoil **6** foul up, mess up, muddle **7** blunder, butcher, do badly, louse up, screw up

bunk 3 bed, cot, rot **4** bull **5** berth, hokum, hooey **6** hot air **7** baloney, blather, bombast, hogwash **8** nonsense

buoyant 3 gay **4** glad **5** happy, jolly, light, merry, peppy, sunny **6** afloat, breezy, bright, elated, lively **7** hopeful **8** animated, cheerful, floating

burden 3 tax, try, vex **4** care, load, onus, pack **5** cargo **6** hamper, hinder, strain, stress, weight **7** afflict, anxiety, freight, oppress, trouble **8** encumber, handicap, hardship, load with, obligate, overload

bureau 6 agency, branch, office **7** cabinet, commode, dresser, service, station **8** division

bureaucrat 8 mandarin, official, politico

burgee 4 flag **6** banner, colors, ensign **7** pennant

burgeon *see* **7 blossom**

burglar *see* **5 thief**

burgundy 3 red **4** wine **5** color

Burgundy
city: 5 Dijon
French: 9 Bourgogne
river: 5 Rhone, Saone

burial 5 rites **7** funeral

burial ground 7 ossuary

8 boneyard, Boot Hill, catacomb, cemetery

Burkina Faso
capital/largest city: 11 Ouagadougou
river: 8 Red Volta

burlap 3 bag **4** hemp, jute **5** cloth **6** fabric **8** material

burlesque 5 farce, spoof **6** comedy, parody, satire **7** mockery, takeoff **8** ridicule, travesty

burly *see* **6 brawny**

Burma *see* **7 Myanmar**

burn 3 nip, tan **4** bite, char, fire, glow, hurt, pain, sear, skin **5** be hot, blaze, brown, chafe, flame, flare, scald, singe **6** abrade, bronze, ignite, scorch **7** blister, consume, cremate, flicker, oxidize, smolder, sunburn, swelter

burnish 3 wax **4** buff **5** rub up, shine **6** polish, smooth

burnoose 4 cape, robe **5** cloak **6** mantle **7** pelisse

burn out 3 pop **4** blow **7** exhaust

burp 5 belch, eruct

Burr, Aaron 13 vice president
event: 4 duel
killed: 8 (Alexander) Hamilton

burro 3 ass **4** mule **6** donkey, onager **7** jackass

Burroughs, Edgar Rice
creator of: 6 Tarzan

burrow *see* **6 furrow**

bursa 3 bag, sac **5** pouch, purse **6** cavity

burst 3 fly, pop, run **4** bang, bust, rend, rush **5** barge, blast, break, crack, erupt, split, spout **6** blow up, detach, divide, sunder **7** explode, rupture

Burundi
capital/largest city: 9 Bujumbura
lake: 7 Rugwero **10** Tanganyika
highest point: 8 Nyarwana
religion: 5 Islam **7** animism **9** Christian

bury 4 hide **5** cache, cover, inter **6** encase, engulf, entomb **7** conceal, cover up, enclose, immerse **8** submerge, submerse

bush 4 veld **5** brush, hedge, plant, shrub, woods **6** forest, jungle **7** barrens **9** shrubbery, woodlands

Bush, George Herbert Walker
presidential rank: 10
   forty-first
party: 10 Republican
state represented: 2 TX 5
   Texas
defeated: 7 Dukakis
defeated by: 7 Clinton
vice president: 6 Quayle
political career:
   ambassador to: 2 UN
   head of: 3 CIA
vice president under: 6
   Reagan
notable events of lifetime/
  term: 7 Gulf War
   Supreme Court
    appointments: 6
    Souter, Thomas
   invasion of: 6 Panama
wife: 7 Barbara
children: 4 John, Neil 5
   Robin 6 George, Marvin
   7 Dorothy

Bush, George Walker
presidential rank: 10
   forty-third
party: 10 Republican
state represented: 2 TX 5
   Texas
defeated: 4 Gore 5 Kerry
vice president: 6 Cheney
political career: 8
   governor (TX)

civilian career: 3 oil 8
   baseball
notable events of lifetime/
  term: 7 Iraq War,
  Katrina
   Supreme Court
    appointments: 5 Alito
   7 Roberts
father: 6 George
mother: 7 Barbara

bush country 5 scrub, wilds
  7 outback

bushed *see* 5 **tired**

bushy 5 hairy 6 fluffy,
  shaggy 7 hirsute 9
  overgrown

business 3 job 4 case, duty,
  firm, line, shop, task,
  work 5 chore, field, place,
  point, store, topic, trade 6
  affair, career, living,
  matter, office 7 affairs,
  calling, company, concern,
  mission, pursuit, venture 8
  commerce, industry,
  vocation

businesslike 7 careful,
  correct, orderly, regular,
  serious 8 diligent,
  sedulous, thorough

bus station 5 depot 8
  terminal, terminus

bust *see* 9 **apprehend**

bustle *see* **6 hustle**

busy 4 full **6** active, employ, engage, intent, occupy **7** engaged, toiling, working **8** absorbed, bustling, employed, laboring, occupied

busybody 3 pry **5** snoop **6** gossip **7** blabber, meddler, Paul Pry **8** telltale

but 3 yet **4** save, than that **5** if not, still **6** except, saving, unless **7** however, outside, that not

butcher 4 goof, kill, muff, ruin, slay **5** botch, purge, spoil **6** boggle, bungle, fumble, hack up, hit man, killer, mess up, murder **7** louse up, screw up **8** decimate, massacre

butt 3 end, hit, jab, ram, rap **4** buck, bump, bunt, dupe, goat, mark, push, slap, stub **5** knock, shank, shove, smack, stump, thump **6** bottom, buffet, jostle, object, strike, target, thrust, thwack, victim **8** blunt end

buttercup 10 Ranunculus

butterfingered *see* **6 clumsy**

butterfly
 pupa: 9 chrysalis

butter up 4 coax **6** cajole **7** flatter, wheedle **8** soft-soap

buttocks *see* **8 backside**

buttonhole 4 halt, slit, stop **6** accost, waylay **7** solicit **8** approach, confront

buttress 4 arch, prop, stay **5** boost, brace, shore, steel **6** prop up **7** bolster, support **8** shoulder

buxom 5 plump **6** bosomy, chesty, robust, zaftig

buy 3 get **4** deal, gain **5** bribe **6** obtain, pay for **7** acquire, bargain, procure **8** invest in, purchase

buzz 3 hum **4** whir **5** drone **6** murmur **7** whisper

by 4 near, over, past **5** along **6** beside, beyond, during, toward **7** through

bygone 4 past **5** olden **6** former, gone by, of yore **7** ancient, earlier **8** obsolete, previous

by itself 4 solo **5** alone, aloof, apart **8** isolated

bypass 4 go by **5** avert, avoid, dodge **8** go around

by-product 8 offshoot

bystander *see* **7 witness**

**by the skin of one's teeth
6** barely, hardly **8** only
just, scarcely

byway 4 lane **5** alley **6**
detour, street **8** shunpike

byword *see* **5 maxim**

Byzantine 6 complex **8**
scheming

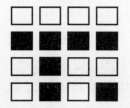  

cab 4 hack, taxi **7** taxi cab

cabal 4 band, plan, plot, ring **5** junta **6** design, league, scheme **7** faction

cabaret 4 cafe, club **6** bistro

cabin 3 hut **4** room **5** lodge, shack **6** shanty **8** bungalow, quarters

cable 4 cord, line, rope, wire **5** chain, wires **6** hawser **7** mooring

cache 4 heap **5** hoard, stock, store **8** hideaway

cachet 4 mark, seal **5** stamp, wafer **6** design, slogan **7** capsule

cackle 7 chatter
sound made by: 3 hen **4** chicken

cacophony 3 din **5** noise **7** discord

cad 3 cur, rat **4** heel, lout **5** churl, knave, louse, rogue **6** rascal, rotter **7** bounder, caitiff, dastard, villain

cadaver 4 body **5** stiff **6** corpse **7** remains **8** dead body, deceased

caddy 3 box, can, tin **5** chest **6** coffer

cadence 4 beat, lilt **5** meter, pulse, tempo **6** rhythm **7** measure

cadet 5 plebe **7** recruit, student

cadge 3 beg, bum **5** mooch **6** hustle, peddle, sponge **7** solicit, scrounge

caesar, Caesar 5 ruler **6** despot, kaiser, tyrant **7** emperor **8** dictator

Caesar, Julius
adopted son: 8 Octavian
conquered: 4 Gaul
crossed: 7 Rubicon (river)
defeated: 6 Pompey
lover: 9 Cleopatra
murdered by: 5 Casca **6** Brutus **7** Cassius
other triumvirs: 6 Pompey **7** Crassus
wife: 7 Pompeia **8** Cornelia **9** Calpurnia

caesura 5 break, pause **6** hiatus

cafe 3 bar, inn **5** diner **6** bistro, eatery **7** automat, beanery

cage 3 pen **4** coop **6** lock up, shut in **7** confine, impound **8** imprison

Cagliari
   capital of: 8 Sardinia

Cain
   father: 4 Adam
   mother: 3 Eve
   brother: 4 Abel, Seth
   home: 4 Eden
   killed: 4 Abel

Cairo
   capital of: 5 Egypt
   river: 4 Nile

cajole 4 coax **7** wheedle **8** blandish, inveigle, persuade

cake 3 dry **4** lump, mass **5** crust, tort **6** eclair, gateau, harden **7** congeal, thicken **8** compress, solidify

cakewalk 5 cinch, dance

calaboose 3 pen **4** jail, stir **6** prison **7** slammer **8** hoosegow

calamity 3 ill, woe **4** blow, ruin **6** mishap **7** failure, ill wind, scourge, tragedy, trouble **8** disaster, distress, downfall, hardship

calculate 4 plan **5** add up, aim at, count, judge, sum up **6** devise, figure, reckon **7** compute, measure, surmise, work out **8** estimate

calculating 3 sly **4** foxy, wily **6** artful, crafty **7** cunning, devious **8** plotting, scheming

Calcutta
   alternate name: 7 Kolkata
   river: 7 Hooghly

Calder, Alexander
   sculptures: 7 mobiles **8** stabiles

caldron, cauldron 3 pot **6** boiler, kettle

calendar 4 list **5** chart, table **6** agenda, docket **8** register, schedule

calf 4 veal **5** dogie **6** weaner **7** leg part
   young of: 3 cow **4** bull, seal **5** whale **8** elephant

caliber 4 bore, rank **5** merit, power, scope, worth **6** repute, talent **7** quality, stature **8** capacity, eminence, position

California
  abbreviation: 2 CA **3** Cal
  5 Calif
  nickname: 6 Golden
  capital: 10 Sacramento
  largest city: 10 Los
    Angeles
  feature:
    island prison: 8
      Alcatraz
  lake: 5 Tahoe **6** Havasu,
  Shasta
  mountain: 5 Coast **6**
  Shasta **7** Cascade,
  Mammoth, Whitney **10**
  San Jacinto **12** Sierra
  Nevada
  highest point: 7 Whitney
  physical feature:
    desert: 6 Mohave,
    Mojave **7** Sonoran **8**
    Colorado
    fault: 10 San Andreas
    sea/ocean: 6 Cortez **7**
    Pacific
    tar pits: 6 La Brea
    tree: 7 redwood,
    sequoia
    valley: 5 Death

call 3 ask, bid, cry, dub, tag
4 bawl, buzz, hail, name,
need, plea, ring, yell **5**
cause, claim, phone, rally,
shout, visit **6** appeal, ask
for, bellow, charge,
clamor, cry out, decree,
holler, know as, muster,
notice, summon **7** contact,
declare, grounds, refer to
8 announce, appeal to,
entreaty, identify, instruct,
look in on, petition,
proclaim

calling 3 job **5** craft, field,
forte, trade **6** career,
metier **7** mission, passion
8 business, devotion,
function, vocation

callous 4 cold, hard **5**
cruel, tough **6** inured **8**
hardened

callow 3 raw **5** crude **7**
artless, awkward, puerile,
shallow, untried **8**
childish, ignorant,
immature, juvenile

call to order 4 open **6**
muster **7** convene,
convoke

calm 4 cool, ease **5** allay,
bland, quell, quiet, still **6**
gentle, lessen, pacify,
placid, sedate, serene,
soothe, subdue **7** assuage,
compose, halcyon, mollify,
placate, relaxed **8**
mitigate, peaceful, tranquil

calumny 4 barb, slur

5 libel, smear **6** malice **7** slander **8** innuendo

calvados
  type: 6 brandy

Calvary 8 Golgotha

Calydonian boar
  sent by: 5 Diana
  killed by: 8 Meleager

Calypso
  form: 5 nymph
  father: 5 Atlas
  detained: 8 Odysseus

calyx 4 husk **5** sepal

cam 3 cog **4** disk **8** cylinder **10** projection

camaraderie 7 jollity **8** bonhomie, good will

Cambodia
  other name: 8 Cambodge **9** Kampuchea
  capital/largest city: 8 Pnom-Penh **9** Phnom Penh, Phnum Penh
  head of state: 4 king
  lake: 8 Tonle Sap
  highest point: 10 Phnom (or Phnum) Aoral (or Aural)
  river: 6 Mekong **8** Tonle Sap
  physical feature:
    gulf: 4 Siam **8** Thailand

  places:
    ruins/temple: 6 Angkor **9** Angkor Wat
  Communist group: 10 Khmer Rouge
    leader: 6 Pol Pot

Cambria *see* **5 Wales**

cambric 5 cloth, linen **6** cotton, fabric **8** material

camel
  chews: 3 cud
  kind: 7 Arabian **8** Bactrian **9** dromedary
  type of: 8 ruminant
  young: 4 calf

camera 3 APS, SLR **4** 35 mm, view **7** digital **8** panorama, Polaroid, twin lens **9** automatic **11** range finder **13** point-and-shoot

Cameroon
  capital: 7 Yaounde
  largest city: 6 Douala
  lake: 4 Chad
  highest point: 8 Cameroon, Cameroun
  physical features:
    gulf: 6 Guinea

camisole 3 top **4** slip **6** jacket

camouflage 4 hide, mask, veil **5** blind, cloak, cover, front **6** shroud **7** conceal, cover up **8** disguise

camp 4 tent **7** bivouac, lodging, rough it **8** barracks

campaign 3 run **4** push **5** drive, stump **6** action, effort **7** crusade **8** endeavor, movement

campanile 6 belfry

Campari
  type: 7 bitters **8** aperitif

can 3 tin **4** buns, fire, rump, seat **5** fanny, put up **6** bottom **8** backside, buttocks, preserve

Canaan
  father: 3 Ham
  brother: 4 Cush
  grandfather: 4 Noah

Canada
  capital: 6 Ottawa
  largest city: 8 Montreal
  division: 3 PEI **5** Yukon **6** Quebec **7** Alberta, Nunavit, Ontario **8** Manitoba **10** Nova Scotia
  lake: 4 Erie **5** Huron **6** Louise **7** Ontario **8** Manitoba, Superior, Winnipeg
  mountain: 5 Coast, Green, Rocky **9** Mackenzie, Vancouver **10** Laurentian

highest point: 5 Logan

sea/ocean: 6 Arctic **7** Pacific **8** Atlantic, Labrador

physical feature:
  canal: 3 Soo **7** Welland
  falls: 7 Niagara

feature:
  emblem: 9 maple leaf

canal 4 duct, Erie, Kiel, Suez, tube **5** Grand **6** Panama **7** channel, conduit

Canary Islands
  named for: 3 dog **5** canis **6** canine
  capital/largest city: 9 Las Palmas

Canberra
  capital of: 9 Australia

cancel 4 undo, void **5** abort, annul **6** delete, recall, repeal, revoke **7** rescind, retract, vitiate **8** abrogate

cancer 3 rot **4** crab **6** plague **7** sarcoma, scourge **8** neoplasm, sickness

Cancer
  symbol: 4 crab
  planet: 4 Moon
  rules: 4 home **6** family
  born: 4 July, June

candelabrum **7** menorah **8** dikerion

candid **4** just, open **5** blunt, frank, plain **6** direct, honest **7** sincere, unposed **8** truthful

candidate **7** hopeful, nominee **8** aspirant

Candide
author: **8** Voltaire

candle **3** dip, wax **5** light, taper **6** bougie, cierge, tallow

candy **3** bar **4** kiss **5** cream, fudge, jelly, taffy **6** bonbon, comfit, nougat, sweets, toffee **7** brittle, caramel, fondant, gumdrop

cane **3** hit, rap, rod, tan **4** beat, drub, flog, lash, whip **5** baste, flail, smite, staff, stick, whack **6** strike, thrash, wallop

canine **3** cur, dog, fox, pup **4** mutt, wolf **5** hound, hyena, puppy, tooth **6** coyote, cuspid, jackal **7** mongrel **8** eyetooth

canker **4** sore **5** ulcer **6** blight, cancer, lesion

cannon **3** bit, gun **5** carom **6** mortar **7** battery **8** field gun, howitzer

canoe **4** boat **5** bungo, kayak **6** dugout **7** pirogue

canon **3** law **4** code, rule **5** dogma, edict, model, order **6** decree **7** pattern, precept, statute **8** doctrine, standard

canopy **4** hood **5** cover **6** awning, tester **8** covering

cant **4** sham, talk **5** argot, lingo, slang **6** jargon **8** parlance, pretense

cantabile
music: **7** flowing, singing **8** songlike

cantaloupe **5** fruit, melon

cantankerous *see* **5** **surly**

canteen **2** PX **4** club **5** flask **6** bottle

canter **4** gait, lope, pace, trot **6** gallop, singer, whiner

Canterbury Tales, The
author: **7** (Geoffrey) Chaucer
starting point: **9** Southwark, Tabard Inn
goal:
tomb of: **6** Becket

cantor of a synagogue
Hebrew: **5** hazan **6** chazan

Cantos
   author: 5 (Ezra) Pound

canvas 4 duck **8** painting

canvass 4 poll, scan, sift **5** study, tally **6** survey **7** analyze, examine, explore, inquire, inspect **8** analysis

canyon 3 col, cut, gap **4** draw, pass, wadi, wash **5** break, chasm, cleft, crack, gorge, gulch, gully, notch **6** arroyo, coulee, ravine, valley **7** fissure

cap 3 fez, lid, tam, top **4** acme, seal **5** beret, cover, limit, outdo **6** better, exceed, top off **7** surpass **8** headgear, out-strip

capable 3 apt **4** able, deft **5** adept **6** adroit, clever **7** skilled **8** masterly, talented

capacious 3 big **4** huge, vast, wide **5** ample, broad, large, roomy **7** mammoth, massive **8** gigantic

capacity 4 mind, role, room, size **5** gifts, limit, range, scope, space **6** extent, talent, volume **7** ability, faculty **8** position, sagacity, strength

cape 4 spit **5** cloak, manta, point, shawl **6** mantle, poncho, serape, tabard, tongue **7** pelisse

capital 4 cash **5** great, money, super **6** riches, superb, wealth

capitalize 4 back, fund **5** stake **7** finance, trade on, utilize **8** profit by

capitulate 5 yield **6** accede, give in, give up, relent, submit **7** succumb

Capp, Al
   creator/artist of: 8 Li'l Abner

caprice 3 fad **4** lark, whim **5** antic, caper, craze, fancy, fling, prank, quirk, spree, stunt **6** notion, oddity, vagary **7** impulse **8** crotchet, escapade

Capricorn
   symbol: 4 goat
   planet: 6 Saturn
   rules: 6 career
   born: 7 January **8** December

capsize 5 upset **6** invert **7** tip over **8** flip over, keel over, overturn, turn over

capsule 4 case, pill **6** ampule **7** cockpit

captain 4 boss, head

5 chief, pilot **6** leader, master, old man **7** headman, skipper

famous: 4 Ahab, Andy, Hook, Kirk, Nemo

caption 5 title **7** heading, subhead **8** headline, subtitle

captivate 4 lure **5** charm **6** dazzle, enamor, seduce **7** attract, bewitch, enchant

captive 3 POW **5** caged **6** penned **7** hostage **8** confined, enslaved, locked up, prisoner

capture 3 bag, nab **4** bust, grab, snag, take, trap **5** catch, grasp, pinch, seize, snare **6** arrest **7** bagging, procure

car 4 auto, heap **5** buggy, coach, diner, motor **6** boxcar, hot rod, jalopy, wheels **7** flivver, machine, sleeper, vehicle **8** carriage

kind: 4 coal **5** cable, horse, motor **6** cattle, dining, parlor, street **7** baggage, freight, Pullman, railway

Caracas
  capital of: 9 Venezuela

carafe 5 flask **6** bottle, vessel

carapace 4 case **5** shell **6** lorica, shield **7** carapax **8** calipash, covering

caravan 4 band, file, line **5** queue, train, troop **6** coffle, column, convoy, parade, string **7** company, cortege, retinue, trailer

caravansary 3 inn **5** hotel

carbohydrate
  kinds: 5 sugar **6** simple, starch, xylose **7** complex, glucose, lactose, maltose, sucrose **8** dextrose, fructose **9** cellulose

carbon 4 coal, coke, copy **8** charcoal

carbon copy 5 clone **7** replica

carcass 4 body, bouk, husk, wall **5** shell, stiff, trunk **6** corpse **7** cadaver, carrion, remains **8** dead body, fireball, skeleton

carcinoma 5 tumor **6** cancer **8** neoplasm

card 4 bill **6** ticket **7** program **8** postcard

card game 3 loo, war **4** brag, faro, fish, skat, vint **5** ombre, poker, rummy, whist **6** Boston, bridge, casino, chemmy, ecarte, euchre, go fish, hearts, memory, piquet, pocher **7** bezique, canasta, cooncan, Old Maid, plafond, primero **8** baccarat, conquian, cribbage, gin rummy, napoleon, patience, pinochle, slapjack

suits: 4 club **5** heart, spade **7** diamond

Cardiff
capital of: 5 Wales

cardigan 5 corgi **6** jacket, wampus **7** sweater

cardinal 3 key, top **4** head, main **5** basic, chief, first, prime, vital **7** central, deep-red, highest, primary, scarlet **8** dominant, foremost, greatest

care 3 TLC **4** heed, load, mind, want, wish **5** grief, pains, worry **6** desire, regard **7** caution, concern, control, custody, keeping

careen 3 tip, yaw **4** lean, list, sway, tilt, veer **5** slant, slope **7** capsize **8** overturn

career 3 job **4** line, work **7** calling, pursuit **8** activity, business, lifework, vocation

carefree 3 gay **4** glad **5** happy, jolly, sunny **6** breezy, elated, jaunty, joyous **7** gleeful, relaxed **8** cheerful, jubilant

careful 4 fine, nice, wary **5** alert, chary, exact, fussy **7** heedful, mindful, on guard, precise, prudent, tactful **8** accurate, cautious, diligent, vigilant

caress 3 hug, pat, pet **5** clasp, touch **6** cuddle, fondle, stroke **7** embrace, petting, toy with **8** fondling, stroking

caretaker 6 keeper, porter, warden **7** curator, janitor

cargo 4 load **5** goods **6** burden, lading **7** freight **8** shipment

Caribbean 3 sea
channel: 7 Yucatan
Indian: 5 Carib **6** Arawak

caricature 4 mock **6** parody, satire **7** lampoon, takeoff **8** satirize

Carmen
author: 7 (Prosper) Merimee
opera by: 5 Bizet

carmine 3 red **6** cherry

7 crimson, deep red, scarlet **8** blood red

carnal 4 lewd **6** erotic, impure, sexual, sinful, wanton **7** lustful, sensual **8** sensuous, unchaste

carnelian
  species: **6** quartz

carnival 4 fair, fete, gala **6** circus **7** jubilee **8** festival, jamboree

carnivore 3 cat, dog, fox **4** bear, lion, lynx, mink, puma, wolf **5** civet, dingo, fossa, hyena, otter, panda, skunk, tayra, tiger **6** badger, bobcat, coyote, ferret, grison, hyaena, jackal, jaguar, marten, olingo, weasel **7** polecat, raccoon, suricat **8** aardwolf, kinkajou, mongoose

carol 4 hymn, noel, sing **5** paean **6** warble **8** canticle

carom 6 bounce, strike **7** collide, rebound, **8** billiard, ricochet

carouse 5 drink, party, quaff, revel **6** guzzle, imbibe, tipple **7** roister, wassail **8** live it up

carp 3 nag **5** cavil, chide,

decry, knock **6** deride, impugn, pick on **8** belittle

carpal
  bone of: **5** wrist

carpenter 6 fitter, joiner **7** builder **8** repairer

carper 6 critic **7** caviler

carpet 3 mat, rug **4** shag **5** cover, layer **7** blanket, matting

carriage 3 air, rig **4** mien **5** buggy, coach, poise, wagon **6** aspect, manner **7** bearing, posture, vehicle **8** attitude, behavior, demeanor, presence

carrion 5 bones, offal, waste **6** corpse, refuse **7** cadaver, carcass, garbage, remains, wastage **8** crowbait, dead body, leavings

carrousel 4 ride, tray **8** conveyor

carry 3 lug, run **4** bear, cart, haul, lift, move, prop, ship, take, tote **5** brace, bring, fetch, offer, stock **6** hold up, supply, uphold **7** display, sustain **8** maintain, shoulder, transfer, transmit

cart 3 gig, lug **4** bear, dray, haul, move, take, tote,

trap **5** bring, carry, fetch, truck, wagon **6** barrow, convey **7** schlepp, trundle, tumbrel **8** curricle, transfer, transmit
kind: 2 go **3** dog, tip **4** dump, hand, push

carte blanche 7 license

cartel 4 OPEC, pool **5** chain, trust **7** combine **8** monopoly

Carter, James Earl, Jr
presidential rank: 11 thirty-ninth
party: 10 Democratic
state represented: 2 GA **7** Georgia
defeated: 4 Ford **8** McCarthy
vice president: 7 Mondale
political career: 8 governor (GA)
notable events of lifetime/
term: 9 Love Canal
  hostages taken in: 4 Iran
  prize: 5 Nobel, peace
  scandal: 6 Abscam **9** Koreagate
wife: 8 Rosalynn
children: 3 Amy **4** John (Jack) **5** James (Chip) **6** Donnel (Jeff)

Carthage *see* **7 Tunisia**

carton 3 box **4** case **5** crate

cartoon 5 comic **6** sketch **7** drawing, funnies, picture **8** animated

cartridge 3 dud **4** case, tape **5** blank, shell **6** holder **7** capsule, package **8** cassette, cylinder

carve 3 hew, saw **4** etch, form, hack, mold, rend, turn, work **5** cleve, cut up, model, shape, slash, slice, split **6** chisel, incise, sculpt **7** engrave

carving 5 cameo **8** intaglio, triptych

caryatid 6 column

Casablanca
director: 6 (Michael) Curtiz
cast: 5 (Peter) Lorre, (Claude) Rains **6** (Humphrey) Bogart, (Dooley) Wilson **7** (Ingrid) Bergman, (Paul) Henreid **11** (Sydney) Greenstreet

Casanova 3 cad, rip **4** beau, lech, roue, wolf **5** lover, Romeo, swain, wooer **6** chaser, lecher, suitor **7** admirer, bounder, Don Juan, gallant, rounder

8 cavalier, Lothario, lover boy, paramour

cascade 4 fall, gush, pour, rush **5** chute, falls, surge **6** plunge, rapids, tumble **7** Niagara **8** cataract

case 3 bin, box **4** plea, suit, tray **5** chest, cover, crate **6** action, affair, appeal, carton, debate, jacket, matter **7** dispute, episode, example, hearing, lawsuit, overlay **8** envelope, incident

cash 5 bills, bread, coins, dough, money **6** change **8** currency, exchange

casing 4 skin **5** frame

cask 3 keg, tub, tun, vat **4** butt, pipe **6** barrel **8** hogshead

casket 4 case, pall **5** chest **6** coffer, coffin

Cassandra 7 seeress
  father: 5 Priam
  mother: 6 Hecuba
  brother: 5 Paris
  concubine of: 9 Agamemnon
  son: 6 Pelops **9** Teledamus
  cursed by: 6 Apollo
  violated by: 4 Ajax

casserole 4 dish, food, mold **6** tureen, vessel **8** saucepan

cast 3 set, sow **4** fire, form, hurl, look, mien, mint, mold, pick, shed, toss **5** fling, heave, model, throw **6** actors, assign, choose, direct, launch, let fly, propel, spread, troupe **8** catapult

castaway 3 bum **4** hobo, waif **5** exile, leper, nomad, rover, stray **6** outlaw, pariah **7** Ishmael, vagrant **8** deportee, derelict, renegade, vagabond, wanderer

caste 4 rank **6** status **7** lineage, station **8** position
  Hindu: 5 sudra, varna **6** vaisya **7** brahman

castigate 5 chide, scold **6** berate, punish, rebuke **7** chasten, chew out, reprove, upbraid **8** admonish, chastise, reproach

castle 4 hall, keep, rook **5** manor, tower, villa **6** palace **7** chateau, citadel, mansion **8** fortress

Castor and Pollux
  also: 6 Gemini **8** Dioscuri

form: 5 twins
mother: 4 Leda
father: 4 Zeus
sister: 5 Helen
members of: 9 Argonauts

casual 4 cool, so-so **5** blase, vague **6** chance, random, sporty **7** offhand, passing, relaxed **8** informal

casualty 4 loss **6** injury, victim **7** injured **8** fatality

cat 3 pet **4** puss, whip **5** kitty, tabby **6** feline, mouser
anatomy: 3 paw **4** loin, nape, rump, tail **5** break, flank, shank **6** feeler **7** dewclaw, leather, whisker **8** vibrissa
family: 7 Felidae
fastest: 7 cheetah
genus: 5 Felis
grinning: 8 Cheshire
tailless: 4 Manx
young: 6 kitten

cataclysm 4 blow **7** debacle **8** calamity, disaster, upheaval

catacomb 4 tomb **7** ossuary **8** cemetery

catafalque 3 box **4** pall **6** casket, coffin

catalog, catalogue 4 file, list, post, roll **5** index **6** record, roster **8** classify, register

catapult 4 cast, hurl, toss **5** fling, heave, pitch, shoot, sling, throw **6** hurtle, onager, propel

cataract 5 falls, flood **6** deluge, rapids **7** cascade, torrent **8** downpour

catastrophe 4 blow **5** havoc **6** mishap, ravage **7** debacle, scourge, tragedy **8** calamity, disaster

catcall 3 boo **4** gibe, hiss, hoot, jeer, razz **7** whistle **8** heckling

catch 3 bag, bat, get, hit, nab **4** bait, bust, dupe, find, fool, grab, hoax, hook, lock, snag, snap, spot, take, trap **5** break, charm, clasp, get to, grasp, hitch, latch, prize, reach, seize, sense, smack, smite, snare, trick, yield **6** arrest, collar, corner, corral, expose, fasten, kicker, snatch, unmask **7** attract, bewitch, capture, closure, deceive, ensnare, gimmick, mislead, rasping **8** contract, overtake

Catcher in the Rye, The
author: 8 (J D) Salinger

character: 8 (Holden) Caulfield

Catch-22
author: 6 (Joseph) Heller
character: 9 Yossarian

catchword 5 motto **6** byword, cliche, slogan, war cry **8** password

categorical 4 flat, sure **7** certain, express **8** absolute, definite, emphatic, explicit

category 5 class, group **8** division, grouping

cater 5 humor **6** pamper, pander, please **7** gratify, indulge, satisfy

caterwaul 3 cry **4** bawl, howl, wail, yelp **5** whine **6** clamor, scream, shriek, squawk, squeal **7** screech

catharsis 7 purging, release, venting

cathedral 6 church **7** lateran **8** basilica, official
Italian: 5 duomo

cathouse 4 stew **5** house **6** bagnio **7** brothel **8** bordello

catnap 3 nap **4** doze **6** siesta, snooze

Cat on a Hot Tin Roof
author: 8 (Tennessee) Williams
director: 6 (Richard) Brooks
cast: 4 Ives (Burl) **6** Carson (Jack), Newman (Paul), Taylor (Elizabeth) **8** Anderson (Judith)

cats-eye
source: 8 Sri Lanka

cat's paw 4 dupe, pawn, tool **5** patsy **7** fall guy

cattle 4 cows, kine, oxen **5** beefs, bulls, stock **6** beeves, calves, dogies, steers
family: 7 Bovidae
group of: 5 drove
kind: 2 ox **3** yak **4** Zebu **5** Angus **6** Ankole, Jersey **7** Brahman **8** Ayrshire, Guernsey, Hereford, Highland, Holstein
young: 4 calf **6** heifer **8** yearling

catty 4 mean **8** spiteful

caucus 6 parley, powwow **7** council, meeting, session **8** assembly, conclave

caudal 4 back, tail **7** tail-end

cauldron *see* **7** caldron

cause 4 goal, make, root,

side **5** ideal, impel, tenet **6** belief, create, effect, incite, motive, origin, reason, source **7** genesis, grounds, incline, inspire, purpose **8** stimulus

caustic 3 lye **4** tart **5** acrid, harsh, sharp **6** biting, bitter **7** burning, cutting, erosive, gnawing **8** scathing, stinging

caution 4 care, heed, warn **5** alarm, alert **6** advise, caveat, tip-off **7** thought, warning **8** admonish, forewarn, prudence, wariness

cavalier 3 fop **4** beau **5** blade, cocky, dandy, swell **6** hussar, lancer **7** cursory, dragoon, gallant, haughty, offhand, playboy **8** arrogant, courtier, gay blade, horseman, uncaring

cave 3 den **4** lair, sink **6** burrow, cavern, cavity, dugout, grotto, hollow

caveat 5 alarm, alert, aviso **6** tip-off **7** caution, red flag, warning

cave in 6 buckle, fall in, give up, submit **7** crumple, give way, implode **8** collapse

cavernous 4 huge, vast **5** roomy **6** gaping **7** chasmal, immense, yawning **8** cavelike, enormous, spacious

cavity 3 dip, pit **4** bore, dent, hole, sink **5** basin, niche **6** hollow, pocket, tunnel **7** opening, orifice, vacuity **8** aperture

cavort 4 play, romp **5** bound, caper, frisk **6** frolic, gambol, prance

CE 9 Common Era

cease see **3 end**

cease-fire 5 truce

cedar 6 Cedrus

cede 4 give **5** grant, leave, yield **6** tender **7** abandon, deliver, release **8** hand over, transfer

ceiling 3 top **4** roof **5** limit **6** canopy, cupola **7** maximum

**Celebes
also: 8** Sulawesi
location: 9 Indonesia

Celebes ox 4 anoa

celebrate 4 laud **5** bless, cheer, exalt, extol, honor **6** hallow, praise, revere **7** acclaim, applaud, commend, glorify

celebrity 3 VIP **4** fame, name, note, star **5** glory, wheel **6** bigwig, renown **7** big shot, notable, stardom **8** eminence, luminary

celerity 5 haste, hurry, speed **6** hustle **8** alacrity, dispatch, fast clip, fastness, legerity, rapidity

celestial 3 sky **5** solar **6** astral, divine **7** angelic, elysian, stellar **8** ethereal, heavenly

celestial being 3 god **5** angel, deity **7** goddess **8** divinity

celibate 4 pure **5** unwed **6** chaste, single **8** bachelor, spinster, virginal

cell
  part: 7 nucleus **8** membrane **9** cytoplasm

cellar 3 den **4** cave **6** dugout **8** basement **10** downstairs **14** wine collection

Celt 4 Gaul, Kelt, Manx, Pict, Scot **5** Irish, Welsh **6** Breton, Briton **8** Scottish

cement 3 fix, set **4** bind, fuse, glue, join, seal, weld **5** paste, stick, unite **6** mortar, secure **8** concrete

cemetery 7 ossuary **8** boneyard, Boot Hill, catacomb

cenobite 4 monk **7** ascetic **8** celibate

censor 4 blip, edit **5** amend, bleep, judge, purge **6** critic, delete, excise **7** Bowdler, clean up **8** suppress

censure 3 pan, rap **5** chide, scold **6** berate, rebuke **7** condemn, reprove, upbraid **8** admonish, reproach

census 3 tax **4** data, list, poll **5** count **6** amount

Centaur
  form: 3 man **5** horse **7** monster
  famous: 6 Chiron

center 3 fix, hub, mid **4** axis, core, crux **5** focus, heart, pivot, point **6** direct, gather, middle **7** address, essence, nucleus **8** converge, interior

centigrade 5 scale **6** degree **7** celcius

centipede 4 boat **5** shrub **6** earwig, insect **8** chilopod, multiped

Central African Republic
  capital/largest city: 6 Bangui
  lake: 4 Chad
  river: 6 Ubangi

Central America
  land form: 7 isthmus
  countries: 6 Belize, Panama **8** Honduras **9** Costa Rica, Guatemala, Nicaragua **10** El Salvador
  lake: 5 Gatun **6** Izabal **7** Atitlan, Managua
  gulf: 7 Fonseca, Nicaya, Panama **8** Mosquito, Honduras

cephalopod 5 squid **7** mollusk, octopus **8** nautilus

ceramic ware 5 china, glass **7** pottery **8** crockery

ceratopsid
  type of: 8 dinosaur

Cerberus
  form: 3 dog
  number of heads: 5 three

cereal 4 bran, corn, oats, rice, seed **5** grain, grass, gruel, plant, wheat **6** barley, pablum **7** oatmeal, pabulum **8** porridge

cerebellum
  part of: 5 brain

controls: 7 balance **8** movement

cerebrum
  part of: 5 brain
  controls: 6 seeing **7** hearing, tasting **8** deciding, feelings, learning, smelling, thinking, touching

ceremonial 4 rite **6** formal, ritual **7** liturgy, service

ceremony 4 rite **6** custom, nicety, ritual **7** amenity, decorum, pageant, service **8** function, protocol

Ceres
  origin: 5 Roman
  corresponds to: 7 Demeter

certain 4 sure **5** valid **6** secure **7** assured, express, settled, special **8** absolute, cocksure, definite, positive, reliable, specific

certificate 4 deed **6** permit **7** diploma, license, voucher **8** document, warranty

certify 4 aver **5** swear, vouch **6** assure, attest, ratify, verify **7** confirm, endorse **8** notarize, sanction, validate

cerulean 4 blue 5 azure 6 cobalt 7 sky blue

Cervantes Saavedra, Miguel de
author of: 10 Don Quixote (de la Mancha)

cessation 3 end 4 halt, stay, stop 5 pause 6 ending, recess 7 ceasing, halting, respite 8 quitting, stopping, surcease

cetacean 4 apod, orca 5 whale 6 beluga, mammal 7 cetacea, dolphin, dowfish, grampus, narwhal 8 porpoise, sturgeon

Ceylon *see* 8 **Sri Lanka**

Chad
capital/largest city: 8 Fort-Lamy, N'Djamena
lake: 4 Chad
highest point: 9 Emi Koussi

chafe 3 rub 4 boil, burn, foam, fume, rage, rasp 6 abrade, rankle, scrape, seethe 7 scratch

chagrin 5 shame 6 dismay 8 distress

chains 3 tie 4 bind, lash 5 bonds, irons 6 fasten, fetter, secure, string, tether

7 bondage, manacle, shackle

chair 4 seat 5 bench, couch, sedan stool 6 chaise, lounge, rocker, settee, throne 7 ottoman

chairman 4 head 5 chair, emcee 6 leader 7 manager, preside, speaker 8 director

chaise 3 gig 4 shay 5 chair 6 daybed, lounge 7 calesin 8 carriage, duchesse

chalcedony 3 gem 4 onyx, opal, sard 5 agate, prase 6 jasper, plasma, quartz, silica 7 catseye, mineral, opaline, sardius 8 hematite, sardonyx

Chaldean 4 seer 5 magic 6 Syriac 7 Aramaic, semitic 8 magician

chalice 3 cup 5 grail 6 goblet, vessel

chalk 4 draw 6 crayon, pastel, sketch

chalk up 4 earn 5 score 6 attain, charge, credit 7 achieve, ascribe

chalky 3 wan 4 pale 5 ashen, white 6 pallid 7 powdery 8 blanched

challenge 3 bid, tax, try

4 dare, defy, gage, test **5** doubt, trial **6** demand, impute **7** defiant, dispute, summons **8** question

chamber 4 diet, hall, room **5** board, court, house, salon **6** office, parlor **7** bedroom, boudoir, council **8** assembly, congress

chameleon 4 newt **6** lizard **8** renegade, turncoat

champagne 4 fizz **6** bubbly
type: 4 wine
measure: 6 magnum **8** jeroboam, rehoboam **9** balthazar

championship 3 cup **5** crown, title **7** backing, defense, support, winning **8** advocacy, espousal

chance 3 try **4** fall, fate, luck, risk **5** lucky, occur **6** gamble, happen, hazard, random **7** attempt, destiny

change 4 swap, turn, vary **5** alter, coins, shift, trade **6** modify, mutate, recast, reform, silver, switch **7** convert, novelty, remodel, replace, restyle, shuffle, variety, veering **8** pin money, swapping, transfer

channel *see* **5** canal

chant 2 om **3** ode **4** hymn, lied, sing, song **5** carol, croon, dirge, elegy, psalm, theme, trill, troll **7** chanson, chorale, descant

chaos 4 mess **5** furor **6** bedlam, jumble, muddle, tumult, uproar **7** turmoil **8** disorder, upheaval

chap 3 boy, dry, guy, jaw, lad, man, rap **4** chop, gent **5** bloke, buyer, crack, split **6** fellow, redden **7** roughen

chapeau 3 hat

chapel 6 church, shrine **7** oratory **9** sanctuary

chaperon, chaperone 5 guard, watch **6** duenna, escort **7** oversee **8** guardian, shepherd

chaplain 4 abbe **5** padre, rabbi, vicar **6** cleric, curate, father, parson, pastor, priest, rector **7** Holy Joe **8** minister, preacher, reverend

Chaplin, Charlie
nickname: 5 (Little) Tramp
wife: 6 (Oona) O'Neill **7** (Paulette) Goddard
daughter: 9 Geraldine

chapter 3 era **4** body, part, span, unit **5** group, phase **6** branch **7** episode, section **8** division

char 4 burn, sear **5** singe **6** scorch

character 4 part, role, self **5** being, honor **6** makeup, nature, person, traits, weirdo

characteristic 4 mark **5** trait **6** aspect **7** earmark, feature, quality, typical **8** property, symbolic

charge 3 ask, bid, fee **4** cost, duty, lade, levy, load, pack, rate, rush, toll **5** beset, blame, debit, order, price, stack, storm, stuff **6** accuse, amount, assail, come at, enjoin, impute, indict, sortie, summon **7** ascribe, assault, control, custody, expense, payment

charger 5 horse, mount, steed **6** vessel **7** accuser, platter **8** warhorse

chariot 3 car **5** buggy **7** phaeton, vehicle **8** carriage

charisma 5 charm **6** allure, appeal **7** glamour **8** presence, witchery

charity 3 aid **4** alms, fund, gift, help, love **6** bounty, giving **7** handout **8** altruism, donating, good will, goodness, humanity, kindness, offering, sympathy

charlatan 4 fake **5** cheat, fraud, quack **7** cozener **8** deceiver, imposter, impostor, swindler

Charleston 5 dance
capital of: 9 W Virginia

Charlotte's Web
author: 7 E B White
Charlotte: 6 spider
saved: 6 Wilbur (piglet)

charm 4 draw, grip, lure, take **5** magic, spell **6** allure, amulet, bauble, cajole, engage, please, seduce, turn on **7** attract, beguile, bewitch, conjure, delight, enchant, gratify, sorcery, trinket, win over **8** charisma, enthrall, entrance, ornament, talisman

Charon
occupation: 8 ferryman
river: 4 Styx

chart 3 map, pie **4** plan, plot **5** draft, graph, table **6** design, draw up, lay out, map out, scheme, sketch **7** diagram, outline

charter 3 let **4** deed, hire, rent **5** grant, lease **6** employ, engage, permit **7** compact, license **8** contract, sanction

Charybdis
form: 7 monster
father: 8 Poseidon
mother: 4 Gaea
identified with: 9 whirlpool

chase 3 dog **4** hunt, oust, rout, shoo, tail **5** drive, evict, hound, quest, stalk, track, trail **6** dispel, follow, pursue, shadow **7** cast out, go after, hunting, pursuit, repulse, scatter **8** pursuing, run after, send away, stalking, tracking

chasm 3 gap, pit **4** gulf, hold, rift **5** abyss, break, cleft, crack, gorge, gulch, split **6** breach, cavity, crater, divide, ravine **7** fissure **8** crevasse

chaste 4 pure **5** clean **6** decent, modest, severe, strict **7** austere, sinless **8** virginal, virtuous

chasten see **5 scold**

chat 3 gab, rap **4** talk

5 prate **7** palaver, prattle **8** converse

chateau 4 wine **6** castle, estate **7** mansion

chatter 3 gas **4** blab, talk **5** clank, click, prate **6** gossip **7** blabber, blather, prattle, talking

chauffeur 6 driver

chauvinism 8 jingoism

cheap 4 base, easy, mean, poor **5** close, gaudy, petty, tacky, tight **6** common, shabby, shoddy, sordid, stingy, trashy **7** ignoble

cheat 3 con, gyp **4** bilk, dupe, fake, foil, fool, gull, hoax, rook, take **5** cozen, crook, fraud, quack, trick **6** delude, dodger, fleece **7** deceive, defraud, mislead, swindle

check 3 bar, end, fit, gag, tab **4** curb, halt, hold, jibe, mesh, rein, slow, stay, stop, test **5** block, brake, choke, limit, probe, stall, study, tally **6** bridle, impede, peruse, review, search, thwart **7** examine, inhibit, inspect, perusal, prevent **8** hold back, look into, look over, restrain, suppress

checkered 4 pied **6** fitful, motley, seesaw, uneven, varied **7** checked, dappled, mottled, piebald

cheek 4 jowl **5** brass, nerve **8** audacity, boldness, temerity

cheep 4 peep **5** chirp, tweet **7** chirrup, chitter, twitter

cheer 3 cry, fun, joy, ole, rah **4** glee, hail, hope, root, warm, yell **5** bravo, shout **6** gaiety, hooray, hurrah **7** animate, comfort, delight, enliven, gladden, hearten **8** brighten, vivacity

cheese
French: **7** fromage

chemical compound 4 acid, base, enol **5** amide, amine, ester, imide **6** isomar, ketone **8** aldehyde

chemise 4 slip **5** dress, shift, shirt, smock **6** blouse **7** garment **8** camisole, lingerie, unbelted

cheri, cherie 4 dear

cherish 4 love **5** honor, nurse, prize, value **6** dote on, esteem, revere, succor

7 care for, idolize, nourish, nurture, shelter, sustain **8** hold dear, treasure, venerate

Cherokee
associated with: **5** (Trail of) Tears
scholar: **7** Sequoya

cherry brandy 6 kirsch

Cherry Orchard, The
author: **7** (Anton) Chekhov

cherub 4 amor **5** angel, child, cupid, youth **6** moppet **8** amoretto

chess
horizontal rows: **4** rank
international chess federation: **4** FIDE
piece: **4** king, pawn, rook **5** queen **6** bishop, castle, knight **8** chessman, material
vertical rows: **4** file

chesterfield 4 coat, sofa **5** couch **8** overcoat

chestnut 8 Castanea

chestnut-colored 6 auburn, russet, sienna **8** cinnamon, nut-brown

chew 4 gnaw **5** champ, crush, grind, munch **6** crunch, nibble **8** ruminate

chew out 5 scold **6** berate, rail at, rebuke **7** reprove, upbraid **8** reproach

chew the fat 3 gab, gas, jaw, rap, yak **4** blab, chat, chin, talk **5** prate **6** gossip, patter **7** blather, chatter, palaver, prattle, twaddle **8** chitchat, converse, talk idly

chic 4 tony **5** natty, ritzy, smart, swank **6** classy, modish, snazzy, swanky **7** elegant, stylish, voguish

Chicago
  airport: 5 O'Hare **6** Midway
  baseball team: 4 Cubs **8** White Sox
  basketball team: 5 Bulls
  downtown area: 4 Loop
  football team: 5 Bears
  fort: 8 Dearborn
  hockey team: 10 Black Hawks
  lake: 8 Michigan
  mayor: 5 Daley
  nickname: 9 Windy City
  river: 7 Chicago **10** Des Plaines

chicanery 4 ruse, wile **5** craft, fraud, guile **6** deceit, duping **7** cunning, gulling, roguery **8** trickery, villainy

chichi 4 arty **5** fussy, showy **6** flashy, frilly, garish, prissy, vulgar **7** finical, pompous, splashy **8** affected, gimcrack, overnice, precious, sissyish

chick
  group of: 5 brood **6** clutch

chicken, chickenhearted 3 hen **4** cock, fowl **5** layer, timid **6** afraid, coward, craven, pullet, scared, yellow **7** caitiff, fearful, gutless, rooster **8** cowardly, timorous

chide *see* **5 scold**

chief 3 key **4** boss, head, lord, main **5** first, major, prime, ruler **6** leader, master **7** captain, monarch, primary, supreme **8** director, dominant, foremost

chiffonier 6 bureau **7** dresser **8** cupboard

chignon 3 bun **4** knot, roll **6** hairdo

child 3 boy, kid, lad, son, tad, tot **4** baby, girl, lass, tyke **5** youth **6** infant, moppet, rug rat **7** toddler **8** daughter, juvenile

child prodigy 7 quiz kid, whiz kid

Chile
  capital/largest city: 8 Santiago
  island: 6 Easter **13** Juan Fernandez **14** Tierra del Fuego
  mountain: 5 Andes, Coast
  highest point: 4 Ojos (del Salado)
  physical feature:
    channel: 6 Beagle **8** Cockburn, Moraleda
    desert: 7 Atacama
    strait: 6 Nelson **8** Magellan
  feature:
    cowboy: 5 huaso
  food:
    meat pie: 8 empanada
    soup: 7 cazuela **8** caldillo

chill, chilly 3 icy, nip, raw **4** bite, cold, cool, keen **5** aloof, brisk, crisp, harsh, nippy **6** arctic, biting, bitter, frigid, frosty **7** coolish, hostile, iciness

chime 4 gong, peal, ring, toll **5** knell, sound **6** jingle, tinkle **7** pealing, ringing **8** carillon, ding-dong, tinkling, tollings **10** set of bells

chimera 5 dream, fancy **6** bubble, mirage **7** fantasy, monster, phantom **8** daydream, delusion, idle whim, illusion

Chimera
  form: 7 monster
  breathes: 4 fire

chimney 4 flue, tube, vent **5** cleft, gully, spout, stack **6** funnel, hearth **7** opening

chimpanzee 3 ape **6** animal, baboon, monkey

chin 3 gab, jaw, rap **4** chat, talk **7** chatter, palaver **8** chitchat, converse

China
  capital: 6 Peking **7** Beijing
  largest city: 8 Shanghai
  island: 5 Macau **6** Hainan, Xiamen **8** Hong Kong, Zhoushan
  river: 4 Amur **7** Hwang Ho, Yangtze **10** Chang Jiang **11** Heilong Jiang **12** Songhua Jiang
  sea: 6 Yellow **9** East China **10** South China
  physical features:
    desert: 4 Gobi
    dry lake: 6 Lopnor

peninsula: 6 Leichu **7** Luichow **8** Liaotung

plateau: 5 Loess **7** Tibetan

strait: 6 Hainan, Taiwan **7** Formosa

language: 7 Chinese **8** Mandarin **9** Cantonese

place:

palace: 6 Summer **8** Imperial **9** Forbidden (City)

square: 9 Tiananmen

wonder: 9 Great Wall

feature:

boat: 4 junk

military academy: 7 whompoa

chinaware 6 dishes, plates **7** pottery **8** crockery

chine 5 spine **6** dorsum **8** backbone

chink 3 cut, gap **4** gash, hole, rent, rift, ring, slit **5** crack, fault, split **6** breach, rattle, tinkle **7** crevice, fissure, opening

chintzy 5 cheap, tacky **6** frumpy, shabby, sleazy

chip 3 bit, cut, hew **4** chop, gash, hack, nick **5** flake, scrap, shred, split **6** chisel, morsel, paring, sliver **8** fragment, splinter

Chippewa (Ojibwa, Ojibway)

tribe: 4 Cree **6** Ottawa **8** Chippewa

leader: 7 Pontiac

Chiron

form: 7 centaur

father: 6 Cronos

chirp 4 peep, sing **5** cheep, chirr, tweet **7** chirrup, chitter, peeping, twitter

chisel 3 cut, gyp **4** gull, hoax, rook, tool **5** blade, cheat, slice **6** incise

type: 4 cape, cold, wood **7** v-shaped

chit 3 IOU, tab **4** note **5** check **7** voucher

chitchat 3 gab **4** chat **5** prate **6** drivel, gossip **7** chatter, prattle **8** converse

chivalrous 6 polite **7** courtly, gallant **8** mannerly

chloride 7 muriate **8** chemical, compound

chocolate 5 brown, candy, cacao, cocoa

Choctaw

related to: 9 Chickasaw

choice 3 say **4** A-one, best, fine, pick, vote **5** array, elite, prime, prize, stock, store, voice **6** option

7 display, special, variety **8** decision

choir *see* **6 chorus**

choke 3 dam, gag **4** clog, plug **5** block **6** arrest, bridle, hamper, hinder, impede, stifle **7** congest, garrote, inhibit, repress, smother **8** obstruct, restrain, strangle, throttle

choler 3 ire **4** fury, rage **5** anger, wrath **6** temper

choose 3 opt **4** like, pick, take, wish **5** adopt, elect **6** decide, desire, intend, opt for, prefer, see fit, select **7** call out, embrace, espouse, extract, fix upon, pick out, resolve **8** decide on, settle on

chop 3 cut, hew, hit, lop **4** blow, chip, crop, cube, dice, hack **5** cut up, mince, split, swipe, whack **6** cleave

choral ode
  Greek: 7 parodos **8** stasimon

chord 4 line, note, tone **5** music, triad **6** string, tendon **7** cadence, harmony

chore 3 job **4** duty, task,

work **5** stint **6** burden, errand

choreography 5 dance

chortle 5 laugh **7** chuckle

chorus 5 choir, unity **6** accord, unison **7** concert, concord, refrain **8** glee club, one voice, response

chosen 5 elite **6** picked, sorted **7** elected **8** selected

Christ, the *see* **5 Jesus**

christen 3 dip **4** name **6** launch **7** baptize, immerse **8** dedicate, sprinkle

Christiania
  capital of: 6 Norway
  now called: 4 Oslo

Christmas
  also: 4 Noel, Yule **8** Yuletide
  feature/symbol: 4 bell, star, tree **5** angel, gifts, holly **6** candle, carols, creche, manger, sleigh, wreath **8** presents

Christmas Carol, A
  author: 7 (Charles) Dickens

chronic 7 abiding, lasting **8** constant, enduring, habitual, periodic

chronicle 3 log **4** epic, list, note, post, saga **5** diary, enter, story **6** annals, docket, record, relate, report **7** account, history, journal, narrate, recount

chronological 5 dated **6** serial **7** ordered, sequent

chronometer 5 clock **8** horologe

chrysolite 4 iron, lava **5** beryl, green, stone **6** yellow **7** mineral, olivine, peridot **8** silicate

chubby 3 fat **5** buxom, plump, podgy, pudgy, stout, tubby **6** chunky, flabby, fleshy, portly, rotund, stocky, zaftig **7** paunchy **8** heavyset

chuckle 5 cluck, laugh **6** clumsy **7** cackle, chortle, snicker

chum 3 pal **4** bait **5** buddy, crony **6** cohort, friend **7** comrade **8** intimate, playmate, sidekick

chump 4 dolt, dupe, fool, goof, goon, head **5** champ, munch **6** sucker

chunk 3 gob, wad **4** clod, hunk, lump, mass **5** batch, block, piece **6** nugget, square

church 4 cult, sect **5** faith **6** belief, chapel, mosque, temple **7** service **8** basilica, religion

churchman 5 vicar **6** bishop, cleric, curate, deacon, parson, pastor, priest, rector **7** prelate **8** chaplain, minister, preacher

churlish *see* **5 surly**

churn 4 beat, foam, rage, roil, roll, toss, whip **5** heave, shake, swirl, whisk **6** stir up **7** agitate, disturb, pulsate

chute 5 rapid, slide, slope **7** incline, passage

chutzpa, chutzpah 4 gall **5** brass, cheek, nerve **8** audacity, boldness, temerity

ciao 2 hi **5** hello **6** so long **7** goodbye

cigar 4 toby **5** claro **6** corona, havana, maduro, stogie **7** cheroot **8** panatela, perfecto
part: 6 binder, filler **7** wrapper
kept in: 7 humidor

cigarette, cigaret 3 cig, fag **4** biri, rett, weed **5** smoke **6** gasper, grette, reefer

ingredient: 3 tar **7** menthol, tobacco **8** nicotine

cinch 4 band, snap **5** girth **6** clinch, ensure, girdle, shoo-in **8** lead-pipe

cinder 3 ash **4** slag **5** ashes, dross, ember **6** embers, scoria **8** clinkers, iron slag

Cinderella
coach: 7 pumpkin
horses: 4 (white) mice
footman: 4 frog
loses: 7 (glass) slipper

cinema 5 films **6** flicks, movies **7** theater

cinnamon 5 spice
variety: 6 cassia, Ceylon

cipher 3 nil, zip **4** code, zero **5** aught **6** naught, nobody **7** anagram, nothing

Circe
turned men into: 4 pigs **5** swine

circle 3 orb, set **4** halo, hoop, loop, ring **5** arena, curve, hem in, orbit, pivot, round **6** border, clique, corona, region, sphere **7** enclose, envelop, revolve, ringlet

8 dominion, province, sequence, surround

circuit 3 lap, run **4** area, beat, edge, tour, trek, walk **5** jaunt, limit, round, route **6** border, bounds, course, margin, sphere **7** compass, confine, journey **8** circling, frontier, orbiting, pivoting

circulatory system
part: 4 vein **5** heart **6** artery **9** capillary
carries: 6 plasma **9** platelets

circumcision
Hebrew: 4 Bris, Brit **5** Berit, Brith **6** Berith
performed by: 5 Mohel

circumference 3 rim **4** edge **5** girth **6** border, bounds, fringe, girdle, limits, margin **7** outline **8** boundary

circumlocution 8 rambling, verbiage

circumnavigate 5 skirt **6** bypass, circle **8** encircle, go around

circumscribe 3 fix **4** curb **5** check, hem in, limit **6** bridle, circle, corset, define, impede **7** confine, enclose, outline **8** encircle, restrain, restrict, surround

circumspect 4 sage, wary **5** alert **7** careful, guarded, prudent **8** cautious, discreet, vigilant, watchful

circumstance 4 fact, item **5** event, point, thing **6** detail, factor, matter **7** element **8** incident

circumvent 4 miss, shun **5** avoid, dodge, elude, evade, skirt **6** bypass, circle, escape, outwit, thwart **8** go around

circus 4 ring **5** arena **6** big top, circle, uproar **8** carnival, coliseum
  act: 5 clown, flyer **7** acrobat, juggler, trapeze **8** side show

cistern 3 box, tub, vat **4** tank, well **6** cavity, vessel **8** aqueduct

citadel 4 fort **7** bastion, rampart **8** fortress

cite 4 name, note **5** honor, quote **6** praise **7** commend, mention, present, refer to, specify **8** document, indicate

citizen 6 native **7** denizen **8** national, resident

Citizen Kane
  director: 11 (Orson) Welles
  cast: 6 Cotten (Joseph), Sloane (Everett), Welles (Orson) **9** Moorehead (Agnes)
  sled: 7 Rosebud

citrine
  species: 6 quartz
  color: 6 yellow

citron 3 rue **4** lime, rind **5** lemon **6** orange, yellow

city 4 burg, town **7** big town **8** denizens, township

city slicker 4 dude **8** urbanite

Ciudad Trujillo
  capital of: 9 Dominican (Republic)

civic 5 local **6** public **8** citizen's, communal

civil 3 lay **4** city **5** civic, state **6** genial, polite, public **7** affable, amiable, citizen, cordial, secular **8** communal, decorous, gracious, mannerly, obliging

clad 6 garbed **7** arrayed, attired, clothed, dressed

claim 3 ask **4** avow, call, plea, take **5** exact, right, title **6** affirm, allege, assert, avowal, charge, pick up **7** command, declare, profess, request

clairvoyant 7 psychic **8** divining, oracular

clam 4 vise **5** clamp, clasp **6** dollar, marine **7** bivalve, mollusk
   part: 4 foot, palp **5** gills, shell, valve **6** mantle, siphon **7** sinuses **8** ligament
   relative: 6 mussel, oyster

clammy 3 wet **4** damp **5** pasty **6** sticky, sweaty

clamor 3 cry, din **4** call, howl, yell **5** blast, chaos, noise, shout, storm **6** bellow, cry out, racket, rumpus, tumult, uproar **7** call out **8** brouhaha, shouting

clamp 4 clip, grip, vise **5** brace, clasp **6** clench, clinch, fasten, secure **7** bracket **8** fastener

clan 4 gang, knot, line, ring **5** breed, cabal, crowd, group, guild, house, party, stock **6** circle, league, strain **7** company, dynasty, lineage, society **8** alliance, pedigree

clandestine 6 covert, hidden, masked, secret, veiled **7** cloaked, furtive, private **8** secluded, sneaking, stealthy

clang 3 din **4** bong, gong, peal, toll **5** chime, clank, clash, knell **6** jangle **7** clangor, resound, ringing, tolling **8** clashing

clank 5 chink, clang, clash, clink **6** jangle, rattle **7** clangor, clatter **8** clashing

clap 3 bat, hit, rap, tap **4** bang, bump, cast, cuff, dash, hurl, peal, push, roar, rush, slam, slap, swat, toss **5** smack, smite, thump, whack **6** buffet, propel, strike, thrust, thwack, wallop **7** applaud, clatter

claret 3 red **5** blood **7** carmine, deep red, red wine **8** blood-red, Bordeaux, cardinal

clarify 5 clear, purge, solve **6** purify, refine **7** clear up, explain, lay open, resolve

clarinet 4 wind **8** woodwind
   mouthpiece: 4 reed
   musician: 7 (Benny) Goodman

clarion 5 acute, clear, sharp **6** shrill **7** blaring, ringing **8** distinct, piercing, resonant, sonorous

clarity 6 purity **8** lucidity, radiance

clash 4 bang, boil, feud, fray, tiff **5** argue, fight **6** battle, combat, fracas, jangle, rattle, tussle **7** contend, contest, discord, dispute, quarrel **8** conflict, friction, struggle

clasp 3 hug **4** bolt, clip, grip, hasp, hold, hook, link, lock, snap **5** catch, clamp, grasp, latch, press **6** buckle, clinch, clutch, fasten, secure

class 3 set **4** form, kind, rank, rate, size, sort, type **5** brand, breed, caste, genus, grade, group, index, label, order, state **6** course, lesson, status **7** section, species, station, variety **8** category, division, pedigree, position

classic, classical 4 epic **5** model **6** heroic **7** paragon **8** absolute, enduring

classify 3 tag **4** list, rank, rate, size, sort, type **5** brand, grade, group, index, label, order **6** assort **7** arrange, catalog **8** organize

clatter 4 bang **5** clack, clang, clank, clash, clink, clump, crash **6** clamor, jangle, racket, rattle **7** chatter **8** crashing, rattling

clause 4 term **7** article, proviso **8** covenant

claw 3 paw **4** foot, grip, maul, tear **5** seize, slash, talon **6** clutch, pincer, scrape **7** scratch **8** lacerate

Clay, Cassius former name of: 3 (Muhammad) Ali

clean 3 mop **4** dust, fine, neat, pure, tidy, trim, wash **5** bathe, clear, fresh, moral, order, scour, scrub, sweep **6** neaten, tidy up, vacuum, washed **7** launder, scoured, shampoo **8** decorous, sanitary, scrubbed, spotless, unsoiled

clear 3 rid **4** fair, free, keen, make, open **5** alert, clean, empty, lucid **6** acquit, bright, remove, serene, unstop, wholly **7** absolve, audibly, certain, evident, glowing, halcyon, hop over, obvious, plainly, unblock **8** apparent, unhidden

clearance 4 room, sale **6** margin, permit **7** removal

clearing 5 glade

cleat 5 block, chock, spike, wedge **6** batten **7** bollard

cleave 3 cut, hew **4** chop, fuse, hack, hold, open, part, plow, rend, rive, slit, tear **5** cling, crack, halve, sever, slash, slice, split, stick, unite **6** adhere, be true, bisect, cut off, detach, divide, furrow, sunder, uphold **7** abide by, chop off, disjoin, lay open, stand by **8** be joined, break off, hold fast, separate

cleft *see* **7 fissure**

clement 4 kind, mild, warm **5** balmy **6** benign, gentle, humane **7** lenient **8** merciful, tolerant

clench 3 set **4** grip **5** clasp, tense **6** clinch, clutch **7** stiffen, tighten **8** fasten on, hold fast

Cleopatra
  queen of: 5 Egypt
  father: 7 Ptolemy
  brother/husband: 7 Ptolemy
  lover: 6 (Mark) Antony, (Julius) Caesar
  death by: 3 asp **7** suicide

clergyman 5 padre, rabbi **6** cleric, father, parson, pastor, priest **7** prelate **8** chaplain, minister, preacher, reverend, sky pilot

clerical 6 cleric, filing, office, typing **7** clerkly **8** churchly

Cleveland, Grover
  first name: 7 Stephen
  presidential rank: 12 twenty-second, twenty-fourth
  party: 10 Democratic
  state represented: 2 NY **7** New York
  defeated: 4 Wing **6** Butler, Weaver, Blaine, St John **7** Bidwell **8** Lockwood, Harrison
  vice president: 9 Hendricks, Stevenson
  political career:
    mayor of: 7 Buffalo
    governor of: 7 New York
  notable events of lifetime/

term:
   strike: 7 Pullman

clever 4 able, cute, deft, keen **5** acute, quick, sharp, smart, witty **6** adroit, artful, astute, bright, crafty, expert, shrewd **8** creative, humorous, original

cliche 3 saw **7** bromide **8** banality, old story

click 3 tap **4** clap, snap **5** clack, clink, crack **6** rattle **7** crackle

client 5 buyer **6** patron **7** advisee, shopper **8** customer **9** purchaser

cliff 3 tor **4** crag **5** bluff, ledge **8** palisade

climactic 7 crucial **8** critical, dramatic

climate 3 air **4** mood, tone **5** pulse **6** spirit, temper **7** quality, weather **8** ambience, attitude

climax 4 acme, apex, peak **5** crown **6** crisis, height, summit **8** pinnacle

climb 4 go up, rise **5** mount, scale **6** ascend, ascent, come up

clinch 3 cap, fix, win **4** bind, bolt, grip, nail **5** cinch, clamp, clasp, close, crown, grasp, screw **6** clutch, fasten, obtain, secure, settle, verify **7** confirm **8** complete, conclude

cling 3 hug **4** fuse, grip, hold **5** clasp, grasp, stick **6** adhere, clutch **8** hang on to, hold fast

clink 4 ting **5** clack, clank, click **6** jangle, jingle, rattle, tinkle

Clinton, William Jefferson
original last name: 6
   Blythe
presidential rank: 11
   forty-second
party: 10 Democratic
state represented: 2 AR
   8 Arkansas
defeated: 4 Bush, Dole
vice president: 4 Gore
political career:
   governor of: 8 Arkansas
notable events of lifetime/
   term: 5 NAFTA **10** Whitewater **11** impeachment
   affair: 8 (Monica) Lewinsky
   Supreme Court
      appointments: 6 Breyer **8** Ginsburg

wife: 7 Hillary
child: 7 Chelsea

Clio
muse of: 7 history

clip 3 bob, cut, fix **4** crop, grip, hook, snip, trim **5** clamp, clasp, shear **6** attach, fasten, staple

clique 3 set **4** clan, gang **5** crowd, group **6** circle **7** coterie, faction

cloak 4 cape, hide, mask, robe, veil, wrap **5** cover, tunic **6** mantle, screen, shield, shroud **7** conceal, curtain, pelisse, secrete

clobber 3 hit **4** beat, belt, drub, lick, maul, rout, slug, sock **5** pound, punch, whack **6** batter, beat up, strike, thrash, wallop **7** trounce

clock 5 watch **8** horologe

clod 3 oaf, wad **4** boor, dolt, dope, glob, lout, lump, rube **5** dunce, moron, yokel **8** imbecile, numskull

clog 4 stop **5** block, check, choke, close, dam up **6** stop up **7** barrier, congest **8** blockage, obstacle, obstruct, stoppage

cloister 4 stoa, walk **5** abbey, aisle **6** arcade, closet, coop up, friary, hole up, immure, shut up, wall up **7** conceal, confine, convent, embower, gallery, nunnery, passage, portico, seclude, walkway

clone 4 copy **5** robot **6** double **7** android, replica

close 3 end, hot, pen **4** akin, clog, fast, fill, firm, fuse, halt, join, near, plug, shut, stop, trim **5** block, cease, tight **6** allied, at hand, clog up, coop up, ending, finale, finish, jammed, narrow, nearby, next to, stop up, windup **7** adjourn, compact, confine, cramped, crowded, devoted, dismiss, seal off, shut off, similar, suspend **8** attached, conclude, familiar, friendly, intimate, obstruct

closed-minded 5 rigid **7** adamant, uptight **8** obdurate, stubborn

closefisted 4 mean **5** cheap, close, mingy, tight **6** stingy **7** miserly **8** grudging

close-fitting 4 snug **5** tight

close of day 3 eve **4** dusk, even **6** sunset **7** evening, sundown **8** eventide, gloaming, twilight

closet 2 WC **4** eury, safe **5** ambry, cuddy **6** covert, hidden, locker pantry, secret, toilet **7** armoire, cabinet, private **8** coatroom, cupboard, imprison, secluded

clot 3 gob **4** lump, mass **7** congeal, thicken **8** embolism, solidify, thrombus

cloth 5 goods **6** fabric **7** textile **8** dry goods, material

clothe 3 don **4** case, coat, deck, garb, robe, veil, wrap **5** array, cloak, cloud, cover, drape, dress **6** attire, bedeck, encase, enwrap, outfit, rig out, screen, shroud **7** bedizen, costume, deck out, sheathe

clothes 4 duds, garb, rags, togs, wear **5** dress **6** attire, finery **7** apparel, costume, raiment, regalia **8** clothing, ensemble, garments, wardrobe

clotheshorse 3 fop **4** dude **5** dandy, model

cloud 3 dim, mar **4** blur, hide, veil **5** blind, cloak, cover **6** darken, impair, muddle, shadow, shroud **7** conceal, distort, eclipse

clout *see* **5 punch**

clover 9 Trifolium

clown 3 wag, wit **4** card, fool, jest, joke, mime, zany **5** comic, cut up, joker **6** jester, madcap **7** buffoon

cloy 3 gag **4** bore, glut, pall, sate, tire **5** choke, weary **6** benumb, overdo **7** exhaust, satiate, surfeit **8** nauseate, saturate

club 3 bat, hit **4** bash, beat, flog, slug **5** flail, group, guild, lodge, stick **6** batter, buffet, cudgel, league, pommel, pummel, strike **7** society **8** alliance, bludgeon, sorority

clue 3 cue, key **4** clew, hint, mark, sign **5** guide, scent, trace **7** glimmer, inkling, pointer **8** evidence

clumsy 5 bulky, crude, gawky, inept, rough **6** klutzy **7** awkward

8 bungling, ungainly, unwieldy

cluster 4 heap, herd, knot, mass, pack, pile **5** batch, block, bunch, clump, crowd, flock, group, swarm **6** gather, throng **7** collect **8** assemble, converge

clutch 3 hug **4** grip, hold **5** clasp, grasp **6** clench **7** cling to, embrace, squeeze

clutter 4 mess, pile **5** chaos, strew **6** jumble, litter, tangle **7** scatter **8** disarray, disorder

Clytemnestra
mother: 4 Leda
brother: 6 Castor, Pollux
sister: 5 Helen **8** Timandra
husband: 9 Agamemnon
son: 7 Orestes
daughter: 7 Electra, Erigone **9** Iphigenia
killed: 9 Agamemnon
killed by: 7 Orestes

coach 3 bus **5** drill, guide, sedan, stage, teach, train, tutor **6** advise, direct, mentor **7** omnibus, trainer **8** carriage, instruct

coachman 3 fly **4** jehu, whip **5** pilot **6** driver

coagulate 3 gel, set **4** clot, jell **6** curdle, harden **7** congeal, thicken **8** solidify

coal 4 ash, bass, char, coke, coom, culm, dust, fuel, slag, smut, swad **5** ember **6** cannel, cinder **7** lignite, clinker **8** charcoal
box: 3 hod **7** scuttle
made from: 6 carbon
mining method: 4 deep **5** strip **8** opencast
mine: 5 drift, shaft, slope, strip
size: 3 egg, nut, pea **5** stove

coalesce 3 mix **4** ally, form, fuse, join, meld **5** blend, merge, unify, unite **6** cohere **7** combine

coarse 4 lewd, rude, vile **5** crass, crude, gross, harsh, rough **6** common, vulgar **7** boorish, bristly, brutish, ill-bred, loutish, prickly, uncouth **8** scratchy

coast 4 skim, slip, waft **5** drift, float, glide, shore, slide, sweep **6** strand **7** seaside **8** glissade, littoral, seaboard, seacoast, seashore

coat 3 fur **4** hair, hide, pelt, wrap **5** cover, glaze, layer, paint, smear **6** blazer, enamel, encase, jacket, spread **7** encrust, envelop, lacquer, overlay, plaster, topcoat **8** laminate, overcoat, raincoat

coax 6 cajole **7** wheedle **8** butter up, inveigle, soft-soap, talk into

cobalt 4 blue **5** azure **7** element, sky blue
chemical symbol: 2 Co

cobbler 3 pie

cobra
also: 3 asp **5** mamba
enemy: 8 mongoose

cocktail 5 drink, fruit, horse **6** shrimp

cocktail lounge 3 bar **6** saloon, tavern **7** gin mill, taproom

cocky 5 brash, saucy **6** jaunty **8** arrogant, cocksure, impudent

cocoon
covering for: 5 larva
stage: 5 pupal
made of: 4 silk

coddle 3 pat, pet **4** baby **5** humor, spoil **6** caress, cuddle, dote on, fondle, pamper **7** indulge

code 4 laws **5** rules **6** cipher **7** statute **8** precepts

codger 5 crank, miser **6** geezer, oddity, old man

codify 4 rank, rate **5** grade, group, index, order **7** arrange, catalog **8** classify, organize, tabulate

coelenterate 5 coral, hydra, polyp **6** Medusa **7** acaleph, radiate **8** acalephe

coerce 3 cow **4** make **5** bully, drive, force **6** compel, oblige **7** dragoon **8** browbeat, bulldoze, pressure, threaten

coffee 6 Coffea
beverage: 5 decaf, latte **6** kahlua **8** espresso

coffer 3 box **4** case **5** chest

coffin 3 box **4** pall **6** casket

cog 3 cam, lie **4** gear **5** cheat, cozen, tenon, tooth, wedge, wheel **8** small boat

cogent 5 sound, valid **6** potent **7** weighty **8** forceful, powerful

cogitate 5 study, think, weigh **6** ponder **7** reflect **8** meditate, ruminate

cognac
type: 6 brandy **7** liqueur

cognate **4** akin, like **5** close **7** kindred, related, similar **8** familial, parallel

cognition **7** knowing

cognizance **4** heed, note **5** grasp **6** notice, regard **8** scrutiny

cognoscenti **6** judges **7** experts **8** insiders

coherent **5** clear, lucid **7** logical, orderly **8** rational

cohesive **3** set **5** solid **6** sticky **7** viscous **8** cemented, sticking

cohort **3** pal **4** chum **5** buddy, crony **6** fellow, friend **7** comrade **8** follower, myrmidon

coif **3** cap **4** hood, veil **6** beggin, burlet, hairdo **8** biggonet, coiffure

coil **4** curl, loop, ring, roll, wind **5** braid, twine, twist **6** circle, spiral, writhe **7** entwine **8** encircle

coin **4** mint **5** hatch, money, piece **6** change, create, devise, invent, make up, silver, strike **7** concoct **8** conceive

coincide **3** fit **4** jibe, meet **5** agree, cross, match, tally **8** converge, dovetail

coincidence **4** fate, luck **6** chance **8** accident

Cointreau type: **7** liqueur

cold **3** icy, old **4** cool **5** aloof, brisk, chill, crisp, cruel, nippy, polar **6** arctic, biting, bitter, chilly, cooled, frigid, frosty, frozen, inured, numbed, severe, wintry **7** chilled, distant, frosted, glacial, nipping, passive, unmoved **8** reticent, uncaring, unheated

coliseum **4** bowl **5** arena **6** circus **7** stadium, theater

collaborate **4** join **5** unite **6** assist, team up **7** collude

collapse **4** coma, fail, fall, flop, fold **5** faint, swoon **6** attack, buckle, cave-in, fizzle **7** crumple, failure, give way, seizure **8** downfall

collar **3** nab **4** eton, grab **5** catch, fichu, pinch, seize **6** arrest, bertha **7** capture

collate **5** order **6** bestow, verify **7** compare **8** assemble, organize

collateral **4** bond **5** extra **6** pledge, surety **7** warrant

8 parallel, security, warranty

colleague 4 mate **6** fellow **7** partner **8** confrere, co-worker, teammate

collect 3 get **4** calm, meet **5** amass, raise, rally **6** gather, heap up, muster, obtain, summon **7** call for, compile, compose, marshal, receive, solicit **8** assemble, gather up, scrape up

college 7 academy **8** seminary

collide 3 hit **4** meet **5** clash, crash, smash **7** crack up, diverge, run into **8** bump into

colloquial 5 homey, plain **6** casual, chatty, common, folksy **8** everyday, familiar, informal

colloquy 4 chat, talk **6** caucus, parley **7** council, palaver, seminar **8** commerce, congress, converse, dialogue

collude 4 plot **7** connive **8** conspire, intrigue

cologne 5 scent **7** essence, perfume

Colombia
 capital/largest city: 6 Bogota
 mountain: 5 Andes
 highest point: 14 Cristobal Colon
 river: 6 Amazon **7** Orinoco **8** Guaviare
 sea: 7 Pacific **9** Caribbean
 physical feature:
  plains: 6 Ilanos
 feature:
  dance: 7 bambuco **8** merengue
  woven hat: 5 jipas

Colombo
 capital of: 8 Sri Lanka

colonnade 3 row **4** stoa **5** porch **6** arcade, piazza **7** portico, terrace **8** cloister

colony 3 set **4** band, body **5** flock, group, swarm **7** mandate **8** dominion, province

colophon 6 design, device, emblem **8** insignia

color 3 dye, hue **4** bias, burn, cast, glow, mood, tint, tone **5** bloom, blush, paint, shade, slant, taint, tinge **6** affect, crayon, redden, spirit **7** distort,

pigment, redness, skin hue
8 dyestuff, rosiness

Colorado

abbreviation: 2 CO **4** Colo

capital/largest city: 6 Denver

feature: 11 Four Corners **17** Continental Divide

mountain: 5 Rocky **9** Pikes Peak

highest point: 6 Elbert

physical feature:
  canyon: 5 Black
  plains: 5 Great
  wind: 7 Chinook
  river: 5 Snake, White **6** Fraser **7** Laramie **8** Arkansas, Colorado

colors 4 flag, jack **6** banner, ensign, pennon **7** pennant **8** standard

colossal 4 huge, vast **5** giant, grand, great **6** mighty **7** extreme, immense, mammoth, massive, titanic **8** enormous, gigantic

Colossus of Rhodes
  statue of: 6 Apollo

colt 4 foal **5** horse **6** novice **8** equuleus, yearling
  constellation of: 8 Equuleus

column 3 row **4** file, line, post **5** pylon, queue, shaft **6** pillar **7** caravan, phalanx, support, upright **8** pilaster

columnist 6 writer **7** analyst

comatose 3 lax **4** dull, idle, lazy **5** inert **6** leaden, torpid **7** drugged, languid **8** indolent, lifeless, slothful

comb 4 card, tuft **5** curry, dress, groom, plume, scour, style **6** search **7** arrange, explore, panache, ransack, topknot **8** head tuft, hunt over, untangle

combat 5 clash, fight **6** action, attack, battle, oppose, resist **7** contest, go to war, wage war **8** conflict, fighting, skirmish, struggle

combine 3 mix **4** fuse, join, pool **5** blend, merge, unify, unite **6** couple, league, mingle **8** compound

combustion 6 firing **7** burning, flaming **8** ignition, kindling

come 2 be, go **3** bud **4** fall, loom, rise **5** occur, range, reach **6** appear, arrive, be made, drop in, emerge, extend, follow, happen, impend, show up, spread, spring, turn up **7** advance, descend, emanate **8** approach

come clean 4 sing **5** own up **7** confess

comedian 3 wag **4** fool, zany **5** clown, comic, cutup, joker **6** jester, madcap **7** buffoon **8** humorist, jokester

comedy 3 fun, wit **5** farce, humor **6** banter, joking, pranks, satire **7** foolery, jesting **8** drollery, raillery, travesty

come face to face with 4 meet **8** confront

comely 4 fair, nice **5** bonny **6** pretty, proper **7** sightly, winning, winsome **8** becoming, blooming, charming, fetching, pleasing

come-on 4 bait, hook, lure, trap **5** decoy, snare **6** magnet

comestibles 5 foods **7** edibles **8** victuals

come to light 4 dawn **5** arise **6** appear, crop up, emerge, evolve, show up,

turn up, unfold **7** develop, surface, turn out

come to pass 5 ensue, occur **6** arrive, befall, follow, happen

come to terms 5 agree, yield **6** give up, settle **7** succumb **8** contract, cry quits

come unglued 6 detach, loosen **8** separate

comfit 5 candy, sweet

comfort 4 calm, ease, help **5** peace, quiet **6** luxury, relief, solace, soothe, succor, warmth **7** console, hearten **8** coziness, pleasure, reassure, serenity, snugness

comic, comical 4 rich **5** droll, funny, merry, silly, witty **6** absurd, jocose, jovial **7** amusing, jocular, risible **8** farcical, humorous, mirthful

coming 4 next **6** advent, future, in view, to come **7** arrival, nearing **8** approach, arriving, imminent, on the way

command 3 bid, get **4** boss, call, draw, fiat, head, hold, lead, rule **5** edict, evoke, grasp, guide **6** adjure, behest, charge, decree, demand, direct, elicit, enjoin, govern, manage, ordain, prompt **7** conduct, control, extract, inspire, provoke, receive, require **8** instruct, motivate

commemorate 4 hail, mark **5** extol, honor **6** hallow, revere, salute **7** acclaim, glorify, observe **8** venerate

commence 5 begin, start **8** get going, initiate

commend 2 OK **4** back, give, laud **5** extol **6** commit, confer, convey, praise **7** acclaim, approve, consign, endorse, entrust, stand by, support **8** delegate, give over, hand over, transfer

commensurate, commensurable 4 even, meet **5** equal **7** fitting **8** balanced, in accord, parallel, relative, suitable

comment 4 note, word **6** remark **7** clarify, discuss, explain, expound

commerce 5 trade **6** barter **7** trading, traffic **8** business, exchange, industry

god of: 6 Hermes **7** Mercury

commingle 3 mix **4** fuse **5** blend, merge, unify **7** combine

commiserate 7 feel for **8** show pity

commission 3 act, bid, cut, fee **4** duty, hire, name, rank, role, task **5** board, order, piece, proxy, trust **6** agency, assign, charge, direct, employ, engage, office **7** appoint, certify, charter, council, empower, license, mandate, portion, rake-off, stipend, warrant **8** contract, delegate, dividend

commit 2 do **3** act, put **4** bind, pull **5** enact, place **6** assign, decide, effect, engage, intern, pursue **7** confine, consign, deliver, deposit, entrust, execute, perform, pull off, resolve **8** carry out, give over, obligate, practice, transact, transfer

committee 4 body, jury **5** bench, board, group, junta, table **6** bureau, soviet **7** cabinet, council

commode 6 bureau, toilet **7** cabinet, dresser

commodious 5 ample, large, roomy **8** spacious

commodity 4 ware **5** asset, goods, stock **6** staple **7** holding, product **8** property

common 4 base **5** brash, cheap, crass, crude, joint, lowly, minor, plain, stock **6** brazen, normal, old-hat, public, shared, simple **7** average, boorish, general, ignoble, loutish, obscene, obscure, popular, prosaic, regular, routine, settled, uncouth, unknown, worn-out **8** communal, everyday, familiar, frequent, mediocre, middling, ordinary, plebeian, standard

commonwealth 5 state **6** nation **8** republic

commotion 3 ado **4** fuss, stir, to-do **5** furor **6** bustle, racket, ruckus, tumult, uproar **7** turmoil

commune 3 gab, rap, yak **4** chat, chin, farm, talk, town **5** visit **6** babble, confer, gossip, parley, powwow **7** chatter, palaver, prattle **8** converse, schmooze

communicable 8 catching

communicate 3 say **4** give, show, talk, tell **5** state, write **6** convey, impart, notify, pass on, relate **7** declare, divulge, mention **8** announce, converse, disclose, proclaim, transmit

communion, Communion 6 accord **7** concord, harmony, rapport, sharing **8** affinity, sympathy

Communist 3 red **6** soviet **7** comrade, marxist **8** Leninist

commute 4 ride, trip **5** alter **6** adjust, change, redeem, soften, switch, travel **7** convert, journey, replace, reverse **8** diminish, exchange, mitigate

Comoros
capital/largest city: 6 Moroni
monetary unit: 5 franc
island: 6 (Grande) Comoro **7** Mayotte
sea: 6 Indian

compact 4 bond, cram, snug, tidy **5** close, dense, press, small **6** little, treaty

7 bargain, crammed, pressed, squeeze, stuffed **8** compress

companion 3 pal **4** chum, mate **5** buddy, crony **6** escort, friend, helper **7** comrade

company 3 mob **4** band, firm, gang **5** bunch, group, guest, party **6** people, throng **7** callers, friends, society, visitor **8** assembly, comrades, presence, visitors

compare 5 equal, liken, match **6** be up to, equate, relate **7** vie with **8** approach, contrast

compare notes 6 confer **7** consult **8** talk over

compartment 3 box, pew **4** brig, cell, crib, hole, nook, room **5** berth, booth, cabin, crypt, niche, stall, vault **6** closet **7** chamber, cubicle, section

compass 5 bound, range, reach, scope, sweep **6** domain, extent **8** boundary, province

compassion 4 pity **5** heart **7** empathy, feeling **8** humanity, sympathy

compatibility 6 accord **7** concord, harmony, rapport **8** affinity

compatible 3 apt, fit **6** seemly **7** fitting **8** in accord, suitable

compelled 4 must **5** bound, urged **6** driven, forced **7** coerced, obliged, pressed **8** commanded, dragooned, pressured, required

compendium 4 list **5** brief **6** apercu, digest, precis, survey **7** abstract, capsule, catalog, epitome, summary **8** syllabus, synopsis

compensate 3 pay **5** cover, repay **6** make up, offset, redeem, square **7** balance, pay back, redress

compete 3 vie **5** fight, rival **6** battle, combat, oppose **7** contend, contest

competent 3 fit **6** expert, versed **7** skilled, trained **8** skillful

competition 4 game **5** event, match, rival **7** contest, rivalry, tourney **8** conflict, struggle

compile 5 amass **6** garner, gather, muster **7** collate, collect, marshal **8** assemble

complacent 4 smug **6** at ease **7** content

complain 3 nag **4** beef, carp, moan **5** cavil, gripe, whine **6** grouch, grouse, squawk **7** grumble

complaisant 4 warm **7** affable, amiable, cordial **8** friendly, gracious, obliging, pleasant, pleasing

complement 3 cap **5** crown, match, total, whole **7** balance, perfect **8** ensemble, entirety, parallel, round out

complete 3 cap, end **4** full **5** total, utter, whole **6** entire, finish, intact, settle, wrap up **7** achieve, execute, fulfill **8** achieved, conclude, executed, round out, thorough, unbroken

complex 4 maze **5** mixed **6** knotty, system **7** network, tangled **8** compound, involved, manifold, multiple, puzzling

complexion 3 hue **4** look, tone **5** color, image, slant **7** outlook **8** coloring

compliant 8 flexible, yielding

complicate 4 knot **5** ravel, snarl **6** muddle, tangle **7** confuse, involve **8** confound, entangle

complicity 8 abetment, intrigue, plotting, schemery, scheming

compliment 5 honor, kudos **6** homage, praise **7** tribute **8** flattery

complimentary 4 free **6** gratis **8** admiring, praising

comply 3 bow **4** bend, meet, mind, obey **5** defer, yield **6** accede, adhere, follow, give in, submit **7** abide by, conform, fulfill

component 4 item, part **5** piece **6** detail, module **7** element, segment

compose 4 calm, form, lull, make **5** frame, quell, quiet, relax, shape, write **6** create, devise, make up, pacify, settle, soothe **7** fashion **8** comprise

compound 3 mix **4** fuse, make **5** add to, alloy, blend, boost, mixed, union, unite **6** fusion, mingle **7** amalgam, augment, blended, combine, complex, concoct, enlarge, magnify, mixture **8** increase

comprehend 3 dig, get **5** catch, grasp, savvy **6** absorb, digest, fathom **8** conceive, perceive

comprehensive 4 full **5** broad **7** copious, general, overall **8** complete, sweeping, thorough

compress 4 cram, pack **5** press **6** reduce, shrink **7** abridge, bandage, compact, curtail, plaster, shorten, squeeze **8** condense, dressing

comprise 4 form **6** make up **7** compose, contain, include **8** be made of

compromise 4 risk **5** agree, truce **6** settle **7** balance, compact, imperil **8** endanger, undercut

comptroller 7 auditor

compulsive 6 driven, hooked **7** driving, fanatic **8** addicted, habitual

compulsory 7 binding **8** coercive, enforced, forcible, required

compunction 5 demur,

qualm, shame **6** regret, unease **7** anxiety, concern, remorse, scruple

compute 3 add **5** sum up, tally, total **6** figure, reckon **7** count up, work out

computer

  language: 3 Ada, APL, XML **4** Java, LISP, HTML, LOGO, SGML **5** ALGOL, BASIC, COBOL **6** Pascal **7** FORTRAN

  term: 2 PC **3** bit, bug, bus, CAD, CAM, CPU, DOS, FAQ, PDA, pdf, RAM, ROM, web, www **4** beta, blog, boot, byte, chip, file, hack, icon, Java, link, spam, Unix **5** CD-Rom, crash, debug, drive, e-mail, input, Linux, modem, mouse, pixel, pop-up, queue, virus **6** adware, analog, applet, avatar, backup, cookie, cursor, domain, glitch, hacker, laptop, memory, online, output, read me, server, window, wizard **7** ActiveX, blogger, browser, digital, keyword, network, offline, program, spyware

8 banner ad, bookmark, chat room, database, download, emoticon, firewall, handheld, hardware, homepage, internet, lightpen, notebook, printout, software, terminal, wireless
see also **8 Internet**

comrade 3 pal **4** ally, chum **5** buddy, crony **6** friend **7** partner **8** confrere, co-worker, intimate

comte 5 count

con 3 gyp **4** anti, bilk, coax, fool, gull, hoax, lure, rook **5** cheat, cozen, felon, trick **6** delude **7** beguile, convict, defraud, mislead, swindle **8** hoodwink

Conakry
   capital of: 6 Guinea

concave 6 hollow, sunken **8** indented

conceal 4 hide, mask **5** cloak, cover **6** screen, shield **7** cover up, obscure, secrete **8** disguise

concede 3 own **4** cede **5** admit, agree, allow, yield **6** accept, give up, resign **7** abandon **8** hand over

conceit 3 ego **5** pride **6** vanity **7** ego trip, egotism **8** bragging, self-love

conceivable 8 credible, knowable, possible

conceive 4 form **5** frame, hatch, start **6** create, ideate, invent **7** concoct, dream up, imagine, produce **8** contrive, envision, initiate

concentrate 4 mass **5** amass, bunch, focus **6** center, gather, reduce **7** close in, cluster, pay heed, thicken **8** assemble, attend to, condense, converge

concept 4 idea, view **5** image **6** belief, notion, theory **7** opinion, thought

concern 3 job **4** care, duty, firm, heed **5** chore, house, store, worry **6** affair, matter, regard **7** anxiety, apply to, company, disturb, involve, mission, trouble **8** distress

concert 5 union, unity **6** accord, settle **7** concord, harmony **8** teamwork

concert hall 5 odeum **6** lyceum **7** theater

concession 5 lease 6 assent 8 giving in, yielding

conciliate 6 pacify 7 appease, placate

concise 5 brief, pithy, short, terse 7 compact 8 succinct

conclave 6 parley, powwow 7 council, meeting, session 8 assembly

conclude 3 end 4 halt, stop 5 close, infer, judge 6 deduce, finish, gather, reason, settle 7 arrange, resolve, surmise 8 break off, carry out, complete

conclusive 5 clear 6 patent 7 certain, obvious 8 absolute, decisive, definite, manifest, palpable

concoct 3 mix 4 brew 5 frame, hatch 6 cook up, create, devise, invent, make up 7 think up 8 compound, contrive

concord 5 amity, peace 6 accord 7 harmony 8 goodwill

concourse 7 joining, linkage, meeting 8 junction

concrete 4 real 5 solid 6 cement 7 express, factual, precise 8 definite, distinct, material, tangible

concur 5 agree, match, tally 6 square 7 conform 8 coincide, hold with

concussion 3 jar 4 blow, bump 5 clash, shock 6 buffet, impact

condemn 4 damn, doom 5 decry 6 rebuke 7 censure 8 denounce, sentence

condense 3 cut 4 trim 6 digest, reduce 7 abridge, compact, liquefy, shorten, thicken 8 compress, contract, pare down

condescend 5 deign, stoop 6 submit, unbend 7 descend, disdain

condiment 4 herb 5 sauce, spice 8 dressing, seasoner

condition 3 fit 4 term 5 adapt, equip, ready, shape, state, train 6 fettle, malady, status, tone up 7 ailment, prepare, proviso 8 position, standing

conditional 7 limited

condolence 4 pity 6 solace 7 comfort 8 sympathy

condone 6 excuse, forget, ignore, pardon, wink at

7 absolve, forgive, justify, let pass **8** overlook

conducive 7 helpful **8** salutary **9** favorable, promotive

conduct 3 act **4** lead, rule, ways **5** carry, deeds, enact, guide, pilot, steer, usher **6** behave, convey, convoy, direct, govern, manage, manner **7** comport, control, marshal, operate, perform **8** dispatch, regulate

conduit 4 duct, main, pipe, tube **5** canal, drain **6** gutter, trough **7** channel, passage **8** aqueduct

cone 5 bevel, shape, spire **6** bobbin, conoid, funnel **7** pyramid, volcano
kind: 3 fir **4** pine **5** larch **7** conifer, retinal **8** ice cream

confabulate 4 chat, talk **6** confer, patter **7** chatter, discuss **8** chitchat, converse, talk idly

confection 3 jam **5** candy **6** pastry **7** dessert **8** conserve, delicacy

confederacy, Confederacy 3 CSA **4** band, bloc **5** guild, union **6** fusion, league **7** combine, society **8** alliance, the South

confederate 4 ally **5** merge, unite **6** cohort, helper **7** abettor, comrade, partner **8** coalesce, coworker

confer 4 give **5** award **6** accord, parley **7** consult, discuss, palaver **8** converse

conference 4 talk **6** parley **7** council, meeting, seminar **8** conclave

confess 3 own **4** avow, sing **5** admit **6** expose, reveal **7** divulge **8** disclose

confide 6 impart, reveal **7** confess, divulge, lay bare, let in on, let know **8** disclose

confident 4 bold, sure **5** cocky **6** daring, secure **7** assured, certain **8** cocksure, intrepid, positive

confidential 5 privy **6** secret **7** private **8** hush-hush

configuration 4 form **6** design, makeup

confine 3 pen, tie **4** bind, cage, hold, jail, keep **5** limit **6** coop up, lock up, shut in **7** impound

8 imprison, regulate, restrain, restrict

confirm 5 prove **6** accept, clinch, ratify, uphold, verify **7** agree to, approve, bear out, certify, sustain **8** make firm, validate

confiscate 4 take **5** seize **7** impound, possess, preempt **8** take over

conflagration 4 fire **5** blaze **7** inferno

conflict 4 fray **5** clash, fight, melee **6** action, battle, combat, fracas, oppose, strife, tussle **7** discord, warfare **8** disagree, division, friction, variance

confluence 5 union **7** conflux, joining, linkage, meeting **8** junction, juncture

conform 3 fit **4** obey **5** adapt **6** adjust, follow **8** adhere to, jibe with, submit to

confound 5 mix up **6** baffle, puzzle, rattle **7** astound, confuse, fluster, mystify, nonplus, perplex, startle **8** astonish, bewilder, dumfound

confrere 3 pal **4** ally, chum **5** buddy **6** friend **7** brother, comrade, partner

confront 4 dare, defy, face, meet **5** brave

confuse 5 addle, befog, mix up, stump **6** baffle, muddle, puzzle, rattle **7** fluster, mistake, mystify, nonplus, perplex **8** befuddle, bewilder, confound, unsettle

confute 4 deny **5** rebut **6** impugn, oppose, refute **7** counter, gainsay

congeal 3 set **4** clot, jell **6** curdle, freeze, harden **7** stiffen, thicken **8** solidify

congenial 4 like **6** genial, social **7** affable, cordial, related, similar **8** agreeing, amenable, pleasant

congenital 6 inborn, inbred, innate, native **7** natural **8** inherent

congestion 3 jam, mob **4** mass **5** snarl **6** pile-up **8** crowding

conglomerate 4 heap, mass, pile **5** amass, blend, stack **7** mixture **8** assemble

Congo, Democratic Republic of

other name: 5 Zaire **12** Belgian Congo
capital/largest city: 8 Kinshasa
lake: 4 Kivu **5** Mweru **6** Albert, Edward
highest point: 7 Stanley **8** Ngaliema
river: 5 Congo, Ebola, Kasai **6** Ubangi
physical feature:
  falls: 7 Stanley
  valley: 4 Rift
Congo, Republic of
other name: 11 French Congo
capital/largest city: 11 Brazzaville
lake: 6 Albert, Nyanza **7** Leopold
highest point: 6 Leketi
river: 5 Congo
congratulate 4 hail **6** salute
congregate 4 mass **5** amass, flock, swarm **6** gather, throng **7** cluster, collect **8** assemble
congress, Congress 4 diet **6** caucus **7** council **8** assembly
congruous 4 meet **6** seemly **7** apropos **8** becoming, relevant, suitable
conjecture 4 idea, view

5 fancy, guess, infer, judge, think **6** notion, reckon **7** presume, suppose, surmise **8** judgment, theorize
conjoined 6 joined, linked, united **7** knitted, meeting **8** combined, touching
conjugate 4 join, pair, yoke **5** mated, unite **6** couple **7** connect, related
conjunction 3 and, but **5** union **7** joining, meeting
conjure 5 allay, charm, raise **6** invoke, summon **7** bewitch, enchant **8** call upon
connected 4 tied **6** joined, merged, united **7** coupled **8** attached
Connecticut
abbreviation: 2 CT **4** Conn
nickname: 6 Nutmeg **12** Constitution
capital/largest city: 8 Hartford
feature: 10 Charter Oak
  casino: 8 Foxwoods **10** Mohegan Sun
  seaport: 6 Mystic
highest point: 8 Frissell
river: 6 Thames **11** Connecticut

connection 3 kin, tie 4 bond, link 5 nexus 7 contact, kinfolk, kinsman, linkage 8 affinity, alliance, junction

Connery, Sean role: 4 (James) Bond

connive 3 aid 4 abet, plan, plot 5 allow 6 wink at 7 collude 8 conspire

connoisseur 5 judge, maven, mavin 6 expert 7 epicure, gourmet

connote 5 imply 6 hint at 7 suggest 8 intimate

connubial 6 wedded 7 marital, nuptial 8 conjugal

conquer 4 beat, best, drub, lick, rout, rule, trim, whip 5 floor, quell 6 defeat, master, thrash 7 possess, win over 8 overcome

conquest 3 fan 4 sway 5 lover 6 adorer, defeat 7 captive, mastery, triumph, victory, winning

conscience 8 scruples

conscience-stricken 6 guilty 7 ashamed 8 contrite, penitent

conscientious 5 exact 6 honest 7 careful, dutiful, ethical, upright

conscious 5 aware, alert, awake 8 noticing, sensible, sentient

consecrate 5 bless 6 hallow 7 glorify 8 sanctify

consecutive 6 in turn, serial 8 unbroken

consensus 6 accord 7 concord

consent 5 agree, allow, yield 6 accede, accept, permit, ratify 7 approve, concede, confirm 8 approval, sanction

consequence 3 end 4 note 5 fruit, value, worth 6 result, upshot 7 gravity, outcome

consequent 7 ensuing 8 eventual

consequently 2 so 4 ergo, then 5 and so, hence, later

conservative 5 quiet 6 square 8 cautious, moderate, undaring

conserve 4 save 5 guard 7 cut back, husband, use less 8 maintain, preserve

consider 4 deem, hold, note 5 judge, opine, study, think, weigh 6 ponder, regard, review 7 believe, examine **8** appraise, hold to be, mull over

considerable 4 tidy **5** ample, great, large **7** notable, sizable

considerate 4 kind **6** kindly **7** mindful **8** obliging

consign 5 remit **6** remand **7** deliver, entrust **8** delegate, hand over, transfer

consist 3 lie **6** reside **7** contain, include

consistent 4 meet **6** steady **7** regular, unified **8** agreeing, constant

console 4 calm, ease **5** cheer **6** soothe, succor **7** comfort, support, sustain

consolidate 4 fuse, join **5** merge, unify, unite **7** combine, fortify **8** compress, condense, federate, solidify

consomme 4 soup **5** broth

consonance 5 amity, unity **6** accord, unison **7** concord, oneness

consort 3 mix **4** club, mate, wife **6** mingle, spouse **7** hang out, husband, partner **8** sidekick

conspicuous 5 clear, overt, plain **6** patent **7** eminent, evident, notable, obvious **8** distinct, manifest, renowned

conspire 5 unite **6** scheme **7** collude, combine, connive

constant 4 even, true **5** fixed, loyal **6** stable, steady, trusty **7** regular, staunch, uniform **8** enduring, faithful, resolute, unvaried

constellation 4 host **5** group, rally **6** circle, galaxy, nebula, spiral, throng **7** cluster, company, pattern

consternation 5 alarm, panic, shock **6** dismay, fright, horror, terror

constituent 4 atom, part **5** piece, voter **6** factor, member **7** elective, element **8** electing, integral, making up

constitute 4 form, make, name **6** create, invest, make up **7** appoint, produce

constrain 4 curb, urge **5** crush, force, quash **6** oblige, subdue **7** confine, repress, squelch **8** hold

back, restrain, restrict,
suppress

constrict 4 bind **5** choke,
cramp, pinch **6** shrink
7 squeeze **8** compress,
contract, strangle

construct 4 form, make **5**
build, erect, frame **6**
create, design, devise **7**
arrange, fashion

construe 4 read, take **7**
explain, make out **8**
decipher

consul 5 envoy **8** emissary,
minister, diplomat **14**
foreign officer,
representative

consult 6 confer, parley,
regard **7** refer to **8**
consider, talk over

consume 3 eat **4** gulp **5**
drain, eat up, spend, use
up, waste **6** absorb,
devour, expend, guzzle,
ravage **7** deplete, destroy,
drink up, engross, exhaust
8 demolish, lay waste,
squander

consummate 2 do **5** sheer,
total, utter **6** finish **7**
achieve, fulfill, perfect,
perform, realize, supreme
8 absolute, complete

contact 4 join, meet **5**
reach, touch, union
7 connect **8** junction,
touching

contagion 7 disease **8**
epidemic, outbreak

contagious 8 catching

contain 4 curb, hold **5**
check **7** embrace, enclose,
include, inhibit, involve,
repress **8** hold back,
restrain, suppress

container 3 bag, box, can,
jar, vat **4** pail **6** barrel,
bottle, bucket, carton,
holder, vessel

contaminate 4 foul, soil **5**
dirty, spoil, taint **6** befoul,
blight, debase, defile,
infect, poison **7** corrupt,
pollute **8** besmirch

contemplate 4 note, plan,
scan **5** weigh **6** ponder,
regard, survey **7** imagine,
observe, project, stare at,
think of **8** aspire to,
envision, mull over,
ruminate

contemporary 3 new **4** late
6 modern, recent, with-it
7 current **8** advanced,
brand-new, up-to-date

contempt 4 hate **5** scorn,

shame **7** disdain, disgust
8 aversion, derision,
distaste, ignominy,
loathing

contend 3 vie, war **4** aver,
avow, hold, spar **5** argue,
claim, clash, fight **6** allege,
assert, battle, combat,
debate, tussle **7** contest,
declare, dispute, grapple,
quarrel **8** maintain,
propound, struggle

content 4 area, core, gist,
load, size, text **5** cheer,
happy, heart, ideas, peace
6 at ease, matter, serene **7**
appease, comfort, essence,
gratify, insides, meaning,
pleased, satisfy, suffice,
unmoved **8** capacity,
serenity

contention 5 clash, fight **6**
battle, combat, strife **7**
discord, dispute, rivalry **8**
argument, conflict,
friction, skirmish, struggle,
variance

conterminous 8 abutting,
adjacent, touching

contest 3 war **4** bout, game
5 fight, match **6** battle,
combat, debate, oppose **7**
dispute, rivalry, tourney **8**
conflict, struggle

context 6 milieu **7** climate,
meaning, setting **8**
ambience

continent 4 pure **6** chaste
8 celibate, land mass,
mainland, virginal

contingency 7 urgency **8**
accident

continue 4 go on, last, stay
5 abide **6** drag on,
endure, extend, remain,
resume **7** carry on, persist,
proceed

contort 4 bend, warp **5**
twist **6** deform **7** distort

contour 4 form **5** lines,
shape **6** figure **7** outline,
profile

contract 3 get **4** pact, take
5 agree, incur **6** absorb,
assume, narrow, pledge,
reduce, shrink, treaty **7**
acquire, develop, dwindle,
shorten, tighten **8**
compress, condense

contradict 4 deny **5** belie,
rebut **6** impugn, oppose,
refute **7** counter, dispute,
gainsay **8** disprove

contraption 6 device, gadget

contrary 5 balky **6** ornery **7**
adverse, counter, hostile,
opposed, willful

8 converse, inimical, opposite, stubborn

contrast **6** depart, differ **7** deviate, diverge **8** variance

contravene **4** deny **5** annul, fight, spurn **6** abjure, breach, combat, disown, negate, oppose **7** disobey, nullify **8** abrogate, disclaim

contribute **4** give **5** endow, grant **6** bestow, confer, donate, lead to **7** advance, forward, hand out, present

contrite **6** rueful **7** humbled **8** penitent

contrive **4** plan, plot **6** create, design, devise, invent, manage, scheme **7** concoct **8** maneuver

control **4** rule, sway **5** brake, steer **6** bridle, charge, govern, manage **7** command, contain, repress **8** regulate, restrain, restrict

controversy **6** debate **7** dispute, quarrel, wrangle **8** argument, squabble

contumacious **6** unruly **7** froward **8** contrary, factious, insolent, mutinous, perverse

contusion **4** hurt, mark, sore **5** mouse **6** bruise, injury, shiner **7** blemish **8** abrasion, black eye

conundrum **5** poser, rebus **6** enigma, puzzle, riddle **7** arcanum, mystery, paradox, problem, puzzler, stopper, stumper

convalesce **4** mend **5** rally **6** revive **7** improve, recover, restore **8** progress

convene **6** gather, summon **7** collect, convoke, round up **8** assemble

convenience **3** use **4** ease **6** chance **7** comfort, service, utility **8** facility, pleasure

convent **7** nunnery **8** cloister

convention **4** code **6** caucus, custom **7** meeting, precept **8** assembly, practice, propriety, protocol, standard

converge **4** meet **5** focus **8** approach

conversant **4** up on **5** aware **6** au fait **7** erudite, privy to, skilled **8** informed

conversation **3** rap **4** chat,

talk **7** gabfest, palaver **8** chit-chat, dialogue

convert 4 turn **6** change, modify, novice **8** neophyte

convex 7 bulging, rounded

convey 4 bear, cede, give, move, tell, will **5** bring, carry, grant **6** impart **7** deliver, divulge **8** disclose, dispatch, transfer, transmit

conveyance 3 bus, car, van **4** cart **5** buggy, truck, wagon **7** vehicle **8** carriage

convict 3 con **4** doom **5** felon **7** condemn **8** jailbird, prisoner, yardbird

conviction 4 view, zeal **5** ardor, creed, dogma, faith, tenet **6** belief **7** opinion **8** doctrine, position

convince 4 sway **6** assure **7** satisfy, win over **8** persuade

convivial 5 merry **6** genial, jovial **7** affable, festive **8** friendly, sociable

convoke 4 meet, open **6** gather, muster **8** assemble, converse

convolute 4 coil, wave, wavy, wind **5** twirl, twist

6 coiled, rolled, spiral, tangle **7** contort, twisted

convoy 5 fleet, usher **6** column, escort **7** conduct

convulse 4 rock, stir **5** laugh, shake, spasm **7** agitate, disturb, perturb

coo 4 bill **6** babble, gurgle, murmur

cook 3 fix **4** chef, fire, heat, make **5** occur **6** cookie, doctor, happen, seethe **7** concoct, prepare, process
method: 3 fry **4** bake, boil, brew, sear, stew **5** baste, broil, grill, poach, roast, saute, scald, shirr, steam **6** braise, coddle, simmer **7** parboil, stir-fry **8** barbecue

cookie 3 bar, gal, gul **4** cake, cook **5** wafer **6** person **7** biscuit, brownie

cooking term 3 a la, cut, dot, fry **4** bake, beat, boil, chop, coat, cube, dice, dust, flan, fold, lard, roux, sear, snip, stew, toss, whip **5** aspic, au jus, baste, blend, bread, broil, brush, candy, cream, crepe, devil, dough, flake, glace, glaze, grate, grill, knead, plank, puree, roast, saute, scald, score, shirr, steep, stock, swear, torte **6** au lait, blanch, braise, coddle, devein, dredge, fillet, flambe, fondue, render, simmer, skewer, sliver **7** a la mode, compote, crouton, garnish, goulash, liquefy, parboil, precook, preheat, rissole, scallop, stir-fry **8** aperitif, au gratin, barbecue, conserve, consomme, julienne, marinate, pot roast

cool 3 icy **4** calm, cold **5** aloof **6** chilly, frosty, serene **7** distant, not warm **8** composed, reserved

Coolidge, Calvin
  first name: 4 John
  nickname: 9 Silent Cal
  presidential rank: 9 thirtieth
  party: 10 Republican
  state represented: 2 MA
  succeeded: 7 Harding
  defeated: 5 Davis, Faris, Johns **6** Foster **7** Nations, Wallace **10** La Follette
  vice president: 5 Dawes
  political career: 13 vice president
    governor of: 2 MA

  notable events of lifetime/ term:
    Act: 8 Volstead
    flight by: 9 Lindbergh
    trial: 6 Scopes

coop 3 mew, pen, sty **4** auto, cage, cote **5** cramp, hutch, roost **6** encase **7** confine **8** imprison

cooperate 4 join **5** unite **7** go along, pitch in, share in **8** take part

coordinate 4 mesh **5** equal, match, order **6** relate **7** arrange, coequal **8** organize, parallel

cop 3 bag, nab, rob, win **4** bull, grab, take **5** bobby, catch, pinch, snare, steal, swipe **6** pilfer, snatch **7** capture **8** gendarme

cope 4 face, spar **6** handle, hurdle, manage, strive, tussle **7** contend, wrestle

copious 4 full **5** ample **6** lavish **7** liberal, profuse **8** abundant, generous

copy 3 ape **4** fake, sham **5** clone, mimic, Xerox **6** follow, mirror, parody, repeat **7** emulate, imitate, replica **8** likeness

coquette 4 vamp **5** flirt, tease

coral 3 red **4** fire, pink, rose **5** horny, polyp, snake **6** orange, sea fan **8** hydrozoa

cord, cordon 5 braid, twine **8** thin rope

cordial 4 warm **6** genial, hearty **7** affable, amiable, sincere **8** friendly

cordon bleu 4 bird **5** finch **7** waxbill

   school for: 5 chefs **7** cooking

core 3 nub **4** crux, gist, guts, meat **5** heart **6** center **7** essence, nucleus

coriander

   flavor: 4 sage **5** cumin **7** caraway

cork 3 bob, oak **4** bark, bung, plug, seal, stop **5** check, close **7** confine **8** restrain, suppress

corker 3 ace **4** lulu, oner, whiz **7** stopper **8** clencher, striking, top notch

corkscrew 4 coil, curl **5** twist **6** spiral **7** winding

corn 4 cure **5** grain **6** callus **7** Zea Mays **8** schmaltz

corner 3 fix, jam, nab **4** bend, grab, hole, nail, nook, spot, trap **5** angle, seize **6** plight, scrape **7** dead end, dilemma

cornerstone 4 base **5** basis

cornet 4 cone, horn **7** trumpet

Cornhusker State

   nickname of: 8 Nebraska

corny 5 banal, hokey, inane, stale, tired, trite, vapid **6** jejune **7** insipid **8** bromidic

corona 4 halo, ring **5** cigar **6** circle, nimbus

coronet 5 tiara **6** diadem **7** chaplet, circlet

corporal 3 NCO **6** bodily **8** physical

corps 4 band, crew, team **5** force, party, squad, troop **6** outfit

corpse 5 stiff **7** cadaver, remains **8** dead body

corpulent *see* **3 fat**

corral 4 herd **5** pen in **6** shut in **7** enclose, fence in, round up

correct 3 fit, fix **4** true **5** alter, amend, emend, right **6** adjust, change, modify, proper, remedy, repair, revamp **7** factual, fitting, improve, precise, rectify **8** accurate, regulate, suitable

correlate 7 compare, connect **8** parallel

correspond 3 fit **4** jibe, suit **5** agree, match **6** accord, concur, equate **7** conform **8** coincide, dovetail, parallel

correspondence 4 mail **7** analogy, letters **8** epistles, missives, relation

corridor 3 way **4** hall, road **5** aisle **6** artery **7** hallway, passage **8** approach

corroborate 4 back **5** prove **6** affirm, uphold, verify **7** certify, confirm, endorse, support, sustain **8** validate

corrosive 4 acid **7** burning, caustic, erosive, mordant **8** abrasive

corrugated 6 fluted, ridged **7** creased, grooved, pleated **8** crinkled, furrowed, puckered

corrupt 3 low **4** base, evil, mean **5** shady **6** debase, poison, seduce, sinful, wicked **7** crooked, debased, debauch,

deprave, immoral, pervert, subvert **8** depraved

corset 5 laces **6** girdle **8** corselet

Corsica 6 island
  capital: 7 Ajaccio
  birthplace of: 8 Napoleon

corundum
  variety: 4 ruby **8** sapphire, star ruby

Cosi fan tutte
  opera by: 6 Mozart

cosmetic 5 blush, liner, paint, rouge **6** makeup, powder **7** mascara, surface **8** artifice, eyeliner, lipstick

cosmic 4 vast **7** immense **8** colossal, enormous, infinite

cosmopolitan 5 suave **6** urbane **7** worldly **8** traveler

cosmos 5 stars **8** universe
  book by: 5 Sagan

Cossack 7 czarist, Russian, trooper **8** horseman

cosset 3 pet **6** caress, coddle, fondle, pamper

cost 3 fee, run, tab **4** bill, loss, take, toll **5** fetch, go for, price, value, worth **6** amount, burden, charge, come to, outlay

7 expense, penalty, sell for, set back **8** amount to

Costa Rica
  capital/largest city: 7 San Jose
  lake: 6 Arenal
  highest point: 8 Chirripo
  feature:
    bird: 7 quetzal
    plantation: 5 finca
  food:
    rice and beans: 10 gallo pinto
    bar snacks: 5 bocas

costume 4 garb **5** dress **6** attire, livery, outfit **7** apparel, clothes, raiment, uniform **8** clothing, garments

cot 3 bed, hut, pen **4** coop, crib **5** cover, stall

coterie 3 set **4** band, camp, clan, club, crew, gang **5** crowd, group **6** circle, clique **7** faction

cottage 3 hut **5** lodge, shack **6** chalet **8** bungalow

cotton
  varieties: 3 bog **4** tree, wild **6** kidney, levant, upland **8** lavender

cotton gin
  invented by: 7 (Eli) Whitney

couch 3 put **4** sofa, word **5** divan, draft, frame, state, utter, voice **6** daybed, draw up, lounge, settee

cougar 3 cat **4** lion, puma **7** panther

cough 4 hack **6** tussis

cough up 3 pay **5** eject, expel **7** deliver **8** hand over

council 5 board, panel **7** cabinet **8** assembly, colloquy, conclave, congress, ministry

counsel 4 urge, warn **6** advice, advise, lawyer **7** call for, caution, suggest **8** admonish, advocate, attorney, guidance, instruct

count 4 deem, hold, lord, rate, tell **5** add up, noble, tally, total **6** impute, number, regard **7** ascribe, include **8** consider, estimate, numerate

countenance 3 aid, air **4** back, face, look, mien **5** build, favor **6** aspect, permit, traits **7** profile, promote, support **8** advocate, auspices, champion, contours, features, presence, sanction

counter 3 bar, man **4** defy, disk **5** piece, stand, table **6** buffet, contra, offset, oppose, resist **7** against **8** contrary, opposite

counterfeit 4 copy, fake, sham **5** bogus, fraud, phony **6** ersatz, forged **7** feigned **8** spurious

countermand *see* **8 overrule**

counterpart 4 copy, mate, twin **5** equal, match **6** double, fellow **8** parallel

countless 6 myriad, untold **7** endless **8** infinite

count on 6 expect **7** hope for

country 4 area, farm, land **5** realm, rural, state **6** nation, people, public, region, rustic **7** boonies, farming, kingdom, natives, scenery, terrain **8** citizens, district, homeland, populace

count up 3 add **5** tally, total **6** reckon **7** compute

count upon 6 expect **7** foresee

coup 3 act **4** blow, deed, feat **6** stroke

coup d'etat 6 mutiny **8** uprising

couple 3 duo, tie **4** bind, join, link, pair, yoke **5** hitch **6** fasten **7** connect, doublet, twosome

courage 4 grit, guts, sand, bold **5** nerve, pluck, spunk, valor **6** daring, mettle **7** bravery

courier 4 mule **5** envoy **6** herald, legate, runner **7** Gabriel, mailman, Mercury, postman **8** emissary

course 3 run, way **4** flow, gush, path, race, road **5** orbit, route, track **6** action, circle, method, policy, stream **7** channel, circuit, classes, lessons, subject **8** lectures

court 3 bar, woo **4** hall, quad, seek, suit, yard **5** bench, manor, plaza, staff, train **6** atrium, invite, palace, pursue, wooing **7** address, attract, cortege, council, flatter, hearing, session **8** assembly

courtesy 5 favor **7** manners, regards, respect **8** civility, kindness

courtier 4 beau **7** gallant **8** cavalier

courtly 5 suave **6** polite **7** elegant, genteel, refined, stately **8** debonair, mannerly, polished

courtyard 4 area, quad **6** atrium

cousin 7 kinsman **8** relation, relative

cove 3 bay **5** inlet **6** lagoon **7** estuary

covenant 3 vow **4** bond, oath, pact **6** pledge, treaty **7** bargain, promise

cover 3 cap, lid, top **4** case, hide, hood, mask, veil, wrap **5** cloak **6** clothe, defend, refuge, report, screen, sheath, shield, shroud **7** blanket, conceal, envelop, include, involve, obscure, overlay, protect, put over, shelter **8** disguise, envelope, pass over, traverse

covert 6 hidden, secret, veiled **7** sub rosa, unknown

covetous 6 greedy **7** craving, envious, jealous, lustful, selfish **8** desirous, grasping, yearning

covey 4 bevy **5** flock, group **6** family

cow 4 beef **5** abash, Bossy, bully, deter, Elsie, scare **6** bovine, cattle, dismay **7** terrify

    young: 4 calf **6** heifer

coward 3 cad **5** sissy **6** craven **7** caitiff, chicken, dastard, milksop **8** poltroon

cowboy 6 drover, gaucho **7** vaquero **8** buckaroo

cower 5 crawl, quail **6** cringe, flinch, grovel, recoil, shrink **7** tremble, truckle

cowl 4 cope, hood **5** cloak

coxcomb 3 fop **4** beau **5** dandy **8** popinjay

coy 3 shy **5** timid **6** demure, modest **7** bashful, prudish **8** blushing

cozen 3 con, gyp **4** bilk, coax, dupe, rook **5** cheat, trick **6** fleece **7** deceive, swindle, wheedle

cozy 4 easy, snug **5** comfy, homey **7** restful

8 homelike, relaxing
French: 6 intime

CPA 7 auditor

crab 4 carp **5** crank, gripe, grump **6** grouch, grouse **8** complain, sourball
constellation of: 6 Cancer

crack 3 gag, jab, pop **4** chip, gibe, jest, joke, quip, rift **5** break, burst, cleft, split **6** cleave, insult, report **7** crevice, fissure, rupture **8** fracture, splinter

crackerjack 2 A-1 **3** ace **4** fine **5** super **6** superb, tip-top **8** splendid, terrific

crackle 4 snap **5** craze, crink

cradle 3 hug **4** crib, font, rock **6** cuddle, enfold, origin, source, spring **7** nursery, snuggle **8** bassinet, fountain

craft 3 art **4** boat, ruse, ship, wile **5** guile, knack, plane, skill, trade **6** deceit, vessel **7** ability, calling, cunning, know-how, perfidy **8** deftness, industry, trickery, vocation

craftsman 4 hand **5** smith

6 worker, wright **7** artisan **8** mechanic

crafty 3 sly **4** foxy, wily **5** canny, sharp **6** artful, astute, shifty, shrewd, tricky **7** cunning, devious **8** scheming

crag 3 tor **4** rock **5** bluff, cliff

cram 3 jam **4** fill, pack **5** crowd, force, grind, press, stuff **7** congest, squeeze **8** compress

cramp 4 pang **5** block, check, crick, limit, spasm **6** hamper, hinder, stitch, stymie **7** prevent, seizure **8** restrain, restrict

crane 4 bird, boom **5** davit, heron **7** derrick
constellation of: 4 Grus

cranium 4 head **5** skull, brain **6** noggin

crank 4 turn, whim **5** brace, winch **6** grouch, handle **7** fanatic **8** crotchet

cranny 3 gap **4** nook, slit **5** break, chink, cleft, crack, notch, split **7** crevice, fissure **8** cleavage

crash 3 din **4** bang, boom, bump, dash, ruin **5** smash, wreck **6** pileup, plunge, racket, topple, tumble **7** clangor, clatter, collide, failure, hitting, intrude, shatter, smashup

crass 5 crude, cruel, gross **6** coarse, oafish, vulgar **7** boorish **8** uncaring

crate 3 box, car **4** auto, case, pack **5** plane **6** jalopy, pallet **8** airplane

crater 3 pit **4** hole **6** cavity

cravat 3 tie **5** ascot, scarf, stock **7** necktie

crave 4 need, want **5** covet **6** desire **7** hope for, long for, pine for, require, sigh for, wish for **8** yearn for

crawl 4 drag, inch, poke, worm **5** creep, mosey **6** squirm, wiggle, writhe **7** slither, wriggle

crayon 5 chalk, draft **6** pastel, pencil, sketch **7** drawing **8** charcoal

crazy 3 mad, odd **4** gaga, nuts, wild **5** rabid, silly, weird **6** absurd, far-out, insane, stupid, unwise **7** berserk, bizarre, cracked, idiotic, strange, unusual **8** demented, deranged, maniacal, peculiar

creak 4 rasp **5** grate, grind

6 scrape, screak, squeak **7** screech

cream 3 top **4** beat, best, drub **5** elite **6** choice, flower **7** the pick, trounce **8** greatest, off-white

crease 4 fold **5** crimp, pleat, ridge **6** furrow, pucker, ruffle, rumple **7** crimple, crinkle, wrinkle

create 4 form, make, mold **5** cause, erect, found, set up **6** design, devise, invent **7** concoct, fashion **8** conceive

creature 3 man **4** bird, fish **5** beast, human **6** animal, insect, mammal, mortal, person **7** critter, reptile

credence 5 faith, trust **6** belief, credit **8** reliance

credentials 6 permit **7** diploma, license, voucher

credenza 5 shelf, table **6** buffet **8** bookcase

credible 6 likely **7** tenable **8** reliable

credit 3 buy **4** time **5** glory, honor, trust **6** esteem **7** acclaim, ascribe, believe, fall for, swallow

credo 4 code, rule **5** maxim, motto, tenet **8** doctrine

credulous **5** naive **8** gullible, trusting

creed **5** dogma **6** belief, canons, gospel **8** doctrine

creek **3** run **4** rill **5** brook **6** branch, spring, stream **7** freshet, rivulet

creep **4** inch, worm **5** crawl, sneak, steal **6** dawdle, squirm, writhe **7** slither, wriggle

creepy **4** eery **5** eerie, scary **6** crawly, spooky, uneasy

cremate **4** burn, char, fire, sear **5** roast **6** ignite, kindle, scorch **8** enkindle

creme de cacao
  type: **6** brandy **7** liqueur

creme de la creme **3** top **4** best **5** cream, elite **6** choice, flower **8** choicest

creme de menthe
  type: **7** liqueur
  flavor: **4** mint

Creole **6** patois **7** criollo, dialect, Haitian

Creon
  king of: **6** Thebes **7** Corinth
  sister: **7** Jocasta

crescent **3** arc, bow **4** arch **5** curve **8** half-moon

crest *see* **6** summit

crestfallen **8** dejected, downcast

Cretan bull
  son: **8** Minotaur
  captured on: **5** Crete
  captured by: **8** Hercules
  recaptured by: **7** Theseus

Crete
  capital/largest city: **5** Canea **8** Iraklion
  division of: **6** Greece
    ruins: **7** Knossos (Palace)

crevice *see* **7** fissure

crew **3** men, mob **4** band, body, herd, pack, team **5** corps, force, group, squad, troop **6** seamen **8** mariners

crib **3** bed, bin, cot, hut, key **4** pony, trot **5** cheat, shack, stall, steal **6** creche, manger **8** bassinet

cricket
  players/team: **6** eleven
  equipment: **3** bat **4** bail, ball **5** stump **6** wicket
  period of play: **4** over **7** innings

crime **3** sin **4** tort **5** wrong **6** felony **7** misdeed, offense, outrage **8** foul play, iniquity, villainy

criminal 4 hood **5** crook, felon, wrong **6** outlaw **7** culprit, lawless **8** culpable, offender, unlawful

crimp 4 curl, fold, kink, wave **5** clamp, flute, frill, frizz **7** crinkle, frizzle, wrinkle **8** obstacle

crimson 3 red **4** ruby **5** blush, flush **6** redden **7** carmine, scarlet

cringe 4 duck **5** cower, dodge, quail, toady **6** blench, flinch, grovel, recoil, shrink **7** truckle

crinkle 5 crush **6** rumple, rustle **7** crumple, wrinkle

crinoline 4 hoop **5** skirt

cripple 4 gimp, halt, harm, maim, stop **6** damage, impair **7** disable **8** make lame, paralyze

crisp 5 brisk, fresh, nippy, terse **6** chilly, snappy **7** brittle, crunchy

criterion 3 law **4** rule **5** gauge, model **7** example, measure **8** standard

critic 5 judge, mavin **6** carper, censor, expert **7** analyst, arbiter,

knocker, reviler **8** reviewer, vilifier

criticize 4 carp, fuss, pick **5** cavil, nag at **7** censure, nitpick, reprove **8** denounce, reproach

croak 3 caw, die **4** kill, moan, roup **7** grumble, kick off

Croatia
  capital/largest city:
   5 Zagreb
  sea: 8 Adriatic
  people: 5 Serbs **6** Croats
   9 Yugoslavs

crock 3 jar, pot **4** olla

crockery 5 china **6** dishes, plates **7** pottery

crocodile 4 croc **6** cayman, gavial, lizard **7** reptile, asurian

crone 3 hag **5** witch **6** beldam **7** beldame

Cronus
  also: 6 Cronos, Kronos
  form: 5 Titan
  father: 6 Uranus
  son: 4 Zeus **5** Hades **8**
   Poseidon
  daughter: 4 Hera **6** Hestia
   7 Demeter
  corresponds to: 6 Saturn

crony 3 pal **4** ally, chum,

mate **5** buddy **6** bunkie, cohort, friend **7** comrade **8** sidekick

crook 3 arc, bow **4** bend, hook, thug, turn **5** angle, cheat, curve, knave, thief, twist **6** bandit, outlaw, robber **7** burglar **8** criminal, swindler

croon 3 hum **4** sing **6** murmur, warble

crop 3 bob, cut, lop **4** clip, snip, trim **5** prune, glean, shear, yield **6** growth **7** harvest, reaping **8** cut short

crop up 5 arise, ensue **6** appear **7** develop, surface

croquet
  equipment: 4 ball, hoop **6** mallet, wicket

Crosby, Bing
  real name: 5 Harry (Lillis) Crosby
  partner: 4 Hope (Bob)
  nickname: 8 Der Bingle

cross 3 mad, mix, tau **4** crux, ford, meet, rood **5** angry, blend, erase, gruff, surly, testy, trial **6** burden, cranky, go over **7** grouchy, oblique, peevish **8** contrary, crucifix, pass over, petulant, snappish

crossing 4 pass **7** mixture, passage **8** blocking, opposing, traverse

cross swords 5 clash, fight **6** battle, combat, tussle **8** skirmish

crotchet 3 tat **4** bent, whim **5** habit, quirk, trait **6** foible, hang-up, oddity, vagary, whimsy **7** caprice

crotchety 3 odd **5** fussy **6** cranky **7** erratic, grouchy **8** contrary, peculiar

crouch 4 bend, duck **5** cower, squat, stoop **6** cringe, recoil, shrink

crow 3 daw, jay, kae **4** blow, brag, rook **5** boast, crake, exult, gloat, raven, strut, vaunt **6** cackle, corbie, magpie **7** jackdaw, triumph, trumpet

crowbar 3 bar, pry **5** jimmy, lever

crowd 3 jam, mob, set **4** cram, gang, herd, host, mass, push **5** flock, group, horde, surge, swarm **6** gather, huddle, legion, throng **7** cluster, coterie, squeeze **8** assemble

crown 3 cap, top **4** acme, apex, head, pate, peak

5 crest, tiara **6** climax, noggin, summit, zenith **7** chaplet, circlet, coronet, fulfill, garland **8** monarchy, pinnacle

crown of thorns 4 bane **5** cross **6** burden, ordeal **7** torment **8** vexation

crow over 5 gloat

crucial 5 grave **6** urgent **7** serious, weighty **8** critical, decisive, pressing

crude 3 raw **5** crass, gross, rough **6** coarse, vulgar **7** obscene, sketchy, uncouth

cruel 6 brutal, savage **7** vicious **8** pitiless, ruthless, sadistic

cruet 3 jar, jug **6** bottle **7** urceole

cruise 4 sail, scud, skim **5** coast, drift, float, glide, sweep **6** stream, voyage **7** seafare **8** navigate

crumble 5 crush, decay, grate, grind **6** powder **8** fragment, splinter

crummy 5 awful, lousy **6** rotten **8** terrible

crumple 4 fall **5** crush **6** cave in, crease, pucker, rumple **7** crimple, crinkle, wrinkle **8** collapse

crunch 4 chew, gnaw **5** chomp, gnash, grind, munch

crusade 5 drive, rally **8** campaign, movement

Crusader 6 knight, zealot **7** pilgrim, Templar **8** champion

Crusades
  foe: 4 Turk **7** infidel, Saladin, saracen
  named: 9 Children's

crush 4 mash **5** break, press, quash, quell, smash **6** squash **7** crumple, shatter, squelch **8** overcome

crust 4 coat, gall, hull, rind, scab **5** brass, nerve, shell **6** harden **7** coating **8** chutzpah, covering

crustacean 4 crab, flea **5** louse, prawn **6** isopod, shrimp **7** lobster **8** barnacle, crawfish

crux 3 nub **4** core, gist **5** basis, heart **7** essence

cry 3 beg, sob, sue **4** bawl, call, hawk, plea, wail, weep, yell, yelp **5** mourn, plead, shout, utter **6** blazon, boohoo, clamor, lament, snivel **7** blubber,

crypt

call out, exclaim, implore, whimper **8** entreaty, petition

crypt 4 tomb **5** vault **8** catacomb

cryptic 4 dark **5** vague **6** arcane, occult, secret **7** obscure, strange **8** esoteric, puzzling

crystal 3 ice **5** clear, flake, glass, lucid **6** quartz **7** diamond **8** stemware

crystallize 3 gel **4** firm **5** candy **6** harden **8** solidify

cub 3 boy, pup **4** bear, lion **5** scout, whelp **6** novice

Cuba
  capital/largest city: 6 Havana **8** Le Habana
  island: 5 Pines, Pinos **8** Camaguey
  highest point: 8 Turquino
  physical feature:
    bay: 4 Nipe, Pigs
    peninsula: 6 Zapata
  places:
    castle: 5 Morro
  feature:
    dance: 5 conga, rumba **6** rhumba
    peasant: 7 guajiro
    witch doctor: 7 nanigos

cubbyhole 4 nook **5** niche **6** cranny

cubicle 3 bay **4** cell, nook **5** booth **6** alcove, carrel

cuckoo 3 ani **4** bats, bird, fool, gaga, nuts **5** balmy, batty, crazy, daffy, dotty, goofy, loony, nutty, silly, wacky **6** screwy **7** idiotic

cuddle 3 hug, pet **5** clasp **6** caress, fondle, huddle, nestle, nuzzle **7** embrace, snuggle

cudgel 4 club **5** baton, staff, stick **8** bludgeon

cue 3 key, tip **4** clue, hint, sign **6** signal **7** inkling

cuff 3 box, hit, rap **4** blow **5** clout, smack, thump, whack **6** thwack, wallop

cuisine 4 fare, food, menu **5** table **6** viands **7** cookery, cooking, edibles **8** victuals, vittles

cul-de-sac 6 pocket **7** dead-end, impasse

culminate 3 cap, end, top **5** crown, end up **6** climax, finish, result, top off, wind up **8** complete, conclude

culpable 6 guilty, liable **7** at fault, to blame **8** blamable

culprit 5 felon **6** sinner

8 criminal, evildoer, offender

cult 4 sect **7** faction, zealots **8** admirers, devotees, devotion **9** disciples, followers **10** admiration

cultivate 3 dig, hoe, sow **4** farm, grow, plow, seek, till, weed **5** plant, spade **6** enrich, garden **7** develop, elevate, enhance, improve

culture 3 art **5** music **7** the arts **8** learning

cumbersome 5 bulky, hefty **6** clumsy **7** awkward **8** ungainly, unwieldy

cumin
    family: 7 parsley
    symbol of: 5 greed

cumulative 7 amassed, piled up **8** additive, heaped up

cunning *see* **6 crafty**
    god of: 6 Hermes

cup 3 cup **5** glass, grail, stein **6** beaker, goblet, vessel **7** chalice, tankard **8** half pint, schooner

cupbearer of gods 8 Ganymede

cupboard 6 buffet, bureau, closet **7** armoire, cabinet

Cupid 6 cherub
    origin: 5 Roman

    god of: 4 love
    mother: 5 Venus
    corresponds to: 4 Eros
    features: 3 bow **5** arrow, wings

cupidity 5 greed **7** avarice, avidity **8** rapacity

cupola 4 dome, roof **5** tower, vault **6** belfry, turret **7** ceiling

curate 5 vicar **6** cleric, deacon, parson, pastor, priest, rector **8** minister, preacher

curative 4 balm **7** healing

curator 5 doyen **6** keeper **7** steward **8** director, overseer

curb 3 rim **4** edge, rein **5** brink, check, ledge, limit **6** halter, retard, slow up **7** control, harness, inhibit **8** moderate, restrain, restrict, suppress

curdle 3 rot **4** clot, curd, sour, turn **5** decay, go bad, spoil **7** congeal, ferment, putrefy

cure 3 dry **4** heal, salt **5** smoke **6** remedy **8** antidote, make well

curio 7 bibelot, trinket

curious 3 odd **4** nosy, rare

5 funny, novel, queer, weird 6 prying 7 bizarre, strange, unusual 8 peculiar, snooping

curl 4 coil, lock, wave, wind 5 crimp, frizz, swirl, twirl, twist 6 spiral 7 frizzle, ringlet, scallop 8 curlicue

curmudgeon 4 crab 5 crank, grump 6 grouch 8 grumbler, sourball

currant 5 Ribes

currency 4 cash, coin 5 bills, money, vogue 6 specie 7 coinage

current 3 now 4 flow, flux, mood, tide 5 trend 6 modern, spirit, stream 7 in vogue, popular, present 8 existing, up-to-date

curse 3 vex 4 bane, cuss, damn, oath 5 swear 6 burden, ordeal, plague, whammy 7 afflict, evil eye, scourge, swear at, torment 8 swearing, vexation

cursory 5 brief, hasty, quick, swift 6 casual, random 7 hurried, offhand, passing 8 careless

curt 4 rude 5 bluff, blunt, gruff, short, terse 6 abrupt, snappy 7 brusque 8 petulant

curtain 3 end 4 mask, veil 5 blind, cover, drape, shade 6 screen, shroud 7 conceal, drapery 8 portiere

curtsy, curtsey 3 bob, bow, dip 5 honor 6 homage

curve 3 arc, bow, ess 4 arch, bend, coil, hook, loop, turn, wind 5 crook, twist 6 spiral, swerve

curving inward 6 hollow, sunken 7 concave 8 hollowed

curving outward 5 bowed 6 convex 7 bulging, rounded 8 bellying

cushion 3 mat, pad 4 damp 5 quiet 6 dampen, deaden, muffle, pillow, soften, stifle 7 bolster 8 suppress

cusp 4 apex, barb, horn, peak 5 angle, point, tooth 6 corner

custard 4 flan, fool 5 creme 6 junket 7 dessert, pudding 8 flummery

custodian 6 duenna, keeper, warden 7 janitor 8 guardian, watchman

custody 4 care **5** watch **6** charge

custom 4 form, mode **5** habit, usage **7** fashion

customer 5 buyer **6** client, patron **7** habitue, shopper

customs 4 duty, levy, toll **6** excise, tariff

cut 3 mow, saw **4** chop, clip, crop, cube, dice, fall, gash, hack, move, nick, pare, part, rent, rive, slit, snip, snub, trim **5** carve, cross, lance, mince, piece, prune, sever, share, shave, shear, slash, slice, split, wound **6** bisect, incise **7** abridge, curtail, dissect, portion, section, segment **8** condense, diminish, incision, lacerate

cut and run 4 bolt, flee, skip **6** escape **7** abscond, get away, make off, run away **8** slip away

cute 5 sweet **6** dainty, pretty **7** darling, lovable **8** adorable, precious

cutlet 3 cut **4** chop **5** slice **9** cotelette, croquette

cutter 4 boat **5** blade, hewer, knife **6** sledge, sleigh, tailor

cutting 3 raw **4** acid, cold **5** harsh, nasty, sharp **6** biting, bitter **7** acerbic, caustic

cutting remark 3 dig **4** gibe, jeer **5** taunt

cycle 3 run **6** series **8** sequence

cyclone 4 gale, gust, wind **5** storm **7** tornado, twister, typhoon

Cyclops, Cyclopes
 form: 5 giant
 number of eyes: 3 one
 father: 6 Uranus
 mother: 2 Ge
 blinded by: 8 Odysseus

cylinder 3 can, tin **4** drum, pipe, roll, tube **5** spool **6** barrel, column, pillar, piston, platen, roller

cynic 7 scoffer, skeptic

cypress 8 Taxodium **9** Cupressus

Cyprus
 biblical name: 6 Kittim
 capital/largest city: 7 Nicosia
 highest point: 7 Olympus
 physical feature:
  peninsula: 6 Karpas
  plain: 8 Mesaoria

language: 5 Greek **7** Turkish

cytology
  study of: 5 cells

czar, tsar 4 king **5** ruler **6** caesar, despot, tyrant **7** emperor, monarch **8** dictator, overlord

czarina 7 empress

Czechoslovakia/Czech Republic *see also* **8** Slovakia
  capital/largest city: 5 Praha **6** Prague
  others: 4 Brno **5** Plzen **7** Ostrava
  monetary unit: 6 koruna

mountain: 7 Sudeten
highest point: 6 Snezka
river: 4 Elbe, Oder **6** Morava
physical feature:
  plateau: 8 Bohemian
place:
  castle: 8 Hradcany
  resort/spa: 8 Carlsbad **9** Marienbad
feature:
  dance: 5 polka
food:
  beer: 6 pilsen
  dumpling: 7 knedlik
  sausage: 5 parky **6** vursty

D

dab 3 bit, pat, tap **6** stroke **7** smidgen, soupcon

dabble 5 slosh **6** fiddle, putter, splash **7** spatter, toy with **8** sprinkle

dad 2 da, pa **3** pop **4** papa, pops, sire **5** daddy, pappy, pater **6** father, parent

Daedalus
   son: 5 Iapyx **6** Icarus
   built: 9 labyrinth
      for: 5 Minos
   made: 5 wings

daft *see* **5 crazy**

dagger 4 dirk, snee **5** blade, knife **6** weapon **7** poniard **8** stiletto

Dahomey *see* **5 Benin**

daily 7 diurnal, per diem

dainty 4 fine **5** fussy, tasty **6** choice, choosy, lovely, pretty, savory **7** choosey, elegant, refined **8** delicate

dais 5 stage **6** podium **7** rostrum **8** platform

daisy 6 Bellis

Dakar
   capital of: 7 Senegal

Dakota (Sioux)
   language family: 6 Siouan
   tribe: 5 Teton **6** Lakota, Santee **7** Yankton

dale 4 dell, dene, glen, vale **6** dingle, hollow, valley

Dallas
   basketball team: 4 Mavs **9** Mavericks
   football team: 7 Cowboys
   hockey team: 5 Stars
   river: 7 Trinity
   stadium: 6 Cotton (Bowl)
   university: 3 SMU

dally 3 toy **4** play **5** flirt **6** dawdle, loiter, trifle

dam *see* **5 block**

damage, damages 3 mar **4** cost, harm, hurt, loss **6** impair, injure, ravage

Damascus
   capital of: 5 Syria

damn 4 doom **5** blast **6** rail at **7** censure, condemn **8** denounce

Damon
  friend: **7** Pythias

damp 3 wet **4** curb, dank, dash, dewy, dull, mist **5** check, foggy, humid, misty, moist, muggy, rainy, soggy, spoil **6** clammy, deaden, hamper, hinder, reduce, soaked, sodden **7** depress, drizzly, inhibit, sopping, wettish **8** dankness, diminish, dripping, humidity, moisture, restrain

damsel 4 girl, lass **6** maiden

Danae
  form: **6** maiden
  lover: **4** Zeus
  son: **7** Perseus

dance 3 hop, jam **4** ball, jump, leap, prom, reel, skip **5** lindy, party, polka, twist **6** bounce, cavort, frolic, gambol, prance, square **7** fox-trot, perform *see also* **6 ballet**

dander 3 ire **5** anger, Irish **6** temper

dandy 3 fop **4** beau, dude, fine **5** beaut, great, super, swell **6** beauty, superb **7** coxcomb, peacock

dangerous 5 hairy, risky **6** chancy, unsafe **8** menacing, perilous

danger signal 5 alarm, alert **7** red flag, warning

dangle 3 sag **4** drag, hang, sway **5** droop, swing, trail **6** depend **7** draggle, hang out, suspend

dank 3 wet **4** cold, damp **5** humid, moist, muggy, soggy **6** chilly, clammy, sodden, sticky

dankness 4 damp **7** wetness **8** dampness, humidity

Dante (Alighieri) *see* **12 Divine Comedy**

dapper 4 neat, trim **5** natty, smart **6** jaunty, modish, spiffy, sporty, spruce **7** stylish

dapple 3 dab, dot **4** spot **6** mottle

dare 3 bet **4** defy **5** taunt

daredevil 4 bold, rash **5** risky **8** heedless, reckless, stuntman

daring 4 bold, game **5** brave **6** plucky **7** bravery, courage, gallant, valiant **8** audacity, boldness, intrepid

dark 3 dim **4** deep, evil, inky **5** angry, black,

bleak, dingy, dusky, murky, night, shady **6** dismal, dreary, gloomy, hidden, opaque, secret, somber, sullen, wicked **7** evening, joyless, obscure, ominous, shadowy, sunless **8** eventide, frowning, hopeless, overcast, sinister

darling 4 cute, dear, love **5** loved, sweet **6** adored, lovely **7** beloved, dearest, lovable **8** adorable, charming, precious

darn 4 damn, dang, dash, drat, mend **5** blast, patch, sew up **6** hang it, stitch **7** consarn, doggone, goldang

dart 3 run **4** bolt, dash, flit, jump, leap, race, rush, tear **5** bound, fling, hurry, spear, spurt **6** hasten, spring, sprint **7** javelin, missile

Darwin, Charles
theory of: 9 evolution
ship: 6 Beagle

dash 3 bit, run, zip **4** bolt, dart, drop, elan, foil, hurl, race, ruin, rush, slam, tear, zeal **5** bound, crash, flair, fling, hurry, oomph, pinch, smash, speed, spoil, throw, touch, verve, vigor

6 dampen, energy, hasten, pizazz, spirit, splash, sprint, thrust, thwart **7** a little, panache, shatter, soupcon, spatter **8** splatter, splinter, vivacity

dastard 3 cad **6** coward, craven **7** bounder, caitiff, chicken **8** poltroon

data 4 dope, info **5** facts, input **7** dossier, figures

date 3 age, era **5** court, epoch, stage **6** escort, period **7** partner, take out

dated 5 passe **6** old hat **8** obsolete, outmoded

daub 4 blot, coat, soil, spot **5** cover, dirty, paint, smear, stain **6** blotch, smirch, smudge **7** splotch

daunt 3 cow **4** dash, faze **5** abash, alarm, scare **6** deject, dismay, menace, subdue **7** depress, unnerve **8** affright, browbeat, frighten, threaten

David
king of: 6 Israel
son: 5 Amnon **7** Absalom, Chileab, Solomon **8** Adonijah
killed: 7 Goliath
wrote: 6 Psalms

David Copperfield
  author: **7** Dickens

Da Vinci, Leonardo
  artwork: **8** Mona Lisa

dawdle **4** idle, loaf **5** dally, delay **6** loiter

dawn **4** rise **5** begin, birth, occur, start, sunup **6** advent, appear, Aurora, emerge, origin, strike, unfold **7** develop, sunrise **8** commence, daybreak

day **3** age, era **4** date, time **5** epoch **6** period

daybed **5** couch **6** lounge

day book **3** log **5** diary **6** agenda **7** journal **8** calendar, schedule

daybreak **4** dawn, morn **5** sunup **7** sunrise

daydream **4** muse **5** fancy **7** fantasy, imagine, reverie

day's end **3** een, eve **4** dusk, even **6** sunset **7** evening, sundown **8** gleaming, twilight

daze **4** numb, stun **5** amaze, shock **6** benumb, dazzle, excite, muddle, stupor **7** astound, confuse, stagger, startle, stupefy **8** astonish, bewilder, surprise

dazzle **3** awe **4** blur, daze **5** blind **6** excite **7** confuse

deacon **6** cleric **9** churchman, clergyman

dead, the dead **4** beat, cold, dull, flat **5** depth, exact, midst, quiet, spent, tired, total, utter, vapid **6** entire, middle, unused **7** defunct, expired, extinct, insipid, precise, useless, utterly, worn-out **8** abruptly, absolute, complete, deceased, entirely, inactive, lifeless, obsolete, perished

dead body **5** stiff **6** corpse **7** cadaver, remains

deadlock **7** impasse **8** standoff

deadpan **5** sober **8** detached

dead ringer **4** copy, mate, twin **6** double

dead weight **7** ballast **9** inert mass

deal **3** act **4** give, hand **5** round, see to, trade, treat **6** behave, handle, market **7** bargain, concern, deliver, dole out, give out, mete out, oversee

dear **4** love **5** angel, loved **6** costly **7** beloved, darling

8 esteemed, precious
French: 5 cheri **6** cherie

dearth 4 lack **7** paucity **8** scarcity, shortage

death, Death 5 dying **6** demise **7** decease, passing

death-dealing 5 fatal **6** lethal, mortal **7** killing

death-defying 4 bold, rash **5** risky **6** daring **8** reckless

deathlike 3 wan **4** pale **5** ashen **6** pallid **7** ghastly

Death of a Salesman author: 6 (Arthur) Miller

debacle 4 rout, ruin **5** havoc, wreck **8** collapse, disaster, downfall

debark 4 land

debase 5 lower **6** befoul, defile **7** corrupt, degrade **8** disgrace, dishonor

debate 5 argue **6** ponder **7** discuss, dispute, reflect **8** argument, cogitate, consider, hash over

debauched 4 lewd **6** wanton **7** corrupt, debased, immoral **8** degraded, depraved, perverse, vitiated

debilitated 5 frail **6** feeble,

infirm **7** worn out **8** delicate, weakened

debit 4 debt **6** red ink **7** account, payable

debonair 5 suave **6** dapper, jaunty, urbane **7** buoyant, elegant, genteel, refined **8** carefree, charming, gracious, well-bred

debris *see* **7 garbage**

debt 4 bill **5** debit **7** arrears

debunk 4 bare **5** strip **6** expose, send up, show up, unmask **7** deflate, lampoon, take off, uncloak, uncover **8** ridicule, satirize

decadent 7 corrupt, debased, immoral **8** decaying, depraved, perverse

Decameron, The author: 9 Boccaccio

decamp 7 move off, run away, take off **8** march off, sneak off

decant 4 pour **7** draw off, pour out

decanter 6 bottle, carafe

decay 3 rot **5** spoil **7** corrode, putrefy, rotting

deceive 3 con **4** fool

5 cheat, put on, trick **6** delude **7** defraud, mislead, swindle

December
event: 8 (Winter) Solstice (21, 22) **11** Pearl Harbor (7)
flower: 5 holly
gem: 4 ruby **6** zircon **9** turquoise
holiday: 7 Kwanzaa (26-Jan 1) **8** Hanukkah **9** Boxing Day (26), Christmas (25)
Zodiac sign: 9 Capricorn **11** Sagittarius

decent 4 fair, nice **5** ample **6** modest, proper, seemly **7** correct, fitting **8** adequate, gracious, obliging, suitable

decide 4 rule **5** elect, judge **6** choose, decree, select, settle **7** resolve

decided 4 firm **7** certain **8** clear-cut, definite, emphatic, resolute

decimate 6 reduce **7** destroy **8** massacre

decipher 4 read **5** solve **6** decode, deduce, render **7** decrypt, dope out, explain, make out, unravel **8** construe, untangle

decision 6 decree, ruling **7** finding, outcome, purpose, resolve, verdict **8** judgment

deck 4 garb, trim **5** adorn, array, dress, prank **6** clothe, doll up, enrich, outfit, tog out **7** apparel, bedizen, festoon, furbish, garnish, gussy up **8** accouter, beautify, ornament, spruce up

declaim 4 rail **5** orate **6** recite **7** inveigh

declare 4 show **6** affirm, reveal **7** express **8** announce, proclaim

decline 3 ebb **4** drop, fail, flag, sink, wane **5** decay, slump, spurn **6** balk at, eschew, lessen, refuse, reject, weaken, worsen **7** dwindle **8** decrease, diminish, downfall

decompose 3 rot **5** decay, spoil **7** putrefy **8** separate

decontaminate 6 purify

decorate 4 trim **5** adorn, array, award, honor **7** festoon, garnish **8** ornament

decorous 3 fit **6** decent, polite, proper, seemly

7 correct **8** becoming, mannerly, suitable

decoy **4** bait, lure **5** plant, snare **6** allure, come-on

decrease **4** drop, ease, loss **5** abate, taper **6** lessen, reduce **7** cutback, decline, dwindle, fall-off, slacken, subside **8** diminish

decree **3** law **5** edict, order **6** dictum, ruling **7** command, mandate, statute **8** proclaim

decrepit **7** rickety **8** battered

decry **7** censure, condemn **8** denounce

dedicate **6** commit, devote, launch, pledge **7** address, present **8** inscribe

deduce **5** infer **6** gather, reason **8** conclude

deduct **4** take **6** remove **8** subtract, take from, withdraw **10** decrease by

deed **3** act **4** feat **5** title **6** action, effort

deem **4** hold, view **5** judge, think **6** regard **7** believe

deep **3** far, sea **4** dark, late, lost, rich, wise **5** far in, midst, ocean, vivid **6** astute, strong **7** extreme, intense, learned **8** absorbed, immersed, involved, profound, resonant, sonorous

deep water **3** jam **4** mess **5** ocean **6** pickle **7** trouble **8** distress

deer
young: **4** fawn
female: **3** doe
male: stag

de-escalate **5** limit **6** lessen, narrow **8** contract, minimize

deface **3** mar **4** mark, scar **5** spoil **6** bruise, damage

de facto **4** real **6** actual, really **8** actually

defamation **5** libel **7** calumny, slander

defeat **4** foil, loss, rout **5** cream, crush, elude, quell **6** baffle, thwart **7** conquer, setback, shellac, trounce **8** confound, overcome, vanquish

defect **4** flaw, scar, spot **5** break, crack, fault, stain **6** blotch, foible **7** blemish, default, failing, frailty **8** omission, weakness

defend **5** guard **6** secure, shield, uphold **7** endorse, protect, shelter, stand by, support, sustain **8** advocate, champion, maintain, preserve

defense 4 care **5** guard **7** custody, support **8** advocacy, security

defer 4 obey **5** delay, table, yield **6** accede, give in, put off, shelve, submit **7** respect, suspend **8** postpone

defiant 4 bold

deficiency 4 flaw **6** defect **7** failing, frailty **8** shortage, weakness

defile 4 soil **5** dirty, smear, spoil, stain, taint **6** befoul **7** degrade, profane, tarnish **8** besmirch, disgrace, dishonor

define 5 state **7** clarify, explain, specify **8** describe, spell out

definite 3 set **4** sure **5** exact, fixed **7** certain, precise **8** clear-cut, positive

definition 6 limits **7** clarity, purpose

deflate 6 reduce **7** flatten **8** contract

deflect 6 divert, swerve

deform 3 mar **4** maim **5** twist **6** mangle **7** blemish, contort, distort

defraud 3 con **4** bilk, rook **5** cheat **6** fleece, rip off **7** swindle

defray 3 pay **5** cover

deft 3 apt **4** able, sure **5** quick **6** adroit, expert **8** skillful

defunct 4 dead **7** extinct

defy 5 spurn **6** oppose, resist **7** disdain **8** confront

degenerate *see* **4 vile**

degrade 5 lower, shame **6** debase, demote **7** corrupt **8** disgrace, dishonor

degree 4 mark, step, unit **5** grade, level, order, phase, point, stage **8** division

dehydrated 3 dry **7** parched, thirsty **8** dried-out

deify 5 exalt **7** glorify, idolize, worship

deign 4 deem **5** stoop **6** see fit **7** consent **8** think fit

deity, the Deity 3 god **4** idol **7** goddess, godhead, Jehovah **8** Almighty, divinity, immortal, Olympian

deja vu 11 already seen

dejected 3 low, sad **4** blue, down **7** doleful, unhappy **8** desolate

Delaware
　abbreviation: 2 DE **3** Del
　nickname: 5 First **7** Blue Hen
　capital: 5 Dover
　largest city: 10 Wilmington
　physical feature:
　　bay: 8 Delaware
　river: 8 Delaware
　feature:
　　company: 6 du Pont

delay *see* **6 detain**

delectable 5 tasty, yummy

delegate 3 rep **4** give, name **5** agent, envoy, proxy **6** assign, charge, deputy **7** entrust **8** give over, transfer

delete 3 cut **4** omit **5** erase **6** cancel, remove

deleterious 7 harmful, hurtful, ruinous

deliberate 4 easy, slow, wary **5** weigh **6** confer, debate **7** careful, discuss, examine, express, planned, prudent, willful **8** cautious, cogitate, consider, measured, meditate, mull over

delicate 4 fine, soft **5** frail, muted **6** ailing, dainty, feeble, flimsy, infirm, minute, savory, sickly, touchy, unwell **7** careful, elegant, fragile, refined, subdued, tactful **8** detailed, luscious, tasteful, ticklish, weakened

delicious 5 tasty, yummy **6** joyful, savory **8** charming, luscious, pleasant

delight 3 joy **5** amuse, charm, cheer, revel **6** please **7** enchant, gratify, rapture **8** pleasure

Delilah
　lover: 6 Samson
　betrayed: 6 Samson

delineate 4 draw **5** draft **6** define, depict, design, lay out, sketch **7** outline, portray **8** describe

delinquent 3 due **4** late **6** remiss **7** hoodlum, misdoer, overdue **8** derelict

delirium 5 fever **6** frenzy, raving **7** madness **8** insanity

deliver 3 aim, say **4** bear,

deal, free, give, save **5** bring, carry, throw, utter **6** convey, direct, launch, rescue, strike **7** release, set free **8** give over, hand over, liberate, proclaim

deliver up 4 cede, give **5** grant, yield **8** fork over, hand over, transfer

dell 4 dale, dene, glen, vale **5** glade **6** dingle, hollow

Delphic oracle
   oracle of: 6 Apollo
   located at: 6 Delphi
   priestess: 6 Pythia

delude 3 con **4** dupe, fool **5** put on, trick **7** deceive, mislead

deluge 4 bury, glut **5** drown, flood, spate, swamp **6** engulf **7** barrage, torrent **8** inundate, submerge

deluxe 4 fine, posh **5** grand **6** choice, classy **7** elegant **8** splendid

delve 5 probe **6** search **7** examine, explore **8** look into

demagogue 6 ranter **7** hothead, spouter **8** agitator, fomenter

demand 4 call, need, want **5** exact, order **7** command, require

demean 5 lower, shame **6** debase, humble **7** degrade **8** disgrace

demeanor 4 mien **6** manner **7** bearing, conduct **8** behavior, presence

demented *see* **5 crazy**

demesne 4 land **5** realm **6** domain, estate **8** property

Demeter
   origin: 5 Greek
   goddess of: 5 earth **9** fertility
   protectress of: 8 marriage
   father: 6 Cronus
   mother: 4 Rhea
   daughter: 10 Persephone
   corresponds to: 5 Ceres

demise 3 end **4** fall, ruin **5** death **7** decease, passing

demobilize 7 disband, release

democracy 8 equality, fairness

Democratic Party
   symbol: 6 donkey

demoiselle 4 girl

demolish 4 raze, ruin **5** level, total, wreck **7** destroy

demon 3 imp **4** jinn, ogre **5** afrit, devil, fiend, genie, harpy, jinni, lamia, satan, troll **6** afreet, dybbuk, goblin **7** incubus, monster, vampire, warlock **8** go-getter, succubus

demonstrate 4 show **5** march, prove, teach **6** parade, picket, reveal **7** display, exhibit, explain **8** describe, manifest

demote 4 bust **5** abase **7** degrade

demur 5 qualm **6** object **7** protest, scruple **8** disagree

demure 3 shy **4** prim **6** modest **7** bashful **8** reserved

den 4 lair **5** haunt, study **6** hotbed **7** hangout, library, retreat, shelter

denial 7 refusal **9** disavowal, disowning, rejection **10** disclaimer

denigrate *see* **7** degrade

denizen 7 dweller **8** resident

Denmark
   capital/largest city: 9 Kobenhavn **10** Copenhagen
   island: 3 Fyn **5** Faero, Faroe, Funen **7** Faeroes, Falster, Lolland, Zealand **8** Bornholm **9** Greenland, Sjaelland
   sea/ocean: 5 North **6** Baltic **8** Atlantic
   physical feature:
      peninsula: 7 Jutland
      strait: 7 Otesund **8** Kattegat
   feature:
      drink: 5 glogg
      park: 6 Tivoli **8** Legoland
   food:
      cheese: 4 Blue **7** Havarti

denomination 4 name, sect, size **5** class, value **8** category, grouping

denote 4 mark, mean, name **6** signal **7** signify **8** indicate

denouement 3 end **6** finale, upshot **7** outcome **8** solution

denounce 6 accuse, vilify **7** censure, condemn

dense 4 dull, dumb, slow **5** close, heavy, thick **6** stupid **7** compact, crowded, intense **8** ignorant **9** dimwitted

dent 3 pit **4** nick **6** hollow

denude 4 bare **5** strip **6** divest **7** lay bare

denunciation 7 censure

deny 6 refuse, refute **7** disavow **8** disallow, disclaim

departed 4 dead, gone, late, left, past, went **6** at rest, bygone **7** gone off

department 4 unit **6** branch, bureau, sector **7** section **8** district, division, province

depend 4 rely, rest **5** count, hinge **6** hang on

depict 4 draw, limn **5** carve, chart, draft, paint **6** define, detail, map out, recite, record, relate, sculpt, sketch **7** diagram, narrate, picture, portray, recount **8** describe

depleted 5 empty, spent, waste **6** barren, used up **7** drained, emptied, reduced, worn out **8** bankrupt, consumed, expended

deplore 5 mourn **6** bemoan, bewail, lament **7** censure, condemn

deport 3 act **4** oust **5** carry, exile, expel **6** banish, behave **7** cast out

deposit 3 put **4** pile **5** place **7** put down, set down **8** sediment

depot 4 dump **7** station **8** terminal, terminus

depraved 4 vile **6** wicked **7** corrupt, debased

deprecate 6 insult **7** condemn, protest **8** belittle, play down

depreciate 5 scorn **7** run down **8** belittle, diminish

depredation 4 sack **6** rapine, ravage **7** looting, pillage, plunder, sacking

depress 5 lower **6** deject, lessen, reduce, sadden, weaken **7** cut back **8** diminish, dispirit

deprive 5 strip **6** divest **8** take from

depths 4 deep **6** bowels **8** interior, recesses

deputy 4 aide **5** agent, envoy, proxy **6** second **8** delegate, emissary

derail 3 bar **4** balk, foil **5** block, check, spike **6** hinder, impede, thwart **7** inhibit, prevent **8** obstruct

deranged 3 mad **5** crazy **6** insane **8** demented

derelict 3 bum **4** hobo **5** tramp **6** remiss **7** outcast, vagrant **8** deserted

derision 5 scorn **7** disdain, mockery **8** ridicule, sneering

derivation 5 stock **6** origin, source **7** descent, getting, lineage **8** ancestry, deriving, heritage

dermatitis 4 rash **6** eczema

derogate 4 blot **5** taint **6** smirch **8** disgrace

derrick 3 rig **5** crane, hoist, tower

dervish 5 fakir **6** Muslim

descend 3 dip **4** drop, pass **5** slant, slope, swoop **6** go down, invade **7** incline **8** come down, inherited

describe 4 draw **5** trace **6** depict, detail, recite, relate **7** explain, mark out, narrate, outline, portray, recount, speak of

desecrate 6 defile **7** profane, violate **8** dishonor

desert 3 dry **4** arid, quit, wild **5** leave, waste **6** barren **7** abandon, forsake **8** desolate, untilled
watering spot: 5 oasis

deserts 3 due **5** worth **6** reward **7** payment

deserve 4 rate **5** merit **7** warrant

desiccate 5 dry up, parch **6** wither **7** shrivel

design 3 aim, end **4** draw, form, goal, plan, plot **5** draft, motif, set up **6** devise, intend, scheme, sketch, target **7** destine, diagram, drawing, fashion, outline, pattern, project, purpose **8** conceive

designate 4 call, name, term **5** elect, label **6** assign, choose, select **7** appoint, signify, specify **8** identify, indicate, nominate, pinpoint

desire 3 yen **4** need, urge, want, wish **5** crave **6** ask for, hunger, thirst **7** craving, longing, long for, request **8** yearning

desist 4 stop **5** cease **6** lay off **7** suspend **8** leave off

desolate *see* **5 empty**

despair 5 gloom, trial **6** burden, ordeal

desperado 4 thug **5** rowdy **6** bandit, gunman, outlaw **7** brigand, convict, hoodlum, ruffian **8** criminal, fugitive, hooligan

desperate 4 dire, rash, wild **5** grave, great **6** daring, urgent **7** extreme, frantic, serious **8** critical, hopeless, reckless, wretched

despicable 4 base, mean, vile

despise 5 abhor, scorn **6** detest, loathe **7** disdain, dislike

despoil 3 rob **4** loot **6** ravage **7** pillage, plunder

despondent 3 low **4** blue, down **8** dejected, downcast, hopeless

despot 4 czar, tsar **6** tyrant **8** autocrat, dictator

dessert 3 pie **4** cake, nuts, tart **5** fruit, sweet, treat **6** pastry **7** cobbler **8** ice cream

destination 3 aim, end **4** goal, plan **6** object, target **7** purpose **8** ambition

destiny 3 lot **4** fate **5** karma, moira **6** future, kismet **7** fortune

destitute 4 poor **5** broke, needy **6** busted **8** indigent

destroy 4 ruin **5** waste,

wreck **6** ravage **8** demolish

destroyer 4 bane **6** blight, killer **7** gunboat, warship

destructive 7 harmful, hurtful, ruinous **8** damaging

desultory 4 idle **6** casual, chance, fitful, random **7** aimless, cursory

detached 4 fair **5** aloof **7** distant, neutral, severed **8** reserved, unbiased

detachment 4 unit **5** force **8** coolness, fairness

detail 4 fact, iota, item **6** aspect, relate **7** appoint, feature, itemize, recount, respect, specify

detain 4 hold, slow, stop **5** delay **6** arrest, hinder, retard, slow up **7** confine

detect 3 see **4** espy, note, spot **5** catch **6** notice **7** observe, uncover **8** discover, perceive

detective 2 PI **3** tec **6** shamus, sleuth **7** gumshoe

deter 4 stop **5** daunt **6** divert, hinder, impede **7** prevent **8** dissuade

deteriorate 3 ebb **4** fade,

wane **5** decay, lapse **6** worsen **7** crumble, decline

determination 4 grit **5** pluck, power, spunk **6** fixing **7** finding, resolve, verdict **8** boldness, decision, judgment, settling, solution, tenacity

determine 5 learn **6** affect, decide, detect, settle **7** control, find out, resolve **8** conclude, discover

deterrent 4 curb **5** check

detest 4 hate **5** abhor **6** loathe **7** despise

dethrone 4 oust **6** depose, unseat

detonate 4 fire **5** blast, burst, erupt, go off, shoot **6** blow up, ignite, report, set off **7** explode

detour 5 skirt **6** bypass, byroad, divert **7** digress

detract 5 lower **6** lessen, reduce **8** diminish

detriment 4 harm, loss **6** damage, injury

devalue 5 lower, taint **6** debase, defile, infect **7** cheapen, corrupt, degrade, pervert, pollute, revalue **8** mark down

devastate 4 ruin **5** level, spoil, waste, wreck **6** ravage **7** despoil, destroy **8** demolish, desolate

develop 4 grow **5** print, ripen **6** evolve, expand, finish, flower, mature, pick up, unfold **7** acquire, advance, amplify, augment, broaden, build up, convert, enlarge, improve, process, turn out **8** contract, energize

deviant 4 warp **5** shift **7** deviate, pervert **8** aberrant, abnormal

deviate 4 part, vary, veer **5** stray **6** depart, swerve, wander **8** go astray

device 4 plan, plot, ploy, ruse, wile **5** angle, trick **6** design, gadget, scheme **7** gimmick **8** artifice

devil, the Devil 3 guy **5** rogue, Satan, thing **6** Azazel, fellow, wretch **7** hellion, Lucifer, ruffian, serpent, villain **8** creature

devious 3 sly **4** wily **6** sneaky, tricky **7** crooked

devise 4 plot **5** forge, frame **6** design, invent, map out **7** concoct, prepare, think up **8** block out, conceive, contrive

devoid 5 empty **6** barren **7** lacking, wanting, without

devote 5 apply **6** direct **7** address, utilize **8** dedicate

devour 7 stuff in **8** bolt down, gobble up, gulp down, wolf down

devout 5 pious **6** ardent **7** earnest, fervent, intense, serious, zealous **8** orthodox, reverent

dewy 4 damp **5** moist

dexterous *see* **6 nimble**

diabolic, diabolical *see* **4 evil**

diadem 4 halo **5** crown, tiara **7** circlet, coronet **8** headband

diagnosis 5 study **8** analysis, scrutiny

diagonal line 4 bias **5** angle, slant

diagram 3 map **4** plan **5** chart **6** sketch **7** drawing, outline

dialect 5 argot, idiom, lingo **6** accent, jargon, patois

dialogue, dialog 4 talk **5** lines **6** parley, speech

diamond
    characteristic: 7 hardest
    color: 4 blue, pink
    6 canary
    element: 6 carbon
    weight: 5 carat, point

Diana
    origin: 5 Roman
    goddess of: 4 moon **7** hunting
    protectress of: 5 women
    corresponds to: 7 Artemis

diaphanous 5 filmy, gauzy, lucid, sheer **6** flimsy, limpid **8** gossamer

diary 3 log **7** daybook, journal

diatribe 6 tirade

dice 4 chop, cube **5** bones, cubes, cut up, mince
    singular: 3 die

dicker *see* **4 deal**

Dick Tracy
    creator: 5 Gould

dictate 4 rule **5** edict, order **6** decree, dictum, direct, enjoin, impose, ordain, ruling, urging **7** bidding, counsel, lay down, mandate **8** set forth

diction 7 wording **8** delivery, rhetoric, verbiage

dictum *see* **5 maxim**

didactic 7 donnish, preachy **8** academic, edifying, pedantic, tutorial

die 3 ebb, rot **4** ache, fade, fail, long, pass, stop, wane **5** croak, yearn **6** depart, expire, go flat, pass on, perish, recede, run out, wither **7** be eager, decline, die away, go stale, run down, subside **8** fade away, melt away, pass away, pass over

diet 5 board, synod **7** edibles, nurture **8** congress, victuals

Diety 3 Bel, God **4** Baal **6** Marduk, Molech, Moloch, Yahweh **7** Jehovah

different 4 rare **6** divers, sundry, unique, unlike **7** bizarre, diverse, foreign, several, strange, unusual, various **8** aberrant, atypical, distinct, peculiar, separate, singular, uncommon

difficult *see* **7 arduous**

diffident *see* **3 shy**

diffuse 5 wordy **7** verbose **8** rambling

dig 3 jab **4** gibe, jeer, like, poke, prod, slur **5** aside, drive, gouge, punch, taunt **6** exhume, thrust **7** put-down, salvage, unearth **8** disinter, excavate, pinpoint, retrieve, scoop out

digest 3 dig **5** grasp **6** absorb, fathom, precis, resume **7** realize, summary **8** abstract, synopsis

dig in 3 eat **4** root **5** begin, embed, imbed, plant **6** anchor **7** pitch in **8** entrench, go to work

digit 3 toe **4** unit **5** light **6** cipher, figure, finger, number **7** integer, numeral

dignified 5 proud **6** august, proper **7** upright **8** decorous, reserved

dignitary 3 VIP **7** notable **8** luminary

dignity 5 honor **7** decorum, majesty, station

digress 5 stray **6** back up, wander **7** deviate

dike 4 bank **5** levee, ridge

dilapidated *see* **3 old**

dilate 5 swell, widen **6** expand, extend **7** broaden, distend, enlarge, inflate, puff out

dilatory 4 lazy, slow **5** tardy **6** remiss **8** dawdling, indolent, slothful, sluggish

dilemma 4 bind **6** crunch,

plight **7** impasse, problem **8** deadlock, quandary

dilettante 7 amateur, dabbler, trifler

diligent 6 active **7** careful, earnest, patient, zealous **8** plodding, sedulous, thorough, untiring

dillydally 3 lag **4** idle, loaf **5** dally, delay **6** dawdle, loiter **8** kill time

dilute 4 thin, weak **6** reduce, temper, watery, weaken **7** diffuse, diluted, thin out **8** decrease, diminish, make weak, mitigate, weakened

dim 3 low **4** hazy, soft, weak **5** dusky, faint, foggy, murky, muted, vague **6** blurry, feeble, gloomy, remote **7** blurred, clouded, muffled, shadowy **8** darkened, nebulous

DiMaggio, Joe
   nickname: 7 Jolting (Joe)
   wife: 6 (Marilyn) Monroe

dime-a-dozen 6 common **7** humdrum **8** ordinary

dimension, dimensions 4 bulk, mass, size **5** range, scope, width **6** extent, height, length, volume, weight **7** measure

diminish *see* **6 reduce**

diminutive *see* **4 tiny**

dimwit *see* **5 idiot**

din 4 stir, to-do **5** bruit **6** babble, clamor, hubbub, racket, ruckus, tumult, uproar **7** clangor

dine 3 eat, sup **4** feed **5** feast, lunch **6** fall to, supper **7** banquet, partake

dingy 4 dull **5** dusty, grimy, murky, tacky **6** dismal, dreary, gloomy, shabby

dinosaur
   fictional: 4 Puff **6** Barney

dint 4 push, will **5** drive, force, labor, might, power **6** charge, effort, energy, strain, stress **8** endeavor, exertion, strength, struggle

diocese 3 *see* **7** eparchy
   jurisdiction of: 6 bishop

Dionysus *see* **7 Bacchus**

Dioscuri *see* **15 Castor and Pollux**

dip 4 bail, dish, dunk, sink, skim, soak **5** droop, ladle, scoop, slope, spoon **6** dabble, dish up, peruse, shovel **7** decline, descend, dish out, run over **8** drop down, submerge

diplomat 5 envoy **6** consul **7** attache **8** emissary, minister

dipsomaniac *see* **5 drunk**

dire *see* **6 crucial**

direct 3 aim **4** head, lead, urge **5** blunt, clear, focus, frank, guide, order, pilot, usher **6** advise, candid, charge, enjoin, handle, head-on, honest, manage **7** address, command, conduct, control, oversee, pointed **8** explicit, instruct, navigate

direction 3 aim, ENE, ESE, NNE, NNW, SSE, SSW, way, WNW, WSW **4** bent, care, east, path, west **5** drift, north, order, route, south, track, trend **6** charge, course, recipe **7** bearing, command, control, current **8** guidance

directive 5 ukase **8** bulletin

directly 4 soon **6** at once, openly **7** exactly, frankly **8** candidly, honestly, in person, promptly, straight

director 4 boss, head

5 chief **6** leader, master **7** curator, foreman, manager **8** chairman, governor, overseer

dirge 6 lament **7** requiem **8** threnody

dirk 3 sny **4** snee, stab **5** knife, skean **6** dagger, skiver **7** poniard

dirt 3 mud **4** dust, loam, mire, muck, scum, slop, smut, soil, soot **5** dross, earth, filth, grime, humus, offal, rumor, slime, trash **6** gossip, ground, refuse, sludge, smudge **7** garbage, rubbish, scandal, slander **8** impurity, leavings, vileness

dirt-cheap 6 a steal **7** bargain

dirty 4 base, foul, hard, lewd, mean, soil, spot, vile **5** grimy, messy, muddy, nasty, smear, stain, sully **6** filthy, grubby, muck up, rotten, shabby, slop up, smudge, smutty, soiled, sordid, untidy, vulgar **7** blacken, corrupt, crooked, devious, illegal, illicit, immoral, low-down, muddied, obscene, pollute, squalid, sullied, tarnish, unclean **8** prurient, scabrous, unwashed

disable 6 damage, hinder, impair, weaken **7** cripple **8** handicap

disadvantage 4 flaw **6** burden **7** trouble **8** drawback, handicap, hardship, nuisance, weakness

disaffirm 4 deny **5** annul **6** disown **7** decline, disavow **8** abnegate, disclaim, forswear, renounce

disagree 4 vary **5** clash, upset **6** depart, differ **7** deviate, diverge **8** conflict

disallow *see* **4 deny**

disappear 2 go **3** end **4** exit, fade, flee **5** leave **6** be gone, depart, die out, retire, vanish **8** be no more, fade away, melt away, withdraw

disappointment 3 dud **4** bomb, loss **6** defeat, fiasco, fizzle **7** failure, letdown, setback, washout **8** disaster

disapprove 4 veto **5** decry **6** refuse, reject **7** censure, condemn, deplore, dislike

8 denounce, disallow, object to, turn down

disarm 4 move, sway **5** charm **6** entice **7** attract, bewitch, enchant, win over **8** convince, persuade

disarray 5 chaos, mix-up, upset **6** jumble **7** clutter **8** disorder, scramble, shambles

disassemble 7 disband, scatter **8** disperse

disaster 4 harm **5** wreck **6** blight, fiasco **7** scourge, tragedy, trouble **8** accident, calamity

disavow 4 deny **6** abjure, disown, recant, reject **7** gainsay, retract **8** denounce

disband 7 adjourn, dismiss, scatter **8** disperse, dissolve

disbelief 5 doubt **7** dubiety **8** distrust, mistrust

disburse 6 lay out, pay out **7** fork out **8** allocate

discard 4 drop, dump, junk, shed **5** scrap **6** remove, shelve **7** abandon **8** get rid of, jettison, throw out

discern 3 see **4** espy **6** behold, descry, detect,

notice **7** make out, observe **8** perceive

discharge *see* **4 emit**

disciple 3 nut **5** freak, pupil **7** admirer, convert, devotee, pursuer, student **8** adherent, believer, follower, neophyte

Disciples *see* **8 Apostles**

discipline 5 drill, prime, rigor, train **6** method, punish **7** break in, chasten, regimen **8** chastise, drilling, instruct, practice, training

disclaim 4 deny **6** disown **7** decline, disavow **8** abnegate, renounce

disclose 4 bare, leak, show, tell **6** expose, impart, reveal, unveil **7** divulge, lay bare, publish, uncover

disco 4 club **5** a-go-go, dance **7** cabaret

discoloration 4 blot, mark, spot **5** smear, stain **6** blotch, bruise, smudge **7** blemish

discomfort 3 try **4** ache, hurt, pain **5** trial **6** misery **7** malaise, trouble **8** disquiet, distress, hardship, nuisance, soreness, vexation

disconcerted 5 fazed, upset **7** annoyed, rattled, ruffled **8** agitated, confused, troubled

disconsolate *see* **3 sad**

discontinue *see* **3 end**

discord 6 strife **7** dispute **8** clashing, conflict, disunity, division, friction

discount 3 cut **5** break **6** rebate **7** cut rate

discourage 4 do in **5** daunt, deter, unman **6** deject, dismay **7** depress, unnerve **8** decimate, dispirit, dissuade, keep back, restrain

discourse 3 gab **4** chat, talk **5** essay **6** confer, sermon, speech **7** address, discuss, lecture, oration **8** colloquy, converse, dialogue, treatise

discourteous *see* **4 rude**

discover 3 see **4** find, spot **5** dig up **6** detect, locate, notice **7** discern, find out, learn of, realize, root out, uncover, unearth **8** come upon, perceive

discredit *see* **10 defamation**

discreet **6** polite **7** careful, politic, prudent, tactful **8** cautious

discrepancy **3** gap **8** variance

discretion **4** tact **6** acumen, option **8** judgment, prudence, volition

discrimination **4** bias **5** taste **6** acumen **7** bigotry **8** inequity, judgment, keenness, sagacity

discursive **7** diffuse **8** rambling

discussion **3** rap **4** talk **6** debate, parley, powwow, review **7** inquiry **8** analysis, argument, colloquy, dialogue

disdain *see* **7** **despise**

disease **6** malady **7** ailment, illness **8** sickness

disembark **4** land **7** deplane, detrain, pile out

disenchant **6** put off **7** turn off **8** alienate, disabuse

disengage **5** sever **6** detach **7** disjoin **8** separate

disentangle **4** free **6** detach, loosen, remove **7** unravel

disfigure *see* **6** **deface**

disgorge **4** spew **5** eject, expel, spout, vomit **6** cast up, spew up **7** cough up, throw up **8** dislodge

disgrace **4** blot **5** abase, shame, stain, taint **6** debase, smirch **7** blemish, degrade, eyesore, scandal, tarnish **8** contempt, derogate, disfavor, dishonor, ill favor

disgruntled **5** sulky, testy, vexed **6** grumpy, shirty, sullen **7** grouchy, peevish

disguise **4** garb, hide, mask, pose, sham, veil **5** blind, cloak, cover, feign, getup, guise **6** facade, muffle, screen, shroud, veneer **7** conceal, cover-up, dress up, falsify **8** pretense

disgust **5** repel **6** appall, hatred, offend, put off, revolt, sicken **7** dislike **8** aversion, contempt, distaste, loathing, nauseate

dish **4** dole, fare, food **5** ladle, place, plate, scoop, serve, spoon **6** recipe, saucer, vessel **7** bowlful, dishful, edibles, helping, platter, portion, serving **8** dispense, plateful, transfer, victuals

dishabille **7** undress

8 bathrobe, disarray, disorder, informal

dishearten 4 dash, faze **5** abash, crush, daunt **6** deject, dismay, sadden **7** depress **8** dispirit

disheveled 5 messy **6** blowsy, frowzy, mussed, sloppy, untidy **7** ruffled, rumpled, tousled, unkempt **8** uncombed

dishonest 5 false **7** corrupt, crooked **8** cheating, spurious, two-faced

dish up 3 dip **5** ladle, serve, spoon **7** dish out, serve up

disillusion 6 clue in **8** disabuse

disinclined 5 loath **6** averse **8** hesitant

disinfect 6 purify **7** cleanse **8** sanitize

disinherit 6 cut off, disown

disintegrate 7 break up, crumble, shatter **8** splinter

disk, disc 3 cam **4** aten, coin, dial, face, plow, puck **5** plate, wafer, wheel **6** harrow, record, sequin **7** discuss **8** diskette
 type: 4 hard **5** fixed **6** floppy **8** magnetic

dislike *see* **4 hate**

dislocate 6 uproot **7** unhinge **8** disjoint, disunite, separate

dislodge 4 oust **5** eject, expel **6** dig out, dispel, remove, uproot **7** disturb **8** displace, force out

disloyal 6 untrue **8** recreant

dismal *see* **8 dreadful**

dismantle 5 strip **6** denude, divest

dismay 3 cow **5** abash, alarm, daunt, dread, panic, scare **6** appall, fright, horror, put off, terror **7** anxiety, concern, horrify, unnerve **8** affright, distress, frighten

dismember 4 limb **6** hack up **8** disjoint

dismiss *see* **4 free**

disobedient 6 unruly **7** defiant, forward, haughty, wayward **8** contrary, mutinous, perverse, stubborn

disorder 4 mess, riot **5** chaos **6** fracas, jumble, malady, muddle, ruckus, uproar **7** ailment, clutter, disease, illness, turmoil **8** disarray, sickness

disorganized 5 messy, upset

7 chaotic, jumbled, mixed-up, muddled **8** confused, rambling

disoriented 7 mixed-up **8** confused, unstable

disown 4 deny **6** reject **7** cast off, disavow, forsake **8** denounce, disclaim, renounce

disparage *see* **4 mock**

disparity 3 gap **8** contrast, imparity, variance

dispassionate 4 calm, cool, fair **6** serene **7** neutral, unmoved **8** composed, detached, unbiased

dispatch 4 item, kill, post, slay **5** flash, haste, piece, speed, story **6** finish, letter, murder, report, settle, wind up **7** bump off, execute, forward, message, missive, send off **8** alacrity, bulletin, carry out, celerity, massacre, rapidity

dispel 4 rout **5** allay, expel, repel **6** banish, remove **7** diffuse, dismiss, resolve, scatter **8** drive off

dispense 6 confer **7** dole out, mete out **8** allocate

disperse 4 rout **6** dispel

7 diffuse, disband, scatter, send off **8** drive off

dispirited *see* **3 sad**

displace *see* **4 move**

display 4 show **6** reveal **7** exhibit **8** manifest

displease 3 irk **5** annoy, pique **6** offend **7** disturb, incense, provoke **8** irritate

dispose 4 rank **5** array, order, place **7** arrange, deal out, incline **8** get rid of

disposition 6 nature, spirit **7** control **8** bestowal, grouping, tendency

dispossess 4 oust **5** evict, expel **8** take away

disproportionate 7 unequal

dispute *see* **7 quarrel**

disqualify 7 disable

disquieting 6 vexing **8** annoying

disregard 6 ignore

disreputable 5 shady **8** infamous, shameful, shocking

disrespect 6 insult **8** contempt, dishonor, rudeness

disrobe 5 strip **7** undress

disrupt 5 upset

dissatisfied 7 unhappy

dissect 5 study **7** analyze, lay open **8** cut apart, separate

dissemble 4 hide, mask **5** feign **7** conceal **8** disguise

disseminate 6 spread **7** diffuse, scatter **8** disperse

dissent 6 object, oppose **7** discord, protest **8** disagree

dissertation 6 memoir, thesis **8** tractate, treatise

disservice 4 harm, hurt **5** wrong **6** injury **7** bad turn

dissipate 5 waste **6** dispel **7** carouse, deplete, scatter **8** disperse, squander

dissolve 3 end, run **4** fade, melt, thaw, void **5** annul, sever **6** finish, render, soften, vanish **7** break up, disband, liquefy, thaw out **8** abrogate, conclude

dissonant *see* **7 hostile**

distance 3 gap **4** span **7** reserve, stretch **8** coldness, coolness, interval

distaste 7 disgust, dislike **8** aversion

distended 4 full, taut **5** puffy, tumid **7** blown up, bloated, dilated, swelled, swollen **8** enlarged, expanded, inflated

distill 7 draw out, extract **8** condense, vaporize

distinct 5 clear, lucid, plain **7** diverse, supreme **8** clear-cut, definite, explicit

distinguish 6 decide, define **7** discern **8** set apart

distorted 4 awry **5** askew **6** belied, loaded, warped **7** altered, colored, crooked, twisted **8** cockeyed, deformed, wrenched

distract 5 amuse, craze, worry **6** divert, madden **7** agitate, confuse, disturb, perplex, torment, trouble **8** bewilder, disorder

distraught 3 mad **7** anxious, frantic **8** agitated, frenzied

distress 4 need, pain, want **5** agony, upset **6** danger, grieve **7** anguish, disturb, torment, torture, trouble

distribute 5 allot, class **6** divide, parcel **7** arrange, catalog, deliver, dole out, give out, scatter **8** classify, dispense, disperse

district 4 area, ward **6** parish, region **8** precinct

distrust 5 doubt **7** suspect

disturb *see* **5 upset**

ditch 3 pit **4** junk **5** scrap **6** hollow, trench **7** abandon, discard **8** get rid of

dither 4 flap, fuss **5** tizzy, waver, whirl **6** bother, flurry, lather, quiver, shiver, thrill **7** fluster, tremble, twitter **8** hesitate

ditty 3 lay **4** song, tune **6** ballad **7** refrain

divan 4 book, hall, poem, room, salon, seat, sofa **5** couch, court **6** canape, daybed, leewan, lounge, settee **7** ottoman

dive 4 dash, fall, jump, leap **5** lunge **6** plunge

divergence 7 parting **8** conflict, rambling, straying, variance

diverse 6 sundry, varied **8** eclectic, far-flung, opposite

divest 3 rid **4** free **5** strip **7** deprive, disrobe, peel off, take off **8** get out of

divide 4 part, sort **5** share, split **7** arrange, deal out, divvy up **8** allocate, classify, disunite, separate

divine 4 holy **5** guess **6** fathom, sacred **7** predict, surmise, suspect **8** forecast, foretell, heavenly

Divine Comedy
  author: 5 Dante
  part: 7 Inferno **8** Paradiso **10** Purgatorio
  guide: 6 Virgil **8** Beatrice

divinity 3 god **5** deity **7** goddess **8** holiness

division 4 part, unit, wing **5** split **6** branch **7** discord, divider, section **8** disunion, variance

divorce 4 rift **5** split **6** breach, divide **7** rupture **8** disunite, separate

divulge 4 tell **6** impart, relate, reveal **8** disclose

dizzy 5 fleet, giddy, quick, rapid, shaky, swift **6** whirly **7** confuse, reeling **8** bewilder, unsteady

Djibouti
  capital/largest city: 8 Djibouti
  highest point: 9 Moussa Ali
  sea: 3 Red
  physical feature:
    gulf: 4 Aden
  religion: 5 Islam

do 3 act **4** fare **5** clean, cover, get on, serve, visit

6 behave, finish, look at, stop in **7** achieve, arrange, carry on, conduct, execute, fulfill, make out, perform, prepare, proceed, suffice **8** carry out, complete

docile 4 tame **7** willing **8** obedient, obliging

dock 4 crop, join, pier, quay **5** berth, wharf **6** couple, cut off, deduct, hook up **7** landing **8** cut short

docket 4 bill, card, list **5** slate **6** agenda, lineup, roster **7** program **8** calendar, schedule

doctor 2 GP, MD **3** PhD **5** alter, treat **6** change **7** dentist, falsify, surgeon

Doctor Zhivago
  director: 4 (David) Lean
  author: 8 (Boris) Pasternak
  cast: 6 Sharif (Omar) **7** Chaplin (Geraldine), Steiger (Rod) **8** Christie (Julie), Guinness (Alec) **9** Courtenay (Tom)

doctrine 5 dogma, tenet **6** belief, gospel **7** precept **8** teaching

document 6 back up, record, verify **7** certify, support

doddering 4 weak **6** feeble, senile **7** shaking **8** decrepit

dodge 4 duck, wile **5** avoid, elude, evade, hedge, trick **6** device, swerve **7** fend off **8** sidestep

Dodoma
  capital of: 8 Tanzania

doff *see* **6 remove**

dog 3 cur, pup **4** heel, mutt **5** beast, puppy **6** canine **7** mongrel, villain
  groups: 3 toy **5** hound **7** herding, terrier, working **8** sporting **11** nonsporting
  anatomy: 3 hip, lip, pad, paw, toe **4** arch, back, hock, loin, rump, stop **5** cheek, crest, croup, flews, skull **6** carpus, dewlap, muzzle, stifle, tarsus **7** brisket, cushion, knuckle, occiput, pastern, withers **8** heelknob, shoulder
  Alaskan: 5 husky **8** malamute, malemute
  Australian: 5 dingo **8** warragal
  barkless: 7 basenji
  Bill Clinton's: 5 Buddy
  Charles, Nick and Nora's: 4 Asta

coach: 9 dalmatian

combining form: 3 cyn **4** cani, cyno

constellation: 5 Canis (Majoris)

Dorothy's: 4 Toto

family: 7 Canidae

FDR's: 4 Fala **5** Falla

genus: 5 Canis

George Bush's: 4 Spot **6** Barney

Little Orphan Annie's: 5 Sandy

movie/TV: 4 Asta, Lady **5** Benji, Tramp **6** Lassie **9** Old Yeller, Rin Tin Tin

mythical: 8 Cerberus

Richard Nixon's: 8 Checkers

star: 6 Sirius **8** Canicula

wild: 5 adjag, dhole, dingo, guara, rabid

young: 3 pup **5** puppy, whelp

dogged 8 stubborn

dogma 5 credo, tenet **7** beliefs **8** doctrine

dogmatic 6 biased **8** stubborn

do in 4 kill **6** murder **7** destroy, exhaust, tire out

dolce vita 9 sweet life

doldrums 5 blues, dumps, gloom

dole 4 deal, give **5** share **6** parcel **7** charity, handout, welfare

doleful *see* **3 sad**

doll 5 dolly, dummy, honey **6** beauty, puppet **7** darling, rag doll **8** baby doll, figurine, golliwog

dollar 3 one **4** bean, bill, buck, coin, note, skin, yuan **5** money, tater, token **6** single **7** ironman, smacker **8** cartwheel

dollop 3 dab **4** blob, dash, lump

Doll's House, A
   author: 5 (Henrik) Ibsen

dolorous *see* **3 sad**

dolt *see* **5 idiot**

domain 4 area, fief, land **5** field **6** empire, estate, region, sphere **7** kingdom **8** dominion, property, province

domestic 4 cook, maid, tame **6** au pair, butler, native **7** endemic, servant

dominate 4 rule **5** dwarf **6** direct, govern **7** command, control **8** domineer

Dominican Republic capital/largest city:

12 Santo Domingo
island: 10 Hispaniola
highest point: 6 Duarte
feature:
  dance: 8 merengue
  sport: 8 baseball
food:
  stew: 8 sancocho

dominion 4 land, rule **5** realm **6** domain, empire, region **7** command

Donald Duck
  creator: 7 (Walt) Disney
  character:
    girlfriend: 5 Daisy
    nephew: 4 Huey **5** Dewey, Louie
    uncle: 7 Scrooge

donate 4 give **6** bestow **7** present **8** bequeath

done 5 ready **8** finished, prepared

done for 4 dead, gone, over, sunk **5** all up, ended, kaput, spent **6** beaten, doomed, ruined **7** through **8** finished

done in *see* **5 tired**

Don Giovanni
  also: 7 Don Juan
  opera by: 6 Mozart

Don Juan *see* **6 suitor**

donkey 3 ass **4** fool, mule **5** burro, idiot **7** jackass

donnish 7 preachy **8** academic, didactic, pedantic

donnybrook 3 row **4** fray **5** brawl, fight, melee, set-to **6** dustup, fracas, ruckus, rumpus **7** scuffle **8** skirmish

do-nothing 5 idler **6** loafer

Don Quixote de la Mancha
  author: 9 Cervantes

doodad 5 gizmo **6** device, gadget **8** ornament

doom 3 end, lot **4** fate, ruin **5** death, judge **7** condemn, convict, destiny, portion

do one's best 3 try **6** strive **7** attempt **8** endeavor

door 4 exit **5** entry **6** egress, portal **7** hallway, ingress **8** entrance

dope *see* **5 idiot**

dope fiend 4 head, user **5** doper, freak **6** addict, junkie **7** hophead **8** cokehead

dormant 4 idle **8** inactive, sleeping

dose 2 OD **3** cut, nip **4** dram, pill, shot, slug

5 quota, share, slice **6** amount, needle, ration, tablet **7** capsule, measure, portion, section, segment **8** overdose, quantity

dossier 4 file **5** brief **6** record

dot 3 dab **4** mark, spot **5** fleck, point, speck **6** dapple, period **7** stipple

dotage 8 senility

dote on 5 adore, prize, spoil, value **6** pamper **7** cherish, indulge **8** fuss over, treasure

double 4 dual, twin **5** clone **6** paired **7** replica, two-part **8** two-sided

double-cross *see* **6 betray**

double-dealing 5 false **6** deceit, sneaky, tricky **7** crooked, devious, perfidy **8** bad faith, betrayal

doublet 4 pair **5** tunic **6** couple, jacket

double-talk *see* **8 nonsense**

doubt 5 qualm **6** wonder **7** suspect **8** distrust, mistrust, question

doucement
  music: 6 gently

dough 4 cash, duff, spud

5 bread, crust, money, paster **6** batter, change, leaven, noodle

doughnut 4 cake, tire **5** bagel **6** dunker, sinker **7** beignet, cruller

doughty 4 bold **5** brave **6** strong **8** fearless, intrepid, unafraid

dour 4 sour **6** gloomy, morose, solemn, sullen

douse 4 soak **5** souse **6** drench **7** immerse **8** saturate, submerge

dovetail 4 jibe, join **5** match, tally, unite **8** coincide

dowager 5 widow **6** relict **7** elderly

dowdy 4 drab **5** tacky **6** frumpy, shabby, sloppy

dowel 3 peg, pin, rod **4** pole **5** stick **7** spindle

down 3 ill **4** blue, deck, drop, fell, gulp, sick **5** drink, floor **6** ailing **7** put away, swallow **8** dejected, downcast, feathers

downfall 4 fall, ruin **6** shower **8** collapse, downpour

downright *see* **6 honest**

downstairs **5** below **6** cellar **8** basement

down the drain **4** gone, lost

down-to-earth **5** crass, plain, sober, solid **6** casual, coarse, earthy, simple **7** relaxed **8** informal, sensible

downturn see **4** drop

Down Under see **9** Australia

downy **4** soft **5** fuzzy, nappy, plumy, quiet **6** fleecy, fluffy **8** feathery

do wrong **3** err, sin

doze **3** nap **6** catnap, siesta, snooze

drab **4** dull, gray **5** dingy **6** dismal, dreary, gloomy, somber

Dracula
author: **6** (Bram) Stoker

draft **4** drag, gulp, haul, pull, wind **5** drink **6** breeze, induct, sketch **7** diagram, outline, swallow

drag **3** lug **4** bore, haul, pull **5** bring, crawl, trail **6** dredge **7** be drawn

drag one's feet **5** crawl, creep **6** dawdle

dragoon **5** bully, force **6** coerce, compel **7** trooper **8** browbeat, bulldoze, cavalier, horseman, pressure

drag through the mud see **8** disgrace

drain **3** sap **4** drag, pipe, tube **5** empty, sewer, use up **6** outlet, strain **7** channel, conduit, debouch, deplete, flow out, pump off **8** empty out

drama **4** play **6** acting

dramatic **8** striking

dramatis personae **4** cast **6** actors **7** players

drape **4** deck, garb, veil, wrap **5** adorn, array, cloak, cover, dress **6** attire, bedeck, enrobe, enwrap, shroud, swathe, wrap up **7** apparel, bedight, envelop, festoon, sheathe, swaddle

drastic **4** dire, rash **7** bizarre, extreme, radical

draw **3** get, tie, tow **4** drag, etch, haul, limn, lure, pick, pull, take **5** charm, draft, drain, evoke, infer, write **6** allure, come-on, deduce, elicit, entice, extend, make up, siphon, sketch **7** attract, distort, draw out, extract, make out, pick out, pull out, pump out, stretch, suck dry, take out, wrinkle **8** deadlock, elongate

drawers 5 pants **6** shorts **7** panties **8** bloomers, calzoons, trousers

drawing room 5 salon **6** parlor

draw the line 5 limit **8** contrast, separate

draw up 3 map **5** draft **6** make up, map out **7** charter, diagram, outline

dray 4 cart **5** wagon **7** tipcart, tumbrel

dread *see* **4 fear**

dreadful 5 awful **6** tragic **7** fearful **8** alarming, horrible, shocking, terrible

dream 3 joy **4** goal, hope, muse, wish **5** think **6** desire, vision **7** delight, fantasy, hope for, reverie, think up **8** consider, pleasure, prospect

dreary 3 sad **4** drab **5** bleak **6** dismal, gloomy **7** forlorn **8** mournful

dregs 6 rabble **7** deposit, grounds, residue **8** canaille, riffraff, sediment

drench 3 wet **4** soak **5** douse **8** saturate

dress 4 curl, deck, do up, garb, gown, robe, trim **5** adorn, frock, groom, treat **6** attire **7** apparel, arrange, bandage, cleanse, clothes, comb out, costume, garnish **8** clothing, decorate, ornament

dresser 6 bureau **7** cabinet, commode **8** cupboard

dressing-down 6 rebuke **7** censure, chiding, reproof **8** reproach, scolding

dribble 4 drip, kick **6** bounce **7** drizzle, trickle

drift 3 aim **4** flow, gist, heap, mass, pile **5** amass, amble, sense **6** course, gather, object, pile up, ramble, stream, wander **7** current, meander, meaning, purpose, scatter

drifter 3 bum **4** hobo **5** idler, tramp **6** loafer **8** derelict, vagabond

drill 4 bore **5** punch, train **6** pierce **8** exercise, practice, puncture, training, work with
type: 4 hand **5** twist **8** electric

drink 3 sip **4** gulp, swig **5** booze, taste, toast **6** absorb, imbibe, ingest, salute **7** alcohol, swallow **8** beverage, libation

drink in 6 absorb, digest, soak up, take in

drip 3 ass **4** bore, jerk, nerd **5** creep, dummy, klutz **6** splash **7** dribble, drizzle, trickle **8** sprinkle

drive 4 goad, lead, mean, move, prod, push, ride, rush, spur, urge **5** force, guide, impel, motor, press, steer, surge **6** coerce, compel, incite, intend, outing **7** advance, conduct, go by car, impulse, operate, suggest **8** ambition, campaign, motivate

drivel 5 drool **6** babble, ramble, slaver **7** dribble, slobber **8** babbling, nonsense, rambling

drizzle 3 fog **4** mist, rain **7** dribble **8** sprinkle

Dr Jekyll and Mr Hyde author: 9 Stevenson

droll 5 funny **7** offbeat, strange **8** humorous

drone 3 hum **4** buzz, whir

5 idler **6** loafer **7** vibrate **8** parasite

drool 6 drivel, slaver **7** dribble, slobber **8** salivate

droop 3 dim, sag **4** flag, sink **5** lower **6** weaken, wither **8** hang down

drop 3 can, dab **4** bead, dash, deck, dive, drip, fall, fell, fire, omit, sack, sink, tear **5** abyss, floor, leave, lower, pinch, slide, slope, smack, trace **6** give up, lessen, plunge **7** abandon, decline, descend, descent, dismiss, dwindle, forsake, globule, plummet, slacken, smidgen, trickle **8** decrease, diminish, leave out

drop anchor 4 dock, moor **5** tie up

drop in *see* **5 visit**

drought, drouth 4 lack, need, want **6** dearth **7** aridity, paucity **8** scarcity, shortage

drover 6 cowboy, driver **7** cowpoke **8** herdsman, shepherd

drown 4 soak **5** flood **6** deluge, drench, engulf

drowsy   **224**

7 immerse **8** inundate, overcome, submerge

drowsy *see* **5 tired**

drub 3 hit **4** beat, cane, flog, whip **5** whale **6** thrash

drudge 4 grub, hack, plod, toil **5** labor, slave **6** lackey, menial, toiler **7** grubber **8** inferior

drum 3 din, keg, rap, tap, tub **4** beat, cask, roar, roll **5** expel, force **6** barrel, harp on, rumble, tattoo **7** dismiss, pulsate **8** drive out, hammer at

drunk 3 sot **4** bust, lush, soak **5** binge, rummy, souse, tipsy, toper **6** barfly, bender, looped, sodden, soused, stewed, zapped, zonked **7** smashed **8** besotted, carousal

dry 4 arid, blot, dull, wipe **5** droll **6** boring, low-key **7** deadpan, parched, tedious, thirsty **8** rainless

dry goods 5 cloth, goods **6** fabric **8** material

dual 6 double **7** twofold, two-part

dub 4 call, name **5** label

6 knight **7** baptize **8** christen, nickname

Dubai *see* **18 United Arab Emirates**
part of: 3 UAE

dubious 5 shady **6** unsure **7** suspect **8** doubtful

Dublin
brewery: 8 Guinness
capital of: 7 Ireland
park: 7 Phoenix
river: 6 Liffey
rising: 6 Easter
university: 7 Trinity

Dubliners
author: 5 (James) Joyce

duce, il duce 6 despot, leader, tyrant **8** dictator

duck
male: 5 drake
group of: 5 brace

duct 4 pipe, tube **6** vessel **7** channel, conduit

ductile *see* **7 elastic**

dud 3 dog **4** bomb, bust, flop, hash **5** botch, lemon, loser **6** bummer, fiasco, fizzle **7** clinker, debacle, failure, washout

dude 3 fop **4** beau **5** dandy **7** peacock

due 4 owed **5** ample, owing **6** enough, proper, unpaid

7 fitting, merited **8** adequate, becoming, deserved, expected, plenty of, rightful, suitable

duet 3 duo, two **4** pair **6** couple **7** twosome

dugout 3 den **4** cave **5** canoe **6** cavity, hollow **7** shelter

dulcet 7 lyrical, musical, tuneful **8** pleasing, sonorous

dull 4 slow **5** blunt, dense, muted, quiet, thick, trite, vapid **6** boring, obtuse, stupid **7** muffled, not keen, prosaic, subdued, vacuous **8** inactive

duly 6 on time **8** properly, suitably

dumb 3 mum **4** dull, mute **5** dense, dopey **6** silent, stupid **7** foolish, aphasic

dumbbell *see* **5 idiot**

dumbfound, dumfound 4 stun **5** amaze **7** startle **8** astonish

dump 3 hut **4** hole, toss **5** empty, hovel, shack **6** shanty, unload **8** get rid of, junkyard

dunce *see* **5 idiot**

dune 4 bank **5** mound

dunk 3 dip, sop **4** duck, soak **5** bathe, douse, drown, slosh, souse, steep **6** deluge, drench, engulf, plunge **7** baptize, immerse **8** inundate, submerge

duo 4 pair **5** combo **6** couple **7** twosome

dupe *see* **5 trick**

duplicate 4 copy **5** clone, match **6** repeat **7** replica **8** parallel

durable 5 sound, tough **6** strong, sturdy **7** lasting

duration 4 term **6** extent, period

duress 5 force **6** threat **8** coercion, pressure

dusk 6 sunset **7** sundown **8** twilight

dust 4 dirt, lint **5** brush, motes **8** sprinkle

Dutch Guiana *see* **8 Suriname**

duty 3 tax **4** levy, onus, task **6** charge, excise, tariff **7** customs **8** business, function

dwarf 3 dim, elf, imp **4** baby, tiny **5** fairy, gnome, pixie, pygmy, small, troll **6** bantam, goblin, petite, sprite **8** diminish

dwelling 4 home **5** abode, house **8** domicile

dwell on 6 accent, stress **7** feature, iterate

dwindle 4 fade, wane **6** lessen, shrink **7** decline **8** decrease, diminish

dye 4 tint **5** color, shade, stain **8** coloring

dynamic 5 vital **6** active **7** driving **8** forceful, powerful, vigorous

dynamite 4 raze, ruin **5** blast, trash, wreck **6** blow up, charge **7** destroy, shatter, wipe out **8** decimate, demolish

dynasty 4 line **5** crown, reign **6** regime **7** lineage, regency **8** dominion, hegemony, monarchy

dyspeptic *see* **7 grouchy**

each 3 per **4** a pop **5** every **6** apiece **7** that one, this one **8** everyone, separate

eager 3 hot **4** agog, avid, keen **6** ardent, fervid, intent, raring **7** athirst, earnest, excited, fervent, intense, longing, zealous **8** desirous, diligent, resolute, spirited, yearning

ear
  section: 5 inner, outer **6** middle
  part: 4 drum **5** anvil, canal **6** hammer **7** cochlea, stirrup

earl 4 lord, peer **5** noble **8** nobleman
  wife: 8 countess

early 5 first **6** primal **7** ancient, archaic, betimes, initial, too soon, very old **8** primeval

earmark 3 tag **4** band, hold, sign **5** allot, label, stamp, token, trait **6** aspect, assign, dog-ear **7** feature, put away, quality, reserve **8** allocate, set aside

earn 3 get, net **4** draw, gain, make, rate, reap **5** clear, merit **6** attain, pick up, secure **7** achieve, collect, deserve, realize

earnest 4 firm **5** eager, fixed, grave, sober, staid **6** ardent, fervid, honest, intent, sedate, solemn, stable, steady, urgent **7** devoted, fervent, intense, serious, sincere, zealous **8** constant, diligent, resolute, spirited, vehement

earnings 3 pay **5** wages **6** income, salary **7** payment, profits **8** proceeds

ear-splitting 7 blaring **8** piercing

earth 3 sod **4** clay, dirt, dust, land, loam, soil, turf **5** terra **6** ground **7** topsoil

earthenware 5 china **7** pottery **8** clayware, crockery

earthquake 5 quake, seism, shock **6** tremor **8** tremblor, upheaval

ease 4 calm, rest, slip **5** abate, allay, poise, quiet, slide, still **6** aplomb, lessen, luxury, pacify, plenty, relief, repose, solace, soothe **7** assuage, comfort, console, leisure, lighten, mollify, relieve **8** diminish, facility, maneuver, mitigate, palliate, serenity

easel 5 frame, stand

easily 5 by far **6** freely, surely **7** clearly, handily, lightly, plainly, readily **8** facilely, smoothly

East, the 4 Asia **6** Orient **7** Far East **8** Near East

East Germany *see* **7 Germany**

easy 4 calm, mild, open, soft **5** cushy, frank, light, naive **6** benign, calmly, candid, docile, easily, gentle, secure, serene, simple **7** lenient, natural, not hard, relaxed, restful, wealthy **8** carefree, composed, friendly, gracious, gullible, informal, outgoing, peaceful, pleasant, serenely, tranquil, yielding

eat 3 sup **4** bolt, dine, feed, gulp, rust, take **5** feast, lunch **6** devour, gobble, ingest, nibble **7** consume, corrode **8** wear away, wolf down

eaves 8 overhang

eavesdrop 3 bug, pry, spy, tap **5** snoop **6** attend, harken **7** monitor, wiretap **8** listen in, overhear

ebb 5 abate, go out **6** go down, lessen, recede, shrink, weaken **7** decline, dwindle, retreat, slacken, subside **8** decrease, diminish, fade away, move back, withdraw

ebony 3 jet **4** dark, inky **5** black, raven, sable **8** hardwood

ebullient 6 elated, joyful, joyous

eccentric *see* **5 weird**

ecclesiastic, ecclesiastical 5 rabbi, vicar **6** cleric, curate, deacon, parson, pastor, priest, rector **7** prelate **8** chaplain, churchly, clerical, minister, pastoral, preacher

echelon 4 file, line, rank, rung, tier **5** grade, level **6** office **8** position

Echidna 8 anteater
   feature: 5 snout

echo 3 ape **4** copy, ring **5** match **6** follow, mirror, parrot, repeat **7** imitate, reflect, resound **8** simulate

Echo
   loved: 9 Narcissus
   loved by: 3 Pan
   changed into: 4 echo

eclair 6 pastry **7** dessert

eclat 4 fame, pomp **5** glory, honor **6** praise, renown, repute **7** acclaim

eclipse *see* **4 hide**

eclogue 4 idyl, poem **5** idyll **7** bucolic **8** dialogue, pastoral

economical 5 chary, cheap **6** frugal, modest, saving **7** careful, prudent, sparing, spartan, thrifty

economics
   term: 3 GNP **5** labor **7** capital, Marxism, surplus **8** property

ecstasy *see* **3 joy**

Ecuador
   capital: 5 Quito
   largest city: 9 Guayaquil
   island: 9 Galapagos
   mountain: 5 Andes
   feature:
      animal: 6 vicuna
      dictator: 8 caudillo
      estate: 8 hacienda
   food:
      marinated raw shrimp/ fish: 7 ceviche, seviche

ecumenical 6 global **7** general **8** catholic

eczema 4 rash **8** eruption

Eden 8 Paradise

edentate 5 manis, sloth **7** antbear **8** aardvark, anteater **9** armadillo

edge 3 hem, rim **4** bind, inch, line, side, trim **5** bound, brink, creep, limit, sidle, slink, sneak, steal, verge **6** border, fringe, margin **7** contour, outline

edict *see* **3 law**

edifice 8 building

edify 5 teach **6** inform **7** educate, improve **8** instruct

Edinburgh
   capital of: 8 Scotland

edit 5 adapt, emend **6** censor, polish, redact, revise **7** abridge, clean up, correct, expunge, rewrite

8 condense, copy-edit, rephrase

edition 4 book, copy, kind **5** issue **6** number **7** imprint, version **8** printing

educate 5 coach, edify, teach, train, tutor **6** inform, school **7** develop **8** civilize, instruct

eel 6 conger
    young: 5 elver

eerie *see* **5 weird**

efface 4 raze **5** erase **6** cancel, delete, excise, rub out **7** blot out, destroy, expunge, wipe out

effect, effects 4 fact, gist, make **5** cause, drift, force, goods, power, tenor, truth **6** action, assets, attain, create, impact, import, intent, result, sequel, things, upshot, weight **7** achieve, essence, execute, meaning, outcome, perform, produce, purport, reality, realize **8** carry out, efficacy, function, holdings, movables

effeminate 7 unmanly **8** sissyish, womanish

effervescence 3 zip **4** dash,

fizz, life **5** froth, vigor **6** gaiety, spirit **7** foaming **8** bubbling, vitality

effete 5 spent **6** barren, wasted **7** sterile, worn-out **8** decadent, depraved

efficient 3 apt **7** capable **8** skillful

effigy 4 doll **5** dummy, image **6** puppet, statue **8** likeness, straw man

effluent 5 waste **6** efflux, sewage **7** outflow

effort 3 try **4** toil, work **5** force, labor, pains, power **6** energy, strain, stress **7** attempt, travail, trouble **8** endeavor, exertion

effrontery 4 gall **5** brass, cheek, nerve **8** audacity, temerity
    Yiddish: 7 chutzpa **8** chutzpah

effusive 5 gushy **6** lavish **7** copious, gushing, profuse

eft 4 newt **5** again **6** lizard

egg 3 ova, roe **4** bomb, goad, mine, oval, ovum, seed, spur **6** embryo, fellow, incite, person **7** albumen

egg on 4 abet, back, goad,

spur **6** exhort, incite **8** talk into

egotism 6 vanity **7** conceit **8** bragging, smugness

egregious 5 gross **7** extreme, glaring, heinous **8** flagrant, grievous, shocking

egress 4 exit, vent **5** issue **6** escape, outlet, way out **7** leakage **8** aperture

Egypt
  other name: 3 UAR
  capital/largest city: 5 Cairo
  lake: 6 Bitter, Nasser
  river: 4 Nile
    Nile branch: 7 Rosetta **8** Damietta
  sea: 3 Red
  physical feature:
    desert: 6 Libyan, Nubian, Sahara **7** Arabian
    gulf: 4 Suez **5** Aqaba
    isthmus: 4 Suez
    peninsula: 5 Sinai
  place:
    dam: 5 Aswan
    pyramids: 4 Giza **5** Khufu **6** Cheops
    ruins: 6 Sphinx, Thebes **7** Memphis
  feature:

peasant: 6 fellah **8** fellahin
sailboat: 7 felucca

Egyptian cross 4 ankh

Egyptian Mythology
  goddess of fertility: 2 Io **4** Isis
  god of creation: 4 Ptah
  god of dead/Nile: 6 Osiris
  god of sun: 2 Ra, Re **5** Horus
  god of tombs/embalming: 6 Anubis
  god of wisdom/magic/ learning: 5 Thoth
  judge/king of dead: 6 Osiris
  king of gods: 4 Amen, Amon **5** Ammon **6** Amen Ra, Amon Ra

eiderdown 4 puff **5** cover, quilt **8** coverlet

Eire *see* **7 Ireland**

Eisenhower, Dwight David
  nickname: 3 Ike
  presidential rank: 12 thirty-fourth
  party: 10 Republican
  state represented: 2 NY
  defeated: 9 Stevenson
  vice president: 5 Nixon
  born: 2 TX **7** Denison
  civilian career:
    university president:

8 Columbia
military service: 7 general
supreme commander of:
4 NATO **6** Allies
notable events of lifetime/
term: 4 D-Day, NATO
invasion: 8 Normandy
wife: 5 Marie
nickname: 5 Mamie

ejaculate 4 howl, yell, yelp
5 shout **6** bellow, cry out
7 exclaim

eject 4 emit, oust, spew **5**
evict, exile, expel, exude,
spout **6** banish, bounce,
deport, remove **7** cast out,
kick out, spit out, turn
out **8** disgorge, drive out,
force out, throw out

eke 3 add **4** also **7**
augment, enlarge, stretch
8 increase, lengthen

elaborate 5 fancy, gaudy,
showy **6** expand, flashy,
garish, ornate **7** clarify,
complex, elegant, labored,
specify **8** involved

elan 4 dash, zeal **5** flair,
verve, vigor **6** energy,
spirit **8** vivacity

eland 3 elk **8** antelope

elapse 4 go by, pass **5** lapse
6 pass by, roll by, slip by
7 glide by, slide by

elastic 6 pliant, supple **7**
pliable, rubbery, springy **8**
flexible, tolerant, yielding

elated *see* **5 happy**

elbow grease 4 work **5**
force, labor **6** effort,
energy, muscle **8** exertion,
hard work

elder 4 head **5** older **6**
senior **8** old-timer

elect 4 pick **5** adopt **6**
choose, opt for, select,
take up **7** embrace,
espouse, fix upon, pick
out **8** decide on, settle on

election 4 poll, vote **6**
choice, option, voting **7**
resolve **8** decision

Electra
brother: 7 Orestes
sister: 9 Iphigenia
husband: 7 Pylades

electric 7 dynamic, rousing
8 exalting, exciting,
spirited, stirring

electricity measure 3 ohm
4 volt, watt **5** joule **6**
ampere

elegance 5 class, grace,
taste **6** purity **7** balance **8**
grandeur, richness

elegant 4 fine, rich **5** grand
6 classy, dapper, lovely,

ornate, polite, urbane **7** classic, courtly, genteel, refined, stylish **8** artistic, charming, debonair, graceful, gracious, handsome, polished, tasteful

elegiac 3 sad **8** funereal, mournful

elegy 7 requiem, sad poem

element, elements 3 air **4** fire **5** earth, water **6** basics, member, milieu **7** essence, factors, origins

elementary 4 easy **5** basal, basic, crude, first, plain **6** simple **7** primary

elephant
  group of: 4 herd
  types: 5 Asian **7** African
  features: 5 trunk, tusks
  famous: 5 Babar, Dumbo
  elephant boy: 4 Sabu **6** mahout
  extinct: 7 mammoth **8** mastodon

elephantine *see* **4 huge**

elevate *see* **4 lift**

elevator 4 cage, lift, silo, wing **5** hoist **7** granary
  inventor: 4 Otis

elf 4 puck **5** fairy, gnome, pixie, troll **6** goblin, sprite **7** brownie, gremlin

elfin 3 fey, wee **4** tiny **7** pixyish

elicit 5 cause, educe, evoke, fetch, wrest **6** derive, extort **7** draw out, extract

elide 4 omit, slur **5** annul **6** delete **7** neglect **8** suppress

eligible 6 proper **7** fitting **8** suitable

Elijah 7 prophet

eliminate 4 drop, omit, oust **5** eject, erase, exile, expel **6** banish, cut out, delete, except, reject, remove, rub out **7** abolish, cast out, dismiss, exclude, weed out **8** get rid of, leave out

elite 3 top **4** best **5** cream **6** choice, flower **7** bigwigs, society, wealthy **8** big shots, notables

elixir 6 potion, remedy **7** essence, extract, panacea, spirits **8** tincture

Elizabeth I
  queen of: 7 England
  father: 5 Henry (Tudor)
  mother: 4 Anne (Boleyn)
  sister: 4 (Bloody) Mary
  brother: 6 Edward

suitor: 5 Essex **6** Dudley **9** Leicester

Elizabeth II
father: 6 George
mother: 9 Elizabeth
husband: 6 Philip
son: 6 Andrew, Edward **7** Charles
daughter: 4 Anne
daughter-in-law: 5 Diana, Sarah (Fergie) **6** Sophie **7** Camilla

Ellice Islands *see* **6 Tuvalu**

elocution 6 speech **7** diction, oratory

elongated 4 long **8** drawn out, extended

eloquent 5 vivid **6** moving, poetic **8** emphatic, forceful, spirited, stirring

El Salvador
capital/largest city: 11 San Salvador
highest point: 8 Santa Ana
feature:
    estate: 5 finca
    musical instrument: 7 caramba

else 3 and, too **4** also, more **5** if not, other **7** besides, instead

elsewhere 4 away **6** except **7** absence, not here

elucidate 6 detail **7** clarify, clear up, explain, expound **8** describe, spell out

elusive *see* **4 wily**

elysian 7 sublime **8** blissful, empyreal, empyrean, ethereal, heavenly

emaciated *see* **5 gaunt**

emanate 4 flow, rise, stem, well **5** exude, issue **6** spring **7** give off, proceed **8** come from

emancipate 4 free **7** manumit, release, set free, unchain **8** liberate

emasculate 4 geld **5** alter **6** soften, weaken **8** castrate

embankment 4 bank, dike, wall **5** levee

embargo 3 ban **8** shutdown, stoppage

embark 5 begin, board, start **6** launch, set out **7** enplane, entrain **8** commence, go aboard

embarrass 4 faze **5** abash, shame, upset **6** rattle **7** agitate, chagrin, fluster, mortify, nonplus **8** distress

embattled 8 fighting

embed **3** fix, set **4** bond **5** plant **6** fasten **8** ensconce

embellish **4** gild **5** adorn, color **6** set off **7** dress up, enhance, garnish, gussy up **8** beautify, decorate, ornament

ember **3** ash **4** slag **6** cinder **7** clinker **8** live coal

embezzle **4** bilk, rook **5** cheat, filch **6** fleece **7** defraud, swindle

embitter **4** sour **6** rankle

emblem **4** sign **5** badge **6** design, device, symbol **8** hallmark, insignia

embody **4** fuse **5** blend, merge **6** typify **7** collect, contain, embrace, express, include, realize **8** manifest

embolden **7** fortify, hearten, inspire **8** inspirit

emboss **4** knob, knot, stud **5** adorn, chase **6** indent **7** engrave, exhaust

embrace **3** hug **5** adopt, clasp, cover, grasp **6** accept, embody **7** contain, espouse, include, involve

embroider **5** color **7** dress up

embroil **4** trap **6** enmesh **7** ensnare, involve **8** entangle

embryo **3** bud, egg **4** germ **5** fetus, larva, ovule **6** budding, source

emend *see* **4** **edit**

emerald
   species: **5** beryl
   color: **5** green

Emerald Isle **7** Ireland

emerge **3** run **4** dawn, emit, flow, gush, loom, pour, rise **5** arise, issue **6** appear, come up, crop up, escape **7** surface

emergence **4** dawn **7** dawning

emergency **5** pinch **6** crisis **7** urgency **8** exigency

emigrate **4** move, quit **5** leave **6** depart, remove **7** migrate

eminent *see* **6** **famous**

emir **4** amir, Arab, Turk **5** chief, emeer, ruler **6** leader, prince

emissary **5** agent, envoy **6** deputy, herald, legate **7** courier **8** delegate

emit **4** beam, give, shed, vent **5** expel, issue **7** cast out, excrete, secrete, send out **8** dispatch, throw out

Emmanuel 5 Jesus **6** Christ **7** Messiah

emollient 3 oil **4** balm **5** balmy, cream, salve **6** lotion **7** calming, easeful, healing, unguent **8** allaying, ointment, soothing

emolument *see* **6 income**

emotion 4 fear, hate, heat, love, zeal **5** anger, ardor, pride **6** fervor, sorrow, warmth **7** concern, despair, passion, sadness **8** jealousy

emperor, empress 4 czar, king, shah **5** queen, ruler **6** caesar, kaiser, mikado, sultan **7** czarina, monarch

emphasize 6 accent, stress **7** dwell on, feature, iterate, point up

emphatic *see* **8 definite**

empire 4 rule **5** realm **6** domain **8** dominion

Empire State
  nickname of: 7 New York

employ 3 use **4** hire **5** apply **6** devote, engage, occupy, retain, take on **7** service, utilize **8** exercise

emporium 5 store **6** bazaar, market

empower 4 vest **5** allow, endow **6** enable, invest, permit **7** license **8** delegate, sanction

empty 4 bare, dump, flow, idle, void **5** banal, drain, inane **6** futile, hollow, vacant **7** aimless, debouch, insipid, pour out, shallow, trivial, vacuous **8** evacuate

emu
  form: 4 bird
  habitat: 9 Australia

emulate 3 ape **4** copy **5** mimic, rival **6** follow **7** imitate

enable 3 aid **5** allow **6** assist, permit **7** benefit, empower, qualify, support

enact 4 pass **6** decree, ratify **7** approve **8** proclaim, sanction

enamel 4 coat **5** paint **7** coating

enamor 5 charm **6** allure, attach, draw to, excite **7** bewitch, enchant **8** enthrall, entrance

encampment 4 camp **5** tents **7** bivouac **8** tent city

encase 4 wrap 5 cover 6 enfold, enwrap 7 enclose, envelop, sheathe

enchant 3 hex 5 charm 7 bewitch, delight 8 enthrall, entrance

enclose, inclose 4 ring 6 circle, girdle, insert, wall in 7 close in, fence in, include 8 encircle, surround

encomium 5 kudos, paean 6 eulogy 7 plaudit, tribute 8 citation

encounter 4 bout, face, meet 5 brush, clash, fight 6 affray, battle, combat, endure, fracas, suffer 7 run into, sustain, undergo 8 come upon, confront, meet with, skirmish

encourage *see* 6 **prompt**

encroach 6 invade 7 impinge, intrude, overrun, violate 8 infringe, overstep, trespass

encumber 3 tax 4 lade, load 6 burden, hinder, impede, saddle 8 handicap, obstruct

end 3 aim 4 edge, goal, halt, kill, ruin, stop 5 cease, close, death, issue, limit, scrap 6 border, demise, design, effect, ending, finale, finish, object, result, run out, upshot, windup 7 destroy, outcome, purpose, remnant 8 boundary, conclude, terminus

endanger 4 risk 6 expose, hazard 7 imperil

endeavor *see* 3 **try**

endorse, indorse 2 OK 4 back, sign 6 affirm, ratify, second 7 approve, certify, support 8 advocate, champion, sanction, validate, vouch for

endowment 4 gift 5 award, flair, grant 6 legacy, talent 7 ability, bequest, faculty 8 aptitude, donation

endure 4 bear, last, live 5 brave, brook, stand 6 live on, remain, suffer 7 persist, prevail, sustain, undergo, weather 8 continue, cope with, tolerate

enemy 3 foe 5 rival 7 nemesis 8 armed foe, attacker, opponent

energy 2 go 3 pep, vim, zip 4 elan, zeal, zest 5 drive, force, power, verve, vigor

6 hustle **8** dynamism, vitality, vivacity

enervated 5 spent **6** effete, wasted **7** languid, worn-out **8** fatigued, listless, sluggish, unmanned, unnerved, weakened

enforce 5 apply, exact **6** defend, impose **7** execute, support **8** carry out

engage 4 hire **6** absorb, combat, employ, occupy, pledge, retain, secure, take on **7** betroth, involve, partake **8** affiance, embark on, take part

engineer 5 pilot **6** driver, hogger **7** builder, planner **8** motorman, operator

England
  other name: 6 Albion **7** Britain **9** Britannia
  capital/largest city: 6 London
  island: 3 Man **4** Holy **5** Wight **6** Scilly **7** Channel **8** Anglesey, Holyhead
  mountain: 7 Pennine
  highest point: 7 Scafell
  river: 4 Tyne **5** Trent **6** Humber, Mersey, Severn, Thames
  sea: 5 Irish, North **8** Atlantic
  physical feature:
    chalk cliffs: 5 Dover
    point: 6 Lizard **8** Lands End
  place:
    fortification/wall: 8 Hadrian's
    tower: 6 London
  food:
    dessert: 6 trifle
    drink: 3 tea **6** squash

engrave 3 cut **4** etch **5** carve, stamp **6** chisel **7** decorate, stipple

engrossed 4 busy, deep **6** intent **7** engaged **8** absorbed, immersed, involved, occupied

engulf 4 bury **5** swamp **6** deluge **7** envelop, immerse, overrun **8** inundate, submerge

enhance 4 lift **5** add to, boost, raise **7** augment, elevate, magnify **8** heighten, redouble

enigma 6 puzzle, riddle, secret **7** mystery **8** question

enjoin *see* **9 prescribe**

enjoy 3 own **4** have, like **5** eat up, fancy, savor **6** admire, relish **7** possess

enlarge 4 grow **5** add to, swell, widen **6** expand, extend **7** amplify, augment, broaden, develop, expound, inflate, magnify **8** elongate, increase, lengthen

enlighten 5 edify **6** advise, inform, wise up **7** apprise, clarify, educate **8** civilize

enlist *see* **4 join**

enliven 4 fire **5** pep up, renew **6** excite, vivify, wake up **7** animate, cheer up **8** brighten, vitalize

en masse 7 in a body **8** as a group, as a whole, in a group, together

enmity 6 animus, hatred, malice, rancor, strife **7** ill will **8** acrimony, bad blood

ennui 6 apathy, tedium **7** boredom, languor

enormous 4 huge, vast **7** immense, mammoth, massive, titanic **8** colossal, gigantic

enough 5 ample, amply **6** plenty **7** copious **8** abundant, adequate

enraged *see* **7 furious**

enrapture 5 charm **6** thrill

7 beguile, bewitch, delight, enchant **8** enthrall, entrance, hold rapt

enrich 5 adorn, endow **6** refine **7** elevate, enhance, fortify, improve, upgrade **8** make rich

enroll 4 join **5** admit, enter **6** accept, engage, enlist, join up, sign up, take on **7** recruit **8** register

ensconce 4 bury, hide, seat **5** lodge **6** settle **7** conceal, secrete, shelter

ensemble 5 getup **6** attire, outfit, troupe **7** company, costume **8** assembly, entirety, grouping, totality

ensign *see* **6 symbol**

enslave 6 addict, subdue **7** capture, control, enchain, shackle **8** dominate, enthrall

ensue 6 derive, follow, result **7** succeed

ensure, insure 5 guard **6** assure, clinch, secure **7** protect, warrant

entangle *see* **4 trap**

entente 4 pact **6** accord, treaty **7** compact **8** alliance, covenant

enter 4 go in, join, list, post

6 arrive, come in, record
8 enlist in, enroll in,
inscribe, pass into

enterprise 4 push, task, zeal
5 drive, vigor **6** daring,
effort, energy, spirit **7**
attempt, program, project,
venture **8** ambition,
boldness, campaign,
endeavor, industry

entertain 4 heed **5** admit,
amuse, charm **6** absorb,
divert, foster, harbor,
please, ponder, regale **7**
beguile, delight, dwell on,
engross, imagine, nurture,
support **8** consider,
enthrall, interest, muse
over, play host

enthrall, enthral 5 charm,
rivet **6** seduce, thrill **7**
beguile, bewitch, enchant,
enslave **8** entrance,
intrigue, transfix

enthusiasm 4 love, rage,
zeal, zest **5** ardor, craze,
hobby, mania **6** fervor,
relish **7** elation, passion **8**
devotion, interest

entice 4 coax, lure **5** tempt
6 allure, incite, induce,
seduce **7** attract, beguile,
wheedle **8** inveigle

entire 4 full **5** gross, total,

whole **6** in toto, intact **8**
absolute, complete

entitle 3 dub, tag **4** call,
name **5** allow, label, style,
title **6** enable, permit **7**
qualify

entity 4 body **5** being, thing
6 matter, object **7** article
8 creature, quantity

entourage 5 court, staff,
suite, train **6** convoy,
escort **7** cortege, retinue

entrails 4 guts **5** offal **6**
bowels **7** innards, insides,
viscera

entrance 4 door, gate **5**
charm, entry, way in **6**
access, entree, portal **7**
beguile, bewitch, delight,
doorway, gateway,
gladden, ingress, opening
8 approach

entrap *see* **4 trap**

entreat *see* **7 beseech**

entree 4 pull **5** entry **6**
access **7** ingress **8**
entrance, main dish

entrench, intrench 3 fix,
set **5** dig in, embed, plant
6 anchor **7** implant, install
8 ensconce

entrust, intrust 5 trust **6**
assign, commit **7** consign

8 delegate, hand over, turn over

entry *see* **8 entrance**

enumerate *see* **3 add**

enunciate **5** sound, speak, voice **8** vocalize

envelop *see* **4 hide**

envelope **5** cover **6** jacket **8** covering, wrapping

enviable **5** lucky **8** salutary

environment **5** scene **6** locale, medium, milieu **7** climate, element, habitat, setting **8** ambience

environs **6** exurbs **7** suburbs **8** vicinity

envisage **5** fancy **7** dream of, dream up, imagine, picture **8** conceive

envoy *see* **8 delegate**

envy **5** greed, spite **6** resent **8** begrudge, grudging, jealousy

enzyme **7** protein **8** molecule
function: **8** catalyst

eon **3** age, era **8** eternity, long time

ephemeral **5** brief **7** passing **8** fleeting, flitting, fugitive

epic **4** saga **5** drama, great, noble **6** fabled, heroic

7 exalted, storied **8** fabulous, majestic

epicure **7** glutton, gourmet **8** gourmand, hedonist, sybarite

epidemic **4** rife **6** plague **7** rampant, scourge **8** outbreak, pandemic

epigram **4** quip **5** adage, maxim **6** bon mot **8** aphorism, apothegm

epilogue **4** coda **5** rider **7** codicil **8** addendum

episode **4** part **5** event, scene **6** affair, period **7** chapter **8** incident

epistle **6** letter **7** message, missive

epithet **5** curse **6** insult **8** nickname

epitome **4** peak **5** ideal, model **6** height **7** essence

epoch **3** age, era **4** time **6** period **8** interval

equable *see* **4 calm**

equal **4** even, like, peer **5** match **7** matched, the same, uniform **8** balanced, be even to, equalize, jibe with, of a piece, parallel

Equatorial Guinea
capital: **6** Malabo

largest city: 4 Bata
division: 5 Bioko **7** Rio Muni
physical feature:
  bay: 6 Biafra
  gulf: 6 Guinea

equilibrium 7 balance **8** symmetry

equip 3 rig **5** stock **6** fit out, outfit, supply **7** appoint, furnish, provide

equity 4 cash **5** value **6** assets, profit **7** justice **8** fairness, justness

equivalent 4 even, peer **5** equal, match **8** parallel

equivocal 4 hazy **5** vague **7** dubious **8** doubtful

era 3 age **4** time **5** epoch **6** period **8** interval

eradicate 5 erase **6** remove **7** abolish, blot out, destroy, expunge, wipe out

erase 6 delete, remove, rub out **7** expunge, scratch

erect 5 build, put up, raise, rigid, stiff **6** unbent **7** stand up, upright **8** straight, vertical

Eritrea
  capital/largest city: 6 Asmara

formerly division of: 8 Ethiopia
  sea: 3 Red

ermine 3 fur **4** duty, rank **6** weasel **7** ermalin **8** position

erode 3 eat **5** spoil, waste **6** ravage **7** corrode, despoil, eat away **8** wear away

Eros
  origin: 5 Greek
  god of: 4 love
  mother: 9 Aphrodite
  corresponds to: 5 Cupid

erotic 3 hot **4** lewd, sexy **5** bawdy, lusty **6** ardent, carnal, impure, ribald, risque, sexual, wanton **7** amorous, raunchy **8** immodest, indecent, unchaste

err 3 sin **6** mess up, slip up **7** blunder, do wrong **8** go astray

errand 4 duty, task **6** office **7** mission

erratic 3 odd **5** queer **6** fitful **7** strange, unusual, wayward **8** aberrant, abnormal, peculiar, shifting, unstable, variable

error 4 flaw **5** boner, botch, fault **6** boo-boo, bungle, howler **7** blooper, fallacy, mistake

ersatz 4 fake, sham **5** bogus, phony

Erse 4 Celt, Gael, Scot **5** Irish **6** Celtic, Gaelic **7** Ireland **8** Scottish

erstwhile 2 ex **4** past **6** bygone, former **7** onetime **8** previous

erudite 4 wise **7** learned, sapient **8** cultured, literate, well-read

erupt 4 emit, gush, vent **5** eruct **6** blow up **7** explode **8** break out, throw off

escadrille 6 armada **8** flotilla, squadron

escalate *see* **4 rise**

escape 3 lam **4** bolt, exit, flee, flow, gush, leak, seep, shun, skip **5** avert, avoid, dodge, elude, issue, skirt **6** efflux, egress, emerge, eschew, exodus, flight, stream **7** abscond, emanate, getaway, leakage, make off, outflow, outpour, run away, seepage **8** breakout, slip away, steal off

escarpment 4 bank, crag

5 bluff, cliff, ridge, slope **8** headland, palisade

eschew 4 shun **5** avoid, forgo **6** give up **7** forbear

escort 4 date, take **5** guard, guide, train, usher **6** squire **7** company, conduct, cortege, retinue

escutcheon 4 arms **5** crest **6** shield
see also **8 heraldry**

Eskimo
tribe: 5 Aleut

esoteric *see* **7 obscure**

especially 6 really **7** notably

esplanade 4 mall, path, walk **5** drive

espouse *see* **3 wed**

essay 3 try **5** paper, theme, tract **6** effort, take on **7** article, attempt, venture **8** critique, endeavor, treatise

essence 4 core, germ, gist, pith, soul **5** heart, point, scent **6** elixir, nature, spirit **7** cologne, extract, meaning, perfume, spirits

essential, essentials 3 key **4** main **5** basic, vital **6** basics, needed **7** crucial, leading **8** cardinal

establish 3 fix **4** form, open, show **5** begin, found, prove, set up, start **6** create, settle, uphold, verify **7** confirm, implant, install, justify, situate, sustain, warrant **8** initiate, organize, validate

estate 4 rank, will **5** class, grade, manor, money, order, state **6** assets, legacy, status, wealth **7** bequest, fortune, station **8** compound, holdings, property

esteem *see* **6 admire**

Esther
  Persian name of: 8 Hadassah
  holiday: 5 Purim

esthetic 7 refined **8** artistic

estimable 4 good **6** prized **7** admired **8** laudable

estimate 4 view **5** assay, guess, judge, opine, think, value **6** assess, belief, figure, reckon **7** believe, opinion, surmise **8** appraise, conclude, consider, evaluate, judgment, thinking

Estonia
  capital/largest city: 7 Tallinn
  lake: 5 Pskov **6** Peipus
  sea: 6 Baltic
  physical feature:
    gulf: 4 Riga **7** Finland

estranged 5 aloof **6** cut off **7** distant **8** detached, divorced

estuary 5 firth, inlet

etc (&c) 4 et al **7** and so on, whatnot **8** et cetera, whatever

etch 3 cut, fix **5** carve, stamp **7** corrode, engrave

eternal 7 abiding, endless **8** constant, immortal, infinite, timeless, unending

eternity 4 Zion **6** Heaven **7** forever, nirvana **8** infinity, paradise

ethereal 4 airy, rare **6** aerial **7** elusive, refined, sublime **8** rarefied

ethical 4 fair, just **5** moral, right **6** decent, kosher, proper **7** correct, fitting, upright **8** virtuous

ethics, ethic 8 morality

Ethiopia
  Biblical name: 4 Cush
  other name: 9 Abyssinia
  capital/largest city: 10 Addis Ababa
  river: 8 Blue Nile

sea: 3 Red
physical feature:
　valley: 4 Rift
etiquette 5 usage **7** decorum, manners **8** behavior, courtesy, good form, protocol
Etruscan
　native of: (ancient) **7** Etruria
　location: 7 Tuscany
　king: 7 Tarquin
eulogy 5 paean **6** homage **7** plaudit, tribute **8** encomium
euphoria 7 ecstasy, elation, rapture
Europa
　brother: 5 Cilix **6** Cadmus **7** Phoenix
　son: 5 Minos **8** Sarpedon
　daughter: 5 Crete
　abducted by: 4 Zeus
Europe
　island: 5 Crete, Malta **6** Faeroe, Sicily **7** Corsica, Iceland, Ireland **8** Balearic, Sardinia
　mountain range: 4 Alps **5** Urals **7** Balkans **8** Caucasus, Pyrenees
　highest point: 6 Elbrus
　lowest point: 10 Caspian Sea

European Union 2 EU
　currency: 4 euro
　predecessor organizations: 3 EEC
evacuate 4 quit **5** leave **6** desert, remove, vacate **7** abandon, forsake, move out, take out **8** order out
evade 4 duck, shun **5** avoid, dodge, elude, hedge, parry **6** escape, eschew **8** sidestep
evaluate 4 rate, test **5** assay, gauge, judge, value, weigh **6** assess, size up **8** appraise, estimate
evanesce 6 vanish **8** fade away, pass away
evangelist 7 apostle **8** disciple, minister, preacher, reformer
evaporate 5 dry up **6** dispel, vanish **7** scatter **8** dissolve, evanesce, fade away, melt away, vaporize
evasive 6 shifty **7** devious, dodging, elusive, elusory
Eve
　husband: 4 Adam
　son: 4 Abel, Cain, Seth
　home: 4 Eden
even 4 calm, fair, flat, just, true **5** equal, flush, level,

plane, plumb **6** placid, smooth, square, steady **7** balance, equable, flatten, regular, the same, uniform **8** balanced, constant, equalize, matching, parallel, straight, unbiased

evening 3 e'en, eve **4** dusk, even **6** sunset **7** day's end, sundown **8** eventide, gloaming, twilight

event 4 bout, game **7** contest, episode **8** incident, occasion

eventful 7 crucial, epochal, fateful, notable, weighty **8** critical, exciting, historic

eventual 5 final, later **6** coming, future **7** ensuing **8** upcoming

ever 5 at all **6** always **7** forever

Everglade State
nickname of: 7 Florida

evergreen 3 fir, yew **4** pine **5** heath, holly **6** laurel, myrtle, privet **7** arbutus, conifer, juniper **8** hawthorn, rosemary

everyday *see* **8 ordinary**

everywhere 7 all over

evict 4 oust **5** eject, expel

6 remove **7** kick out, turn out **8** dislodge

evidence 4 fact, sign **5** proof, token **7** exhibit

evident *see* **7 obvious**

evil 3 bad, sin **4** base, vice, vile **5** venal **6** sinful, wicked **7** heinous, immoral, vicious **8** baseness, iniquity, sinister

evoke 4 stir **5** rouse, waken **6** arouse, awaken, call up, elicit, excite, induce, invite, invoke, summon **7** produce, provoke, suggest

evolution 4 rise **6** change, growth **8** fruition, increase
theory: 6 Darwin

ewer 3 jug, urn **5** basin **6** vessel **7** pitcher

exacerbate 3 irk **5** anger **6** deepen, worsen **7** inflame, magnify, provoke, sharpen **8** heighten, irritate

exact 4 take, true **5** claim, force, mulct, right, wrest **6** compel, demand, extort, strict **7** careful, correct, extract, literal, precise, require, squeeze **8** accurate, clear-cut, exacting, explicit, specific

exaggerate 5 boast

6 overdo **7** amplify, lay it on, magnify, stretch

exalt 4 laud **5** cheer, elate, extol, honor **6** praise, uplift **7** acclaim, applaud, commend, elevate, ennoble, glorify, inspire, magnify, worship **8** venerate

examine 4 pump, quiz, scan, test, view **5** audit, grill, probe, query, study **6** peruse, ponder, review, survey **7** explore, inspect, observe **8** consider, look into, look over, question

example 5 ideal, model **6** sample **7** paragon, pattern **8** exemplar, specimen, standard

exasperate *see* **3 vex**

Excalibur 5 sword
  drawn from: 5 stone
    by: 6 Arthur

excavate 3 dig **4** mine **5** dig up, gouge **6** burrow, cut out, dig out, furrow, groove, quarry, tunnel **7** unearth **8** scoop out

exceed 4 pass **5** excel **6** go over, outrun, overdo **7** outpace, outrank, surpass **8** go beyond, outreach, outstrip, surmount

excel 5 outdo **6** exceed **7** prevail, surpass **8** outrival, outstrip

except 3 ban, bar, but **4** omit, save **6** enjoin, excuse, exempt, reject, remove, saving **7** barring, besides, exclude, shut out **8** count out, disallow

exceptional 3 odd **4** rare **5** great, queer **6** unique **7** special, strange, unusual **8** aberrant, abnormal, atypical, freakish, peculiar, singular, superior, terrific

excerpt 4 part **5** piece **7** extract, portion, section **8** abstract, fragment

excess 4 glut **5** extra, flood, spare **7** residue, surfeit, surplus, too much **8** fullness, overflow

excessive 5 undue **6** excess **7** extreme, profuse, too much **8** needless

exchange 4 swap **5** trade **6** barter, switch **8** bandying, trade off

excise *see* **3 tax**

excite 4 fire, move, whet **5** evoke, pique, rouse, waken **6** arouse, awaken, elicit, foment, incite, kindle, spur on, stir up, thrill **7** agitate, animate, inflame **8** energize

exclaim **4** howl, yell **5** shout **6** bellow, cry out **7** call out **8** proclaim

exclude **3** ban, bar **4** omit, oust **5** eject, evict, expel **6** banish, except, forbid, refuse, reject, remove **7** boycott, keep out, rule out, shut out **8** disallow, leave out, prohibit

exclusive **4** full, posh, sole **5** aloof, total **6** closed, entire, single **7** private **8** absolute, clannish, cliquish, snobbish

excommunication **3** ban **6** ouster **8** anathema

excoriate **4** flay **5** curse **6** berate, revile **7** censure **8** denounce, execrate

excrescence **4** bump, hump, knob, knot, lump **5** bulge, gnarl **6** nodule **8** swelling

excrete **4** void **5** expel **8** evacuate

excruciating **5** acute **6** fierce, severe **7** cutting, extreme, intense, racking

exculpate **5** clear **6** acquit, excuse, pardon **7** absolve

excursion *see* **4 trip**

excuse **4** free **5** alibi, clear, spare **6** acquit, defend, exempt, let off, pardon, reason **7** absolve, condone, defense, explain, forgive, indulge, justify, release **8** argument, bear with, mitigate, overlook, palliate, pass over

execrable **4** vile **5** awful **8** dreadful, terrible

execute **2** do **3** act **4** kill, play, slay **5** enact **6** effect, murder, render **7** achieve, enforce, fulfill, perform, realize, sustain **8** carry out, complete, massacre

executive **3** CEO, CFO **4** suit **7** manager **8** chairman, director

exemplify **6** depict, embody, typify **8** instance

exempt **4** free **5** clear, freed, spare **6** except, excuse, immune, pardon, spared **7** absolve, cleared, excused, release, relieve **8** absolved, excepted, relieved

exercise **3** use **4** show **5** apply, drill, exert, teach, train, tutor, wield **6** employ, school, warm-up **7** break in, develop, display, execute, exhibit, perform, prepare, program, utilize, workout **8** accustom, aerobics, carry out, ceremony, movement, practice

exert 3 use **5** apply, wield **6** employ, expend **7** utilize **8** exercise, put forth

exhale 4 huff, pant, puff **6** expire **7** breathe, respire

exhaust 3 fag, tax **4** bush, poop, tire **5** drain, empty, spend, use up **6** expend, finish, strain, weaken **7** consume, deplete, disable, draw off, draw out, fatigue, wear out **8** enervate, overtire

exhibit 3 air **4** show **6** flaunt, parade, reveal, unveil **7** display

exhilarate 4 lift **5** cheer, elate **6** excite, perk up **7** animate, delight, enliven, gladden, hearten, quicken

exhort 3 bid **4** goad, prod, spur, urge **5** egg on, press **6** advise, enjoin **7** beseech, implore **8** admonish, advocate, appeal to

exhume 5 dig up **8** disinter

exigency 3 fix, jam **5** needs, pinch **6** crisis, pickle, plight, scrape, strait **7** demands **8** hardship

exile 2 DP **4** oust **5** eject, expel **6** banish, deport, emigre, pariah **7** outcast, refugee **8** drive out

exist 4 last, live, stay **5** abide, ensue, occur **6** endure, happen, obtain, remain **7** breathe, survive

exit 4 blow **5** go out, leave, split **6** cut out, depart, egress, escape, exodus, way out **7** retreat

exodus 4 exit **5** exile **6** flight, hegira

exonerate 4 free **5** clear **6** acquit **7** absolve, forgive

exorbitant 4 dear **5** undue **6** costly **7** extreme

exorcise 5 expel **7** cast out **8** get rid of

exotic 5 alien **6** quaint, unique **7** foreign, strange, unusual **8** colorful, peculiar, striking

expand 4 grow, open **5** swell, widen **6** dilate, evolve, extend, fatten, spread, unfold, unfurl, unroll **7** amplify, augment, develop, distend, enlarge, inflate, magnify, stretch, unravel **8** heighten, increase

expatriate 2 DP **5** exile **6** emigre, pariah **7** outcast, refugee

expect 5 guess, trust **6** assume, demand, plan on, reckon **7** believe, count on, foresee, hope for, imagine, look for, presume, require, suppose, surmise **8** envision, reckon on, rely upon

expedient 4 help, wise **5** means **6** resort, tactic, useful **7** benefit, helpful, measure, politic, selfish

expedite *see* **5 hurry**

expedition 4 trek **6** voyage **7** journey, mission **8** campaign, voyagers

expel 4 fire, oust, sack, spew, void **5** eject, evict, exile **6** banish, bounce, remove **7** cashier, cast out, dismiss, drum out, excrete **8** dislodge, drive out, evacuate, force out

expend 3 pay **4** give **5** drain, empty, spend, use up **6** donate, lay out, pay

out **7** consume, exhaust, fork out, wear out **8** disburse, squander

expense 4 cost, rate **5** drain, price **6** amount, charge, figure, outlay

experience 3 see **4** bear, feel, know, meet, view **5** doing, event, sense **6** affair, behold, endure, suffer **7** episode, observe, sustain, undergo **8** incident, practice, training

experiment 4 test **5** assay, flier, trial **6** feeler, try out **7** analyze, examine, explore **8** analysis

expert 3 ace, apt, pro, wiz **4** able, deft, whiz **5** adept, crack, doyen, maven, mavin, shark **6** adroit, artist, facile, master, wizard **7** perfect, skilled, trained, veteran **8** masterly, virtuoso

expire 3 die, end **5** cease, lapse **6** finish, perish, run out **7** decease, kick off, succumb **8** pass away

explain 6 fathom **7** clarify, clear up, justify, resolve **8** describe, spell out

explicit *see* **5 clear**

explode **5** belie, blast, burst, erupt, go off **6** blow up, refute, set off **8** detonate

exploit **4** feat **5** abuse **6** misuse **7** utilize **8** profit by, put to use

explore **3** try **5** plumb, probe, scout **6** survey, try out **7** analyze, examine, feel out, pry into **8** look into, research, traverse

explosive **3** TNT **5** shaky, tense **6** touchy **7** cordite, keyed up **8** critical, dynamite, perilous, strained, unstable, volatile

exponent **6** backer **8** advocate, champion, defender, promoter

export **7** send out **8** dispatch

expose **4** bare, risk, show **5** brand, offer, strip **6** betray, denude, divest, hazard, let out, reveal, submit **7** display, divulge, exhibit, imperil, let slip, subject, uncover, unearth **8** denounce, disclose

exposition **4** expo, fair, mart, show **6** bazaar, market **7** display, exhibit

expostulate **5** argue

6 enjoin, exhort, object, reason **7** caution, protest

expression **4** look, mien, term, tone, word **5** idiom, style **6** airing, aspect, phrase, saying **7** emotion, meaning, stating, telling, venting, voicing, wording **8** language, phrasing, relating, speaking

expropriate **4** take **5** seize **8** take over

expulsion *see* **5 expel**

expunge *see* **5 erase**

expurgate **3** cut **4** blip, edit **5** bleep, purge **6** censor, cut out, delete, excise, remove **8** bleep out

exquisite **4** fine **5** dainty **6** choice, lovely, superb **7** elegant, perfect **8** delicate, flawless, peerless, precious

extant **6** living **7** present **8** existent, existing

extemporaneous **5** ad-lib **7** offhand

extend **4** give **5** grant, offer, widen **6** bestow, expand, impart, put out, spread, submit **7** advance, amplify, augment, prolong, stretch **8** continue, elongate, lengthen, protract, reach out

extent 4 area, size, time **5** range, reach, scope, sweep **6** amount, degree, length **7** breadth, compass, expanse, stretch

exterior 4 face, skin **5** alien, outer, shell **6** exotic, facade, finish, manner **7** bearing, coating, foreign, outside, outward, surface **8** demeanor, external

exterminate *see* **7 destroy**

extinct 4 dead, gone, lost **6** put out **7** defunct, died out, gone out **8** vanished

extinguish *see* **7 destroy**

extol 4 laud **6** praise **7** acclaim, applaud, commend, glorify

extortion 5 force, graft **6** payola, ransom **7** threats, tribute **8** coercion

extra 4 more **5** spare **7** adjunct, further, surplus

extract 3 get **4** cite, cull **5** educe, evoke, exact, gleen, juice, quote, wrest **6** choose, deduce, derive, elicit, obtain, pry out, remove, select **7** copy out, distill, draw out, essence, excerpt, passage, pull out, root out, take out **8** abstract, bring out, citation, pluck out, press out, separate

extraordinary 3 odd **4** rare **5** queer **6** unique **7** amazing, notable, strange, unusual **8** uncommon

extraterrestrial 2 ET **3** Alf **6** cosmic

extravagant 4 wild **6** absurd, costly, unreal **7** foolish **8** fabulous, lavishly, prodigal, spending, wasteful

extreme 3 end **5** depth **6** excess, height, severe **7** intense, radical, unusual **8** advanced, boundary, farthest, uncommon

extremity 3 arm, end, leg, tip, toe **4** edge, foot, hand, limb **5** bound, brink, limit, reach **6** border, finger, margin **7** confine, extreme **8** boundary, terminus

extricate 4 free **5** loose **6** get out, rescue **7** deliver, release **8** liberate, untangle

extrovert 7 show-off

extrude 4 spew **5** eject,

expel **7** project, push out **8** force out, protrude

exuberant *see* **8 abundant**

exude 4 drip, emit, ooze **5** sweat **7** secrete

exult 4 crow **5** gloat, glory **7** rejoice **8** be elated

eye 3 orb **4** scan, view **5** sight, study, taste, watch **6** behold, gaze at, look at, peeper, regard, survey, take in, vision **7** inspect, observe, stare at

part: 4 iris, lens, rods **5** cones, nerve, pupil **6** cornea, muscle, retina

eyeglass, eyeglasses 4 lens **5** specs **6** eyecup, lenses **7** goggles, monocle **8** bifocals, cheaters, contacts, pince-nez

fable 3 fib, lie **4** hoax, myth, tale, yarn **6** legend **7** fiction, parable, untruth, whopper **8** allegory

fabric 5 cloth, frame, stuff **6** makeup **7** textile **8** dry goods, material

fabricate 4 fake, form, make **5** build, erect, feign, forge, frame, hatch, shape **6** design, devise, invent, make up **7** compose, concoct, falsify, fashion, produce, trump up **8** contrive, simulate

fabulous 5 great **6** fabled, superb **7** amazing, storied **8** fanciful, invented, mythical, smashing

facade 4 face, mask **6** veneer **8** frontage

face 3 air, mug, pan **4** coat, gall, grit, look, pout, puss, sand **5** brass, cheek, cover, front, image, nerve, pluck, spunk **6** aspect, daring, facade, kisser, mettle, repute, visage **7** bravado, dignity, grimace, obverse, surface **8** boldness, confront, features, prestige

facet 3 cut **4** part, side **5** angle, phase, plane **6** aspect **7** surface

facetious *see* **5** funny

facile *see* **6** clever

facilitate *see* **4** ease

facsimile 3 fax **4** copy **5** clone, Xerox **7** replica, reprint **8** likeness

fact 3 act **4** deed **5** event, truth **6** verity **7** reality **8** incident, specific

faction 3 set **4** bloc, gang, ring, sect, side, unit **5** cabal, clash, group, split **6** breach, circle, clique, schism, strife **7** combine, coterie, section **8** division, minority

factor 4 part **5** agent, cause **6** reason **7** element

factory 4 mill, shop **5** plant, works **8** workshop

factual *see* **4 true**

faculty, faculties *see* **6 talent**

fad 4 mode, rage, whim **5** craze, fancy, mania, vogue **6** whimsy **7** fashion

fade 3 die, dim, ebb **4** blur, dull, fail, flag, pale, wane **5** droop, taper **6** bleach, lessen, recede, whiten, wither **7** crumble, decline, dwindle, fall off, grow dim, shrivel **8** diminish, dissolve, languish, melt away

Faerie Queene, The author: 7 Spenser

fag 4 bush, butt, poop, tire, weed **5** weary **6** tucker **7** exhaust

fail 3 die, ebb **4** bomb, flag, flop, fold, wane **5** abort, crash, droop, flunk **6** desert, slip up **7** decline, dwindle, forsake, founder, give out, go under, let down, misfire **8** be in vain, collapse, miscarry

faint 3 dim, low **4** pale, soft, thin, weak **5** dizzy, faded, frail, giddy, muted, small, swoon, timid **6** dulcet, feeble, little, meager, remote, slight, subtle, torpid **7** fearful, fragile, obscure, pass out **8** black out, collapse, delicate, drooping, fatigued

fair 4 fine, just, pale, so-so **5** blond, bonny, sunny **6** blonde, bright, comely, creamy, decent, honest, justly, kosher, lovely, medium, pretty, proper, square **7** average, cricket, legally, not dark, upright **8** adequate, carnival, mediocre, middling, moderate, ordinary, pleasant, squarely, unbiased

fairy 3 elf **5** pixie **6** sprite

fairy tale 3 fib **4** myth **5** fable **6** legend **7** fantasy, fiction **8** tall tale

faith 4 sect **5** creed, trust **6** belief, church, fealty **7** loyalty, promise **8** credence, fidelity, reliance, religion, security

fake 4 hoax, ruse, sham **5** bogus, dodge, dummy, faker, false, feign, forge, fraud, phony, put-on, quack, trick **6** deceit, forged, humbug, poseur, pseudo **7** falsify, forgery, not real, pretend, trump up **8** artifice, contrive, deceiver, delusion, imposter, invented, simulate, specious, spurious

falcon 4 eyas **5** hobby, saker **6** desert, lanner, merlin **7** goshawk, kestrel, prairie, shaheen, tiercel **cover eyes: 4** seel

falconry 7 hawking **equipment: 4** lure **5** cadge **6** jesses **7** creance

fall, falls 3 die, ebb, err, sin **4** drop, plop, ruin, slip, wane **5** droop, lapse, occur, slope, slump, spill **6** autumn, crop up, defeat, happen, perish, plunge, topple, tumble **7** be slain, be taken, capture, cascade, crumple, decline, descend, descent, falling, plummet, sinking, succumb **8** collapse, diminish, disgrace, hang down

fallacious *see* **5 false**

fall apart 5 decay **7** break up, crumble, shatter **8** fragment, splinter

fall back 6 recede **7** back off, retreat

fall for 7 believe, swallow

fall guy 4 dupe, pawn, tool **5** patsy **7** cat's-paw

fallible 5 frail, human **6** faulty, mortal, unsure

falling out 4 spat **7** dispute, quarrel **8** argument, squabble

fallow 4 arid, idle **5** inert **6** barren, unused **7** dormant, unsowed, worn out **8** depleted, inactive

fall short 6 be less, fail at, give up

false 4 fake, sham **5** bogus, phony, wrong **6** ersatz, faulty, forged, pseudo, tricky, unreal, untrue **7** devious, feigned, inexact, invalid, unsound **8** mistaken, spurious, two-faced

falter 3 lag **4** halt, reel **5** demur, waver **6** dodder, mumble, shrink, teeter, totter **7** shamble, shuffle, stagger, stammer, stumble, stutter **8** hesitate

fame 4 note **5** eclat, glory **6** renown, repute **7** laurels **8** eminence, prestige

familiar 3 pal **4** bold, chum, cozy, free, snug **5** buddy, close, crony, known, stock, usual **6** chummy, common, friend **7** forward, general **8** accepted, amicable, at home in, everyday, frequent, friendly, habitual, informal, intimate, ordinary, seasoned, versed in

family 3 kin, set **4** clan, kind, line, race, sept **5** blood, breed, brood, class, group, house, issue, order, stock, tribe **7** dynasty, kinfolk, kinsmen, lineage, progeny **8** ancestry, category, division, kinsfolk

famine 4 lack, want **6** dearth, hunger **7** paucity, poverty **8** scarcity

famished 6 hungry **7** starved

famous 5 noted **7** eminent, notable **8** far-famed, renowned, well-known

fan 3 bug, nut **4** buff **5** fiend, freak **6** addict, rooter, zealot **7** booster **8** follower, partisan

fanatic 5 crazy **6** maniac, zealot **7** hothead, radical **8** activist, militant

fancy 3 yen **4** fine, idea, like, want **5** crave, dream,

enjoy, favor, opine, showy, taste, think **6** custom, deluxe, desire, notion, ornate, rococo, take it, vagary, vision **7** baroque, caprice, conceit, dream of, elegant, gourmet, imagine, long for, picture, presume, reverie, special, suppose, surmise, suspect **8** be fond of, crotchet, daydream, fondness, penchant, yearn for

fang 4 claw, nail, root, take, tang, tusk **5** prong, seize, tooth **6** obtain **7** capture, procure **8** eyetooth

fanny *see* **8 backside**

fan out 7 scatter **8** disperse

fantastic 3 mad, odd **4** huge, wild **5** antic, crazy, great, queer, weird **6** absurd, superb **7** amazing, bizarre, extreme, strange **8** enormous, fabulous, fanciful, freakish, illusory, quixotic, romantic, terrific

fantasy 4 mind **5** dream, fancy **6** mirage, notion, vision, whimsy **7** caprice, chimera, fiction, figment, phantom, reverie **8** daydream, illusion

far 4 afar, much **6** deeply, remote, way-off, yonder **7** distant, greatly

farce 4 sham **6** parody **7** mockery **8** nonsense, pretense, travesty

fare 2 do **3** fee **4** diet, food, menu **5** board, get on, rider, table **6** charge, client, manage **7** make out, perform, regimen, turn out **8** customer, get along, victuals

farewell 6 so long **7** good-bye, parting

far-fetched 7 dubious **8** doubtful, strained, unlikely

farm 3 sow **4** plow, reap **5** plant, ranch, tract **6** grange, spread **7** harvest

far-out 3 mad **4** wild **5** crazy, weird **7** bizarre, strange

far side 4 back **7** reverse **8** back side

Far Side, The creator/artist: **6** (Gary) Larson

farsighted 4 wise **5** acute **6** shrewd **7** prudent

farthest 3 end **4** most **7** extreme, longest **8** furthest, remotest, ultimate

fascia 4 band, sash **5** board, strip **6** fillet, girdle, ribbon, tissue **7** bandage **8** membrane

fascinate *see* **6 absorb**

fascism 6 Nazism

fashion 3 air, fad, hew, way **4** form, make, mode, mold, rage **5** carve, craze, forge, frame, habit, shape, style, tenor, trend, usage, vogue **6** create, custom, design, devise, manner **7** compose, pattern, produce **8** attitude, behavior, contrive, demeanor

fast 4 firm, taut, true, wild **5** ahead, brisk, fleet, fully, hasty, loose, loyal, quick, rapid, rigid, swift, tight **6** famish, firmly, flying, rakish, secure, speedy, stable, starve, steady, wanton, winged **7** fixedly, hastily, hurried, immoral, quickly, rapidly, swiftly **8** reckless, resolute, speedily, unfading

fasten 3 bar, fix, pin, tie, wed **4** bind, bolt, clip, fuse, hold, hook, join, lash, link, lock, moor, snap, weld, yoke **5** affix, clamp, clasp, dowel, focus, hitch, close, latch, rivet, screw, stick, truss, unite **6** adhere, anchor, attach, button, cement, couple, direct, secure, tether **7** connect **8** dovetail

fastidious 5 fussy, picky **6** choosy, dainty, proper, queasy **7** finicky **8** exacting, precious

fat 4 full, oily **5** beefy, fatty, flush, heavy, obese, palmy, plump, pudgy, stout, suety **6** chubby, fleshy, grease, greasy, portly, rotund **7** copious, fertile, lumpish, paunchy, replete, stuffed **8** abundant, blubbery, chockful, fruitful, thickset

fatal 6 deadly, lethal, mortal **7** ruinous **8** terminal, virulent

fate 3 lot **4** doom **5** karma, moira **6** effect, future, kismet, upshot **7** chances, destiny, fortune, outcome, portion **8** prospect

father 3 dad, pop **4** abbe, cure, papa, sire **5** beget, begin, daddy, found, hatch, maker, padre, pater

6 author, create, design, old man, parson, pastor, priest **7** creator, founder **8** ancestor, begetter, designer, engender, forebear, inventor

fathom 5 probe **6** divine, follow **7** root out, uncover **8** discover

fatigue 3 fag **4** bush, tire **5** drain, weary **6** tedium, tucker, weaken **7** exhaust, languor, wear out **8** enervate, overtire

fatuous *see* **5 silly**

faucet 3 tap **4** cock **5** spout, valve **6** nozzle, outlet, spigot **7** bibcock

fault 3 bug, sin **4** flaw, slip, snag **5** blame, crime, error, guilt, stain, taint, wrong **6** defect, foible, glitch, impugn **7** blemish, blunder, censure, failing, frailty, misdeed, mistake, offense, reprove **8** drawback, weakness

faun
  form: 5 deity, satyr **7** goat-man

Faust
  author: 6 (Johann) Goethe
  opera by: 6 Gounod

faux pas 4 goof **5** boner, error, gaffe, lapse **6** boo-boo, howler, slip-up **7** blooper, blunder, mistake

favela 4 slum

favor 3 aid **4** abet, back, gift, help, like **5** be for, fancy, humor **6** assist, esteem, foster, oblige, pamper, prefer, succor, uphold **7** endorse, go in for, indulge, kind act, present, service, support **8** advocacy, approval, courtesy, espousal, largesse, look like, resemble, sanction, side with

favorite 3 pet **5** fancy, jewel **6** choice **7** darling, special

favoritism 4 bias

fawn 5 toady **6** pander **7** flatter, truckle **8** pay court

faze 4 fret **5** abash, daunt, upset, worry **6** bother, flurry, rattle **7** disturb, fluster, perturb

fealty 7 loyalty **8** devotion, fidelity

fear 3 awe **4** care **5** alarm, bogey, dread, panic, qualm, worry **6** dismay, esteem, fright, horror, phobia, revere, terror, threat, wonder **7** anxiety, bugaboo, bugbear, concern, quaking, specter

feasible 6 doable, viable **7** fitting, politic **8** possible, suitable, workable

feast 4 dine, fete **5** festa, gorge **6** bounty **7** banquet, holiday, jubilee, surplus **8** festival

feat 3 act **4** deed, task **6** action, stroke **7** exploit, triumph **8** maneuver

feather 4 down, kind, sort **5** adorn, eider, pinna, plume, quill **7** bristle, plumage, variety

feature, features 3 see **4** mark, star **5** fancy, trait **6** aspect, play up, visage **7** display, earmark, imagine, picture, present, quality

February
  birthday: 7 Lincoln **10** Washington
  event: 3 Ash (Wednesday) **4** Lent **5** Purim **8** Leap year **9** Groundhog (Day), Mardi Gras
  flower: 6 violet **8** primrose
  gem: 8 amethyst
  holiday: 10 President's

(Day), Valentine's (Day 14)

place in year:
Gregorian: 6 second
Roman: 7 twelfth
Zodiac signs: 6 Pisces **8** Aquarius

feckless 3 lax **5** slack **6** remiss **8** careless, heedless

federation 5 union **6** league **7** combine **8** alliance

fee 4 fare, hire, toll, wage **5** price **6** charge, salary, tariff **7** payment, stipend

feeble *see* **4 weak**

feed 3 eat **4** fare, fuel, mash **5** cater, feast, graze **6** devour, fodder, forage, foster, viands **7** augment, bolster, consume, gratify, nourish, nurture, pasture, satisfy, support, sustain

feeder 6 branch **7** channel

feel 3 paw, see **4** know **5** grope, press, probe, reach, sense, think, touch **6** finger, fumble, handle, makeup, notice **7** believe, discern, feeling, observe, palpate, texture **8** perceive

feeler 7 antenna **8** proposal, tentacle

feet 4 dogs, pads, paws

5 hoofs **6** hooves **8** gunboats, tootsies

feign *see* **4 fake**

felicitous *see* **5 happy**

fell 4 raze **5** level **7** cut down, destroy, hew down **8** demolish

fellow 3 boy, guy, mac, man, pal **4** chap, chum, dude, gent, mate, peer **5** equal **6** friend **7** comrade, consort **8** coworker

felon 5 crook, cruel, thief **6** fierce, outlaw, wicked **7** convict, illegal, villain **8** criminal, gangster, jailbird, murderer

female 3 cow, dam, hen, sow **4** girl, mare **5** bitch, tabby, woman **6** heifer **7** distaff, womanly **8** feminine, ladylike

femme fatale 4 vamp **5** siren **7** charmer

fen 3 bog **4** moor, sump **5** marsh, swale, swamp **6** bottom, morass, slough **7** wetland **8** quagmire

fence 3 pen **4** coop, duel, gird, rail **5** hedge, hem in **6** corral, secure, wall in **7** barrier, confine, palings

8 encircle, palisade, stockade, surround

fencing
 equipment: 4 epee, foil, mask **5** saber, sword **8** plastron
 deceptive move: 5 feint
 movement: 5 lunge, parry **6** thrust **7** riposte

fend 2 do **5** avert, avoid, parry, repel, shift **6** manage **7** keep off, make out, provide, repulse, ward off **8** push away

fender 3 pad **4** curb **5** guard **6** buffer, bumper, shield **7** cushion, railing

feral 4 wild **6** brutal, deadly, ferine, fierce, savage **7** bestial, vicious

Ferdinand the Bull
 author: 4 (Munro) Leaf

ferment 4 foam, mold, sour, turn **5** froth, yeast **6** enzyme, fester, leaven, seethe, tumult, unrest, uproar **7** agitate, inflame, smolder, turmoil **8** bubble up, disquiet

ferocious see **6 savage**

fertile 4 rich **5** loamy **6** fecund **8** creative, fruitful, original, prolific

fertilizer 4 dung, muck **5** guano, niter **6** manure, potash **7** compost **8** bonemeal, dressing

fervor 4 fire, zeal, zest **5** ardor, gusto, piety, verve **6** warmth **7** passion

fester see **8 irritate**

festive 3 gay **4** gala **5** jolly, merry **6** festal, joyous **7** larkish, playful **8** sportive

festoon 3 lei **4** swag **5** chain, curve **6** wreath **7** garland, hanging **8** decorate

fetch 3 get **4** cost **5** bring, go for, yield **6** afford, obtain **7** procure, realize, sell for **8** retrieve

fete 4 gala **5** feast, party, treat **6** regale **7** banquet, holiday **8** carnival, festival

fetid see **6 putrid**

fetish 4 idol, joss **5** charm, craze, image, mania, totem **6** amulet, scarab **7** passion **8** talisman

fetter see **7 confine**

feud see **7 quarrel**

fever 4 fire, heat **5** ardor, craze, flush, furor **6** desire, frenzy, warmth

7 ferment, illness, pyrexia **8** delirium, sickness

few 4 rare, some, thin **5** scant **6** meager, paltry, scanty, scarce, skimpy, sparse, unique **7** handful, limited, not many, several, unusual **8** piddling, sporadic

fiance, fiancee 8 intended, promised

fiasco 4 bomb, flop **5** botch **6** fizzle **7** debacle, washout **8** disaster

fiat *see* **3 law**

fib 3 lie **5** hedge **7** fiction, untruth **8** white lie

fiber 4 hemp, jute, silk **5** fibre, linen, nylon, rayon, shred, sinew, sisal **6** cotton, dacron, manila, nature, strand, thread **7** quality, texture **8** filament

fickle 5 giddy **6** fitful **7** erratic, flighty **8** shifting, unstable, unsteady, variable, volatile, wavering

fiction 3 fib, lie **4** play, tale, yarn **5** fable, novel **7** fantasy, novella, romance **8** tall tale

fiddle 3 bow, saw, toy **4** fool **5** cheat, dally, fraud **6** dawdle, monkey, potter, putter, tamper, trifle, violin **7** falsify, finagle, fritter, swindle

Fidelio
opera by: 9 Beethoven

fidelity 5 honor **6** fealty **7** honesty, loyalty, probity **8** accuracy, devotion

fidget 4 fret, fuss, jerk, stew, toss **5** chafe, worry **6** jiggle, squirm, twitch, wiggle, writhe **7** wriggle

fief 4 land **6** domain, estate

field 3 lea **4** area, grab, lawn, line, mead, turf, yard **5** arena, catch, court, front, glove, green, heath, lists, orbit, range, reach, realm, scope, sward, sweep **6** circle, common, course, domain, extent, meadow, pick up, region, sphere **7** acreage, calling, diamond, expanse, pasture, run down, stretch **8** clearing, province, retrieve

fiend 5 beast, brute, demon, devil, Satan **6** dybbuk **7** incubus, monster, villain

fierce *see* **6 savage**

fiery 5 afire, angry, irate **6** ablaze, alight, ardent, fervid, fierce, red-hot, torrid **7** blazing, burning, febrile, fervent, fevered, flaming, glaring, glowing, peppery, pyretic, violent, zealous **8** choleric, feverish, flashing, headlong, inflamed, spirited, vehement, wrathful

fiesta 4 fete, gala **5** feast, party **8** carnival, feast day, festival, jamboree

fight 3 box, row, war **4** bout, duel, feud, fray, grit, spar, spat, tiff, tilt, wage **5** argue, brawl, brush, clash, event, joust, match, melee, pluck, round, scrap, set-to **6** battle, bicker, combat, engage, fracas, mettle, oppose, resist, spirit, strife, tussle **7** carry on, conduct, contend, contest, discord, dispute, go to war, quarrel, repulse, scuffle, tourney, wage war, wrangle **8** confront, dogfight, gameness, skirmish, squabble, struggle

figment 5 fable, fancy, story **6** canard **7** fantasy, fiction, product **8** creation

figurative 6 florid, ironic, ornate **7** flowery **8** humorous, symbolic

figure, figures 3 cut, man, sum **4** body, cast, cost, foot, form, mark, plan, rate, sign, sums **5** add up, adorn, build, count, digit, force, frame, guess, judge, motif, price, shape, think, total, tot up, value, woman **6** amount, assess, cipher, design, device, factor, leader, number, person, reckon, schema, symbol **7** believe, compute, count up, diagram, drawing, imagine, notable, numeral, outline, pattern, presume, suppose **8** appraise, be placed, eminence, estimate, ornament, physique, presence

Fiji
  capital/largest city: 4 Suva
  island: 8 Viti Levu **9** Vanua Levu
  highest point: 8 Tomanivi, Victoria
  sea: 4 Koro **7** Pacific

filament 4 hair, line, wire **5** fiber, fibre **6** cilium, ribbon, strand, string, thread

filch **3** cop, rob **4** copy, crib, hook, lift **5** boost, heist, steal, swipe **6** pilfer, pirate **7** purloin

file **3** row **4** data, line, list, rank, tier **5** apply, chain, index, put in, queue, store **6** drawer, folder, record, stacks, string **7** catalog, dossier, put away, records, request **8** archives, classify, petition
    type: **4** mill, nail, rasp, wood **5** round

filial **7** dutiful, sonlike

fill **3** act **4** cram, glut, lade, load, meet, pack, puff, sate **5** crowd, gorge, lay by, lay in, serve, stock, store **6** assign, blow up, dilate, do duty, expand, infuse, occupy, outfit, supply **7** distend, execute, furnish, inflate, pervade, preside, satiate, satisfy, suffuse, surfeit **8** function, permeate

fillet **4** band **5** slice, strip **6** ribbon **7** bandeau, circlet

Fillmore, Millard
    presidential rank: **10** thirteenth

    party: **4** Whig
    state represented: **2** NY
    succeeded upon death of: **6** Taylor
    born: **2** NY **5** Locke
    notable events of lifetime/ term: **10** Compromise (of 1850)
        act: **13** Fugitive Slave

film, films **4** cine, coat, haze, mist, skin, veil **5** cloud, flick, movie, sheet, shoot **6** cinema, flicks, movies, screen **7** coating **8** membrane

filter **4** leak, ooze, seep **5** drain, exude, sieve **6** effuse, purify, refine, screen, strain **7** clarify, cleanse, dribble, trickle, well out **8** filtrate, strainer

filth *see* **4** dirt

finagle **3** con, gyp **4** plot, rook **5** cheat, mulct, trick **6** chisel, fleece, scheme, wangle **7** defraud, swindle **8** intrigue, maneuver

final *see* **4** last

finance **6** pay for **7** banking **8** accounts

financier **5** angel **6** backer, banker, broker **7** rich man

find **3** get, see, win **4** earn,

espy, gain, meet, rule, spot **5** award, catch, dig up, judge, learn **6** attain, come by, decide, decree, detect, expose, locate, regain **7** achieve, acquire, adjudge, bargain, bonanza, discern, get back, godsend, good buy, hit upon, procure, recover, uncover, unearth **8** bump into, come upon, discover, disinter, lucky hit, meet with, retrieve, windfall

fine 4 airy, chic, fair, keen, neat, nice, rare, thin **5** bonny, clear, dandy, gauzy, mulct, nifty, sharp, sheer, silky, small, smart, sunny, swell **6** assess, bonnie, bright, charge, choice, comely, dainty, flimsy, ground, lovely, minute, modish, pretty, silken, slight, spiffy, subtle, superb **7** damages, elegant, forfeit, fragile, penalty, perfect, precise, refined, slender, stylish **8** cobwebby, delicate, ethereal, flawless, penalize, pleasant, polished, skillful, splendid, superior

finesse 4 ruse, tact, wile **5** craft, dodge, guile, savvy

7 cunning **8** artifice, delicacy, intrigue, trickery

finger 3 paw **4** feel, poke, ring **5** digit, index, punch, thumb, touch **6** caress, feeler, handle, middle, pinkie, pollex **7** pointer, squeeze, toy with, twiddle **8** identify, play with

finicky 5 fussy, picky **6** choosy **8** niggling

finish 3 end **4** coat, face, gild, goal, kill, last, seal, stop **5** cease, close, glaze, use up **6** clinch, defeat, devour, ending, finale, settle, veneer, wind up **7** achieve, coating, consume, curtain, destroy, fulfill, get done, lacquer, realize, surface, varnish **8** carry out, complete, conclude, dispatch, epilogue, exterior, get rid of

finite 7 bounded, limited **8** confined, temporal

Finland
other name: 5 Suomi
capital/largest city: 8 Helsinki
island: 5 Aland
lake: 6 Saimaa
sea: 6 Baltic **8** Atlantic
physical feature:

gulf: 7 Bothnia, Finland
isthmus: 7 Karelia
place:
  memorial: 8 Sibelius
  north: 7 Lapland

Finn
  also: 5 Fionn
  origin: 5 Irish
  king of: 4 gods
  son: 6 Ossian

Finnegans Wake
  author: 5 (James) Joyce

fiord, fjord 5 firth, inlet **7** estuary

fir 4 pine **5** cedar, larch **6** alpine, balsam, linden, spruce **7** conifer, cypress, douglas

fire 3 can, vim **4** bake, boot, burn, cook, dash, dump, elan, hurl, oust, sack, stir **5** ardor, blaze, eject, flame, flare, flash, force, gusto, let go, light, power, punch, rouse, shoot, spark, verve, vigor **6** arouse, excite, fervor, foment, genius, ignite, incite, kindle, luster, spirit, stir up, vivify, volley **7** bombard, bonfire, cashier, dismiss, inferno, inflame, inspire, project, quicken, sniping, trigger **8** radiance, vivacity

firearm 3 gun, rod **5** piece, rifle **6** pistol **7** shotgun **8** revolver

firefly 8 glowworm, lampyrid

firm 4 bent, fast, grim, hard, taut **5** close, dense, fixed, house, rigid, rocky, solid, stiff, stony, tight, tough **6** dogged, flinty, intent, moored, rooted, secure, stable, steady, steely **7** compact, company, dead set, decided, settled, staunch **8** anchored, business, constant, definite, obdurate, resolute

firmament 3 air, sky **5** ether, space, vault **6** canopy, welkin **7** heavens, the blue, the void

first 4 head, main **5** basic, prime, start, vital **6** before, eldest, maiden, outset, primal **7** highest, leading, premier, primary, ranking, supreme **8** earliest, foremost, original, superior

firsthand 6 direct **8** personal

first-rate *see* **4 best**

firth 5 fjord, inlet **7** estuary

fish 3 net **4** cast, hook, hunt **5** angle, grope, seine, trawl, troll **6** ferret, search **7** rummage

fish
    class: 7 Agnatha
    fin: 4 anal, tail **6** caudal, dorsal, median, paired, pelvic **7** adipose, ventral **8** pectoral
    part: 3 fin **4** gill **5** scale **6** cirrhi

fisherman 5 eeler **6** angler, caster, jacker, netter, seiner **7** trawler, troller **8** piscator

Fishes
    constellation of: 6 Pisces

fishy *see* **5 weird**

fissure 3 gap **4** rift, slit **5** chink, cleft, crack, gully, split **6** breach, cranny, groove, hiatus **8** aperture, cleavage

fit 4 able, good, hale, meet, ripe, suit, well, whim **5** adapt, agree, alter, burst, equal, equip, hardy, match, ready, right, shape, sound, spasm, spell, train **6** access, accord, adjust, become, concur, enable, in trim, mature, primed, proper, robust, seemly, strong, timely, worthy **7** adapted, apropos, capable, caprice, conform, correct, empower, fashion, healthy, prepare, qualify, rectify, seizure, toned up, trained **8** apposite, coincide, eligible, graduate, outbreak, outburst, paroxysm, prepared, relevant, suitable

fitful *see* **4 weak**

fix 3 jam, put, set **4** bind, make, mend, mess, moor, spot **5** place, rivet **6** adjust, anchor, attach, decide, fasten, harden, impose, muddle, pickle, plight, repair, scrape, secure, settle **7** congeal, connect, correct, dilemma, impasse, implant, patch up, prepare, rebuild **8** assemble, hot water, make fast, make firm, quandary, regulate, renovate, set right, solidify

fixation 5 quirk **6** fetish **7** complex **8** crotchet, delusion

fizzle *see* **4 fail**

flabbergast *see* **5 amaze**

flabby 4 lame, limp, soft,

weak **5** baggy, slack **6** doughy, effete, feeble, flimsy, floppy, spongy **7** flaccid **8** impotent, listless

flag 3 ebb, sag **4** fade, fail, pall, sink, tire, wane, warn, wave, wilt **5** abate, faint, slump **6** banner, colors, dodder, emblem, ensign, signal, totter **7** decline, give way, pennant, subside, succumb **8** grow weak, languish, Old Glory, standard, streamer

flagon *see* **3 gun**

flagrant 5 gross, sheer **6** arrant, brazen, crying **7** blatant, glaring, heinous, obvious **8** immodest

flail 4 beat, lash, whip **5** swing **6** thresh **7** scourge

flair 4 bent, dash, feel, gift **5** knack, style, taste, touch, verve **6** genius, talent **7** faculty, feeling, panache **8** aptitude

flake 3 bit **4** chip, peel **5** fleck, layer, patch, scale, sheet, strip **7** chip off, crumble, peel off, shaving

flaky 4 bats, gaga, nuts **5** balmy, batty, crisp, daffy, dotty, goofy, loony, nutty, scaly, short, wacky

6 scabby, screwy, scurfy **8** scabious, squamous

flamboyant 4 wild **5** gaudy, jazzy, showy **6** flashy, florid, garish, ornate, rococo **7** baroque, dashing **8** colorful, exciting

flame 4 beau, fire, glow **5** ardor, blaze, blush, flare, flash, flush, glare, gleam, light, lover, spark, swain **6** fervor, ignite, warmth **7** passion **8** fervency

flan 3 pie **4** gust, puff, tart **6** expand, pastry **7** custard, dessert

flank 3 hip **4** edge, line, loin, side, wing **5** cover, skirt **6** border, fringe, haunch, screen, shield

flap 3 bat, fly, tab **4** bang, beat, flop **5** apron, shake, skirt **6** lappet **7** agitate, banging, flutter, vibrate

flare 4 burn, glow **5** blaze, erupt, flame, flash, glare, gleam, taper, torch, widen **6** blow up, dilate, expand, ignite, signal, spread **7** distend, stretch **8** boil over, break out

flash 4 glow, wink **5** blaze, blink, burst, flame, flare, glare, gleam, jiffy, shake, shine, spark, touch, trice **6** minute, moment, second, streak **7** flicker, glimmer, glisten, glitter, instant, sparkle **8** instance, outburst, radiance

flask 6 bottle **7** canteen

flat, flats 3 low **4** dead, dull **5** clear, equal, flush, level, marsh, plain, plane, prone, shoal, shoes, stale, total, vapid **6** direct, planar, smooth, supine **7** blowout, exactly, insipid, laid low, loafers, prairie, shallow **8** absolute, definite, lowlands, puncture

flatfish 3 ray **4** sole **5** brill, fluke **6** turbot **7** halibut, sunfish **8** flounder

flatter 4 fool, laud **5** court, extol, honor, toady **6** become, cajole, delude **7** adulate, beguile, deceive, wheedle **8** bootlick, butter up, soft-soap

flaunt *see* **4 brag**

flavor 4 aura, lace, soul, tang, tone **5** gusto, imbue, savor, spice, style, tenor **6** aspect, infuse, lacing, relish, season, spirit **7** essence, instill **8** piquancy

flaw 3 mar **4** blot, harm, spot, vice **5** error, fault, speck, stain **6** blotch, deface, defect, foible, impair, injure, injury, smudge **7** blemish, failing, frailty, mistake **8** weakness

flay 4 bark, pare, peel, skin **5** scalp, scold, strip **6** assail, fleece, punish, rebuke **7** plunder, upbraid

fleck *see* **4 iota**

fledgling 4 tyro **6** novice **8** beginner, freshman

flee 4 shun, skip **5** avoid, dodge, elude, evade, split **6** decamp, desert, vanish **7** abscond, fly away

fleece *see* **5 cheat**

fleet 3 run **4** band, fade, fast, flow, navy, skim, spry, swim, unit **5** agile, array, brief, creek, drift, float, hasty, inlet, light, quick, rapid, shift, ships, short, swift **6** abound, active, armada, nimble, number, speedy, sudden, vanish **7** hurried **8** flotilla, squadron

flesh 3 fat **4** meat, pulp **5** brawn, power **6** people **7** fill out, realize **8** physique

flesh and blood 3 kin **4** real **6** family **7** kindred **8** children

flexible 4 mild, soft **5** lithe **6** docile, genial, gentle, limber, pliant, supple **7** amiable, ductile, elastic, plastic, pliable, springy **8** bendable, yielding

flicker 4 flit, glow, sway **5** blaze, flame, flare, flash, gleam, glint, shake, spark, throb, trace, waver **6** quaver, quiver **7** flutter, glimmer, glitter, pulsate, shimmer, sparkle, tremble, vestige, vibrate

flicks 5 films **6** cinema, grazes, movies, sweeps, whisks **7** brushes

flier 4 bill **5** pilot **6** notice **7** aviator, leaflet, venture **8** brochure, bulletin, circular, handbill

flight 4 rout, rush, wing **5** flock **6** escape, exodus, flying, hegira **7** fleeing, retreat, soaring **8** squadron

flighty 5 dizzy, giddy **6** fickle **8** quixotic, reckless, unstable, volatile

flimsy *see* **5 frail**

flinch 3 fly, shy **4** jerk **5** cower, quail, quake, start, wince **6** blench, cringe, falter, quaver, quiver, recoil, shiver, shrink **7** contort, grimace, shudder

fling 2 go **3** try **4** ball, bash, cast, dash, emit, hurl, lark, toss **5** eject, expel, heave, pitch, sling, spree, trial **6** let fly, propel **7** attempt

flinty 4 cold, hard **5** cruel, harsh, stern, stony **6** inured, steely **7** callous

flip 3 tap **4** bold, pert, spin, toss, turn **5** brash, flick, fresh, throw, thumb **6** cheeky, fillip **8** impudent, insolent, turn over

flirt 3 toy **4** play, vamp **5** dally, tease **6** trifle **8** coquette

flit 4 dart, scud, skim, wing **5** speed **6** hasten, scurry **7** flicker, flutter

flivver 3 car **4** auto, heap **6** jalopy, wheels **7** vehicle

float 3 bob **4** waft **5** drift, hover, slide **6** buoy up, hold up **8** levitate

flock *see* **5 crowd**

flog 4 beat, cane, club, cuff,

drub, hide, lash, maul, whip **5** birch, flail, smite, strap **6** cudgel, paddle, strike, switch, thrash **7** scourge **8** lambaste

flood 4 flow, glut, gush, tide **6** deluge, drench, shower, stream **7** cascade, current, torrent **8** downpour, flow over, inundate, saturate, submerge

floor 4 base, deck, fell, tier **5** level, stage, story **6** bottom, ground **7** minimum, parquet **8** flooring, pavement

flop 4 bomb, bust, drop, fail, fold, plop **5** close **6** fiasco, fizzle, topple, tumble, turkey **7** failure, go under, shutter, washout **8** disaster, lay an egg

floral 6 bloomy **7** verdant **8** blossomy

florid 4 rosy **5** gaudy, ruddy, showy **6** blowsy, hectic, ornate, rococo **7** baroque, flowery, flushed, reddish **8** inflamed, rubicund, sanguine

Florida
   abbreviation: 2 FL **3** Fla
   nickname: 8 Sunshine
   capital: 11 Tallahassee
   largest city: 12 Jacksonville
   explorer: 11 Ponce de Leon
   island: 4 Keys **7** Captiva, Sanibel **8** Biscayne
   physical feature:
      bay: 8 Biscayne
      cape: 7 Kennedy **9** Canaveral
      gulf: 6 Mexico
      swamp: 10 Everglades, Okefenokee

flotilla 5 fleet **6** armada

flotsam 4 junk **6** debris, refuse **7** garbage

flounce 3 hem **4** edge, leap, skip, trim, trip **5** bound, caper, frill, stamp, stomp, storm, strut **6** bounce, edging, fringe, gambol, prance, ruffle, sashay, spring **7** valance **8** furbelow, ornament, skirting, trimming

flounder *see* **6 falter**

flourish 4 curl, dash, grow, pomp, rant, show, turn **5** bloom, bluff, get on, shake, strut, sweep, swing, swish, twirl, twist, wield **6** flaunt, flower, hot air, parade, splash, thrive, waving **7** blossom, bravado, burgeon, fanfare, glitter, prosper, succeed, swagger **8** brandish, fare well, get ahead

flout 3 rag **4** defy, mock, twit **5** chaff, scorn, spurn, taunt **6** gibe at, insult

flow 3 jet, run **4** flux, gush, pass, pour, rush, seep, tide **5** drain, drift, float, flood, glide, issue, spout, spurt, surge, sweep, swirl, train **6** abound, course, deluge, efflux, effuse, filter, plenty, rapids, stream **7** cascade, current, debouch, torrent **8** effusion, millrace

flower 3 bud **4** best, blow, open, pick, posy **5** bloom, cream, elite, ripen **6** mature **7** blossom, bouquet, burgeon, develop, nosegay, prosper

flower arranging
   Japanese: 7 ikebana

fluctuate *see* **6 falter**

flue 3 net **4** barb, down, pipe, tube, vent **5** fluff, fluke, shaft **6** funnel **7** channel, chimney, passage

fluent 4 glib **5** vocal **6** facile **7** voluble **8** eloquent

fluff 3 err, nap **4** down, flub, fuzz, lint, miss, puff, slip, soft **5** botch, floss, froth, primp **6** forget **7** blunder **8** feathers

fluid 6 liquid, watery **7** unfixed **8** flexible, floating, shifting, solution

fluke 3 hap **5** freak **6** chance **7** miracle **8** accident, windfall

flunky 6 lackey, menial, minion **7** servant

flurry 3 ado **4** fuss, gust, heat, puff, stir **5** alarm, fever, flush, haste, panic **6** breeze, bustle, pother, rattle, shower, squall, tumult **7** agitate, confuse, disturb, fluster, flutter

flush 4 even, glow, swab, tint, wash **5** bloom, blush, color, elate, flood, level, rinse, scour, scrub, shock, spray **6** access, dampen, deluge, douche, drench, excite, puff up, quiver, redden, sponge, thrill, tremor **7** animate, flutter, glowing, impulse, moisten, wash out **8** rosiness, squarely, strength

fluster *see* **7 confuse**

flute 4 fife, fold, pipe, roll,

flutter

tube, wind **5** crimp **6** furrow, groove **7** piccolo, whistle **8** recorder

flutter 3 bob **4** flap, flit, soar, stir, wave, wing **5** hurry, shake, throb **6** flurry, quiver, ripple, thrill, tremor, wobble **7** beating, flitter, fluster, pulsate, tremble, twitter **8** flapping, tingling

flux 4 flow, tide **5** flood **6** course, motion, stream, unrest **7** current **8** shifting

fly 4 flap, flee, sail, skip, soar, wave, wing **5** coast, float, glide, hover, hurry, split, swoop **6** hasten, hustle **7** flutter, run away, take off, vibrate **8** take wing, undulate

fly-by-night 5 shady **6** shifty **7** crooked **8** unstable, untrusty

fly the coop 4 bolt, flee **6** escape, run off **7** abscond, make off, take off

foal 4 colt **5** filly, young

foam 4 fizz, head, scum, suds **5** froth, spume **6** lather **7** sparkle

fob 5 chain, medal, strap **6** ribbon **8** ornament

focal 3 key **4** main **5** chief **7** central, pivotal

focus 3 aim, fix, hub **4** core **5** haunt, heart **6** adjust, center, direct, middle, resort **7** nucleus, retreat

fodder 4 feed, food **6** forage, silage **7** rations

foe 5 enemy, rival **8** attacker, opponent

fog 3 dim **4** daze, haze, smog, soup **5** cloud **6** darken, muddle, stupor, trance **7** confuse, obscure, pea soup, perplex

foible 4 kink **5** quirk **6** defect, whimsy **7** failing **8** crotchet, weakness

foil *see* **7 prevent**

foist 6 impose, unload **7** palm off, pass off

fold 3 hug, lap, pen, sty **4** bend, sect, tuck, wrap, yard **5** clasp, close, flock, group, layer, pleat **6** corral, crease, dog-ear, double, encase, enfold, furrow, gather, parish, ruffle, wrap up **7** embrace, entwine, envelop, flounce, overlap, wrinkle **8** barnyard, compound, doubling, stockade

foliage 6 leaves **7** verdure

folklore 5 myths **6** fables **7** legends

folks 3 kin **6** family, people **7** kinsmen, parents **8** everyone

follow 3 dog **4** copy, heed, hunt, mind, note, obey, tail **5** aim at, chase, grasp, hound, stalk, trace, track, trail, watch **6** attend, notice, pursue, regard, shadow, take up **7** cherish, emulate, imitate, observe, replace, succeed **8** practice, supplant

folly 6 idiocy, levity **7** inanity, mistake **8** nonsense, trifling

foment 4 goad, spur, urge **5** rouse **6** arouse, excite, foster, incite, kindle, stir up **7** agitate, inflame, promote, provoke, quicken **8** irritate

fond 5 naive **6** ardent, doting, loving, tender **7** amorous, devoted **8** desirous, enamored, harbored, held dear

fondle 3 hug, neck, pet **4** neck **5** spoon **6** caress, cuddle, nestle, nuzzle, smooch, stroke **7** embrace, make out **8** canoodle

food 4 chow, feed, grub **5** board, manna **6** fodder, forage, viands **7** edibles, nurture, pasture, rations **8** eatables, victuals

fool *see* **3 oaf**

fool around 3 toy **4** idle **5** clown, dally **6** dawdle, loiter, trifle

foolhardy 4 rash **5** brash, hasty **6** madcap **8** careless, heedless, reckless

foot *see* **4 feet**

football
  term: 3 end **4** bomb, down, draw, flat, punt, sack **5** blitz, guard, zebra **6** center, fumble, option, pocket, safety, tackle **7** audible, bootleg, flanker, holding, kickoff, lateral, offside, platoon, reverse, rollout, shotgun **8** clipping, gridiron, halfback, turnover

footfall 3 pad **4** pace, step **5** tread **8** footstep

footloose 4 free **8** carefree

footpad 5 thief **6** bandit, mugger, outlaw, robber

footpath 4 lane, ramp 5 jetty, trail 8 sidewalk

footstool 6 buffet 7 hassock, ottoman

fop 4 beau, dude 5 dandy, swell 7 coxcomb

forage *see* 4 hunt

foray 4 raid 5 sally 6 attack, inroad, invade, ravage, thrust 7 pillage, plunder, venture

forbear *see* 4 stop

forbid 3 ban, bar 4 veto 5 taboo 6 enjoin, hinder, impede, oppose, refuse, reject 7 exclude, gainsay, inhibit, obviate, prevent 8 disallow, obstruct, preclude, prohibit, restrain

force 3 pry, vim 4 army, body, coax, crew, drag, gang, make, pull, push, team, unit, urge 5 break, clout, corps, drive, group, impel, might, power, press, value, vigor, wrest 6 coerce, compel, duress, effect, elicit, energy, enjoin, impact, impose, induce, oblige, propel, stress, thrust 7 intrude, potency, require, squeeze, stamina 8 coercion, division, efficacy, emphasis, momentum, pressure, strength, violence, vitality

ford 4 span, wade 5 cross, shoal 6 bridge, stream 8 crossing

Ford, Gerald Rudolph
  born: 17 Leslie Lynch King Jr
  nickname: 5 Jerry 7 Mr Clean
  presidential rank: 12 thirty-eighth
  party: 10 Republican
  state represented: 2 MI
  vice president: 11 Rockefeller
  born: 2 NE 5 Omaha
  political career: 5 House 13 vice president
  notable events of lifetime/ term:
    talks: 4 SALT
  wife: 9 Elizabeth
    nickname: 5 Betty

fore 5 front 7 frontal 8 anterior, headmost

forearm 4 ulna 5 prime, ready 7 prepare

foreboding 4 omen 5 dread 6 augury 7 portent

forecast 5 augur 6 augury, divine, expect 7 outlook,

portend, predict, presage, project **8** envisage, envision, prophesy

foreign 5 alien **6** exotic, remote **7** distant, strange, unknown, unusual **8** imported

foreman 4 boss **7** manager **8** chairman, overseer

foremost 4 head, main **5** chief, vital **7** capital, leading, supreme

foresee *see* **8 forecast**

forest 4 bush, wood **5** copse, grove, stand, woods **6** jungle **7** thicket **8** wildwood, woodland

forever 6 always

forfeit 4 fine, miss **5** waive, waste, yield **6** waiver **7** damages, default, let slip, penalty **8** squander

forge 4 copy, form, make **5** clone, shape **6** devise, hearth, smithy **7** falsify, fashion, furnace, imitate, produce, turn out **8** contrive, simulate

forget 6 slight **7** neglect **8** overlook, pass over

forgive 5 clear **6** acquit, excuse, pardon **7** absolve, condone, release, set free **8** overlook, reprieve

forgo 4 skip **5** waive, yield **6** eschew, give up **8** abnegate, renounce

fork 4 bend, stab **5** angle, elbow, split **6** branch, crotch, divide, impale, pierce, ramify, skewer **7** diverge, trident

forlorn *see* **6 lonely**

form 3 cut, hew, way **4** body, cast, kind, make, mode, mold, plan, rite, rule, sort, trim, type **5** being, brand, build, carve, class, forge, found, frame, genre, genus, guise, habit, image, model, order, phase, set up, shape, stamp, style, usage **6** aspect, chisel, create, custom, design, devise, figure, matrix, person, sculpt **7** anatomy, compose, conduct, contour, decorum, develop, fashion, manners, outline, pattern **8** comprise, contract, likeness, physique, symmetry

formal 4 cool, prim **5** aloof, fancy, fixed, grand, legal,

Page 278

rigid, smart, stiff **6** dressy, lawful, proper, solemn, strict **7** distant, pompous, regular, settled, stilted, stylish **8** decorous, definite, explicit, external, official, reserved, starched

formality 4 rite **6** custom, motion, ritual **7** decorum, reserve **8** ceremony

formation 3 set **6** makeup **8** building, creation

former 2 ex **4** gone, past **5** olden, prior **6** bygone, gone by, lapsed **7** ancient, earlier, elapsed, old-time **8** previous

formidable 6 taxing **7** awesome, fearful, mammoth, onerous **8** alarming, imposing, menacing, terrific

Formosa *see* **6 Taiwan**

formula 4 cant, plan, rule **5** chant **6** cliche, recipe, saying, slogan **7** precept

forsake 4 deny, drop, flee, quit **5** leave, spurn, waive, yield **6** abjure, depart, desert, give up, reject, resign, vacate **7** abandon, cast off, disavow, discard, lay down **8** abdicate, disclaim, jettison, part with, renounce

fort 4 base, camp **5** tower **6** castle **7** bastion, bulwark, citadel, station **8** garrison

forte 4 bent **5** knack, skill **6** talent **8** strength
music: 4 loud

forthcoming 5 handy, on tap **6** at hand **7** helpful

forthright *see* **6 candid**

forthwith 4 ASAP, stat **6** at once, pronto **7** quickly **8** directly, promptly

fortify 4 lace **5** boost, brace, cheer **6** buoy up, enrich, harden, secure, shield **7** build up, hearten, protect, shore up, stiffen, support, sustain **8** buttress, reassure

fortissimo
music: 8 very loud

fortuitous 5 happy, lucky, stray **6** casual, chance

fortune, fortunes 3 lot **4** doom, fate, luck, mint, pile, star **5** karma, means **6** chance, estate, income, kismet, riches, wealth **7** bonanza, capital, destiny, godsend, portion, revenue **8** gold mine, good luck, opulence, property, treasure, windfall

fortuneteller 4 seer **5** augur, Gypsy, sibyl **6** medium, oracle **7** palmist, prophet **8** magician

forty winks 3 nap **4** doze **6** catnap, snooze

forum 6 medium, outlet **7** rostrum, seminar **8** platform

forward, forwards 3 out **4** back, bold **5** ahead, brash, fresh, relay, sassy **6** assist, brazen, cheeky, hasten, onward, pass on, send on, spread **7** advance, further, promote **8** immodest, impudent, insolent

fossil 4 fogy, rock **5** fogey, oldie, relic, stone

foster 3 aid **4** back, feed, rear, tend **5** favor, nurse, raise **6** foment, harbor, mother, rear up, take in **7** advance, bring up, care for, cherish, further, nourish, nurture, promote, protect, support **8** advocate, befriend, sanction, treasure

foul 3 wet **4** base, clog, evil, lewd, soil, vile **5** dirty, foggy, grimy, gross, gusty, misty, muddy, murky, nasty, rainy, sully, taint **6** coarse, defile, filthy, grubby, odious, putrid, smelly, smutty, soiled, sordid, stormy, tangle, vulgar **7** abusive, begrime, ensnare, hateful, impeded, obscene, pollute, profane, smeared, squalid, stained, sullied, tangled, unclean **8** besmirch, blustery, ensnared, entangle, indecent, infamous, stinking

foul play 5 crime **6** murder

found 4 base, rear, rest **5** build, erect, raise, set up, start **6** create, ground, locate, settle **7** develop, sustain **8** colonize

foundation 3 bed **4** base, foot, fund, rock, root **5** basis, cause **6** bottom, cellar, ground, origin, reason, source **7** support **8** creation

founder 4 fall, limp, reel, sink, trip **5** abort, drown, lurch, swamp **6** go down, go lame, hobble, perish, plunge, sprawl, topple, tumble **7** break up, builder, capsize, creator, go under, stagger, stumble, succumb **8** collapse

fountain 3 jet **4** flow, gush, well **5** birth, cause, spout **6** cradle, feeder, origin, source, spring **7** genesis

Fountainhead, The author: 4 (Ayn) Rand

fourth dimension 4 time

fourth estate 5 press

fowl 3 hen **4** cock, duck, game **5** banty, capon, chick, goose, quail **6** bantam, grouse, pigeon, turkey **7** chicken, cornish, leghorn, poultry

fox
    young: 3 kit, pup
    group of: 5 leash, skulk

foxglove 9 digitalis

foxy *see* **6 clever**

foyer 4 hall **5** lobby **6** loggia **8** anteroom

fracas 3 row **4** fray, to-do **5** brawl, broil, clash, fight, melee, scrap **6** battle, ruckus, rumpus, strife, uproar **7** scuffle

fraction 3 bit, few **4** chip **5** crumb, piece, ratio, scrap **6** morsel, trifle **7** cutting,

portion, section, segment, shaving **8** fragment, particle, quotient

fracture 4 rend, rift **5** break, crack, fault, sever, split **6** breach, cleave **7** disrupt, rupture, shatter **8** cleavage, division

fragile 4 soft, weak **5** crisp, frail **6** dainty, feeble, flimsy, infirm, sleazy, slight, tender **7** brittle, crumbly, friable, rickety, shivery **8** decrepit, delicate

fragment 3 bit **4** chip, snip **5** crumb, cut up, piece, scrap, shard, shred, trace **6** chop up, divide, morsel **7** break up, crumble, portion, section, segment, shatter **8** fraction, separate, splinter

fragrant 5 balmy, spicy **7** odorous **8** aromatic, perfumed, redolent

frail 4 puny, weak **6** feeble, flimsy, infirm, sleazy, slight, weakly **7** brittle, crumbly, fragile, rickety, shivery **8** decrepit, delicate, fallible

frame 3 rim, set **4** body, case, cast, form, make, mold, mood, plan **5** build, draft, hatch, humor, set up, shape, state **6** border, casing, design, devise, edging, figure, indite, invent, map out, nature, scheme, sketch, system, temper **7** anatomy, backing, chassis, concoct, contour, housing, outline, setting **8** attitude, conceive, contrive, mounting, organize, physique, skeleton

frame of mind 4 mood **7** climate **8** attitude

France
  ancient name: 4 Gaul
  capital/largest city: 5 Paris
  island: 4 Cite **7** Corsica **10** Saint-Louis
  lake: 6 Geneva
  mountain: 4 Alps, Jura **6** Vosges **8** Ardennes, Pyrenees
  highest point: 5 (Mont) Blanc
  river: 5 Loire, Rhine, Rhone, Seine
  sea: 5 North **8** Atlantic **13** Mediterranean
  physical feature:
    bay: 6 Biscay
    channel: 7 English **8** La Manche
  place:
    museum: 6 Louvre
    palace: 6 Elysee **10** Versailles
    prison: 8 Bastille
  feature:
    dance: 6 cancan
    tower: 6 Eiffel
  food:
    dish: 4 pate **5** crepe **6** quiche **7** soufflee **8** escargot, pot au feu
    drink: 6 cognac **9** champagne

franchise 5 grant, right **6** ballot **7** charter, freedom, license **8** suffrage

frank *see* **6 candid**

Frankenstein
  author: 7 (Mary) Shelley

frantic 3 mad **4** wild **5** crazy, rabid **6** hectic, insane **7** excited, furious, nervous, violent **8** agitated, frenetic, frenzied

fraternity 4 clan, club **5** union **6** circle, clique, league **7** company, coterie, kinship, society **8** alliance

fraud 4 fake, hoax, hype, ruse, sham **5** cheat, craft, guile, knave, quack, rogue, trick **6** deceit, humbug, rascal **7** swindle **8** artifice, cheating, cozenage, impostor, swindler, trickery

fraught 4 full **5** heavy, laden **6** filled, loaded **7** charged, replete, teeming

fray *see* **5 fight**

freak 3 fad, odd **4** kink, turn, whim **5** craze, fancy, humor, queer, quirk, sport, twist **6** marvel, oddity **7** anomaly, bizarre, erratic, monster, strange, unusual **8** mutation

free 3 big, lax **4** able, bold, easy, idle, idly, open, save **5** clear, extra, let go, loose, rid of, spare **6** daring, devoid, exempt, giving, gratis, lavish, parole, ransom, redeem, unbond, uncage, wanton **7** allowed, assured, forward, liberal, loosely, manumit, release, unchain, unleash **8** careless, devoid of, informal, let loose, liberate, released, unfasten

freedom 4 play **5** range, scope, sweep, swing **6** candor, margin **7** abandon, license **8** autonomy, openness

free-for-all 3 row **4** fray

5 brawl, fight, melee, scrap **6** fracas, ruckus, tussle **7** rhubarb, wrangle

freeze 3 nip **4** bite, cool, halt, stop **5** chill, frost, sting **6** benumb, harden **7** ceiling **8** solidify

freight 4 haul, lade, load, ship **5** cargo, carry, goods **6** burden, charge, convey **7** baggage, luggage

frenzy 3 fit **4** fury **5** craze, furor, mania, state **6** access **7** mad rush, madness, seizure, turmoil **8** delirium, hysteria

frequent 5 daily, haunt, usual **6** common, wonted **7** regular **8** constant, everyday, familiar, habitual, numerous

fresh 3 fit, hot, new **4** bold, cool, fair, keen, late, pert, pure, rare, rosy, rude **5** alert, brisk, chill, clear, green, nervy, novel, ready, ruddy, sassy, saucy, stiff, sweet **6** active, biting, brassy, brazen, cheeky, lively, modern, recent, snotty, unique **7** bracing, cutting, forward, glowing, just out, nipping, uncured, untried, unusual

8 brand-new, creative, flippant, gleaming, impudent, insolent, original, up-to-date

fret *see* **5 worry**

Freya
  also: 5 Freia
  origin: 8 Teutonic
  goddess of: 4 love **6** beauty
  leader of: 9 Valkyries

friction 6 strife **7** chafing, discord, grating, quarrel, rubbing **8** abrasion, bad blood, conflict, fretting

Friday
  from: 5 Freya, Frigg
  heavenly body: 5 Venus

friend 3 pal **4** ally, beau, chum, date, mate **5** amigo, buddy, crony, lover **6** backer, cohort, escort, fellow, intime, minion, patron **7** brother, comrade, partner **8** advocate, coworker, defender, favorite, follower, intimate, mistress, paramour, partisan, playmate, sidekick, soulmate

Friendly Islands *see* **5 Tonga**

Frigg
  also: 3 Fri **5** Frija
  origin: 8 Teutonic
  goddess of: 3 sky **8** marriage
  husband: 4 Odin

fright 4 fear, funk **5** alarm, dread, panic, scare **6** dismay, horror, terror, tremor **7** anxiety, concern, quaking **8** cold feet

frigid 3 icy, raw **4** cold, cool, prim **5** aloof, bleak, gelid, stiff **6** biting, bitter, chilly, formal, frosty **7** distant, glacial **8** freezing

fringe *see* **4 edge**

frisk 3 hop **4** jump, lark, leap, romp, skip, trip **5** bound, caper, cut up, dance, sport **6** bounce, cavort, frolic, gambol, prance, search, spring **7** disport, examine, inspect, ransack **8** look over

fritter 4 blow **5** use up, waste **7** deplete, pancake **8** idle away, squander

frivolous 4 airy, vain **5** barmy, dizzy, empty, inane, light, minor, petty, silly **6** flimsy, frothy, slight **7** fatuous, flighty, foolish, trivial, witless

8 careless, flippant, piddling, trifling

frock 4 coat, gown, robe, suit **5** cloak, dress, smock **6** blouse **7** cassock

frog 3 pad, pod **4** knot, wood **5** hitch, track **6** holder, peeper, toggle **7** croaker, cushion, leopard, tadpole **8** bullfrog, pollywog

frolic 3 fun **4** lark, play, romp, skip **5** act up, antic, caper, frisk, mirth, prank, sport, spree **6** cavort, gaiety, gambol **7** disport, jollity, make hay

front 3 air **4** face, fore, head, lead, mask **6** facade, regard **7** bearing, initial **8** anterior, carriage, demeanor, presence, pretense, trenches

frontier 4 edge **5** march, verge **6** border, limits **7** extreme, marches **8** boundary, confines

frost 4 rime **5** chill **7** iciness **8** coolness, distance

froth 4 fizz, foam, fume, head, scum, suds, surf **5** spume **6** lather **7** bubbles, rubbish **8** flummery,

frippery, nonsense, whitecap

frown 4 fret, mope, muse, pout, sulk **5** glare, scowl **6** glower, ponder

frozen *see* **6 freeze**

frugal 4 slim **5** scant, tight **6** skimpy, stingy **7** ascetic, sparing, thrifty

fruit 4 crop **5** award, issue, yield, young **6** effect, profit, result, reward **7** benefit, harvest, outcome, produce, product, progeny

fruition 8 maturity, ripeness

frumpy 4 drab **5** dowdy **8** slovenly

frustrate 3 bar **4** balk, foil **5** block, check, upset **6** baffle, cancel, defeat, hinder, impede, thwart **7** cripple, fluster, inhibit, prevent **8** obstruct

fry 4 cook **5** brown, grill, saute **7** frizzle

fry 4 fish **5** child, young **8** children, small fry

fudge 3 lie **4** bosh, fake **5** candy, cheat, evade, hedge, hunch, patch **7** penuche **8** divinity

fuel 3 fan, gas, oil **4** coal, feed, fire, wood **5** light, means, stoke **6** charge, fill up, fodder, ignite, incite, kindle **7** impetus, inflame **8** activate, energize, gasoline, material

fugitive 4 hobo **5** brief, exile, hasty, nomad, rover, short, tramp **6** errant, fading, flying, loafer, outlaw **7** elusive, erratic, escaped, escapee, fleeing, hurried, passing, refugee, runaway, vagrant **8** deserter, fleeting, flitting, renegade, vagabond, wanderer

fuhrer 4 Nazi **6** Hitler, leader, tyrant **8** dictator

fulfill 2 do **4** heed, keep, meet, obey, suit **6** answer, effect, follow, redeem **7** achieve, execute, observe, perform, realize, satisfy

full 3 big **4** rich, very, wide **5** ample, broad, flush, laden, large, plump, quite, round, sated, total, whole **6** entire, gorged, intact, loaded, mature, packed, rotund **7** crammed, glutted, heaping, maximum, perfect, replete, shapely, stuffed, teeming

8 brimming, bursting, complete

full of life 5 vital **8** animated, spirited, vigorous

fulminate 4 boil, rage, rant **7** explode **8** denounce

fulsome 3 fat **4** foul **5** suave **6** lavish, odious **7** cloying, lustful, noisome, obscene **8** unctuous

fumble 3 err, mar **4** blow, muff **5** grope, spoil **6** bobble, bungle, mess up **7** butcher, screw up

fume 3 gas **4** boil, burn, emit, foam, haze, puff, rage, rant, rave, reek, waft **5** exude, scent, smell, smoke, stink, vapor **6** billow, exhale, seethe **7** explode, flare up, smolder

fun 3 gas **4** ball, game, jest, lark, play, romp, trip **5** antic, blast, cheer, mirth, prank, sport, spree **6** frolic, gaiety, joking **7** jollity, revelry **8** good time, pleasure

function 3 act, job **4** duty, fete, gala, help, role, task, work **5** feast, field, niche, party, place, power, range, scope, serve **6** affair, behave, do duty, office, soiree, sphere **7** banquet, benefit, concern, faculty, operate, perform, purpose **8** activity, business, ceremony, occasion

fund 3 pot **4** bank, foot, lode, mine, pool, vein, well **5** endow, float, fount, hoard, kitty, stock, store **6** pay for, spring, supply **7** finance, nest egg, reserve, savings

fundamental 3 key **4** ABC's, base, main **5** axiom, basic, basis, chief, first, major, vital **7** central, crucial, element, primary **8** cardinal

funds 4 cash, jack **5** bread, dough, lucre, means, money, moola **6** assets, income, wealth **7** capital, scratch **8** finances

funeral 4 wake **5** rites **6** burial **7** requiem

funeral song 5 dirge, elegy **6** lament **7** requiem **8** threnody

fungus, fungi 4 mold, myco, rust, smut **5** ergot, yeast **6** mildew **7** truffle **8** mushroom

funnel 4 cone, duct, flue, pipe, pour **5** focus, shaft **6** direct, filter, siphon **7** channel, chimney, conduit

funny 3 odd **5** antic, comic, droll, merry, queer, weird, witty **6** absurd, jocose **7** amusing, bizarre, comical, curious, jesting, jocular, offbeat, strange, unusual, waggish **8** farcical, humorous, mirthful, peculiar

fur 3 fox **4** down, hair, lamb, mink, pelt, seal **5** coney, otter, sable **6** beaver, fleece, jaguar, nutria, rabbit **7** cheetah, leopard, muskrat, opossum, raccoon **8** squirrel

furbish 4 buff **5** renew, shine **6** polish **7** burnish **8** renovate

furious 3 mad **4** wild **5** angry, fiery, irate, rabid **6** enrage, fierce, fuming, raging, stormy **7** violent **8** frenetic, frenzied, heedless, maddened, provoked, reckless, vehement, wrathful

furl 4 coil, curl, fold, roll, wrap **6** spiral

furnace 4 kiln, oven **5** forge, stove **6** boiler, heater

furnish 3 arm, rig **4** gird, give, vest **5** array, dress, endow, equip, favor, fit up, grant, stock **6** fit out, outfit, purvey, render, supply **7** appoint, indulge, prepare, provide **8** bestow on, decorate

furniture 7 effects **8** chattels, movables, property

furor 3 fad **4** flap, rage, to-do, word **5** craze, mania, noise **6** fervor, frenzy, hoopla, lunacy, raving, uproar **7** madness, passion **8** brouhaha

furrow 3 cut, dig, rut **4** knit, line, plow, rift, seam **5** cleft, crack, ditch, ridge, track **6** crease, groove, trench, trough **7** channel, crevice, fissure

further 3 aid, new, too, yet **4** also, back, help, more **5** again, extra, favor, fresh, other, spare, speed **6** abroad, assist, back up, beyond, foster, hasten, oblige, to boot, yonder **7** advance, afar off, farther, forward, promote, quicken, stand by **8** expedite

furtive *see* **6 secret**

fury 3 fit, hag, ire, pet **4** gall, huff, rage, snit **5** force, might, shrew, vixen, wrath **6** attack, choler, frenzy, spleen, virago **7** assault, bluster, dudgeon, tantrum **8** acrimony, ferocity, outburst, severity, spitfire

fuse *see* **4 join**

fusillade 4 hail, rain **5** salvo, spray **6** volley **7** barrage, battery **8** drumfire, enfilade

fuss 3 ado, nag **4** carp, fool, fret, fume, pomp, spat, stew, stir, tiff, to-do **5** annoy, cavil, labor, set-to, worry **6** bother, bustle, excite, fidget, flurry, hubbub, hustle, niggle, pester, putter, tinker **7** agitate, confuse, dispute, fluster, nitpick, quibble, perturb, trouble, turmoil

futile 4 idle, vain **5** petty **7** useless **8** abortive, bootless, trifling

future 4 hope **5** after, later

6 coming, latter, to come **7** by-and-by, ensuing **8** eventual, prospect, tomorrow

fuzzy 3 dim **4** hazy **5** downy, foggy, linty, misty, murky, vague, wooly **6** fluffy, frizzy, woolly **7** blurred, obscure, shadowy, unclear **8** confused

gab 3 jaw, rap, yak **4** blab, chat **5** prate **6** babble, gibber, gossip, jabber, patter **7** baloney, blarney, blather, chatter, prattle **8** chitchat, idle talk

gable 4 edge, peak, roof, wall **6** detail, dormer, pinion **7** aileron **8** pediment, triangle

Gabon
   capital/largest city: 10 Libreville
   sea: 8 Atlantic

Gaborone
   capital of: 8 Botswana

Gabriel 9 archangel
   spoke to: 4 Mary

gadget 4 tool **6** device, doodad, jigger **7** gimmick, novelty

Gaea
   also: 2 Ge **4** Gaia
   origin: 5 Greek
   goddess of: 5 earth
   husband: 6 Uranus

Gaelic
   branch: 4 Erse **6** Celtic
   subgroup: 4 Manx **5** Irish **8** Scottish

gaffe 4 goof **5** boner **6** boo-boo **7** blunder

gag *see* **4 hoax**

gaiety, gayety *see* **3 fun**

gain, gains 3 add, bag, get, hit, net, win **4** jump, leap, plus, reap **5** bloom, bonus, fetch, glean, put on, reach, wages, yield **6** attain, come to, gather, income, obtain, pick up, profit, secure **7** achieve, acquire, capture, collect, improve, procure, produce, prosper, recover **8** addition, dividend, earnings, flourish, increase, overtake, proceeds, winnings

gainsay 4 deny **6** abjure, oppose, refute **7** dispute

gait 4 pace, step, walk **5** tread **6** stride **7** bearing

gala 3 gay **5** grand, party

7 benefit, festive, opulent **8** festival, majestic, splendid
French: 4 fete

Galahad
  father: 8 Lancelot
  mother: 6 Elaine
  quest: 5 (Holy) Grail
  symbol of: 6 purity **8** nobility

gale 4 blow, gust **6** squall, tumult **7** tempest **8** outbreak, outburst

gall 3 bug, irk, vex **4** bile, flay, fret, miff, rile **5** anger, annoy, brass, chafe, cheek, gripe, nerve, score, sting, venom **6** abrade, bruise, enrage, harass, injure, nettle, offend, rancor, ruffle, spleen **7** affront, incense, provoke, rub sore **8** acrimony, boldness, temerity

gallant *see* **7 valiant**

gallery 4 stoa **5** salon **6** arcade, loggia **7** passage **8** cloister, corridor

gallivant, galavant 3 gad **4** kite, roam, rove **5** jaunt, range, stray **6** ramble, travel, wander **7** meander, traipse

gallop 3 fly, hie, jog, run **4** bolt, dart, dash, flit, race, rush, scud, skim, trot, whiz **5** bound, hurry, speed **6** hasten, scurry, sprint **7** mad dash **8** fast clip, fast gait

gallows 4 rope **5** noose **6** gibbet, halter **8** scaffold

galore 7 aplenty, to spare

galvanize 4 fire, move, stir, wake **5** rally, rouse, treat **6** arouse, awaken, charge, excite, spur on **7** inspire, quicken **8** activate, energize, vitalize

Gambia
  capital: 6 Banjul
  largest city: 9 Serekunda
  river: 6 Gambia
  sea: 8 Atlantic

gambit 4 ploy, ruse **5** feint, trick **6** scheme **8** artifice, maneuver

gamble 3 bet **4** back, risk **5** flyer, wager **6** chance, hazard, toss-up **7** trust in, venture

gambol *see* **6 frolic**

game 3 bad, fun **4** halt, lame, lark, play, prey, romp **5** antic, brave, cocky, gimpy, match, sport, spree **6** daring,

frolic, gaiety, gambol,
heroic, plucky, quarry,
spunky **7** contest,
crooked, gallant, pastime,
tourney, valiant, willing **8**
crippled, deformed,
disabled, fearless,
hobbling, intrepid,
resolute, spirited, valorous

gamut 3 ken **5** reach, scope,
sweep **6** extent **7** compass,
purview

gang 3 mob **4** band, body,
crew, pack, pals, ring,
team **5** chums, crowd,
flock, group, party **6**
clique, outfit **7** buddies,
coterie, cronies, friends **8**
comrades

gap *see* **4 hole**

gape 4 gasp, gawk, gaze,
ogle, part, peer, yawn **5**
split, stare **6** cleave,
expand **7** fly open **8** wide
open, separate

garb *see* **7 clothes**

garbage 4 dirt, junk **5** offal,
swill, trash, waste **6**
debris, litter, refuse **7**
carrion, rubbish

garble 5 mix up **6** jumble **7**
confuse, distort **8**
fragment

garden 4 Eden, lawn, plot,
yard **8** paradise

Garfield, James Abram
presidential rank: 9
twentieth
party: 10 Republican
state represented: 2 OH
vice president: 6 Arthur
born: 2 OH **6** Orange **8**
log cabin
assassinated by: 7
Guiteau
wife: 8 Lucretia
nickname: 5 Crete

gargantuan 4 huge, vast **5**
great **7** hulking, immense,
mammoth, massive, titanic
8 colossal, enormous,
gigantic

garish 4 loud **5** cheap,
gaudy, showy **6** brassy,
bright, flashy, tawdry,
tinsel, vulgar **7** glaring

garland 3 bay, lei **4** halo **5**
crown **6** corona, diadem,
wreath **7** chaplet, circlet,
coronet, festoon **8**
headband

garlic
charm against: 7 poverty,
witches

garment, garments *see* **7**
clothes

garner 4 reap **5** amass,

hoard **6** gather, heap up **7** acquire, collect **8** assemble

garnet
month: 7 January

garnish 4 deck, gild, trim **5** adorn, array **6** bedeck, doll up **7** festoon, smarten **8** ornament, spruce up, trimming

garret 4 loft **5** attic

garrison 4 fort **5** guard **6** patrol, secure **7** battery, bivouac, station

garrulous 5 gabby, windy, wordy **6** chatty **7** gossipy, prating, verbose, voluble **8** babbling, chattery, effusive

gas 4 fuel, fume **5** vapor **6** petrol **7** essence

gash 4 hack, rend, rent, slit, tear **5** carve, cleft, crack, lance, slash, wound **6** cleave, incise **7** dissect, fissure **8** lacerate

gasp 4 gulp, pant, puff **5** blurt **6** suck in, wheeze

gastronome 7 epicure, gourmet

gastropod 4 slug **5** cowry, snail, whelk **6** cowrie, limpet, nerite **7** abalone, mollusk **8** univalve

gate 3 tap **5** crowd, house, valve **6** portal, sluice **7** doorway **8** audience

gatekeeper 5 guard **6** porter **7** St. Peter **8** watchman

gather 4 fold, mass **5** amass, group, infer, learn, pleat, stack **6** assume, deduce, muster, pile up **7** cluster, collect, convene, marshal, observe **8** assemble, conclude

gauche 5 inept **6** clumsy, oafish **7** awkward, boorish, ill-bred, uncouth **8** bungling, tactless

gaudy 4 loud **5** cheap, showy, vivid **6** flashy, flimsy, garish, tawdry **7** glaring **8** colorful, dazzling, striking

gauge, gage 4 rate, size **5** guess, judge, meter **6** assess **7** adjudge, measure **8** appraise, estimate, evaluate, standard

gaunt 4 bony, grim, lank, lean, slim, thin **5** bleak, lanky, spare **6** barren, meager, skinny, wasted **7** haggard, pinched, scrawny, slender, starved **8** raw-boned, skeletal

gauzy 5 filmy, sheer **6** flimsy, sleazy

gawky 6 clumsy, klutzy **7** awkward, lumpish **8** bungling, fumbling, lubberly, ungainly

gay *see* **6 genial**

gaze 3 eye **4** gape, ogle, peek, peer, scan **5** glare, lower, stare, study, watch **6** behold, glance, glower, peruse, regard, survey **7** examine, inspect, observe

gear 3 cam, rig **4** duds, garb, togs **5** dress, tools **6** attire, outfit, tackle, things **7** apparel, clothes, rigging **8** clothing, cogwheel, flywheel, garments

gelatin 4 agar, glue **5** aspic, gelee, jelly **6** glutin, pectin **7** protein, sericin

geld 5 alter **8** castrate

gelid 3 icy **6** frigid, frozen **8** freezing

gem 4 dear, doll, rock **5** beaut, bijou, jewel, peach, prize **6** marvel, wonder

Gemini
   symbol: 5 twins
   planet: 7 Mercury
   born: 3 May **4** June
   twins: 6 Castor, Pollux

gender 3 sex **4** kind, male, sort, type **5** class **6** female

genealogy 4 line **5** birth, house, stock **7** lineage **8** ancestry, pedigree

general 5 basic, broad, usual, vague **6** common, normal, public **7** blanket, generic, natural, overall, popular, regular, typical **8** everyday, frequent, ordinary, sweeping

generate 4 form, make **5** beget, breed, cause, frame **6** create, evolve, father, induce, invent **7** develop, fashion, produce **8** contrive

generation 3 kin **4** clan, line, race **5** breed, house, issue, stock, tribe **6** family, growth, strain **7** genesis, lineage, progeny **8** breeding, creation

generic 6 common **7** general **8** sweeping

generous 5 ample, large, lofty, noble **6** humane, lavish **7** copious, liberal **8** abundant, effusive, obliging, princely, prodigal

genesis 4 rise, root **5** birth **6** origin **8** creation

genial

genial **3** gay **4** glad, kind, warm **5** civil, happy, jolly, merry, sunny **6** bright, cheery, hearty, jaunty, jovial, joyful, joyous, kindly, lively **7** affable, amiable, cordial, festive **8** cheerful, friendly, gracious, pleasant, sociable

genius **3** ace, wit **4** bent, gift, mind, whiz **5** brain, flair, knack **6** expert, master, wisdom **7** faculty, insight, prodigy **8** judgment, sagacity

genre **4** kind, sort, type **5** breed, class, genus, group, order, style **6** school **7** fashion, species, variety **8** category, division

genteel **4** tony **5** civil, elite, ritzy, swank, swell **6** poised, polite **7** courtly, elegant, refined, stylish **8** cultured, decorous, ladylike, polished, well-bred

gentile
  Yiddish: **3** goy
  man: **7** shegetz
  woman: **6** shiksa

gentle **3** low **4** calm, easy, kind, meek, mild, soft,

tame **5** balmy, bland, light, quiet **6** benign, broken, docile, kindly, placid, serene, slight, smooth, tender **7** lenient, pacific, subdued **8** moderate, peaceful, tolerant, tranquil

gentleman **3** don, guy, man, one **4** chap, gent **5** swell **6** fellow, person, squire **7** esquire, hidalgo **8** cavalier

gentry **5** elite **7** society **8** nobility

genuflect **4** bend **6** kowtow

genuine **4** open, pure, real, true **5** frank, naive, plain, solid **6** actual, candid, honest, proven, simple **7** artless, earnest, natural, sincere **8** bona fide, sterling, true-blue

genus **4** kind, sort, type **5** class, group **7** variety **8** category, division

Georgia
capital/largest city: **7**
  Tbilisi
mountain: **8** Caucasus
sea: **5** Black
Georgia
abbreviation: **2** GA
nickname: **5** Peach
capital/largest city:

7 Atlanta
island: 3 Sea **6** Jekyll
mountain: 5 Stone **7**
   Lookout **8** Kennesaw
physical feature:
   springs: 4 Warm

Georgia Peach
   nickname of: 6 Ty Cobb

germ 3 bud, bug, egg **4**
ovum, root, seed **5** ovule,
spark, spore, virus **6**
embryo, origin, source,
sprout **7** microbe, nucleus,
seed bud **8** bacillus,
offshoot, rudiment

German 3 Hun **4** Goth **5**
boche, heine, jerry, kraut,
Saxon **8** Prussian,
Teutonic
   empire: 5 reich
   thank you: 5 danke
   toast: 6 prosit

germane 3 apt, fit **6** native,
proper **7** apropos, fitting,
related **8** material,
relative, relevant, suitable

Germanic Mythology
   chief of gods: 5 Wotan
   goddess of clouds/sky/
      marriage: 3 Fri **5** Frigg,
      Frija **6** Frigga
   goddess of love/beauty/
      fecundity: 5 Freya
   hero: 6 Sigurd **9** Siegfried

heroine: 6 Gudrun,
   Kudrun **7** Guthrun **8**
   Brunhild
maidens: 9 Valkyries
nymph: 7 Lorelei, Lurelei

Germany
   capital/largest city: 6
   Berlin
   mountain: 4 Alps, Harz
   lake: 7 Wannsee **9**
   Constance
   river: 3 Inn **4** Elbe, Lech,
   Main, Oder, Ruhr **5**
   Rhine **6** Danube **7**
   Moselle
   physical features:
      canal: 4 Kiel
      forest: 5 Black
      sea: 5 North **6** Baltic
   feature:
      china: 7 Dresden
   food:
      sausage: 5 wurst

Germany, East
   capital/largest city: 10
   East Berlin

Germany, West
   capital: 4 Bonn
   largest city: 10 West
   Berlin

Germinal
   author: 4 (Emile) Zola

germinate 3 bud **4** blow,
open **5** bloom, shoot

6 flower, push up, sprout
7 blossom, burgeon,
develop **8** generate, spring
up

gesture 3 nod **4** sign, wave,
wink **5** nudge, shrug,
touch **6** beckon, motion,
signal **8** high sign

get 3 bag, fix, net, win **4**
beat, coax, earn, gain,
grab, grip, grow, have,
hear, move, take, turn **5**
catch, fetch, grasp, learn,
reach, seize, sense **6**
attain, become, collar,
come by, come to,
fathom, follow, obtain,
pick up, pocket, secure,
snatch, take in, turn to **7**
achieve, acquire, capture,
ensnare, go after, inherit,
prepare, realize, receive **8**
contract, perceive,
persuade

getaway 6 escape, exodus,
flight

get even 6 avenge **7**
counter, hit back, pay
back, revenge

get the upper hand
6 master **7** conquer **8**
dominate, overcome,
surmount

get-together 2 do **3** bee

4 meet **5** agree, party,
visit **6** affair, gather,
hobnob **7** meeting **8**
assembly

getup 3 rig **6** attire, outfit **7**
costume **8** disguise,
ensemble

get used to 5 adapt, inure
6 adjust **8** accustom

gewgaws 7 baubles,
doodads, trifles **8** trinkets

Ghana
other name: 9 Gold Coast
capital/largest city:
5 Accra, Akkra
lake: 5 Volta
river: 5 Volta
sea: 8 Atlantic
physical feature:
gulf: 6 Guinea
feature:
national dress: 5 kente
UN leader: 4 Kofi **5**
Annan

ghost 4 hint **5** demon,
shade, spook, trace **6**
goblin, shadow, sprite,
wraith **7** banshee,
chimera, phantom, specter

ghoulish 5 eerie, scary,
weird **7** demonic, hellish,
macabre, ogreish, satanic
8 diabolic, fiendish,
gruesome, infernal, sinister

giant 3 big **4** huge **5** titan

7 Goliath, whopper **8** behemoth, colossus

gibberish *see* **8 nonsense**

gibe, jibe 3 rag **4** jeer, mock, quip, razz, twit **5** chaff, flout, knock, toast, scoff, sneer, taunt **6** deride, needle **7** poke fun **8** brickbat, derision, ridicule

Gibraltar
government: 6 colony (UK)
mountain: 6 Misery
physical feature:
   cliffs: 7 Pillars (of Hercules)

giddy 5 dizzy, faint, silly **6** fickle, fitful **7** awesome, erratic, flighty, muddled, reeling **8** careless, fanciful, reckless, unsteady, volatile, whirling

gift 3 aid, dot, fee, sop, tip **4** alms, bent, boon, dole, help, turn **5** award, bonus, bribe, craft, dower, dowry, favor, flair, forte, graft, grant, knack, power, prize, skill **6** genius, legacy, talent, virtue **7** bequest, faculty, handout, largess, premium, present, quality, tribute **8** aptitude,

capacity, donation, facility, gratuity, offering

gig 3 job **4** trap **6** chaise **7** dogcart **8** carriage

gigantic *see* **4 huge**

giggle 6 cackle, hee-hee, simper, tee-hee, titter **7** chuckle, snicker, snigger

Gilbert Islands *see* **8 Kiribati**

gild 4 bend **5** slant, twist **7** cover up, touch up

Gilgamesh
origin: 8 Sumerian
king of: 4 Uruk **5** Erech

gimcrack 5 bijou, curio **6** bauble, gewgaw **7** trinket, whatnot **8** ornament

gimmick 4 plan, ploy, ruse, wile **5** angle, dodge, stunt **6** design, device, gadget, scheme **7** wrinkle

ginger 3 pep, tan **5** brown, spice **6** energy

gingerly 6 warily **7** charily, timidly **8** daintily

gingham 5 cloth **6** cotton, fabric, striped **8** chambray

giraffe
kin: 5 okapi

girder 4 beam **5** brace, truss **6** binder, rafter **7** support

girdle **3** hem **4** band, belt, ring, sash **5** girth, hedge, stays **6** bodice, circle, corset **7** baldric, circlet, contour **8** boundary, cincture, corselet

girl **4** bird, cook, help, lass, maid, minx, miss **5** angel, chick, nymph, wench **6** damsel, lassie, maiden, virgin **7** baggage, colleen, darling, fiancee, ingenue, nymphet **8** daughter, domestic, mistress, scullion

girlfriend **6** steady **7** beloved, sweetie

Girl Scouts
founded by: 3 (Juliette) Low

girt **4** belt, bind, gird, ring **5** bound, girth **6** belted, circle, girdle, ringed **7** circled, girdled

gist **3** nut **4** core, crux, meat, pith **5** drift, force, heart, sense, tenor, theme **6** burden, center, effect, import, kernel, marrow, spirit **7** essence, purport

give **3** buy, pay, tip **4** bend, ease, emit, hire, lend, show, sink **5** admit, allot, allow, apply, award, bribe, deign, endow, grant, issue, leave, offer, relax, voice, yield **6** afford, assign, attach, bestow, commit, confer, convey, devote, donate, enable, enrich, hand to, impart, loosen, notify, open on, permit, recede, relent, render, shrink, supply, tender **7** concede, consign, deliver, entrust, fork out, furnish, hand out, present, provide, retreat, slacken **8** announce, bequeath, collapse, dispense, exchange, fork over, hand over, lead on to, move back, shell out

give a leg up **3** aid **4** help, lift **5** boost, hoist, raise **6** assist **7** elevate

give in **5** defer, yield **6** accede, cave in, submit **7** succumb

give one's word **3** vow **5** swear **6** assure, pledge **7** certify, promise, warrant

give rise to **4** sire **5** breed, cause **6** lead to **7** produce **8** engender, generate, occasion

give up the ghost **3** die **6** expire, pass on, perish **7** decease **8** pass away

give way 4 fall **6** buckle, cave in **7** crumple **8** collapse

gizmo 4 tool **6** device, doodad, gadget **7** whatsis

glacial 3 icy, raw **4** cold **5** chill, gelid, polar **6** arctic, biting, bitter, frigid, frosty, frozen, wintry **7** hostile **8** freezing, inimical, piercing

glad 5 happy **6** elated, joyful, joyous **7** elating, gleeful, pleased, tickled **8** blissful, cheerful, cheering, pleasing, rejoiced

glade 4 dell, glen, lawn, vale, wood **5** grove, marsh, vista **6** hollow **7** opening **8** clearing

glad rags 5 array **6** attire, finery

glamor, glamour 5 charm, magic **6** allure **7** glitter, romance **8** illusion

glance 4 kiss, peek, peep, scan, skim, slip **5** brush, graze, shave, touch **6** bounce, careen, squint **7** glimpse **8** ricochet

gland
  type: 4 duct **8** ductless
  kind: 3 oil **5** sweat

7 adrenal, thyroid **8** pancreas **9** pituitary

glare 4 glow **5** blaze, flame, flare, flash, gleam, glint, gloss, lower, scowl, sheen **6** dazzle, glower **7** flicker, glimmer, glisten, glitter, radiate, shimmer, sparkle, twinkle **8** radiance

glass 6 beaker, goblet **7** chalice, tumbler

glasshouse 7 nursery **8** hothouse

glaze 4 blur **5** gloss **6** enamel, finish **7** grow dim, varnish **8** film over

gleam 3 bit, jot, ray **4** beam, drop, glow, hint, iota **5** blink, flare, flash, glare, glint, gloss, grain, sheen, shine, spark, speck, trace **6** luster, streak **7** flicker, glimmer, glimpse, glisten, glitter, inkling, shimmer, sparkle, tiny bit, twinkle **8** radiance

glean 4 cull **5** amass **6** gather, pick up **7** harvest

glebe 3 sod **4** clod, land, plot, soil **5** earth, field

glee *see* **3** joy

glib **4** oily **5** gabby, quick, ready, suave **6** facile, fluent, smooth **7** devious, voluble **8** slippery

glide **3** run **4** flow, roll, sail, skim, slip, soar **5** coast, drift, float, issue, skate, slide, steal **6** elapse, stream **7** proceed

glimmer *see* **7** **glitter**

glimpse **3** see, spy **4** espy, peek, peep, spot **6** glance, peek at, peep at, squint

glint *see* **6** **glance**

glisten **4** glow **5** flash, gleam, glint, shine **7** flicker, glimmer, glister, glitter, radiate, shimmer, sparkle, twinkle

glitter **4** fire, glow, pomp, show **5** flare, flash, gleam, glint, sheen, shine **6** luster, thrill, tinsel **7** glamour, glimmer, glisten, radiate, sparkle, twinkle **8** radiance, splendor

gloaming **4** dusk **7** evening **8** twilight

gloat **4** bask, brag **5** exult, strut, vaunt **7** revel in, swagger, triumph **8** crow over

globe **3** orb **4** ball **5** Earth, world **6** planet, sphere **7** globule **8** spheroid

globule **4** ball, bead, bleb, blob, drop **5** globe **6** bubble, pellet, sphere **7** blister, droplet **8** spheroid

gloom *see* **6** **misery**

gloomy **3** dim, sad **4** dark, dour, down, dull, glum, grim, mopy, sour **5** dusky, moody, mopey, murky, shady **6** cloudy, dismal, dreary, morbid, morose, shaded, somber **7** doleful, forlorn, shadowy, sunless, unhappy **8** dejected, desolate, downcast, frowning, funereal, overcast

glory **4** fame, mark, name **5** boast, honor, revel, vaunt **6** esteem, homage, praise, renown, repute **7** dignity, majesty, worship **8** blessing, eminence, grandeur, nobility, prestige, splendor

gloss **4** glow, mask, veil **5** cloak, color, glaze, gleam, japan, sheen, shine **6** enamel, excuse, luster, polish, veneer **7** cover up, lacquer, shimmer, varnish

8 annotate, disguise, mitigate, radiance

glove 3 kid **4** cuff, mitt **5** catch, thumb **6** gusset, mitten **8** gauntlet

glow 4 fill, heat **5** ardor, bloom, blush, color, flush, gleam, gusto, shine **6** fervor, thrill, tingle, warmth **7** flicker, glimmer, glisten, glitter, radiate, shimmer, smolder, twinkle **8** radiance

glower 4 pout, sulk **5** frown, glare, scowl, stare

glue 3 fix, gum **5** affix, epoxy, paste, putty, stick **6** adhere, cement, fasten, mortar **7** plaster, stickum **8** adhesive, fixative, mucilage

glum 6 gloomy, morose **8** dejected **9** cheerless

glut 4 bolt, clog, cram, drug, fill, gulp, jade, load, sate **5** choke, flood, gorge, stuff **6** burden, deluge, devour, excess, gobble **7** congest, overeat, satiate, surfeit, surplus **8** overdose, overfeed, overload, plethora, saturate

glutinous 5 gluey, bummy, mucid, ropey, slimy, tacky, thick **6** sticky, viscid **7** viscous **8** adhesive

glutton 3 hog, pig **8** gourmand

gnarled 6 knotty, rugged, snaggy **7** crooked, knotted, nodular, twisted **8** leathery, wrinkled

gnat 7 no-see-um
group of: 5 cloud, horde

gnaw *see* **4 chew**

gnome 3 elf **4** pixy **5** dwarf, troll **6** goblin, sprite

gnostic 4 sage, wise **6** clever, shrewd **7** knowing **8** mandaean, simonian

gnu 7 brindle **8** antelope

go 3 act, end, fit, fly, pep, run, try, vim **4** blow, dash, elan, fare, flee, flow, jibe, lead, life, pass, quit, stir, turn, wend, work **5** agree, begin, be off, blend, drive, force, get on, lapse, leave, reach, scram, slide, split, steam, tally, trial, verve, vigor, whirl **6** accord, beat it, be used, belong, chance, decamp, depart, effort, elapse, energy, expire, extend, pass by, repair, result, retire, spirit **7** advance, attempt, fall out, glide by, move out, operate, perform, proceed, slip off, take off, turn out, vamoose, work out **8** function, move away, progress, slip away, sneak off, spread to, start for, steal off, vitality, withdraw

goad *see* **8 persuade**

goal 3 aim, end **4** home, mark, wire **5** point, score, tally **6** design, intent, object, target **7** end line, purpose **8** ambition, goal line, terminus

goat 3 kid **4** buck, butt **5** billy, nanny **6** victim **7** fall guy
combining form: 4 aego **5** capri
family: 7 Bovidae
female: 3 doe **5** capra, nanny **7** doeling
genus: 5 Capra
goat-boy: 5 Giles
goat-man: 5 satyr
god: 3 Pan **5** satyr
group of: 4 herd **5** tribe
male: 4 buck **5** billy
meat: 7 cabrito
young: 3 kid

gob 3 dab, tar **4** clot, glob, lump, mass **6** sailor **7** Jack Tar

go back 6 return **7** retreat

gobble 3 caw **4** bolt, gulp, wolf **5** raven, stuff **6** cackle, devour, gabble, gaggle **8** bolt down, cram down, gulp down

go-between 5 agent, envoy, fixer, proxy **6** deputy, second **7** arbiter **8** emissary, mediator

goblet 3 cup **5** glass **6** vessel **7** chalice

goblin 4 ogre **5** bogey, demon, troll **7** gremlin **8** bogeyman

go by 4 pass **6** elapse, pass by, roll by, rush by, slip by **7** glide by, slide by

go-cart 4 cart **5** buggy **6** barrow **8** carriage, handcart, pushcart

God, god 4 Lord **5** Allah, deity **6** Elohim, Jahveh, Yahweh **7** Holy One, Jehovah, Skaddai **8** divinity, the Deity

Godfather, The
author: 4 (Mario) Puzo

family: 8 Corleone
members: 4 Vito **5** Fredo,
Sonny **6** Connie **7**
Michael
director: 7 (Francis Ford)
Coppola
cast: 4 (James) Caan **5**
(Talia) Shire **6** (Marlon)
Brando, (John) Cazale,
(Robert) Duvall, (Diane)
Keaton, (Al) Pacino
godforsaken 5 bleak **6**
lonely, remote **8** deserted,
desolate, wretched
go down 3 ebb **4** drop,
fade, wane **5** abate, lower,
slide **6** lessen, plunge,
reduce, weaken **7** descend,
plummet, slacken, subside
8 decrease, moderate
go-getter 4 doer **7** hustler **8**
achiever, live wire
gold 3 bar **4** gilt **5** aurum,
ingot **6** beauty, nugget,
purity, yellow **7** bullion
Gold Coast *see* **5** Ghana **11**
Sierra Leone
Golden Fleece
kept at: 7 Colchis
kept by: 6 (King) Aeetes
stolen by: 5 Jason **9**
Argonauts
accomplice: 5 Medea

goldfinch
group of: 5 charm
golf
**average number strokes to
complete a hole: 3** par
club: 4 iron, wood **5**
wedge **6** driver, putter
club carrier: 6 caddie
**hole scored in one stroke:
3** ace **9** hole-in-one
**one stroke less than par:
6** birdie
**one stroke more than par:
5** bogey
**two strokes less than par:
5** eagle
uprooted turf: 5 divot
warning cry: 4 fore
Golgotha 7 Calvary
Goliath 5 giant
slain by: 5 David
weapon: 5 sling
Gomorrah
destroyed with: 5 Sodom
6 Zeboim
gone 3 ago, out **4** away,
dead, left, lost, past **6**
absent, ruined, used up **7**
defunct, died out, extinct,
missing **8** departed,
finished, vanished
Gone With the Wind
author: 8 (Margaret)
Mitchell

character: 5 Mammy,
Rhett (Butler) **6** Ashley
(Wilkes), Gerald
(O'Hara), Prissy **7**
Melanie (Wilkes) **8**
Scarlett (O'Hara)
director: 7 (Victor)
Fleming
cast: 5 (Clark) Gable,
(Vivien) Leigh **6** (Leslie)
Howard **7** (Butterfly)
McQueen **8** (Hattie)
McDaniel **10** (Olivia) de
Haviland
good 3 ace, fit, new **4** best,
boon, fine, full, gain,
kind, pure, real **5** ample,
crack, favor, great, large,
merit, moral, pious, prize,
right, solid, sound, sunny,
valid, value, worth **6**
adroit, choice, devout,
entire, genial, honest,
kindly, lively, profit,
proper, seemly, select,
tiptop, useful, virtue,
wealth **7** benefit, capable,
capital, dutiful, fitting,
genuine, godsend, healthy,
sizable, skilled, success,
upright **8** adequate,
becoming, blessing,
cheerful, complete,
innocent, kindness,
obedient, obliging,

pleasant, precious,
reliable, salutary, skillful,
sociable, splendid,
thorough, topnotch,
valuable, virtuous,
windfall
Good Book 5 Bible
good breeding 5 grace **6**
polish **7** manners
goodby, goodbye 3 bye **6**
bye-bye, bye now, so long
7 parting, send-off **8**
farewell, Godspeed
good deed 8 kindness
Hebrew: 7 mitsvah,
mitzvah
good-for-nothing 5 idler **6**
loafer **7** useless
good-natured 4 warm **5**
sunny **6** genial, kindly **7**
affable, amiable **8**
cheerful, friendly, pleasant
good opinion 6 esteem,
regard **7** respect
goods 4 gear **5** cloth, stock,
wares **6** fabric, things **7**
effects, fabrics **8** chattels,
material, movables,
property, textiles
good sense 6 brains,
wisdom **8** judgment
goof *see* **5 error**

goose
  young: 7 gosling
  group of: 5 flock, skein **6** gaggle

go over 5 audit, check **6** review **7** examine, inspect

gore 5 blood **7** carnage **8** butchery

Gore, Albert
  wife: 6 Tipper
  political career: 2 VP **5** House **6** Senate **13** vice president
  ran for: 9 president
  party: 8 Democrat

gorge 3 gap, ire **4** bolt, cram, craw, dale, dell, fill, glen, glut, gulp, pass, sate, vale **5** abyss, anger, blood, chasm, cleft, gulch, gully, mouth, stuff, wrath **6** canyon, devour, gobble, gullet, hatred, hollow, ravine, throat **7** indulge, overeat, satiate **8** crevasse

gorgeous 4 fine, rich **5** grand **6** bright, costly, lovely **7** elegant, opulent, shining **8** dazzling, glorious, imposing, splendid, stunning

Gorgons
  form: 7 maidens **8** monsters

  best-known: 6 Medusa
  hair of: 6 snakes
  hands of: 5 brass
  turned viewers to: 5 stone

gorilla
  group of: 4 band

gospel 5 credo, creed **8** doctrine

gossamer 5 filmy, gauzy, sheer **8** cobwebby

gossip 4 news **6** babble, report, tattle **7** comment, hearsay, prattle

go through 4 bear **6** endure, suffer **7** sustain, undergo

go to pieces 5 break, crack **7** break up, crack up, crumble, give way, shatter **8** splinter

gouge 5 carve, drill, scoop **6** chisel, extort

go under 4 fail, fall, sink

gourmand 7 glutton

gourmet 7 epicure

govern 3 run **4** boss, curb, form, head, lead, rule, tame **5** check, guide, pilot, steer **6** direct, manage **7** command, control, oversee **8** dominate, restrain

government 3 law **4** rule **5** state **6** regime

7 command, control **8** dominion, guidance
absence of: 7 anarchy
absolute: 7 tyranny

gown 4 robe **5** dress, frock

grab 3 bag, nab **4** grip, hold, pass **5** catch, clasp, grasp, lunge, pluck, seize **6** clutch, collar, snatch **7** capture

grace 4 deck, love, tact, trim **5** adorn, charm, endow, exalt, favor, honor, mercy, merit, piety, skill, taste **6** beauty, bedeck, enrich, polish, set off, virtue **7** charity, decorum, dignify, dress up, enhance, glorify, manners **8** beautify, elegance, felicity, fluidity, holiness, lenience, ornament, reprieve

Graces
  goddesses of: 6 beauty
  father: 4 Zeus

grade 4 bank, even, hill, mark, ramp, rank, rate, sort, step **5** brand, caste, class, level, order, pitch, place, slope, stage, value **6** degree, rating, status **7** flatten, incline **8** classify,

gradient, position, standing

grade-A *see* **5** great

gradual 4 slow **6** gentle, steady **7** regular **8** measured

graduate 5 grade **6** alumna **7** alumnus, mark off

Graduate, The
  director: 7 (Mike) Nichols
  cast: 4 (Katharine) Ross **7** (Dustin) Hoffman **8** (Anne) Bancroft

Graeae
  goddesses of: 3 sea
  sisters: 7 Gorgons
  three shared: 6 one eye **8** one tooth
  eye stolen by: 7 Perseus

graft 3 bud **4** join, last, slip, swag **5** booty, infix, inset, plant, scion **6** bribes, payola, splice, spoils **7** bribery, implant, payoffs, plunder, rake-off **8** kickback

Graiae *see* **6** **Graeae**

grain 3 bit, dot, jot, rye **4** atom, corn, dash, iota, mite, oats, seed, whit **5** crumb, grist, maize, pinch, spark, speck, touch, trace, wheat **6** barley, cereal, kernel, millet, morsel, pellet **7** granule **8** fragment

grand 3 big **4** fine, full, good, head, huge, keen, main **5** chief, fancy, great, large, lofty, noble, regal, royal, showy, super, swell **6** august, choice, kingly, lordly, superb **7** dashing, elegant, exalted, haughty, mammoth, opulent, queenly, stately, sublime, supreme **8** arrogant, complete, fabulous, glorious, imperial, imposing, majestic, palatial, princely, smashing, splendid, striking, terrific

grant 4 boon, cede, gift, give **5** admit, allot, allow, award, endow, favor, yield **6** accord, assign, bestow, confer, donate, permit **7** agree to, bequest, concede, consent, deal out, largess, present, subsidy, tribute **8** accede to, allocate, bestowal, donation, offering

Grant, Ulysses Simpson
real first name: 5 Hiram
nickname: 3 Sam **4** Lyss

presidential rank: 10 eighteenth
party: 10 Republican
vice president: 5 Ferry **6** Wilson, Colfax
born: 2 OH **13** Point Pleasant
notable events of lifetime/ career: 8 Civil War
wife: 5 Julia

granulate 5 crush **6** powder

graphic 4 seen **5** clear, drawn, lucid, vivid **6** visual **7** painted, printed, visible, written **8** distinct, explicit, forcible, lifelike, pictured, striking

grapple 4 face, grip, hold, meet **5** catch, clasp, fight, grasp, seize **6** clutch, combat, engage, fasten, tackle, take on **7** contend, wrestle **8** confront, make fast, struggle

grasp 3 get, ken **4** grab, grip, hold, sway, take **5** catch, clasp, infer, range, reach, savvy, seize, sense, skill, sweep **6** clinch, clutch, deduce, fathom, follow, master, snatch, take in **7** catch at, compass, control, embrace, grapple, mastery, seizing, seizure **8** clutches, gripping, perceive

grassland 3 lea **4** farm, vale, veld **5** field, pampa, plain, range, veldt **6** meadow **7** pasture, prairie, savanna **8** flatland, savannah

grate *see* **3 vex**

grateful 7 obliged **8** beholden, indebted, thankful

Grateful Dead
  leader: 6 (Jerry) Garcia
  fan: 8 Deadhead

Gratiae *see* **6 Graces**

gratify 4 suit **5** amuse, favor, humor **6** coddle, divert, pamper, please, regale, soothe, thrill, tickle **7** appease, delight, enchant, flatter, gladden, indulge, refresh, satisfy

gratuitous 4 free **6** gratis, wanton **7** donated, willing **8** baseless, unproven

gratuity 3 tip **4** gift **8** donation

grave 4 dour, sage, tomb **5** acute, crypt, mound, quiet, sober, staid, vault **6** gloomy, solemn, somber **7** crucial, earnest, ossuary,

serious, subdued, weighty **8** catacomb, cenotaph, critical, frowning

gravity 4 pull **6** danger, import, moment **7** concern, dignity, urgency **8** calmness, enormity, grimness, serenity, sobriety

gray, grey 3 dun **4** ashy, dark, drab, pale **5** ashen, foggy, hoary, misty, murky, slate **6** cloudy, dismal, gloomy, silver, somber **7** clouded, grayish, grizzly, neutral, silvery, sunless **8** overcast

graze 3 rub **4** crop, rasp, skim, skin **5** brush, grind, swipe **6** abrade, browse, bruise, glance, scrape **7** pasture, scratch **8** abrasion, eat grass

grease 3 fat, oil **4** balm, lard **5** salve **6** anoint, tallow **7** unguent **8** ointment

great 3 apt, big **4** able, a-one, cool, fine, good, high, huge, kind, many, phat, vast, well **5** chief, crack, grand, grave, gross, heavy, large, noble, super, swell **6** choice, expert, famous, loving, strong, superb **7** awesome, crucial, decided, eminent, extreme, immense, mammoth, notable, serious, titanic **8** abundant, colossal, critical, enormous, esteemed, fabulous, gigantic, glorious, renowned, skillful, smashing, splendid, superior, terrific

Great Gatsby, The
  author: 16 F Scott Fitzgerald

Great Lake 4 Erie **5** Huron **7** Ontario **8** Michigan, Superior

grebe 4 bird, fowl, loon **5** diver **6** dipper **7** henbill

Greece
  capital/largest city: 6 Athens
  highest point: 7 Olympus
  island: 5 Crete, Delos, Samos **6** Euboea, Ithaca Lemnos, Lesbos, Rhodes **8** Cyclades
  sea: 5 Crete **6** Aegean, Ionian **13** Mediterranean
  physical feature:
    gulf: 7 Corinth, Saronic
    isthmus: 7 Corinth
    peninsula: 6 Balkan

    place:
      port: 7 Piraeus
  feature: 8 Olympics
  food:
    dish: 4 gyro **7** baklava, mousaka **8** moussaka, souvlaki
    liquor: 4 ouzo

greed 7 avarice, avidity, craving **8** cupidity, rapacity

Greek Mythology
  afterworld of the blessed: 7 Elysium
  drink of the gods: 6 nectar
  enchantress: 5 Circe
  female warrior: 6 Amazon
  goddess of the earth: 2 Ge **4** Gaea, Gaia
  goddess of earth/fertility: 7 Demeter
  goddess of earth/Hades: 6 Hecate, Hekate
  goddess of the hearth: 6 Hestia
  goddesses of literature/the arts: 5 Muses
    muse of history: 4 Clio
    muse of poetry/epic: 8 Calliope
  goddess of love/beauty: 9 Aphrodite
  goddess of wisdom/ fertility/arts/warfare:

6 Athena
**god of fire/metalworking/
handicrafts: 10**
Hephaestus, Hephaistos
god of the heavens: 4
Zeus
god of sea: 8 Poseidon
**god of shepherds/flocks/
pastures/forests: 3** Pan
god of war: 4 Ares
**god of wine/fertility/
drama: 7** Bacchus **8**
Dionysus
messenger of gods: 6
Hermes
**moon goddess/huntress/
virgin: 7** Artemis
one-eyed giant: 7 Cyclops
queen of heaven: 4 Hera,
Here
race of gods: 6 Titans
river in Hades: 4 Styx **5**
Lethe **7** Acheron,
Cocytus
 ferryman: 6 Charon
seven sisters: 8 Pleiades
sorceress: 5 Medea
three-headed dog: 8
Cerberus
underworld: 5 Hades,
green 3 raw **4** jade, lawn,
lime, turf **5** crude, heath,
olive, rough, sward, young
6 callow, campus,
common, tender, unripe

7 awkward, emerald,
verdant, verdure **8**
gullible, ignorant,
immature, unsmoked,
untanned
greenback 4 bill **8**
banknote
greenhorn *see* **6 novice**
Greenland
capital/largest city: 4
Nuuk **8** Godthaab
greet 4 hail, meet **5** admit
6 accept, accost, salute **7**
receive, speak to, welcome
gregarious 6 genial, lively,
social **7** affable **8** friendly,
outgoing, sociable
gremlin 3 imp **5** demon,
gnome **6** goblin
Grenada
other name: 5 (Isle of)
Spice
capital/largest city: 9 St
Georges
island: 8 Windward **9**
Carriacou **10** Grenadines
sea: 9 Caribbean
Greystoke, Lord
real identity of: 6 Tarzan
griddle cake *see* **7 pancake**
grieve 3 cry, rue, sob **4**
moan, pain, wail, weep **5**
be sad, mourn **6** bemoan,

deject, harass, lament, sadden, sorrow **7** afflict, agonize, depress, oppress, torture **8** disquiet, distress

griffin
    also: 7 griffon, gryphon
    form: 7 monster
    head/wings of: 5 eagle
    body of: 4 lion

grill 3 fry **4** cook, grid, pump, quiz, sear **5** broil, query **7** broiler, grating, griddle **8** question

grim 4 foul, hard, ugly **5** cruel, harsh, lurid, stern, sulky **6** brutal, fierce, gloomy, grisly, grumpy, horrid, morose, odious, severe, somber, sullen **7** austere, ghastly, hideous, inhuman, macabre, squalid, vicious **8** dreadful, fiendish, gruesome, horrible, resolute, scowling, shocking, sinister

grimace 4 face **5** scowl, smirk, sneer **6** glower **7** wry face
    French: 4 moue

grime *see* **4 dirt**

grim reaper 5 death

grin 4 beam **5** smile, smirk

grind 4 file, grit, mill, rasp, whet **5** chore, crush, gnash, grate **6** abrade, drudge, polish, powder, scrape **7** crammer, plodder, sharpen, slavery **8** bookworm

grip 3 bag **4** grab, hilt, hold **5** clasp, grasp, rivet, seize **6** clench, clutch, handle, retain, snatch, valise **7** attract, control, impress, mastery, satchel **8** hold fast, suitcase

gripe, gripes 4 beef, carp, fret, kick, pain, pang, rail **5** cavil, colic, spasm, whine **6** cramps, grouch, grouse, kvetch, mutter, squawk **7** grumble, protest, whining **8** complain

grisly 4 foul, gory, grim **5** lurid **6** horrid, odious **7** ghastly, hideous, macabre **8** dreadful, gruesome, horrible, shocking, sinister

grit 3 rub **4** guts, sand **5** gnash, grate, nerve, pluck, spunk **6** crunch, mettle, scrape **7** courage, stamina **8** backbone, tenacity *see also* **4 dirt**

groan 4 howl, moan, roar, wail **5** bleat, crack, creak, whine **6** bellow, bemoan, lament, murmur **7** grumble, whimper **8** complain

groggy 5 dazed, dizzy, dopey, shaky, woozy **6** punchy **7** muddled, reeling, stunned **8** confused, sluggish, unsteady

groom 4 comb, wash **5** boots, brush, curry, dress, drill, preen, prime, primp, train, valet **6** flunky, lackey, spouse **7** clean up, consort, develop, educate, footman, freshen, husband, prepare, refresh, servant **8** initiate, make neat, spruce up

groove 3 cut, rut, use **4** rule **5** flute, habit, score, usage **7** channel, cutting, scoring

grope 3 paw **5** probe **6** finger, fumble **7** fish for, venture

gross 3 bag, big, fat **4** bulk, earn, huge, lewd, mass, rank, reap, vast **5** crude, great, heavy, large, obese, total, utter, whole **6** carnal, coarse, earthy, entire, ribald, smutty, sordid, take in, vulgar **7** glaring, immense, lump sum, massive, obscene, obvious, uncouth **8** colossal, complete, enormous, flagrant, gigantic, improper, indecent, unseemly

grotto 4 cave **6** burrow, cavern, hollow, recess, tunnel **8** catacomb

grouchy 5 cross, testy **6** crabby, cranky, grumpy, touchy **8** snappish **10** ill-humored, out of sorts

ground, grounds 3 set, sod **4** area, base, call, dirt, farm, land, loam, soil, turf, yard **5** acres, basis, beach, cause, dregs, drill, earth, field, lawns, realm **6** campus, domain, estate, motive, reason, secure, settle, sphere **7** deposit, educate, founder, gardens, habitat, prepare, support, terrain **8** district, exercise, initiate, instruct, premises, property, sediment

groundless 4 idle **5** empty, false **6** faulty, flimsy, unreal, untrue **8** baseless, needless, unproved

group 3 set 4 band, clan, file, gang, herd, pack, sift, size, sort 5 align, bunch, class, crowd, flock, grade, hoard, index, party, place, range, swarm, tribe, troop 6 assign, branch, circle, clique, family, league, line up, throng 7 arrange, cluster, combine, company, coterie, faction, section 8 classify, division, graduate, organize

grouse *see* 8 **complain**

grove 4 bosk 5 brake, copse 6 forest, pinery, timber 7 coppice, orchard, thicket

grovel 4 fawn 5 cower, crawl, toady 6 cringe, kowtow 7 truckle

grow 3 bud, sow, wax 4 boom, farm, rise, till 5 bloom, breed, plant, raise, ripen, surge, swell, widen 6 become, expand, extend, flower, garden, mature, spread, sprout, thrive 7 advance, amplify, blossom, develop, enlarge, fill out, improve, produce, prosper, stretch, succeed 8 flourish, fructify, increase, mushroom, progress, vegetate

growl *see* 8 **complain**

grown-up 3 big, man 4 lady 5 adult, woman 6 mature, senior 7 worldly

grub 3 bum, dig 4 food, toil, worm 5 cadge, larva, mooch 6 drudge, sponge 7 rummage

grubby *see* 5 **dirty**

grudge 4 envy 5 pique, spite 6 animus, hatred, malice, rancor, resent 7 dislike, ill will 8 aversion

grueling 4 hard 6 brutal, tiring 7 racking

gruesome 4 gory, grim 5 awful 6 grisly, horrid 7 ghastly, hideous, macabre 8 shocking, terrible

gruff 4 curt, rude, sour, tart 5 bluff, blunt, harsh, husky, raspy, rough, sharp, short, stern, sulky, surly 6 abrupt, croaky, crusty, grumpy, hoarse, ragged, sullen 7 bearish, brusque, caustic, crabbed, cracked, grouchy, peevish, throaty, uncivil 8 churlish, impolite, snarling

grumpy *see* **7 grouchy**

grunt 3 cry **4** bark, call, gasp, howl **5** croak, groan, snort, utter **6** grouch, mumble, murmur, mutter **7** howling

gryphon *see* **7 griffin**

Guam
  capital: 5 Agana
  largest city: 8 Tamuning
  part of: 7 Mariana (islands)
  sea: 7 Pacific
  explorer: 8 Magellan

guarantee, guaranty 4 avow, bail, bond, pawn, word **5** swear **6** affirm, allege, assure, attest, avowal, insure, pledge, surety **7** endorse, promise, sponsor, voucher, warrant **8** contract, covenant, security

guard 4 mind, save, tend **5** watch **6** attend, convoy, defend, escort, patrol, picket, screen, secure, sentry, shield, warder **7** conduct, defense, protect, shelter **8** defender, garrison, guardian, keep safe, preserve, security, sentinel, watchdog

Guatemala
  capital/largest city: 13 Guatemala City
  highest point: 9 Tajamulco
  lake: 6 Izabal
  physical feature:
    gulf: 8 Honduras
  feature:
    bird: 7 quetzal

guess 4 deem, view **5** fancy, judge, opine, think **6** assume, belief, deduce, gather, reckon, regard, theory **7** believe, imagine, opinion, predict, suppose, surmise, suspect, venture **8** conclude, estimate, theorize

guest 5 diner **6** caller, client, friend, inmate, lodger, patron, roomer **7** boarder, company, visitor **8** customer

guide 4 lead, rule **5** model, pilot, steer, usher **6** beacon, convoy, direct, escort, govern, handle, leader, manage, marker, master, mentor **7** adviser, command, conduct, control, example, marshal, monitor, oversee, pattern, steerer, teacher **8** chaperon, director, maneuver, regulate, shepherd

guild 5 hansa, hanse, order, union **6** league **7** company, society

guile 5 craft, fraud **6** deceit, tricks **7** cunning, slyness **8** artifice, trickery, wiliness

guilty 5 sorry, wrong **6** erring, sinful **7** ashamed, corrupt **8** criminal, culpable, penitent, sheepish

Guinea
   capital/largest city: 7 Conakry
   river: 5 Niger **6** Gambia **7** Senegal

Guinea-Bissau
   capital/largest city: 6 Bissau

Guinevere
   husband: 6 Arthur
   lover: 8 Lancelot

guise 4 garb, mode **5** dress, habit **6** attire **7** apparel, clothes, costume, fashion **8** clothing, pretense

gulch 3 gap **4** rift **5** abyss, chasm, cleft, crack, gorge,

gully, split **6** arroyo, breach, divide, ravine

gulf 4 cove, rent, rift **5** abyss, chasm, cleft, firth, fjord, inlet **6** canyon, lagoon **7** estuary, opening

gull 3 gyp **4** dupe, rook **5** cozen, trick **7** deceive, defraud, sea bird, swindle

gullet 3 maw **4** craw, crop **5** belly, gorge, tummy **6** dewlap, throat **7** abdomen, stomach

gullible 5 green, naive **6** simple **8** innocent, trustful, trusting

Gulliver's Travels
   author: 5 (Jonathan) Swift

gully 3 gap **5** ditch, gorge, gulch **6** defile, furrow, gutter, ravine, trench

gulp 4 bolt, swig **5** quaff, swill **6** devour, guzzle **7** swallow **8** mouthful

gummy 5 gluey, gooey, gunky **6** gloppy, sticky, viscid **7** rubbery, viscous **8** adhesive

gumption 3 zip **4** dash, push **5** drive, spunk, verve **6** energy, hustle, pizazz, spirit **7** courage

gumshoe 4 dick **6** shamus

gun 3 aim, gat, rod, try **4** Colt, hunt, iron **5** piece, rifle, shoot **6** cannon, mortar, musket, pistol **7** attempt, carbine, firearm, go after, shotgun **8** howitzer, revolver

gunman 6 bandit, outlaw, robber, sniper **7** hoodlum

Gunsmoke
  cast: 5 (Amanda) Blake, (Milburn) Stone **6** (James) Arness, (Dennis) Weaver
  setting: 5 Dodge (City)

gurgle 5 plash **6** babble, bubble, burble, murmur

guru 5 guide **6** leader, master **7** teacher

gush 3 gab, gas, jet, run **4** blab, bull, rush, well **5** issue, prate, spout, spurt **6** babble, burble, drivel, hot air, splash, squirt, stream **7** baloney, blabber, chatter, pour out, torrent, twaddle **8** outburst, rattle on

gussy up 5 adorn **7** dress up, enhance **8** beautify, decorate, ornament

gust 3 fit **4** blow, puff, wind **5** blast, burst, draft **6** breeze, flurry, squall, zephyr

gusto 3 joy **4** zeal, zest **5** savor **6** fervor, relish **7** delight **8** pleasure

gut 4 raze **5** belly, clean, level, tummy **6** bowels, paunch, ravage **7** abdomen, stomach, viscera

guts *see* **7 courage**

guttural 3 low **4** deep **5** gruff, harsh, husky, raspy, thick **6** hoarse **7** throaty **8** croaking

guy 3 boy, joe, kid, man **4** body, chap, dude, gent, rope **5** bloke, human, joker **6** fellow, hombre, person

Guyana
  formerly: 6 (British) Guiana
  capital/largest city: 10 Georgetown

Guys and Dolls
  based on story by: 6 (Damon) Runyon
  cast: 4 (Stubby) Kaye **6** (Vivian) Blaine, (Marlon) Brando **7** (Jean) Simmons, (Frank) Sinatra

guzzle 4 bolt, gulp, swig

5 quaff, swill **6** devour, imbibe, tipple

gymnasium 5 arena **6** circus **7** stadium

gyp *see* **4 hoax**

gyrate 5 swirl, twirl, wheel, whirl **6** circle, rotate, spiral **7** revolve

habiliments *see* **7 clothes**

habit 3 rut, way **4** garb, gear, robe, rule, wont **5** dress, trait, usage **6** attire, custom, groove, livery, manner, outfit **7** apparel, clothes, costume, garment, leaning, raiment, routine, uniform, vesture **8** clothing, nun's wear, practice

habitat 3 pad **4** digs, home, spot, zone **5** abode, haunt, place, range, realm, roost **6** domain, locale, milieu, region **7** housing, lodging, setting, terrain **8** domicile, dwelling

hack 3 cab, cut, hew, nag **4** bark, chip, chop, gash, plug, rasp, slit, taxi **5** cut up, slash, slice, whack **6** cleave, mangle **7** taxicab **8** mutilate

hackle 3 peg **4** card, comb, hack, hook, ruff **5** curry, plume **7** bristle, feather

hackneyed *see* **8 ordinary**

Hadassah 6 Esther

Hades 4 hell
   god of: 5 Orcus, Pluto
   goddess of: 6 Hecate

hag 3 bat, nag **4** drab, fury **5** biddy, crone, frump, harpy, shrew, vixen, witch **6** gorgon, ogress, virago **8** battle-ax, harridan

Hagar
   servant of: 5 Sarah
   husband: 7 Abraham
   son: 7 Ishmael

haggard *see* **5 tired**

haggle 6 barter, bicker, dicker **7** bargain, dispute, quarrel, quibble, wrangle

hail 3 ave **4** call **5** cheer, exalt, extol, greet, hello, honor, shout **6** accost, call to, esteem, salute **7** acclaim, address, applaud, commend, glorify, receive, shout at, usher in, welcome **8** cry out to, eulogize, greeting

Hail Mary
  Latin: 8 Ave Maria

hair 3 fur, mop **4** coat, down, iota, mane, pelt, wool **5** bangs, curls, locks **6** fleece **7** tresses
  loss: 8 alopecia, baldness

haircut, hairdo 3 bob, bun, cut **4** Afro, clip, crop, fade, perm, shag, trim, updo **5** bangs, braid, butch, swirl **6** boogie, mohawk **7** beehive, buzzcut, chignon, cornrow, crewcut, flattop, natural, page boy, pigtail, tonsure, upsweep **8** bouffant, coiffure, ducktail, ponytail

hair-raising 5 eerie **7** bristle **8** exciting

hairsplitting 4 fine **6** minute, subtle **7** carping **8** caviling, delicate, niggling

hairy 5 bushy, furry, wooly **6** fleecy, shaggy **7** hirsute

Haiti
  capital/largest city: 12 Port-au-Prince
  sea: 8 Atlantic **9** Caribbean
  island: 6 Gonave **7** Tortuga

feature:
  belief: 6 voodoo

halcyon see **4 calm**

hale 3 fit **4** well **5** hardy, sound **6** hearty, robust, rugged, sturdy **7** healthy, in shape **8** vigorous

Hale-Bopp 5 comet

half 4 part, some **6** all but, barely, fairly, feebly, in part, meager, partly, rather, weakly **7** divided, limited, partial, portion **8** middling, moderate, passably

half-hearted 4 cold, cool, tame **5** blase, faint **7** languid, passive **8** listless, lukewarm

half-wit 4 dolt, dope, fool **5** dummy, dunce, idiot, moron, ninny **6** dimwit, nitwit **7** dullard **8** imbecile, numskull

hall 5 entry, foyer, lobby **6** arcade **7** chamber, gallery **8** anteroom, corridor, entrance

hallmark 4 sign **5** badge, stamp **6** device, emblem, symbol

hallow 5 bless **7** respect **8** dedicate, sanctify, venerate

hallucination 5 dream **6** mirage, vision **7** fantasy **8** delusion, illusion

halo 6 aurora, corona, luster, nimbus **7** aureole, dignity, majesty **8** grandeur, radiance, sanctity, splendor

halt 3 end **4** balk, curb, foil, quit, rest, stay, stem, stop, wait, whoa **5** abate, block, brake, break, cease, check, close, crush, delay, pause, quash, quell **6** defeat, draw up, hamper, hinder, impede, linger, pull up, rein in, scotch, subdue, thwart **7** inhibit, prevent, put down, squelch, suspend, time out **8** break off, breather, choke off, knock off, overturn, prohibit, restrain, restrict, shut down, suppress

hamlet 4 burg **7** village **8** hick town, tank town

Hamlet
  author: 11 (William) Shakespeare
  character: 7 Horatio, Laertes, Ophelia **8** Claudius, Gertrude, Polonius

  castle: 8 Elsinore
  setting: 7 Denmark

hammer 3 hit, tap **4** bang, form, make, nail **5** drive, forge, knock, pound, punch, shape, whack **6** pummel, strike **7** fashion
  type: 4 claw, jack, tack **5** gavel, steam **6** mallet, sledge **8** ballpeen

hamper 3 gag **4** balk, curb, stem **5** block, check, stall **6** fetter, hinder, hog-tie, hold up, impede, retard, thwart **7** inhibit, prevent **8** encumber, handicap, obstruct

hamstring 6 impair, muscle, tendon **7** cripple, disable **8** handicap

hand, hands 3 man, paw **4** care, give, help, hold, lift, mitt, pass **5** guide, power, reach **6** assist, convey, helper, script, worker **7** command, control, custody, deliver, keeping, laborer, ovation, present, support, workman **8** employee, guidance, handyman, hired man, meat-hook

handbag 3 bag **4** grip

5 purse **6** clutch, valise **7** satchel **8** reticule

handcuffs 5 cuffs, irons **6** chains **7** fetters **8** manacles, shackles

hand down 4 will **5** leave **6** hand on, pass on **8** bequeath

handgun 3 rod **5** piece **6** pistol, weapon **7** firearm **8** revolver

handicap 4 curb **5** limit **6** burden, defect, hamper, hinder, impede, retard, thwart **7** barrier, inhibit **8** drawback, encumber, hold back, obstacle, restrain, restrict

handle 3 paw, ply, run, tag, use **4** feel, grip, hilt, hold, knob, name, poke, pull, sell, work **5** carry, grasp, guide, knead, pilot, pinch, shaft, shank, steer, swing, touch, treat **6** caress, deal in, fondle, manage, pick up, stroke **7** care for, command, conduct, control, moniker, operate, paw over, trade in, utilize **8** cognomen, deal with

handout 4 alms, dole **7** freebie

hand over 4 cede **5** grant, yield **6** give up, tender **7** release **8** transfer

handsome 4 fair **5** bonny, noble **6** benign, comely, lovely, pretty **7** elegant, sightly, sizable **8** abundant, generous, gracious, imposing, princely, splendid, stunning, tasteful

handy 4 deft, near **5** adept **6** adroit, clever, expert, useful **7** capable, helpful, skilled **8** skillful

hang 3 bow, sag **4** drop, gist, rest **5** affix, droop, hinge, knack, lie in, lower, lynch, point **6** append, attach, dangle, depend **7** incline, meaning, suspend, thought **8** lean over, string up

hangdog 6 abject **7** ashamed **8** defeated, degraded, hopeless, resigned, wretched

hanger-on 7 admirer, groupie **8** follower

hang out 4 live **5** dwell **6** hobnob, loiter, mingle, reside **7** consort

hankering *see* **6 desire**

Hanoi
  capital of: 7 Vietnam

haphazard 6 casual, chance, fitful, random **7** aimless, chaotic **8** careless, slapdash, sporadic

hapless 6 cursed, jinxed, no-good, rotten, woeful **7** forlorn, unhappy, unlucky **8** accursed, hopeless, ill-fated, luckless, wretched

happen 5 arise, ensue, occur **6** appear, befall, betide, crop up, result **7** turn out **8** become of, spring up

happenstance 4 luck **6** chance **8** accident, fortuity

happy 4 glad, meet **5** lucky **6** elated, joyful, joyous, timely **7** content, fitting, gleeful, pleased, tickled **8** blissful, cheerful, ecstatic, exultant, jubilant, pleasant

harangue 5 scold **6** speech, tirade **7** lecture **8** diatribe

harass 3 cow, irk, vex **4** bait, ride **5** annoy, beset, bully, harry, hound, tease, worry **6** attack, badger, bother, heckle, hector, pester, plague **7** assault, torment **8** browbeat, distress, irritate

harbinger 4 clue, omen **5** token **6** herald, symbol **7** portent **8** signaler

harbor 3 bay **4** cove, dock, feel, goal, hide, hold, keep, pier, port, quay **5** basin, haven, house, inlet, lodge, wharf **6** asylum, billet, refuge, retain, shield, take in **7** care for, conceal, nurture, protect, retreat, shelter **8** keep safe, maintain, terminus

hard 3 sad **4** cold, firm, mean, ugly **5** cruel, eager, harsh, heavy, rigid, rough, solid, stern, stiff, stony, tight, tough **6** bitter, brutal, fierce, firmly, severe, steely, strict, strong, thorny, unkind **7** arduous, callous, complex, earnest, harmful, heavily, hostile, hurtful, inhuman, intense, onerous, solidly **8** critical, diligent, exacting, forceful, intently, pitiless, powerful, rocklike, ruthless, severely, spirited, steadily, strongly, stubborn, untiring

harden 3 dry, gel, set **4** cake, fire, firm **5** inure **6** freeze, temper **7** calcify, callous, fortify, petrify, stiffen, toughen **8** solidify

hard feelings 5 anger **6** grudge, hatred, rancor **7** ill will **8** acrimony

hardhearted 4 cold, hard, mean **5** cruel, stony **7** callous **8** pitiless, ruthless, uncaring

Harding, Warren Gamaliel
presidential rank: 11 twenty-ninth
party: 10 Republican
state represented: 2 OH
vice president: 8 (Calvin) Coolidge
born: 2 OH **7** Corsica
notable events of lifetime/ term:
   scandal: 10 Teapot Dome
wife: 8 Florence
mistress: 3 Nan (Britton)

hardly 4 just, only **6** barely, rarely **7** faintly **8** not often, not quite, scarcely

hardship 3 woe **4** load **5** agony, grief **6** burden, misery, ordeal **7** travail, trouble **8** handicap

hard times 4 bust **5** slump

hard to grasp 6 arcane **7** complex, elusive

8 abstruse, baffling, puzzling, slippery

hard to please 5 fussy, picky **7** exigent, finicky **8** critical

hardworking 8 diligent, sedulous

hardy 3 fit **4** hale **5** tough **6** hearty, mighty, robust, rugged, strong, sturdy **7** healthy **8** vigorous

Hardy, Oliver
partner: 6 (Stan) Laurel

harebrained 5 silly, wacko, wacky **7** asinine, flighty, foolish **8** skittish

harem 5 serai, wives **6** purdah, serail **8** love nest, seraglio
guard: 6 eunuch

harlot *see* **5 whore**

harm 3 ill, mar, sin **4** evil, hurt, maim, pain, ruin, vice **5** abuse, agony, havoc, spoil, wound, wrong **6** damage, deface, impair, injure, misuse, trauma **7** blemish, cripple, degrade, scourge **8** aggrieve, calamity, iniquity, maltreat, villainy

harmony *see* **5 peace**

harness 4 curb, rein, tugs,

yoke **5** lines, reins, rig up
6 bridle, collar, employ,
halter, muzzle, straps,
tackle, traces **7** exploit,
hitch up, utilize **8** restrain

harp on 7 dwell on

Harpy
form: **7** monster
head of: **5** woman
body of: **4** bird

harridan 3 hag **5** crone,
shrew, witch **6** virago **8**
battle-ax

harried 5 upset **7** worried **8**
harassed, troubled

Harrison, Benjamin
nickname: **3** Ben **9** Little
Ben
presidential rank: **11**
twenty-third
party: **10** Republican
state represented: **2** IN
vice president: **6** Morton
born: **2** OH **9** North Bend
notable events of lifetime/
term:
tariff: **8** McKinley

Harrison, William Henry
nickname: **6** Old Tip
presidential rank: **5** ninth
party: **4** Whig
state represented: **2** OH
vice president: **5** Tyler
born: **2** VA

political career:
territorial governor of: **7**
Indiana
military service: **3** War
(of 1812)
battle: **10** Tippecanoe

harrowing 7 fearful, painful
8 alarming, chilling

harry 3 irk, vex **4** bait, raid,
ride **5** annoy, haunt,
hound, worry **6** badger,
bother, harass, heckle,
hector, pester **7** disturb,
torment, trouble **8**
distress, irritate

Harry Potter (Series)
author: **7** (J K) Rowling
evil wizard: **9** Voldemort
non-magical people: **7**
Muggles
school: **8** Hogwarts

harsh 4 hard, mean **5** cruel,
raspy, rough, sharp, stern
6 bitter, brutal, hoarse,
severe, shrill, unkind **7**
abusive, caustic, grating,
jarring, rasping **8** pitiless,
ruthless, strident, ungentle

harum-scarum 5 giddy **6**
wildly **7** erratic, foolish **8**
careless, confused

harvest 3 cut, mow **4** crop,
gain, pick, reap **5** amass,
fruit, pluck, yield

6 gather, haying, mowing, output, result, return, reward **7** benefit, collect, produce, reaping **8** proceeds

hash out 6 review **7** discuss **8** consider, talk over

hasp 4 lock **5** catch, clasp, latch **7** closure **8** fastener

hassle *see* **3 vex**

hassock 4 boss, seat, tuft, weed **5** bunch, chair, group **6** plants, tuffet **7** ottoman, tussock

hasten 3 fly, run **4** bolt, dart, dash, flit, jump, race, rush **5** egg on, hurry, impel, speed, whisk **6** hustle, incite, scurry, sprint, urge on **7** advance, drive on, hurry on, hurry up, promote, quicken, scamper, scuttle, speed up **8** expedite, make time

hatch 4 plan, plot **5** frame **6** cook up, create, design, devise, evolve, invent, make up **7** concoct, dream up, fashion, produce, think up **8** conceive, contrive

hate 5 abhor, dread, venom **6** animus, detest, enmity, hatred, loathe, malice, rancor **7** be sorry, despise, dislike **8** acrimony, aversion, loathing

haughty 5 aloof **6** lordly, snooty, uppish, uppity **7** high-hat, stuck-up **8** arrogant, scornful, snobbish

haul 3 bag, lug, tow, tug **4** cart, drag, draw, gain, jerk, move, pull, swag, take, tote, yank **5** booty, bring, carry, catch, fetch, yield **6** convey, remove, reward, spoils

haunches 4 buns, rear, rump, seat **5** nates **7** rear end **8** buttocks

haunt 3 vex **5** beset, worry **6** obsess, plague, prey on **7** disturb, terrify, torment, trouble **8** distress, frequent

haunts 3 den **4** cave, hole, lair, nest **6** burrow **7** hangout **8** hideaway

Havana
capital of: 4 Cuba

have 3 buy, eat, get, own, use **4** gain, hold, host, keep, make, must **5** carry, enjoy, force, grasp, ought **6** accept, affirm, compel, harbor, obtain, permit, retain, suffer **7** achieve, acquire, defraud, possess, realize, receive **8** comprise, maintain, manifest, perceive

have faith in 5 trust **6** rely on

haven 4 port **5** cover **6** asylum, harbor, refuge **7** hideout, retreat, shelter

havoc 4 ruin **5** chaos **8** calamity, disaster, disorder, upheaval

Hawaii
abbreviation: **2** HI
nickname: **5** Aloha
capital/largest city: **8** Honolulu
mountain: **8** Mauna Loa
highest point: **8** Maunakea
sea: **7** Pacific
island: **4** Maui, Oahu **5** Kauai, Lanai **6** Hawaii **7** Molokai
physical feature:
beach: **7** Waikiki
harbor: **5** Pearl
promontory: **11** Diamond Head
volcano: **7** Kilauea **8** Mauna Kea, Mauna Loa **9** Haleakala

feature:
dance: **4** hula
feast/festivity: **4** luau
gift: **3** lei
greeting: **5** aloha
musical instrument: **3** uke **7** ukelele, ukulele
native woman: **6** wahine

Hawaii
author: **8** (James) Michener

hawk 4 bird, sell, vend **6** falcon, peddle **8** militant
young: **4** eyas
group of: **4** cast

Hawkeye State
nickname of: **4** Iowa

hawser 4 line, rope **5** cable **7** mooring

Hayes, Rutherford Birchard
nickname: **3** Rud
presidential rank: **10** nineteenth
party: **10** Republican
vice president: **7** Wheeler
born: **2** OH **8** Delaware
political career:
governor of: **4** Ohio
wife: **4** Lucy

hayseed 4 hick, rube **5** yokel **6** rustic **7** bumpkin

hazard 3 bet **4** dare, luck, risk **5** fluke, guess, offer, peril, stake, wager

6 chance, danger, expose, gamble, menace, mishap, submit, threat **7** imperil, pitfall, suppose, venture **8** accident, jeopardy, theorize

hazel 3 nut **4** tree **5** brown, shrub, tawny **8** brownish

hazy *see* **5 fuzzy**

head 3 aim, CEO, end, tip, top **4** acme, apex, boss, czar, font, fore, gift, king, lead, main, mind, peak, rise, rule, tsar, turn, well **5** begin, brain, chief, crest, crown, first, front, guide, pilot, prime, queen, ruler, steer **6** climax, crisis, direct, genius, honcho, launch, leader, manage, origin, ruling, source, spring, summit, talent, zenith **7** ability, admiral, captain, command, conduct, control, general, go first, highest, leading, make for, manager, marshal, monarch, precede, premier, primary, proceed, supreme, topmost **8** aptitude, big wheel, capacity, chairman, dictator, director, dominant, foremost,

fruition, initiate, judgment, pinnacle, start off, superior, suzerain

headache 5 trial **6** strain, stress **7** problem, trouble **8** migraine, nuisance

headgear 3 cap, fez, hat, tam **4** hood, kepi, topi **5** beret, busby, crown, derby, miter, shako, snood, terai, tiari, topee, toque **6** beanie, boater, bonnet, bowler, cloche, fedora, helmet, panama, trilby, turban **7** bicorne, biretta, chapeau, hardhat, homberg, pillbox, porkpie, stetson, **8** babushka, mantilla, skullcap, sombrero, tarboosh, tricorne, yarmulke

headlong 6 abrupt **8** abruptly, heedless, pell-mell, reckless

headstrong *see* **8 stubborn**

heal 4 cure, knit, mend **5** right, salve, treat **6** remedy, settle, soothe **7** compose, get well, improve, recover, relieve

health 5 vigor **7** fitness, stamina **8** strength, vitality

heap 4 fill, gobs, hunk,

load, lots, lump, mass, mess, pack, pile, slew **5** amass, award, batch, bunch, flood, group, mound, ocean, stack **6** accord, assign, bundle, deluge, gather, jumble, oceans, oodles, plenty **7** barrels, cluster **8** inundate, pour upon

hear 4 heed **5** admit, favor, grant, judge, learn **6** attend, be told, gather, look on **7** approve, concede, examine, find out, receive, witness **8** accede to, discover, listen to

hearing 5 probe, sound **6** review **7** council, earshot, inquiry **8** audience

hearken to 4 heed, mark, mind **6** attend **8** listen to

hearsay 4 talk **5** rumor **6** gossip, report **8** idle talk

heart 3 hub, nub **4** base, core, crux, guts, meat, mood, pith, root, soul **5** pluck, spunk, valor **6** center, kernel, middle, nature, source, spirit **7** bravery, charity, courage, essence, nucleus **8** backbone, boldness,

feelings, fondness, gameness, interior, main part, sympathy
part: 5 aorta, valve **6** atrium **7** chamber **9** ventricle

heartbreaker 4 vamp **5** flirt, tease **8** coquette

hearten see **7 comfort**

hearth 4 home **5** abode, house **8** fireside

hearty 4 hale, warm, well **5** ample, hardy, sound **6** lively, robust, strong **7** cordial, genuine, healthy, profuse, sincere, zestful **8** effusive, vigorous

heat 3 fry **4** bake, boil, cook, sear, stew, warm, zeal **5** ardor, broil, roast, steam **6** braise, climax, fervor, height, simmer, stress, thrill, warmth, warm up **7** passion, rapture, swelter **8** fervency, warmness

heathen 5 pagan **6** savage **7** atheist, gentile, infidel **8** agnostic, idolator

heat up 3 fan, zap **4** goad, nuke, warm, whet **6** arouse **7** enhance, sharpen **8** increase

heave 3 peg, pry, sob **4** arch, blow, cast, emit, fire, haul, hurl, lift, moan, pant, puff, pull, toss, yank **5** boost, bulge, chuck, eject, fling, groan, hoist, lever, pitch, raise, retch, sling, surge, swell, throw, vomit **6** dilate, drag up, exhale, expand, launch, let fly, propel **7** elevate

heaven, Heaven, the Heavens 4 Zion **5** bliss, glory, mercy, space **6** my oh my, utopia **7** delight, ecstasy, Elysium, nirvana, Olympus, rapture **8** boy oh boy, goodness, paradise, Valhalla
   god of: 4 Jove, Zeus **7** Jupiter

heavy 3 big, fat, sad **4** full, slow **5** broad, bulky, dense, grave, gross, harsh, hefty, large, obese, plump, stout, thick **6** clumsy, deadly, dreary, gloomy, leaden, pained, portly, solemn, strong, sturdy, woeful **7** complex, copious, intense, joyless, lumpish, massive, notable, onerous, serious, tedious, weighty **8** abundant, burdened, crushing, damaging, dejected, forceful, imposing, mournful, profound, sluggish, unwieldy

Hebe
   goddess of: 5 youth **6** spring
   father: 4 Zeus
   mother: 4 Hera
   husband: 8 Hercules

heckle 4 bait, hiss, hoot, mock, razz, ride **5** annoy, bully, chivy, harry, hound, taunt **6** badger, harass, hector, jeer at, needle **7** provoke

hectic 3 mad **4** wild **6** stormy **7** chaotic, frantic, furious **8** feverish, frenetic, frenzied

hector *see* **6 heckle**

Hector
   father: 5 Priam
   mother: 6 Hecuba
   brother: 5 Paris
   sister: 9 Cassandra
   hero of: 9 Trojan War
   killed by: 8 Achilles

Hecuba
   father: 5 Atlas
   husband: 5 Priam
   son: 5 Paris **6** Hector
   changed into: 3 dog

hedge *see* **5 dodge**

hedonistic 7 sensual

heed 4 care, mind, obey **5** bow to, pains, study **6** concur, follow, hold to, notice, regard **7** defer to, observe, respect, yield to **8** accede to, consider, listen to, prudence, submit to

heel 3 cad, cur, end, rat **4** list, rind, tilt **5** churl, crust, louse **6** rotter **7** bounder, caitiff, dastard

hefty 3 big **5** beefy, bulky, burly, heavy, husky, large, stout **6** brawny, hearty, mighty, robust, rugged, strong, sturdy **7** hulking, massive, weighty **8** muscular, powerful, stalwart, thickset

hegira 6 exodus, flight **7** journey

height 4 acme, apex, hill, peak, rise **5** bluff, cliff, crest, knoll, limit, mound, tower **6** apogee, heyday, summit, zenith **7** hilltop, maximum **8** altitude, eminence, highland, mountain, palisade, pinnacle

heinous *see* **8 dreadful**

Helen
    father: 4 Zeus
    mother: 4 Leda
    brother: 6 Castor, Pollux
    husband: 8 Menelaus
    abducted by: 5 Paris
    abduction caused: 9 Trojan War

helicopter 8 autogyro **9** eggbeater

hell, Hell 5 agony, grief, Hades **6** misery **7** anguish, despair, inferno, remorse, torment

hellion 5 devil, rogue, scamp

hellish 4 foul, vile **5** awful **6** brutal **7** hateful **8** accursed, damnable, dreadful, horrible, infernal

hello
    French: 7 bonjour
    German: 8 guten tag
    Hebrew: 6 shalom
    Italian: 4 ciao
    Latin: 3 ave

help 3 aid **4** back, calm, care, cure, ease, gift, save **5** allay, emend, force, guide, hands, salve, serve, staff **6** advice, assist, give to, relief, remedy, rescue, soothe, succor **7** advance, backing, correct, endorse, further, improve, nurture, promote, rectify, relieve, support, welfare **8** advocate, befriend, champion, guidance, maintain, mitigate, retrieve, side with

helplessness 8 weakness

Helsinki
  capital of: 7 Finland

hem 3 box, rim **4** bind, brim, edge, welt **5** bound, brink, skirt, verge **6** border, edging, fringe, impede, margin, turn up **7** confine, enclose, stammer, stutter **8** encircle, restrain, surround

hen
  young: 6 pullet **7** lobster

henchman 4 goon, thug **6** flunky, lackey, minion, stooge **7** gorilla **8** hireling, retainer

henna 3 dye **5** rinse **6** auburn, russet **8** cinnamon

henpecked 4 meek **5** timid **6** docile **8** obedient

Hephaestus
  father: 4 Zeus
  mother: 4 Hera
  god of: 4 fire

  vocation: 5 smith
  wife: 9 Aphrodite

Hera
  origin: 5 Greek
  queen of: 6 Heaven
  father: 6 Cronus
  mother: 4 Rhea
  brother/husband: 4 Zeus

Heracles *see* **8 Hercules**

herald 4 clue, omen, sign **5** crier, envoy, token, usher **6** augury, inform, report, reveal, symbol **7** courier, divulge, portent, usher in, warning **8** announce, forecast, foretell, proclaim

heraldic emblem 4 arms, coat (of arms) **5** crest **8** blazonry, insignia

heraldry
  band: 3 bar **4** bend, fess, orle
  black: 5 sable
  blue: 5 azure
  colors: 8 tincture
  divided diagonally: 7 per bend
  divided vertically and horizontally: 9 quartered
  gold/yellow: 2 or
  green: 4 vert
  horizontal band: 4 fess
  left part: 8 sinister

main figure: 6 charge **8** ordinary

red: 5 gules

right part: 6 dexter

surface/background: 5 field

vertical band: 4 pale

white/silver: 6 argent

herb 4 drug **5** plant, spice **6** annual, physic **7** herbage, perfume **8** aromatic, biennial, medicine

herculean, Herculean *see* **6** strong

Hercules

also: 8 Heracles, Herakles

father: 4 Zeus

mother: 7 Alcmene

wife: 4 Hebe **6** Megara **8** Deianira

teacher: 6 Chiron

performed: 6 labors

number of labors: 6 twelve

herd 3 lot, mob **4** army, band, body, gang, goad, host, lead, mass, pack, spur **5** array, bunch, crowd, drive, drove, flock, force, group, guide, horde, party, press, rally, swarm, tribe, troop **6** gather, huddle, legion, muster, number, throng **7** company, round up **8** assemble

herdsman 6 cowboy, driver, drover **8** shepherd

hereafter 5 limbo **6** heaven **8** paradise

hereditary 6 inborn, inbred **7** genetic

heretic 7 skeptic **8** apostate, recreant, recusant, renegade

heritage 6 estate, legacy **7** portion

Hermes

origin: 5 Greek

messenger of: 4 gods

father: 4 Zeus

invented: 4 lyre

sandals had: 5 wings

hermetic 6 mystic, occult **7** obscure **8** abstruse, airtight, esoteric, mystical

hermit 7 recluse **8** cenobite, monastic, solitary

hermitage 5 abbey **6** friary, priory **7** convent, retreat **8** cloister

hero, heroine 4 idol, star **7** gallant **8** champion

Hero

priestess of: 9 Aphrodite

lover: 7 Leander

death by: 7 suicide **8** drowning

hesitate 4 balk, halt **5** delay, pause, shy at, waver **6** falter **7** scruple, stick at **8** be unsure, hang back

Hestia
origin: 5 Greek
goddess of the: 6 hearth
father: 6 Cronos
mother: 4 Rhea

heterogeneous 5 mixed **6** motley, unlike, varied **7** diverse, jumbled **8** assorted

hew 2 ax **3** cut, lop **4** chop, form, hack, mold **5** carve, model, prune, sever, shape **6** chisel, devise

hex 4 harm, jinx, sign **5** curse, spell, witch **6** hoodoo, voodoo, whammy **7** bewitch, enchant, evil eye, ill wind, possess

heyday 4 acme **5** bloom, crest, flush, prime, vigor **6** zenith

hiatus 3 gap **4** void **5** blank, break, lapse, space **6** lacuna, vacuum **7** interim **8** interval

hibernate 5 sleep **6** retire

hick 4 boor, rube **5** yokel **6** rustic **7** hayseed

hide 4 mask, pelt, skin, veil **5** cache, cloak, cloud, cover **6** lie low, screen, shroud **7** conceal, curtain, leather, obscure, seclude, secrete **8** disguise

hideous 4 grim, ugly, vile **5** awful **6** horrid, odious **7** ghastly, macabre **8** dreadful, gruesome, horrible, shocking

high 3 gay, top **4** main, tall **5** aloft, chief, far up, grand, great, jolly, lofty, noble, prime, sharp **6** august, elated, jovial, shrill **7** capital, eminent, exalted, excited, extreme, leading, notable, soaring **8** elevated, exultant, foremost, imposing, jubilant, mirthful, piercing, superior, towering

highbred 5 noble, regal **6** lordly **7** refined **8** wellborn

highbrow 4 snob **5** brain **7** bookish, egghead, elitist, scholar **8** cultured, mandarin

high-hat 5 aloof **6** formal, la-di-da, snooty **7** haughty **8** snobbish

highjinks, hijinks 6 antics, capers, pranks, stunts

highland, Highlands 4 rise **7** heights, plateau, uplands **8** headland
refers especially to: 8 Scotland

highlight 4 peak **6** accent, climax, stress **7** feature, point up

high-minded 4 fair, just **5** lofty, moral, noble **6** honest, worthy **7** ethical, sincere, upright **8** virtuous

High Noon
director: 9 (Fred) Zinnemann
cast: 5 (Grace) Kelly **6** (Gary) Cooper **7** (Lloyd) Bridges **8** (Thomas) Mitchell

high point *see* **6 height**

high society 5 elite **6** jet set **9** haut monde, top drawer
French: 9 haut monde

high-strung 4 edgy **5** jumpy, moody, tense **6** uneasy **7** jittery, nervous, uptight **8** neurotic, restless, skittish

highway 7 freeway, parkway, thruway **8** speedway, turnpike

highwayman 5 crook, thief **6** bandit, outlaw, robber **7** brigand, footpad

hike 4 rise, roam, trek, walk **5** march, tramp **6** draw up, hoof it, ramble, trudge, wander **7** hitch up, raise up **8** addition, increase

hilarious 3 gay **5** jolly, merry, noisy **6** jocund, jovial, joyful, joyous, lively **7** comical, gleeful, riotous **8** mirthful

hill *see* **6 height**

Himalayas 9 mountains
peak: 7 Everest **9** Annapurna
native: 6 sherpa
legendary creature: 4 yeti

hinder 3 bar **4** curb, foil, stay, stop **5** block, check, delay, deter, stall **6** detain, fetter, hamper, hobble, hold up, impede, retard, stifle, stymie, thwart **7** inhibit **8** hold back, obstruct, restrain

hindquarters *see* **8 backside**

hinge 4 hang, rest, turn **5** pivot, swing **6** depend

hint 3 bit, jot, tip **4** clue, idea, iota **5** imply, pinch, tinge, touch, trace, whiff **6** notion **7** inkling, pointer, signify, suggest, whisper **8** allusion, indicate, intimate

hinterland 6 sticks **7** boonies, country **8** interior

hippodrome 5 arena **6** circus **7** stadium **8** coliseum

Hippolyte
   also: 7 Antiope **9** Hippolyta
   queen of: 7 Amazons
   husband: 7 Theseus

hire 3 fee, get, let, pay **4** cost, gain, rent **6** charge, employ, engage, retain, reward, salary, secure **7** charter, procure **8** earnings, receipts

hireling 4 goon, thug **6** flunky, lackey, menial, minion, stooge **7** gorilla **8** henchman, retainer

hirsute 5 bushy, downy, hairy, nappy, wooly **6** shaggy, woolly **7** bearded, bristly, prickly, unshorn

hiss 3 boo **4** mock, razz **6** deride, heckle, hoot at, jeer at, revile **7** catcall, scoff at, sneer at

histology
   study of: 6 tissue

historical period 3 age, era **4** date, time **5** epoch, stage

history 4 epic, saga, tale **5** story **6** annals, change, growth, record, resume, review **7** account, the past **8** old times

histrionics 4 fuss **6** acting, tirade **7** bluster, bombast **8** outburst

hit 3 bat, jab, lob, rap, tap **4** bang, bash, beat, belt, blow, boon, bump, butt, clip, club, coup, cuff, damn, drub, find, flog, hurt, move, pelt, poke, slam, slap, slug, sock, stir, swat **5** abash, baste, clout, crack, crush, flail, knock, paste, pound, punch, reach, rouse, smack, smash, smite, thump, whack **6** assail, attack, attain, batter, cudgel, effect, incite, revile, strike, thrash, thwack, wallop **7** achieve, assault, clobber, execute, shatter, success, triumph **8** bang into, blessing, lambaste

hitch 3 tie, tug **4** curb, draw, halt, haul, hike, jerk, knot, loop, pull, snag, stop, yank, yoke **5** catch, check, clamp, delay, raise, tying **6** attach, couple, fasten, mishap, secure, tether **7** bracket, connect, mistake, problem, trouble **8** make fast, obstacle

hither 2 on **4** here, near **5** close **6** nearer, onward **7** close by, forward

hit man 6 killer, slayer **8** assassin, hired gun, murderer

hit-or-miss 6 casual **7** aimless, cursory **8** slapdash

hive 3 hub **5** heart **6** center, colony **7** cluster

hoard 4 fund, heap, mass, pile **5** amass, buy up, cache, lay up, store **6** save up, supply **7** acquire, collect, lay away, reserve

hoarse 5 gruff, harsh, husky, raspy, rough **6** croaky **7** cracked, rasping, raucous, throaty **8** gravelly, guttural, scratchy

hoary *see* **3 old**

hoax 3 gyp **4** bilk, dupe, fake, fool, gull, yarn **5** bluff, cheat, cozen, fraud, prank, spoof, trick **6** delude, humbug **7** deceive, defraud, fiction, mislead, swindle **8** hoodwink

Hobbit, The
author: 7 (J R R) Tolkien

hobble 4 bind, gimp, halt, limp **5** block, check, cramp **6** fetter, hamper, hinder, hog-tie, impede, lumber, stymie, thwart, toddle **7** inhibit, manacle, shackle, shamble, shuffle, stagger **8** encumber, handicap, hold back, restrain, restrict

hobby 7 pastime, pursuit **8** sideline

hobgoblin 3 imp **4** ogre **5** bogey **6** goblin **7** bugaboo, bugbear

hobnob 3 mix **4** club **6** mingle **7** consort, hang out

hobo 3 beg, bum **5** stiff, tramp **6** beggar, cadger, loafer **7** drifter, migrant, moocher, vagrant **8** derelict, vagabond

Ho Chi Minh City
formerly: 6 Saigon
river: 6 Saigon
delta: 6 Mekong

hocus-pocus 4 bosh, bull, hoax, sham **5** chant, charm, cheat, magic, spell **6** bunkum, deceit, fakery, humbug **7** con game, hogwash, rubbish, swindle **8** delusion, flimflam, tommyrot, trickery

hodgepodge, hotchpotch 3 mix **4** hash, mess, olio **6** jumble **7** melange, mixture **8** mishmash

hog 3 pig, sow **4** arch, boar **5** swine **6** porker **7** glutton, take all

hogshead 3 keg, tun, vat **4** butt, cask, drum **6** barrel

hogwash *see* **10** **hocus-pocus**

hoi polloi 6 rabble **8** canaille, populace, riffraff

hoist 4 lift **5** heave, raise, run up **6** bear up, pull up, take up, uplift **7** elevate, raise up

hold 4 bind, bond, curb, deem, grip, have, lock, prop, rule, stay, sway, take, urge **5** block, brace, carry, check, cling, grasp, guard, limit, offer, stall, stand, stick, think **6** affirm, assert, assume, clutch, deduct, detain, direct, handle, manage, occupy, reckon, retain, submit, tender **7** believe, command, confine, contain, control, declare, embrace, enclose, enforce, possess, prevent, profess, protect, reserve, support, suspend **8** advocate, conclude, maintain, put forth, restrain, restrict

hold a candle to 5 equal, match **6** be up to **7** compare **8** approach

holdings 6 assets **8** property

holdup 3 rob **5** heist, steal, theft **6** hijack **7** robbery, stickup

hole 3 den, gap, pit **4** brig, cage, cave, flaw, keep, lair, rent, slit, slot **5** break, crack, fault, shaft **6** burrow, cavern, cavity, crater, defect, pocket, tunnel **7** dungeon, opening, orifice, slammer **8** aperture, puncture

holiday 4 fete, gala **6** fiesta, junket, outing **7** holy day, jubilee **8** feast day, festival, vacation

Holland *see* **11 Netherlands**

holler 4 bark, roar, yell **5** gripe, shout **6** bellow, cry out, grouse **8** complain

hollow 3 dip, low, rut **4** cave, dale, deep, dell, dent, dull, glen, hole, sink, vain, vale, void **5** ditch, empty, false, muted **6** cavern, crater, dig out, groove, pocket, sunken, valley **7** channel, concave, useless **8** crevasse, excavate, gouge out, indented, scoop out, specious

holly 4 Ilex

Holmes, Sherlock
  address: 5 Baker (Street)
  author: 5 (Arthur Conan) Doyle
  brother: 7 Mycroft
  femme fatale: 5 Irene (Adler)
  foe: 8 (Professor) Moriarty
  hobby: 6 violin
  housekeeper/landlady: 6 (Mrs) Hudson

  sidekick: 6 (Dr John) Watson

holocaust 5 havoc **6** ravage **7** carnage, inferno, killing **8** butchery, genocide, massacre

holy 4 pure **5** godly, moral, pious **6** adored, devout, divine, sacred, solemn **7** angelic, blessed, from God, revered, saintly, sinless **8** faithful, heavenly, virtuous

holy war
  Arabic: 5 jehad, jihad

homage 5 honor **6** esteem, praise, regard **7** respect, tribute **8** devotion

home 5 abode, haunt, haven, house **6** asylum, cradle, refuge **7** habitat, hangout **8** domicile, dwelling, hospital

Homer
  author of: 5 Iliad **7** Odyssey

homespun 5 plain **6** folksy, homely, modest, native, simple **7** artless, natural

homicide 6 killer, murder, slayer **7** slaying **8** foul play, murderer

homily 6 sermon **7** lecture

homogeneous 4 akin, pure **7** kindred, similar, uniform, unmixed **8** all alike, constant, of a piece

Honduras
  capital/largest city: 11 Tegucigalpa
  highest point: 8 Las Minas
  sea: 7 Pacific **8** Atlantic **9** Caribbean
  physical feature:
    coast: 8 Mosquito
    gulf: 7 Fonseca **8** Honduras
  feature:
    musical instrument: 7 caramba, marimba

hone 4 tool, whet **5** strop **6** sharpen

honest 4 fair, just, open, real, true **5** blunt, frank, legal, plain, valid **6** candid, decent, lawful, proper **7** artless, ethical, genuine, sincere, upright **8** bona fide, clear-cut, faithful, innocent, reliable, straight, truthful, virtuous

honeybee
  live in: 4 hive **6** colony
  headed by: 5 queen
  male: 5 drone
  laborer: 6 worker
  gather: 6 nectar, pollen
  produce: 5 honey
  pertaining to: 5 apian
  keeper: 8 apiarist

honeyed 4 kind **5** sweet **6** sugary **7** cloying, fawning

Honeymooners, The
  cast: 6 (Art) Carney **7** (Jackie) Gleason, (Audrey) Meadows **8** (Joyce) Randolph
  Ralph's job: 9 bus driver
  Ed's job: 5 sewer
  lodge: 8 Raccoons

Hong Kong
  part of: 5 China
  capital: 8 Victoria
  formerly governed by: 7 Britain
  mountain: 6 Castle **8** Victoria
  river: 5 Pearl **6** Canton
  sea: 10 South China
  physical feature:
    bay: 7 Kowloon, Repulse
    peninsula: 7 Kowloon
  feature:
    houseboat: 6 sampan

honk 4 toot **5** blare, blast **7** trumpet

honky-tonk 4 dive **7** gin mill

honor 3 pay **4** cash, fame,

laud, take **5** adore, exalt, extol, favor, glory, right, truth, value **6** accept, admire, credit, esteem, homage, praise, redeem, regard, renown, repute, revere, virtue **7** acclaim, commend, dignify, liberty, respect **8** eminence, fairness, goodness, justness, look up to, make good, pleasure, venerate

hood 4 cowl, lout, punk **5** bully, rowdy, tough **6** vandal **7** hoodlum, ruffian **8** hooligan

hoodlum 4 hood, punk, thug **5** crook, rowdy, tough **6** gunman **7** bruiser, gorilla, mobster, ruffian **8** criminal, gangster, hooligan, plug-ugly

hoodwink 3 gyp **4** dupe, fool, gull, hoax **5** cheat, trick **7** deceive, defraud, mislead, swindle

hook 3 arc, bag, bow, nab, net **4** arch, bend, bill, curl, gaff, grab, loop, take, trap, wind **5** angle, catch, fluke, hitch, latch, seize, snare **6** buckle, collar, fasten, secure

7 capture, ensnare, grapnel, grapple **8** crescent

hooligan *see* **4 hood**

hoopla 4 hype **8** ballyhoo

hoot 3 boo, din **4** bawl, blow, hiss, honk, howl, jeer, moan, mock, razz, wail, yelp **5** shout, sneer, taunt, whoop **6** bellow, chorus, cry out, deride, outcry, shriek, shrill, tumult, uproar **7** catcall, scoff at, screech, sing out, ululate

Hoover, Herbert Clark
presidential rank: 11 thirty-first
party: 10 Republican
state represented: 2 CA
vice president: 6 Curtis
born: 2 IA **10** West Branch
notable events of lifetime/ term:
   crash of: 11 stock market
wife: 3 Lou

hop 3 bob **4** ball, jump, leap, prom, romp, skip, step **5** bound, caper, dance, mixer **6** bounce, gambol, prance, soiree

hope 3 yen **4** help, wish

5 crave, dream, faith, fancy, trust **6** aspire, belief, chance, desire, expect, hunger, rescue **7** believe, longing **8** ambition, daydream, optimism, prospect, yearning

horde 3 mob **4** band, gang, host, pack **5** bunch, crowd, crush, party, swarm, tribe **6** throng

horizon 4 area **5** field, range, realm, scope, vista **6** bounds, domain **7** expanse, stretch **8** frontier

horizontal 4 even, flat **5** flush, level, plane, plumb, prone **6** supine

hormone 4 ACTH **5** auxin **6** cortin **7** estrone, insulin, steroid **8** endocrin, estrogen, galactin, lactogen, secretin

horn 4 tusk **5** cornu, point, spike **6** antler
brass instrument: 4 oboe, tuba **5** bugle **6** cornet **7** bassoon, trumpet **8** alto horn, baritone, clarinet, trombone

Horn of Africa *see* **7 Somalia**

horny 4 hard **5** tough **7** callous, lustful **8** callused, hardened

horoscope *see* **9 astrology**

horrible 3 bad **4** foul, rank, vile **5** awful, nasty **6** grisly, horrid, odious **7** ghastly, hideous **8** dreadful, gruesome, shocking, terrible

horrify 5 daunt, repel, shock **6** appall, dismay, sicken **7** petrify, terrify **8** frighten, nauseate

horror 4 fear **5** alarm, crime, dread, panic **6** dismay, hatred, misery, terror **7** anguish, cruelty, disgust, dislike, outrage, torment **8** atrocity, hardship

hors d'oeuvre 3 dip **6** canape, relish, tidbit

horse 4 colt, foal, hack, jade, mare, plug, pony, sire, stud **5** bronc, filly, mount, pacer, pinto, steed **6** bronco, dobbin, equine, nellie **7** cavalry, charger, gelding, hackney, mustang, palfrey, trotter **8** galloper, stallion, yearling
castrated: 7 gelding
combining form: 4 eque, equi **5** hippo

family: **7** Equidae
female: **3** dam **4** mare
 5 filly
gear: **3** bit **4** rein, tack **6**
 saddle **7** blinder, harness,
 snaffle
Gene Autry's: **8** Champion
genus: **5** equus
kind: **3** cob **4** race **6**
 bronco, hunter, jumper **7**
 charger, mustang,
 palfrey, quarter, trotter **8**
 destrier
Lone Ranger's: **6** Silver
male: **4** colt **8** stallion
measure: **4** hand
pace: **4** lope, trot **5** amble
 6 canter, gallop
pair of: **4** span, team **6**
 tandem
riding show: **8** gymkhana
Roy Rogers': **7** Trigger
small: **4** pony
Tom Mix's: **4** Tony
Tonto's: **5** Scout
winged: **7** Pegasus
young: **4** colt, foal **5** filly
 8 yearling
horse collar **3** zip **4** zero **5**
 aught, zilch **6** cipher,
 naught **8** goose egg
horseman **5** groom, rider **6**
 hussar, jockey, lancer,
 ostler **7** cossack, dragoon,
 hostler, trainer, trooper

horseplay **6** pranks **7**
 foolery
Horus
 origin: **8** Egyptian
 god of: **3** sun
 symbol: **6** falcon
 mother: **4** Isis
 father: **6** Osiris
hosannas **4** yeas **5** kudos **6**
 bravos, cheers, paeans **7**
 acclaim, hurrahs, huzzahs,
 yippees **8** applause
hospitable *see* **6** genial
hospital **4** home **6** asylum,
 clinic **7** sick bay
host, hostess **3** lot, mob **4**
 army, band, body, crew,
 gang, mess **5** array,
 crowd, emcee, group,
 horde, party, swarm **6**
 throng **8** hosteler, hotelier,
 landlord
hostage **6** pledge **7** captive
 8 prisoner
hostel **3** inn **4** hall **5** hotel,
 lodge **7** hospice, lodging,
 shelter **8** hospital, hostelry
hostile **3** icy **4** cold, mean,
 ugly **5** angry, at war,
 enemy **6** at odds, bitter,
 chilly, cranky, malign,
 touchy, unkind **7**
 opposed, vicious, warring

8 battling, clashing, contrary, fighting, opposing, spiteful, venomous

hot 3 new, top **4** good, late, live, warm **5** fiery, fresh, sharp **6** ardent, baking, fervid, fierce, heated, hectic, latest, molten, raging, recent, red-hot, stormy, sultry, torrid **7** boiling, burning, excited, furious, intense, melting, peppery, popular, pungent, searing **8** agitated, animated, broiling, feverish, frenzied, roasting, scalding, sizzling, steaming

hot air 7 bombast **8** rhetoric

hothouse 6 tender **7** fragile, nursery **8** delicate

hound 3 dog, fan, nag, nut, pup **4** bait, hunt, mutt, tail **5** annoy, chase, freak, pooch, puppy, stalk, track, trail **6** addict, badger, canine, follow, harass, hector, keep at, needle, pester, pursue **7** bedevil

group of: 3 cry **4** mute, pack

hour 3 day **4** span, time **5** space **6** period **8** interval

house 4 clan, firm, hall, home, line **5** abode, board, lodge, put up **6** billet, church, family, garage, harbor, temple **7** company, contain, dynasty, lineage, quarter, shelter, theater **8** ancestry, assembly, audience, building, business, domicile, dwelling

household gods 5 lares **7** penates

house of worship 6 chapel, church, mosque, temple **8** basilica

housewife 4 wife **8** hausfrau

hovel 3 hut **4** dump, hole **5** cabin, shack **6** shanty

hover 4 flit, hang **5** float, haunt, pause, poise **6** falter, seesaw **7** flutter

howl 3 bay, cry **4** bark, hoot, roar, wail, yell, yelp, yowl **5** groan, shout, whine **6** bellow, clamor, cry out, outcry, scream, shriek, uproar **7** ululate

hub 3 nub **4** axis, core

5 focus, heart, pivot **6** center, middle

hubbub *see* **5 noise**

Huckleberry Finn
author: **5** (Mark) Twain

huckster 5 adman **6** badger, hawker, kidder, seller, vendor **7** haggler, peddler

huddle 4 heap, herd, mass, mess **5** bunch, crowd, group **6** cuddle, curl up, jumble, medley, muddle, nestle **7** cluster, collect, snuggle **8** converge

hue 4 cast, tint, tone **5** color, shade, tinge **8** tincture

hue and cry 4 call, howl, roar, yell, yowl **5** alarm, alert, shout **6** clamor, hubbub, outcry, uproar

huffy *see* **7 grouchy**

hug 4 hold **5** clasp **6** clutch, cuddle, nestle **7** cling to, embrace, snuggle, squeeze

huge 4 vast **5** giant, great, jumbo **6** mighty **7** immense, mammoth, massive, titanic **8** colossal, enormous, gigantic

hulk 4 ship **5** giant, wreck **8** behemoth

hull 3 pod **4** case, husk, peel, rind, skin **5** shell, shuck **7** coating **8** carapace

hullabaloo 3 din **4** stir **5** babel **6** bedlam, clamor, hubbub, ruckus, tumult, uproar

hum 4 buzz, purr, whir **5** croon, drone, thrum **6** be busy, bustle, intone, murmur, thrive **7** vibrate **8** whirring

human 3 man **6** gentle, humane, kindly, mortal, person **7** hominid **8** merciful, personal

humane 4 kind **5** human **6** kindly, tender **7** pitying **8** merciful

humble 3 low **4** meek, poor **5** abase, crush, lower, plain, shame **6** common, debase, demean, demure, gentle, modest, shabby, simple, subdue **7** chasten, conquer, degrade, obscure, put down **8** bring low, ordinary, plebeian, pull down, wretched

humbug 3 fib, gyp, lie **4** bull, bunk, dupe, fake, fool, gull, hoax, liar, lies, sham **5** cheat, cozen, dodge, faker, fraud, hokum, lying, quack, spoof, trick **6** deceit, fibber **7** beguile, blather, cheater, deceive, falsify, fiction, forgery, mislead, rubbish, swindle **8** claptrap, flimflam, flummery, hoodwink, nonsense, pretense, swindler, trickery

humdinger 4 lulu **5** dandy, doozy **6** beauty, hummer, marvel **8** superior

humdrum *see* **8 ordinary**

humid 4 damp, dank **5** muggy **6** clammy, steamy, sticky, sultry

humiliate 5 abash, crush, shame **6** debase, humble, subdue **7** chagrin, chasten, degrade, mortify, put down **8** belittle, bring low, disgrace, dishonor

humility 7 modesty, shyness **8** meekness, timidity

hummock 4 hill, rise **5** knoll, mound **7** hillock, tussock

humor 3 wit **4** gags, mood, puns **5** farce, jests, jokes **6** cajole, comedy, joking, pamper, parody, satire, soothe, temper **7** appease,

flatter, fooling, indulge, jesting, mollify, placate **8** drollery, jocosity, nonsense, raillery, ridicule, tolerate

humorist 3 wag, wit **4** card **5** comic **8** comedian

hump 4 arch, bend, bump, knob, lift, lump, rise **5** bulge, hunch, knurl, mound, put up, tense **8** swelling

hunch 4 clue, idea **7** feeling, glimmer, inkling

hunched 4 bent **7** crooked, slumped, stooped

Hungary
  capital/largest city: 8 Budapest
  lake: 7 Balaton
  river: 5 Drava, Tisza **6** Danube **7** Vistula
  feature:
    dog: 4 puli
  food:
    dish: 6 gulyas **7** goulash
    wine: 5 Tokay

hunger 3 yen **4** itch, love, lust, want, wish **5** crave, greed **6** desire, famine, relish, thirst **7** burn for, craving, long for

8 appetite, fondness, yearning

hunk 3 gob, wad **4** clod, glob, lump, mass **5** block, chunk, piece **7** portion

hunt 4 seek **5** chase, probe, shoot, stalk, trace, track, trail **6** course, follow, pursue **7** explore, go after, look for **8** drive out

Hunting
goddess of: 5 Diana **7** Artemis

hurdle 4 jump, leap, snag, wall **5** bound, clear, fence, hedge, vault **6** hazard **7** barrier **8** surmount

hurl *see* **5 throw**

hurly-burly 4 stir **5** furor **6** action, bustle, hubbub, hustle, uproar **8** activity

hurrah, hurray 4 fine, good **5** bravo, cheer, great, huzza **6** huzzah, salute **7** acclaim, hosanna

hurricane 7 cyclone, monsoon, tempest, typhoon

hurry 4 bolt, dart, dash, fuss, goad, prod, rush, whiz **5** egg on, haste, speed **6** hasten, hustle, scurry, tumult, urge on

7 drive on, press on, scuttle, speed up **8** pressure, scramble, step on it

hurt 3 cut, mar **4** ache, burn, harm, lame, maim, mark, maul, pain, scar **5** agony, check, grief, limit, smart, sting **6** bruise, damage, deface, dismay, grieve, hamper, hinder, impair, impede, injure, mangle, miffed, misery, narrow, offend, oppose, piqued, reduce, retard, thwart, weaken **7** agonize, bruised, chagrin, cripple, disable, exclude, inhibit, scratch, torment, torture, trouble, wounded **8** decrease, diminish, distress, hold back, minimize, mutilate, obstruct, preclude, restrain, soreness, wretched

hurtle 4 bolt, dart, dash, race, rush, tear, whiz **5** bound, scoot, shoot, speed, whisk **6** charge, gallop, plunge, scurry **7** scamper

husband 3 man **4** keep, mate, save **5** amass,

hoard, hubby, store
6 retain, save up, spouse **7**
consort **8** conserve,
maintain, preserve

hush 4 calm **5** quell, quiet,
shush, still **6** shut up,
soothe **7** be quiet, be still,
keep mum, mollify, silence
8 pipe down, quietude

hush money 5 bribe **6**
payoff, payola **7** tribute

husky 3 big **5** beefy, burly,
gruff, harsh, hefty, plump,
rough, solid, stout, thick
6 brawny, coarse, hoarse,
robust, stocky, strong,
sturdy **7** rasping, raucous
8 croaking, guttural,
muscular, powerful,
thickset

hussy 4 bawd, jade, minx,
slut, tart **5** wench, whore
6 harlot, wanton **7**
baggage, trollop **8**
strumpet

hustle 3 ado, fly **4** bolt,
dart, dash, fuss, prod,
push, rush, stir, toss **5**
elbow, hurry, nudge,
scoot, shove, throw **6**
bounce, bustle, hasten,
hubbub, scurry, tumult **7**
scuttle, speed up, turmoil
8 scramble, step on it

hustler 4 doer **6** con man,
hooker **8** go-getter,
swindler

hut 4 shed **5** cabin, hutch,
shack **6** lean-to, shanty **7**
cottage, shelter

hutch 3 pen, sty **4** cage,
coop, crib, shed

hybrid 5 cross **7** amalgam,
mixture

Hydra
  form: 7 (water) serpent
  number of heads: 4 nine
  killed by: 8 Hercules

hydrophobia 6 rabies
  fear of: 5 water

hygienic 4 pure **5** clean **7**
aseptic, healthy, sterile **8**
germ-free, salutary

hymn 5 paean, psalm **6**
anthem

hyper 7 keyed-up

hyperbolize 6 overdo **7**
amplify, magnify, stretch

Hyperion
  also: 6 Helios
  form: 5 Titan
  father: 6 Uranus
  mother: 4 Gaea
  son: 6 Helios

hypocrisy 6 deceit, fakery **7**
falsity

hypocrite 5 phony **8** deceiver

hypothesis 6 theory, thesis **7** premise, theorem **8** proposal

hypothetical 7 assumed, dubious **8** possible, supposed

hysterical 5 crazy, droll **6** absurd, crazed, raving **7** amusing, comical **8** farcical, frenzied

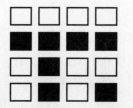

Iberian Peninsula
  comprising: 5 Spain **8** Portugal

Icarus
  father: 8 Daedalus
  built: 5 wings
  flew too near: 3 sun

ice 3 gem **4** berg, floe, gems, rime **5** chill, frost, glace **6** freeze, icicle, jewels **7** crystal, dessert, glacier, iceberg, jewelry, sherbet **8** diamonds

ice cream 7 dessert, sherbet **4** soda **5** glace **6** frappe, sundae **7** dessert, parfait, sherbet, spumoni, tortoni

Iceland
  capital/largest city: 9 Reykjavik
  mountain/volcano: 7 Surtsey
  sea: 8 Atlantic
  feature:
    literary genre: 4 saga

icky 5 gluey, gooey, gross, gucky, gummy, mushy, nasty, tacky, weepy **6** sticky, syrupy, viscid **7** maudlin, viscous

icon, ikon 4 idol **5** image **6** effigy, figure, statue **7** picture **8** likeness

iconoclast 5 rebel **7** radical, upstart

Idaho
  abbreviation: 2 ID **3** Ida
  nickname: 3 Gem
  capital/largest city: 5 Boise
  mountain: 5 Rocky **6** Tetons
  highest point: 5 Borah
  river: 5 Boise, Snake, St Joe **6** Salmon
  physical feature:
    divide: 11 Continental
    valley: 3 Sun

idea 4 clue, hint, view **6** belief, notion **7** concept, feeling, inkling, insight, opinion, thought **8** approach, proposal, solution

ideal 3 aim **4** hero, idol **5** dream, model **7** epitome,

idealist 7 dreamer, utopian 8 romantic

optimal, pattern, perfect 8 exemplar, paradigm, standard, ultimate

identification 2 ID 5 badge, label 6 dogtag 7 license 8 passport

identify 4 know 5 place 6 finger, verify 7 combine, pick out, specify

identity 4 name, self 6 accord 7 harmony, oneness, rapport

ideology 5 dogma, ethos 6 ideals, theory 7 program 8 doctrine

idiom 5 argot, lingo, slang 6 brogue, jargon, patois, phrase, speech 7 dialect 8 language, localism

idiosyncrasy 3 tic 5 quirk 6 oddity 7 anomaly

idiot 3 ass 4 boob, dolt, dope, fool, jerk 5 cluck, dummy, dunce, moron, ninny 6 cretin, dimwit, nitwit 7 halfwit 8 dumbbell, numskull

idle *see* 4 **lazy**

idolize 5 adore, deify, honor, prize 6 admire,

revere 7 worship 8 treasure, venerate

idyllic 6 rustic, sylvan 7 bucolic 8 pastoral, peaceful, romantic

if 6 though 7 whether 8 although, provided

iffy 4 moot 5 risky 6 chancy, unsure 7 dubious 8 arguable, doubtful

ignite 4 burn, fire 5 flame, light 6 blow up 7 explode, inflame 8 touch off

ignoble 3 low 4 base, foul, mean, vile 6 craven 7 debased, heinous 8 cowardly, indecent, infamous, shameful, unworthy

ignorant 4 dumb 5 naive 6 stupid 7 asinine, blind to, fatuous, shallow, unaware 8 innocent, untaught

ignore 4 omit, skip, snub 5 scorn 6 eschew, slight 7 neglect 8 overlook

Iliad, The
author: 5 Homer
subject: 9 Trojan War

ill, ills 3 woe 4 evil, foul, harm, sick, vile 5 surly 6 ailing, injury, laid up, malady, malice, plague, poorly, sickly, sorrow, unkind, unwell **7** ailment, disease, failing, harmful, invalid, ominous, outrage, trouble, unsound **8** diseased

ill-advised 4 dumb, rash **5** hasty, silly **6** myopic, stupid, unwise **7** foolish

illegal 5 wrong **6** banned **7** illicit **8** criminal, not legal, outlawed, unlawful

illegible 7 unclear **8** obscured

illegitimate 7 bastard, illegal, illicit, lawless, natural **8** baseborn, improper, unlawful

illicit *see* **7** illegal

Illinois
  abbreviation: 2 IL **3** Ill
  nickname: 7 Prairie
  capital: 11 Springfield
  largest city: 7 Chicago
  highest point: 12 Charles Mound
  lake: 8 Michigan
  river: 4 Ohio **6** Wabash **7** Chicago **8** Illinois **11** Mississippi

illiterate 7 witless **8** childish, ignorant

ill-natured 4 sour **5** cross, nasty, surly **6** bitter, cranky, malign **7** caustic, grouchy, peevish **8** churlish, spiteful

illuminate 5 edify, light **7** clarify, enhance, explain, light up **8** brighten, illumine, instruct, spell out

illusion 5 error, fancy **6** mirage, vision **7** chimera, fallacy **8** delusion

illustrate 4 show **6** define **7** clarify, explain, picture, point up, portray

illustrious 5 famed, great, noted **6** famous **7** eminent, honored, notable **8** glorious, lustrous, peerless, renowned, splendid

ill will 4 gall **5** anger, spite **6** animus, enmity, hatred, malice, rancor, spleen **7** dislike **8** acrimony, aversion, loathing

I Love Lucy
  cast: 4 Lucille (Ball) **5** (Desi) Arnaz

image 4 copy, icon, idea, idol **6** double, effigy, fetish, figure, memory, simile, statue, symbol, visage **7** concept, picture, replica **8** likeness, metaphor, portrait

imaginary 4 sham **5** fancy, phony **6** made-up, unreal **7** fancied, fiction, figment

imagine 5 fancy, guess, infer, judge **6** assume, gather **7** believe, dream up, picture, presume, pretend, project, suppose, surmise, suspect **8** conceive, envision

imbecile *see* **5 idiot**

imbibe 4 swig, tope **5** drink, quaff **6** guzzle, ingest, tipple **7** partake **8** toss down, wash down

imbroglio *see* **5 fight**

imbue 4 fill, fire, tint **5** bathe, color, endow, steep, tinge **6** arouse, infuse **7** animate, impress, ingrain, inspire, instill, pervade, suffuse **8** permeate

imitation 4 fake, mock, sham **5** aping, phony **6** ersatz, parody **7** man-made, mimicry, takeoff **8** travesty

immaculate 4 pure **5** clean, ideal **6** chaste, intact, virgin **7** perfect, sinless **8** flawless, innocent, spotless, virginal

immaterial 7 ghostly, shadowy, trivial **8** bodiless, ethereal, mystical, noumenal, spectral, trifling, unbodied

immature 5 green, young **6** callow, unripe **7** kiddish, puerile **8** childish, juvenile, youthful

immediate 4 near, next, nigh **5** close, hasty, local, swift **6** abrupt, nearby, prompt, recent, speedy, sudden **7** express, instant, nearest **8** adjacent

immense 4 huge, vast **5** great **7** mammoth, massive **8** colossal, enormous, gigantic

immerse 3 dip **4** duck, dunk, sink, soak **5** bathe, douse, lower, steep **6** absorb, engage, occupy, plunge **8** submerge

immigrant 5 alien **7** migrant, settler **8** colonist, newcomer

imminent 4 near **7** looming **8** menacing, perilous

immobile 4 fast **5** fixed, quiet, rigid, stiff, still

6 at rest, laid up, rooted, secure, static **7** riveted

immodest 4 lewd, vain **5** gross, loose **6** brazen, coarse, risque, wanton **7** pompous **8** boastful, braggart, indecent, inflated, unchaste

immoral 4 evil, lewd **5** dirty, wrong **6** sinful, wicked **7** corrupt, heinous, obscene, raunchy, vicious **8** depraved, indecent, infamous, prurient

immortal 3 god **6** divine **7** abiding, eternal, undying **8** enduring

immovable 3 icy, set **4** cold, fast **5** fixed **6** dogged, secure, steely, stolid **7** adamant, settled **8** detached, fastened, immobile, obdurate, resolute, stubborn

immune 4 free, safe **5** clear **6** exempt

immure 3 hem, pen **6** entomb, wall in, wall up **7** confine, enclose **8** cloister, imprison

immutable 4 firm **5** fixed, solid **6** stable **7** lasting **8** constant, enduring

imp 3 elf **4** brat **5** demon, devil, gnome, pixie, scamp **6** goblin, hoyden, rascal, sprite, urchin **7** upstart

impact 4 jolt **5** brunt, crash, force, shock, smash **6** burden, effect, thrust **7** contact

impair 3 mar **4** harm, hurt **6** damage, hinder, injure, lessen, reduce, weaken **7** cripple, subvert, vitiate **8** decrease, enfeeble

impale 3 fix, pin **4** gore, stab, tack **5** affix, stick **8** transfix

impart 4 give, lend, tell **5** grant, offer, share **6** accord, afford, pass on, relate, render, report, reveal **7** confide, consign, deliver, divulge, mention **8** bestow on, dispense

impartial 4 fair, just **7** neutral **8** detached, unbiased

impasse 4 snag **7** dead end **8** deadlock, standoff

impassioned *see* **5 eager**

impassive 4 calm, cool **5** aloof, stony **6** sedate, stolid **7** stoical, unmoved

impatient 4 edgy **5** fussy,

hasty, itchy, rabid, tense, testy **6** ardent, touchy **7** annoyed, anxious, brusque, hurried, nervous, peevish, restive **8** agitated, feverish, restless

impeach 4 slur **6** accuse, assail, attack, charge, impugn, indict **7** arraign, slander **8** belittle

impeccable 7 perfect **8** flawless

impecunious 4 poor **5** broke, needy **6** hard-up **8** bankrupt, indigent

impede *see* **5 block**

impel 4 goad, prod, push, spur, urge **5** drive, force **6** compel, incite, induce, prompt **7** require

impending 4 near **6** coming **7** brewing, looming **8** imminent, oncoming

impenetrable 5 dense, solid, thick **6** sealed **7** obscure

imperative 6 urgent **7** crucial, needful **8** critical

imperceptible 5 minor, scant, small **6** hidden, minute, slight, subtle **7** minimal **8** academic

imperfect 6 faulty, flawed

8 deformed, fallible, impaired

imperious 5 bossy, lofty **6** lordly **7** haughty **8** arrogant, despotic, imperial

imperishable 6 stable **7** durable, lasting

impermanent 7 passing **8** fleeting

impermeable 5 dense, solid, tight **6** opaque

impersonal 4 dead **6** remote **7** general, inhuman, neutral **8** detached, lifeless, soulless

impersonate 3 ape **4** copy, mime **5** mimic **6** pose as **7** imitate, portray

impertinence 4 sass **5** cheek, sauce **7** affront **8** boldness, rudeness

imperturbable 4 calm, cool **6** sedate, serene **8** composed

impetuous *see* **6 abrupt**

impetus *see* **6 motive**

impinge 7 intrude, obtrude, violate **8** encroach, infringe, trespass

implant 3 fix, set, sow **4** root **5** embed, graft, inlay

6 infuse, insert **7** impress, instill

implement 4 tool **5** begin, enact, piece, start **6** device **7** achieve, article, fulfill, realize, utensil **8** activate, carry out

implicate 7 connect, embroil, ensnare, involve

implicit 5 total **6** hinted, innate **7** certain, implied, staunch **8** absolute, inferred, inherent

implore *see* **7 beseech**

imply 4 hint, mean **6** denote **7** connote, presume, signify, suggest **8** indicate, intimate

impolite 4 rude **7** uncivil

import 6 burden, moment, thrust **7** meaning

important 5 great, major **7** leading, notable, seminal, serious, weighty **8** creative, esteemed

imported 5 alien **6** exotic **7** foreign

importune *see* **7 beseech**

impose 3 set **4** levy **5** apply, enact, foist, force, lay on **6** slap on **7** inflict, palm off, place on

impossible 8 stubborn

impostor 4 sham **5** cheat, duper, fraud, phony, quack **6** con man

impotent *see* **4 weak**

impound 3 pen **4** cage **5** seize **6** coop up, lock up, shut in **7** confine

impoverish 4 bust, ruin **5** break, drain **6** beggar, pauper, reduce **7** deplete, exhaust **8** bankrupt

imprecation 5 curse

impregnable 6 mighty, potent, strong, sturdy **8** powerful

impregnate 3 wet **4** soak **5** steep **6** dampen, drench, imbrue, infuse **7** moisten, suffuse **8** inundate, permeate, saturate

impresario 7 manager, sponsor **8** director

impress 4 grab, move, stir, sway **5** reach, touch **6** affect, excite, sink in, strike **8** bedazzle

impression 4 idea, mark, mold, view **5** hunch, stamp, trace, track **6** belief, effect, impact, notion **7** contour, feeling, impress, imprint, opinion, outline, surmise

imprint 3 fix **4** etch, mark, sign **5** infix, press, stamp, title **6** indent **7** engrave, impress **8** inscribe

improbable 8 doubtful, unlikely

impromptu 6 sudden **7** offhand

improper 4 lewd **5** inapt, unfit **8** indecent, off-color, unseemly

improve 4 help **5** rally **6** better, enrich, repair **7** correct, develop, enhance

improvised 5 ad-lib **7** devised, offhand

imprudent 4 rash **5** crazy, dopey **6** unwise **7** foolish **8** heedless, mindless

impudent *see* **4 rude**

impugn 4 deny **5** knock, libel **6** assail, attack, berate, negate, oppose **7** asperse, slander **8** denounce, question

impulse 4 bent, goad, push, spur, urge, whim **5** drive, fancy, force **6** desire, motive, notion, thrust, whimsy **7** caprice, impetus **8** instinct, stimulus

impure *see* **5 dirty**

inaccuracy 4 goof, slip **5** error, fault, wrong **6** boo-boo **7** blunder, erratum, fallacy, mistake

inactive 4 dull, idle, lazy **5** inert, quiet, still **6** static, torpid **7** dormant, languid **8** indolent, slothful, sluggish

inadequate 5 inept, short, unfit **6** meager, scanty, too raw **7** lacking, not up to, wanting **8** below par, unfitted

in advance 6 before, in time, sooner **7** earlier

inadvertent 7 unmeant

inadvisable 5 risky **6** chancy, unwise

inalienable 6 sacred **8** absolute, inherent

inamorata 4 lady, love **5** lover **7** beloved, darling **8** mistress, paramour

inane *see* **6 stupid**

inanimate 4 cold, dead, dull **5** inert **6** asleep, stolid **8** lifeless, soulless

inappropriate 5 inapt **8** ill-timed, improper, unsuited

inarticulate **4** dumb, mute **7** babbled, blurred, garbled, mumbled **8** confused, wordless

inattentive **7** unaware **8** careless, heedless

inaugurate **5** set up, start **6** induct, launch **7** kick off, usher in **8** initiate

inauspicious **7** unlucky

inborn **5** basic **6** inbred, innate, native **7** natural **8** inherent

Inca
> **language family:** **7** Quechua
> **leader:** **7** Huascar **8** Topa Inca **9** Atahualpa
> **conquered by:** **7** Pizarro

incandescent **7** dynamic, glowing, radiant **8** electric, magnetic, white-hot

incantation **3** hex **4** jinx **5** chant, charm, magic, spell **6** voodoo **7** sorcery **8** wizardry

incapacitate **4** maim, undo **5** lay up **7** cripple, disable **8** enfeeble, handicap, paralyze, sideline

incarcerate **4** jail **6** commit, coop up, intern, lock up **7** confine **8** imprison

incendiary **8** agitator, arsonist

incensed *see* **3 mad**

incentive **4** lure, spur **6** come-on **8** stimulus

inception **5** birth, debut, onset, start **6** origin, outset **7** arrival

incessant **8** constant, unbroken, unending

inchoate **7** budding, nascent **8** formless, unformed, unshaped

incident **5** clash, event, scene **6** affair **7** episode, related **8** occasion

incineration **6** firing **7** burning, flaming **8** ignition, kindling

incipient **7** budding, nascent **8** inchoate

incision *see* **3 cut**

incisive **4** curt, keen **5** acute, brisk, crisp, sharp **6** biting, shrewd **7** cutting, express, precise, probing **8** analytic, piercing

incite *see* **7 provoke**

inclement **3** raw **4** foul

5 harsh, nasty, rough **6** bitter, severe, stormy

inclination 3 bow, dip, nod **4** bend, bent, hill, rake, rise **5** grade, pitch, slant, slope **6** liking **7** leaning **8** penchant, tendency

include 5 cover **6** enfold, entail, take in **7** contain, embrace, involve

incognito 7 unknown, unnamed **8** nameless

incoherent 7 muddled, unclear **8** confused

income 5 wages **6** salary **7** revenue **8** earnings

incompetent 5 inept, unfit

incomplete 6 broken **7** partial, wanting

incomprehensible 7 obscure **8** abstruse, baffling

incongruous 3 odd **6** far-out **8** contrary

inconsequential 5 petty **6** slight **7** trivial **8** nugatory, picayune, piddling, trifling

inconsiderate 4 rash, rude **6** remiss, unkind **7** uncivil **8** careless, impolite, tactless, uncaring

inconsistent 6 fickle **7** erratic, wayward

8 contrary, notional, unstable, variable

inconsolable 7 crushed **8** dejected, desolate

inconspicuous 3 dim **5** faint, muted **6** modest

inconvenient 7 awkward, unhandy **8** annoying, tiresome, untimely

incorporated 6 united **8** embodied, included

incorrect 5 false, wrong **6** untrue **7** inexact **8** mistaken

incorrigible 6 unruly **8** hardened, hopeless

incorruptible 4 pure **6** honest **8** reliable

increase 3 wax **4** grow **5** add to, swell **6** enrich, expand **7** advance, augment, enhance, enlarge **8** multiply

incredible 6 absurd **7** amazing, awesome

incredulous 7 dubious **8** doubtful

increment 4 gain, rise **5** raise **6** growth, profit **8** addition, increase

incriminate 5 blame **6** accuse, charge, indict

incubate 3 set, sit **4** plot **5** breed, brood, clock, cover, hatch **6** scheme **7** develop, gestate **8** generate

inculcate 5 drill, imbue, infix, teach, train **6** impart, infuse **7** implant, impress, instill **8** instruct

incur 6 arouse, assume, incite, stir up **7** acquire, bring on, involve, provoke

incursion 4 push, raid **5** foray **6** attack, inroad, sortie **7** assault **8** invasion

indebted 5 bound **8** beholden, grateful

indecent *see* **6 vulgar**

indecision 5 doubt **6** acrisy **7** dilemma, swither **8** wavering

indeed 5 truly **6** in fact, really **7** for sure, in truth **8** actually, to be sure

indefatigable 6 dogged **8** diligent, tireless

indefensible 8 improper, vincible

indefinite 3 dim **5** vague **6** unsure **7** inexact, obscure, unknown **8** doubtful

indelible 4 fast **5** fixed, vivid **7** lasting **8** deep-dyed

indelicate *see* **6 vulgar**

indemnity 7 redress **8** coverage, security

indentation 3 bay, cut, pit **4** dent, nick **5** gouge, inset, niche, notch **6** cavity, pocket, recess

indenture 4 bind **8** contract

independent 4 free **7** solvent, well-off **8** affluent, separate, unallied, well-to-do

index 4 clue, mark, sign **5** proof, token **7** catalog, symptom **8** evidence, glossary, register

India
  capital: 5 Delhi **8** New Delhi
  largest city: 6 Bombay, Mumbai
  mountain: 9 Himalayas, Nanda Devi
  highest point: 12 Kanchanjanga
  river: 5 Indus **6** Ganges
  sea: 6 Indian **7** Arabian
  island groups: 7 Andaman, Nicobar
  physical feature:
    bay: 6 Bengal
    desert: 4 Thar
    plateau: 6 Deccan
    rains: 7 monsoon

valley/vale: 7 Kashmir
religion: 4 Sikh **5** Hindu, Islam **7** Jainist **8** Buddhism
feature:
  dance: 6 nautch
  movie center: 9 Bollywood
  shrine: 5 stupa
food:
  bread: 7 chapati
Indiana
  abbreviation: 2 IN **3** Ind
  nickname: 7 Hoosier
  capital/largest city: 12 Indianapolis
  lake: 5 Clear **8** Michigan
  river: 4 Ohio **6** Maumee, Wabash **8** Kankakee
indicate 4 mean, show, tell **5** imply **6** denote, evince, record, reveal **7** bespeak, point to, signify, specify, suggest **8** point out, register, stand for
indict 4 cite **6** accuse, charge, have up, impute, pull up **7** arraign, bring up, impeach
indifferent *see* **5 aloof**
indigenous 6 native **7** endemic **8** domestic
indigent 4 poor **5** needy **6** hard-up, in need

indignant 3 mad **4** sore **5** angry, huffy, irate, riled **6** fuming, miffed, peeved, piqued **8** incensed, offended, provoked, steaming, wrathful
indigo 3 dye **4** blue
indirect 5 vague **6** remote, zigzag **7** crooked, devious, evasive, oblique, winding **8** tortuous
indiscreet 4 rash **6** unwise **7** foolish **8** careless, tactless
indiscriminate 6 motley, random **7** aimless, chaotic, jumbled **8** confused, slapdash
indispensable 5 basic, vital **6** needed **7** crucial, needful **8** required
indisposed *see* **4 sick**
indisputable 4 sure **7** assured, certain, decided, evident, obvious **8** absolute, apparent, clear-cut, definite, positive
indistinct *see* **5 faint**
individual 6 person, unique **7** one's own, private, special, unusual **8** distinct, especial, original,

personal, separate, singular, specific

Indochina 9 peninsula
  includes: 4 Laos **6** Malaya **7** Myanmar, Vietnam **8** Cambodia, Thailand

indoctrinate 5 brief, drill, teach, train, tutor **6** infuse, school **7** educate, implant, instill **8** initiate

indolent *see* **4 lazy**

indomitable 6 dogged **7** doughty, staunch, valiant **8** fearless, intrepid, resolute, stalwart, stubborn

Indonesia
  capital/largest city: 7 Jakarta **8** Djakarta
  sea: 4 Java **5** Banda, Timor **6** Indian **7** Celebes, Molucca, Pacific
  island: 4 Bali, Java **5** Timor **6** Borneo **7** Celebes, Sumatra **8** Moluccas, Sulawesi **9** New Guinea
  physical feature:
    volcano: 8 Krakatoa
  feature:
    cloth: 5 batik
    lizard: 6 Komodo (dragon)

indubitable 4 sure **7** certain

induce *see* **7 provoke**

induct 5 crown, draft, frock **6** enlist, invest, lead in, ordain, sign up **7** bring in, install, instate, usher in **8** enthrone, initiate, register

indulgent 4 kind **6** benign, tender **7** clement, lenient, patient, sparing **8** humoring, obliging, tolerant, yielding

industry 2 go **4** toil, zeal **5** field, labor, trade **6** bustle, energy, hustle **8** activity, business, commerce

inebriated *see* **5 drunk**

ineffective 4 vain, weak **6** futile **7** useless **8** impotent

inefficient 5 inept, slack **6** futile **8** slipshod

inept 5 inane, silly, unapt **6** clumsy **7** asinine, awkward, foolish **8** bungling

inequality 8 imparity, inequity

inert 4 dull, numb **5** slack, still **6** leaden, static, supine, torpid **7** languid, passive **8** immobile, inactive, listless, sluggish

inevitable 4 sure 5 fated 7 certain 8 destined

inexact 3 off 6 faulty, sloppy 8 careless, slovenly

inexhaustible 7 endless 8 infinite, tireless, unending

inexorable 4 firm 5 cruel, stiff 6 dogged 7 adamant 8 pitiless, ruthless

inexpensive 5 cheap 8 moderate

inexperienced 5 fresh, green, naive 6 callow 7 untried 8 unversed

inexplicable 8 abstruse, baffling, puzzling

infallible 4 sure 7 assured, certain, perfect 8 positive, reliable, surefire, unerring

infamy 4 evil 5 odium, shame 7 scandal 8 contempt, disgrace, dishonor, ignominy

infant 3 kid 4 babe, baby 5 child 7 neonate, newborn, preemie 8 suckling

infantryman 7 dogface, dragoon 8 chasseur, doughboy

infatuated 7 charmed, smitten 8 beguiled, enamored, obsessed

infect 4 ruin 5 spoil, taint, touch 6 blight, damage, poison 7 afflict, corrupt

infer 4 deem 5 glean, guess, judge, opine 6 deduce, gather, reason, reckon 7 presume, suppose, surmise

inferior 4 poor 6 junior 8 low-grade, mediocre 9 secondary 10 low-quality, second-rate, subsidiary 11 indifferent, subordinate, subservient, substandard 12 not up to snuff

infernal *see* 8 **dreadful**

inferno 4 hell, oven 5 abyss, Hades 7 furnace 8 hellfire, hellhole, scorcher

infertile 4 arid, bare 6 barren, effete, fallow 7 drained, sterile 8 depleted, desolate, impotent

infest 4 team 5 beset, crawl, creep, swarm 6 abound, infect, plague, ravage 7 overrun, torment

infidel 5 pagan 6 savage 7 atheist, heathen, heretic 8 agnostic, apostate

infiltrate 4 leak, seep 5 imbue, steep 6 absorb, seep in 7 pervade 8 colonize, permeate

infinite 4 vast **5** great **7** endless, immense **8** enormous

infinitesimal 3 wee **4** puny, tiny **6** minute

infirm *see* **3 ill**

inflame 4 fire, rile **5** craze, rouse **6** arouse, enrage, excite, heat up, ignite, incite, kindle, madden, stir up, work up **7** agitate, incense, provoke **8** enkindle

inflate 5 bloat, swell **6** blow up, dilate, expand, fill up, pump up **7** distend, improve, puff out

inflection 4 tone **5** tenor **6** accent

inflexible 4 firm, hard, taut **5** fixed, rigid, solid, stiff **6** dogged, mulish **7** adamant **8** obdurate, stubborn

inflict 4 dump **5** lay on, wreak **6** impose, unload **7** put upon

influence 4 hold, move, pull, stir, sway **5** clout, guide, impel, power **6** arouse, effect, incite, induce, prompt, weight **7** act upon, actuate, control, dispose, incline, inspire,

potency **8** dominion, leverage, persuade, pressure, prestige

influx 5 entry **6** inflow **7** arrival, indraft, ingress

inform 3 rat **4** fink, tell **5** edify **6** advise, clue in, notify, snitch, squeal, tattle, tell on, tip off **7** apprise, let know **8** acquaint, denounce

informal 4 easy **6** casual, simple **7** natural, offhand **8** familiar

information 4 data, news **5** facts, notes **6** notice, papers, report **7** account, tidings **8** briefing, bulletin, evidence, material

informer 3 rat **4** fink **5** Judas **6** canary **7** blabber, stoolie, tattler, traitor **8** betrayer, squealer

infraction 6 breach **8** trespass

infrastructure 4 base, root **5** basis **6** bottom, fabric, ground **7** bedrock, footing, support

infrequent 3 few **4** rare **6** fitful, seldom, unique **7** unusual **8** sporadic, uncommon

infringe 5 break 6 butt in, invade 7 disobey, impinge, intrude 8 encroach, overstep, trespass

infuriate 3 vex 4 gall, rile 5 anger, chafe 6 enrage, madden, offend 7 incense, inflame, outrage, provoke 8 irritate

infuse 5 imbue 7 fortify, implant, inspire, instill 8 impart to, pour into

ingenious 4 deft 6 adroit, artful, clever, crafty, expert, shrewd 7 cunning 8 skillful, stunning

ingenuous 4 open 5 frank, naive 6 direct, honest 7 artless, genuine 8 trusting

ingest 3 eat 4 gulp, take 5 drink 6 absorb, devour, imbibe, take in 7 consume, swallow

ingot 3 bar 5 block

ingrained 4 deep, firm 5 fixed 6 inborn, inbred, innate, rooted 8 inherent

ingratiating *see* 6 **genial**

ingredient 4 part 6 aspect, factor 7 element, feature

ingress 5 entry, way in 6 access 8 entrance

inhabitant 6 inmate, native, renter, tenant 7 boarder, citizen, denizen, dweller, settler 8 occupant, resident

inhale 5 sniff, snuff 6 suck in 7 inspire, respire

inherent 6 inborn, inbred, innate, native 7 natural

inheritance 6 devise, estate, legacy 7 bequest 8 bestowal, heritage

inhibit 3 bar, gag 4 curb, stop 5 block, check 6 arrest, enjoin, forbid, hinder, impede, muzzle 7 control, harness, prevent, repress, smother 8 hold back, obstruct, prohibit, restrain, restrict, suppress

inhospitable 4 cold, cool, rude 5 aloof 6 unkind 7 distant, hostile 8 impolite

inhuman 5 cruel 6 brutal, savage 7 brutish, satanic, vicious 8 barbaric, demoniac, fiendish, pitiless, ruthless

inimical *see* 7 **hostile**

inimitable 4 rare 6 unique 7 supreme 8 peerless

iniquitous *see* 4 **evil**

initial 5 first 6 maiden,

primal **7** opening **8** germinal, original, starting

initiate *see* **8 commence**

initiative 4 lead

inject 3 put **4** pump **5** force, imbue, infix **6** infuse, insert **7** instill, throw in **8** intromit

injection 4 hypo, shot **7** booster, vaccine

injudicious *see* **6 stupid**

injunction 4 writ **5** edict, order **7** command

injure 3 mar **4** harm, hurt, lame, maim **5** abuse, sting, wound, wrong **6** bruise, damage, debase, deform, impair, mangle, offend **7** afflict, blemish, violate **8** lacerate, mutilate

injurious 7 abusive, adverse, harmful, hurtful, noxious, ruinous **8** damaging

injury 3 cut **4** blow, gash, harm, hurt, stab **5** wound **6** bruise, damage, lesion **7** scratch

injustice 3 sin **4** bias, evil **5** wrong **6** injury **7** bigotry, offense, tyranny **8** foul play, inequity, iniquity

inkling 3 cue, tip **4** clue,

hint, idea **6** notion **7** glimmer

inky 3 jet **4** dark **5** black, raven, sable **7** stygian

inlet 3 bay **4** cove, gulf **5** bight, fiord, firth, fjord **6** harbor, strait **7** estuary, narrows **8** waterway

inmate 3 con **5** felon **6** lodger, tenant **7** convict **8** prisoner, resident

inn 5 hotel, lodge, motel, serai **6** hostel, imaret, tavern **7** pension **8** hostelry

innards 4 guts **6** bowels, vitals **7** gizzard, insides, viscera

innate 6 inborn, inbred, native **7** natural **8** inherent

inner 6 hidden, inside, inward, mental, middle **7** central, private, psychic **8** esoteric, interior, internal, personal

innkeeper 4 host, oste **6** tapper, venter **7** padrone **8** hosteler, hotelier, landlord, publican

innocent 3 tot **4** baby, naif, open, pure, tyro **5** clean, naive **6** chaste, honest, novice, simple **7** artless, ingenue, sinless, upright **8** harmless, pristine, spotless, virginal, virtuous

innocuous 4 dull, mild **5** banal, empty, trite, vapid **6** barren **7** insipid **8** harmless, innocent

innovation 5 shift **7** novelty

innuendo 4 hint **7** whisper

innumerable 6 myriad **8** numerous

inoculate 5 imbue, shoot **6** inject **7** implant, instill **8** immunize

inoffensive 4 mild, safe **5** bland **7** neutral **8** harmless, innocent

inopportune 7 awkward **8** ill-timed, untimely

in order 2 OK **4** neat, tidy **6** proper **7** correct, perfect **8** all right

inordinate *see* **7 extreme**

inorganic 4 dead **7** mineral **8** lifeless

in plain sight 7 exposed, obvious

inquest 5 probe **7** autopsy, delving, hearing, inquiry

inquire *see* **3 ask**

inquisitive 4 nosy **6** prying, snoopy **8** meddling

insane *see* **5 crazy**

inscription 5 motto, title **6** legend, rubric **7** address, caption, epigram, epitaph, heading, titulus, writing **8** colophon, epigraph, graffiti

inscrutable 6 arcane, hidden, masked, veiled **7** deadpan, elusive **8** baffling, puzzling

insect
    young: 4 grub, pupa **5** larva, nymph **6** larvae, maggot **9** chrysalis

insectivore 4 mole **5** shrew **6** desman, tenrec **7** moon rat **8** anteater, hedgehog

insecure 4 weak **5** frail, risky, shaky **6** infirm, unsafe, unsure, wobbly **7** dubious, exposed, rickety **8** doubtful, perilous, unstable, unsteady

insensate 4 cold **5** cruel **6** brutal **8** inhumane

insensibility 4 coma **5** swoon **6** apathy, torpor, trance **8** blackout, dullness, lethargy, numbness, obduracy

insensitive 4 cold, dead, numb **5** blase **7** callous **8** hardened

insert 3 add **5** embed, enter, imbed, infix, inlay, inset, pop in, put in, set in **6** infuse, inject, push in, tuck in **7** implant, intrude, place in, slide in, stuff in **8** thrust in

inset 5 embed, imbed, inlay, panel **6** insert

inside 2 in **5** inner **6** inmost, inward, secret **7** private **8** cliquish, esoteric, interior, internal, intimate

insidious *see* **7 devious**

insignia 3 bar **4** mark, sign **5** badge, medal, patch **6** emblem, stripe, symbol **7** chevron, epaulet

insignificant *see* **6 paltry**

insincere 5 false, lying **6** untrue **7** devious, evasive **8** guileful, two-faced, uncandid

insinuate *see* **5 imply**

insipid *see* **6 stupid**

insist 4 aver, hold, urge, warn **5** claim, vouch **6** assert, demand, exhort, repeat, stress **7** caution, command, contend, require **8** maintain

insolent *see* **4 rude**

insolvent 5 broke **6** ruined **8** bankrupt, wiped out

insouciant *see* **6 casual**

inspect 3 eye **4** scan **5** probe, study **6** peer at, peruse, review, survey **7** examine, explore, observe

inspire 4 fire, stir **5** cause, exalt, impel, rouse **6** arouse, excite, induce, prompt, vivify **7** animate, enliven, hearten, produce, promote, provoke, quicken **8** embolden, engender, enkindle, illumine, inspirit, motivate

install, instal 3 lay **4** seat **5** crown, embed, imbed, lodge, plant **6** induct, invest, locate, move in, ordain **7** arrange, emplace, situate, usher in **8** coronate, initiate

instance 4 case, time **6** sample **7** example **8** occasion, specimen

instant 5 flash, jiffy, quick, trice **6** abrupt, minute, moment, second, sudden

instead 6 in lieu, rather

instigate *see* **7 provoke**

instill, instil 4 pour **5** mix in, teach **6** impart, induce **7** implant, inspire

instinct 4 gift **5** knack **6** genius, nature **7** faculty **8** aptitude, tendency

institute 4 pass **5** begin, enact, found, set up, start **8** commence, initiate

institution 4 rite **6** custom, prison, school **7** academy, college, company, fixture **8** madhouse, nuthouse, seminary

instruct *see* **7 educate**

instrument 4 deed, tool **5** agent, grant, means, paper **6** agency, device, gadget **7** charter, machine, utensil, vehicle **8** contract

instrumental 5 vital **6** active, useful **7** crucial, helpful **8** a means to, decisive, valuable

insubordination 6 mutiny, revolt **8** sedition

insubstantial 4 airy, weak **5** frail, shaky, small **6** flimsy, modest, paltry, slight, unreal **7** fragile, trivial, unsound

8 bodiless, delicate, ethereal, trifling, unstable

insufferable 7 hateful **8** dreadful

insufficient 6 scanty, skimpy, sparse **7** lacking, wanting **8** impotent

insulate 5 cover **6** cut off, detach, enisle, shield **7** cushion, isolate, protect, seclude **8** separate

insult 3 cut **4** slap **5** abuse, cheek, scorn **6** deride, offend, slight **7** affront, offense, outrage **8** be rude to, belittle, rudeness

insurance 6 policy **8** coverage, security, warranty

insurrection 4 riot **6** mutiny, revolt, rising **8** outbreak, uprising

intact 4 safe **5** sound, whole **6** unhurt **7** perfect **8** complete, integral, unbroken, unharmed

intangible 5 vague **7** elusive, shadowy **8** abstract, ethereal, fleeting

integer 5 digit, whole **6** entity, figure, number **7** numeral

integral 4 full **5** basic, total,

whole **6** entire, intact **7** perfect **8** complete, finished, inherent

integrate *see* **3 mix**

integrity 5 unity **6** purity, virtue **7** decency, honesty, probity **8** cohesion, morality, strength

intellectual 4 sage **5** brain **6** brainy, mental, pundit, savant **7** bookish, egghead, scholar, thinker **8** abstract, academic, cerebral, highbrow, mandarin, rational

intelligent 4 keen, sage, wise **5** alert, canny, quick, sharp, smart **6** astute, brainy, bright, clever, shrewd **7** knowing, prudent **8** informed, sensible, thinking

intelligible *see* **5 clear**

intemperate 5 harsh **6** brutal, rugged, severe **7** extreme **8** uncurbed

intend 3 aim **4** mean, plan, wish **6** aspire, design, expect **7** propose, resolve

intense 4 deep, keen **5** acute, sharp **6** ardent, potent, strong **7** burning, earnest, extreme, fervent,

violent **8** emphatic, forceful, forcible, powerful, vehement

intent 3 aim, end, set **4** bent, gist, plan **5** drift, fixed **6** burden, design, import, steady **7** earnest, intense, meaning, purport, purpose **8** absorbed, piercing, resolved

inter 4 bury **5** inurn **6** entomb, inhume **7** inearth, lay away

interact 4 join, mesh **5** coact, unite **6** engage **7** combine, conjoin **8** dovetail

intercede 5 plead **6** step in **7** mediate, speak up

intercept 3 nab **4** grab, stay, stop, take **5** catch, seize **6** ambush, arrest, cut off, detain **7** deflect, reroute

interchange 4 swap **5** shift **6** switch **7** trading **8** exchange, junction, transfer

intercourse 4 talk **5** trade **6** coitus, parley **7** pairing, traffic **8** colloquy, commerce, congress, coupling, dealings

interdict *see* **6 forbid**

interest, interests 4 gain, good, part **5** share, stake, touch, yield **6** affect, behalf, engage, notice, profit, regard **7** attract, benefit, concern, holding, pastime, portion, pursuit **8** dividend

interfere 3 jar, mix **6** butt in, horn in, meddle, rush in, step in **7** counter, intrude **8** conflict

interim 7 stopgap **8** interval, meantime, temporal

interior 4 bush **5** inner **6** inside, inward **8** internal

interject 5 put in **6** inject, insert, slip in **7** force in

interlope 6 invade, meddle **7** intrude, obtrude **8** encroach, infringe, trespass

interlude 5 break, event, letup, pause **6** recess **7** episode, respite **8** incident, interval

intermediate 3 mid **4** fair, mean, so-so **6** median, medium, middle, midway **7** average, halfway,

mediate **8** mediocre, middling, moderate

interminable 6 prolix **7** endless **8** infinite

intermingle *see* **3 mix**

intermission 3 gap **4** halt, rest, stop **5** break, pause **6** hiatus, recess **8** interval

intermittent 6 fitful **8** on and off, periodic, sporadic

intern 6 commit, detain **7** confine, impound **8** imprison, restrain

internal 5 inner, state **8** domestic, interior

Internet terms: 3 AOL, DSL, FAQ, FTP, GIF, ISP, net, PDF, RDF, URL, USI, web, WWW **4** baud, blog, chat, host, HTML, Java, link, post, SMTP, spam, wi-fi, worm, VOIP **5** ASCII, cyber, e-mail, flame, virus, Yahoo **6** applet, cookie, dial-up, domain, Google, online, server, web log **7** browser, netizen, spiders, spyware, Website **8** bookmark, download, firewall

interpolate 3 add **5** put in

6 inject, insert, work in **7** implant, intrude, stick in, throw in, wedge in **8** sandwich

interpose 6 butt in, impose, inject, insert, meddle, step in **7** intrude, mediate

interpret 3 see **4** read, take **6** accept, define, render, reword **7** clarify, explain, make out, restate, unravel **8** construe, decipher

interrogate 3 ask **4** test **5** grill, probe, query **7** examine **8** question

interrupt 4 stop **5** sever **7** cut in on, disjoin, disturb **8** break off

intersect 4 meet **5** cross **6** bisect, divide **7** overlap **8** crosscut, transect, traverse

intersperse 3 dot, mix **5** strew **6** mingle, pepper **7** bestrew, scatter, wedge in **8** disperse, sprinkle

interstice 4 slit, slot **5** crack, space **7** opening **8** aperture, interval

interval 3 gap **4** gulf, rest, rift **5** break, cleft, pause, space, spell **6** breach, hiatus, recess, season **7** interim, opening

intervene 4 pass **6** befall, butt in, step in **7** break in, intrude, mediate

interview 4 chat, talk **6** parley **7** meeting **8** audience

intestines 4 guts **6** bowels **7** insides, viscera **8** entrails

intimate 3 pal **4** chum, dear, deep, hint **5** bosom, buddy, close, crony, imply, rumor **6** allude, direct **7** guarded, private, special, suggest **8** detailed, familiar, indicate, personal, thorough

intimation 4 clue, hint, sign **5** rumor **7** inkling, portent **8** allusion, innuendo

intime 4 cozy **8** intimate

in time 6 before, sooner **7** earlier

intimidate 3 cow **5** alarm, bully, daunt, scare **6** coerce, menace, subdue **7** buffalo, terrify **8** browbeat, frighten

into 2 in, to **5** among **6** inside, toward, within

intolerable 7 hateful, racking

intolerant **7** bigoted, hostile, jealous

intonation **4** tone **5** pitch **6** accent **8** chanting

in toto **5** in all, uncut **6** entire, wholly **7** totally **8** as a whole, entirely, outright

intoxicated *see* **5 drunk**

intractable **6** mulish, ornery, unruly **7** froward, willful **8** obdurate, perverse, stubborn

intransigent **7** diehard **8** obdurate, stubborn

intrepid **4** bold **5** brave **6** daring, heroic **7** doughty, valiant **8** fearless, resolute

intricate **6** knotty, tricky **7** complex **8** involved

intrigue **3** spy **4** fire, plot **5** amour **6** absorb, arrest, scheme **7** attract, collude, romance **8** conspire, enthrall, scheming

intrinsic **5** basic **6** inborn, inbred, innate **7** natural **8** inherent

introduce **3** add **4** show, urge **5** begin, offer, put in, start **6** create, expose, import, inform, insert **7** advance, kick off, lead off, present, propose, sponsor **8** acquaint, initiate, lead into

introduction **6** change **7** novelty, opening, preface, prelude **8** foreword, preamble, prologue

introvert **5** loner **7** brooder, thinker

intrude **4** push **6** butt in, impose, meddle, thrust **8** encroach, trespass

intrusive **4** nosy **5** pushy **6** prying, snoopy **8** in the way, invasive

intuition **5** flash, hunch **7** insight, surmise **8** instinct

Inuit *see* **6 Eskimo**

inundate **4** glut **5** drown, flood, swamp **6** deluge, drench, engulf **8** overflow, saturate, submerge

inure **5** adapt, train **6** adjust, custom, harden, temper **7** toughen **8** accustom

invade **4** raid **4** flood, limit **6** assail, attack, engulf, infect, infest **7** assault, overrun, violate **8** restrict, trespass

invalid **4** null, sick, void, weak **5** false **6** ailing, infirm, sickly, unwell **7** amputee, cripple, unsound, useless **8** disabled

invalidate 5 annul **6** cancel, refute, repeal, weaken **7** nullify, vitiate **8** abrogate

invaluable 4 rare **6** choice

invariable 7 uniform **8** constant

invective 4 rant **5** venom **6** insult **7** censure, railing, sarcasm **8** diatribe

inveigh *see* **5 scold**

inveigle *see* **6 seduce**

invent 4 coin **6** cook up, create, devise, make up **7** concoct, develop, fashion, think up, trump up **8** conceive, contrive

invention 3 lie **4** fake, sham **6** design, device, gadget **7** fiction **8** creation

inventive 6 bright, clever

inventory 4 roll **5** goods, index, stock **6** roster, supply **7** catalog **8** register, schedule

inverse *see* **8 backward**

invest 4 fill, garb, give **5** adorn, allot, array, color, cover, dress, endow,

imbue **6** clothe, devote, enable, enrich, infuse, supply **7** appoint, license

investigate *see* **7 explore**

investment 4 ante, risk **5** share, stake **7** venture **8** offering

inveterate 6 inured **7** adamant, chronic, diehard **8** constant, habitual

invidious 7 vicious **8** spiteful

invigorate 4 stir **5** brace, cheer, liven, pep up, renew, rouse, zip up **6** jazz up, vivify **7** animate, enliven, fortify, refresh, restore **8** energize, vitalize

inviolate 4 pure **6** intact, sacred, secret **8** hallowed

invisible 6 covert, hidden, unseen, veiled **7** obscure

invite 3 bid **4** call, lure, urge **5** tempt **6** entice, induce **7** attract, solicit, welcome

invocation 4 plea **6** appeal, orison, prayer **8** petition

invoke *see* **7 beseech**

involuntary 6 forced, reflex **7** coerced

involve 5 imply, mix up

6 commit, engage, entail, wrap up **7** contain, embroil, include **8** comprise, entangle

inward, inwards 5 inner **6** mental, toward **7** going in, ingoing, private **8** incoming, interior, inwardly, personal

ion
  part of: 8 molecule
  loses or gains: 8 electron

iota 3 bit, jot **4** atom, spot, whit **5** shred, spark, speck **7** smidgin **8** particle

IOU 4 chit, debt, note **6** marker

Iowa
  abbreviation: 2 IA
  nickname: 7 Hawkeye
  capital/largest city: 9 Des Moines
  lake: 5 Clear, Storm **6** Spirit
  river: 4 Iowa **8** Missouri **11** Mississippi

Iphigenia
  father: 9 Agamemnon
  brother: 7 Orestes
  sister: 7 Electra
  saved by: 7 Artemis

Iran
  other name: 6 Persia
  capital/largest city:
  6 Tehran **7** Teheran
  mountain: 6 Elburz, Zagros
  highest point: 8 Damavand, Demavend
  sea: 7 Arabian, Caspian
  island: 7 Abu Musa
  physical feature:
    gulf: 4 Oman **7** Persian
    strait: 6 Hormuz
  feature:
    clothing: 6 chador **7** chawdar
    throne: 7 Peacock

Iraq
  capital/largest city: 7 Baghdad
  mountain: 6 Zagros
  river: 6 Tigris **9** Euphrates
  physical feature:
    desert: 6 Syrian
    gulf: 7 Persian
  place:
    ancient gardens: 7 Hanging
    ruins: 2 Ur **7** Babylon
    Sumerian temple tower: 8 Ziggurat

irascible *see* **7** grouchy

ire 4 fury, rage **5** anger, wrath **6** choler **7** outrage, umbrage **8** vexation

Ireland
  other name: 4 Eire, Erin
  capital/largest city: 6
    Dublin
  river: 5 Boyne **6** Liffey **7**
    Shannon
  sea: 5 Irish **8** Atlantic
  island: 4 Aran **6** Achill **8**
    Aranmore, Inisheer
  physical feature:
    bay: 5 Sligo **6** Bantry,
      Dingle, Galway, Tralee
      7 Donegal, Dundalk
  feature:
    ancient book: 5 Kells
    castle: 4 Tara **7**
      Blarney
    military group: 3 IRA
    political movement: 8
      Sinn Fein
    stone: 7 Blarney

iridescent 5 shiny **7**
  glowing **8** colorful

Irish 4 Erse **4** Celtic,
  dander, Gaelic, temper
  accent: 6 brogue
  flower: 8 shamrock
  girl: 7 colleen
  king: 9 Brian Boru
  saint: 7 Patrick

Irish Mythology
  cats: 8 Kilkenny
  hero: 10 Cuchulainn
  king: 4 Bres **5** Ronan

    9 Conchobar
  king of gods: 4 Finn **5**
    Fionn

irk 3 bug, vex **4** gall **5**
  annoy **6** bother, pester,
  ruffle **7** provoke **8** irritate

ironic, ironical 3 odd **5**
  funny, weird **6** biting **7**
  abusive, caustic, curious,
  cutting, mocking, strange
  8 derisive, sardonic

irons 5 bonds **6** chains **7**
  fetters, presses, smooths **8**
  manacles, shackles

Iroquois
  tribe: 6 Cayuga, Mohawk,
    Oneida, Seneca **8**
    Onondaga **9** Tuscarora

irrational 6 absurd **7**
  foolish, unsound

irregular 3 odd **5** bumpy,
  queer, rough **6** broken,
  uneven **7** crooked,
  unusual **8** aberrant,
  abnormal, improper,
  peculiar, singular

irrelevant 5 inapt **7** foreign,
  off base

irrepressible 7 vibrant **8**
  bubbling, galvanic

irresistible 8 alluring,
  enticing

irresolute 4 weak **6** fickle,

unsure **8** doubtful, hesitant, unsteady, wavering

irresponsible 4 rash **7** foolish **8** careless, immature, reckless

irreverent 5 saucy **6** brazen **7** impious, profane **8** critical, impudent

irrevocable 5 final

irritable *see* **7 grouchy**

irritate 3 irk, vex **5** anger, annoy, chafe, peeve **6** nettle, worsen **7** inflame, provoke **8** make sore

irruption 4 raid **5** break, foray **6** inroad **7** upsurge **8** bursting, invasion

Isaac
    father: 7 Abraham
    mother: 5 Sarah
    brother: 7 Ishmael
    wife: 7 Rebekah
    son: 4 Esau **5** Jacob
    blessed: 5 Jacob
    sacrificed at: 6 Moriah

Iscariot *see* **5 Judas**

Ishmael
    father: 7 Abraham
    mother: 5 Hagar
    brother: 5 Isaac

Ishtar
    origin: 8 Assyrian
    goddess of: 3 war **4** love

Isis
    origin: 8 Egyptian
    goddess of: 9 fertility
    husband: 6 Osiris
    son: 5 Horus

Islam
    adherent: 4 Sufi **5** Shiah, Sunni **6** Moslem, Muslim, Shiite, Wahabi **7** Sunnite
    deity: 5 Allah
    fasting month: 7 Ramadan
    flight from Mecca: 6 hegira
    founder/prophet: 8 Mohammed, Muhammad
    holy city: 5 Mecca **6** Medina
    holy war: 5 jahad, jihad
    house of worship: 6 mosque
    Islamic school: 8 madrassa, madressa
    legal verdict: 5 fatwa
    pilgrimage to Mecca: 4 hadj, hajj
    holy building: 5 Kaaba
    religious leader: 4 imam
    scripture: 5 Koran

island 4 isle **5** atoll, haven,

islet, oasis **6** refuge **7** enclave, retreat, shelter

isle, islet 3 ait, cay, key **4** holm **5** atoll, islet **6** island

isolate 6 banish, detach, enisle **7** seclude **8** insulate, separate, set apart

Israel
  former name: 5 Jacob
  wrestled with: 5 angel

Israel
  other name: 4 Zion **6** Canaan **9** Palestine
  capital/largest city: 9 Jerusalem
  lake: 7 Dead Sea, (Sea of) Galilee **8** Tiberias
  river: 6 Jordan
  sea: 3 Red **4** Dead **7** Galilee **13** Mediterranean
  physical feature:
    desert: 5 Negev, Sinai
    gulf: 5 Aqaba
    plain: 5 Judea **6** Sharon
  place:
    mount: 4 Zion **6** Olives, Scopus
  feature:
    collective village: 7 kibbutz
    cooperative village: 6 moshav
    dance: 4 hora
    movement: 7 Zionism

    Palestinian uprising: 8 intifada
    scrolls: 7 Dead Sea

Israel, tribes of 3 Dan, Gad **4** Levi **5** Asher, Judah **6** Joseph, Reuben, Simeon **7** Zebulun **8** Benjamin, Issachar, Naphtali

Israelite 3 Jew **6** Hebrew, Jewish, Semite **7** Judaist **8** Hebraist
  descended from: 5 Jacob

issue 4 gush, rise, stem **5** allot, arise, ensue, erupt, go out, heirs, spout, yield **6** emerge, follow, number, result, spring **7** dispute, emanate, flow out, give out, outcome, outflow, pass out, problem, proceed, product, progeny **8** children, dispense, drainage, eruption, granting, question

isthmus 4 neck, spit **5** point, strip **6** narrow, strait, tongue **7** narrows

Italy
  capital/largest city: 4 Roma, Rome
  mountain: 4 Alps, Etna **9** Apennines, Dolomites
  volcano: 4 Etna

8 Vesuvius
highest point: 9 Mont
   Blanc
lake: 4 Como **5** Garda **8**
   Maggiore
river: 2 Po **4** Arno **5**
   Tiber **7** Rubicon
sea: 6 Ionian **8** Adriatic
   13 Mediterranean
island: 4 Elba **5** Capri **6**
   Sicily **8** Sardinia
physical feature:
   bay: 6 Naples
   lagoon: 6 Venice
   pass: 7 Brenner,
     Simplon
   resort: 7 Riviera
   strait: 6 Sicily **7**
     Messina, Otranto
place:
   leaning tower: 4 Pisa
   opera house: 7 La Scala
   palace: 5 Doges
   road: 9 Appian Way
food:
   cheese: 8 parmesan **9**
     provolone
   dish: 5 pizza **6** scampi
     7 lasagna, ravioli,
     risotto
   wine: 7 Chianti
itch 3 yen **4** ache, long,
   pine **5** crave, crawl, creep,
   yearn **6** desire, hanker,

hunger, thirst **7** craving **8**
have a yen, yearning
item 4 unit **5** entry, piece,
point, story, thing **6**
detail, matter, notice **7**
account, article, feature,
subject
itemize 6 detail **7** specify **8**
spell out
iterate 6 repeat **7** restate
itinerant 5 nomad, rover **7**
migrant, nomadic,
roaming, vagrant **8**
vagabond, wanderer
itinerary 3 log **5** diary,
route **6** course **7** account,
circuit, journal **8** schedule
It's a Wonderful Life
   director: 5 (Frank) Capra
   cast: 4 (Donna) Reed **7**
     (James) Stewart **9**
     (Lionel) Barrymore
itsy-bitsy *see* **4** tiny
Ivanhoe
   author: 5 (Sir Walter)
     Scott
ivory 4 tusk **6** dentin
   source: 6 walrus **8**
     elephant
Ivory Coast
   French name: 11 Cote
     d'Ivoire
   largest city: 7 Abidjan

sea: 8 Atlantic
physical feature:
   gulf: 6 Guinea
ivory towered
   6 remote **8** academic,
   romantic
Ivy League 4 Penn

(Pennsylvania), Yale **5**
Brown **7** Cornell,
Harvard **8** Columbia **9**
Dartmouth, Princeton
IWW 5 (labor) union **8**
   Wobblies
   leader: 4 Debs **7**
   Haywood

J

jab *see* **3** hit

jabber *see* **8** nonsense

jackass 3 ass **4** fool, mule
5 burro, dummy, idiot **6**
donkey

jacket 4 case, coat **5** cover
6 blazer, casing, folder,
sheath **7** wrapper **8**
envelope, mackinaw

Jackson, Andrew
  nickname: 10 Old
    Hickory
  presidential rank: 7
    seventh
  party: 10 Democratic
  state represented: 2 TN
  defeated: 4 Clay **5**
    Adams
  vice president: 7 Calhoun
    8 Van Buren
  born: 2 SC **6** Waxhaw
  military career:
    defeated: 6 Creeks **9**
      Cherokees
    military governor of: 7
      Florida

  **notable events of
  lifetime/term:**
    battle: 5 Alamo **10**
      New Orleans
    Trail of: 5 Tears
  wife: 6 Rachel
Jackson, Jesse Louis
  title: 8 Reverend
  religion: 7 Baptist
  connected with: 4 PUSH,
    SCLC **7** Rainbow
    (Coalition)
Jackson, Michael
  siblings: 4 Tito **5** Janet,
    Randy **6** Jackie, La
    Toya, Marlon **7**
    Maureen **8** Jermaine
  ranch: 9 Neverland
  trademark: 5 glove **8**
    moonwalk
Jacob
  father: 5 Isaac
  mother: 7 Rebekah
  brother: 4 Esau
  wives: 4 Leah **6** Rachel
  concubines: 5 Bilah **6**
    Zilpah
  dream of: 6 ladder

wrestled with: 5 angel
name changed to: 6 Israel

jacuzzi 4 bath

jaded 5 blase, bored, sated, spent, stale, tired, weary **6** cloyed, dulled, fagged **7** glutted, satiate, spoiled, wearied, worn-out **8** fatigued, overused, shopworn

jagged *see* **6 zigzag**

jaguar 3 cat **5** tiger **6** feline **7** panther **8** uturuncu

jail 3 bag, can, jug, nab, pen **4** book, brig, bust, cell, keep, stir **5** seize **6** arrest, collar, cooler, lockup, prison, take in **7** bring in, capture, confine, dungeon, slammer **8** bastille, big house, imprison, stockade

jalopy 3 car **4** auto, heap **5** motor **6** wheels **7** flivver, machine, vehicle

jam 3 fix, mob, ram, sea **4** army, cram, herd, host, mess, pack, push, stop **5** block, cease, crowd, crush, drove, flock, horde, pinch, press, shove, stall, stick, stuff, swarm, wedge **6** edge in, pickle, plight, scrape, thrust **7** dilemma,

force in, squeeze, trouble **8** hot water, obstruct, quandary

Jamaica
capital/largest city: 8 Kingston
highest point: 4 Blue
sea: 8 Atlantic **9** Caribbean
feature:
guerilla fighters: 7 Maroons
music: 7 calypso
witch doctor: 8 obeah man
food:
drink: 3 rum **8** tia maria
meat: 4 jerk

jamboree *see* **5 party**

James 7 apostle
brother: 4 John, Levi **5** Judas
disciple of: 5 Jesus
killed by: 5 Herod (Agrippa)

Jane Eyre
author: 6 (Charlotte) Bronte

jangle *see* **6 jingle**

janitor 5 super **6** porter **8** handyman

January
flower: 8 snowdrop

9 carnation
gem: 6 garnet
holiday: 7 Kwanzaa (1, last day) **8** Epiphany (6), New Year's (Day, 1)
origin of name: 5 Janus
place in year:
   Gregorian: 5 first
   Julian/Roman: 8 eleventh
Zodiac sign: 8 Aquarius **9** Capricorn

Janus
   origin: 5 Roman
   god of: 8 doorways

Japan
   other name: 5 Nihon **6** Nippon
   capital/largest city: 3 Edo **5** Tokyo
   highest point: 4 Fuji **7** Fujisan
   sea: 5 Japan **6** Inland **7** Pacific
   island: 6 Honshu, Kyushu, Ryukyu **7** Okinawa, Shikoko **8** Hokkaido
   physical feature:
     bay: 3 Ise **4** Miku, Tosa, Yedo **5** Osaka, Tokyo **9** Kagoshima
     divine wind: 8 kamikaze
   feature:
     bed: 5 futon

     clothing: 3 obi **6** kimono
   flower arranging: 7 ikebana
   paper-folding art: 7 origami
   poem: 4 waka **5** haiku, tanka
   puppet theater: 7 bunraku
   rush floor covering: 6 tatami
   sport: 4 judo, sumo (wrestling) **6** karate
   theater: 2 no **3** noh **6** kabuki
   tree: 6 bonsai
   way of the warrior: 7 bushido
   food:
     beverage: 4 sake **8** green tea
     dish: 5 sushi **7** sashimi, tempura **8** sukiyaki, teriyaki, yakitori

jape 4 gibe, joke **5** antic, caper, prank **7** mockery

jar 3 din, jug, pot, urn **4** bong, bray, buzz, daze, faze, jolt, rock, stir, stun **5** blare, blast, brawl, clang, clank, crash, crock, flask, quake, shake, shock, upset **6** beaker, bottle, impact, racket, rattle,

vessel **7** agitate, astound, clangor, clatter, perturb, shake up, startle, stupefy **8** bewilder, canister, disquiet, unsettle
Spanish: 4 olla

jargon 4 bosh, bull, bunk, cant **5** argot, fudge, hooey, idiom, lingo, prate, usage **6** babble, brogue, drivel, patois, pidgin, piffle **7** blabber, blather, dialect, prattle, rubbish **8** malarkey, nonsense, parlance, verbiage

Jason
  leader of: 9 Argonauts
  teacher: 6 Chiron **7** centaur, Cheiron
  retrieved: 6 (Golden) Fleece
  ship: 4 Argo
  loved by: 5 Medea

jaunty 4 airy, neat, trim **5** natty, perky **6** blithe, bouncy, breezy, dapper, lively, sporty, spruce **7** buoyant **8** carefree, debonair

javelin 4 dart **5** lance, shaft, spear **10** projectile

jaw 3 gab, rap **4** chat, chin, talk **7** jawbone, palaver **8** chitchat, mandible

Jaws
  author: 8 (Peter) Benchley
Jayhawker State
  nickname of: 6 Kansas

jealous 4 wary **7** anxious, envious, mindful **8** covetous, grudging, watchful

jeer 3 boo, bug, dig, rap **4** barb, hiss, hoot, mock, razz, slam, slur **5** abuse, flout, hound, knock, scoff, scorn, sneer, taunt, whoop **6** deride, harass, heckle, hector, insult, revile **7** catcall, laugh at, mockery, obloquy **8** derision, ridicule, scoffing

Jefferson, Thomas
  presidential rank: 5 third
  party: 20 Democratic-Republican
  state represented: 2 VA
  defeated: 5 Adams **8** Pinckney
  vice president: 4 Burr **7** Clinton
  born: 2 VA **8** Shadwell
  education: 14 William and Mary
  political career:
    secretary of: 5 State
    minister to: 6 France

notable events of lifetime/term:
  expedition of: 13 Lewis and Clark
  importation prohibited of: 6 slaves
  purchase: 9 Louisiana
mother: 4 Jane
wife: 6 Martha
associated with: 5 Sally (Hemings)

jehad *see* **5 jihad**

Jehovah 3 god **4** YHWH **5** diety

jejune 4 dull **5** banal, inane, stale, trite, vapid **7** humdrum, insipid, puerile **8** ordinary

jell 3 gel, jam, set **4** clot, firm **5** jelly **7** congeal, thicken

jellyfish 5 hydra, polyp, softy **6** coward, medusa, nettle **7** sunfish **8** weakling

jeopardy *see* **5 peril**

jerk *see* **5 idiot**

jerky 4 beef, meat **5** jolty, jumpy **6** choppy, elboic, jouncy **7** biltong, charqui, fidgety, twitchy

jerry-built *see* **5 frail**

jersey 3 cow **5** maillot, shirt **6** tricot **7** sweater **8** camisole, pullover

jest *see* **4 joke**

jester *see* **5 clown**

Jesus
also called: 6 Christ **7** Holy One, Messiah **8** Nazarene, Son of God
mother: 4 Mary
stepfather: 6 Joseph
birthplace: 9 Bethlehem
lived in: 8 Nazareth
death place: 9 Jerusalem
buried by: 6 Joseph (of Arimathea)
disciples: 4 John, Jude **5** James, Judas (Iscariot), Peter, Simon **6** Andrew, Philip, Thomas **7** Matthew **12** Bartholomew (Nathanael)
secret follower: 9 Nicodemus

jet 4 gush **5** flush, issue, shoot, spout, spray, spurt, surge, swash **6** effuse, nozzle, rush up, squirt, stream **7** syringe **8** atomizer, fountain, Spritzer

jetty 4 dike, dock, mole, pier, quay, slip **5** black, ebony, groin, levee, raven, sable, wharf **6** bridge **7** sea wall **8** buttress

Jew 6 Essene, Hebrew, Judean, Semite **7** Edomite, Judaist, Moabite **8** Hebraist, Sephardi **9** Israelite

jewel 3 ace, gem, pip **4** bead, dear, find, ring, whiz **5** honey, pearl, prize, stone, tiara **6** bangle, bauble, brooch, locket, winner **7** earring, pendant, trinket **8** bracelet, necklace, ornament, pure gold, treasure

Jewish 6 Hebrew, Judaic **7** Hebraic, Semitic
  bread: 5 matzo **6** matzoh **7** challah
  candelabrum: 7 menorah
  coming of age: 10 bar mitzvah, bat mitzvah
  dietary laws: 7 kashrut **8** kashruth
    fit to eat: 6 kosher
    not fit to eat: 4 tref
  holy day/festival: 5 Purim, seder **6** Sukkot **7** Shavuot **8** Chanukah, Hanukkah, Passover **9** Yom Kippur **12** Rosh Hashanah
  law/scripture: 5 Torah **6** Gemara, Talmud, Tanach **7** Mishnah
  marriage canopy: 6 chupah
  prayerbook: 6 mahzor, siddur **7** machzor
  quarter: 6 ghetto, mellah
  school: 5 heder **6** cheder
  skullcap: 5 kipah **8** yarmulka
  synagogue: 4 shul **5** schul
  toast: 8 mazel tov

jib 3 arm, shy **4** balk, boom, sail, tack **5** demur, gigue, stick **6** recoil **7** scruple

jibe *see* **5 agree**

jiffy *see* **7 instant**

jigger 4 dram, shot **5** glass **6** device, doodad, gadget, object **7** gimmick, measure

jiggle *see* **5 shake**

jihad 6 strife **7** holy war **8** struggle

jilt 5 leave **6** betray, desert **7** forsake, let down

jimmy 3 bar, pry **5** force, lever **7** crowbar

jingle 4 ring **5** clang, clank, clink, ditty **6** jangle, tinkle **7** clatter, ringing **8** doggerel, facetiae, limerick

jinx   386

jinx *see* **3 hex**

jitney 3 bus, cab

jitterbug 5 dance, lindy **8**
lindy hop

job 3 lot **4** care, duty, part,
role, spot, task, work **5**
chore, craft, field, place,
quota, share, stint, trade,
trust **6** affair, career,
charge, errand, living,
metier, office, output **7**
calling, mission, product,
pursuit **8** activity,
business, capacity,
contract, function,
position, province,
vocation

Job 8 sufferer
father: 8 Issachar
friend: 5 Elihu **6** Bildad,
Zophar **7** Eliphaz

Jocasta
queen of: 6 Thebes
brother: 5 Creon
husband: 5 Laius **7**
Oedipus
son: 7 Oedipus **8** Eteocles
9 Polynices
daughter: 6 Ismene **8**
Antigone
death by: 7 hanging,
suicide

Jochebed
son: 5 Aaron, Moses

jocose *see* **3 fun**

jocular *see* **6 jovial**

jog 3 bob, jar, tug **4** jerk,
pull, rock, stir, trot, yank
5 nudge, shake, twist **6**
bounce, jiggle, jostle,
jounce, prompt, twitch,
wrench **7** actuate, animate
8 activate, energize

John
father: 7 Zebedee
brother: 5 James
son: 5 Peter

Johnny-come-lately 8
newcomer

Johnson, Andrew
presidential rank: 11
seventeenth
party: 10 Democratic
state represented: 2 TN
succeeded: 7 Lincoln
born: 2 NC **7** Raleigh
died: 2 TN **14** Carter's
Station
political career:
first president to be: 9
impeached
governor of: 2 TN
notable events of lifetime/
term: 14 Reconstruction
purchase of: 6 Alaska

Johnson, Lyndon Baines
nickname: 3 LBJ

presidential rank: 11 thirty-sixth
party: 10 Democratic
state represented: 2 TX
succeeded: 7 Kennedy
defeated: 9 Goldwater
vice president: 8 Humphrey
born: 2 TX **9** Stonewall
notable events of lifetime/ term:
  act: 11 Civil Rights **12** Voting Rights
  assassination of: 4 King **7** Kennedy
  capture of: 6 Pueblo
  war: 7 Vietnam
  wife: 7 Claudia
    nickname: 8 Lady Bird
  children: 4 Luci **5** Lynda

John the Baptist
  descendant of: 5 Aaron
  precurser of: 5 Jesus

join 3 hug, mix **4** abut, ally, band, bind, fuse, glue, link, meet, pool **5** affix, brush, chain, enter, graze, marry, merge, paste, reach, skirt, stick, touch, unify, unite **6** attach, bridge, couple, fasten, solder, splice **7** combine, connect **8** border on, enroll in, federate, hold fast

joint 4 hock, knee, knot, link **5** elbow, hinge, nexus **6** common, mutual, shared, united **7** knuckle, unified **8** junction, juncture
  kind:
    ball and socket: 3 hip **8** shoulder
    fused: 5 skull
    hinged: 4 knee **5** elbow
    unfused: 3 hip, jaw **4** knee **5** elbow **8** shoulder

joist 4 beam **5** brace **6** timber **7** support

joke 3 gag, pun, wit **4** butt, dupe, fool, gibe, goof, gull, jape, jest, josh, lark, mock, quip **5** antic, caper, cinch, clown, farce, prank, put-on, roast, tease, trick **6** banter, bon mot, deride, frolic, gambol, jeer at, parody, satire, take in, whimsy **7** chortle, lampoon, laugh at, scoff at, smile at, snicker **8** repartee, ridicule, town fool

jolly *see* **5 happy**
jolt *see* **5 shake**

Jonah
  swallowed by: 4 fish **5** whale

jonquil 4 bulb, lily **8** daffodil **9** narcissus

Jordan
  capital/largest city: 5 Amman
  highest point: 8 Jabal Ram
  river: 6 Jordan
  sea: 3 Red **4** Dead **7** Galilee **13** Mediterranean
  physical feature:
    desert: 6 Syria
    gulf: 5 Aqaba
    wind: 7 Khamsin
  place:
    ruins: 5 Petra
  feature:
    headdress: 8 kaffiyeh
    village headman: 7 mukhtar
  food:
    dessert: 7 baklava

Joseph
  father: 4 Bani **5** Aseph, Jacob **10** Mattathias
  mother: 6 Rachel
  wife: 4 Mary **7** Asenath
  stepson: 5 Jesus
  buried: 5 Jesus

josh *see* **4 joke**

Joshua
  succeeded: 5 Moses
  captured: 7 Jericho, Lachish

jostle 3 jab **4** bump, butt, poke, prod, push **5** elbow **7** collide **8** shoulder

jot 3 bit, dot **4** iota, list, mite, note, snip, whit **5** enter, speck, trace **6** record, trifle **7** modicum, one iota, put down, set down, smidgen, snippet **8** flyspeck, particle, register, scribble, take down

jounce 3 bob **6** bounce **7** rebound **8** ricochet

journal 3 log **5** album, daily, diary, paper, sheet **6** annual, ledger, memoir, record, weekly **7** almanac, daybook, gazette, history, logbook, monthly **8** calendar, notebook, register

journey *see* **6 voyage**

joust 4 tilt **5** combat, jostle **7** contend, contest, tourney **8** run a tilt

Jove *see* **7 Jupiter**

jovial 3 gay **5** jolly, merry, sunny **6** blithe, cheery, hearty, jocose, jocund

7 gleeful, jocular, playful, zestful **8** humorous, laughing, mirthful, sportive

jowl 3 jaw **5** cheek, chops **6** muzzle **8** mandible

joy 3 gem **4** glee **5** jewel, pride, prize **6** gaiety **7** delight, ecstasy, elation, rapture **8** gladness, pleasure, treasure

jubilant *see* **7 radiant**

jubilee *see* **5 party**

Judah, tribes of *see* **14 Israel, tribes of**

Judas
    brother: 5 James
    also called: 8 Thaddeus
    disciple of: 5 Jesus

Judas Iscariot 8 betrayer
    disciple of/betrayed: Jesus
    betrayed: 5 Jesus
    replaced by: 8 Matthias

judge 3 try **4** deem, find, hear, rank, rate **5** fancy, gauge, guess, infer, juror, value, weigh **6** assess, critic, decide, deduce, expert, review, rule on, settle, size up, umpire **7** analyze, arbiter, discern, justice, referee, resolve, suppose, surmise

8 appraise, conclude, consider, official, reviewer

Judgment Day 8 doomsday

judicial 5 legal **8** imposing, juristic, majestic, official

judiciary 5 bench, court

judicious *see* **6 astute**

jug 3 jar, urn **4** ewer **5** crock, stein **6** bottle, carafe, flagon, vessel **7** pitcher, tankard **8** decanter, demijohn

juggle 4 redo **5** alter **6** modify **7** falsify **8** disguise, fool with

juicy 3 wet **4** lush, racy **5** fluid, lurid, moist, pulpy, runny, sappy, spicy, vivid **6** fluent, liquid, watery **7** flowing **8** dripping, exciting, luscious

Julius Caesar
    author: 11 (William) Shakespeare

July
    flower: 8 larkspur
    holiday: 11 Bastille Day (14), Dominion Day (1) **15** Independence Day (4) **16** Saint Swithin's Day (15)
    gem: 4 ruby

place in year:
  Gregorian: 7 seventh
  Roman: 5 fifth
Zodiac sign: 3 Leo **6**
  Cancer

jumble *see* **3 mix**

jumbo *see* **4 huge**

jump 3 hop **4** buck, leap, pass, skip **5** boost, bound, pitch, start, surge, vault, wince **6** ambush, attack, bounce, flinch, gambol, go over, hurdle, prance, spring, upturn **7** maunder, overrun, upsurge **8** fall upon

jumpy *see* **7 anxious**

junction 6 linkup **7** conflux, joining

juncture 4 pass, seam **5** joint **6** crisis, linkup, moment **7** closure, joining, meeting **8** interval, occasion

June
  characteristic: 8 weddings
  event: 8 (summer) Solstice
  flower: 4 rose
  gem: 5 pearl
  holiday: 4 Flag (Day) **7** Father's (Day)
  place in year:
    Gregorian: 5 sixth

    Roman: 6 fourth
  Zodiac sign: 6 Cancer, Gemini

jungle 4 bush, wild **5** woods

Jungle Books, The
  author: 7 (Rudyard) Kipling

junior 5 later, lower, minor, newer **6** lesser **7** younger **8** inferior

junk 4 dump **5** scrap, trash, waste **6** debris, litter, refuse **7** clutter, discard, garbage, rubbish

junket 4 tour, trip **7** journey

Juno
  origin: 5 Roman
  queen of: 6 heaven
  father: 6 Saturn
  brother: 7 Jupiter
  husband: 7 Jupiter
  son: 4 Mars
  protectress of: 5 women **8** marriage
  corresponds to: 4 Hera, Here

junta 5 cabal **7** council

Jupiter
  also: 4 Jove
  god of: 5 light **7** heavens, weather
  corresponds to: 4 Zeus

Jupiter
  position: **5** fifth
  satellite: **2** Io **6** Europa **8**
  Amalthea, Callisto,
  Ganymede
  characteristic: **7** red spot
jurisdiction **3** say **4** area,
  beat, rule, sway, zone **5**
  field, range, reach, scope
  6 bounds, domain, sphere
  7 circuit, command,
  compass, control, quarter
jury **5** panel, peers **6** assize,
  twelve
just **3** but, due **4** fair, firm,
  good, only, sane **5** fully,
  moral, quite, solid, sound
  6 at most, barely, decent,
  hardly, honest, merely,
  proper, worthy **7** ethical,

merited, only now, upright
8 adequate, balanced,
deserved, narrowly,
recently, scarcely,
unbiased

justice **5** honor, right, truth
  6 amends, equity, the law,
  virtue **7** honesty, payment,
  penalty, probity, redress **8**
  fair play, fairness,
  goodness, legality
justification *see* **6 excuse**
justify *see* **8 validate**
jute
  varieties: **5** Bimli, China,
  Tossa, white **7** bastard
juvenile *see* **5 young**
juxtaposed **6** next to **8**
  adjacent, touching

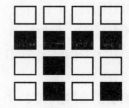

kabob 5 cabab, cabob, kabab, kebab, kebob **7** shaslik **8** shashlik

kahlua
    type: 6 brandy

kaiser 5 ruler **7** emperor, Wilhelm **8** autocrat

kaleidoscopic 6 mobile, motley **7** protean **8** shifting, unstable, variable

Kali
    also: 3 Uma **5** Durga **7** Parvati
    husband: 4 Siva **5** Shiva
    festival: 6 dewali
    goddess of: 5 death **7** disease

kangaroo
    young: 4 joey
    group of: 3 mob **5** troop

Kansas
    abbreviation: 2 KS **4** Kans
    nickname: 9 Jayhawker
    capital: 6 Topeka
    largest city: 7 Wichita
    highest point: 9 Sunflower
    river: 6 Kansas, Saline **8** Arkansas, Cimarron, Missouri **10** Republican
    physical feature:
        plains: 5 Great, Osage

karma 3 act **4** aura, deed, duty, fate, rite **5** force, power **6** action, kismet, spirit **7** destiny

Katzenjammer Kids
    creator: 5 (Rudolph) Dirks

Kazakhstan
    capital/largest city: 7 Alma-Ata
    sea: 4 Aral **7** Caspian
    physical feature: 7 steppes

kazoo 5 bazoo, zarah **6** hewgag

keel over 5 faint, swoon, upset **7** capsize, tip over **8** collapse, fall down, fall flat, flip over, overturn, turn over

keen 4 avid, fine **5** acute, alert, eager, sharp **6** ardent, astute, clever, fervid, fierce, shrewd

7 earnest, excited, fervent, intense, zealous **8** incisive

keep 3 bar **4** clog, fort, have, heap, hold, mind, pile, stay **5** abide, block, carry, cramp, delay, deter, guard, honor, lay in, place, stack, stall, stand, stick, stock, store, tie up, tower **6** castle, detain, endure, hamper, hinder, impede, pay for, remain, retain, retard **7** care for, carry on, furnish, inhibit, observe, possess, prevent, shackle, sustain **8** conserve, continue, hang on to, hold back, maintain, preserve, restrain

keep an eye on 5 watch **7** oversee

keep company 4 date **5** court **7** consort, hang out **8** go around, go steady

keeper 5 guard, nurse **6** duenna, escort, jailer, sentry, warden **7** curator **8** chaperon, guardian, retainer, sentinel

keep in mind 8 consider, remember

keepsake 5 relic, token **6** emblem, memory, symbol

7 memento **8** memorial, reminder, souvenir

keg 3 tub, tun, vat **4** butt, cask, drum, tank **6** barrel **7** rundlet **8** hogshead, puncheon

Keller, Helen
in childhood: 4 deaf **5** blind
teacher: 8 (Anne) Sullivan

Kelly, Grace
husband: 7 (Prince) Rainier

Kelly, Walt
creator of: 4 Pogo

kelp 3 ash **4** agar, alga, leag **5** varec, varic, wrack **7** seaweed
source of: 4 soda **6** iodine

Kennedy, John Fitzgerald
nickname: 3 JFK **4** Jack
presidential rank: 11 thirty-fifth
party: 10 Democratic
state represented: 2 MA
defeated: 5 Nixon
vice president: 3 LBJ **7** Johnson
born: 2 MA **9** Brookline
died by: 13 assassination
assassinated by: 6 Oswald
military service: 6 US Navy

commander of: 6 PT boat
notable events of lifetime/ term: 9 Bay of Pigs **10** Berlin Wall, Peace Corps **13** missile crisis
  march: 11 Civil Rights
wife: 10 Jacqueline
  nickname: 6 Jackie
  second marriage to: 7 Onassis
children: 4 John **7** Patrick **8** Caroline

Kentucky
abbreviation: 2 KY
nickname: 9 Bluegrass
capital: 9 Frankfort
largest city: 10 Louisville
highest point: 5 Black **8** Big Black
river: 4 Ohio **5** Green **8** Big Sandy, Kentucky **9** Tennessee
physical feature:
  basin: 9 Bluegrass
  cave: 7 Mammoth
  gap: 10 Cumberland
feature:
  fort: 4 Knox
  race: 5 (Kentucky) Derby
  trail: 10 Wilderness

Kenya
capital/largest city: 7 Nairobi

highest point: 5 Kenya
lake: 6 Rudolf **8** Victoria
sea: 6 Indian
physical feature:
  plain: 4 Kano
  valley: 9 Great Rift
feature:
  round house: 6 shamba
  secret organization: 6 Mau Mau
  tree: 6 ayieke, baobab

kerchief 5 cloth, scarf **7** muffler **8** babushka, bandanna, kaffiyah, neckwear

kernel 3 nub, nut, pip, pit **4** core, germ, gist, pith, seed **5** grain, stone **6** center, marrow **7** nucleus

Ketcham, Hank
creator of: 6 Dennis (the Menace)

kettle 3 pan, pot, tub, vat **6** boiler, teapot, tureen **8** cauldron, crucible, saucepan

key 3 cue, fit **4** clue, gear, mode, suit **5** adapt, light, point, scale **6** adjust, answer, direct, opener **7** address, finding, meaning, pointer **8** indicant, solution, tonality

Key, Ted
  creator of: **5** Hazel
keyboard instrument 5
  organ, piano **6** spinet **8**
  psaltery, virginal
keyed up 5 tense **7** excited,
  nervous **8** volatile
Key Largo
  director: **6** (John) Huston
  based on story by: **8**
    (Maxwell) Anderson
  cast: **6** (Lauren) Bacall,
    (Humphrey) Bogart,
    (Claire) Trevor **8**
    (Edward G) Robinson **9**
    (Lionel) Barrymore
keynote *see* **7 essence**
keystone 4 base, crux, root
  5 basis **8** gravamen,
  linchpin
khaki 5 cloth **6** fabric **7**
  uniform
khan, kahn 3 inn **4** lord **5**
  chief, ruler **6** prince **7**
  emperor
  famous: **3** Aga, Ali **4**
    Yuan **6** Kublai **7**
    Genghis **8** Ghenghis
Khayyam, Omar
  author of: **8** Rubaiyat
kibitzer 3 pry **5** prier,
    snoop **6** butt-in **7** advisor,

meddler, snooper, watcher
  8 busybody, onlooker
kick 3 fun, hit, out, pep,
  vim **4** beef, boot, dash,
  fret, fume, fuss, life, punt,
  snap, tang, zest **5** eject,
  force, gripe, growl, power,
  punch, verve, vigor **6**
  flavor, grouch, grouse,
  object, recoil, remove,
  return, strike, stroke, thrill
  7 boot out, cast out,
  grumble, fly back, protest,
  rebound, sparkle, turn out
  8 backlash, complain,
  jump back, piquancy,
  pleasure, pungency,
  reaction, throw out,
  vitality
kickback 3 cut **5** bribe,
  graft, share **6** boodle,
  payoff, payola
kickoff 5 start **7** opening
kicks 3 fun **7** thrills **8**
  pleasure
kid *see* **4 joke**
Kiddush 6 prayer **8** blessing
kidnap 5 seize, steal **6**
  abduct, hijack, snatch **7**
  bear off, capture, impress,
  skyjack **8** bear away,
  carry off, shanghai

Kidnapped
    author: 8 (Robert Louis) Stevenson

kill 4 beat, do in, halt, hang, ruin, slay, stay **5** break, check, drown, erase, lynch, quell, shoot, waste **6** behead, defeat, murder, poison, rub out, stifle **7** bump off, butcher, cut down, destroy, execute, garrote, silence, smother, squelch, wipe out **8** blow away, dispatch, get rid of, knock off, massacre, strangle, string up

killer whale 4 orca **7** grampus

killjoy 6 grouch **8** grumbler, sourball, sourpuss

kill time 4 idle **6** dawdle

Kilmer, Joyce
    author of: 5 Trees

kiln 3 ost **4** bake, burn, fire, oast, oven **5** drier, glaze, stove, tiler **7** furnace **8** calciner, limekiln

Kim
    author: 7 (Rudyard) Kipling

kimono 4 gown, robe
    traditional costume of:
    5 Japan
    sash: 3 obi
    ornament: 7 netsuke

kin 4 akin, clan, kith, race **5** folks, tribe **6** family, people **7** kinfolk, kinsmen, related **8** clansmen, kinfolks

kind 3 ilk **4** cast, make, mold, sort, type **5** brand, breed, caste, civil, class, genre, genus, style **6** benign, gentle, kidney, kindly, nature, polite, strain, tender **7** amiable, cordial, variety **8** amicable, friendly, generous, gracious, merciful, obliging

kindle 4 fire, goad, prod, stir, urge, whet **5** awake, light, rouse, waken **6** arouse, excite, foment, ignite, incite, induce, stir up **7** agitate, animate, inflame, inspire, provoke, quicken, sharpen **8** enkindle

kindred 4 akin, like **5** alike **6** allied, united **7** related, similar **8** agreeing, familial, matching

kine 4 cows, oxen **6** cattle

king 3 HRH **5** liege, ruler

7 monarch **8** suzerain
Latin: 3 rex

King, Martin Luther
 born: 7 Atlanta, Georgia
 died: 7 Memphis **9**
  Tennessee
 wife: 7 Coretta (Scott)

King and I, The
 director: 4 (Walter) Lang
 cast: 4 (Deborah) Kerr **6**
  (Martin) Benson, (Rita)
  Moreno **7** (Yul) Brynner

kingdom 4 land **5** duchy,
 field, realm, state **6**
 domain, empire, nation,
 sphere **7** country,
 dukedom **8** dominion,
 monarchy

King Kong
 director:
  1933: 6 (Merian C)
   Cooper
  1976: 10 (John)
   Guillermin
 cast:
  1933: 4 (Fay) Wray **5**
   (Bruce) Cabot **6**
   (James) Flavin **7**
   (Noble) Johnson **9**
   (Robert) Armstrong
  1976: 5 (Jessica) Lange
   6 (Charles) Grodin **7**
   (Jeff) Bridges **8** (John)
   Randolph

King Lear
 author: 11 (William)
  Shakespeare

king of gods 4 Amen,
 Amon, Finn, Zeus **5**
 Ammon, Enlil, Fionn,
 Wotan **6** Marduk **7**
 Jupiter **8** Merodach

kink 4 coil, flaw, knot, pang
 5 cramp, crick, crimp,
 frizz, gnarl, hitch, quirk,
 snarl, spasm, twist **6**
 defect, foible, glitch,
 oddity, tangle, twinge,
 vagary **7** crinkle, frizzle **8**
 crotchet

kinky 3 odd **4** sick, wiry **5**
 kooky, queer **6** frizzy,
 matted, quirky, twisty **7**
 bizarre, deviant, frizzly,
 knotted, strange, tangled,
 twisted, unusual **8**
 aberrant, abnormal,
 crinkled, freakish, frizzled,
 peculiar, perverse

kinsman 3 sib, son **4** aunt,
 heir **5** child, uncle **6**
 cousin, father, mother,
 parent, sister **7** brother **8**
 daughter, landsman,
 relation, relative

Kirghiz *see* **10 Kyrgyzstan**
Kiribati
 other name: 7 Gilbert

(Islands)
capital/largest city: 6 Tarawa
island: 5 Flint, Ocean **6** Banaba, Canton, Malden, Tarawa **7** Abemama, Fanning, Gilbert, Marakei, Nonouti, Phoenix, Vostock **8** Caroline, Starbuck
sea: 7 Pacific

kismet 3 end, lot **4** doom, fate **5** karma, moira **7** destiny, fortune, portion **8** God's will

kiss 4 buss, neck **6** smooch, salute **8** osculate

kit 3 rig **4** gear **5** tools **6** outfit, tackle, things **7** devices **8** supplies, utensils

kitchen 6 bakery, cocina, galley **7** cuisine **8** cookroom, scullery

kittenish 3 coy **7** playful

klutzy 4 dumb **6** clumsy, stupid **7** awkward

knack 4 bent, gift, turn **5** flair, forte, skill **6** genius, talent **7** ability, faculty, finesse **8** aptitude, capacity, facility

knave 3 cad, cur, dog, rat **4** jack (cards) **5** phony, rogue, scamp **6** con man, rascal, rotter, varlet, wretch **7** bounder, culprit **8** scalawag, swindler

knee breeches 8 breeches, jodhpurs, knickers

kneel 3 bow **6** curtsy, kowtow, salaam **7** bow down

knell 4 peal, ring, toll **5** chime, sound **6** stroke **7** pealing, ringing, tolling

knickknack, nicknack 3 toy **6** bauble, gewgaw, trifle **7** bibelot, trinket **8** frippery, gimcrack

knife 3 cut **4** dirk, shiv, stab **5** blade, slash, wound **6** cutter, pierce **7** cut down, cutlery **8** cut apart, lacerate, mutilate
type: 3 pen **4** jack **5** bowie, bread, putty, table **6** dagger, paring, pocket **7** butcher, carving, hunting, machete, palette, pruning, scalpel **8** skinning, stiletto, surgical

knight 4 hero **7** fighter, gallant, paladin, soldier, Templar, warrior **8** cavalier, champion, defender, guardian, horseman, Lancelot

knit 3 tat **4** ally, bind, draw, join, knot, link **5** braid, plait, twist, unify, unite, weave **6** attach, crease, fasten, furrow, stitch **7** connect, crochet, wrinkle

knob 3 nub **4** bulb, bump, grip, hold, hump, knot, knur, lump, node, snag **5** bulge, gnarl, knurl, latch, lever, swell **6** handle, nubbin **8** handhold, swelling, tubercle

knock 3 bat, hit, pat, rap, tap **4** bang, beat, belt, blow, bomb, bump, clip, cuff, dash, kick, lick, push, slam, slap, sock, swat, thud **5** abuse, cavil, clout, crack, crash, decry, pound, punch, smack, smash, smite, thump, whack **6** batter, carp at, defeat, hammer, jostle, murder, peck at, pummel, strike, stroke, thwack, wallop **7** censure, condemn, failure, setback **8** belittle, lambaste

knockout 2 KO **4** doll

5 beaut, Venus **6** beauty, eyeful **7** stunner

knoll 4 hill, rise **5** mound

knot 3 bun **4** bump, frog, heap, hump, loop, lump, mass, pack, pile, star, tuft **5** braid, bunch, clump, group, hitch, knurl, plait, twist **6** bundle, circle **7** cat's-paw, chignon, cluster, epaulet, rosette **8** ornament

type: 3 bow, top **4** flat, slip **5** slide **6** double, single, square **7** running **8** hangman's, overhand, shoulder, surgeon's

know 3 see **6** be sure, be wise, notice **7** be smart, discern, make out, realize **8** identify, perceive

know-how 3 art **4** bent, gift **5** craft, flair, knack, savvy, skill **6** talent **7** ability, mastery **8** aptitude, capacity, deftness

know-it-all 5 brash

knowledge 3 ken, tip **4** data, hint, lore, news **5** sense **6** memory, notice, report, wisdom **7** inkling, mention, tidings **8** learning

knuckle under 5 yield

6 give in, submit **7** bow down

knurled 5 bumpy, lumpy **6** gnarly, knobby, knotty, knurly, nubbly, ridged **7** bulging, gnarled, knotted, nodular

koala
  family: 9 marsupial
  habitat: 9 Australia
  kin of: 6 wombat

Kon-Tiki
  author: 9 (Thor) Heyerdahl

kook 3 nut **5** crazy, flake, loony, wacko **6** cuckoo, weirdo **7** dingbat **8** crackpot

Koran 5 Islam, Quran
  revelations to: 8 Mohammed
  division: 4 sura
  dictated by: 7 Gabriel **9** archangel

Korea
  other name: 6 Chosen
  capital:
    North Korea: 9 Pyongyang
    South Korea: 5 Seoul
  largest city: 5 Seoul
  highest point: 6 Paektu **9** Paektusan

river: 3 Han **4** Yalu **5** Tumen
  sea: 5 Japan **6** Yellow **9** East China
  physical feature:
    valley: 7 Naktong
  feature:
    clothing: 5 chima
    martial art: 9 tae-kwon-do
    musical instrument: 6 chaing **7** kayagum, komungo
  food:
    bean curd: 4 tubu
    hot pickle: 6 kimchi

kosher 5 right **6** proper **7** ethical **8** fit to eat

kowtow 4 bend, fawn **5** cower, stoop, toady **6** bow low, cringe, curtsy, grovel, salaam **7** truckle **8** bootlick, butter up, softsoap

Kronos *see* **6 Cronus**

Kubla Khan
  author: 9 (Samuel) Coleridge
  city: 6 Xanadu

kudos 4 fame **5** award, glory, honor, prize **6** esteem, praise, renown, repute **7** acclaim, plaudit **8** citation, prestige

Kuwait
name means: 9 small fort
capital/largest city: 10
  Kuwait City
head of state: 4 emir
physical feature:
  duststorm: 4 kaus
  gulf: 7 Persian
ruling family: 5 Sabah

Kwanzaa
alternate form: 6 Kwanza

word origin: 7 Swahili
  (first fruits)
celebrated in: 7 January
  8 December

Kyrgyzstan
formerly: 7 Kirghiz (SSR)
capital/largest city: 6
  Frunze **7** Bishkek
government: 8 republic
mountain: 8 Tian Shan

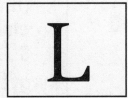

label 3 tag **4** mark, name, note, seal, sign, slip **5** brand, stamp, tally, title **6** define, docket, ticket **7** earmark, mark off, sticker **8** classify, describe

labor, labour 4 plod, toil, work **5** slave, sweat **6** drudge, effort, suffer **7** agonize, travail, workers, workmen **8** exertion, manpower, struggle

labyrinth *see* **4 maze**

Labyrinth
　form: 4 maze
　location: 5 Crete
　built by: 8 Daedalus
　for: 5 (King) Minos
　challenged by: 7 Theseus
　housed: 8 Minotaur

lace 3 tie **4** beat, bind, cane, dope, lash, whip **5** braid, cinch, close, flail, spank, spike, strap, tie up, truss **6** dope up, fasten, flavor, infuse, punish, secure, switch, tether, thrash **7** fortify, spice up, suffuse, tighten

Lacedaemon
　founder of: 6 Sparta
　father: 4 Zeus
　wife: 6 Sparta
　daughter: 8 Eurydice
　descendants: 5 Helen **6** Castor, Pollux **8** Dioscuri

lacerate *see* **3 cut**

lachrymose *see* **3 sad**

lack 4 miss, need, want **6** dearth **7** absence **8** omission, scarcity, shortage

lackadaisical 4 idle **7** languid, loafing **8** lifeless, listless, mindless

lackey *see* **7 servant**

lackluster *see* **4 dull**

LA Confidential
　director: 6 (Curtis) Hanson
　cast: 5 (Russell) Crowe **6** (Guy) Pearce, (Kevin)

Spacey **8** (Kim) Basinger, (James) Cromwell

laconic *see* **7 concise**

lacquer 4 coat **5** glaze **7** coating, shellac, varnish

lacrimoso
music: 7 tearful

lacrosse
Indian name: 9 bagataway
circle around goal: 6 crease
played with: 5 stick **6** crosse

lacuna 3 gap, pit **4** gulf, hole, void **5** blank, break, crack, ditch, pause, space **6** breach, cavity, hiatus **7** caesura, fissure, interim, opening, vacancy **8** interval, omission

lacy 4 fine **5** filmy, gauzy, meshy, netty, sheer, webby **6** barred, frilly, netted, porous, webbed **7** gridded, netlike **8** delicate, filigree, gossamer, retiform

lad 3 boy, kid **5** sprig, youth **6** shaver, sprout **8** juvenile, young man

Ladino
spoken by: 9 Sephardim
script: 6 Hebrew **7** mestizo

La Dolce Vita
director: 7 (Federico) Fellini
cast: 4 (Nadia) Gray **6** (Anouk) Aimee, (Lex) Barker, (Anita) Ekberg **11** (Marcello) Mastroianni

ladrone 5 thief **6** bandit, outlaw

lady 4 wife **5** woman **6** female, matron, spouse **7** duchess, peeress **8** baroness, countess

Lady Chatterley's Lover
author: 8 (D H) Lawrence

Lady of the Lake, The
author: 5 (Sir Walter) Scott

Laertes
son: 8 Odysseus

lag *see* **4 drag**

lagniappe, lagnappe *see* **5 bonus**

laic 3 lay **5** civil **7** amateur, popular, profane, secular, worldly **8** temporal

lair 3 den, lie, mew **4** hole, nest **5** cover, haunt **6** burrow, cavern, covert **7** hideout, retreat

laissez-faire, laisser-faire 8 hands off

Laius
  king of: **6** Thebes
  wife: **7** Jocasta
  son: **7** Oedipus
  killed by: **7** Oedipus

lama **4** monk **6** priest
  in: **7** Lamaism
  high priest: **9** Dalai Lama
  locale: **5** Tibet

lambaste *see* **5 scold**

lambent *see* **7 radiant**

lame **4** game, halt, weak **5**
  sorry **6** clumsy, feeble,
  flimsy, infirm, maimed;
  uncool **7** failing, limping
  8 crippled, deformed,
  disabled

lamebrain *see* **5 idiot**

lament *see* **5 mourn**

lamp **4** bulb **5** light, torch **6**
  beacon **7** blinker, lantern

lampoon *see* **6 parody**

lanai **4** deck **5** porch **7**
  terrace, veranda

lance **4** gaff, pike **5** shaft,
  spear **7** assegai, halberd,
  harpoon, javelin

Lancelot, Launcelot
  father: **3** Ban
  son: **7** Galahad
  lover: **6** Elaine **9**
    Guinevere

lancer **8** cavalier, horseman

land **3** get, lea, nab, net **4**
  area, dirt, dock, gain,
  grab, lawn, loam, moor,
  park, soil, take, ward,
  zone **5** acres, catch, earth,
  grass, put in, realm, seize,
  shire, snare, state, tract **6**
  anchor, clinch, colony,
  county, debark, domain,
  empire, fields, ground,
  meadow, nation, realty,
  region, secure **7** acreage,
  capture, country, descend,
  grounds, kingdom,
  pasture, section, set down,
  subsoil **8** come down,
  district, dominion, make
  port, province, republic

landmark **8** keystone,
  monument, signpost

Land of Enchantment
  nickname of: **9** New
    Mexico

Land of Lincoln
  nickname of: **8** Illinois

Land of Opportunity
  nickname of: **8** Arkansas

**Land of Ten Thousand
Lakes**
  nickname of: **9** Minnesota

Land of the Midnight Sun
  nickname of: **6** Alaska

lane *see* **4 path**

language 4 cant, jive **5** argot, idiom, lingo, prose, slang, words **6** jargon, patois, tongue **7** dialect, diction, wording **8** parlance, rhetoric, verbiage

language, artificial 6 Lincos, Loglan **7** Volapuk **8** Solresol **9** Esperanto

language, extinct 6 Dacian, Hattic, Lycian, Lydian, Palaic **7** Cornish, Elamite, Hittite, Hurrian **8** Etruscan, Illyrian, Phrygian, Sumerian, Thracian, Urartian

languid *see* **4 lazy**

languish 3 ebb **4** fade, fail, flag, wane, wilt **5** covet, droop, faint, yearn **6** desire, hunger, sicken, thirst, wither **7** dwindle, long for, pine for **8** diminish

languor *see* **5 ennui**

lanky *see* **6 skinny**

Laocoon
  vocation: 6 priest
  father: 5 Priam
  mother: 6 Hecuba
  warned: 7 Trojans
  warned of: 5 (Trojan) horse
  killed by: 8 (sea) serpents

Laos
  capital/largest city: 9 Viengchan, Vientiane
  highest point: 7 Phou Bia
  river: 6 Mekong
  physical feature:
    plain: 4 Jars **9** Vientiane
  feature:
    Buddhist priest: 5 bonze
    Communist guerrilla group: 9 Pathet Lao
    temple: 3 wat
    trail: 9 Ho Chi Minh

lap *see* **4 lick**

lapidary
  expert in: 4 gems

lapis lazuli 9 azure-blue

Lapland
  region of: 6 Norway, Sweden **7** Finland
  peninsula: 4 Kola
  native: 4 Lapp
  herders of: 8 reindeer

lapse 3 gap, sag **4** drop, fall, flaw, go by, loss, sink, slip, stop, wane **5** boner, break, cease, droop, error, fault, pause, slump **6** breach, expire, hiatus, period, recede, recess, wither **7** blunder, decline, descent, failure, faux pas, interim, passage, respite **8** interval, omission, slip away

larboard 8 left side
same as: 4 port

larceny *see* **5 fraud**

larder 5 cuddy **6** pantry, spence **7** buttery

lares
form: 7 spirits
watched over: 5 house **6** hearth
single member: 3 lar
companions: 7 penates
correspond to: 8 Dioscuri

large 3 big, fat **4** high, huge, vast, wide **5** ample, broad, grand, great, heavy, hulky, obese, plump, roomy **6** portly, rotund **7** copious, immense, liberal, massive, sizable **8** colossal, enormous, gigantic, imposing, towering

largess, largesse *see* **7 charity**

lark *see* **5 antic**

larva
insect stage after: 3 egg
insect stage before: 4 pupa

legless: 6 maggot

lascivious *see* **6 vulgar**

lash *see* **6 strike**

lass, lassie 4 girl, maid, miss **5** wench **6** damsel, female, lassie, lovely, maiden, pretty, virgin **7** colleen

Lassie
type of dog: 6 collie

lassitude *see* **5 ennui**

lasso 4 lash, rope **5** catch, noose, riata **6** lariat

last 3 end **4** go on, keep, live, stay, wear **5** abide, after, exist, final, stand **6** behind, endure, extend, finale, finish, remain **7** extreme, outlive, outwear, persist, survive, tailing **8** at the end, continue, farthest, hindmost, maintain, rearmost, terminal, terminus, trailing, ultimate

Last of the Mohicans, The
author: 6 (James Fenimore) Cooper

last part 3 end **6** ending, finale, finish **8** third act

Last Picture Show, The
director: 11 (Peter) Bogdanovich

based on story by: 8
(Larry) McMurtry
cast: 7 (Jeff) Bridges,
(Timothy) Bottoms,
(Ellen) Burstyn, (Ben)
Johnson **8** (Cloris)
Leachman, (Cybil)
Shepherd

La Strada
director: 7 (Federico)
Fellini
cast: 5 (Anthony) Quinn
6 (Giulietta) Masina **7**
(Aldo) Silvana **8**
(Richard) Basehart

latch 3 bar **4** bolt, clip,
hasp, hook, lock, loop,
shut, snap **5** catch, clamp,
close **6** buckle, button,
clinch, fasten, secure

late 3 new **4** dead, gone,
slow **5** fresh, tardy **6** held
up, put off, recent **7**
delayed, newborn,
overdue, tardily **8**
departed, detained,
dilatory, passed on

latent *see* **7 dormant**

later 4 next **5** since **6**
behind, in time, mature **7**
ensuing, tardily **8** in a
while, in sequel

lateral 4 side **5** sided

7 flanked, oblique, sloping
8 edgeways, edgewise,
flanking, sidelong,
sideward, sideways,
sidewise, skirting, slanting

lather 4 foam, head, scum,
soap, suds **5** froth, spume,
sweat **6** soap up

Latino, Latina 8 Hispanic

latitude 5 range, scope,
sweep **6** leeway, margin **7**
license **8** free play

latter *see* **4 last**

lattice 4 fret, grid **5** frame,
grate **6** grille, screen **7**
framing, grating, network,
trellis, webwork

Latvia
capital/largest city: 4
Riga
highest point: 11
Gaizinkalns
river: 5 Gauja, Venta **7**
Daugava
sea: 6 Baltic
physical feature:
gulf: 4 Riga

laud 5 extol, honor **6** praise
7 acclaim, commend,
glorify

laudable 5 model, noble **8**
sterling

laugh 4 glee, ha-ha, ho-ho,

howl, roar **5** mirth **6** cackle, giggle, guffaw, titter **7** break up, chortle, chuckle, snicker, snigger

laughingstock *see* **3 oaf**

launch 4 fire, hurl **5** begin, eject, float, found, impel, shoot, start, throw **6** let fly, propel, unveil **7** fire off, project **8** catapult, initiate, premiere

launder 4 soak, wash **5** clean, rinse, scour, scrub **7** cleanse, wash out

laurels *see* **5 kudos**

lavender 4 herb, mint **5** aspic, behen, lilac, spick, spike **6** purple **7** inkroot **8** amethyst, stichado
represents: 6 purity
uses: 6 sachet **7** perfume **8** medicine

lavish *see* **7 copious**

law 3 act **4** bill, code, fuzz, rule, writ **5** axiom, canon, dogma, edict, model, truth **6** decree, policy **7** justice, mandate, precept, statute, theorem **8** standard

Law and Order
creator: 4 (Dick) Wolf
cast: 4 (Steven) Hill, (Chris) Noth, (Elisabeth)

Rohm **5** (Benjamin) Bratt **6** (Angie) Harmon, (Jesse) Martin, (Jerry) Orbach **8** (Fred) Thompson **9** (S Epatha) Merkerson, (Sam) Waterson

lawn 4 park, turf, yard **5** glade, grass, sward **7** grounds, terrace

Law of Moses 5 Torah

Lawrence of Arabia
director: 4 (David) Lean
cast: 5 (Anthony) Quinn, (Claude) Rains **6** (Jose) Ferrer, (Peter) O'Toole, (Anthony) Quayle, (Omar) Sharif **7** (Jack) Hawkins **8** (Alec) Guinness

lawyer 6 jurist, legist **7** counsel, shyster **8** advocate, attorney

lax *see* **6 casual**

lay 3 air, bet, put, set **4** bear, fell, fine, form, give, laic, lend, levy, make, plan, poem, raze, rest, seat, song, tune **5** align, allot, apply, ditty, exact, floor, hatch, level, offer, place, stage, wager **6** assess, assign, ballad, charge, demand, depict, devise, gamble, ground, hazard, impose, impute, laical, layout, locate, melody, repose, strain **7** amateur, arrange, concoct, contour, deposit, dispose, forward, present, produce, profane, proffer, refrain, secular, set down, situate, station **8** allocate, assemble, beat down, give odds, inexpert, organize, oviposit, position

lay bare *see* **6 expose**

layer 3 bed, lap, ply **4** coat, fold, leaf, seam, slab, tier, zone **5** level, plate, scale, sheet, stage, story **6** lamina **7** stratum

layman 4 laic **6** sister **7** amateur, brother

layout *see* **7 outline**

lay waste *see* **7 destroy**

Lazarus 6 beggar
　means: 8 God helps
　sister: 4 Mary **6** Martha
　hometown: 7 Bethany
　resurrected by: 5 Jesus

lazy 3 lax **4** idle, slow **5** inert, slack **6** torpid **7** laggard, languid

8 inactive, indolent, listless, slothful, sluggish

lead 2 go **3** aim, top **4** clue, draw, edge, have, head, hero, hint, live, lure, pass **5** charm, excel, guide, model, outdo, pilot, steer, tempt **6** allure, convey, direct, entice, extend, induce, manage, margin, pursue, seduce **7** bring on, command, conduct, control, example, go first, marshal, precede, surpass **8** go before, moderate, outstrip, persuade, priority, shepherd, star part
　ore: 6 galena, pyrite

leaden *see* **6 gloomy**

leaf 4 flip, foil, page, skim **5** blade, bract, folio, frond, green, inset, petal, sheet, thumb **6** browse, glance, insert, needle **7** foliole, lamella, leaflet
　edge: 5 erose **7** crenate, dentate
　angle: 4 axil
　aperture: 5 stoma
　kind: 5 calyx, petal, sepal **7** corolla

leaflet *see* **8 brochure**

league 4 ally, band **5** cabal,

group, guild, merge, union **6** cartel **7** combine, compact, company, network, society **8** alliance

leak 3 ebb, rip **4** blab, gash, hole, ooze, rent, rift, seep, vent **5** break, chink, cleft, crack, drain, exude, fault, spill **6** breach, efflux, escape, filter, let out, reveal, take in **7** confide, divulge, dribble, fissure, let slip, opening, outflow, seepage **8** aperture, disclose

lean 3 aim, bow, tip **4** bend, cant, lank, list, poor, rely, rest, slim, tend, thin, tilt **5** gaunt, lanky, lurch, scant, slant, slope, small, spare, weedy **6** barren, depend, meager, modest, nonfat, prefer, scanty, skinny, sparse, svelte **7** angular, count on, recline, scrawny, slender, willowy **8** exiguous

Leander
  loved: 4 Hero
  swam nightly: 10 Hellespont
  death by: 8 drowning

leap 3 hop **4** jete, jump, romp, rush, skip **5** bound, caper, frisk, vault **6** bounce, cavort, frolic, gambol, hasten, hurtle, prance, spring **7** hop over

learn 3 con **4** hear **6** detect, master, pick up **7** find out, uncover, unearth **8** discover, memorize

leash *see* **4 rein**

leatherneck 6 gyrene, marine

Leather-Stocking Tales
  author: 6 (James Fenimore) Cooper
  hero of: 6 (Natty) Bumppo, Trapper **7** Hawkeye **10** Deerslayer

leave 2 go **3** fly **4** cede, exit, flee, jilt, keep, quit, will **5** allot, be off, cause, endow, forgo, going, split, waive, yield **6** assign, decamp, depart, desert, eschew, forego, give up, legate, move on, recess, resign, retain, set out **7** abandon, abscond, bequest, consign, deposit, forsake, holiday, parting, produce, respite, retreat, sustain, take off **8** bequeath, farewell, furlough, maintain, shove off, vacation

Leaves of Grass
  author: 7 (Walt) Whitman

Lebanon
  ancient name: 9 Phoenicia
  capital/largest city: 6
    Beirut **8** Beyrouth
  mountain: 6 Hermon **7**
    Lebanon
  river: 6 Litani **7** Orontes
  sea: 13 Mediterranean
  physical feature:
    valley: 5 Beqaa **6**
      al-Biqa
  feature:
    Shia Islamic
      organization: 9
      Hezbollah
    tree: 5 cedar
  place:
    ruins: 7 Baalbek
  food:
    dish: 6 hommos,
      hummus, kibbeh **7**
      falafel
    drink: 4 arak **6** arrack

Le Carre, John
  real name: 8 (David)
    Cornwell

lecherous *see* **4 lewd**

lecture 4 talk **5** chide, scold, speak **6** homily, preach, rail at, rebuke, sermon, speech **7** address, expound, oration, reprove, upbraid **8** admonish, harangue, reproach

Leda
  lover: 4 swan, Zeus
  son: 6 Castor, Pollux **8**
    Dioscuri
  daughter: 5 Helen **6**
    Phoebe **8** Philonoe,
    Timandra

Leda and the Swan
  author: 5 (W B) Yeats

ledge 4 sill, step **5** ridge, shelf **6** mantel, offset **8** foothold, shoulder

leek 18 Allium ampeloprasum
  emblem of: 5 Wales

leer 4 ogle **5** fleer

leery *see* **4 wary**

leeway 4 play **5** scope, slack **6** margin **7** cushion, headway, reserve **8** headroom, latitude

leftover *see* **6 excess**

left-wing 7 leftist, liberal, radical

leg 3 gam, lap, pin **4** limb, part, post, prop **5** brace, femur, shank, stage, stump, tibia **6** column, fibula, member, pillar

7 portion, section, segment, stretch, support, upright

legacy 4 gift **6** devise, estate **7** bequest, vestige **8** heirloom, heritage, leftover, survivor

legal 4 fair **5** licit, of law, valid **6** kosher, lawful **7** cricket **8** forensic, judicial, juristic, rightful

legal tender 4 cash **5** money **8** currency

legatee 4 heir **7** heiress

legend *see* **5 fable**

Legend of Sleepy Hollow, The
   author: 6 (Washington) Irving

legerdemain 7 cunning **8** deftness, jugglery, juggling, trickery

legible 4 neat **5** clear, plain **7** visible **8** clear-cut, distinct, readable

legion *see* **5 horde**

leg irons 5 bonds, irons **6** chains **7** fetters **8** shackles

legislation 3 act **4** bill **6** ruling **7** measure, statute

legitimate *see* **5 legal**

leisure *see* **4 calm**

lend 4 give, loan **6** impart, in vest, supply **7** advance, furnish

length 3 run **4** span, term, time **5** piece, range, reach **6** extent, period **7** compass, measure, portion, section, segment, stretch **8** distance, duration, end to end

leniency *see* **5 mercy**

Lennon, John
   wife: 7 Cynthia, Yoko Ono
   sons: 4 Sean **6** Julian
   killer: 7 (Mark) Chapman
   see also **7 Beatles**

Leo
   symbol: 4 lion
   planet: 3 Sun
   rules: 7 romance
   born: 4 July **6** August

leopard 3 cat **7** panther **10** spotted cat
   group of: 4 leap

lepidoptera
   group: 4 moth **9** butterfly

leprechaun 3 elf, imp **5** dwarf, gnome **6** sprite

Lerner, Alan J.
   born: 7 New York
   partner: 5 (Frederick) Loewe

Lesbos
  island in: 6 Aegean
  home of: 6 Sappho
Lesotho
  other name: 10
    Basutoland
  capital/largest city: 6
    Maseru
  head of state: 4 king
  river: 6 Orange
  physical feature:
    gorge: 5 Oxbow
  feature:
    blanket: 4 kobo
    house: 8 rondavel
less 5 fewer **6** barely, little
  7 smaller **8** meagerly
lessen *see* **6 reduce**
lesson 5 class, drill, guide,
  model, moral, study **6**
  caveat, notice, rebuke **7**
  example, message **8**
  exercise, homework
let 4 make, rent **5** admit,
  allow, cause, grant, lease,
  leave **6** enable, permit,
  sublet, suffer **7** approve,
  charter, concede,
  empower, endorse,
  warrant **8** sanction,
  sublease
let fly *see* **5 throw**
lethal *see* **5 fatal**

lethargic *see* **4 lazy**
Lethe
  form: 5 river
  location: 5 Hades
  son: 6 Apollo
  consort: 4 Zeus
  daughter: 5 Diana **7**
    Artemis
let slip *see* **6 betray**
Let's Make a Deal
  host: 4 (Monty) Hall
  announcer: 7 (Jay)
    Stewart
letter 4 note **7** epistle,
  message, missive **8**
  dispatch, document
lettuce 7 Lactuca
  varieties: 3 cos **5** chalk,
  frog's, lamb's, water **6**
  Boston, garden, miner's
  7 iceberg, prickly,
  romaine **8** escarole
letup *see* **6 relief**
levee 3 dam **4** bank, dike,
  pier, quay, wall **5** ditch,
  jetty, ridge, wharf
level 3 aim, bed **4** even,
  flat, rank, raze, tied,
  vein, zone **5** align, floor,
  flush, grade, layer, plane,
  point, stage, story, wreck
  6 direct, height, reduce,
  topple **7** even out,

flatten, stratum **8** equalize, make even, position, tear down

level-headed *see* **6 steady**

lever 3 bar, pry **5** jimmy, raise **7** crowbar

Levi
father: 5 Jacob **6** Melchi, Symeon
mother: 4 Leah
son: 6 Kohath, Merari **7** Gershom
brother: 3 Dan, Gad **5** Asher, Judah **6** Joseph, Reuben, Simeon **7** Zebulun **8** Benjamin, Issachar, Naphtali
sister: 5 Dinah
violated: 5 Dinah
also called: 7 Matthew
descendant of: 6 Levite

Leviathan 6 dragon

Leviathan
author: 6 (Thomas) Hobbes

Levitch, Joseph
real name of: 5 (Jerry) Lewis

levity 3 fun **5** mirth **6** joking, whimsy **8** hilarity, trifling

levy *see* **3 tax**

Levy, Marion
real name of: 7 (Paulette) Goddard

lewd 5 bawdy **6** ribald, risque, vulgar, wanton **7** immoral, lustful, obscene **8** indecent, prurient

Lewis, Jerry
real name: 7 (Joseph) Levitch
partner: 6 (Dean) Martin

lexicon 5 gloss, index **8** glossary, synonymy, wordbook, wordlist

Lhasa
capital of: 5 Tibet

liable 3 apt **4** open **5** prone **6** likely **7** exposed, ripe for, subject **8** disposed, inclined

liaison 4 bond, link **5** amour, union **7** contact **8** alliance, intrigue, mediator

liar 6 fibber **8** perjurer

libation *see* **8 beverage**

libel 4 slur **5** smear **6** defame, malign, revile, vilify **7** asperse, blacken, calumny, obloquy, slander

liberal 5 ample, broad **6** casual, lavish **7** leftist, lenient **8** abundant, advanced, flexible,

generous, handsome,
left-wing, prodigal,
reformer, tolerant,
unbiased

liberate *see* **4 free**

Liberia
  capital/largest city: 8
    Monrovia
  highest point: 6 Wutivi
  sea: 8 Atlantic
  physical feature:
    wind: 9 harmattan
    leader: 3 Doe **6**
      Tubman **7** Roberts,
      Tolbert
  feature:
    clothing: 5 lappa
    noted for: 6 rubber

liberties 6 misuse **7** license

libertine *see* **4 lewd**

liberty *see* **7 freedom**

Libra
  symbol: 6 scales **7** balance
  planet: 5 Venus
  rules: 8 marriage
  born: 7 October **9**
    September

Libya
  capital/largest city: 7
    Tripoli
    summer capital: 8
      Benghazi
  highest point: 5 Bette
    (Peak)

  sea: 13 Mediterranean
  physical feature:
    desert: 6 Libyan,
      Sahara
    gulf: 5 Bomba, Sidra,
      Sirte
    wind: 6 ghibli
    leader: 5 Idris **7**
      Qadhafi, Qaddafi
  feature:
    clothing: 5 lanaf
    Islamic law: 6 sharia
  food:
    dish: 8 couscous

license 3 let **4** pass, visa **5**
  allow, grant, leave, right **6**
  enable, laxity, permit **7**
  anarchy, approve, certify,
  endorse, freedom, liberty,
  warrant **8** accredit,
  passport, sanction

licentious *see* **6 vulgar**

licit 5 legal, legit, valid **6**
  kosher, lawful

lick 3 bit, dab, hit, jot, lap
  4 beat, blow, drub, fire,
  hint, iota, rout, slap, snip,
  sock, suck, whip **5** crack,
  punch, sally, shred, spank,
  speck, taste, touch, trace
  6 defeat, master, sample,
  stroke, subdue, thrash,
  tongue, wallop **7** clobber,
  conquer, modicum,

smidgen, trounce **8** overcome

lid 3 cap, top **4** cork, curb, plug **5** cover, limit **7** ceiling, maximum, stopper, stopple

lie *see* **7 deceive**

Liechtenstein
capital/largest city: 5 Vaduz
ancient province: 6 Rhaeti **7** Rhaetia
mountain: 4 Alps
river: 5 Rhine
feature:
    wine: 7 Vaduzer

lie down 6 retire **7** go to bed, recline **8** take a nap

life 4 path, soul, zest **5** being, human, plant, story, verve, vigor **6** animal, career, course, energy, memoir, person, spirit **8** organism, vitality, vivacity
French: 3 vie

life jacket 7 Mae West

Life Magazine
founder: 4 (Henry) Luce

lifework 6 career **7** calling **8** vocation

lift 4 high, palm, pick, rear, rise, soar, take **5** boost, climb, exalt, filch, heave, hoist, pinch, raise, steal, swipe **6** ascend, ascent, pilfer, remove, revoke, snatch, thieve **7** elation, elevate, purloin, rescind

ligament
holds: 5 bones

light 3 gay **4** airy, beam, easy, fair, fall, find, fire, glow, lamp, land, pale, puny, side, soft, stop **5** aglow, blaze, blond, faint, flame, funny, glare, guide, happy, jolly, match, model, perch, petty, put on, roost, shine, small, spare, sunny, torch **6** beacon, blithe, bright, candle, gentle, get off, ignite, kindle, luster, settle, simple, slight, turn on **7** buoyant, chipper, gleeful, insight, lantern, not dark, paragon, radiant, radiate, sparkle, sunbeam, trivial **8** brighten, carefree, cheerful, come upon, discover, ethereal, exemplar, gossamer, graceful, illumine, jubilant, luminous, moderate, moonbeam, not heavy, paradigm, sportive, untaxing

god of: 6 Apollo **7** Mithras, Phoebus, Pythius **8** Heimdall
measurement: 7 candela

lighthearted *see* **5 merry**

light sleep 3 nap **4** doze **6** catnap, snooze

light wind 4 waft **6** breeze, zephyr

like 4 akin, care, dote, same, wish **5** enjoy, equal, fancy, favor, savor **6** admire, allied, choose, esteem, relish **7** approve, cognate, endorse, matched, related, similar, support, uniform **8** be fond of, think fit

likely 3 apt, fit **4** able **6** liable, proper **8** credible, destined, inclined, probable, probably, rational, reliable, suitable

likeness *see* **5 image**

likewise 3 and, eke, too **4** also **5** ditto **6** as well **7** besides, equally, the same **8** moreover

Li'l Abner
creator: 4 (Al) Capp

lilac 7 Syringa

lilliputian *see* **4 tiny**

lily 6 Lilium

lily-livered *see* **6 afraid**

Lima
capital of: 4 Peru

limb 3 arm, gam, leg, pin **4** part, spur, twig, wing **5** bough, shoot, sprig **6** branch, member

limber *see* **6 nimble**

lime
varieties: 3 key **4** wild **7** Mexican, Persian, Rangpur, Spanish **8** Mandarin

Limerick
county in: 7 Ireland
gave name to: 8 nonsense (poem)
rhyme scheme: 5 aabba
popularized by: 4 (Edward) Lear

limits 3 rim, top **4** curb, edge **5** bound, check, quota **6** border, define, fringe, margin, narrow **7** ceiling, confine, maximum **8** frontier, restrain, restrict

limn 4 draw **6** sketch **7** picture

limp 3 lax **4** gimp, halt, soft, weak **5** crawl, loose, skulk, slack **6** droopy, falter, flabby, floppy, hobble **7** flaccid

limpid *see* **5 clear**

Lincoln, Abraham
  nickname: 9 Honest Abe
  presidential rank: 9
    sixteenth
  party: 4 Whig **10**
    Republican
  state represented: 2 IL
  defeated: 4 Bell **8**
    Fremont, Douglas **9**
    McClellan **12**
    Breckinridge
  vice president: 6 Hamlin
  7 Johnson
  born: 8 log cabin
  died: 12 Fords Theater
  died by: 13 assassination
    assassinated by: 5
      Booth
  notable events of lifetime/
    term: 8 Civil War
      Act: 9 Homestead,
      Judiciary
      Address/speech: 10
        Gettysburg
      debated: 7 Douglas
  wife: 4 Mary
  children: 6 Edward,
    Robert, Thomas **7**
    William

lindy 5 dance **8** lindy hop

line, lines 4 card, cord,
  dash, draw, file, idea,
  mark, note, part, race,
rank, rope, rule, tier, word
5 align, array, breed,
cable, craft, front, house,
model, queue, range,
score, slash, stock, trade **6**
border, column, crease,
family, furrow, letter,
method, metier, policy,
series, stance, strand,
streak, stripe, system,
thread **7** calling, circuit,
conduit, contour, lineage,
pattern, purpose, pursuit,
wrinkle **8** ancestry,
business, dialogue,
ideology, postcard,
vanguard, vocation

linen
  fabric: 6 canvas, damask
    7 butcher, cambric **8**
    birds-eye
  plant: 4 flax

linger 3 lag **4** idle, last,
stay, wait **5** dally, delay,
tarry, trail **6** dawdle, hang
on, loiter, remain **7**
persist, survive

lingo *see* **6 jargon**

linguist 8 polyglot

liniment 4 balm **5** salve **7**
unguent **8** ointment

link 3 tie **4** bind, bond,
fuse, loop, ring **5** group,
joint, tie in, unite

6 couple, relate, splice **7** combine, connect, liaison **8** junction

lion 3 cat **6** cougar **7** wildcat
group of: 5 pride
constellation of: 3 Leo

lionhearted *see* **7 valiant**

lionize *see* **6 admire**

lion's share 4 bulk, most **8** majority

lip 3 lap, rim **4** brim, edge, kiss, lick, wash **5** apron, mouth, spout, utter **6** labial, labium, margin **8** backtalk, labellum

Lipizzaner 5 horse
bred in: 7 Austria
color: 5 white
used in: 8 dressage

liqueur 5 booze, drink, hooch **7** alcohol, potable, spirits **8** beverage
almond: 8 amaretto
anise: 8 absinthe
apple: 8 calvados
caraway: 6 kummel **7** aquavit
coffee: 6 Kahlua
herb: 6 pernod **7** raspail
honey: 8 Drambuie
orange: 6 strega **7** curacao
raspberry: 9 framboise

liquid 5 drink, fluid **6** melted, thawed **7** potable **8** beverage, solution

liquidate *see* **7 destroy**

liquor 3 gin, rum, rye **5** booze, broth, hooch, juice, sauce, vodka **6** brandy, liquid, redeye, rotgut, Scotch **7** bourbon, extract, spirits, whiskey
measure: 4 pint, pony, shot **5** fifth, quart **6** jigger, magnum

Lisbon
capital of: 8 Portugal

lissome *see* **6 nimble**

list 3 tip **4** bend, heel, lean, roll, tilt **5** index, slant, slate, slope, table **6** careen, muster, record, roster **7** catalog, in cline, leaning **8** register, schedule, tabulate

listen 4 hark, hear, heed, list **6** attend **7** give ear, hearken **8** overhear

listless *see* **4 lazy**

litany 4 list **7** account, catalog, recital

literacy 7 culture **8** learning

literal *see* **8 tangible**

literate 7 learned **8** cultured, educated,

lettered, literary, schooled, well-read

literature 4 lore **5** books, works **6** papers, theses **7** letters **8** classics, writings

lithe *see* **6 nimble**

Lithuania
  other name: 5 Litva **7** Lietuva
  capital/largest city: 5 Vilna **6** Kaunas **7** Vilnius
  highest point: 9 Juozapine
  lake: 8 Vistytis
  river: 5 Neman, Neris, Venta **6** Nieman, Sesupe **7** Nemunas
  sea: 6 Baltic

litigation 4 suit **7** contest, dispute, lawsuit

litter 3 bed **4** heap, junk, lair, mess, nest, pile **5** issue, strew, trash, young **6** debris, jumble, pallet, refuse **7** bedding, clutter, kittens, progeny, puppies, rubbish, scatter **8** leavings

little 3 bit, dot, jot, wee **4** dash, drop, hint, iota, mean, mild, tiny, whit **5** brief, crumb, elfin, faint, fleet, hasty, never, petty, pinch, pygmy, quick, scant, short, small, speck, trace **6** bantam, hardly, meager, minute, narrow, paltry, petite, rarely, seldom, skimpy, slight, trifle **7** minimum, modicum, not much, trivial **8** not often, particle, piddling, pittance, scarcely, trifling

Little Bighorn 5 river **7** Wyoming
  battle site of: 5 Sioux **6** Custer, Dakota **8** Cheyenne

Little Caesar
  director: 5 (Mervyn) LeRoy
  cast: 7 (Glenda) Farrell **8** (Edward G) Robinson **9** (Douglas) Fairbanks (Jr)

Little Corporal 8 Napoleon

Little House on the Prairie
  author: 6 (Laura Ingalls) Wilder

little-known 6 unsung **7** obscure, unnoted

Little Lord Fauntleroy
  author: 7 (Frances H) Burnett

Little Lulu
  creator: 9 (Marge) Henderson

Little Mermaid, The
    author: 8 (Hans Christian) Andersen

little one 3 tot **4** babe, baby, tyke **5** child **6** infant, wee one **7** toddler

Little Orphan Annie
    creator: 4 (Harold) Gray

little people 5 elves **6** dwarfs **7** fairies, midgets

Little Tramp
    nickname of: 7 (Charlie) Chaplin

Little Women
    author: 15 Louisa May Alcott

liturgy 4 mass, rite **6** ritual **7** service, worship **8** ceremony, services

livable, liveable 4 cozy, snug **5** comfy, homey **8** bearable, passable, pleasant, suitable

live 2 be **3** hot **4** bunk, feed, stay **5** abide, afire, aglow, alive, dwell, exist, fiery, lodge, quick, stand, vital **6** ablaze, active, aflame, alight, at hand, billet, bodily, endure, hold on, occupy, red-hot, remain, reside, settle **7** animate, at issue, be alive, breathe, burning, current, fleshly, ignited, persist, prevail, subsist, survive **8** have life, physical, pressing, take root

livelihood *see* **6 career**

lively 5 alert, brisk, eager, peppy, perky, vivid **6** active, ardent, bouncy **7** buoyant, excited, fervent, intense **8** animated, spirited, vigorous

liver
    stores: 8 glycogen
    color: 3 red **5** brown
    produces: 4 bile **5** blood (cells)

livery *see* **6 clothes**

livid *see* **5 furious**

living 3 job **4** life, live, work **5** alive, being, quick, trade **6** active, bodily, career, extant, income **7** animate, calling, fleshly, going on, organic, venture **8** business, existent, material, vocation

living quarters 4 home **5** abode, house **6** billet **7** housing, lodging, shelter **8** domicile, dwelling

lizard 3 dab, eft, uma **4** adda, gila, newt, seps,

tegu, uran **5** agama, anole, anoli, gecko, idler, shrink **6** aguana, dragon, iguana, komodo, moloch **7** lounger, monitor, reptile, saurian **8** dinosaur, lacerata, scorpion

characteristic: 6 scales **7** molting

constellation of: 7 Lacerta

llama 6 alpaca, kechua, mammal, vicuna **7** guanaco **8** ungulate

load 3 try, vex **4** care, fill, haul, heap, lade, pack, pile **5** cargo, crush, stack, worry **6** burden, hamper, hinder, lading, misery, strain, weight **7** freight, oppress **8** capacity, contents, encumber, shipment

loads 4 lots, much **5** heaps, piles, scads **6** oodles, plenty

loaf 4 idle, loll **5** dally **6** be lazy **7** goof off **8** kill time, malinger

loafer *see* **3 bum**

loan 4 lend **5** allow **6** credit **7** advance, lending **8** mortgage

loath *see* **7 hostile**

loathe *see* **4 hate**

lobby 5 foyer **8** anteroom, politick

local 6 narrow, native, nearby **7** insular, limited **8** confined, regional

locale *see* **4 area**

locate *see* **4 find**

Loch Ness
  in: 8 Scotland
  home of: 6 Nessie **7** monster

lock 3 bar, dam, pen **4** bang, bolt, cage, coil, curl, grab, grip, hank, hold, hook, jail, join, link, tuft **5** catch, clamp, clasp, grasp, latch, seize, skein, tress, unite **6** clinch, coop up, fasten, secure, shut in **7** confine, embrace, impound **8** imprison

lock horns *see* **5 fight**

lockup 3 jug, pen **4** jail, stir **5** clink, pokey **6** cooler, prison **7** slammer **8** big house, hoosegow

lock up *see* **6 prison**

locust 7 Robinia

locution *see* **6 phrase**

lode 3 bed **4** seam **7** deposit

lodge 3 bed, hut **4** camp, file, room, stay **5** cabin, catch, hotel, house, motel, put up **6** billet, harbor, resort, submit **7** cottage, quarter, shelter, sojourn

Loewe, Frederick
  partner: 6 (Alan J) Lerner

loft 3 lob **5** attic, pop up **6** belfry, garret **7** balcony, gallery, hit high, mansard **8** top floor

lofty *see* **7 haughty**

log 5 block, diary, stump **6** docket, lumber, record, timber **7** account, daybook, journal, logbook **8** calendar, schedule

loges 5 boxes **7** balcony

loggia 5 lanai, porch **6** piazza **7** balcony, gallery

logical 5 clear, sound, valid **6** cogent, likely **7** germane **8** coherent, rational, relevant, sensible

logos 4 word **5** ratio **6** saying, speech **7** thought

logy *see* **5 weary**

Lohengrin
  opera by: 6 Wagner

Lohengrin
  origin: 8 Germanic

knight of: 9 Holy Grail
  father: 8 Parsifal, Parzival

loiter 4 idle, laze, loaf, loll, lurk **5** dally, skulk, slink, tarry **6** dawdle

Loki
  origin: 5 Norse
  god of: 4 fire
  daughter: 3 Hel
  caused death of: 5 Baldr **6** Balder, Baldur

Lolita
  author: 7 (Vladimir) Nabokov
  cast: 4 (Sue) Lyon **5** (James) Mason **7** (Peter) Sellers, (Shelley) Winters

loll *see* **8 languish**

London
  area: 4 Soho **7** Chelsea, Pimlico **8** Vauxhall **9** Belgravia
  capital of: 2 UK (England) **7** (Great) Britain
  river: 6 Thames

lonely 6 remote **7** forlorn **8** deserted, desolate, forsaken, hermitic, isolated, secluded, solitary

Lone Ranger, The
  character: 5 Tonto
  cast: 4 (John) Hart **5** (Clayton) Moore

11 (Jay) Silverheels
horse: 5 Scout **6** Silver
saying: 8 kemo sabe
Lone Star State
nickname of: 5 Texas
long 4 hope, lust, pine, sigh, want, wish **5** covet, crave, yearn **6** aspire, hanker, hunger, thirst **7** lengthy, spun out **8** drawn-out, extended
long-faced *see* **3 sad**
long-wearing 5 tough **6** strong, sturdy **7** durable, lasting **8** enduring
long-winded *see* **7 verbose**
look 3 air, see **4** cast, face, gape, gaze, mien, ogle, peek, peep, scan, seem, show, view **5** front, glare, guise, sight, stare, study, watch **6** behold, glance, regard, survey **7** examine, glimpse **8** demeanor, manifest, once-over, presence, scrutiny
look askance at 7 condemn **8** object to
look down on 7 despise, disdain
Look Homeward, Angel
author: 5 (Thomas) Wolfe
lookout 4 heed **5** guard, scout, vigil **6** patrol, sentry **7** spotter **8** observer, sentinel, watchdog, watchman
look out 4 mind **6** beware **8** take care, watch out
look up to *see* **6 admire**
loom 4 hulk, rise, soar **5** tower **6** appear, ascend, emerge **8** stand out
loop 3 eye **4** bend, coil, curl, furl, ring, roll, turn **5** braid, curve, noose, plait, twirl, twist, whorl **6** circle, eyelet, spiral **7** opening, ringlet **8** aperture, encircle, loophole
loose 4 fast, free, lewd, undo, wild **5** freed, let go, slack, untie, vague **6** undone, untied, wanton **7** immoral, inexact, unbound, uncaged, unchain, unleash, unyoked **8** careless, heedless, not tight, unbridle, unfasten
loot *see* **3 rob**
lop *see* **5 sever**
lopsided 4 awry **5** askew **6** aslant, tipped, uneven **7** crooked, leaning, listing, slanted, tilting **8** cockeyed
loquacious *see* **7 verbose**

lord 4 king **5** chief, crown, ruler **6** leader, master **7** monarch **8** overlord, seignior, superior
   Japanese: 6 daimyo
   Turkish: 3 beg, bey

Lord Jim
   author: 6 (Joseph) Conrad

lordliness 7 disdain **8** contempt

Lord of the Flies
   author: 7 (William) Golding

Lord of the Rings, The
   author: 7 (J R R) Tolkien

lore 7 beliefs, legends **10** traditions

Lorelei
   origin: 8 Germanic
   form: 5 nymph
   dwelling place: 5 cliff, Rhine
   caused shipwrecks by: 7 singing

Los Angeles
   area: 5 Watts **6** Bel Air **8** Pasadena, Westwood **9** Hollywood
   baseball team: 7 Dodgers
   basketball team: 6 Lakers, Sparks **8** Clippers
   hockey team: 5 Kings

   university: 3 USC **4** UCLA **7** Caltech

lose 4 fail, miss **6** forget, ignore, mislay **7** confuse, forfeit **8** misplace

loser 4 flop **7** failure

loss 4 ruin **5** wreck **6** defeat, losing **7** licking, removal, undoing **8** overturn, riddance, wrecking

lost 5 stray **6** absent, astray, killed, ruined, wasted **7** mislaid, missing, misused, strayed, wrecked **8** perished, vanished, wiped out

Lost Horizon
   author: 6 (James) Hilton

lost in thought 7 pensive **8** absorbed

Lost Weekend, The
   author: 7 (Charles) Jackson
   director: 6 (Billy) Wilder
   cast: 5 (Philip) Terry, (Jane) Wyman **7** (Howard) da Silva, (Doris) Dowling, (Ray) Milland

lot 4 fate, lots, many, much, plot **5** field, patch, quota, share, straw, tract

6 oceans, oodles, ration **7** counter, measure **8** beaucoup, property

Lot
> **uncle: 7** Abraham
> **son: 5** Ammon
> **hometown: 5** Sodom
> **rescued by: 6** angels
> **fled to: 4** Zoar

lothario *see* **6 suitor**

lotion 4 balm, wash **5** salve **6** liquid **7** unction, unguent **8** cosmetic, liniment, ointment, solution

lots 4 much **5** heaps, loads, plots, scads

lotus 7 Nelumbo
> **varieties: 4** blue **5** water, white **6** sacred **8** American, Egyptian

loud 5 gaudy, noisy, showy, vivid **6** bright, flashy, garish **7** booming, intense, splashy **8** colorful, sonorous

loud sound 4 bang, boom, clap, honk, howl, peal, roar, slam, toot **5** blare, blast, burst, crash **6** bellow, report, scream, shriek **7** clatter, thunder

Louisiana
> **abbreviation: 2** LA
> **nickname: 5** Bayou **7** Pelican
> **capital: 10** Baton Rouge
> **largest city: 10** New Orleans
> **highest point: 8** Driskill
> **lake: 13** Pontchartrain
> **river: 3** Red **5** Black, Pearl **6** Saline **8** Ouachita **11** Mississippi
> **physical feature:**
>> **gulf: 6** Mexico
> **feature:**
>> **area: 5** bayou
>> **festival: 9** Mardi Gras
>> **hurricane: 7** Katrina
>> **music: 4** jazz
>> **quarter: 6** French
>> **street: 7** Bourbon
> **food:**
>> **broiled beef or veal: 9** grillades
>> **dish: 5** gumbo **9** jambalaya
>> **pastry: 7** beignet

lounge *see* **4 ease**

louse *see* **3 cad**

lousy *see* **3 bad**

lout *see* **3 oaf**

love 3 man **4** beau, bent, dear, girl, mind, turn **5** adore, amity, amour, angel, ardor, enjoy, fancy, flame, honey, lover, savor, taste, woman **6** admire, esteem, fellow, relish **7** cherish, concord, darling, dearest, emotion, passion, rapture, revel in, sweetie **8** affinity, devotion, fondness, goodwill, hold dear, mistress, paramour, penchant, precious, treasure

love child 7 bastard

lovely 4 cute, fine, good **5** sweet **6** comely **7** elegant, lovable, winning, winsome **8** adorable, alluring, charming, engaging, fetching, handsome, pleasant, pleasing

love seat 4 sofa **5** couch **6** settee

lovesick 7 amorous **8** yearning

Love Story
  author: 5 (Erich) Segal

low 4 base, blue, deep, down, evil, glum, mean, soft, vile **5** awful, cruel, dirty, dumpy, faint, gross, lower, lowly, muted, prone, quiet, short, small, squat **6** coarse, common, crummy, gloomy, humble, hushed, little, paltry, scurvy, softly, sordid, stubby, stumpy, sunken, vulgar, wicked **7** coastal, concave, corrupt, doleful, heinous, muffled, obscene, snubbed, squalid, subdued, unhappy **8** degraded, dejected, depraved, downcast, murmured, terrible, trifling, unworthy

low-key *see* **6 subtle**

lowly *see* **6 humble**

loyal 4 firm, true **6** trusty **7** devoted, dutiful, staunch **8** constant, faithful, reliable, resolute, true-blue

lozenge 4 drop, pill **6** tablet, troche **8** pastille

lucid *see* **5 clear**

Lucifer 5 Satan

luck 3 lot **4** fate **5** karma **6** chance, kismet **7** destiny, fortune, success, triumph, victory **8** accident, fortuity, Lady Luck

lucky 4 good **5** happy **6** timely **7** blessed, favored

lucrative 7 gainful **8** fruitful

Lucretia
  husband: 6 Lucius (Tarquinius Collatinus)

raped by: 6 Sextus (Tarquinius)

death by: 7 suicide

Lucullan 4 rich **6** lavish **7** gourmet

ludicrous *see* **6 absurd**

lug 3 tow, tug **4** bear, drag, draw, haul, pull, tote **5** carry, heave

luggage 4 bags, gear **6** trunks **7** baggage, effects, valises

lugubrious *see* **6 somber**

Luke

    companion: 4 Paul

    occupation: 6 doctor

    wrote: 6 Gospel

lukewarm 4 cool, mild, warm **5** aloof, tepid **8** detached, uncaring

lull *see* **5 pause**

lulu 3 pip **4** oner **5** dandy, doozy **8** Jim Dandy

lumber 3 log **4** plod, wood **5** barge, clump, stamp **6** boards, planks, trudge, waddle **7** shamble, shuffle **8** flounder

luminary 3 VIP **5** light, wheel **6** bigwig **7** big shot, notable **8** somebody

luminous *see* **7 radiant**

lump 3 gob, mix **4** bump, cake, clod, fuse, heap, hunk, knob, knot, mass, node, pile, pool **5** amass, batch, blend, bunch, chunk, clump, group, knurl, merge, tumor, unite **6** gather, growth, nodule **7** collect, combine, compile **8** assemble

lunacy 5 folly, mania **6** idiocy **7** madness **8** dementia, insanity

lunatic *see* **6 maniac**

luncheonette 4 cafe **5** diner **7** beanery **8** snack bar

lunge 3 cut, jab **4** dash, dive, pass, rush, stab **5** hit at, lurch, swing, swipe **6** attack, charge, plunge, pounce, thrust **7** set upon **8** fall upon, strike at

lunkhead *see* **5 idiot**

Lupercalia

    origin: 5 Roman

    event: 8 festival

    honoring: 6 Faunus **8** Lupercus

lurch 4 cant, keel, list, reel, roll, sway, tilt, toss **5** lunge, pitch, slant **6** careen, plunge, swerve, teeter, totter **7** incline, stagger, stumble

lure *see* **6 cajole**

lurid *see* **4 grim**

lurk **4** hide **5** prowl, skulk, slink, sneak

luscious **5** tasty **6** savory **7** scented **8** aromatic, fragrant, perfumed

lush *see* **4 rich**

lust **5** covet, crave **6** be lewd **7** craving, lechery, passion **8** lewdness

luster *see* **5 shine**

lusty *see* **6 hearty**

lux **5** *see* **light**

Luxembourg
  capital/largest city: 10 Luxembourg
  mountain: 8 Ardennes
  river: 5 Mosel, Sauer **7** Alzette, Moselle
  physical feature:
    plateau: 8 Ardennes, Lorraine
    valley: 7 Moselle

luxury **5** bliss **6** heaven, riches, wealth **7** delight **8** paradise, pleasure

Lydia
  kingdom in: 9 Asia Minor
  king: 7 Croesus
  capital: 6 Sardis
  conquered by: 8 Persians

lying down **5** in bed, prone **6** supine **7** napping, resting **8** snoozing

lynch **4** hang **6** gibbet **8** string up

lynx **3** cat **6** bobcat **7** wildcat

lyric, lyrical **6** poetic **7** lilting, melodic, musical, singing, tuneful **8** songlike

M

macabre 4 grim **5** eerie, weird **6** grisly, horrid **7** ghastly, ghostly **8** dreadful, gruesome, horrible, horrific

Macao
part of: 5 China
former territory of: 8 Portugal
river: 5 Pearl **6** Canton
sea: 10 South China

Macbeth
author: 11 (William) Shakespeare

Maccabees
title of: 5 Judas
holiday: 8 Hanukkah

mace
from same tree as: 6 nutmeg

Macedonia
formerly part of: 10 Yugoslavia
capital/largest city: 6 Skopje

macerate *see* **4 mash**

Machiavellian 6 amoral, crafty **7** cunning, devious **8** scheming

machination 4 plot, rule, ruse **5** dodge **6** design, device, scheme **8** artifice, intrigue, maneuver

machine 3 set **4** army, body, camp, club, gang, pool, ring **5** corps, crowd, force, group, setup, trust, union **6** device **7** coterie, faction, society

macho 5 he-man, manly **6** strong, virile

Machu Picchu 5 ruins
of: 5 Incas
in: 4 Peru

macintosh, mackintosh 7 slicker **8** raincoat

mackerel
young: 5 spike **6** tinker **7** blinker

macrocosm 6 cosmos, nature **7** heavens **8** creation, universe

mad 4 avid, daft, loco, nuts, wild **5** angry, balmy,

crazy, irate, nutty **6** ardent, crazed, cuckoo, fuming, insane, miffed, screwy, ticked **7** cracked, enraged, fanatic, furious, lunatic, riled up, teed off, touched **8** crackers, demented, deranged, frenzied, incensed, maniacal, unhinged, wrathful

Madagascar
other name: 8 Malagasy
capital/largest city: 10 Tananarive **12** Antananarivo
sea/ocean: 6 Indian

madam, madame 3 Mrs **4** dame, lady **6** matron **7** dowager **8** mistress

Madame Bovary
author: 8 (Gustave) Flaubert

Madame Butterfly
opera by: 7 Puccini

made 5 built **6** formed **7** created **8** produced

Madeira Islands
capital: 7 Funchal
ocean: 8 Atlantic

made-up *see* **5 false**

madhouse 6 asylum,
bedlam, uproar **7** turmoil **8** loony bin, nuthouse

Madison, James
presidential rank: 6 fourth
party: 20 Democratic Republican
state represented: 2 VA
vice president: 5 Gerry **7** Clinton
born: 2 VA **10** Port Conway
notable events of lifetime/ term:
  treaty of: 5 Ghent
  Washington DC burned by: 7 British
wife: 8 Dorothea
  nickname: 6 Dolley

Madrid
capital of: 5 Spain

maelstrom 4 eddy **5** shoot, swirl **6** bedlam, rapids, tumult, uproar, vortex **7** riptide, torrent **8** disorder, madhouse, upheaval

Magdalene *see* **4 Mary**

magenta 6 maroon **7** carmine, crimson, fuchsia

maggot 4 grub, worm **5** larva **8** mealworm

Magi
also called: 7 wise men
followed: 4 Star (of Bethlehem)

visited: 5 Jesus

gifts: 4 gold **5** myrrh **12** frankincense

magic 4 lure **5** charm, spell **6** hoodoo, voodoo **7** sorcery **8** charisma, jugglery, witchery, wizardry

Magic Flute, The
  opera: 6 Mozart

magician 5 magus **6** shaman, wizard **7** juggler **8** conjurer, sorcerer

magistrate 2 JP **5** judge **7** prefect

Magna Carta 7 charter
  forced by: 6 barons
  upon: 8 King John
  at: 7 England

magnate 3 VIP **5** giant, mogul, nabob **6** bigwig, leader, tycoon **7** big shot, notable **8** big wheel

magnetism 4 lure **5** charm **6** allure **8** charisma

magnificent *see* **7 sublime**

magnify 4 laud **5** adore, boost, exalt, extol **6** blow up, double, expand, praise, puff up **7** acclaim, amplify, enlarge, glorify, inflate, stretch, worship **8** maximize

magnitude *see* **4 size**

Magyar 9 Hungarian

mahogany 4 tree, wood **5** brown **8** hardwood

maid 7 servant **8** domestic

mail 4 arms, post **5** armor **7** airmail, letters **8** dispatch, packages

maim *see* **5 wound**

main 4 head **5** chief, prime, vital **6** urgent **7** capital, central, crucial, leading, primary, supreme **8** critical

Maine
  abbreviation: 2 ME
  nickname: 8 Pine Tree
  capital: 7 Augusta
  largest city: 8 Portland
  highest point: 8 Katahdin
  lake: 6 Sebago **8** Rangeley
  river: 4 Saco, York **6** St John **8** Kennebec
  sea: 8 Atlantic
  island: 8 Mt Desert

mainstay 4 prop **6** anchor, pillar **7** bulwark **8** backbone, buttress

maintain 4 aver, avow, hold, keep **5** claim, state, swear **6** affirm, allege, assert, defend, insist, keep up, uphold **7** care for, contend, profess, stand by, support **8** conserve, continue, preserve

maize 4 corn, milo **5** grain **6** cereal, silage, yellow

majestic, majestical *see* **5 royal**

major 4 main **5** chief, prime, vital **6** larger, urgent **7** capital, crucial, greater, leading, primary, ranking, serious, supreme **8** critical, foremost

majority 4 bulk, mass **8** legal age, maturity

make 3 fix **4** form, kind, mark, meet, pass **5** beget, brand, build, catch, cause, enact, erect, force, frame, impel, press, reach, shape, speak, utter **6** attain, compel, create, devise, draw up, effect, render **7** appoint, compose, deliver, fashion, produce, require

make a clean breast of 7 confess, lay bare, own up to **8** blurt out

make a stab at 3 try **5** essay, guess **6** reckon, take on **7** attempt, surmise, venture **8** estimate, give a try

make-believe *see* **4 fake**

make good 5 repay **6** arrive, make it **7** fulfill, succeed

make inroads 6 invade **7** impinge, intrude **8** encroach, infringe, trespass

make light of 8 belittle, minimize, pooh-pooh, sneeze at

make much of 5 honor **6** praise **7** acclaim, applaud, commend, flatter **8** fuss over

make one's blood boil 5 anger **6** enrage, madden **7** incense, inflame

make out 3 see **4** espy **6** behold, descry, detect, fill in, notice **7** discern, observe, pick out **8** get along, perceive, write out

make public 3 air **4** tell **5** print, utter, voice **6** expose, inform, reveal **7** declare, display, divulge, exhibit, express, publish **8** announce, disclose, proclaim

maker, Maker 3 god **4** poet **5** smith **6** author, forger

7 builder, creator, founder
8 inventor, producer

make ready 5 prime **7**
arrange, forearm, prepare

makeshift 6 make-do **7**
standby, stopgap **8**
slapdash

make tracks 2 go **4** scat,
shoo **5** be off, leave,
scram **6** beat it, cut out,
depart, go away

make up 4 form **5** cover **6**
invent **7** arrange, concoct
8 assemble

maladroit 5 inept **6** clumsy,
gauche **7** awkward,
unhandy **8** bumbling,
bungling, tactless

malady 7 ailment, disease,
illness **8** disorder, sickness

malaise 5 throb **6** twinge **7**
anxiety **8** disquiet

Malawi
　other name: 9 Nyasaland
　capital/largest city: 8
　　Lilongwe
　lake: 5 Nyasa **6** Malawi
　river: 5 Shire
　physical feature:
　　highlands: 5 Shire
　　valley: 4 (Great) Rift **5**
　　Shire

Malaysia
　capital/largest city: 11
　　Kuala Lumpur
　highest point: 8 Kinabalu
　sea/ocean: 4 Sulu **6**
　　Indian **7** Celebes **10**
　　South China
　island: 6 Borneo, Penang
　physical feature:
　　peninsula: 5 Malay
　　strait 7 Malacca
　feature:
　　cloth: 5 batik
　　clothing: 6 sarong

malcontent *see* **7 grouchy**

Maldives
　capital/largest city: 4
　　Male
　sea/ocean: 6 Indian **7**
　　Arabian
　feature: coconut fiber: 4
　coir
　　dried coconut: 5 copra

male 3 boy, man, ram, tom
4 bull **5** manly, youth **6**
tomcat **7** rooster **8**
stallion

Male
　capital of: 8 Maldives

male bird 4 cock **5** drake **6**
gander **7** rooster

malediction 5 curse **8**
anathema, diatribe

malefactor 5 felon, knave,

rogue **6** sinner **7** culprit **8** criminal, offender

malevolence *see* **4 evil**

malfeasance 5 crime **8** misdeeds

malfunction 6 glitch, malady **7** problem

Mali
  other name: 11 French Sudan
  capital/largest city: 6 Bamako
  division: 8 Timbuktu
  highest point: 7 Hombori
  river: 5 Niger
  physical feature:
    desert: 6 Sahara
  feature:
    empire: 4 Mali **5** Ghana **7** Bambara, Songhai

malice 4 hate **5** spite, venom **6** enmity, grudge, hatred, rancor **7** ill will **8** acrimony

malignant *see* **4 evil**

malinger 4 loaf **5** dodge, shirk, slack **7** goof off

mall 4 yard **5** court, plaza **6** arcade, circus, piazza, square **8** cloister

malleable 6 docile, pliant **7** ductile, plastic, pliable

8 flexible, moldable, workable

Malta
  capital: 8 Valletta
  largest city: 6 Sliema
  sea: 13 Mediterranean

Maltese Falcon, The
  author: 7 (Dashiell) Hammett
  director: 6 (John) Huston
  cast: 4 (Elisha) Cook **5** (Mary) Astor, (Peter) Lorre **6** (Humphrey) Bogart **11** (Sydney) Greenstreet

malt liquor 3 ale **4** beer **5** stout **6** porter

maltreatment 5 abuse **6** ill-use, injury **7** assault, cruelty

mammon, Mammon 4 gain, gold **5** money **6** profit, riches, wealth

mammoth 4 huge **5** great **6** mighty **7** immense, massive **8** colossal, enormous, gigantic

man 3 boy, guy, one **4** chap, gent, hand, male, soul **5** equip, hubby, human, staff **6** anyone, attend, fellow, fit out, helper, outfit, person, spouse, waiter, worker

7 husband, laborer, mankind, someone **8** employee, garrison, henchman, humanity

Man, first 4 Adam

Man, Isle of
    capital: 7 Douglas
    Manx cat lacks: 4 tail

man about town 5 blade **7** playboy **8** cavalier, gay blade

manacle, manacles 5 bonds, irons **6** chains, fetter **7** shackle **8** handcuff, shackles

manage 4 care, rule **6** bosses, wheels **7** bigwigs, command, conduct, control **8** big shots, guidance, handling, ordering, planning, top brass

manager 4 boss, head **5** agent, chief **7** foreman, planner **8** overseer

Managua
    capital of: 9 Nicaragua

manana 6 future **8** tomorrow

Manchuria
    city: 6 Dairen, Harbin, Mukden

    peninsula: 8 Liaotung
    river: 4 Amur, Liao, Yalu

mandate 5 edict, order **6** behest, charge, decree **7** command, dictate

mandatory 7 binding, exigent, needful **8** required

mandible 3 jaw **4** beak, bill, jowl **7** maxilla

maneuver 4 move, plot, ploy **5** dodge, guide, pilot, steer, trick **6** deploy, device, gambit, scheme, tactic **7** finagle **8** artifice, contrive, intrigue

mangle 3 cut **4** harm, hurt, lame, maim, maul, ruin, tear **5** crush, press, slash **6** damage, impair, injure **7** flatten **8** lacerate, mutilate

manhandle 4 maul **5** abuse **6** batter **7** rough up **8** maltreat, mistreat

maniac 3 ass, nut **4** fool **5** loony **6** cuckoo, madman, nitwit **7** half-wit, lunatic

manic 2 up **4** high **7** excited, frantic, hyped up **8** agitated, frenzied, worked up

manifest *see* **6** candid

manifestation 4 show

7 display, example, symptom **8** evidence

manifesto 4 bull **5** edict, ukase **6** notice

manifold *see* **4 many**

Manila
   capital of: 11 Philippines
   island: 5 Luzon

manipulate 3 pat, ply, use **4** feel, work **5** drive, pinch, wield **6** employ, finger, handle, manage, stroke **7** control, deceive, defraud, massage, operate, squeeze

Manitoba
   abbreviation: 2 MB
   nickname: 7 Prairie **8** Keystone
   capital/largest city: 8 Winnipeg
   highest point: 5 Baldy
   lake: 8 Manitoba, Winnipeg
   river: 3 Red **8** Winnipeg **9** Churchill **11** Assiniboine
   physical feature:
     bay: 6 Hudson

mankind *see* **3 man**

manna 4 boon **5** award **6** reward **7** bonanza

mannequin 4 form **5** dummy, model **6** figure

manner 3 air, way **4** form, kind, make, mode, mold, race, rank, sort, type **5** brand, breed, caste, genre, grade, guise, habit, stamp, style **6** aspect, custom, method **7** bearing, conduct, variety **8** behavior, carriage, demeanor, presence

manners 6 polish **7** decorum **8** behavior, breeding, courtesy

manpower 4 help **5** brawn, labor

manque 6 failed, missed **7** lacking

mansion 5 manor, villa **6** castle, estate, palace **7** chateau

manslaughter 6 murder **7** killing **8** homicide

mantle 4 cape, film, mask, pall, veil **5** cloak, cloud, cover, scarf, tunic **6** canopy, screen, shroud **7** blanket, curtain, wrapper **8** covering, mantilla

manual 6 primer **8** handbook, physical, textbook, workbook

manufacture 4 form, make, mold **5** build, frame

6 cook up, create, devise, invent, make up **7** concoct, fashion, produce, think up, trump up **8** assemble

manumit 4 free **7** set free **8** liberate

manure 4 dung **5** feces **6** ordure **7** compost, excreta **8** dressing

Manx 3 cat
　　cat lacks: 4 tail

many 4 a lot, lots **5** a heap, heaps, piles **6** myriad, scores, sundry **7** numbers, several **8** numerous

Mao Zedong
　　also: 10 Mao Tse-Tung
　　title: 8 Chairman
　　led: 9 Long March

map 4 plan, plot **5** chart, graph, ready **6** design, devise, lay out **7** diagram, prepare **8** organize

mar 4 hurt, maim, mark, nick, ruin, scar **5** botch, spoil, stain, taint **6** damage, deface, defile, impair **7** blemish, scratch **8** diminish **9** disfigure

marauder 6 looter, pirate, ranger **7** corsair, ravager, spoiler **8** pillager

marble 3 jet **4** vein **5** agate **6** basalt, mottle, streak **7** calcite **8** dolomite

march 2 go **4** hike, rise, step, trek, walk **5** tramp **6** file by, growth, parade **7** advance **8** progress

March
　　event: 9 Mardi Gras
　　flower: 7 jonquil **8** daffodil
　　gem: 10 aquamarine, bloodstone
　　holiday: 10 St Patrick's
　　origin of name: 4 Mars
　　　　Roman god of: 3 war
　　place in year:
　　　　Gregorian: 5 third
　　　　Roman: 5 first
　　Zodiac sign: 5 Aries **6** Pisces

Mardi Gras 7 holiday **8** carnival, festival, jamboree
　　king: 3 rex
　　social club: 5 krewe

Marduk
　　origin: 10 Babylonian
　　chief of: 4 gods

margin 3 hem, rim **4** edge, side **5** bound, skirt, verge **6** border, fringe, leeway **7** confine **8** boundary

marijuana, marihuana 3 boo, kif, pot, tea **4** hash,

hemp, herb, weed **5** bhang, blunt, dagga, ganja, grass, joint **6** buddha, moocah, reefer **7** chronic, hashish **8** cannabis, mary jane

marine 3 sea **5** naval **6** gyrene **7** aquatic, oceanic, pelagic **8** maritime, nautical, seagoing

mariner 3 gob, tar **4** salt **5** pilot **6** sailor, sea dog, seaman **7** boatman **8** helmsman, seafarer

marital 6 wedded, wifely **7** married, nuptial, spousal **8** conjugal

mark 3 cut, mar, pit **4** dent, goal, line, mind, nick, note, rate, scar, show, sign, spot **5** badge, brand, grade, judge, label, point, proof, score, stain, stamp, token **6** attend, bruise, deface, emblem, reveal, streak, symbol, target, typify **7** blemish, correct, imprint, measure, scratch, signify, suggest, symptom **8** bull's-eye, indicate, manifest, standard

Mark
also: 8 John Mark
mother: 4 Mary

cousin: 8 Barnabas
wrote: 6 Gospel

marker 3 IOU, peg, run, tab **4** chip, flag, sign **5** score **6** ticket **7** counter **8** monument

market 4 hawk, sell, vend **5** stand **6** bourse, peddle, retail **7** grocery

marketplace 4 mart **5** agora, arena, plaza **6** bazaar, market, square **8** exchange

marksmanship 3 aim **5** skill **8** accuracy

maroon 4 plum, wine **6** desert, strand **7** abandon, magenta **8** cast away

marquee 4 tent **6** awning, canopy

Marriage of Figaro, The
opera: 6 Mozart

married 3 wed **5** mated **6** joined, united, wedded **7** hitched, marital **8** combined, espoused

Mars
origin: 5 Roman
god of: 3 war
mother: 4 Juno

Mars 6 planet
position: 6 fourth
nickname: 9 Red Planet

satellite: 6 Deimos, Phobos

marsh 3 bog, fen **5** swamp **6** morass, slough **7** bottoms, wetland **8** quagmire

marshal *see* **7 collect**

marsupial 5 koala **6** numbat, possum, wombat **7** cuscuse, opossum, wallaby **8** kangaroo

martial 7 hostile, warlike **8** militant, military

martinet 6 despot, tyrant **8** dictator

martyr 5 saint **8** sufferer

marvel 4 gape **6** be awed, rarity, wonder **7** miracle **8** be amazed

marvelous, marvellous *see* **5 great**

Marx Brothers 5 Chico (Leonard), Gummo (Milton), Harpo (Adolph, Arthur) Zeppo (Herbert) **7** Groucho (Julius)

Mary 6 Virgin **7** Madonna **8** Holy Mary
mother: 4 Anna, Anne
husband: 6 Joseph
son: 4 Jude, Mark **5** James (the Less), Jesus, Moses, Simon

sister: 6 Martha
brother: 7 Lazarus **8** Barnabas
home: 8 Nazareth
visitor: 7 Gabriel
flower: 4 lily **8** marigold

Maryland
abbreviation: 2 MD
nickname: 7 Old Line
capital: 9 Annapolis
largest city: 9 Baltimore
mountain: 9 Blue Ridge
highest point: 8 Backbone
river: 3 Wye **7** Potomac
sea/ocean: 8 Atlantic
physical feature:
    bay: 10 Chesapeake
feature:
    fort: 7 McHenry
    horse race: 9 Preakness
    presidential retreat: 9 Camp David

Mary Tyler Moore Show
cast: 5 (Ed) Asner, (Mary Tyler) Moore **6** (Valerie) Harper, (Ted) Knight **7** (Gavin) MacLeod **9** (Cloris) Leachman

masculine 4 bold, male **5** brave, hardy, husky, macho, manly **6** brawny, daring, manful, plucky, robust, strong, sturdy, virile **7** staunch, valiant

8 athletic, forceful, intrepid, muscular, powerful, vigorous

mash 4 mush **5** crush, paste, puree, smash **6** squash **8** mishmash

M*A*S*H (TV Series)
   cast: 4 (Alan) Alda, (Jamie) Farr, (Loretta) Swit **6** (Harry) Morgan, (Wayne) Rogers **7** (Mike) Farrell **8** (Gary) Burghoff, (Larry) Linville **9** (McLean) Stevenson
   war: 6 Korean

masjid 6 mosque

mask 4 hide, veil **5** blind, cloak, cover **6** domino, screen, shroud **7** conceal, cover-up, curtain, obscure **8** disguise

masquerade 4 mask, ruse, veil **5** cloak, cover, guise, trick **6** masque, pose as, screen, shroud **7** cover-up, pretext **8** artifice, pretense

mass, Mass 3 jam, lot, mob **4** body, bulk, cake, clot, heap, host, hunk, knot, lump, pack, pile **5** amass, batch, block, bunch, chunk, clump, corps, crowd, crush, group, horde, press, stack, troop

6 bundle, gather, matter, throng, weight **7** collect, pyramid **8** assemble, main body, majority

Massachusetts
   abbreviation: 2 MA **4** Mass
   nickname: 8 Bay State
   capital/largest city: 6 Boston
   highest point: 8 Greylock
   river: 6 Nashua **7** Charles
   sea/ocean: 8 Atlantic
   island: 9 Nantucket **15** Martha's Vineyard
   physical feature:
      bay: 8 Buzzard's
      cape: 3 Ann
      pond: 6 Walden

massacre 7 butcher, carnage **8** butchery, decimate

massage 3 rub **4** flex **5** chafe, knead **6** finger, handle, stroke **7** rubbing, rub down, stretch **8** kneading, stroking

masses 6 plebes, proles, rabble

massive *see* **4 huge**

mast 4 main, nuts, pole, post, spar **5** spirit, staff, stick, stuff **6** acorns, pillar
   type: 4 fore, main

6 jigger, mizzen
support: 4 bibb

master 3 act **4** able, A-one, boss, curb, head, lord, main, tame, whiz **5** check, chief, grasp, owner, prime, ruler **6** choice, expert, genius, gifted, govern, leader, manage, subdue **7** conquer, control, manager, primary, skilled, skipper, supreme **8** director, dominate, finished, governor, overcome, regulate, virtuoso

master of ceremonies 4 host **5** emcee

masterpiece 5 jewel, prize **7** classic, paragon **8** monument, treasure

masticate 4 chew, gnaw **5** chomp, munch **6** nibble

mat 3 dim, pad, rug **4** dead, dull, flat **5** doily, muted **6** carpet, matrix, tangle **7** bedding, bolster, coaster, cushion, support
Japanese: 6 tatami

match 3 fit **4** game, join, mate, meet, pair, peer, suit, twin, yoke **5** adapt, agree, event **6** couple, double, oppose

7 combine, connect, contend, contest **8** parallel

matchless 4 rare **7** supreme **8** crowning, foremost, peerless, sterling, superior

mate *see* **6 friend**

materialistic 6 greedy **8** covetous, grasping

materialize 4 loom, rise, show **5** bob up, issue, pop up **6** appear, crop up, emerge, turn up

materials 4 data **5** cloth, facts, notes, tools **6** stocks, stores **7** fabrics, figures **8** dry goods, supplies

maternal 4 fond **6** doting **8** motherly

maternity 5 labor **8** delivery

mathematical, mathematic 5 exact, rigid **6** strict **7** precise **8** accurate, rigorous, unerring

matriculate 4 join **5** enter **6** enlist, enroll, sign up **7** check in **8** register

matrimonial 6 bridal **7** marital, married, nuptial, spousal **8** conjugal

matrimony 7 wedlock **8** marriage

matrix 3 die **4** cast, form, mold **5** frame, punch, stamp

matron 4 dame **5** madam **7** dowager **8** forelady, mistress, overseer

matter 3 fix **4** gist, snag, text **5** count, drift, event, sense, stuff, theme, thing, topic **6** affair, crisis, import, moment, object, scrape **7** content, dilemma, essence, purport, signify, subject **8** argument, elements, exigency, material, obstacle

matter-of-fact 4 real **5** blunt, frank **6** candid, direct **7** factual, literal, mundane, natural, prosaic **8** ordinary, sensible

Matthew 7 apostle
also called: 4 Levi
wrote: 6 Gospel

mature 4 ripe **5** adult, bloom, grown, manly, of age, ready, ripen **6** flower, grow up, mellow, nubile, virile **7** blossom, develop, grown-up, matured, womanly **8** finished, maturate, seasoned

maudlin 5 gushy, mushy, teary **6** slushy **7** gushing, mawkish, tearful **8** bathetic

maul 4 beat **5** stomp **6** batter, beat up, bruise, mangle, pummel, thrash **7** rough up

Mau Mau 7 (secret) society
of: 6 Kikuyu
in: 5 Kenya

Mauritania
capital/largest city: 10 Nouakchott
river: 7 Senegal
sea: 8 Atlantic
physical feature:
desert: 6 Sahara

Mauritius
capital/largest city: 9 Port Louis
sea: 6 Indian

mauve 4 plum, puce **5** lilac **6** violet **8** lavender

maverick 5 loner **8** yearling

maw 4 craw, crop, jaws **5** mouth **6** gullet, muzzle, throat

mawkish 5 gushy, mushy, teary **7** maudlin, tearful

maxim 3 saw **4** rule **5** adage, axiom, motto **6** old saw, saying, truism **7** proverb **8** aphorism

maximum 3 top **4** most **6** utmost **7** highest, largest, maximal, optimum, supreme **8** greatest

May
  characteristic: 7 Maypole
  flower: 4 lily (of the valley) **8** hawthorn
  gem: 7 emerald
  holiday: 6 May Day (1) **7** Mother's (Day) **8** Memorial (Day)
  number of days: 9 thirty-one
  origin of name: 4 Maia
    Roman goddess of: 6 spring
  place in year:
    Gregorian: 5 fifth
    Roman: 5 third
  Zodiac sign: 6 Gemini, Taurus

Maya
  location: 6 Belize, Mexico **7** Yucatan **8** Honduras **9** Guatemala

maybe 6 mayhap **7** perhaps **8** feasibly, possibly

mayhem 4 maim **6** felony **7** cripple **8** mutilate, violence

maze 5 snarl **6** jungle, tangle **7** complex, meander, network

McKinley, William
  presidential rank: 11 twenty-fifth
  party: 10 Republican
  state represented: 2 OH
  vice president: 6 Hobart **9** Roosevelt
  born: 2 OH **5** Niles
  died by: 13 assassination
    assassinated by: 8 Czolgosz
  governor of: 4 Ohio
  notable events of lifetime/ term:
    war with: 5 Spain
  wife: 3 Ida

mea culpa 7 my fault

meadow 3 lea **4** mead, park **5** field, green **6** forage **7** herbage, pasture, savanna

meager 4 bare, lean, slim, thin **5** scant, short, spare **6** little, paltry, scarce, skimpy, sparse **7** scrimpy, wanting

meal 4 bran, chow, diet, eats, fare, food, grub, menu **5** feast, flour, grits **6** farina, groats, repast, spread **7** banquet, cooking, cuisine, oatmeal **8** cornmeal, victuals

mean 3 low, par, say **4** base, evil, norm, poor,

vile, want, wish **5** aim at, cheap, cruel, nasty, petty, small, venal **6** flimsy, greedy, intend, malign, medium, menial, normal, paltry, stingy, trashy, unfair **7** average, balance, express, inhuman, miserly, regular, signify, squalid, suggest, trivial, vicious **8** grasping, indicate, inhumane, intimate, pitiless, standard, stand for, uncaring

meander 4 loop, rove, wind **5** snake, stray, twist **6** circle, ramble, spiral, wander, zigzag **8** undulate

meaningless 5 trite **6** absurd, paltry, stupid **7** aimless, fatuous, foolish, idiotic, shallow, trivial, useless **8** baffling, piddling, puzzling

means 3 way **4** jack, mode **5** bread, dough, funds, money **6** avenue, course, income, method, resort, riches, wealth **7** capital, dollars, measure, process, revenue **8** property

measure 3 act, law **4** bill, plan, rule, size, step, time **5** clock, gauge, judge, limit, means, quota, range, scale, scope, share, sound **6** amount, assess, degree, design, extent, scheme, survey **7** portion **8** appraise, evaluate, proposal, quantity

Measure for Measure author: 11 (William) Shakespeare

measurement 4 area, mass, size **5** depth, width **6** extent, height, length, volume, weight **7** breadth, content, gauging **8** capacity, plumbing, sounding

meat 3 nut **4** core, fare, food, gist, grub **5** heart, point **6** kernel **7** edibles, essence, nucleus **8** victuals

mechanic 6 joiner **7** artisan

mechanism 4 tool **5** motor, works **7** machine, utensil

medal 5 award, honor, prize **6** reward, trophy

meddle 5 mix in **6** butt in, horn in, kibitz **7** intrude, pry into

**Medea
form: 9** sorceress
aunt: 5 Circe

lover: 5 Jason
escaped to: 6 Athens
media 2 TV **5** press, radio
singular: 6 medium
median 3 mid, par **4** mean, norm **5** mesne **6** center, medial, medium, middle **7** average, central, halfway **8** midpoint, moderate
mediate 6 pacify, step in, umpire **7** referee **8** moderate
medical 7 healing **8** curative, remedial, salutary
medicine 4 balm, drug, pill **5** salve, tonic **6** remedy **7** nostrum
medieval 8 Dark Ages
mediocre 4 so-so **6** common, meager, medium, normal **7** average **8** ordinary, passable
meditate 4 muse, plan **5** aim at, study, think **6** devise, ponder **7** concoct, propose, reflect **8** cogitate, consider, mull over, ruminate
Mediterranean
coast: 7 Riviera
gulf: 5 Lions, Sidra, Tunis
7 Antalya, Catania, Taranto
island: 4 Elba **5** Capri, Corfu, Crete, Malta **6** Cyprus, Euboea, Rhodes, Sicily **7** Corsica, Majorca, Minorca **8** Balearic, Sardinia
resort: 4 Nice **5** Capri **6** Cannes **7** Riviera
sea: 6 Aegean, Ionian **8** Adriatric, Ligurian
wind: 7 mistral, sirocco
medium 3 way **4** form, mean, mode, tool **5** means, organ **6** agency, avenue, common, milieu, normal **7** average, channel, diviner, psychic, setting **8** moderate
medley 4 hash, mess, olio **6** jumble, mosaic **7** farrago, melange, mixture **8** mishmash, pastiche
medulla
part of: 5 brain
controls: 6 glands **7** muscles
Medusa
form: 6 Gorgon
sisters: 6 Graiae
loved by: 8 Poseidon

sight of her turned people to: 5 stone
killed by: 7 Perseus

meek 4 mild **6** docile, gentle, humble, modest **8** retiring, tolerant, yielding

meet 3 apt, fit **4** abut, face, good, heed, obey **5** cross, equal, greet, match, rally, right **6** adjoin, answer, border, follow, gather, muster, proper, seemly **7** collect, convene, execute, fitting, observe, respect, run into, satisfy, welcome **8** assemble, bump into, confront, converge

Mein Kampf author: 6 (Adolf) Hitler

melancholy *see* **3 sad**

melange 3 mix **4** olio **6** jumble, medley **7** mixture **8** compound, mishmash, pastiche

meld 3 mix **4** fuse, join **5** blend, merge, unite **6** mingle **7** combine **8** coalesce, intermix

melee *see* **5 fight**

mellifluous 4 soft **5** sweet **6** dulcet, mellow, smooth **7** musical **8** resonant

mellow 4 rich, ripe, soft **5** drunk, sweet **6** mature,
soften **7** matured, relaxed **8** luscious, tolerant

melodramatic 5 corny, hammy, hokey, stagy **7** maudlin, mawkish

melody 3 air **4** aria, song, tune **5** ditty, theme **6** ballad, strain, timbre **7** concord, euphony

melt 4 fade, fuse, pass, thaw **5** blend, merge, shade, touch **6** affect, disarm, dispel, soften, vanish **7** appease, dwindle, liquefy, mollify, scatter **8** dissolve

member 3 arm, leg, toe **4** foot, hand, limb, part, tail, wing **5** bough, digit, organ, piece, shoot **6** branch, finger, pinion **7** element, portion, section, segment **8** fragment

membrane 3 web **4** film, skin **6** lining, sheath **7** coating **8** pellicle

memento 5 favor, relic, token **6** record, trophy **8** keepsake, souvenir

memoir 4 life **5** diary **7** journal

memorable 6 famous **7** eminent, notable, salient **8** historic, stirring, striking

memorandum 4 memo, note 5 brief 6 agenda, minute, record 7 jotting

memorial 6 homage 7 tribute 8 monument

memory 4 fame, mark, name, note 5 glory, honor, token 6 esteem, recall, regard, renown, repute 7 memento, respect 8 eminence, keepsake, memorial, prestige, reminder, souvenir

menace 3 cow 4 risk 5 bully, daunt, peril 6 danger, hazard, threat 7 imperil, pitfall, portend, presage, terrify 8 endanger, threaten

mend 3 fix 4 cure, darn, heal, knit 5 amend, emend, patch 6 better, remedy, repair 7 correct, improve, rectify, restore, retouch 8 overhaul

mendacity 5 fraud, lying 6 deceit 7 falsity, perfidy

Mendel, Gregor Johann
founded: 8 genetics

mendicant 6 beggar

Menelaus
king of: 6 Sparta
father: 6 Atreus
mother: 6 Aerope
brother: 9 Agamemnon
wife: 5 Helen

menial 4 mean 5 drone, lowly, slave, toady 6 abject, drudge, flunky, helper, humble, lackey 7 ignoble, servant, servile, slavish 8 cringing

mental *see* 5 **crazy**

mental hospital 6 asylum 8 madhouse

mentality 4 mind 6 acumen, brains, wisdom 8 judgment, sagacity

mention 3 say 4 cite, hint, name, tell 5 imply, state 6 hint at, notice, remark, report, tell of 7 comment, divulge, narrate, observe, recount, refer to 8 allusion, disclose, intimate

mentor 4 guru 5 guide, tutor 6 master 7 adviser, monitor, proctor, teacher

mercantile 5 trade 8 business

mercenary 5 venal 6 greedy 7 selfish 8 covetous, grasping, hireling, monetary

merchandise 4 sell 5 goods,

stock, trade, wares **6** deal in, market

merchant 6 broker, dealer, hawker, jobber, trader, vendor **7** peddler **8** chandler, retailer, salesman

Merchant of Venice, The
author: 11 (William) Shakespeare

mercurial 6 fickle, lively **7** erratic, flighty **8** electric, spirited, unstable, variable, volatile

Mercury
origin: 5 Roman
messenger of: 4 gods
god of: 7 science, thieves **8** commerce

mercy 4 pity **5** grace **7** charity **8** blessing, clemency, humanity, kindness, lenience, leniency, sympathy

merely 3 but **4** just, only **5** quite **6** barely, in part, purely, simply, solely **7** utterly **8** scarcely, wholly

meretricious 4 mock, sham **5** bogus, false, phony **6** pseudo, shoddy, tawdry **8** delusive, spurious

merge 4 fuse, join, weld **5** blend, marry, unify, unite **6** link up **7** combine **8** coalesce, converge

meridian see **6 summit**

merit 4 earn, rate **5** value, worth **6** credit, desert, invite, prompt, talent, virtue **7** ability, benefit, deserve, quality, stature, warrant **8** efficacy

merry 3 gay **5** happy, jolly **6** blithe, cheery, jocund, jovial, joyous, lively **7** festive, gleeful, jocular **8** animated, carefree, cheerful, gladsome, laughing, mirthful, partying, reveling, sportive

Merry Wives of Windsor, The
author: 11 (William) Shakespeare

mesa 4 hill, peak **5** bench, butte, table **7** plateau

mesh 3 fib, net, web **4** grid, jibe, lace **5** agree, sieve, tally **6** engage, enmesh, grille, plexus, screen **7** connect, engaged, netting, network, webbing **8** dovetail, interact

Meshach
former name: 7 Mishael
companion: 6 Daniel

friend: 8 Abednego, Shadrach

mesmerize 5 charm **7** bewitch **8** enthrall, entrance

mess 3 fix **4** hash, stew **5** mix-up, pinch **6** crisis, jumble, litter, muddle, pickle, plight, scrape, strait **7** clutter, dilemma, trouble **8** disarray, disorder, quandary

message 4 news, note, word **5** moral, point, theme **6** letter, notice, report **7** meaning, missive, purport, tidings **8** bulletin, dispatch

messenger 5 envoy **6** bearer, runner **7** carrier, courier **8** delegate, emissary

mess up 3 mar **4** goof, muff, ruin **5** botch, spoil **6** bungle, foul up **7** blunder, butcher, disturb, louse up, screw up

mesto
    music: 8 mournful

metal
    alloy: 5 brass, monel **6** bronze, nickel, niello, pewter, solder
    classification: 5 light, noble **6** alkali, common **7** coinage **8** platinum, precious **9** rare earth
    heaviest: 6 osmium
    lightest: 7 lithium
    liquid: 7 mercury
    worker: 5 smith **6** forger, welder **7** armorer, riveter **8** armourer

metamorphose 6 change, mutate **7** convert

metaphor 5 image, trope **6** simile **7** analogy **8** metonymy, parallel

metaphysical 5 basic, lofty, vague **6** far-out **7** eternal **8** abstract, abstruse, esoteric, mystical, ultimate

mete, mete out 5 allot **6** assign, divide **7** deal out, dole out **8** allocate, disburse, dispense

meteoric *see* **4 fast**

method 3 way **4** form, mode, plan, tack **5** means, order, style, usage **6** course, design, manner, scheme, system **7** fashion, formula, process, program, purpose, routine **8** approach, efficacy

meticulous 4 nice **5** exact, fussy **7** finical, finicky, precise **8** sedulous

metier 3 job **4** area, line, work **5** craft, field, forte, trade **7** calling, pursuit **8** business, vocation

Metis
  member of: 6 Titans
  father: 7 Oceanus
  mother: 6 Tethys
  consort of: 4 Zeus
  daughter: 6 Athena

mettle 3 vim **4** grit, guts **5** nerve, pluck, spunk, valor, vigor **6** spirit **7** bravery, courage, heroism **8** audacity, backbone, boldness, temerity

Mexico
  other name: 8 New Spain
  capital/largest city: 10 Mexico City
  highest point: 7 Orizaba
  river: 6 Grande **8** Colorado
  sea: 7 Pacific **8** Atlantic **9** Caribbean
  island: 6 Cancun **7** Cozumel
  physical feature:
    bay: 8 Campeche
    desert: 7 Sonoran
    gulf: 6 Mexico
    peninsula: 7 Yucatan
  feature:
    Christmas tradition:
    6 pinata
  empire: 5 Aztec, Mayan, Olmec **6** Mixtec, Toltec **7** Zapotec
  large estate: 8 hacienda
  musician: 8 mariachi
  trade agreement: 5 NAFTA
  food:
    corn cake: 8 tortilla
    dish: 4 taco **6** tamale **7** burrito, tostado **8** empanada
    drink: 7 tequila

Mexico City
  capital of: 6 Mexico

Michigan
  abbreviation: 2 MI **4** Mich
  nickname: 9 Wolverine
  capital: 7 Lansing
  largest city: 7 Detroit
  highest point: 5 Arvon
  lake: 4 Erie **5** Huron **8** Michigan, Superior
  river: 5 Flint, Grand, White **7** Detroit
  physical feature:
    bay: 5 Green **7** Saginaw, Thunder
    strait: 8 Mackinac
  feature:
    canal 3 Soo

Mickey Mouse
  creator: 6 (Walt) Disney
  character: 5 Morty **6**
    Ferdie, Minnie

microbe 4 germ **5** virus **6**
  gamete, zygote **8** bacillus,
  parasite

Micronesia
  part of: 7 Oceania
  island: 4 Guam, Truk,
    Wake **5** Nauru **6** Bikini,
    Ellice **7** Gilbert, Mariana
    8 Caroline, Kiribati,
    Marshall

microorganism 3 bug **4**
  germ **5** virus **7** microbe **8**
  bacillus, pathogen **9**
  bacterium

Midas
  king of: 7 Phrygia
  gift: 11 golden touch
  gift from: 7 Silenus

midday 4 noon **7** noonday
  8 meridian, noontime

middle 3 gut, hub, mid **4**
  core, main **5** belly, midst,
  waist **6** center, course,
  medial, median, midway **7**
  central, halfway, midriff,
  nucleus, stomach **8**
  midpoint

middle-class 4 mass **8**
  ordinary

middleman 5 agent **6**
  broker, dealer, jobber **7**
  liaison **8** mediator

middle-of-the-road 8
  moderate

middling *see* **8 ordinary**

midget 4 doll, runt **5** dwarf,
  pygmy **6** peewee, puppet,
  shrimp, squirt **7** manikin
  8 half-pint, munchkin

Midi 5 skirt

midlands 8 interior

midriff 3 gut **4** guts **5** belly,
  tummy **6** paunch **7**
  abdomen, stomach

midst *see* **6 middle**

Midsummer Night's Dream
  author: 11 (William)
    Shakespeare

midterm 4 exam, test **6**
  review

mien 3 air **4** look **5** guise,
  style **6** aspect, manner,
  visage **7** bearing, feature **8**
  demeanor

miff *see* **3 vex**

might 3 may **5** brawn,
  clout, force, power, vigor
  6 energy, muscle **7**
  potency, prowess **8**
  strength

migration 4 trek **6** exodus,

flight, moving **7** passage **8** diaspora, movement

mikado 5 ruler **7** emperor, monarch

mild 4 calm, easy, soft, warm **5** balmy, bland **6** docile, gentle, placid, serene, smooth **7** pacific, summery **8** delicate, moderate, pleasant, soothing, tranquil

mildew 4 mold **6** blight, fungus

milestone 7 jubilee **8** milepost, signpost

milieu 5 scene **7** culture, element, setting **8** ambience, backdrop

military 4 army **5** armed, crisp **6** strict, troops **7** martial, militia, Spartan, warlike **8** generals, soldiers

military force 4 army, navy **5** corps, fleet **6** legion, troops **7** division, legions, militia **8** military, regiment, soldiers, squadron

military storehouse 6 armory **7** arsenal **8** magazine

milksop 4 baby, wimp

5 mouse, pansy, sissy, softy **6** coward **7** crybaby, nebbish **8** mama's boy, poltroon, weakling

mill 4 roam, teem **5** crush, grind, shape, swarm, works **6** finish, groove **7** factory, meander

**Million Dollar Baby
director: 8** (Clint) Eastwood
cast: 5 (Hilary) Swank **7** (Morgan) Freeman **8** (Clint) Eastwood

millstream 3 run **4** race **5** brook, creek, river **6** branch

**Milo, Milos
island of: 6** Greece **8** Cyclades **9** Aegean Sea
found: 5 Venus **6** statue
missing: 4 arms

milquetoast 4 wimp **7** milksop, nebbish

mimic *see* **4 copy**

mince 4 dice, pose **5** grate, shred **6** refine, soften **7** posture, qualify **8** chop fine, hold back, mitigate, moderate, palliate

mince words 5 dodge, hedge, stall

mind 4 hate, heed, note,

obey, tend, will, wits **5** abhor, bow to, brain, focus, sense, watch **6** brains, choice, detest, follow, intent, liking, memory, notice, notion, reason, recall, regard, resent, sanity **7** dislike, observe, opinion, outlook, thought **8** reaction, response, thinking

mine 3 dig, pit **4** fund **5** cache, hoard, shaft, stock, store **6** quarry, supply, tunnel, wealth **7** extract, reserve **8** excavate

Minerva
  origin: 5 Roman
  goddess of: 3 war **4** arts **6** wisdom

mingle 3 mix **4** fuse, join **5** blend, merge, unite **6** hobnob **7** combine, consort **8** coalesce, intermix

miniature *see* **4 tiny**

minimal 5 token **7** minimum, nominal

minister 4 abbe, tend **5** padre, rabbi, serve, vicar **6** answer, cleric, father, oblige, parson, pastor, priest **7** care for, cater to **8** attend to, chaplain, pander to, preacher, reverend

ministration 3 aid **4** care **6** charge **7** comfort

Minnesota
  abbreviation: 2 MN **4** Minn
  nickname: 6 Gopher
  capital: 6 St Paul
  largest city: 11 Minneapolis
  mountain: 6 Mesabi
  highest point: 5 Eagle
  lake: 3 Red **8** Superior, Traverse
  river: 3 Red **5** Snake **7** St Croix, St Louis **11** Mississippi

minor 5 child, light, petty, small, youth **6** infant, lesser, paltry, slight **7** trivial **8** trifling

minor-league 4 punk **5** dinky, seedy, tacky **6** cheesy, common, lesser, shabby **8** inferior

Minos
  king of: 5 Crete
  father: 4 Zeus
  mother: 6 Europa
  wife: 8 Pasiphae
  daughter: 7 Ariadne, Phaedra

Minotaur
  form: 7 monster
  combined: 3 man **4** bull
  father: 10 Cretan bull
  mother: 8 Pasiphae
  home: 9 Labyrinth
  killed by: 7 Theseus

minstrel 4 bard, poet **6** dancer, end man, lyrist, player, singer **8** comedian, songster

mint 7 menthol **9** spearmint

minute 3 wee **4** fine, puny, tiny, wink **5** close, exact, flash, jiffy, petty, scant, shake, teeny, trice **6** breath, little, moment, petite, second, slight, strict **7** careful, instant, minikin, precise **8** detailed
  abbreviation: 3 min

minutiae 6 trivia **7** trifles **8** niceties

minx 4 jade, slut **5** hussy, huzzy, wench **7** baggage

miracle 4 omen, sign **6** marvel, wonder **7** mystery, portent, prodigy

miraculous 6 divine **7** amazing, magical

mirage 5 fancy **7** fantasy **8** delusion, illusion

mire *see* **3** mud

Miriam
  brother: 5 Aaron, Moses

mirror 4 copy, show **5** glass, image, model **7** epitome, example, paragon, reflect **8** exemplar, manifest, paradigm, standard

mirth 4 glee **6** gaiety, levity **7** jollity **8** drollery, hilarity, laughter

mirthless 3 sad **4** dour, glum **6** gloomy, morose **7** joyless, unhappy

misadventure 3 ill **4** slip **6** mishap **7** debacle, failure, reverse, setback **8** bad break, calamity, disaster

misanthropic 4 cold **5** surly **6** morose **7** cynical, distant

misapprehension 5 mixup **7** mistake

misappropriate 4 bilk **5** abuse, cheat, mulct, steal **6** misuse **7** defraud, purloin, swindle **8** embezzle, misapply, peculate

misbehave 5 act up **7** disobey, do wrong

miscalculate 3 err **8** misjudge

miscarry 4 fail **5** abort, botch **6** fizzle, go awry

miscellaneous 5 mixed **6** divers, motley, sundry, varied **7** diverse, various **8** assorted, manifold

mischance 6 mishap **7** bad luck, ill wind **8** accident

mischief *see* **4 evil**

misconduct 7 misdeed, misstep

misconstrue 7 distort, mistake **8** misjudge

miscreant 3 bum **4** heel **5** knave, scamp **6** bad egg, rascal, wretch **7** villain **8** evildoer, scalawag

misdeed 3 sin **4** slip **5** crime, lapse, wrong **6** felony **7** faux pas, offense, outrage **8** atrocity, trespass

misdemeanor 3 sin **5** crime, fault **7** offense, misdeed **8** disorder

miserable 3 sad **4** mean **5** sorry **6** abject, shabby, sordid, woeful **7** abysmal, crushed, doleful, forlorn, hapless, unhappy **8** degraded, dejected, desolate, inferior, mournful, pathetic, pitiable, wretched

Miserables, Les author: 4 (Victor) Hugo

miserly *see* **5 cheap**

misery 3 woe **5** agony, curse, grief, trial **6** ordeal, sorrow **7** anguish, chagrin, despair, sadness, torment, trouble **8** calamity, disaster, distress, exaction, hardship

misfortune 4 blow, loss **6** misery, mishap **7** bad luck, reverse, setback, tragedy, trouble **8** calamity, casualty, disaster, downfall, hard luck, hardship

misgiving, misgivings 4 fear **5** alarm, doubt, dread, qualm, worry **7** anxiety, dubiety **8** disquiet, mistrust

misguided 5 at sea **6** adrift, faulty, misled, unwise **7** in error **8** mistaken

mishap 4 slip, snag **5** botch **6** fiasco, slipup **7** setback **8** casualty, disaster

misjudge 3 err **7** mistake

mislead *see* **7 deceive**

misnomer 8 misusage, solecism

misogynist 5 cynic

misplace 4 lose **5** abuse **6** mislay

misrepresent 7 falsify, mislead **8** disguise

miss 4 blow, girl, lack, lady, lass, lose, loss, maid, muff, skip, slip, want **5** avert, avoid, error, forgo, let go, woman **6** bypass, damsel, forego, lassie, maiden, pass by **7** blunder, colleen, default, failure, let pass, let slip, long for, mistake, neglect, overrun, pine for **8** leave out, omission, senorita, spinster, yearn for

missile 4 ball, dart **5** arrow, lance, shaft, shell, spear, stone **6** bullet, rocket **7** harpoon, javelin

missing 4 AWOL, gone, lost **6** absent **7** lacking, left out **8** avoiding

mission 3 end, job **4** task **5** quest **6** charge **7** calling, mandate, pursuit **8** legation, ministry

Mississippi
abbreviation: 2 MS

4 Miss
nickname: 8 Magnolia
capital/largest city: 7 Jackson
highest point: 7 Woodall
river: 3 Red **5** Pearl, Yazoo **11** Mississippi
physical feature:
  gulf: 6 Mexico

missive 4 note **6** billet, letter **7** epistle, message

Missouri
abbreviation: 2 MO
nickname: 5 Ozark **6** Show-Me
capital: 13 Jefferson City
largest city: 7 St Louis
mountain: 6 Ozarks
river: 8 Missouri **11** Mississippi
physical feature:
  plateau: 5 Ozark

misstep *see* **7** mistake

mist 3 fog **4** haze, murk, smog **5** steam, vapor **7** drizzle

mistake 4 slip **5** boner, error, gaffe, mix-up **6** slipup **7** blooper, blunder, confuse, faux pas, misstep **8** confound, misjudge

mister 3 aga, dom, don, pan, reb, sir **4** agha, babu, herr **5** sahib, senor

6 senhor, signor **7** mynheer **8** monsieur

mistreat 4 harm **5** abuse, bully, hound, wrong **6** harass, ill-use, injure, misuse, molest **7** assault, oppress, outrage, pervert, torment, violate

mistress 3 mrs **4** doxy, lady, miss **5** lover, madam **6** matron **8** ladylove, paramour

mistrust 5 doubt, qualm **7** anxiety, dubiety, suspect **8** distrust, question, wariness

misunderstanding 4 rift, spat **5** set-to **7** discord, dispute, quarrel, wrangle **8** conflict, squabble

mite 3 bit, jot **4** atom, iota, whit **5** scrap, speck **6** spider **7** smidgen **8** arachnid, particle

Mithras
    origin: 7 Persian
    god of: 5 light, truth

mitigate 4 ease **5** allay, blunt **6** lessen, reduce, soften, soothe, temper, weaken **7** assuage, lighten, mollify, placate, relieve **8** moderate, palliate

mitzvah, mitsvah 8 good deed

mix 3 add **4** beat, club, fold, fuse, join, stir, whip **5** admix, alloy, blend, merge, put in, unite **6** commix, fusion, hobnob, mingle **7** combine, consort, include, mixture **8** assembly, coalesce, compound, intermix, mingling

mixture 3 mix **4** hash, stew **5** alloy, blend, union **6** fusion, jumble, medley **7** amalgam, melange **8** compound, mishmash, pastiche

mixup 4 mess, riot **5** fight, melee, snafu **6** fracas, muddle, tangle **7** mistake **8** disorder

moan 3 sob **4** keen, wail **5** groan **6** bemoan, bewail, lament, plaint **7** grumble

moat 5 ditch, fosse, graff **6** gutter, rundel, trench

mob 4 gang, herd **5** crowd, crush, horde, Mafia, swarm **6** masses, rabble, throng **7** flock to **8** assembly, populace

mobile 6 active, motile **7** kinetic, movable,

nomadic **8** portable, rootless

mobster 4 hood **6** hitman **7** hoodlum, Mafioso **8** gangster

Moby Dick author: 8 Melville

mock 3 ape **4** copy **5** belie, mimic, scorn, spurn, taunt **6** deride, insult, jeer at, parody, revile, show up **7** imitate, laugh at, let down, profane, scoff at, sneer at **8** ridicule

mode 3 cut, fad, way **4** form, rage, rule **5** craze, means, style, taste, trend, vogue **6** custom, manner, method **7** process **8** approach, practice

model 4 cast, copy, form, mold, show, type **5** build, dummy, ideal, shape, sport, style **6** design, mirror, mock-up **7** display, example, fashion, outline, paragon, pattern, perfect, replica **8** exemplar, paradigm, peerless, standard

moderate 4 calm, cool, curb, fair, hush, mild, tame **5** abate, chair, sober **6** direct, gentle, lessen, manage, medium, modest, soften, subdue, temper **7** average, careful, conduct, control, oversee **8** diminish, measured, ordinary, passable, rational, regulate, restrain

modern 3 new **6** modish, recent **7** current, in vogue **8** up-to-date

modest 3 coy, shy **4** meek, prim **5** plain, quiet, timid **6** demure, humble, proper, simple **7** bashful, limited **8** blushing, discreet, moderate, reserved

modicum *see* **4 iota**

modify 4 redo, vary **5** adapt, alter, limit, lower, remit **6** adjust, change, narrow, reduce, remold, revise, rework, temper **7** remodel, reshape **8** moderate, modulate, restrain, restrict

modish 4 chic **5** nifty, sharp, smart **6** dapper, snazzy, spiffy, trendy, with it **7** current, faddish, stylish, voguish

modulate 4 pass **5** lower **6** accord, attune, change, reduce, soften, temper

8 moderate, regulate, tone down

Mogadishu, Mogadiscio
  capital of: 7 Somalia

mogul 3 VIP **4** czar, lord **5** baron, power, wheel **6** bigwig, tycoon **7** big shot, magnate **8** big wheel

Mohammed
  also: 7 Mahomet, Prophet **8** Muhammad
  born: 5 Mecca
  daughter: 6 Fatima
  died: 6 Medina
  flight: 4 hadj **6** hegira, hejira
  follower: 6 Moslem, Muslim, Wahbi
  religion: 5 Islam
  shrine: 5 Kaaba
  son: 7 Ibrahim
    adopted: 3 Ali
  successor: 4 imam **5** calif **6** caliph **7** Abu Bakr
  wife: 5 Aisha **6** Ayesha, Safiya **7** Khadija **8** Khadidja, Kadijah

Mohammedan *see* **6 Moslem**

moisture 3 dew, wet **4** damp, mist **5** sweat, vapor **7** drizzle, exudate, wetness **8** dampness, dankness, humidity

mold 3 cut, die, ilk **4** cast, form, kind, line, make, rust, sort, turn, type **5** frame, knead, model, shape, stamp **6** blight, fungus, lichen, matrix, mildew, sculpt **7** develop, fashion, outline, pattern

Moldova
  other name: 8 Moldavia
  capital/largest city: 8 Chisinau, Kishinev
  river: 8 Dniester

molest 3 irk, vex **4** fret, harm, hurt **5** abuse, annoy, beset, harry, worry **6** attack, bother, harass, hector, injure, pester, plague **7** assault, disturb, torment, trouble

mollify 4 calm, curb, dull, ease, lull **5** abate, allay, blunt, check, quell, quiet, still **6** lessen, pacify, reduce, soften, soothe, temper **7** appease, assuage, placate **8** mitigate, moderate, palliate

mollusk 4 clam, slug **5** conch, cowry, murex, snail, squid, whelk **6** chiton, cockle, cowrie, limpet, mussel, oyster, teredo, triton **7** abalone, bivalve, geoduck, octopus, scallop **8** argonaut, nautilus, shipworm

mollycoddle 3 pet **4** baby, wimp **5** sissy, spoil **6** cosset, coward, pamper **7** cater to, crybaby, indulge **8** weakling

molt 4 cast, shed, slip **6** change, slough **7** castoff, discard, ecdysis **8** exuviate

molten 6 melted, red-hot **7** fusible, igneous, smelted

moment 5 flash, jiffy, trice, value, worth **6** import, minute, second, weight **7** concern, gravity, instant

momentum 2 go **4** dash, push **5** drive, force, speed, vigor **6** energy, thrust **7** headway, impetus, impulse **8** velocity

Monaco
    capital: 11 Monaco-Ville
    largest city: 10 Monte Carlo
    head of state: 6 prince
    ruling family: 8 Grimaldi
    physical feature: 9 Cote d'Azur
    prince: 5 Louis **6** Albert **7** Rainier
    princess: 5 Grace **8** Caroline **9** Stephanie

place:
    casino: 10 Monte Carlo

Mona Lisa
    also called: 8 (La) Gioconda
    artist: 7 (Leonardo) da Vinci
    noted for: 5 smile
    museum: 6 Louvre

monarch 4 czar, doge, emir, khan, king, rani, shah, tsar **5** rajah, ruler, queen **6** caesar, kaiser **7** czarina, emperor, empress, majesty, pharaoh

monastery 5 abbey **6** friary, priory **7** convent, nunnery, retreat **8** cloister

Monday
    French: 5 lundi
    German: 6 montag
    heavenly body: 4 moon
    Italian: 6 lunedi
    means: 3 day (of the moon)
    Spanish: 5 lunes

money 4 cash, coin **5** bread, bucks, dough, funds **6** assets, specie **7** capital, coinage, revenue, scratch **8** currency

money-grubbing 5 venal **6** greedy **8** grasping

money lender 6 banker, lender, usurer **7** shylock

Mongolia
  capital/largest city: 9 Ulan Bator
  mountain range: 5 Altai **7** Hangayn, Hentiyn
  physical feature:
    desert: 4 Gobi
    leader: 6 Kublai (Khan) **7** Genghis (Khan)
  feature:
    felt tent: 4 yurt

mongrel 3 cur **4** mutt **5** mixed **6** hybrid **7** bastard **8** offshoot

moniker 3 tag **4** name **5** label, title **6** eponym, handle **8** nickname

monitor 4 tend **5** guide, teach **6** censor, direct, pickup, screen, sensor **7** oversee, proctor **8** watchdog

monkey 3 ape, toy **4** dupe, fool, jerk **5** clown **6** baboon, fiddle, meddle, simian, tamper, tinker **7** buffoon, primate
  group of: 5 troop

monkeyshines 6 antics, capers, pranks **7** hijinks

monocle 4 quiz **5** glass **7** lorgnon **8** eyeglass

monolith 5 stone **6** column, menhir, pillar, statue **7** obelisk **8** monument

monologue, monolog 6 screed, sermon, speech **7** address, lecture, oration

monopoly 4 bloc **5** trust **6** cartel, corner **7** combine, control **8** dominion

monotony 3 rut **5** ennui **6** tedium **7** boredom, humdrum **8** dullness, flatness, sameness

Monroe, James
  presidential rank: 5 fifth
  party: 20 Democratic-Republican
  state represented: 2 VA
  vice president: 8 Tompkins
  born: 2 VA
  political career:
    governor of: 8 Virginia
  notable events of lifetime/ term:
    Compromise: 8 Missouri
    Doctrine: 6 Monroe
    war: 8 Seminole
  wife: 9 Elizabeth
    nickname: 5 Eliza

Monroe, Marilyn
  real name: 9 Norma Jean

(Mortenson Baker)
husband: 8 (Joe)
DiMaggio **6** (Arthur)
Miller

Monrovia
capital of: 7 Liberia

monster 4 Fury, gila, ogre,
yeti **5** argus, beast, brute,
demon, devil, fiend, freak,
ghoul, giant, golem,
harpy, hydra, satyr, titan
6 dragon, gorgon, oddity,
savage, zombie **7** centaur,
chimera, deviant, grendel,
incubus, mammoth,
mermaid, vampire **8**
bogeyman, colossus,
gargoyle, Loch Ness,
succubus, werewolf

Montana
abbreviation: 2 MT **4**
Mont
nickname: 6 Big Sky
capital: 6 Helena
largest city: 8 Billings
mountain: 7 Rockies
river: 6 Powder **7** Bighorn
8 Columbia, Missouri

Montenegro
other name: 4 Zeta **8**
Crna Gora
capital: 7 Cetinje **8**
Titograd **9** Podgorica
lake: 7 Scutari, Shkoder

mountain: 7 Dinaric
(Alps)
sea: 8 Adriatic

Montevideo
capital of: 7 Uruguay

Montezuma
emperor of: 6 Aztecs
in: 6 Mexico
conquered by: 6 Cortez

monument 4 slab **5** token **6**
shrine **7** memento, obelisk
8 cenotaph, memorial,
monolith

monumental *see* **4 huge**

mooch 3 beg, bum **5** cadge
6 hustle, sponge **7** solicit
8 freeload

moody 4 mean **5** sulky,
surly, testy **6** crabby,
dismal, fickle, gloomy,
mopish, morose, sullen **7**
erratic, flighty, peevish,
unhappy **8** brooding,
variable, volatile

moon 4 gape, lamp, luna,
roam **5** dream, month,
stare **6** dawdle, wander **8**
daydream

moonshine *see* **8 nonsense**

moonstone
species: 8 feldspar

moor 3 fen **4** dock, down,
fell, lash, wold **5** affix,

berth, chain, heath, marsh, tie up **6** anchor, attach, fasten, secure, steppe, tether **8** make fast

moot 4 open **7** eristic **8** arguable, disputed

mope 4 fret, pine, pout, sulk **5** brood, worry **6** grieve, grouse, lament, repine **7** grumble **8** languish

moral 3 tag **4** fair, just, pure **5** adage, maxim, motto, noble, right **6** honest, lesson, proper, saying **7** epigram, ethical, message, proverb **8** aphorism, virtuous

morale 4 mood **6** spirit, temper

morass 3 bog, fen **4** mire **5** marsh, swamp **6** slough **8** quagmire, wetlands

morbid 3 sad **4** dour, glum, grim **5** moody **6** gloomy, morose **8** brooding

mordant 6 biting, bitter **7** acerbic, caustic, cutting, waspish **8** incisive, piercing, scathing, scornful, stinging, venomous, virulent

more 5 added, extra, other, spare **6** longer **7** further, reserve

mores 4 code **5** ethos, forms, rules **6** usages **7** customs, rituals

moribund 5 dying **6** doomed, waning

Mormon State
   nickname of: 4 Utah

morning 4 dawn **5** early, sunup **7** sunrise **8** daybreak, daylight, forenoon

Morocco
   capital: 5 Rabat
   largest city: 10 Casablanca
   sea: 8 Atlantic **13** Mediterranean
   physical feature:
      desert: 6 Sahara
      strait: 9 Gibraltar
   feature:
      hat: 3 fez
   food:
      dish: 8 couscous

moron *see* **5** idiot

morose 3 low, sad **4** blue, dour, glum, sour **5** cross, moody, sulky, surly, testy **6** cranky, gloomy, grumpy, mopish, solemn, sullen **7** waspish

8 churlish, downcast, mournful

morsel 3 bit, nip, sip **4** bite, drop, iota, whit **5** crumb, grain, piece, scrap, snack, speck, taste, touch, trace **6** dollop, nibble, sliver, tidbit **7** segment **8** fraction, fragment, particle

mortal 4 deep, type **5** fatal, grave, human **6** deadly, lethal, living, person, severe **7** earthly, mundane **8** temporal

mortar 6 cannon, cement, vessel **7** plaster **8** adhesive

mortify 3 rot **4** deny, fast **5** abash, decay, shame **6** appall, fester **7** chagrin, horrify, putrefy

Moscow
   capital of: 4 USSR **6** Russia
   landmark: 7 Bolshoi, Kremlin **8** Lubyanka **9** Red Square
   river: 5 Volga **6** Moscow
   Russian: 6 Moskva

Moses
   sister: 6 Miriam
   brother: 5 Aaron
   successor: 6 Joshua

mosey 4 poke **5** amble **6** stroll **7** saunter, shuffle

Moslem 4 Moor **5** Islam, Sunni **6** Muslim, Shiite **7** Islamic

most 4 best, very **6** degree **7** maximum

mostly 6 mainly **7** as a rule, chiefly, greatly, largely

mote 3 dot **4** iota **5** speck **8** particle

moth-eaten 5 holey **6** old-hat **7** worn-out **8** outmoded

mother 4 bear, mind, rear, tend **5** beget, breed, nurse, raise **6** origin, source **7** care for, indulge, nurture, produce, protect

mother's helper 6 au pair

motif 4 form, idea **5** shape, style, theme, topic **6** design, figure, thread **7** pattern, refrain, subject

motion 3 cue, nod **4** flow, flux, move, sign, stir **5** drift **6** action, beckon, signal, stream **7** gesture, passage, request **8** mobility, movement

motion picture see **5** movie

motivate 4 goad, move, stir **5** egg on, impel **6** arouse, induce, prompt, stir up, turn on **7** actuate, provoke **8** activate

motive 3 aim, end **4** goal, spur **5** cause **6** design, object, reason **7** grounds, purpose **8** occasion, stimulus, thinking

motley 4 pied **5** mixed, tabby **6** hybrid, sundry, unlike, varied **7** dappled, piebald **8** assorted, brindled, speckled

motor vehicle 3 bus, cab, car, van **4** auto, heap, jeep, limo, taxi **5** motor, sedan, truck, wagon **6** jalopy, jitney, pickup, wheels **7** flivver, hardtop, machine, vehicle

motto *see* **5 maxim**

moue 4 pout **7** grimace

mound 4 bump, dune, heap, hill, pile, rick **5** knoll, mogul, ridge, stack **7** bulwark, hillock, hummock, rampart

mount 3 fit, fix, rig, set, wax **4** go up, grow, rise, soar **5** affix, climb, equip, frame, scale, surge, swell **6** ascend, fit out, outfit, set off **7** augment, climb up, get over, install, set into **8** increase, multiply, straddle

mountain 3 alp **4** peak **5** butte, range **6** height, massif **7** volcano

mountebank 5 cheat, fraud, phony **6** con man **7** hustler **8** huckster, swindler

mourn 3 cry, rue, sob **4** keen, pine, wail, weep **6** bemoan, bewail, grieve, lament, regret, sorrow **7** deplore, despair **8** languish, weep over

mouser 3 cat **4** puss **5** kitty, pussy **6** feline **8** pussycat

mousy 3 shy **4** drab, dull **5** timid, wimpy **7** bashful, fearful **8** timorous

mouth 3 bay, say **4** bell, jaws, lips **5** inlet, speak, voice **6** outlet, portal **7** declare, estuary, opening **8** aperture, propound

mouthpiece 4 reed **6** lawyer **7** counsel **8** advocate, attorney

movable, moveable 4 free **5** loose **6** mobile, motile, moving **8** portable

move 2 go **3** act, ask, get **4** bear, deed, fire, lead, pass, ploy, step, stir, sway, turn, urge **5** begin, budge, carry, cause, drive, impel, plead, rouse, shift, touch **6** action, affect, arouse, attack, excite, exhort, incite, induce, motion, prompt, switch **7** advance, gesture, go ahead, impress, inspire, measure, operate, proceed, propose, provoke, request, suggest **8** interest, maneuver, motivate, persuade, relocate, start off, stirring, transfer, transmit

move out 5 leave **6** depart, vacate **8** evacuate

movie 4 film, show **5** flick **6** cinema **7** feature, picture, showing

moxie 4 grit, guts, sand **5** nerve, pluck, spunk **6** mettle, spirit **7** courage, stamina **8** audacity, backbone

Mozambique
capital/largest city: 6 Maputo
highest point: 5 Binga
river: 7 Limpopo, Zambezi
ocean: 6 Indian

Mr Smith Goes to Washington
director: 5 (Frank) Capra

cast: 5 (Claude) Rains **6** (Jean) Arthur, (Guy) Kibbee, (Edward) Arnold **7** (James) Stewart **8** (Thomas) Mitchell

much 3 far **4** a lot, lots **5** about, ample, heaps, loads, often **6** almost, indeed, nearly, overly, plenty, rather, scores **7** copious, greatly **8** abundant, quantity

Much Ado About Nothing
author: 11 (William) Shakespeare

mucilage 3 gum **4** glue **5** paste **6** cement **8** adhesive

muck 3 mud **4** dirt, dung, gunk, mire, ooze, slop **5** filth, slime **6** sewage, sludge **7** compost, garbage

mud 4 dirt, muck, soil, wire

muddle 3 fog **4** blow, daze, haze, mess, muff, ruin **5** botch, chaos, mix up **6** boggle, bungle, fumble, goof up, jumble, mess up, rattle **7** blunder, clutter, confuse **8** bewilder, confound, disarray, disorder

muddy 4 dull **5** dirty, grimy, vague **6** filthy, grubby **7** obscure **8** begrimed

muff 5 botch, spoil **6** bungle

muffle 3 gag **4** dull, hush, mask, mute, veil, wrap **5** cloak, cover, quell, quiet, still **6** dampen, deaden, shroud, stifle **7** conceal, envelop, silence

mug 3 cup **4** face, puss, toby **5** stein, stoup **6** beaker, flagon, goblet, kisser, visage **7** chalice, tankard, toby jug, tumbler

mugger 8 assailer, attacker

muggy 5 close, humid **6** clammy, steamy, sticky, stuffy, sultry, sweaty **8** steaming, vaporous

mule 3 ass **5** burro **6** donkey **7** jackass
group of: 4 span

mulish 5 balky **6** ornery **8** perverse, stubborn

mull, mull over 5 study, weigh **6** ponder **8** consider, meditate, pore over, ruminate

multifarious 4 many **5** mixed **6** divers, motley, sundry, varied **7** diverse, protean, several, various **8** manifold, numerous

multiply 5 add to, beget, breed, raise **6** extend, spread **7** augment, enhance, enlarge, magnify **8** generate, heighten, increase

multitude 3 mob **4** army, herd, host, mass, pack, slew **5** array, crowd, crush, drove, flock, flood, horde, troop **6** legion, myriad, scores, throng

mum 4 mute **5** quiet, still, tacit **6** silent **8** taciturn, wordless

mumble 5 growl, grunt, mouth **6** murmur, mutter, rumble **7** stammer

mumbo jumbo 3 rot **4** blah, bosh, cant, tosh **5** bilge, hokum, hooey, tripe **6** hot air, humbug **7** baloney

munch 4 chew, gnaw **5** champ, chomp, crush

mundane 5 petty **7** earthly, humdrum, prosaic, routine, worldly **8** everyday, ordinary

municipality 4 city, town **6** parish **7** village **8** township

munificent 4 free **6** kindly, lavish **7** liberal, profuse **8** generous, princely

murder 4 kill, slay **5** abuse,

waste **6** mangle, misuse **7** butcher, corrupt, cut down, killing **8** homicide, knock off

murky *see* **5 fuzzy**

murmur 3 hum **4** buzz, purl, purr, sigh **5** drone **6** lament, mumble, mutter, rumble, rustle **7** grumble, whimper, whisper

muscle 4 grit, thew **5** bicep, brawn, force, might, power, sinew, vigor **6** energy, flexor, tendon **7** potency, prowess, stamina

muscular contraction 3 tic **5** cramp, crick, spasm **6** stitch

muse 4 mull **6** ponder, review **7** reflect **8** cogitate, meditate, ruminate

Muses
  also: 7 the Nine **8** Pierides
  form: 9 goddesses
  father: 4 Zeus

mush 5 slush **6** drivel **8** porridge

mushroom 4 grow **5** burst, fungi **6** blow up, expand, fungus, spread, sprout **7** burgeon, explode, shoot up **8** flourish, increase, spring up

part: 3 cap **4** veil **5** gills, stalk, tubes, volva **6** button, hyphae, spores **7** annulus, basidia
  study of: 8 mycology

mushy 4 soft **5** foggy, misty, pulpy, vague **6** spongy **7** maudlin, mawkish, quishy **8** effusive, romantic

music 4 song, tune **5** score **6** melody **7** euphony, harmony **8** lyricism

musical 5 lyric, sweet **6** dulcet **7** lilting, lyrical, melodic, tuneful

musical instrument
  classification: 4 horn, reed, wind **5** brass **6** string **8** keyboard, woodwind **10** electronic, percussion

musical terms
  agitated: 7 agitato
  all players/singers together: 5 tutti
  continue without a break: 5 segue
  disconnected/each note separate: 8 staccato
  fast: 6 veloce **7** allegro
  gentle: 5 soave
  gently: 9 doucement

gradually getting louder: 9 crescendo

half: 5 mezzo

heavy: 5 lourd

in a low voice: 9 sotto voce

little: 4 poco

loud: 5 forte

more: 3 piu

mournful: 5 mesto

quick/vivacious: 6 vivace

rapid alternation of notes: 5 trill

repeat from beginning: 6 da capo

sliding: 9 glissando

slow: 5 lento **6** adagio

slow dignified tempo: 5 largo

soft: 5 piano

solemn/serious: 5 grave

sweetly: 5 dolce

trembling vibrating effect: 7 tremolo

very: 5 molto

with fire: 8 con fuoco

with spirit: 7 con brio

with style: 8 con gusto

musician 4 bard **5** piper **6** artist, player, singer, violer **7** bandman, cellist, drummer, pianist, twanger **8** minstrel, organist, virtuoso

musing 6 absent, dreamy **7** mulling **8** absorbed

Muslim *see* **6 Moslem**

muss *see* **4 mess**

muster 4 call **5** amass, raise, rally **6** gather, line up, summon **7** collect, company, convene, convoke, marshal, meeting, round up, turnout **8** assemble, assembly, mobilize

musty 3 old **4** damp, dank, worn **5** banal, dirty, dusty, moldy, stale, tired, trite **6** frousy, frouzy, old hat, stuffy **7** worn-out **8** mildewed

mutate 4 turn **5** alter **6** change **7** convert

mute 3 mum **4** dumb **5** quiet, tacit **6** silent **8** nonvocal, reserved

mutilate 4 lame, maim **6** cut off, deform, excise, mangle **7** butcher, cripple **8** amputate, lacerate, truncate

mutiny 4 coup **5** rebel **6** revolt, rise up **8** takeover, upheaval, uprising

mutt 3 cur, dog, pup **5** puppy **7** mongrel

mutter 4 carp **5** gripe, growl, grunt **6** grouch, grouse, kvetch, mumble, murmur, rumble **7** grumble **8** complain

mutual 5 joint **6** common, shared **7** related **8** communal, returned

muzzle 3 gag **4** bind, curb **5** check, quiet, still **6** bridle, rein in, stifle **7** harness, silence **8** suppress

Myanmar
  also called: 5 Burma
  capital/largest city: 6 Yangon **7** Rangoon
  river: 6 Salwin, Yangon **7** Irawadi, Rangoon, Salween **9** Irrawaddy
  sea: 7 Andaman
  place:
    road: 5 Burma
  feature:
    skirt: 6 longyi

My Fair Lady
  director: 5 (George) Cukor
  based on play by: 4 (George Bernard) Shaw (Pygmalion)

cast: 7 (Audrey) Hepburn **8** (Rex) Harrison, (Stanley) Holloway **9** (Wilfrid) Hyde-White

my fault
  Latin: 8 mea culpa

myriad 6 untold **7** endless **8** infinite, manifold

mystery 6 enigma, occult, puzzle, riddle, secret **7** problem, secrecy

mystical, mystic 5 inner **6** hidden, occult **7** cryptic, obscure **8** abstruse, esoteric, ethereal, symbolic

mystify 4 fool **5** elude **6** baffle, puzzle **7** confuse, deceive, mislead, perplex **8** bewilder, confound

myth 3 fib, lie **4** tale, yarn **5** error, fable, story **6** canard, legend **7** fantasy, fiction, hearsay, parable **8** allegory, delusion, illusion, tall tale

mythological, mythologic 6 unreal **8** fabulous, illusory, imagined

nab *see* **5 catch**

nabob 3 VIP **4** lord **5** mogul, nawab **6** deputy, tycoon **7** magnate

nadir 4 base, zero **5** floor **6** apogee, bottom **7** nothing **8** low point

nag 4 fury, goad, harp **5** annoy, devil, harpy, scold, shrew, vixen **6** badger, bicker, harass, hassle, heckle, hector, nettle, peck at, pester, pick at, pick on, plague, rail at, tartar, virago **7** bedevil, upbraid **8** battle-ax, irritate

Naiad
  form: 5 nymph
  location: 5 water

nail 3 fix, pin **4** brad, claw, spad **5** talon **6** fasten, hammer, secure
  part: 3 bed **4** root

Nairobi
  capital of: 5 Kenya

naive *see* **8 gullible**

naked 4 bald, bare, nude, pure **5** bared, frank, plain, sheer **6** patent, simple, unclad **7** blatant, exposed **8** disrobed

Naked and the Dead, The
  author: 6 (Norman) Mailer

namby-pamby *see* **6 jejune**

name 3 dub, tag **4** call, term **5** label, title **6** choose, ordain, select **7** appoint, baptize, epithet, specify **8** christen, cognomen, delegate, deputize, nominate, taxonomy

namely
  Latin: 3 viz **9** videlicet

Name of the Rose, The
  author: 3 (Umberto) Eco

Namibia
  former name: 15 South West Africa
  capital/largest city: 8 Windhoek
  highest point: 9 Brandberg
  river: 6 Orange

7 Zambezi **8** Okavango
sea: 8 Atlantic
physical feature:
   bay: 6 Walvis
   desert: 5 Namib **8**
     Kalahari
   region: 7 Caprivi (Strip)
feature:
   homeland: 9 bantustan
Nammu
   origin: 8 Sumerian
   mother of: 4 gods
   personifies: 3 sea
Nana
   author: 4 (Emile) Zola
Nancy
   creator: 10 (Ernie)
     Bushmiller
nap *see* **4 doze**
napery 5 doily **6** linens,
   napkin
Napoleon Bonaparte
   born: 7 Corsica
   exile to: 4 Elba **6** (Saint)
     Helena
   position: 6 consul **7**
     emperor
   wife: 9 Josephine **11**
     Marie-Louise (of Austria)
narcissism 6 egoism, vanity
   7 conceit **8** self-love
narcissus
   father: 8 Cephisus

mother: 8 Leiriope
loved: 7 himself
loved by: 4 Echo
punished by: 9 Aphrodite
changed into: 6 flower
narcotic 4 drug, morphine
   5 opium **6** herion, opiate
   8 medicine, sedative
narrate *see* **6 recite**
narrow 3 set **4** fine, slim **5**
   close, scant, small, tight **6**
   biased, scanty **7** bigoted,
   cramped, pinched,
   shallow, slender **8**
   confined, dogmatic,
   squeezed
narrows 4 neck, pass **5**
   canal **6** ravine, strait **7**
   channel, isthmus, passage
Nassau
   capital of: 7 Bahamas
nasty *see* **4 vile**
nates 4 buns, rear, rump,
   seat **7** rear end **8**
   buttocks, haunches
nation 4 host, race **5** realm,
   state, tribe **6** empire,
   people **7** country,
   kingdom **8** republic
native 4 home **5** basic,
   local, natal **6** inborn,
   inbred, innate, savage **7**
   citizen, endemic, natural

8 domestic, inherent, national, paternal

Native Americans
major tribes: 3 Ute **4** Crow, Hopi, Iowa, Pima **5** Creek, Aleut, Haida, Kiowa, Lummi, Omaha, Osage, Sioux **6** Apache, Eskimo, Lumbee, Mandan, Mohawk, Navajo, Oneida, Ottawa, Paiute, Pequot, Pueblo, Seneca **7** Bannock, Catawba, Choctaw, Tlingit **8** Arapahoe, Cherokee, Chippewa, Comanche, Kickapoo, Nez Perce, Onondaga, Seminole, Shoshone **9** Blackfoot, Chickasaw, Penobscot, Sac and Fox, Wampanoag, Winnebago

native of Israel
Hebrew: 5 sabra

native soil 8 homeland

Native Son
author: 6 (Richard) Wright

natty *see* **4 chic**

natural 5 plain **6** inborn, native, normal **7** earthly, genuine, regular **8** God-given, inherent
in craps: 5 seven **6** eleven

natural gift *see* **6 talent**

nature 4 bent, kind, mood, sort, type **5** birth, earth, globe, humor, stamp, style, trait **6** cosmos, spirit **7** essence, feature, variety **8** category, creation, instinct, property, universe

naught *see* **4 zero**

naughty *see* **3 bad**

Nauru
capital: 5 Yaren (District)
sea: 7 Pacific
feature: 9 phosphate

nauseate 5 repel, upset **6** offend, revolt, sicken **7** disgust, repulse

nautical 5 naval **6** marine **7** aquatic, boating, oceanic **8** maritime, of the sea, seagoing, yachting

Navajo, Navaho (Dine)
noted for: 6 silver (smithing) **7** weaving
dwelling: 5 hogan

navigate 3 fly **4** ride, sail, ship **5** cross, steer **6** cruise, voyage **8** maneuver, sail over

navy 5 fleet **6** armada, convoy **8** flotilla, warships

navy-blue 6 indigo **8** dark blue, deep blue

nay 4 also, deny, vote **5** never **6** denial, refuse **7** against, refusal **8** negative

Nazi 7 facist

air force: 9 Luftwaffe

collaborator: 8 quisling

leader: 4 Hess **6** Hitler **7** Himmler **8** Goebbels

police: 7 gestapo

trials: 9 Nuremberg

near *see* **5 close**

nearsighted 6 myopic

neat 4 tidy **5** clean, great **6** groovy **7** concise, correct, orderly **8** accurate, exciting, original, straight, striking, succinct

Nebraska

abbreviation: 2 NE **4** Nebr

nickname: 10 Cornhusker

capital: 7 Lincoln

largest city: 5 Omaha

highest point: 13 Panorama Point

river: 4 Loup **5** Logan **6** Platte **7** Elkhorn **8** Missouri

physical feature:

plains: 5 Great

feature:

organization: 8 Boy's Town

nebris

skin of: 4 fawn

Nebuchadnezzar

king of: 7 Babylon

conquered: 9 Jerusalem

destroyed: 6 temple

deported: 4 Jews

into: 7 slavery

nebula 4 Crab, Ring, Veil **5** Great **6** Lagoon **7** Rosette

nebulous *see* **5 vague**

necessary *see* **7 crucial**

necessity, necessities 4 must, need **6** demand, needed **7** urgency **8** exigency, pressure

neck 3 pet **4** kiss, nape, pass **6** caress, cervix, cuddle, fondle, smooth, strait **7** channel, isthmus, make out

necklace 3 tie **5** beads, chain, noose **6** choker, collar, locket, pearls, string **7** jewelry, pendant **8** ornament

necktie 3 bow **4** band **5** ascot, black, scarf **6** cravat, string **7** Windsor

necromancer *see* **6 wizard**

necromancy 5 magic, spell **7** sorcery **8** black art

necrophobia
 fear of: 4 dead (bodies) **5** death

nectar
 drink of: 4 gods
 gives: 4 life

need 4 lack, want, wish **5** crave, exact **6** demand, penury **7** call for, longing, poverty, require, straits **8** distress, exigency

needle *see* **5 tease**

needlework 6 sewing **7** basting, brocade, darning, tacking, tatting **8** applique, knitting, quilting

ne'er-do-well *see* **3 bum**

nefarious *see* **3 bad**

Nefertiti
 queen: 5 Egypt
 husband: 8 Ikhnaton **9** Amenhotep
 nephew: 3 Tut(ankhamen)

negate *see* **6 refute**

negative 4 blue, dark **5** bleak **6** at odds, gloomy **7** dubious, opposed **8** contrary, doubtful, downbeat, inimical, opposing, refusing

neglect *see* **8 overlook**

negligee, neglige 4 robe

6 kimono **7** wrapper **8** bathrobe, peignoir

negligent 3 lax **5** slack **6** remiss, untidy **8** careless, heedless, slovenly

negligible *see* **5 minor**

negotiate 4 cash, make, pass **6** barter, cash in, convey, dicker, haggle, handle, manage, redeem, settle **7** arrange, consign, discuss **8** contract, cope with, deal with, sign over, transact, transfer, transmit, turn over

neigh 5 hinny **6** nicker, whinny

neighbor 4 abut, meet **5** touch **6** adjoin, be near, border, friend **7** conjoin **8** borderer, border on

neighborhood 4 area, part, side, ward **5** place, range **6** locale, parish, region, sphere **7** quarter, section **8** confines, district, environs, precinct, purlieus, vicinity

Nemean lion
 strangled by: 8 Hercules

nemesis *see* **6 rival**

nene 13 Hawaiian goose

neologism, neology 7
coinage

neonate 4 baby **6** infant **7** newborn

neophyte *see* **6 novice**

neoplasm 5 tumor **6** cancer, growth **7** sarcoma

Nepal
other name: **9** Shangri-La
capital/largest city: **8** Katmandu **9** Kathmandu
mountain: **6** Lhotse **9** Annapurna, Himalayas
highest point: **7** Everest
physical feature:
    valley: **5** Nepal **8** Katmandu
feature:
    animal: **3** dzo, yak **7** dzopkyo
    legend: **4** Yeti
    soldiers: **6** Gurkha

nepenthe 4 drug **5** drink, opium **6** heroin, opiate **7** hashish **8** narcotic

ne plus ultra 4 acme **6** finest **8** ultimate

Neptune
origin: **5** Roman
god of: **3** sea
corresponds to: **8** Poseidon

Neptune
position: **6** eighth
satellite: **6** Nereid, Triton
color: **4** blue

neritic 7 aquatic, coastal **8** offshore

Nero
emperor of: **4** Rome
mother: **9** Agrippina
father: **8** Domitius
stepfather: **8** Claudius
tutor: **6** Seneca
wife: **7** Octavia
successor: **5** Galba

nerve *see* **7 courage**

nervous *see* **7 anxious**

nervous system
component: **3** CNS **4** ears, eyes **5** brain, taste, touch **7** ganglia **8** nerve end

nestle 3 lie, pet **4** live, snug, stay **5** clasp, dwell, lodge **6** bundle, coddle, cuddle, enfold, fondle, huddle, nuzzle, occupy, remain, settle **7** embrace, inhabit, snuggle

net 3 web **4** earn, gain, grab, grid, grip, mesh, snag, take, trap **5** catch, clasp, grate, seize, snare **6** clutch, enmesh, gather, grille, obtain, pick up, screen, snap up, take in **7** acquire, bring in, capture, collect, ensnare, grating, lattice **8** entangle, gridiron

nether 5 basal, below, lower, under **6** bottom **8** downward, inferior

Netherlands
  other name: 7 Holland
  capital/largest city: 9 Amsterdam
  seat of government: 8 The Hague
  highest point: 11 Vaalserberg
  lake: 7 Haarlem
  river: 4 Maas, Waal **5** Meuse, Rhine **6** Ijssel **7** Scheldt
  sea: 5 North
  island: 7 Frisian
  physical feature:
    former bay: 9 Zuider Zee
  feature:
    flower: 5 tulip
    pottery: 5 Delft
    reclaimed land: 6 polder
    wooden shoes: 7 klompen
  food:
    cheese: 4 Edam **5** Gouda **6** Leyden

    drink: 3 gin **8** anisette, schnapps

Netherlands East Indies *see* **9 Indonesia**

netherworld 4 hell **5** Hades

nettle *see* **3 vex**

nettle 6 Urtica

network 3 web **4** grid, mesh, trap **5** grate, group, snare **6** grille, scheme, system

neurotic *see* **7 anxious**

neuter 5 fixed **6** barren, fallow, gelded, spayed **7** asexual, sexless, sterile **8** impotent

neutral 4 mean **5** aloof **6** medium, middle, normal, remote **7** average **8** pacifist, peaceful, unbiased

Nevada
  abbreviation: 2 NV **3** Nev
  nickname: 6 Silver **9** Sagebrush
  capital: 10 Carson City
  largest city: 8 Las Vegas
  mountain: 7 Rockies
  highest point: 9 Boundary (Peak)
  lake: 4 Mead **5** Tahoe **7** Pyramid
  river: 7 Truckee **8** Colorado, Columbia,

Humboldt
physical feature: 7 geysers
   basin: 5 Great
   desert: 7 Sonoran
   hot springs: 4 Tule
feature:
   dam: 5 Davis **6** Hoover
   mine: 12 Comstock
   Lode

never 4 ne'er **7** not ever **8** at no time, not at all

nevertheless 3 but, yet **6** anyhow, anyway, even so, though **7** however **8** after all, although

new 4 late **5** fixed, fresh, green, novel **6** modern, reborn, recent, remote, unused **7** current, just out, untried **8** original, up-to-date

New Brunswick
   bay: 5 Fundy
   capital: 11 Fredericton
   channel: 5 Minas
   island: 4 Deer **6** Miscou **7** Machias

New Deal Agency 3 AAA, CCC, CWA, FCA, FHA, FSA, NRA, NYA, PWA, REA, SEC, SSB, TVA, WPA **4** FCIC, FDIC, FERA, HOLC, NLRD, USHA

New Delhi
   capital of: 5 India

New England
   state: 5 Maine **7** Vermont **11** Connecticut, Rhode Island **12** New Hampshire **13** Massachusetts

newfangled 5 novel **6** modern, modish **7** stylish

Newfoundland
   abbreviation: 4 Nfld
   capital: 10 Saint Johns
   mountain: 9 Long Range
   river: 5 Eagle **6** Fraser, Gander **9** Churchill
   section: 8 Labrador

New Guinea
   capital/largest city: 11 Port Moresby
   division:
      western half of island: 9 Indonesia, Irian Jaya
      eastern half of island: 5 Papua (New Guinea)
   sea: 5 Coral **6** Indian **7** Arafura, Pacific, Solomon **8** Bismarck
   feature:
      bird: 9 cassowary
   food:
      dried coconut meat: 5 copra

New Hampshire
abbreviation: 2 NH
nickname: 7 Granite
capital: 7 Concord
largest city: 10
   Manchester
mountain: 5 White
highest point: 10
   Washington
river: 9 Merrimack **11**
   Connecticut
sea: 8 Atlantic
physical feature:
   notch: 7 Kinsman,
    Pinkham **8** Crawford

New Hebrides *see* **7 Vanuatu**

New Jersey
abbreviation: 2 NJ
nickname: 6 Garden
capital: 7 Trenton
largest city: 6 Newark
highest point: 9 High
   Point
river: 6 Hudson **7** Passaic,
   Raritan **8** Delaware
sea: 8 Atlantic
physical feature: 9
   Palisades, Sandy Hook
   bay: 8 Delaware
   cape: 3 May
feature:
   casinos: 12 Atlantic
   City

New Mexico
abbreviation: 2 NM **4** N
   Mex
nickname: 8 Sunshine
capital: 7 Sante Fe
largest city: 11
   Albuquerque
mountain: 6 Sandia **7**
   Rockies
highest point: 7 Wheeler
river: 3 Ute **4** Gila **5**
   Pecos **6** Grande **8**
   Canadian
physical feature:
   caverns: 8 Carlsbad
feature: 11 Four Corners

New Orleans
event: 9 Mardi Gras,
   Sugar Bowl
hurricane: 7 Katrina
noted for: 4 jazz
people: 5 Cajun **6** Creole
   7 Acadian
river: 11 Mississippi
street: 5 Royal **7**
   Bourbon

news 4 dirt, dope, talk,
word **5** flash, libel, piece,
rumor, story **6** babble,
expose, gossip, report **7**
account, article, chatter,
hearsay, lowdown,
mention, message, release,
scandal, slander, tidings **8**
bulletin, dispatch

New Spain *see* **6 Mexico**

newspaper 3 rag **5** daily, paper, sheet **6** herald, weekly **7** courant, gazette, journal, tabloid, tribune

New Testament
  books of: 4 Acts, John, Jude, Luke, Mark **5** James, Peter, Titus **6** Romans **7** Hebrews, Matthew, Timothy **8** Philemon **9** Ephesians, Galatians **10** Colossians, Revelation **11** Corinthians, Philippians **13** Thessalonians

New York
  abbreviation: 2 NY
  nickname: 6 Empire
  capital: 6 Albany
  largest city: 7 New York
  mountain: 7 Catskill **10** Adirondack
  highest point: 5 Marcy
  lake: 4 Erie **6** Cayuga, Finger, George, Oneida, Seneca **7** Ontario, **9** Champlain
  river: 6 Hudson, Mohawk **7** Niagara **8** Delaware **10** St Lawrence **11** Susquehanna
  sea: 8 Atlantic
  island: 4 Long **6** Staten **8** Thousand

  9 Manhattan
  physical feature:
    canal: 4 Erie
    falls: 7 Niagara

New York City
  nickname: 6 Gotham **8** Big Apple
  area: 4 Soho **6** Harlem **7** Chelsea, Midtown, Tribeca **8** Broadway
  baseball team: 4 Mets **7** Yankees
  basketball team: 6 Knicks **7** Liberty
  borough: 5 Bronx **6** Queens **8** Brooklyn, Richmond **9** Manhattan **12** Staten Island
  feature:
    building: 11 Empire State
    park: 7 Central
    square: 5 Times, Union **6** Herald
    statue: 7 Liberty
  football team: 4 Jets **6** Giants
  hockey team: 7 Rangers
  island: 4 City, Long **5** Ellis, Ward's **6** Riker's, Staten **7** Liberty **8** Randall's **9** Governor's, Manhattan, Roosevelt
  river: 4 East **6** Harlem, Hudson

New Zealand
  native's nickname: 4 Kiwi
  capital: 10 Wellington
  largest city: 8 Auckland
  highest point: 4 Cook **6**
    Aoraki
  sea: 6 Tasman **12** South
    Pacific
  island: 4 Cook **5** North,
  South **6** Bounty **7**
  Stewart, Tokelau **8**
  Auckland
  physical feature:
    glacier: 3 Fox **6**
      Tasman
    sound: 8 Doubtful
    strait: 4 Cook **7**
      Foveaux
  feature:
    bird: 3 kea, tui **4** kiwi,
      weka **6** takahe **7**
      apteryx **8** bellbird
    food:
      fish: 4 mako
      fruit: 4 kiwi **9** tamarillo
next to 6 beside **8** abutting,
  adjacent
next world, the 6 Heaven **8**
  eternity, paradise
nib *see* **6 summit**
nibble 3 nip **4** bite, chew,
  gnaw, peck **5** crumb,
  munch, speck, taste

6 crunch, morsel, peck at,
  tidbit **8** fragment, particle
Nibelungenlied
  origin: 8 Germanic
  form: 4 epic
  related to: 8 Volsunga
  inspired: 6 Wagner
Nibelungs, Niblungs
  origin: 8 Germanic,
    Teutonic
  followers of: 9 Siegfried
  race: 6 dwarfs
  possessed: 8 treasure
  captured by: 9 Siegfried
  family of: 7 Gunther
Nicaragua
  capital/largest city: 7
    Managua
  highest point: 7 Mogoton
  lake: 6 Apanas **7**
    Managua **9** Cocibolca,
    Nicaragua
  sea: 7 Pacific **9**
    Caribbean
  physical feature:
    coast: 8 Mosquito
    gulf: 7 Fonseca
  feature:
    dance: 5 sones
    political party: 10
      Sandinista
  food:
    beans: 8 frijoles
    dish: 6 ajiaco

9 picadillo
drink: 5 tiste **7** pinolio

nice 4 deft, fine, good, kind **5** dandy, exact, fussy, great, swell **6** divine, genial, lovely, proper, seemly, strict, subtle **7** amiable, cordial, correct, genteel, likable, precise, refined, winning **8** charming, cheerful, friendly, gracious, jim-dandy, pleasant, skillful, unerring, virtuous, well-bred

niche 4 cove, nook, slot **5** berth, trade **6** alcove, cavity, corner, cranny, metier, recess **7** calling **8** position, vocation

Nicholas Nickleby
author: 7 (Charles) Dickens

nick *see* **3 cut**

nickname 6 handle **7** agnomen, epithet, moniker, pet name **8** baby name, cognomen

Niger
capital/largest city: 6 Niamey
mountain: 3 Air
highest point: 7 Bagzane, Greboun

lake: 4 Chad
river: 5 Benue, Niger **6** Dillia
island: 6 Boubon
physical feature:
 bight: 5 Benin **6** Biafra
 desert: 6 Sahara
 gulf: 6 Guinea
feature:
 empire: 4 Mali **6** Fulani **7** Songhai

Nigeria
capital: 5 Abuja
largest city: 5 Lagos
division: 6 Biafra
highest point: 12 Chappal Waddi
lake: 4 Chad
river: 5 Benin, Benue, Cross, Niger, Oshun **6** Kaduna, Sokoto
sea: 8 Atlantic
physical feature:
 bight: 5 Benin, Bonny **6** Biafra
 delta: 5 Niger
 gulf: 6 Guinea
 highlands: 6 Yoruba
place:
 mosque/walled city: 4 Kano
feature:
 dress: 4 riga **7** agbados
 war: 7 Biafran

niggling *see* **5 petty**

nigh 4 near **5** close, handy **6** almost, at hand, nearly **7** close by **8** adjacent

night 4 dark, dusk **7** bedtime, evening, sundown **8** eventide
goddess of: 3 Nox

nightingale
group of: 5 watch

nightmare 7 incubus **8** bad dream, succubus

nihilist 5 rebel **9** anarchist, terrorist

Nike
origin: 5 Greek
goddess of: 7 victory
father: 6 Pallas
mother: 4 Styx
brother: 5 Zelos
corresponds to: 6 Athena **8** Victoria

nil *see* **4 zero**

Nile
boat: 5 baris **6** cangia, nuggar, sandal **7** felucca, gaiassa **8** dahabeah
cities: 4 Juba **5** Aswan, Asyut, Cairo, Luxor **7** Rosetta **8** Khartoum **10** Alexandria
dam: 5 Aswan (High)
desert bordering: 6 Libyan, Nubian **7** Arabian

feature: 6 Sphinx
pyramid: 4 Giza
temple: 8 Ramses II **9** Abu Simbel
lake: 6 Albert, Edward, Nasser **8** Victoria
plain: 6 Gezira
swamp: 4 Sudd

nimble 4 deft, spry **5** agile, fleet, light, quick, rapid, ready, swift **6** lively, speedy, supple **8** animated, skillful, spirited

nimbus 4 aura, disk, halo **5** cloud, vapor **7** aureole **8** radiance

Nimrod
father: 4 Cush
grandfather: 3 Ham
great grandfather: 4 Noah
famed as: 6 hunter

nincompoop *see* **5 idiot**

Nineteen Eighty-Four
author: 6 (George) Orwell

Ninety-Five Theses
author: 6 (Martin) Luther

ninny *see* **5 idiot**

Ninotchka
director: 8 (Ernst) Lubitsch
cast: 5 (Greta) Garbo **6** (Ina) Claire, (Bela) Lugosi **7** (Melvyn) Douglas

setting: **5** Paris

nip 3 cut, lop **4** bite, clip, crop, dock, grab, grip, ruin, snag, snap, snip **5** blast, check, chill, clamp, clasp, crack, crush, frost, grasp, pinch, quash, seize, sever, shear, snare, tweak **6** cut off, freeze, pierce, snatch, sunder, thwart **7** curtail, shorten, squeeze **8** compress, cut short

nip-and-tuck 5 close

nip in the bud 7 prevent **8** preclude

Nippon *see* **5 Japan**

nippy *see* **4 cold**

nit-pick 4 carp, pick **5** cavil

nitrate 4 salt **5** ester **6** sodium

nitty-gritty 4 core, crux, gist, meat, pith **5** heart **7** essence

nitwit *see* **5 idiot**

Nixon, Richard Milhous
  presidential rank: 13 thirty-seventh
  party: 10 Republican
  state represented: 2 CA
  defeated: 7 Wallace **8** Humphrey
  vice president: 4 Ford

5 Agnew
  born: 2 CA **10** Yorba Linda
  dog: 8 Checkers
  notable events of lifetime/ term:
    first men on: 4 moon
    incident: 11 Wounded Knee
    massacre: 5 Mylai
    pardon of Nixon by: 4 Ford
    resignation of: 5 Agnew, Nixon
    scandal: 9 Watergate
    war: 7 Vietnam
  wife: 8 (Thelma Catherine) Patricia
    nickname: 3 Pat
  children: 5 Julie **8** Patricia (Tricia)

no 3 nay, nix, not **4** none, veto
  French: 3 non
  German: 4 nein
  Russian: 4 nyet

Noah
  father: 6 Lamech
  grandfather: 10 Methuselah
  son: 3 Ham **4** Shem **7** Japheth
  built: 3 ark
  collected: 5 pairs

7 animals
survived: 5 flood
Noah's Ark
landfall: 6 Ararat
nob 4 peer, toff **5** swell
Nobel, Alfred
invented: 8 dynamite
originated: 10 Nobel Prize
noble 3 don **4** high, just, lord, peer **5** famed, grand, great, lofty, moral, regal, royal **6** famous, gentle, honest, knight, lordly, squire, superb, worthy **7** courtly, eminent, exalted, stately, supreme **8** baronial, cavalier, glorious, highborn, imperial, imposing, lordlike, majestic, princely, renowned, selfless, splendid, superior, virtuous
nock 5 notch
in: 5 arrow
nocturnal 4 dark **5** night **7** nightly, obscure
nod 3 bob **4** doze, hail, show, sign **5** agree, greet, lapse, let up **6** assent, beckon, concur, drowse, motion, reveal, salute, signal **7** consent, drop off, fall off, gesture, signify

node, nodule 3 bud **4** bump, burl, hump, knob, knot, lump **5** bulge, joint **6** button **8** swelling
noel, Noel 4 yule **5** carol **8** yuletide **9** Christmas
No Exit
author: 6 (Jean-Paul) Sartre
noggin 3 cup, mug **4** bean, head, pate **5** gourd **6** noodle
noise 3 ado, din **4** bang, blab, boom, echo, pass, roar, stir, wail **5** babel, blare, blast, bruit, rumor, sound, voice **6** bedlam, clamor, hubbub, racket, rumble, tumult, uproar **7** barrage, thunder **8** gabbling, shouting
noisome *see* **6 putrid**
nomad *see* **7 vagrant**
nomadic *see* **7 vagrant**
nom de guerre 5 alias **7** war name
nom de plume 5 alias **7** pen name
nomenclature *see* **6 jargon**
nominal *see* **5 small**
nominate *see* **6 choose**
nonbeliever *see* **5 cynic**

nonce 6 pro tem **7** present

nonchalant *see* **6 casual**

nonentity *see* **4 zero**

no-nonsense *see* **6 somber**

nonpareil 5 elite, ideal, model, super **6** symbol, unique **7** epitome, paragon, pattern, supreme **8** exemplar

nonpartisan 4 fair, just **8** unbiased, unswayed

nonplus 4 balk, faze, foil, halt, stop **5** abash, stump, upset **6** baffle, bother, dismay, muddle, puzzle, stymie **7** astound, confuse, disturb, mystify, perplex **8** astonish, bewilder, confound, deadlock

nonsense 3 rot **4** bosh, bunk **5** folly, trash **6** antics, babble, drivel, joking, piffle **7** baloney, blather, bombast, chatter, fooling, garbage, hogwash, inanity, prattle, rubbish, trifles, twaddle **8** claptrap, flummery

noodle 4 bean, head, pate **5** gourd, pasta **6** noggin **8** practice

nook 3 den **4** cove, lair **5** haven, niche **6** alcove, cavity, corner, cranny, dugout, recess, refuge **7** retreat, shelter **8** hideaway

noon 6 midday, zenith **8** high noon, meridian

noose 3 tie **4** bond, hang, loop **5** catch, hitch, lasso, snare **6** choker, entrap, halter, lariat, tether

Nordic Mythology *see* **Norse Mythology**

noria 10 water wheel

norm *see* **8 standard**

normal 3 fit, par **4** sane **5** sound, usual **6** steady **7** average, healthy, natural, regular, typical, uniform **8** constant, expected, ordinary, reliable, standard

Normandy, Normandie
beach: 4 Gold, Juno, Utah **5** Omaha, Sword
borders: 7 (English) Channel, Picardy **8** Brittany
city: 4 Caen, St. Lo **5** Rouen **7** Le Havre **9** Cherbourg
event: 4 D Day
region of: 6 France
river: 5 Seine

Norse Mythology

abode of man: **7** Midgard
   10 Mithgarthr
afterworld: **6** Manala **7**
   Tuonela
began race of giants: **4**
   Ymir
blacksmith/hero: **9**
   Ilmarinen
bridge of gods: **7** Bifrost
dragon: **6** Fafnir
dwarf: **5** Skuld **7** Andvari
earth is made from: **4**
   Ymir
elf: **4** Norn **8** Verdandi
epic: **8** Kaleva
first god: **4** Buri **7**
   Forsete, Forseti
first man: **3** Ask
first woman: **5** Embla
folk hero: **8** Kalevala
giant: **4** Loki **5** Jotun,
   Thrym **6** Thiazi,
   Thjazi **7** Skrymir
giantess: **3** Urd **5** Thokk
   9 Angerboda,
   Angrbodha, Angurboda
goat: **7** Heidrun
goddesses: **7** Asynjur
goddess of death: **3** Hel
**goddess of marriage/
   peace/prosperity:** **4** Frey
   5 Freyr
goddess of spring: **4** Idun
   5 Iduna, Ithun **6** Ithunn

goddess of the sea: **3**
   Ran
god of beauty: **5** Baldr **6**
   Balder, Baldur
god of dawn: **8** Heimdall
god of farming: **4** Thor
god of fire: **4** Loki
god of knowledge/poetry:
   4 Odin **5** Othin
   **corresponds to
   Germanic:** **5** Wotan
god of justice: **7** Forseti
god of light: **8** Heimdall
god of music: **5** Bragi
god of navigation: **5**
   Niord, Njord
god of prosperity: **5**
   Niord, Njord
god of rain: **4** Thor
god of sea: **5** Aegir,
   Mimir
god of thunder: **4** Thor
god of underworld: **8**
   Niflheim
god of victory: **3** Tyr
god of war: **4** Odin **5**
   Othin
   **corresponds to
   Germanic:** **5** Wotan
god of wind: **5** Niord,
   Njord
god of wisdom: **4** Odin **5**
   Othin
   **corresponds to
   Germanic:** **5** Wotan

home of dead: 3 Hel
nature spirit: 7 Eriking
oak tree: 9 Barnstock, Branstock
Odin's court/hall: 8 Valhalla
Odin's father: 3 Bor
Odin's magic ring: 8 Draupnir
Odin's raven: 5 Hugin, Munin
Odin's spear: 6 Gungni
Odin's wolf: 4 Geri **5** Freki
race of gods: 5 Vanir
saga: 8 Vulsunga
sea monster: 6 Kraken
serpent: 7 Nidhogg
Sigmund's sword: 4 Gram
sorceress: 5 Louhi **8** Grimhild
Thor's hammer: 7 Miolnir
Thor's servant: 7 Thialfi
tree with three roots: 9 Iggdrasil, Yggdrasil
Valkyrie: 8 Brynhild **9** Brunhilde, Sigrdrifa
virgin goddess: 3 Urd **4** Norn **5** Skuld, Urdar **8** Verdandi
warrior: 8 Baresark **9** Berserker
watchdog: 4 Garm
wolf monster: 6 Fenrir, Fenris

north 5 polar, upper **6** arctic
North America *see* **7** America, North
North Carolina
  abbreviation: 2 NC **4** N Car
  nickname: 7 Tar Heel
  capital: 7 Raleigh
  largest city: 9 Charlotte
  mountain: 9 Blue Ridge **10** Great Smoky
  highest point: 8 Mitchell
  river: 3 New **6** Pee Dee, Pigeon **7** Catawba, Roanoke
  sea: 8 Atlantic
  island: 7 Roanoke, **8** Hatteras **10** Outer Banks
  physical feature:
    cape: 4 Fear **7** Lookout **8** Hatteras
    plateau: 8 Piedmont
    sound: 7 Croatan, Pamlico
    swamp: 6 Dismal
North Dakota
  abbreviation: 2 ND **4** N Dak
  nickname: 5 Sioux
  capital: 8 Bismarck
  largest city: 5 Fargo
  highest point: 10 White Butte

river: 3 Red **5** Knife **8** Cheyenne, Missouri
physical feature:
  area: 8 Badlands
  plains: 5 Great
  valley: 8 Red River

Northern Rhodesia *see* **6** **Zambia**

North Korea *see* **5 Korea**

North Vietnam *see* **7 Vietnam**

Northwest Territories
  abbreviation: 3 NWT
  borders: 6 Arctic (Ocean) **7** Alberta, Nunavut **8** Beaufort (Sea) **12** Saskatchewan **15** British Columbia
  city: 11 Yellowknife
  country: 6 Canada
  island: 5 Banks **7** Melville **8** Bathurst, Somerset, Victoria
  lake: 9 Great Bear **10** Great Slave
  mineral: 3 oil **4** gold, lead, zinc **6** silver **8** tungsten **9** petroleum
  native: 5 Inuit **6** Eskimo

Norway
  other name: 5 Norge
    land of the: 11 Midnight Sun
  capital/largest city: **4** Oslo
  highest point: 12 Galdhopiggen
  sea: 5 North **6** Arctic **7** Barents **8** Atlantic **9** Norwegian, Skagerrak
  island: 6, Solund, Vannoy **7** Lofoten **8** Jan Mayen, Svalbard **10** Vesteralen
  physical feature:
    fjord: 4 Oslo **5** Sogne
  feature:
    former colony: 7 Vinland
    literature form: 4 edda, saga
  food:
    cheese: 9 Jarlsberg
    drink: 7 aquavit
    potato dumplings: 5 klubb

Norwegian Mythology *see* **Norse Mythology**

nose
  sense of: 5 smell
  part: 7 nostril

nosegay 4 posy **7** bouquet

nostalgia 6 pining, regret **7** longing

Nostromo
  author: 6 (Joseph) Conrad

nostrum *see* **6 remedy**

nosy, nosey 6 prying,

snoopy 7 all ears, curious **8** snooping

notable 3 VIP **4** name **5** famed, wheel **6** biggie, bigwig, famous, marked **7** eminent, salient **8** luminary, renowned

notation 5 entry

notch 3 cut **4** dent, mark, nick, nock **5** grade, level, score **6** degree **7** scratch

note 4 bill, fame, line, mark **5** bread, draft, enter, green, money, write **6** regard, renown **7** epistle, jot down, lettuce, message, missive, voucher **8** currency, eminence, perceive

notebook 3 log **5** diary **6** record **7** journal

noted 6 famous **7** eminent **8** renowned

nothing *see* **4** zero

notice 3 eye, see **4** dope, heed, info, mark **5** goods **6** poster, rating, regard, review, take in **7** leaflet, mention, observe, warning **8** brochure, circular, pamphlet

notify *see* **6** inform

notion *see* **4** idea

notoriety 4 blot **5** shame, stain **6** infamy, stigma **7** scandal **8** disgrace, dishonor, ignominy

not quite 6 all but, almost, nearly

Nouakchott
capital of: 10 Mauritania

nourish 4 feed **5** nurse **6** suckle **7** nurture, sustain

Nova Scotia
borders: 5 (Bay of) Fundy **8** Atlantic Ocean **12** New Brunswick
city: 5 Truro **7** Halifax **8** Yarmouth
country: 6 Canada
island: 10 Cape Breton
mineral: 3 oil **4** lead, salt, sand, zinc **6** barite, gravel, gypsum, silver **9** celestite, petroleum **10** natural gas
part of: 6 Acadia
river: 4 Avon **5** Clyde **6** LaHave, Medway, Mersey **7** St Mary's

novel 3 new **6** unique **7** unusual **8** original, singular, uncommon

November
event: 11 Election Day
gem: 5 topaz
holiday: 8 All Souls,

Veterans **9** Guy Fawkes
12 Thanksgiving
number of days: 6 thirty
place in year:
    Gregorian: 8 eleventh
    Roman: 5 ninth
Zodiac sign: 7 Scorpio **11**
Sagittarius

novice 4 tyro **5** pupil **7**
amateur, learner, student
8 beginner, disciple,
newcomer

now and then 8 on-and-off,
periodic, sometime,
sporadic

Nox, Nyx *see also* **Nyx, Nox**
goddess of: 5 night

noxious *see* **6 putrid**

nth degree 5 limit **6** utmost
7 extreme

nuance 5 shade, touch **6**
nicety **7** finesse **8** delicacy,
fineness, keenness, subtlety

nub 4 core, crux, gist,
hump, knob, knot, lump,
node **5** bulge, heart **6**
kernel **7** essence **8**
swelling

nucleus *see* **6 center**

nude *see* **5 naked**

nudge 3 jab, jog, nod **4**
bump, jolt, poke, prod,
push **5** elbow, press,
punch, touch **6** jostle

nugatory *see* **6 paltry**

nugget 4 hunk, lump **5**
chunk, piece

nuisance *see* **7 trouble**

null 2 NG **4** void **6** no
good **7** invalid

nullify *see* **4 void**

numb 4 dead **6** frozen **8**
deadened

number 3 mob, sum, tot **4**
army, bevy, book, herd,
host, mass, part **5** array,
bunch, count, crowd,
digit, group, issue, tally,
total **6** amount, cipher,
figure, reckon **7** compute,
edition, foliate, integer,
numeral **8** estimate,
paginate, quantity

numeral 5 digit **6** cipher,
figure, letter, number,
symbol **7** integer

numerous 4 many **6** myriad
7 copious, profuse **8**
abundant

Numidia *see* **7 Algeria**

numskull, numbskull *see* **5**
idiot

Nunavut
    name means: 7 our land

abbreviation: 2 NU
borders: 3 NWT **8** Manitoba **9** Baffin Bay, Hudson Bay
capital/largest city: 7 Iqaluit
country: 6 Canada
island: 5 Devon **6** Baffin **8** Victoria **9** Elizabeth, Ellesmere
mineral: 4 gold, zinc **9** petroleum
people: 5 Inuit

nuncio 5 envoy **6** legate **8** diplomat, minister

nunnery 5 abbey, order **6** priory **7** cenacle, convent **8** cloister

nuptials 7 wedding **8** marriage

nurse 4 feed **5** nanny, treat **6** attend, doctor, foster, harbor, remedy, sister, succor, suckle **7** care for, nourish, nurture, promote **8** attend to, guardian
Hindi/Indian: 4 ayah
Orient: 4 amah
famous: 5 (Sister) Kenny **6** (Edith) Cavell **11** (Florence) Nightingale

nurture 4 feed, mess, rear, tend **5** breed, raise, teach, train, tutor **6** foster, school **7** bring up, develop, educate, nourish, prepare, sustain, victual **8** instruct, maintain

nut *see* **6 maniac**
Nut
    origin: 8 Egyptian
    goddess of: 3 sky

nut-brown 5 tawny **6** auburn, brunet **8** brunette, cinnamon

Nutmeg State
    nickname of: 2 CT

nutrition 4 chow, feed, food, grub **6** fodder, forage, silage **7** edibles, rations **8** eatables

nuzzle *see* **6 fondle**

Nyasaland *see* **6 Malawi**
nyet
    Russian: 2 no

nymph 5 belle, dryad, houri, naiad, nixie, oread, sylph **6** beauty, daphne, kelpie, maenad, nereid, ondine, sprite, undine **7** charmer, galatea **8** Eurydice

Nyx, Nox
    form: 7 goddess
    personifies: 5 night
    originated from: 5 Chaos

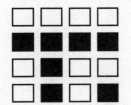  

O

oaf 3 sap **4** boob, boor, clod, dolt, dope, fool, jerk, lout **5** booby, dummy, dunce, idiot, klutz, moron, ninny **6** lummox, nitwit **7** half-wit **8** bonehead, imbecile, numskull

oak 7 Quercus
venerated by: 6 Druids

oar 3 row **4** pole **5** blade, rower, scull **6** paddle, propel **9** propeller
blade: 4 palm, peel
fulcrum: 5 thole **7** oarlock, rowlock
part: 4 loom **5** shaft **6** collar

oasis 5 haven **6** asylum, harbor, refuge **7** retreat, sanctum, shelter

oast 4 kiln, oven

oat, oats 5 Avena
varieties: 3 sea **4** wild **6** potato **8** animated

oath 3 vow **5** curse **6** avowal, pledge **8** cuss word, swearing

oatmeal 6 cereal **7** pottage **8** drammock, porridge

obdurate *see* **8 stubborn**

obeah 5 charm, magic **6** fetish, voodoo **7** sorcery

obedient 5 loyal **6** docile **7** devoted, dutiful **8** amenable, faithful, obeisant, yielding

obeisance *see* **7 respect**

obelisk 5 pylon, shaft, tower **6** column, dagger, needle, pillar **8** memorial, monolith, monument

obese *see* **3 fat**

obey *see* **4 heed**

obfuscate *see* **7 confuse**

obi 4 sash **5** obeah **6** girdle

object 3 aim, end, use **4** body, butt, dupe, form, gist, goal, pith, prey **5** abhor, basis, cause, knock, point, sense, thing **6** balk at, carp at, device, dingus, gadget, intent, loathe, motive, oppose, quarry, reason, target, victim

7 dislike, essence, frown on, mission, protest, purpose, subject **8** be averse, denounce

objection *see* **7 protest**

objective *see* **4 goal**

objet d'art **5** bijou, curio **7** bibelot, trinket

obligation **4** bond, care, debt, duty, oath, onus, word **6** charge, pledge **7** promise **8** contract, guaranty, warranty

oblige **3** aid **4** bind, help, make **5** favor, force, impel, serve **6** assist, coerce, compel **7** require, support **8** obligate

oblique *see* **7 devious**

obliterate *see* **7 destroy**

oblivion **5** limbo **7** the void

obloquy **5** abuse, odium, shame **6** infamy, rebuke **7** calumny, censure, railing **8** contempt, disfavor, disgrace, ignominy

obnoxious **4** foul, vile **5** nasty **6** odious **7** hateful **8** unseemly

oboe family
  instruments: **5** shawm **6** curtal, pommer, racket **7** bassoon, bombard, curtall, hautboy **8** crumhorn, schalmey, tenoroon

obscene *see* **6 vulgar**

obscure **3** dim, fog **4** blur, dark, hide, mask, veil **5** bedim, befog, block, cloak, cloud, cover, dingy, dusky, faint, murky, vague **6** cloudy, darken, hidden, muddle, screen, shadow, shroud, somber, unsung **7** conceal, confuse, cryptic, eclipse, unclear **8** befuddle, confused, disguise

obsequies **5** rites **6** burial **7** funeral

obsequious *see* **6 menial**

observance *see* **4 custom**

observation **4** heed, idea, view **5** probe **6** eyeing, notice, remark, search, seeing, survey, theory

observatory **5** tower **7** lookout

observe **3** eye, say, see **4** espy, heed, keep, mark, note, obey, ogle, spot, view **5** honor, opine, state, watch **6** assert, behold, detect, follow, notice, peer at, regard, remark, size up, survey **7** abide by, comment, declare, fulfill, glimpse, inspect, perform, reflect, respect, stare at **8** carry out, discover, perceive, sanctify, theorize

obsession 5 craze, mania, quirk **6** phobia **8** fixation

obsolete *see* **7 archaic**

obstacle 3 bar **4** curb, snag **5** block, catch, check **6** hurdle **7** barrier, problem **8** blockade, stoppage

obstinate *see* **8 stubborn**

obstreperous 4 loud **5** noisy **6** unruly **8** perverse

obstruct *see* **6 hinder**

obtain *see* **3 get**

obtrusive *see* **4 nosy**

obtuse 4 dull, slow **5** blunt, dense, thick **6** simple, stupid **7** blunted **8** ignorant, not sharp

obverse 4 face **5** front **of coin: 4** head

obviate *see* **5 dodge**

obvious 5 clear, plain **6** patent **7** evident, glaring, visible **8** apparent, distinct, manifest,

palpable, striking, unhidden

ocarina 11 sweet potato **14** wind instrument

occasion 4 base, time **5** basis, cause, event **6** advent, affair, chance, elicit, ground, lead to, motive, prompt, reason **7** episode, inspire, venture **8** incident, instance

occidental 7 Western **8** American, European

occlude *see* **6 hinder**

occult 4 dark **5** magic **6** arcane, hidden, mystic, secret, veiled **7** obscure, private **8** esoteric, mystical, shrouded

occupant 5 owner **6** lessee, lodger, native, renter, roomer, tenant **7** dweller, settler **8** colonist, occupier, resident

occupation *see* **3 job**

occupy 3 use **4** be in, be on, busy, fill, hold **5** amuse, sit in **6** absorb, employ, engage, fill up, room in, take up **7** engross, inhabit, overrun, pervade, possess

8 permeate, reside in, saturate

occur 3 hit **4** rise **5** arise, ensue **6** appear, befall, crop up, emerge, happen, result, strike, turn up **7** be found, come off, develop

ocean 3 sea **4** deep, main, pond **5** flood, water **7** big pond, high sea

  god of: 3 Nun **4** Nanu **7** Neptune, Oceanus **8** Poseidon

Oceania, Oceanica 9 Australia, Melanesia, Polynesia **10** Micronesia

  ocean: 7 (South) Pacific

  island: 4 Cook, Guam, Fiji, Maui, Niue, Wake **5** Aunuu, Bonin, Kauai, Lanai, Tonga **6** Bikini, Futuna, Hawaii, Marcus, Midway, Rurutu, Tahiti, Tubuai, Tuvalu, Wallis **7** Gambier, Gilbert, Iwo Jima, Leeward, Mariana, Molokai, Phoenix, Solomon, Tokelau, Tuamotu, Tutuila, Vanuatu, Volcano **8** Aitutaki, Bismarck, Bora-Bora, Johnston, Kiribati, Marshall, Pitcairn, Windward

oceanic 6 marine **7** aquatic, pelagic **8** seagoing

Oceanid
  form: 5 nymph
  location: 3 sea
  father: 7 Oceanus
  mother: 6 Tethys

Oceanus
  member of: 6 Titans
  father: 6 Uranus
  mother: 4 Gaea
  consort of: 6 Tethys
  father of: 8 Oceanids
  son: 7 Proteus
  form: 6 stream

ocelot 3 cat **7** wildcat

Octavia
  brother: 8 Augustus
  husband: 4 Nero **10** Mark Antony
  grandson: 8 Caligula

October
  flower: 6 cosmos **9** calendula
  gem: 4 opal
  holiday: 8 Columbus (Day, 12) **9** Halloween (31)
  number of days: 9 thirty-one
  origin of name: 4 octo (Latin meaning eight)
  place in year:
    Gregorian: 5 tenth

Roman: 6 eighth
Zodiac sign: 5 Libra **7** Scorpio

Octopus, The
author: **6** (Frank) Norris

odd *see* **7 strange**

Odd Couple (TV), The
cast: **6** (Larry) Gelman **7** (Jack) Klugman, (Tony) Randall **8** (Al) Molinaro

Odd Couple (Movie), The
director: **4** (Gene) Saks
based on play by: **5** (Neil) Simon
cast: **6** (Jack) Lemmon **7** (Herb) Edelman, (John) Fiedler, (Walter) Matthau

oddity 5 freak, sight **6** marvel, rarity, wonder
Latin: **8** rara avis

odds and ends 4 olio **6** scraps **8** remnants

ode 4 epic, hymn, poem **5** lyric, paean, psalm, verse **6** ballad **8** canticle
type: **8** Horatian, Pindaric

Ode on a Grecian Urn
author: **5** (John) Keats

Ode to a Nightingale
author: **5** (John) Keats

Odin
brother: **2** Ve **4** Vili
children: **4** Hodr, Thor **5** Baldr **6** Balder, Baldur
counterpart: **5** Woden, Wotan
court: **8** Valhalla
god of: **3** war **6** poetry, wisdom
grandson: **7** Volsung
origin: **5** Norse
raven: **5** Hugin, Munin
remaining eye: **3** sun
ruler of: **5** Aexir
spear: **7** Gungnir
wife: **3** Fri **5** Frigg, Frija **6** Frigga
wolf: **4** Geri **5** Freki

odious *see* **4 evil**

odor 4 aura **5** aroma, scent, smell, stink **6** flavor, stench **7** bouquet, essence, perfume

Odysseus
also: **7** Ulysses
king of: **6** Ithaca
father: **7** Laertes
hero of: **5** Iliad **7** Odyssey
wife: **8** Penelope **9** Callidice
seduced by: **5** Circe
killed by: **9** Telegonus

Odyssey
author: **5** Homer

Oedipus
king of: **6** Thebes

father: 5 Laius
mother: 7 Jocasta
wife: 7 Jocasta
son: 8 Eteocles **9** Polynices
daughter: 6 Ismene **8** Antigone
killed: 5 Laius
defeated: 6 Sphinx

oenology
  science of: 5 wines

oeuvre 4 work **5** works

of a piece 5 alike, equal **7** matched, the same **8** all in one

of bad character 5 shady **8** unsavory

off 2 by **3** bad, far, ill, odd **4** afar, away, down, from, kill, poor, stop **5** amiss, apart, aside, crazy, wrong **6** absent, begone, lessen, remote **7** distant, further, in error, stopped, tainted **8** abnormal, canceled, inferior, mistaken

offal *see* **5 trash**

off base 5 amiss, wrong **8** improper, mistaken

offbeat *see* **7 strange**

off-color *see* **4 lewd**

off duty 8 inactive

offend *see* **6 insult**

offer 3 bid **6** bestow, extend, render, submit, tender **7** advance, hold out, present, proffer, propose, suggest **8** overture, proposal, put forth

offhand, offhanded 5 ad-lib, hasty **6** casual, chance, random **7** relaxed **8** careless, cavalier

office 3 job **4** post, role **8** capacity, function, position

officer 3 cop **4** head **7** manager **8** director, gendarme, governor

official 5 agent **6** formal, vested **7** manager, officer **8** approved, chairman, director, licensed

official communication 5 edict, order, ukase **6** report **7** release **8** bulletin

officiate *see* **6 direct**

officious 6 prying **7** pompous **8** meddling

offset 6 redeem **7** balance, nullify **8** equalize

offshoot 4 limb **5** scion, shoot **6** branch **7** adjunct

offspring *see* **7 progeny**

off the mark 5 amiss 6 afield, astray

off-the-record 5 privy 6 secret 7 private

off the top of one's head 5 ad-lib 7 offhand

Of Human Bondage
  author: 7 (W Somerset) Maugham

Of Mice and Men
  author: 9 (John) Steinbeck

often 3 oft 4 much 7 usually 8 commonly, ofttimes

ogle 3 eye 6 gape at, gawk at, goggle, leer at 7 stare at 8 goggle at

ogre, ogress 5 brute, demon, fiend, ghoul, harpy 6 despot, tyrant 7 bugbear, monster

Ohio
  abbreviation: 2 OH
  nickname: 7 Buckeye
  capital/largest city: 8 Columbus
  highest point: 8 Campbell (Hill)
  lake: 4 Erie
  river: 4 Ohio 5 Miami 6 Maumee, Wabash 8 Cuyahoga, Sandusky
  physical feature:

  caverns: 4 Ohio, Zane 6 Seneca

oil 4 balm, lard 5 cream, salve 6 anoint, grease, pomade 7 unguent 8 liniment, ointment
  type: 4 corn, fuel, hair 5 crude, motor, olive, whale 6 canola 7 cooking, mineral 9 safflower, vegetable

ointment 4 balm 5 salve 6 lotion, pomade 7 pomatum, unguent 8 liniment

OK 4 fine, good 7 approve, endorse 8 all right, approval
  French: 7 d'accord

Oklahoma
  abbreviation: 2 OK 4 Okla
  nickname: 6 Boomer, Sooner
  capital/largest city: 12 Oklahoma City
  mountain: 6 Ozarks 7 Wichita 8 Ouachita
  highest point: 9 Black Mesa
  river: 3 Red 5 Grand 6 Little 7 Washita 8 Arkansas, Canadian, Cimarron

physical feature: 9
Panhandle

Oklahoma!
director: 9 (Fred)
Zinnemann
cast: 5 (Shirley) Jones **6**
(Eddie) Albert, (Gordon)
MacRae **7** (Gloria)
Grahame, (Rod) Steiger
8 (James) Whitmore **9**
(Charlotte) Greenwood

old 4 aged, used **5** hoary, of
age **6** beat-up, bygone, of
yore **7** ancient, antique,
archaic, elderly, outworn,
rundown, vintage,
wornout **8** decrepit,
obsolete, outdated,
timeworn

Old Dominion
nickname of: 8 Virginia

oldest man 10 Methuselah

old hand 3 pro **6** expert,
master **8** virtuoso

old hat *see* **7 archaic**

Old Line State
nickname of: 8 Maryland

Old Man and the Sea, The
author: 9 (Ernest)
Hemingway

old saw *see* **5 maxim**

Old Testament
first five books:

10 Pentateuch
first six books: 9
Hexateuch
first seven books: 10
Heptateuch
books of: 3 Job **4** Amos,
Ezra, Joel, Ruth **5**
Hosea, Jonah, Kings,
Micah, Nahum, Songs,
Tobit **6** Baruch, Daniel,
Esther, Exodus, Haggai,
Isaiah, Joshua, Judges,
Judith, Psalms, Samuel,
Sirach, Wisdom **7**
Ezekiel, Genesis,
Malachi, Numbers,
Obadiah **8** Habakkuk,
Jeremiah, Macabees,
Nehemiah, Proverbs **9**
Leviticus, Zechariah,
Zephaniah **10** Chronicles
11 Deuteronomy **12**
Ecclesiastes **13** Song of
Solomon **14**
Ecclesiasticus

old-world 6 formal **7**
courtly, gallant, old-line **8**
European, orthodox

oleoresin 3 gum **5** anime,
apiol, elemi **6** balsam **7**
solvent

olio 4 stew **6** jumble,
medley **7** melange,
mixture **8** mishmash

olive-drab 5 khaki
Oliver Twist
   author: 7 (Charles)
   Dickens
olla 3 jar, pot
Olympic Games
   site:
      1896: 6 Athens
      1900: 5 Paris
      1904: 7 St Louis
      1906: 6 Athens
      1908: 6 London
      1912: 9 Stockholm
      1920: 7 Antwerp
      1924: 5 Paris 8
      Chamonix
      1928: 8 St Moritz 9
      Amsterdam
      1932: 10 Lake Placid,
      Los Angeles
      1936: 6 Berlin 21
      Garmisch-Partenkirchen
      1948: 6 London 8 St
      Moritz
      1952: 4 Oslo 8 Helsinki
      1956: 7 Cortina
      (d'Ampezzo) 9
      Melbourne
      1960: 5 Tokyo 11
      Squaw Valley
      1968: 8 Grenoble 10
      Mexico City
      1972: 6 Munich 7
      Sapporo

      1976: 8 Montreal 9
      Innsbruck
      1980: 6 Moscow 10
      Lake Placid
      1984: 8 Sarajevo 10
      Los Angeles
      1988: 5 Seoul 7
      Calgary
      1992: 9 Barcelona 11
      Albertville
      1994: 11 Lillehammer
      1996: 7 Atlanta
      1998: 6 Nagano
      2000: 6 Sydney
      2002: 8 Salt Lake (City)
      2004: 6 Athens
      2006: 5 Turin
      2008: 7 Beijing
      2010: 9 Vancouver
      2012: 6 London
Oman
   other name: 13 Muscat
   and Oman
   capital: 6 Masqat, Muscat
   largest city: 5 Matra 6
   Matrah
   highest point: 6 al-Sham
   sea: 6 Indian 7 Arabian
   physical feature:
      gulf: 4 Oman
      peninsula: 7 Arabian
      strait: 6 Hormuz
   war: 4 Gulf
omega 3 end 4 last 5 final

6 ending **8** terminus
opposite: 5 alpha
omen 4 sign **5** token **6** augury, herald **7** auspice, portent, presage, warning
ominous *see* **4 grim**
omit *see* **6 delete**
omnipotent 6 mighty **7** supreme **8** almighty, powerful, puissant
omniscient 7 all-wise, supreme **8** infinite
on 2 at **4** atop, near, over, upon **5** about, above, ahead, along, anent **7** against, forward, planned **8** abutting, adjacent, attached, intended, touching
on-and-off 6 spotty **8** episodic
once 7 ages ago, long ago, one time **8** formerly, hitherto, years ago
once-in-a-lifetime 6 unique **7** special **8** singular
on cloud nine 6 elated, joyful, joyous **8** ecstatic, euphoric
one 2 an **3** you **4** a man, lone, only, sole **5** a body, a soul, whole **6** a thing, entire, single, unique **7** a

person, someone **8** complete, singular, solitary, somebody
O'Neal, Ryan
daughter: 5 Tatum (O'Neal)
O'Neal, Tatum
father: 9 Ryan (O'Neal)
husband: 7 (John) McEnroe
one and the same 5 equal **7** matched
one by one 6 singly
One Flew Over the Cuckoo's Nest
director: 6 (Milos) Forman
based on story by: 6 (Ken) Kesey
one-of-a-kind *see* **6 unique**
oneology
science of: 5 wines
onerous 5 heavy **6** taxing **7** arduous, painful, weighty **8** crushing, grievous
On Golden Pond
director: 6 (Mark) Rydell
based on play by: 8 (Ernest) Thompson
cast: 5 (Henry, Jane) Fonda **6** (Doug) McKeon **7** (Dabney)

Coleman, (Katharine) Hepburn

onion 6 Allium

only 4 just, lone, sole **5** alone **6** barely, merely, purely, simply, single, singly, solely, unique **7** at least **8** by itself, singular, solitary

on one's uppers 5 broke

onset 4 push, raid **5** birth, sally, start **6** attack, charge, onrush, outset, thrust **7** assault, genesis, infancy, offense **8** founding, invasion, outbreak, storming

onslaught 4 coup, push, raid **5** blitz, foray, onset, sally **6** attack, charge, putsch, thrust **7** assault, offense **8** invasion

on tap 5 handy **6** at hand, on hand

Ontario
  bay: 6 Hudson
  canal: 5 Trent **6** Rideau
  capital: 7 Toronto
  province of: 6 Canada
  river: 6 Ottawa, Thames **7** Niagara **10** St Lawrence

on the alert 4 wary **7** careful, mindful, on

guard **8** cautious, watchful

On the Beach
  author: 5 (Nevil) Shute

on the dot 7 exactly **8** promptly

on the go 4 busy **6** active, mobile **8** in motion

on the nose 5 exact **7** exactly, precise **8** accurate, on target

On the Waterfront
  director: 5 (Elia) Kazan
  cast: 4 (Lee J) Cobb **5** (Eva Marie) Saint **6** (Marlon) Brando, (Karl) Malden **7** (Pat) Henning, (Rod) Steiger **8** (Leif) Erickson

onto 4 atop, upon **5** aware, privy **6** aboard

onus 4 duty, load **5** cross **6** burden, strain, weight

onward, onwards 5 ahead, along **7** forward, ongoing

oodles 4 gobs, lots, many **5** heaps, loads, scads

ooze 4 drip, leak, mire, muck, seep, silt **5** bleed, drain, exude, slime, sweat **6** filter, sludge **7** dribble, leakage, seepage, soft mud, trickle **8** alluvium

opal
  color: 3 red **5** black, white **6** orange
  variety: 8 fire opal

opalescent 5 milky **6** pearly **8** irisated, luminous

opaque *see* **7 obscure**

open 4 ajar, fair, just, wide **5** agape, begin, clear, crack, found, frank, plain, unbar **6** candid, create, direct, expand, gaping, honest, launch, unfold, unlock, unseal, unshut **7** artless, exposed, not shut, sincere, unblock, unclose **8** commence, outgoing, unbiased, unfasten, unlocked, unsealed

open-air 7 outdoor, outside
  Italian: 8 al fresco

openwork 3 net **4** lace **6** eyelet **7** lattice, Madeira, tracery **8** filigree

opera 5 score **7** musical **8** libretto
  comic: 5 buffa **7** comique
  glass: 9 lorgnette
  hat: 5 crush, gibus
  singer: 4 bass, diva **5** basso, buffa, buffo, tenor **7** soprano **8** baritone **9** contralto **10** coloratura, prima donna

12 mezzo soprano
  singular: 4 opus
  solo: 4 aria
  text: 8 libretto

operate 2 go **3** run **4** go in, work **6** behave, manage, open up **7** oversee, perform **8** function

opiate 4 dope **6** downer **7** anodyne **8** hypnotic, narcotic, nepenthe, sedative

opine *see* **7 presume**

opinion 4 idea, view **6** belief, notion, theory **7** surmise **8** estimate, judgment, thinking

opponent 3 foe **5** enemy, rival **8** resister

opportune *see* **5 lucky**

oppose *see* **6 resist**

opposite 5 other **6** facing **7** adverse, counter, reverse **8** contrary, converse

opposition *see* **5 enemy**

oppress *see* **6 burden**

opprobrium 5 shame **6** infamy **8** disgrace, dishonor

opt for *see* **6 choose**

optimistic 6 bright **7** hopeful, roseate

8 buoyed up, cheerful, sanguine

optimum *see* **4 best**

option 4 will **5** voice **6** choice, liking **8** decision, election, free will, pleasure

opulence *see* **6 wealth**

opus 4 work **5** piece **6** effort **7** attempt, product **8** creation

oracle, Oracle 4 sage, seer **5** augur, sibyl **6** wizard **7** adviser, diviner, prophet

oral 5 vocal **6** spoken, verbal, voiced **7** uttered

orangutan, orang-outang 3 ape **4** mias **5** satyr **6** primate

    native land: 6 Borneo **7** Sumatra

oration 4 talk **5** spiel **6** eulogy, sermon, speech **7** address, lecture, recital

orb *see* **6 sphere**

orbit 3 way **4** path **5** cycle, route, track **6** circle, course **7** channel, circuit

orchestra 3 pit **4** band **6** stalls **7** parquet **8** ensemble, parterre

orchestrate 5 adapt, score **7** arrange, compose

ordain 4 name, rule, will **5** elect, enact, frock **6** decree, invest **7** adjudge, appoint, command, dictate **8** delegate, deputize

ordeal *see* **8 calamity**

order 3 bid, law **4** body, book, calm, club, fiat, form, kind, rank, rule, sort, type **5** breed, caste, class, grade, group, guild, house, lodge, quiet, ukase **6** adjure, charge, decree, degree, demand, dictum, direct, engage, enjoin, family, status, stripe, system **7** bidding, caliber, call for, command, control, dictate, harmony, pattern, request, reserve, silence, society, station **8** alliance, division, instruct, neatness, position, purchase, standing, tidiness

ordinance *see* **3 law**

ordinarily 7 as a rule, usually **8** commonly, normally

ordinary 4 dull, so-so **5** usual **6** common, normal **7** average, humdrum, routine, typical

8 everyday, familiar, habitual, standard

ordnance depot 6 armory **7** arsenal

ore 3 tin **4** gold, iron, lead, paco, rock, zinc **5** metal **6** bronze, copper, galena, sulfur **7** halvans, mineral **8** aluminum, cinnabar, hematite
 deposit: 3 bed **4** lode, mine, vein **7** bonanza
 layer: 4 seam **5** stope
 worthless: 4 slag **5** dross, matte

oregano
 botanical name: 8 O vulgare, Origanum
 family: 4 mint

Oregon
 abbreviation: 2 OR **4** Oreg
 nickname: 6 Beaver **7** Webfoot
 capital: 5 Salem
 largest city: 8 Portland
 mountain: 5 Coast **6** Tacoma **7** Cascade, Klamath, Rainier
 highest point: 4 Hood
 lake: 6 Crater
 river: 5 Rogue, Snake **6** Powder **7** Klamath **8** Columbia, Umatilla

 sea/ocean: 7 Pacific
 physical feature:
  bay: 4 Coos
  wind: 7 Chinook

Orestes
 father: 9 Agamemnon
 mother: 12 Clytemnestra
 sister: 7 Electra **9** Iphigenia
 wife: 8 Hermione
 son: 9 Tisamenus
 killed: 9 Aegisthus **12** Clytemnestra
 pursued by: 6 Furies

organ 6 agency **7** journal, vehicle

organic 5 alive, quick **6** living **7** animate, natural, ordered, planned, unified **8** designed, physical

organism 4 cell **5** plant, whole **6** animal, entity, system **7** network, society **8** creature

organization 4 club, firm, sect **5** corps, group, order, party, union **6** design, league, making, outfit **7** company, forming, harmony, pattern, society **8** alliance, assembly, business, grouping, ordering

organize *see* **7** arrange

orgy **7** debauch, wassail **8** carousal **9** bacchanal

orient, the Orient **3** fix, set **4** Asia, find **6** locate, relate, square **7** situate **8** accustom **9** acclimate, reconcile **10** the Far East **11** Eastern Asia, familiarize

oriental **4** Arab, fine, Thai, Turk **5** Asian **6** bright, Indian, Korean **7** Asiatic, Chinese, Eastern, Iranian, shining **8** Japanese, lustrous, precious, superior **10** Vietnamese

animal: **4** zebu **5** rasse

building: **6** pagoda

dish: **5** pilau, pilaw **6** pilaff

drum: **6** tomtom

food fish: **3** tai

garment: **3** aba **6** sarong

inn: **4** Khan **5** serai **6** imaret **11** caravansary

laborer: **6** coolie

market: **3** suk, sug **4** souk **6** bazaar

nurse: **4** amah, ayah

prince: **4** amir, haja

sail: **6** lateen

sash: **3** obi

shrub: **3** tea **5** henna **8** oleander

wagon: **5** araba

weight: **2** mo **4** rotl, tael **5** catty, liang **6** cantar

orifice **3** gap, pit **4** hole, slit, slot, vent **5** cleft, inlet, mouth **6** cavity, cranny, hollow, lacuna, pocket, socket **7** crevice, fissure, opening, passage **8** aperture, entrance

origami

Japanese art of: **12** paper folding

origin **4** base, line, race, rise, root **5** agent, basis, birth, breed, cause, house, stock **6** author, family, father, ground, growth, mother, reason, source, spring, strain **7** creator, descent, genesis, lineage, taproot **8** ancestry, nativity, producer **9** beginning, inception

original **3** new **4** bold **5** basic, basis, first, fresh, novel **6** daring, primal, unique **7** example, initial, pattern, primary, seminal, strange, unusual **8** atypical, creative, earliest, germinal, primeval, singular, uncommon

Original Amateur Hour, The

host: **7** Ted Mack

Origin of Species, The
    author: 13 Charles Darwin

Orion
    form: 5 giant
    vocation: 6 hunter
    pursued: 8 Pleiades
    killed by: 7 Artemis
    became: 13 constellation

Oriya
    language family: 12 Indo-European
    branch: 11 Indo-Iranian
    group: 5 Indic
    spoken in: 5 (northern) India

Orkney Islands
    county seat: 8 Kirkwall
    country: 8 Scotland
    firth: 8 Pentland
    island: 3 Hay **6** Rousay, Sanday **7** Westray **8** Stronsay **14** South Ronaldsay
    largest city: 6 Pomona

Orlando
    author: 13 Virginia Woolf
    character: 5 Sasha **14** Nicholas Greene **28** Archduchess Harriet of Roumania, Marmaduke Bonthrop Shelmerdine

Orlando
    character in:
    11 As You Like It
    author: 11 Shakespeare
    novel by: 13 Virginia Woolf

Orlando Furioso
    author: 7 Ariosto
    character: 6 Rogero **7** Rinaldo **8** Agramant, Angelica, Rodomont **9** Bradamant **11** Charlemagne

Ormazd 10 Ahura Mazda **12** supreme deity
    religion: 14 Zoroastrianism

ormolu 5 alloy, brass, paste **6** bronze **7** gilding **8** ornament
    imitation of: 4 gold
    used to decorate: 5 clock **9** furniture

ornament *see* **8 decorate**

ornamental 4 gilt **5** fancy **6** chichi, rococo **10** decorative
    ball: 4 bead **6** pompom
    button: 4 stud
    grass: 4 neti
    loop: 5 picot
    metal: 5 niello

ornate *see* **5 fancy**

ornery *see* **7 grouchy**

ornithophobia
  fear of: 5 birds

ornithopod
  type of: 8 dinosaur
  member: 9 Iguanodon 10
  Edmontonia, Nodosaurus
  11 Anatosaurus,
  Polacanthus,
  Saurolophus,
  Scolosaurus, Stegosaurus
  12 Ankylosaurus,
  Camptosaurus,
  Lambeosaurus,
  Pisanosaurus 13
  Acanthopholis,
  Corythosaurus,
  Hypsilophodon,
  Palaeoscincus 14
  Thescelosaurus 15
  Parasaurolophus,
  Procheneosaurus 17
  Heterodontosaurus

orotund 4 full, rich 5 clear
  6 strong 7 pompous,
  ringing, vibrant 8
  resonant, sonorous

Orpheus
  vocation: 4 poet 8
   musician
  mother: 8 Calliope
  wife: 8 Eurydice
  member of: 9 Argonauts
  went into: 5 Hades
  killed by: 7 Maenads

ort 3 bit 5 crumb, dregs,
  scrap 6 morsel, refuse,
  trifle 7 remnant 8
  leavings, leftover

orthodox 5 fixed, pious,
  usual 6 devout, narrow 7
  limited, regular, routine 8
  accepted, approved,
  official, ordinary, standard

oryx 5 beisa 6 pickax 7
  gazelle, gemsbok 8
  antelope, leucoryx

oscillate 4 vary 5 pulse,
  swing, waver 6 change,
  seesaw 7 librate, pulsate,
  vibrate 8 hesitate

osier 3 rod 4 wand 5 salix,
  withe 6 willow 7
  dogwood, wilgers 9
  twigwithy
  use: 6 wicker 8 basketry

Osiris
  origin: 8 Egyptian
  god of: 4 dead, Nile
  judge/king of: 4 dead
  wife/sister: 4 Isis
  son: 5 Horus
  brother: 3 Set 4 Seth 5
   Horus
  killed by: 3 Set 4 Seth

Oslo
  capital of: 6 Norway
  former name: 11
   Christiania

ossify 6 harden **7** stiffen

ossuary 8 boneyard

ostensible *see* **8 apparent**

ostentatious 4 loud **5** gaudy, showy **6** flashy, florid, garish **7** pompous **8** affected, overdone

ostracize *see* **4 snub**

Otello
 also: 7 Othello
 opera by: 5 Verdi **7** Rossini

other 4 more **5** added, extra, spare **6** unlike **7** further, reverse **8** contrary, opposite

otherwise 5 if not **6** or else

otherworldly 7 sublime **8** heavenly

otiose *see* **4 lazy**

Ottawa
 capital of: 6 Canada
 early name: 6 Bytown
 river: 6 Ottawa, Rideau **8** Gatineau

ottoman, Ottoman 4 seat, Turk **5** couch, divan, stool **7** sultane, Turkish
 color: 3 red **9** vermilion
 governor: 3 bey, dey **5** pasha
 ruler: 5 Osman **8** Suleiman

Our Town
 author: 6 (Thornton) Wilder

oust 4 fire, sack **5** eject, evict, expel **6** banish, bounce, put out, remove, unseat **7** boot out, cashier, cast out, dismiss, kick out **8** throw out

out 2 ex **4** away **5** aloud, eject, forth, not in, passe **6** absent, begone, excuse, public **7** outside **8** exterior, external, revealed

outbreak 5 burst **7** display **8** epidemic, eruption, invasion, outburst

outburst 5 blast, burst **7** display, thunder **8** eruption, outbreak

outcast *see* **8 fugitive**

outcome *see* **6 result**

outdated 5 passe **7** antique **8** outmoded

outdo 3 top **4** beat, best **5** excel, worst **6** better, defeat, exceed, outfox, outwit **7** eclipse, outplay, outrank, surpass **8** outclass, outshine, outstrip, overcome

outdoor market 5 agora **6** bazaar

outer 6 distal, remote **7** extreme, farther, outside, outward, without **8** exterior, external, outlying

Outer Mongolia *see* **8 Mongolia**

outfit 3 fit, rig **4** gear **5** array, dress, equip, getup, habit, rig up **6** clothe, supply **7** costume, furnish **8** ensemble, wardrobe

outgoing *see* **6 genial**

outing 4 hike, ride, spin, tour, trip, walk **5** drive, jaunt, tramp **6** airing, junket, ramble **7** holiday

outlandish *see* **7 strange**

outlast *see* **5 outdo**

outlaw *see* **6 forbid**

outlay 3 fee **4** cost **5** outgo, price **6** charge **7** expense, payment **8** spending

outlet 3 way **4** door, duct, exit, gate, path, vent **5** means **6** avenue, egress, escape, portal **7** channel, gateway, opening, passage

outline 4 plot **5** brief, trace **6** digest, limits, resume, review **7** contour, diagram, profile, summary, tracing **8** abstract, synopsis

outlook 4 view **5** scene, sight, vista **6** aspect, chance **7** picture, promise **8** attitude, forecast, panorama, prospect

outmoded *see* **7 archaic**

out of hand 4 wild **5** rowdy **6** unruly

out of line 6 unruly

out of one's head *see* **5 crazy**

out of operation 4 dead, down **8** inactive

out of sorts *see* **7 grouchy**

out-of-towner 7 tourist, visitor

outpace *see* **5 outdo**

outpouring 6 deluge **7** barrage, gushing, outflow **8** effusion

output 4 crop, gain, take **5** yield **6** profit **7** harvest, produce, product, reaping, turnout **8** proceeds

outrage 4 evil, gall, rile **5** anger, shock, wrong **6** arouse, enrage, insult, madden, offend, ruffle **7** affront, incense, provoke, steam up **8** atrocity

outre 8 improper

outreach 6 exceed **7** surpass

outright *see* **5 total**

outrival *see* **5 outdo**

outset 4 dawn **5** birth, start **7** dawning

outshine *see* **5 outdo**

outside 4 case, face, skin **5** alien, faint, outer **6** facade, remote, sheath, slight **7** coating, distant, foreign, obscure, outdoor, outward, strange, surface **8** covering, exterior, external, outdoors

outsider 5 alien **7** outcast **8** onlooker, stranger

outskirts 3 rim **4** edge **6** limits, verges **7** borders, fringes, margins, suburbs

outspoken *see* **6 honest**

outstanding *see* **7 notable**

outstrip 4 pass **6** exceed, outrun **7** outpace, surpass

outward 5 outer **7** evident, outside, surface, visible **8** apparent, exterior, external, manifest

outweigh 6 exceed **7** eclipse, surpass **8** override

outwit *see* **5 trick**

ouzo
    type: 7 liqueur
    origin: 6 Greece

oval 5 ovate, ovoid **6** curved, ovular **7** obovate, oviform, rounded

ovation 6 cheers, homage, hurrah, hurray, huzzah **7** acclaim, fanfare, tribute **8** applause, cheering

oven 3 umu **4** kiln, oast **5** baker, range, stove **6** hearth **7** broiler, chamber, kitchen, roaster
    clay: 7 tandoor
    fork: 7 fruggan, fruggin
    mop: 6 scovel

over 3 too **4** also, anew, done, else, gone, past **5** above, again, ended, extra, often **6** afresh, bygone, lapsed, no more, to boot **7** at an end, elapsed, expired, settled, surplus **8** finished, in excess, once more, too great

overall 5 total **6** entire **7** general **8** complete, long-term, sweeping

overbearing *see* **8 dogmatic**

overcast 4 dark, dull, gray, hazy **5** foggy, misty, murky **6** cloudy, dreary, gloomy, leaden **7** sunless **8** lowering

overcharge 3 gyp, pad **4** rook, skin, soak **5** bleed, cheat, gouge, stick, sting, usury **6** extort, fleece **7** exploit

overcoat 3 mac **5** parka **6** duster, poncho, raglan, tabard, ulster **7** oilskin, paletot, topcoat **8** burberry, mackinaw

overcome *see* **6 defeat**

overdo 4 gild **6** expand **7** amplify, magnify, overact **8** overplay

overdue 4 late, slow **5** tardy **7** belated, delayed, past due **8** dilatory

overflow *see* **6 excess**

overgarment 4 cape, coat, robe **5** cloak, habit, parka, shawl, smock **6** blazer, blouse, duster, jacket, kimono, mantle, poncho **7** sweater, topcoat, wrapper **8** cardigan, raincoat

overhang 3 jut **4** eave **5** bulge, drape, eaves, jetty **6** beetle, impend, sadden, shelve **7** project, suspend **8** protrude, threaten

overhaul *see* **8 renovate**

overhead 3 nut **4** atop, roof **5** above, aloft, on top,

upper **6** upward **7** ceiling, topmost **8** superior

overlay 4 coat **5** cover, layer **6** carpet, veneer **7** blanket, coating **8** covering

overload *see* **9 overwhelm**

overlook 4 miss, omit, skip **6** excuse, forget, give on, ignore, pass up, slight, survey **7** forgive, let ride, neglect **8** leave out, pass over

overly 3 too **4** very **6** highly, unduly **7** acutely, too much **8** severely, to a fault, unfairly

overpass 4 span **6** bridge

override 5 crush, quash **7** reverse **8** set aside

overrule 4 deny, veto **5** annul, eject, repel, waive **6** cancel, refuse, reject, revoke **7** dismiss, nullify, outvote **8** override, overturn, preclude, throw out

overrun 4 loot, raid, sack **5** choke **6** deluge, engulf, infest, invade **7** despoil, pillage, plunder, surplus **8** inundate

overseas, oversea 5 alien

6 abroad, exotic **7** foreign **8** external

oversee *see* **6 direct**

overshadow **3** fog **4** hide, mask, veil **5** cover, dwarf, shade **6** darken, screen, shroud **7** conceal, eclipse, obscure **8** outshine

overshoe **3** gum **4** boot **6** arctic, gaiter, galosh, patten, rubber **7** galoshe

overshoot **4** pass **6** exceed, go over **8** go beyond

oversight *see* **7 mistake**

overstep **6** exceed **7** violate

overt *see* **7 obvious**

overtake **4** go by, pass **5** catch, reach **6** befall, gain on **7** run down **8** approach, overhaul

overtax *see* **7 exhaust**

over the hill **3** old **4** aged **5** aging **7** elderly

overthrow *see* **6 defeat**

overtone **3** hue **4** hint **5** drift **8** coloring, innuendo

overture *see* **7 gesture**

overturn *see* **7 conquer**

overweening **5** bossy, cocky, pushy **6** brassy **7** haughty, pompous **8** arrogant, egoistic

overweight *see* **3 fat**

overwhelm **4** beat, bury **5** crush, quash, quell, swamp **6** defeat, engulf **7** conquer, overrun, stagger **8** bowl over, confound, inundate, vanquish

overwrought **4** wild **5** riled **6** touchy, uneasy **7** excited, nervous, ruffled **8** agitated, frenzied, inflamed, wild-eyed, worked up

ovule **3** egg, nit **4** germ, ovum **6** embryo **7** seedlet

ovum **3** egg **4** cell, germ, seed **5** spore **6** gamete **8** oosphere

owed **3** due **5** owing **6** unpaid

own **4** avow, have, hold, keep, tell **5** admit, allow, grant, yield **6** assent, concur, retain **7** concede, possess, private **8** disclose, maintain, personal

own up to *see* **5 admit**

ox **3** oaf **4** bull, clod, musk, urus, zebu **5** aiver, beast, bison, gayal, steer **6** auroch, bantin, bovine **7** banteng, buffalo **10** clodhopper

Cambodian: 7 Kouprey, Kouproh

Celebesian: 3 goa, noa **4** anoa

extinct: 4 urus **7** aurochs

family: 7 bovidae

genus: 3 bos

Indian: 4 gaur

Paul Bunyan's: 4 Babe
   color: 4 blue

team: 4 yoke

Tibetan: 3 yak

wild: 3 ure **4** anoa

young: 4 stot **5** stirk

oxide 8 compound

   calcium: 4 calx, lime

   iron: 4 rust

   sodium: 4 soda

oxidize 4 burn, char, rust **7** corrode

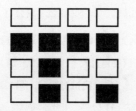 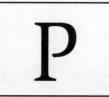 

pa 3 dad, paw, pop **4** papa **5** daddy, pater **6** father
mate: 2 ma

pace 4 clip, flow, gait, rate, step, walk **5** speed **6** motion stride **7** saunter **8** momentum, velocity

Pacelli, Eugenio Maria Giuseppe Giovanni 8 Pope Pius (XII)

pachyderm 5 hippo, rhino **8** elephant, ungulate
characteristic: 4 tusk **5** ivory, trunk
prehistoric: 7 mammoth **8** mastodon

pacific 4 calm **5** quiet, still **6** gentle, placid, serene **8** dovelike, peaceful, tranquil

pack 3 box, jam, kit, lot, mob, set, tie **4** bevy, bind, cram, fill, heap, herd, load, mass **5** crowd, flock, group, horde, swarm **6** bundle, gaggle, throng **7** cluster

package 3 box, kit **4** case, pack, wrap **6** bundle

pact 4 bond **6** treaty **7** compact **8** alliance, contract, covenant

pad 3 mat **4** fill **5** stuff **6** blow up, fatten, tablet **7** bolster, cushion, inflate, protect, puff out

padre 6 cleric, father, priest **8** chaplain

paean 6 anthem, eulogy **7** hosanna
form: 4 hymn, song
characteristic: 6 joyful

pagan 7 atheist, heathen, infidel **8** idolator

page 3 boy, lad **4** beep, call, girl, leaf **5** folio, groom, sheet, youth **6** knight, number, summon **7** callboy, contact **8** announce
blank: 7 flyleaf
left-hand: 5 verso
right-hand: 5 recto

pageant 4 pomp, rite, show

6 parade, ritual **7** display
8 ceremony

Pagliacci, I
  also: 9 The Clowns
  opera by: 11 Leoncavallo
  character: 5 Canio,
    Nedda, Tonio **6** Silvio

Pago Pago
  capital of: 5 (American)
    Samoa

Pahlavi *see* **4 Iran**

pain 3 vex, woe **4** ache,
gall, hurt, pang, rile **5**
agony, annoy, grief,
smart, sting, throb, worry
6 aching, grieve, misery,
sadden, sorrow **7** anguish,
hurting, malaise, sadness,
torment

pain in the neck 4 bane **6**
bother **7** torment **8**
headache, nuisance

painstaking 5 fussy **7**
careful, earnest, finicky,
precise **8** diligent,
exacting, thorough

paint 4 coat, daub, draw,
limn, swab, tint **5** brush,
color, cover, rouge, shade,
stain **6** depict, enamel,
makeup, opaque, sketch **7**
pigment, portray
  tool: 5 brush, easel, knife

6 canvas, roller, sponge
7 palette **8** spraygun

pair 3 duo **4** dyad, team **5**
brace, match, unite **6**
couple **7** combine, match
up, pair off

Pakistan
  capital: 9 Islamabad
  largest city: 7 Karachi
  division: 4 Sind **6** Bengal,
    Punjab **8** Peshawar
    empire: 5 Gupta,
      Mogul **7** British
  mountain ranges: 5 Pamir
    9 Himalayan, Hindu
    Kush, Karakorum
  highest point: 12
    Godwin-Austen (K2),
    Godwin-Austin
  river: 5 Indus, Kabul **6**
    Ganges
  sea: 7 Arabian
  physical feature:
    delta: 6 Ganges
    desert: 4 Sind, Thal,
     Thar
    mountain pass: 6
     Khyber
  food:
    bread: 8 chappati
    dish: 5 kebab, pilaf

pal *see* **4 chum**

palace 5 villa **6** castle **7**
chateau, mansion

8 hacienda
French: 6 palais
Italian: 7 palazzo

palatable 5 tasty **6** savory **8** pleasant

palatial 4 posh, rich **5** grand, noble, plush, regal, ritzy, showy **6** swanky **7** elegant, opulent, stately **8** imposing, splendid

pale 3 pen, wan **4** fold, post **5** ashen, light, pasty, white **6** anemic, sallow, whiten **7** deathly, ghastly

Palermo
capital of: 6 Sicily

Palestine *see* **6 Israel**

palisade 5 close, fence **7** bulwark, rampart **8** stockade

pall 4 cloy, haze, sate **5** gloom **6** shadow, sicken **7** dimness **8** darkness

Pallas *see* **6 Athena**

pallid 3 wan **4** blah, dull, pale **5** ashen, bland, pasty, vapid **6** peaked, sallow **7** ghostly

Palmetto State
nickname of: 13 South Carolina

palpable *see* **7 obvious**

palpitate 4 beat **5** pound, shake, throb **7** tremble, vibrate

palsied 7 quaking, shaking, spastic

paltry 4 poor, puny **6** measly, shabby **7** trivial **8** inferior, picayune, piddling, trifling

pamper 5 humor, spoil **6** coddle, cosset **7** cater to, indulge **8** give in to

pamphlet 5 tract **6** folder **7** booklet, leaflet **8** brochure, bulletin, circular

pan 3 boo, map, mug, pot **4** face, hiss **6** kisser **8** ridicule, saucepot

Pan
also: 7 Sinoeis
origin: 5 Greek
form combined: 3 man **4** goat
god of: 6 flocks **7** forests **8** pastures **9** shepherds
father: 4 Zeus **6** Hermes
loved: 4 Echo **5** Pitys **6** Syrinx
invented: 5 pipes **6** syrinx
corresponds to: 6 Faunus

panacea 6 elixir **7** cure-all, nostrum

panache 4 dash, elan, tuft 5 flair, plume, style, verve

Panama
  capital/largest city: 10 Panama City
  mountain: 6 Darien
  highest point: 4 Baru 8 Chiriqui
  lake: 5 Gatun 6 Bayano
  sea/ocean: 7 Pacific 9 Caribbean
  island: 5 Coiba, Pearl 7 San Blas
  physical feature:
    dam: 5 Gatun
    gulf: 6 Darien, Panama 7 San Blas
    isthmus: 6 Darien, Panama 7 San Blas
  food:
    meat: 6 tazajo
    soup: 8 sancocho

pancake 5 blini, crepe, latke 6 blintz, makeup 7 fritter, hotcake 8 flapjack

pancreas
  produces: 7 insulin

pandemic 4 rife 7 rampant 8 epidemic

pandemonium *see* 5 **chaos**

pander, panderer 4 mack, pimp 7 hustler 8 procurer

Pandora
  form: 10 first woman
  created by: 10 Hephaestus
  presented to: 10 Epimetheus
  given by gods: 3 box
    box contained: 4 hope 5 evils

panegyric 6 eulogy, homage, praise 7 tribute 8 citation, encomium

panel 4 jury, pane 5 board, group, piece 6 insert 7 divider 8 bulkhead

pang 4 ache, pain 5 pinch, smart, stick, sting 6 stitch, twinge

panhandle 3 beg, bum 5 mooch 6 hustle 7 solicit

panic 5 alarm, dread, go ape, scare 6 fright, horror, terror 7 anxiety 8 affright, hysteria

panorama 5 scene, vista 6 survey 7 diorama, picture, scenery, tableau 8 long view, overview, prospect

pansy 5 Viola

pant 4 blow, gasp, huff, puff 6 wheeze

panther 3 cat 6 cougar 7 leopard

pantry 5 ambry, store 6 closet, galley 8 cupboard, scullery

pants 5 jeans **6** denims, shorts, slacks **7** drawers, panties **8** breeches, britches, knickers, trousers

pap 3 rot **4** bosh, junk, mash, mush, pulp, tosh **5** gruel, paste **6** cereal, drivel, Pablum, trivia **7** rubbish

papa 2 pa **3** dad, doc, paw, pop **5** daddy, poppy **6** father, priest
  mate: 4 mama

papal 9 apostolic, of the pope **10** pontifical

paper 4 bond, deed, news, opus, pulp **5** daily, draft, essay, stock, theme **6** record, report, weekly **7** article, gazette, journal, monthly, tabloid, writing **8** document

Papua New Guinea
  formerly: 16 British New Guinea
  capital: 11 Port Moresby
  island: 6 Misima **10** New Britain
  archipelago: 8 Bismarck
  sea: 5 Coral **7** Solomon
  strait: 6 Torres

papyrus 4 pith, reed **5** paper, sedge **6** scroll **7** bulrush **8** document
  accordion pleated: 6 orihon
  genus: 7 Cyperus
  origin: 5 Egypt

par 5 level, usual **6** normal, parity **7** average, balance, the norm **8** equality, evenness, identity, sameness, standard

parable 4 myth, tale **5** fable, story **6** homily, legend **8** allegory, apologue, folk tale

parade 4 line, pomp, show **5** array, march, strut **6** flaunt, review, string **7** caravan, cortege, display, show off

paradigm *see* **7 paragon**

paradise 3 joy **4** Eden **5** bliss **6** heaven, utopia **7** delight, ecstasy, nirvana, rapture **8** pleasure

Paradise Lost
  author: 6 (John) Milton

Paradise Regained
  author: 6 (John) Milton

paradox 5 poser **6** enigma, oddity, puzzle, riddle **7** anomaly

paragon 4 norm **5** ideal, model **6** symbol

7 example, pattern **8** paradigm, standard

Paraguay
  capital/largest city: 8 Asuncion
  highest point: 9 Cerro Pero **14** Cerro Tres Kandu
  lake: 4 Vera, Ypoa
  river: 5 Negro, Plata **6** Parana **8** Paraguay
  island:
    floating island: 8 camalote
  physical feature:
    falls: 6 Guaira
    plains: 5 Chaco
  place:
    dam: 6 Itaipu
  feature:
    bird: 6 toucan
    clothing: 6 poncho **7** rebozos
    dance: 7 Sante Fe
    fish: 7 piranha
  food:
    drink: 4 cana, mate **5** mosto **6** terere
    soup: 8 bori-bori

parallel 4 akin, like, same, twin **5** alike, equal, match **7** be alike, similar **8** analogue, likeness, relation

parallelogram 6 square **7** diamond, rhombus

paralyze 4 stun **6** benumb, deaden, disarm, freeze, weaken **7** cripple, destroy, disable, stupefy

paramount *see* **7 supreme**

paramour 3 man **4** doxy **5** lover, Romeo **6** gigolo **7** Don Juan **8** Casanova, fancy man, lothario, loverboy, mistress

paranoid 4 wary **7** deluded

parapet 7 bulwark, rampart **8** abutment, palisade

paraphernalia 3 rig **4** gear **5** stuff **6** tackle, things **7** regalia **8** fittings, supplies, utensils

paraphrase 5 recap **6** rehash, reword **8** rephrase

parasite 5 leech **6** beggar, loafer **7** moocher, shirker, slacker **8** deadbeat

parasol 5 shade **6** shadow **7** roundel **8** umbrella
  mushroom: 7 lepiota

parboil 4 boil **5** scald **6** blanch **7** precook

parcel 3 lot **4** bale, pack, part, plot **5** allot **6** bundle, divide **7** dole out, package, portion, section, segment **8** allocate, dispense, disperse, division, fraction, fragment

parch 4 bake, burn, char, sear **5** dry up, singe **6** dry out, scorch, sun-dry, wither **7** blister, shrivel

parchment 6 scroll, vellum **7** papyrus **8** goatskin

pardon 5 grace, mercy **6** excuse **7** absolve, amnesty, forgive, indulge, release, set free **8** overlook, reprieve

pare *see* **5** prune

parent 3 dam **4** sire **5** model **6** father, mother **7** creator **8** ancestor, original

parenthetical 5 aside **6** braced, casual **8** inserted

pariah 5 exile, rover, stray **6** outlaw, roamer **7** outcast **8** vagabond, wanderer

Paris
  capital of: 6 France
  city planner: 9 Haussmann
  island: 7 (Ile) St Louis **6** (Ile de) la Cite
  nickname: 11 city of light
  river: 5 Seine
  subway: 5 Metro
  university: 8 Sorbonne

Paris
  father: 5 Priam
  mother: 6 Hecuba
  brother: 6 Hector **9** Polydorus
  sister: 9 Cassandra
  abducted: 5 Helen
  killed by: 11 Philoctetes

parish 4 fold **5** flock, shire **7** diocese, section **8** brethren, district

parity 7 balance **8** equality, sameness

park 4 lawn **5** field, green, grove, woods **6** common, meadow **7** grounds **8** preserve, woodland

parlance 4 talk **5** idiom, lingo **6** speech

parley 4 talk **6** confab, powwow, summit **7** council, meeting, palaver

parliament 4 diet **5** court, house, junta **6** fan-tan, senate, sevens **7** cabinet, council **8** assembly, congress
  British: 5 (House of) Lords **7** (House of) Commons
  Communist: 6 Soviet **9** politburo, presidium

German: 9 Bundesrat, Bundestag, Bolksraad
Greek: 5 Boule
Icelandic: 7 Althing
Israeli: 7 Knesset **8** Knesseth
Scandinavian: 7 Lagting, Riksdag **8** Lagthing, Storting
Spanish: 6 Cortes

parlor 5 salon **6** saloon **8** best room

parochial 5 local, petty, small **6** church **7** insular, limited **8** regional

parody 5 mimic **6** satire **7** lampoon, takeoff **8** satirize, travesty

paroxysm 3 fit **5** spasm, spell **7** seizure

parrot 3 ape **4** bird, echo, lory **5** macaw, mimer, mimic **6** chorus, monkey **7** copycat, imitate **8** cockatoo, imitator, parakeet

parry *see* **5 dodge**
Parsifal
    opera by: 6 Wagner

parsimonious 5 close, tight **6** frugal, saving, stingy **7** miserly, sparing, thrifty

parson *see* **6 priest**
    French: 4 abbe, cure

part 2 go **3** bit, job **4** care, chip, duty, hunk, item, open, rend, role, slit, task, tear, unit **5** break, chore, crumb, guise, leave, piece, place, scrap, sever, shard, share, sherd, shred, slice, split **6** branch, charge, cleave, depart, detach, detail, divide, go away, member, morsel, region, sector, set out, sliver, sunder **7** concern, cutting, disjoin, element, portion, push off, section, segment, snippet **8** fraction, fragment

partake 5 enjoy, savor, share **6** join in, sample **7** share in **8** engage in

partial 6 biased, unfair, unjust **7** limited, slanted **8** one-sided, partisan

participate 5 share **6** join in **7** partake, perform **8** engage in, take part

particle 3 bit, jot **4** atom, iota, mite, snip, whit **5** crumb, grain, scrap, shred, speck, trace **6** morsel, tittle, trifle **7** granule, modicum, smidgen

particular **4** sole **5** exact, fixed, fussy, picky **6** single, strict **7** express, finicky, special **8** concrete, definite, distinct, explicit, personal, separate, specific

partition **4** wall **5** allot, fence, panel **6** assign, divide, screen **7** barrier, deal out, divider

partner **3** aid, pal **4** ally, chum, mate **5** aider, buddy **6** fellow, friend **7** comrade **8** confrere, sidekick

partridge
   group of: **5** covey

parturition **5** birth **8** delivery

party **2** do **4** band, bash, body, crew, fete, gang, team, unit, wing **5** corps, force, group, squad **6** affair, league, soiree **7** accused, blow out, company, coterie, faction **8** alliance

party-pooper **4** drag

parvenu **4** snob **6** nobody **7** upstart **8** arrivist, mushroom

Pasiphae
   father: **6** Helios

   mother: **7** Perseis

   husband: **5** Minos

   daughter: **7** Ariadne, Phaedra **9** Acacallis

   became enamored of: **4** (Cretan) bull

   mother of: **8** Minotaur

pass **2** go **3** cap, die, end, gap, hit, top, use, way **4** best, busy, fill, flow, give, go by, go on, hand, kick, lane, meet, toss **5** gorge, gulch, leave, outdo, route, throw **6** affirm, canyon, convey, decree, depart, elapse, employ, engage, exceed, expend, expire, permit, ratify, ravine, slip by, strait, take up **7** pathway, present, proceed, qualify, satisfy, slide by, surpass **8** transfer, transmit

pass away **3** die **6** depart, expire, pass on, perish **7** decease **8** pass over

passe *see* **8 outdated**

passenger **4** fare **5** rider **8** commuter, stowaway, traveler, wayfarer

passing **5** brief, death, dying **6** demise, fickle **7** decease, passage, pass on **8** adequate, fleeting

passion 4 fire, idol, love, lust, rage, urge **5** ardor, flame, heart **6** desire, fervor, hunger, thirst **7** craving, ecstasy, emotion, feeling, rapture

passive *see* **6 docile**

pass muster 2 do **5** serve **6** answer **8** be enough

pass over 6 ignore, slight **7** neglect **8** overlook

pass up 4 miss **6** ignore, refuse

password 3 key **4** word **6** by word, slogan **7** keyword, tessera

past 2 by **4** gone **5** ended, prior **6** beyond, bygone, former, gone by **7** ancient, earlier, elapsed, expired, history, long ago, through **8** departed, finished, previous

pasta 4 orzo, ziti **6** elbows, shells **7** gnocchi, lasagna, pastina, ravioli, rotelli **8** ditalini, linguini, macaroni, rigatoni, tortelli
ingredient: 3 egg **5** flour

pasta sauce 4 ragu **5** pesto, salsa **6** tomato **7** alfredo **8** mushroom, pomodoro **9** bolognese, carbonara

past due 4 late **5** tardy **7** belated, overdue

paste 3 gum, hit **4** glue, seal **5** affix, stick **6** attach, cement **8** adhesive, mucilage

pastel 3 dim **4** pale, soft **5** chalk, faded, faint, light, muted **6** crayon

pastime 3 fun **4** game, play **5** hobby, sport

past one's prime 3 old **4** aged **5** aging **7** elderly

pastor *see* **6 priest**

pastoral 5 rural **6** rustic **7** bucolic, idyllic **8** arcadian, clerical, priestly

pasty *see* **4 pale**

pat 3 apt, dab, hit, pet, rap, tap **4** cake, daub, easy, glib, slap **5** ready, slick **6** fondle, simple, smooth, stroke **7** fitting, perfect, precise, reliant

patch 3 fix, lot **4** area, darn, mend, plot, spot, zone **5** field, sew up, tract **6** garden, repair, stitch **7** expanse, stretch **8** clearing, insignia

pate 3 pie **4** brow, head **5** brain, crown, paste,

pastry, patty, skull **6** noddle, noggin, noodle

patella
bone of: 7 kneecap

patent 4 bald, bold, open, rank **5** clear, gross, overt, plain **6** permit **7** decided, evident, license, obvious **8** apparent, distinct, flagrant

paternal 4 kind **6** tender **8** fatherly, parental, vigilant, watchful

path 3 way **4** lane, plan, road, walk **5** byway, means, orbit, route, track, trail **6** access, course **7** pathway, process, walkway **8** approach

pathetic 3 sad **6** moving, rueful, woeful **7** doleful, piteous, pitiful **8** dolorous, grievous, pitiable, poignant, touching, wretched

pathogen 3 bug **4** germ **5** virus **7** microbe **8** bacillus

pathophobia
fear of: 7 disease

pathos 3 woe **5** agony **6** misery **7** anguish, feeling, sadness **8** distress

patient 4 case **6** dogged,

serene **8** composed, diligent, enduring

patio 4 deck **5** lanai, porch **6** piazza **7** terrace, veranda

patois 5 argot, idiom, lingo **6** jargon **7** dialect

pat on the back 6 praise **7** plaudit

patriarch 5 elder, ruler **6** father, leader, old man **8** male head

patrician 4 lord, peer **5** noble **6** lordly **7** genteel, stately **8** highborn, imposing, well-bred

Patroclus
friend: 8 Achilles
killed by: 6 Hector

patrol 5 guard, scout, watch **6** ranger, sentry, warden **7** protect **8** sentinel

patron 5 angel, buyer **6** backer, client, friend, helper **7** shopper, sponsor, visitor **8** attender, customer, financer, promoter, upholder

patronize 5 humor **6** shop at **7** buy from **8** deal with, frequent

patsy 4 dupe, pawn, tool **7** cat's-paw, fall guy

patter 3 pad, pat, rap, tap **4** beat, drum **5** pound, thrum **6** tattoo **7** rat-a-tat, spatter, tapping **8** drumming, sprinkle

pattern 4 copy, form, mold, plan **5** draft, guide, ideal, mimic, model, motif, shape **6** design, follow, sample **7** emulate, example, fashion, imitate, paragon

Patton
    director: 9 (Franklin) Schaffner
    cast: 5 (George C) Scott, (Michael) Strong, (Stephen) Young **6** (Karl) Malden

paucity *see* **7 poverty**

Paul
    former name: 4 Saul
    birthplace: 6 Tarsus
    companion: 4 John **5** Silas **7** Timothy **8** Barnabas
    conversion place: 8 (road to) Damascus
    wrote: 8 epistles

paunch 3 gut, pot **5** belly, tummy **7** abdomen, stomach **8** potbelly

pauper 6 beggar **7** almsman **8** bankrupt, indigent

pause 3 gap **4** halt, rest, stop, wait **5** break, cease, delay, let up **6** hiatus **7** interim, time out **8** break off, hesitate, interval

pavement 4 slab **5** brick **6** cement, hearth, street, tarmac **7** asphalt, cobbles, macadam **8** concrete, driveway, sidewalk

pavilion 4 tent, ward, wing **5** arbor, kiosk **6** gazebo **7** pergola

paw 2 pa **3** dad, pop, toe **4** feel, foot, grab, hand, maul, mitt, papa **5** daddy, touch **6** caress, clutch, father, handle, scrape **7** rough up

pawn 4 bond, dupe, hock, tool **5** agent, patsy **6** flunky, lackey, pledge, puppet **8** henchman

Pax
    origin: 5 Roman
    goddess of: 5 peace
    corresponds to: 5 Irene

pay 3 fee **4** foot, give, meet **5** grant, honor, remit, wages, yield **6** ante up, chip in, extend, income, profit, render, return, salary, settle **7** benefit, cough up, proffer, stipend **8** earnings, shell out

payoff 3 end **4** soap **5** bribe, graft **6** climax, crunch, finale, finish, grease, payola, result, upshot, windup **7** outcome **8** clincher

pea 5 Pisum **12** Pisum sativum

peace 4 calm, ease **5** amity, truce **6** accord, repose **7** concord, content, entente, harmony **8** serenity
   Hebrew: 6 shalom
   Russian: 3 mir

peace of mind 8 security, serenity

peach 13 Prunus persica

Peach State
   nickname of: 7 Georgia

peachy 4 fine, keen **5** dandy, super, swell

peacock
   group of: 6 muster

peak *see* **6 summit**

peaked 3 ill, wan **4** lean, pale, thin, weak **5** ashen, drawn, gaunt, spare **6** ailing, infirm, pallid, pointy, sallow, sickly, skinny **7** haggard, tapered

peal 3 din **4** boom, clap, ring, roar, roll, toll **5** blare, blast, clang, crack, crash, knell **6** rumble **7** clangor, resound, ringing

peanut 3 pod, tot **4** puny, seed **5** petty, small **6** goober, legume, measly, paltry **8** earthpea

Peanuts
   creator: 7 (Charles) Schultz

pear 5 Pyrus **13** Pyrus communis

pearl
   grows in: 6 oyster
   genus: 8 Pinctada
   composed of: 5 nacre
   quality: 6 luster
   type: 8 cultured, Oriental (saltwater) **9** simulated

Pearly Gates 7 heaven

peasant 4 boor, esne, peon, serf **5** churl, knave, yokel **6** farmer, rustic, worker **7** laborer, lowlife, villein
   Arabic: 6 fellah
   French: 6 paysan
   Indian: 4 ryot **5** kisan **6** raiyat
   Irish: 4 kern
   Russian: 5 kulak **6** muzhik
   Scottish: 6 cotter

peccadillo 4 slip **5** lapse **6** boo-boo **7** blunder, faux pas, misdeed, misstep

peck 3 pat, rap, tap **4** buss, gobs, lots, mess **5** batch, bunch, heaps, scads, thump **6** nibble, oodles, pick at, strike, stroke, worlds **8** light jab

peculiar *see* **7 strange**

pecuniary 6 fiscal **8** economic, monetary

pedagogue, pedagog 5 tutor **7** teacher **8** academic, educator

pedantic 5 fussy **7** bookish, finicky, pompous **8** academic, didactic

peddle 4 hawk, sell, vend **7** deal out **8** dispense

pedestal 4 base, foot **6** bottom, plinth

pedestrian 6 walker **7** mundane, prosaic, tedious, trekker **8** mediocre, ordinary, stroller

pedigree 4 line **6** family, strain **7** descent, lineage **8** ancestry

peek 3 pry **4** peep, peer **5** watch **6** glance **7** glimpse

peel 4 bark, hull, husk, pare, rind, skin, tear, zest **5** flake, scale, strip **6** remove **7** undress

peep 4 peek, peer, skim, word **5** cheep, chirp, tweet **6** emerge, glance, murmur, mutter, squeak **7** chirrup, glimpse, peeping, peer out, twitter, whimper, whisper

peer 4 gape, gaze, look, lord, peek, peep **5** equal, noble, stare **6** appear, emerge, squint **7** compeer

peerless 7 supreme **8** flawless

peeve *see* **8 irritate**

peewee 4 tiny **5** dwarf, small, teeny **6** little, midget, minute

peg 3 pin **4** nail **5** cleat, dowel, spike, thole **6** skewer, toggle **8** fastener, tholepin

Pegasus
form: 5 horse
characteristic: 6 winged
mother: 6 Medusa

pejorative 7 mocking **8** debasing, negative, scornful

Peking *see* **7 Beijing**

Peleus
brother: 7 Telamon
wife: 6 Thetis **8** Antigone
son: 8 Achilles
daughter: 8 Polydora

Pelican State
  nickname of: 9 Louisiana

pellet 3 pea **4** ball, bead, drop, pill **5** pearl, stone **6** pebble **7** globule

pell-mell 6 rashly **7** hastily **8** slapdash

pelt 3 fur, hit, rap **4** belt, coat, hide, skin, sock **5** pound, punch, whack **6** batter, buffet, fleece, pepper, pummel, strike, thrash, thwack **7** clobber

pen 3 sty **4** cage, coop, crib, fold **5** draft, hutch, pound, quill, stall, write **6** corral, scrawl **7** compose, paddock **8** scribble

penalty 4 fine **7** forfeit **8** handicap

penates
  protectors of: 4 home
  companions: 5 lares

penchant 4 bent, bias, gift, turn **5** fancy, flair, knack, taste **6** liking, relish **7** leaning **8** affinity, fondness, tendency

pendant 3 fob **5** charm **6** locket

pending 8 imminent

pendulous 7 hanging,

pendent **8** dangling, drooping, swinging

Penelope
  husband: 8 Odysseus **9** Telegonus
  fended off: 7 suitors

penetrate 3 get **4** bore **5** catch, enter, prick **6** decode, fathom, invade, pierce, seep in **7** cut into, discern, pervade, unravel **8** decipher, perceive, permeate, puncture, saturate, traverse

penguin 8 great auk

peninsula 4 cape **5** point **8** headland

penitent 5 sorry **6** rueful **7** atoning, devotee, pilgrim **8** contrite

penitentiary 3 can, pen **4** jail, stir **5** joint **6** prison **7** slammer **8** big house

pennant 4 flag, jack **6** banner, burgee, colors, ensign, pennon **7** bunting **8** ensignia, streamer

penniless *see* **4 poor**

Pennsylvania
  abbreviation: 2 PA **4** Penn
  nickname: 8 Keystone
  capital: 10 Harrisburg

largest city: 12 Philadelphia

mountain: 6 Pocono **9** Allegheny **11** Appalachian

highest point: 5 Davis

lake: 4 Erie

river: 4 Ohio **8** Delaware **9** Allegheny **11** Monongahela, Susquehanna

sea: 8 Atlantic

island: 9 Three Mile

feature:
   bell: 7 Liberty

penny 3 sum **4** cent **5** cheap, pence **6** copper, stiver **7** trivial

penny-pinching 5 close, tight **6** stingy **7** miserly

pensee 7 thought

pension 5 grant **6** income, retire **7** annuity, stipend, subsidy

pensive 3 sad **5** grave **6** dreamy, musing, solemn, somber **7** serious, wistful

pent-up 7 boxed-up, checked, stifled **8** hedged-in, held back, penned-in, penned-up, reined in, stored-up

penurious *see* **5 cheap**

penury 4 need, want **7** poverty

peon 4 pawn, serf **5** slave **6** drudge, menial, worker **7** footman, laborer, orderly, peasant, servant

peony 7 Paeonia
   varieties: 4 tree **7** Chinese, Tibetan **8** Majorcan

people 3 kin **5** folks **6** family, humans, the mob **7** mankind, mortals **8** citizens, humanity, populace

pepper 3 dot **6** shower, strafe **7** bombard **8** sprinkle

pepper, peppercorn
   botanical name: 5 Piper **7** Pnigrum **8** Capsicum
   color: 3 red **5** black, green, white

peppery 3 hot **5** fiery, sharp, spicy **7** burning, piquant, pungent

peppy *see* **5 perky**

perambulate 4 pace, tour, walk **5** amble, mosey **6** ramble, stroll **7** meander, saunter

perceive 3 get, see **4** feel, hear, know, note **5** grasp, savvy, sense, smell, taste **6** deduce, detect, gather, notice **7** discern, observe, realize

perceptive 4 keen **5** acute, aware, quick, sharp **6** astute, shrewd

perch 3 sit **4** land, rest, seat **5** eyrie, light, roost **6** alight, settle

percolate 4 boil, brew **6** bubble, seethe

percussion instrument 4 gong **5** anvil, bells, tabor **6** chimes, rattle **7** celesta, cymbals, marimba, taboret, timpani **8** bass drum, side drum, triangle

perdition 4 Hell, ruin **8** hellfire

pere 6 father, senior

Pere Goriot
   author: 6 (Honore de) Balzac

peremptory 5 final **6** biased, lordly **8** absolute, decisive, dogmatic

perennial 5 fixed **7** lasting, undying **8** constant, enduring, timeless

perfect 4 pure, true **5** exact, ideal, whole **6** effect, entire, evolve, strict

7 achieve, develop, fulfill, precise, realize, sublime, supreme **8** flawless, thorough, unerring

perforate *see* **8 puncture**

perform 2 do **3** act **4** meet, play **5** enact **6** attain, depict, effect, finish, render, troupe **7** achieve, execute, fulfill, portray, present, pull off, realize

perfume 4 odor **5** aroma, scent, smell **7** bouquet, cologne, essence, extract, sweeten

perfunctory 3 lax **6** casual **7** cursory, offhand **8** careless, listless, lukewarm

pergola 5 arbor, bower **6** ramada **7** balcony, trellis

perhaps 5 maybe **6** mayhap **8** peut-etre, possibly

perigee 5 depth, nadir **8** low point

peril 4 risk **6** danger, hazard, menace, threat **7** pitfall **8** jeopardy

perimeter 4 edge **6** border, bounds, margin **8** confines

period 3 age, end, eon, era **4** halt, stop, term, time **5** close, epoch, limit **6** finale, finish, season

8 duration, interval
French: 6 siecle

periodical 5 daily, paper **6**
annual, review, weekly **7**
journal, monthly **8**
bulletin, magazine

peripatetic 6 roving **7**
migrant, nomadic,
roaming, walking **8**
rambling, tramping

periphery 4 edge **5** bound **6**
border **7** fringes **8**
boundary

perish 3 die **5** decay **6**
expire, vanish **7** crumble
8 pass away

perk up 4 lift **5** cheer, rally,
renew **6** buoy up, lift up,
revive **7** animate, enliven,
gladden **8** brighten,
vitalize

perky 3 gay **4** pert **5** alert,
brisk, happy, saucy, sunny
6 jaunty, lively **8**
animated, cheerful,
spirited

permanent 3 set **4** perm,
wave **6** stable **7** abiding,
durable, endless, eternal,
lasting, undying **8**
constant, enduring,
immortal, infinite,
unending

permeate 4 fill **5** imbue **6**
infuse **7** pervade **8**
saturate

permission 5 grant, leave **6**
permit **7** consent, license
8 approval, sanction

permit 2 OK **3** let **5** allow
6 endure, suffer **7** agree
to, approve, condone,
endorse, let pass, license,
warrant **8** bear with,
sanction, tolerate

pernicious 5 fatal, toxic **6**
deadly, lethal, mortal **7**
baneful, harmful, noxious

perpendicular 4 sine **5**
erect, plumb, sheer, steep
7 upright **8** vertical

perpetrate 2 do **5** enact **6**
commit, pursue **7** execute,
inflict, perform, pull off **8**
carry out, transact

perpetual *see* **7 eternal**

perplex *see* **7 confuse**

perquisite 3 due **4** gift,
perk **5** right **6** reward **7**
benefit, present

Perry Mason
cast: 4 (Raymond) Burr,
(Barbara) Hale **6**
(William) Hopper,
(William) Talman

persecute 3 vex **4** bait

5 abuse, annoy, bully, harry, hound **6** harass, hector, plague **7** oppress, torment **8** maltreat

Persephone
queen of: 5 Hades
father: 4 Zeus
mother: 7 Demeter
husband: 5 Hades
abducted by: 5 Pluto

Perseus
father: 4 Zeus
mother: 5 Danae
wife: 9 Andromeda
saved: 9 Andromeda
killed: 6 Gorgon, Medusa

persevere 6 hang on, keep on **7** persist **8** keep at it, plug away, work hard

Persia *see* **4 Iran**

Persian Mythology
god of light/truth: 7 Mithras

persist 4 go on, last, stay **6** endure, hang on, remain **7** hold out, survive **8** continue, keep at it, not yield

persnickety 5 fussy **6** choosy **7** finical, finicky **8** picayune

person 4 body, soul **5** being, human **6** mortal **8** creature

personable 4 warm **7** affable, amiable, cordial, likable **8** amicable, friendly, outgoing, pleasant, sociable

personage 3 VIP **5** nabob **6** bigwig **7** big name, big shot, notable **8** big wheel, luminary, somebody

personal 3 own **5** privy **6** bodily, inward, secret **7** private, special **8** intimate

personality 3 ego **4** self **5** charm **6** makeup, nature **8** charisma, identity

persona non grata 9 unwelcome (person)

personnel 4 crew **5** staff **7** members, workers **8** manpower

perspective 4 view **5** scape, scene, vista **7** outlook **8** overview, prospect

perspicacious 4 keen **5** acute, alert, awake, sharp **6** astute, shrewd

persuade 3 get **4** coax, lure, move, sway **5** tempt **6** cajole, entice, induce, prompt **7** wheedle, win over **8** convince

pert 4 flip, spry **5** alert, fresh, nervy, perky, quick **6** brassy, brazen, cheeky, lively, nimble **7** chipper

pertain 2 be **5** apply, touch **6** befall, belong, relate **7** concern, connect

pertinacious 6 dogged **8** stubborn

pertinent 3 apt **4** meet **7** apropos, fitting, germane, related **8** apposite, material, relevant, suitable

perturb 5 upset, worry **6** bother **7** disturb, fluster, trouble **8** disquiet, distress

Peru
  capital/largest city: 4 Lima
  mountain: 5 Andes
  highest point: 9 Huascaran
  lake: 5 Junin **8** Titicaca
  river: 6 Amazon, Pampas **7** Mantaro, Maranon, Pastaza, Ucayali **8** Putumayo
  sea: 7 Pacific
  physical feature:
    current: 6 el nino
    desert: 7 Atacama, Sechura
    gulf: 9 Guayaquil
  place:
    ruins: 5 Huaco **11** Machu-Picchu
  feature:
    animal: 5 llama **6** alpaca, vicuna **7** guanaco
    Inca capital: 5 Cuzco
    tree: 8 cinchona

peruse 3 con **4** read, scan **5** study **6** search, survey **7** examine, inspect

pervade 4 fill **5** imbue **6** infuse **7** suffuse **8** permeate, saturate

pervert 4 warp **5** abuse **6** debase, misuse **7** corrupt, degrade, distort, falsify, subvert **8** misapply

pesky 7 chafing, galling, irksome **8** annoying

pessimistic 6 gloomy **8** hopeless

pester *see* **8 irritate**

pesticide 3 DDT **7** biocide **8** fumigant

pestilence 6 blight, plague **7** disease **8** epidemic
  god of: 4 Irra

pet 3 pat **4** baby, dear **6** caress, choice, fondle, stroke **7** beloved, darling, dearest, favored **8** favorite

Peter 7 apostle

means: 4 rock
also called: 5 Simon **6** Cephas
father: 4 John **5** Jonas
brother: 6 Andrew
disciple of: 5 Jesus
companion: 4 John **5** James
pertaining to: 7 Petrine

Peter and the Wolf
composed by: 9 Prokofiev

peter out 3 ebb **7** decline, dwindle, fall off, give out **8** diminish

Peter Pan
author: 6 (James) Barrie

petite 3 wee **4** tiny **5** small **6** little

petition 3 ask, beg, sue **4** plea, pray, seek, suit, urge **5** press **6** appeal, invoke, orison, prayer **7** beseech, entreat **8** entreaty, proposal

pet name 8 nickname

pet phrase 5 maxim, motto **6** saying, slogan

petrified 4 hard **5** dense, solid, stony **6** frozen **8** hardened, rocklike

Petrified Forest, The
director: 4 (Archie) Mayo

based on play by: 8 (Robert) Sherwood
cast: 5 (Bette) Davis, (Dick) Foran **6** (Humphrey) Bogart, (Leslie) Howard **12** Leslie Howard **14** Humphrey Bogart (Duke Mantee)

Petronius
author of: 9 Satyricon

petty 4 mean **5** minor, small **6** flimsy, paltry, shabby, slight **7** trivial **8** picayune, piddling, trifling

petulant 4 sour **5** cross, gruff, huffy, sulky, surly, testy **6** grumpy, sullen **7** grouchy, peevish

pew 4 seat **5** bench **6** settle

Peyton Place
9 (Grace) Metalious

Phaedra
father: 5 Minos
mother: 8 Pasiphae
sister: 7 Ariadne
husband: 7 Theseus
stepson: 10 Hippolytus
loved: 10 Hippolytus
death by: 7 hanging, suicide

phalanx 6 column, parade

phantom 5 dream, ghost **6** mirage, spirit, vision,

wraith **7** chimera, specter **8** illusion, phantasm

Phantom of the Opera, The
director:
    1925 version: 6 (Rupert) Julian
    1943 version: 5 (Arthur) Lubin
    2004 version: 10 (Joel) Schumacher

pharos 5 light **6** beacon, signal **7** seamark

phase 4 side, step, view **5** angle, facet, guise, level, slant, stage **6** aspect, degree, period **7** feature **8** attitude, juncture

pheasant
    group of: 4 nest, nide

phenomenon 5 thing **6** marvel, rarity, wonder **7** episode, miracle **8** incident, occasion

phial 4 vial **6** bottle, vessel

Philadelphia
    baseball team: 8 Phillies
    bay: 8 Delaware
    football team: 6 Eagles
    founded/planned by: 4 Penn
    hockey team: 6 Flyers
    river: 8 Delaware **10** Schuylkill

    university: 4 Penn **6** Drexel, Temple

Philadelphia Story, The
    director: 5 (George) Cukor
    based on play by: 5 (Philip) Barry
    cast: 5 (Cary) Grant **6** (Ruth) Hussey **7** (Katharine) Hepburn, (James) Stewart

philanderer 3 rip **4** rake, wolf **5** flirt **6** lecher, tomcat, wanton **7** dallier, Don Juan, gallant, swinger, trifler **8** lothario, lover boy, rakehell

philanthropy 6 bounty **7** charity **8** goodness

Philip
    hometown: 9 Bethsaida
    disciple of: 5 Jesus

Philippines
    capital/largest city: 6 Manila
    mountain: 3 Iba **4** Mayo, Taal **6** Pagsan **7** Banahao, Canlaon **8** Pinatubo, Zambales
    highest point: 3 Apo
    sea: 4 Sulu **7** Celebes, Pacific **10** Philippine, South China
    island: 4 Cebu **5** Leyte,

Luzon **7** Mindoro,
Palawan **8** Mindanao
physical feature:
   bay: 6 Manila
   gulf: 4 Moro **5** Davao,
      Leyte **8** Lingayen
   ocean trench: 8
      Mindanao
   peninsula: 6 Bataan
feature:
   animal: 7 carabao,
      tamarau, tarsier
   clothing: 4 saya **6**
      camisa
   guerrilla fighter: 3 huk
   naval base: 6 Cavite
food:
   dish: 3 poi **4** baha,
      sabu, taro
philistine 5 yahoo **6** savage
   7 Babbitt, lowbrow,
   prosaic **8** ignorant
philosophy 4 calm, view **5**
   ideas, logic **6** reason **7**
   beliefs, opinion, thought **8**
   doctrine, thinking
   school of: 7 Sophism **8**
      idealism, Milesian,
      Stoicism **9** Epicurean,
      pantheism, Platonism
phlegmatic 4 calm, cool,
   dull **6** serene **7** languid,
   passive **8** tranquil

Phnom-Penh
   also: 8 Pnom Penh
   capital of: 8 Cambodia **9**
      Kampuchea
   river: 6 Mekong **8** Tonle
      Sap
phobia 5 dread **6** horror,
   terror **7** bugaboo, bugbear
   8 aversion, loathing
Phoenicia *see* **7 Lebanon**
Phoenician Mythology
   goddess of fertility/
      reproduction: 7 Astarte
Phoenix
   baseball team: 12
      Diamondbacks
   basketball team: 4 Suns **7**
      Mercury
   capital of: 7 Arizona
   football team: 9 Cardinals
   hockey team: 7 Coyotes
   river: 4 Salt
Phoenix
   also: 6 Phenix
   origin: 10 Phoenician
   form: 4 bird
   gift: 11 immortality
phonograph 4 hi-fi **5** phono
   6 stereo **8** Victrola
phony, phoney *see* **5 fraud**
photograph 3 pic **4** film,
   snap **5** image, print,
   shoot, still **6** candid,

glossy **7** mugshot, picture, tintype **8** likeness, portrait, snapshot
bath: 5 fixer, toner **7** reducer **9** developer
book: 5 album

photostat 4 copy **7** replica

phrase 3 put, say **4** word **5** couch, idiom, maxim, state, utter, voice, words **6** cliche, dictum, impart, remark, saying, truism **7** declare, express, proverb **8** aphorism, locution

physical 4 real **5** human, solid **6** actual, animal, bodily, carnal **7** fleshly, natural, sensual **8** concrete, corporal, external, material, palpable, tangible

physical checkup 4 exam **8** physical

physical condition 5 shape **7** fitness, stamina

physical disorder 6 malady **7** ailment, disease, illness **8** sickness

physical training 3 gym **6** sports **8** exercise

physician 2 GP, MD **3** doc **5** medic **6** doctor, medico **7** surgeon **8** sawbones

physiognomy 4 face **5** shape **6** facade, visage **7** contour, outline, profile **8** features

pianissimo
  music: 8 very soft
    abbreviation: 2 pp

piano
  music: 4 soft

piazza 5 patio, porch **6** square **7** gallery, portico, veranda

picaresque 6 daring **7** raffish, roguish, waggish **8** devilish, prankish, rascally, scampish

picayune, picayunish *see* **6 paltry**

pick 3 cut **4** crop **5** cream, elect, elite, pluck, prize **6** choice, choose, detach, flower, select **7** harvest, pull off, the best

pickings 4 loot **5** booty **6** scraps, spoils **7** plunder

pickle 3 fix, jam **4** corn, dill, mess, sour **6** crisis, plight, scrape **7** dilemma, gherkin, mustard **8** cucumber, hot water

pick on 5 annoy, bully **6** harass, jibe at **7** torment **8** browbeat

Pickwick Papers
  author: 7 (Charles) Dickens

picky 5 fussy **6** choosy **7** finicky

picture 3 see **4** copy, draw, film **5** fancy, flick, image, model, movie, paint, photo, study **6** cinema, depict, double, mirror, sketch **7** drawing, etching, feature **8** envision, likeness, painting, snapshot

Picture of Dorian Gray, The
  author: 5 (Oscar) Wilde

picturesque 6 exotic, quaint **7** unusual **8** artistic, charming, striking

piddling *see* **6** paltry

pie 4 tart **6** pastry, quiche **7** cobbler, dessert **8** turnover
  liner: 5 crust, shell
  top: 7 lattice **8** meringue

piece 3 bit, cut, fix, pat **4** blob, case, hunk, item, lump, mend, part **5** chunk, essay, scrap, shard, shred, slice, story, study **6** amount, entity, length, member, paring, repair, review, sample, sketch, sliver, swatch **7** article, cutting, patch up, portion, restore, section, segment **8** creation, division, fraction, fragment, quantity

Pied Piper
  source: 6 German, legend
  town: 7 Hamelin
  plague: 4 rats
  charmed by: 6 piping
  led away: 4 rats **8** children

pier 4 anta, dock, mole, quay, slip **5** jetty, levee, wharf **6** pillar **7** landing

pierce 3 cut **4** hurt, pain, stab **5** drill, lance, prick, spear, spike, wound **6** impale **8** distress, puncture

Pierce, Franklin
  presidential rank: 10 fourteenth
  party: 8 Democrat
  state represented: 2 NH
  defeated: 4 Hale **5** Scott
  vice president: 4 King
  born: 2 NH **9** Hillsboro (Hillsborough)
  military service: 6 US Army **7** general
    war: 7 Mexican
  notable events of lifetime/term:
    Manifesto: 6 Ostend

Purchase: 7 Gadsden
wife: 4 Jane

piety 7 loyalty, respect **8** devotion, humility

pig 3 hog **5** piggy, porky, swine **6** porker **7** glutton, guzzler **8** gourmand
male: 4 boar
female: 3 sow
young: 5 shoat **6** farrow, piglet

pigeonhole 4 rank, rate, type **5** brand, cubby, group, label, niche **8** category, classify

pigheaded 6 dogged, mulish **7** willful **8** contrary, obdurate, perverse, stubborn

pigment 3 dye **4** tint **5** color **8** coloring, dyestuff

pigtail 5 braid, plait, queue **8** ponytail

pile 3 nap **4** heap, mass **5** amass, batch, fluff, grain, hoard, mound, plush, stack, store **6** fleece, gather, piling, pillar **7** collect, pyramid, support, surface, upright **8** assemble, quantity

pilfer *see* **5 steal**

pilgrim, Pilgrim 4 haji **5** exile, hadji **6** palmer **7** pioneer, Puritan, settler **8** newcomer, traveler, wanderer, wayfarer

Pilgrim's Progress, The author: 6 (John) Bunyan

pill 3 rob **5** bolus **6** bullet, pellet, tablet **7** capsule **8** medicine

pillage 3 rob **4** loot, raid, sack **5** booty, rifle, strip **6** fleece, maraud, piracy, ravage, spoils **7** despoil, looting, plunder, robbery

pillar 3 VIP **4** pile, post, rock **5** shaft, wheel **6** column **7** obelisk, support **8** mainstay

pillow 3 pad **7** bolster, cushion **8** headrest

pilot 4 lead **5** flyer, guide, steer **6** airman, direct, escort, fly-boy, handle, leader, manage **7** aviator, birdman, conduct, control

pin 4 bind, clip, tine **5** affix, badge, clasp, dowel, medal, prong **6** brooch, fasten, pinion, secure, skewer **8** hold down, hold fast, restrain
type: 3 hat **4** push **5** stick, thole **6** breast,

common, diaper, safety **8** straight

pincer 4 claw **5** chela

pinch 3 bit, cop, jam, jot, nab, nip **4** bust, crib, grab, iota, lift, mite, pain, snip, spot **5** catch, crimp, filch, steal, swipe, trace, trial, tweak **6** arrest, crisis, snatch, snitch, strait **7** purloin, squeeze, tighten **8** compress, exigency, hardship

pinch hitter 5 proxy **7** stand-in **9** alternate

pine *see* **5 yearn**

pin hope on 6 bank on **7** count on, long for, wish for **8** aspire to, yearn for

pink 8 Dianthus

pinnacle *see* **6 summit**

pinochle
derived from: **7** bezique
lowest card: **4** nine

pinpoint 3 dot, jot **4** iota, spot **5** speck **6** detail **8** localize, zero in on

pioneer 5 found, start **6** create, father, herald, invent, leader **7** develop, founder **8** colonist, discover, explorer

pious 4 holy **5** godly

6 devout, divine **7** sainted, saintly **8** faithful, reverent, unctuous

pipe 4 duct, main, peep, sing, tube **5** cheep, chirp, trill, tweet **6** warble **7** conduit, twitter, whistle **8** conveyor

piquant *see* **7 peppery**

pique 3 ire, irk, vex **4** gall, goad, miff, snit, spur, stir **5** annoy, peeve, rouse, spite **6** arouse, excite, kindle, nettle, offend **7** affront, perturb, provoke **8** irritate

pirate 3 rob **5** steal **6** raider, robber, sea dog **7** brigand, corsair, plunder **8** marauder **9** buccaneer, privateer
name: **4** Kidd **6** Morgan **7** Lafitte **10** Blackbeard

Pirates of Penzance, The
comic opera by: **18** Gilbert and Sullivan

Pisces
symbol: **4** fish
planet: **7** Jupiter, Neptune
rules: **7** secrets
born: **13** February-March

pistol (revolver) 3 gat, gun, rod **4** colt, iron **5** luger

6 heater, mauser **7** firearm, sidearm

pit 3 dip, nut **4** dent, hole, nick, pock, scar, seed **5** gouge, gully, match, notch, stone **6** cavity, crater, dimple, furrow, hollow, indent, kernel, oppose, trough **7** scratch **8** contrast, pockmark

Pit and the Pendulum, The author: 3 (Edgar Allan) Poe

pitch 3 bob, dip, fix, lob, set, shy, top **4** apex, cant, cast, fall, fire, hurl, jerk, jolt, peak, rock, tone, toss **5** angle, chuck, crown, erect, fling, grade, heave, level, lurch, place, plant, point, raise, set up, shake, slant, sling, slope, sound, throw **6** degree, height, let fly, plunge, summit, topple, tumble

pitcher 3 jar, jug **4** ewer **6** carafe **8** decanter
  and catcher: 7 battery
  award: 7 Cy Young
  left-hander: 8 southpaw
  reliever: 7 fireman

piteous 3 sad **6** moving, woeful **7** pitiful

8 pathetic, pitiable, poignant, touching

pitfall 4 risk, trap **5** peril, snare **6** ambush, danger, hazard **8** quagmire

pith 4 core, gist, meat **5** heart, point **7** essence, meaning

pithy 5 terse **6** cogent **7** concise **8** forceful, succinct

pitiful 3 sad **4** poor **5** sorry **6** abject, measly, moving, paltry, shabby **7** doleful, forlorn, piteous **8** dreadful, god-awful, mournful, pathetic, pitiable, poignant, touching, wretched

pittance 4 mite **5** crumb **6** little, trifle **7** minimum, modicum, smidgen

Pittsburgh
  baseball team: 7 Pirates
  football team: 8 Steelers
  hockey team: 8 Penguins
  noted for: 5 steel
  river: 4 Ohio **9** Allegheny

pituitary
  located in: 5 brain

pity 5 mercy, shame **6** lament, lenity, regret **7** charity, feel for, weep for

8 bleed for, clemency, humanity, leniency, sad thing, sympathy

pivot 4 axis, axle, hang, rely, spin, turn **5** focus, hinge, twirl, wheel, whirl **6** center, circle, depend, rotate, swivel **7** fulcrum, hinge on, revolve

pixie, pixy 3 elf **5** fairy **6** sprite

pizazz 5 flair, vigor, style **6** energy, spirit **8** vitality

placard 4 bill, sign **6** notice, poster **8** bulletin

placate 4 calm, lull **5** quiet **6** pacify, soothe **7** appease, assuage, mollify

place 3 fix, job, put, set **4** area, city, digs, duty, farm, firm, home, land, plot, post, rank, rest, shop, site, spot, town, zone **5** abode, affix, array, berth, house, lodge, niche, plant, point, ranch, space, stand, state, store, venue **6** assign, attach, county, harbor, invest, locale, locate, office, region, settle **7** appoint, deposit, situate, station **8** location, lodgings, position, premises, property, remember, standing, vicinity
Latin: 4 situ

placid 4 calm, mild **5** quiet **6** gentle, poised, serene, smooth **7** pacific, restful **8** composed, peaceful, tranquil

plague 3 irk, vex, woe **4** bane, evil, fret, gall, pain, pest **5** agony, chafe, curse, harry, haunt, peeve, worry **6** bother, burden, cancer **7** afflict, disturb, perturb, scourge, torment, trouble **8** hardship, pandemic
French: 5 peste

**Plague, The
author: 5** (Albert) Camus

plain 4 bald, bare, open **5** blunt, clear, frank, naked, vivid **6** candid, common, direct, homely, honest, modest, simple **7** average, glaring, obvious, plateau, prairie **8** clear-cut, ordinary

plaintive 3 sad **6** rueful **7** doleful, moaning, piteous, pitiful, tearful **8** dolorous, grievous, mournful

plait 5 braid, queue, twine, twist, weave **7** pigtail

plan 3 aim, map, way **4** form, idea, plot **5** frame, shape **6** design, devise, intend, lay out, map out, method, scheme, sketch **7** diagram, outline, propose, purpose **8** conceive, contrive, organize, strategy

plane 3 jet **4** bird, flat **5** level, plumb **6** degree, status **7** regular, station **8** aircraft, airplane, position, standing

planet, planets 13 celestial body
  first: 7 Mercury
  second: 5 Venus
  third: 5 Earth
    satellite: 4 Moon
  fourth: 4 Mars
    satellite: 6 Deimos, Phobos
    nickname: 9 Red Planet
  fifth: 7 Jupiter
    satellite: 2 Io **6** Europa **8** Amalthea, Callisto, Ganymede
    characteristic: 7 red spot
  sixth: 6 Saturn
    satellite: 4 Rhea **5** Dione, Janus, Mimas, Titan **6** Phoebe, Tethys **7** Iapetus **8** Hyperion **9** Enceladus

    characteristic: 5 rings
  seventh: 6 Uranus
    satellite: 5 Ariel **6** Oberon **7** Miranda, Titania, Umbriel
    color: 9 blue-green
    characteristic: 5 rings
  eighth: 7 Neptune
    satellite: 6 Nereid, Triton
    color: 5 green
  ninth: 5 Pluto
    satellite: 6 Charon

plank 4 deal, deck, slab **5** board, shole, stone **8** platform

plant 4 bush, herb, mill, moss, shop, slip, tree, vine, weed, wort, yard **5** algae, flora, fungi, grass, set in, shrub, works **6** flower, foster, infuse, set out **7** factory, foundry, herbage, implant, inspire, instill, scatter, sow seed **8** seedling

plaster 4 coat, daub, sand **5** grout, smear **6** bedaub, gypsum, lather, stucco **7** overlay, spackle
  mixture of: 4 lime **5** water **6** gypsum

plastered *see* **5 drunk**

plastic 4 soft **6** pliant,

supple **7** ductile, elastic, pliable **8** flexible, formable, shapable

plate 4 dish **6** saucer **7** platter, portion, serving

plateau 4 mesa **5** table **6** upland **8** highland

platform 4 dais, goal, plan **5** creed, plank, stage, stand **6** podium, policy, pulpit, tenets

Plath, Sylvia
author of: 5 Ariel **7** (The) Bell Jar

platitude 3 saw **6** cliche, old saw, truism **7** bromide **8** banality, chestnut

Plato
author of: 7 Apology, Republic

platoon 4 band, body, crew, team, unit **5** corps, force, group

platter 4 dish, disk, lanx **6** salver **7** record **8** trencher

plaudit, plaudits *see* **5 cheer**

plausible 5 sound, valid **6** likely **7** logical, tenable **8** credible, feasible, possible, probable, rational, sensible

play 3 act, fun, toy **4** jest, lark, romp, room, show

5 antic, caper, drama, enact, farce, frisk, revel, space, sport, sweep, swing **6** act out, cavort, comedy, frolic, gambol, leeway, trifle **7** disport, have fun, pageant, perform, skylark, tragedy, vie with **8** pleasure, take part

playboy *see* **6 suitor**

playing field 4 bowl **5** arena **7** diamond, stadium **8** gridiron

play on words 3 pun

playwright 6 author, writer

plea 4 suit **5** alibi **6** appeal **7** apology, begging, defense, request **8** entreaty, petition

plead 3 ask, beg **6** adjure, enjoin **7** beseech, entreat, implore, request, solicit **8** appeal to, petition

please 3 opt **4** like, suit, want, will, wish **5** amuse, charm, elate, elect **6** choose, desire, divert, prefer, thrill, tickle **7** content, delight, gladden, gratify, satisfy **8** enthrall, entrance

pleasure 3 fun, joy **4** like, will, wish **5** bliss, cheer, mirth **6** choice, desire, gaiety, option **7** delight, elation, rapture

pleat 4 fold **5** crimp, frill **6** crease

plebeian 3 low **4** base, mean **5** banal **6** coarse, common, vulgar **7** lowbrow **8** commoner, ordinary

pledge *see* **4 oath**

plenty 4 gobs, lots, slew **5** scads **6** luxury, oceans, oodles, riches, wealth, worlds **8** opulence **9** plenitude
  goddess of: 3 Ops

plethora 4 glut **5** flood **6** excess, wealth **7** overage, surfeit, surplus **8** fullness

pliable 5 lithe **6** limber, pliant, supple **7** elastic, plastic, springy, willing **8** flexible, yielding

plight 3 fix, jam **5** pinch, state, trial **6** crisis, muddle, pickle, scrape **7** dilemma, impasse, straits, trouble **8** distress, exigency

plod 4 drag, grub, moil, plug, slog, toil **5** tramp **6** drudge, lumber, trudge **7** shuffle **8** struggle

plot 3 lot, map **4** area, draw, mark, plan, yarn **5** chart, draft, field, patch, space, story, tract **6** action, design, scheme, sketch **7** diagram, outline **8** conspire, maneuver

plow, plough 3 cut, dig **4** push, till, work **5** break, dig up, drive, forge, press, shove, spade **6** furrow, loosen, plunge, turn up **7** break up **8** bulldoze

ploy 4 game, ruse, wile **5** trick **6** design, scheme, tactic **7** gimmick **8** artifice, maneuver, strategy

pluck 4 draw, grab, grit, guts, jerk, pick, sand, yank **5** spunk, valor **6** daring, mettle, snatch, spirit, uproot **7** bravery, courage **8** boldness, tenacity

plug 4 bung, cork **5** close, stuff **6** stanch, stop up

plum
  varieties: 3 hog **4** Coco, date, Duhr, gage, Java, sand, sloe, wild **5** beach, black, goose, Islay,

Jaman, Lansa, Moxie, nanny, Natal, shore, Simon **6** August, Batoko, Canada, Cheney, cherry, common, Damson, ground, Indian, Jambul, Kaffir, Kelsey, Lomboy, Pigeon, Sapote, Sierra, Sisson **7** apricot, Burbank, Cheston, Jambosa, Malabar, Orleans, Pacific, Spanish, Wickson **8** American, Assyrian, Burdekin, European, Hortulan, Jambolan, Japanese, Oklahoma, Prunello, Victoria

plume 3 pen **4** down **5** egret, pique, preen, pride, prize, quill **7** feather
military: 7 panache

plummet 4 dive, fall **6** plunge, tumble **8** nosedive **12** fall headlong

plump 4 drop, firm, flop, plop, sink **5** blunt, buxom, obese, plunk, pudgy, solid, spill, stout **6** abrupt, chubby, direct, fleshy, portly, rotund, sprawl, stocky, tumble

plunder *see* **7** pillage

plunge 3 dip, fly, run

4 bolt, cast, dart, dash, dive, drop, duck, fall, jerk, roll, jump, leap, push, reel, rock, rush, sink, tear **5** heave, lunge, lurch, pitch, surge **6** charge, hasten, hurtle, thrust **7** descend, immerse, scuttle **8** submerge

plunk 4 pick, thud **5** pluck, plumb, strum, twang **6** dollar **7** exactly **8** squarely

plus 5 added, extra, other, spare **6** useful **7** helpful

plush *see* **5 fancy**

Pluto
    also: 5 Hades
    god of: 10 underworld

Pluto 6 planet
    position: 5 ninth
    satellite: 6 Charon

plutocrat 5 mogul **6** fat cat, tycoon

plutonic 7 abyssal, igneous

poach 3 rob **4** cook **5** shirr, steal **6** plunge, simmer **7** trample **8** encroach, trespass

pocket 3 bag, get, pit **4** gain, lode, sack, vein **5** pouch, purse, pygmy, small, steal, strip, usurp

6 cavity, pilfer **7** compact, handbag, receive **8** arrogate, envelope

pocket-sized 3 wee **4** tiny **5** dwarf, pygmy, small **6** bantam, little, midget, minute, petite **7** compact

pod 4 case, hull, husk **5** shell **6** jacket, sheath **8** pericarp, seed case

podium 4 dais, foot, wall **5** stipe **7** lectern **8** pedestal, platform **9** footstalk

poem 3 lay, ode **4** epic, song **5** elegy, idyll, lyric, rhyme, verse **6** ballad, jingle, sonnet **8** doggerel, limerick, madrigal

Poetics
author: 9 Aristotle

poetry 5 poesy, rhyme, verse
god of: 4 Odin, Ogma **5** Brage, Bragi, Othin **6** Apollo **7** Phoebus, Pythius **9** Musagetes

Pogo
creator: 5 (Walt) Kelly

poignant 3 sad **5** sharp **6** moving, rueful, woeful **7** doleful, piquant, pitiful, pungent, tearful **8** piercing, touching

point 3 aim, end, hit, nib, run, tip, use **4** apex, bend, bode, core, game, gist, goal, item, mark, meat, pike, pith, spur, time, turn, unit **5** level, limit, place, prong, prove, score, spike, stage, tally, value **6** aspect, detail, direct, moment, number, object, reason **7** essence, purpose, suggest **8** indicate, main idea, position, sharp end

point-blank 5 blunt **6** direct

point d'appui 4 prop, stay

point of view 4 side **5** angle, slant **6** aspect **7** outlook **8** attitude

poise 4 calm **5** raise **6** aplomb **7** balance, elevate **8** presence

poison 4 bane, evil, harm **5** curse, taint, toxin, venom **6** cancer, canker, infect, plague, weaken **7** corrode, corrupt, degrade, disease, pollute

poke 3 dig, hit, jab **4** butt, drag, gore, idle, jolt, prod, push, stab **5** dally, delay, mosey, nudge **6** dawdle, fiddle, thrust **7** saunter

poker
derived from: 5 as nas, gilet **6** brelan **7** primero

11 brouillotte

hand: 4 pair, four (of a kind) **5** flush, three (of a kind) **5** flush **8** straight, two pairs **9** full house **13** straight flush

Poland
> **other name: 6** Polska
> **capital/largest city: 6** Warsaw
> **mountain: 5** Tatra **7** Sudeten **10** Carpathian
> **highest point: 4** Rysy
> **lake: Masurian, Niegocin**
> **river: 3** Bug **4** Oder, Styr **6** Neisse, Nieman **7** Vistula **8** Dniester
> **sea: 6** Baltic
> **physical feature:**
>> **gulf: 6** Danzig, Gdansk
>> **lagoon: 7** Stettin
>> **plain: 7** Silesia
> **place:**
>> **7** Casimir
> **feature:**
>> **folk dance: 5** polka **7** mazurka **9** polonaise
>> **medieval capital 6** Cracow, Krakow
>> **union: 10** Solidarity
> **food:**
>> **filled dumpling: 7** pierogi
>> **sausage: 8** kielbasa
>> **soup: 7** barszca

polar 3 icy **6** arctic, frigid, wintry **7** glacial, ice-cold **8** freezing

polaroid 6 camera
> **invented by: 4** Land

pole 3 rod **4** mast, spar **5** shaft, staff, stick **6** tongue **9** pikestaff
> **flax holder: 7** distaff
> **Scottish: 5** caber
> **tribal: 5** totem

police, police officer 4 cops, dick, fuzz, tidy **5** clean, guard **6** neaten, patrol **7** marshal, officer, protect, sheriff **8** blue coat, flatfoot, regulate
> **French: 8** gendarme

policy 3 way **4** plan, rule **5** habit, style **6** custom, design, method, scheme, system **7** tactics **8** platform, practice, strategy

polish 3 oil, wax **4** buff, sand **5** class, glaze, gloss, shine **6** refine, smooth **7** culture, enhance, finesse, sauvity, touch up, varnish **8** elegance

polish off 6 finish **8** complete, get rid of

polite 4 high **5** civil, elite **6** proper **7** elegant, gallant, genteel, refined **8** cultured, mannerly

politic 4 wily, wise **5** chary, suave **6** artful, astute, shrewd, subtle **7** tactful **8** cautious, scheming

political party 3 GOP **4** Tory, Whig **5** Labor **7** faction

Polk, James Knox
  presidential rank: 8 eleventh
  party: 8 Democrat
  state represented: 2 TN
  defeated: 4 Clay **6** Birney
  vice president: 6 Dallas
  born: 2 NC
  notable events of lifetime/ term:
    Proviso: 6 Wilmot
    war: 7 Mexican
  wife: 5 Sarah

polka 5 dance

poll 4 head, vote **5** count, tally **6** census, survey, voting **7** canvass, figures **8** register, sampling

pollutant 5 fumes, smoke, waste **7** exhaust **8** emission, impurity

pollute 4 foul, soil **5** dirty, sully **6** befoul, debase, defile **7** deprave, profane

Pollux *see* **15** Castor and Pollux

polo
  equipment: 6 mallet
  period of play: 7 chukker

poltergeist 5 ghost **6** spirit
  manifestation: 5 knock, noise, prank

poltroon 6 coward, craven **7** caitiff, chicken, dastard

polygon 10 multiangle **11** plane figure
  eight-sided: 7 octagon
  equal angled: 6 isogon
  five-sided: 8 pentagon
  four-sided: 6 square **7** rhombus **8** tetragon **9** rectangle, trapezoid
  nine-sided: 7 nonagon
  seven-sided: 8 heptagon
  six-sided: 7 hexagon
  ten-sided: 7 decagon
  three-sided: 8 triangle
  twelve-sided: 9 dodecagon

polymer 5 dimer, nylon **6** hydrol **7** hexamer **8** oligomer

Polynesia
  name means: 11 many islands
  island: 4 Cook, Line **5** Samoa, Tonga **6** Easter, Ellice, Hawaii, Midway, Tahiti, Tuvalu **7** Austral,

Maupiti, Phoenix, Society, Tokelau, Tuamotu **8** Pitcairn
sea: 7 Pacific
 explorer: 4 Cook **6** Tasman, Wallis **8** Magellan
feature:
 clothing: 5 pareu **6** sarong **8** lavalava
 dance: 4 hula, siva
 priest: 7 kahunas
 supernatural power: 4 mana
food:
 dish: 3 kai, poi **4** taro **8** palusami
 drink: 3 ava **4** kava, kawa
polyp 5 coral, hydra, tumor **6** growth, isopod **7** octopod
polysaccharide 6 insulin, starch **7** dextrin **8** galactin, lichenin
Pomerania
 capital: 7 Stettin
 country: 6 Poland **7** Germany
pommel, pummel 4 beat, hilt, horn, knob, pake **6** finial, strike
pompous *see* **7 haughty**

poncho 4 cape **5** cloak, shawl **6** mantle, serape
pond 4 pool, tarn **5** basin **6** lagoon
ponder 4 muse, mull **5** study **6** wonder **7** reflect **8** cogitate, consider, ruminate
pontiff 4 pope **6** bishop, priest **8** pontifex
pony 3 nag **4** crib, trot **5** glass, horse, pinto **7** mustang
 breed: 6 Exmoor **8** Shetland
pooh-pooh 5 knock **7** disdain, put down, run down, sneer at **8** belittle
pool 3 pot **4** ally, bank, lake, mere, pond, tarn **5** group, kitty, merge, share, union, unite **6** puddle, splash, stakes **7** combine
poop 3 fag **4** bush, deck, do in, tire **7** exhaust, fatigue, wear out **8** enervate
poor 3 sad **4** bare, dead, vain, worn **5** broke, empty, needy, sorry **6** meager, paltry, wasted **7** forlorn, unhappy, unlucky, wanting **8** badly off, bankrupt, beggarly,

depleted, grieving, inferior, pathetic, pitiable, strapped

Poor Richard's Almanack
  author: 8 (Benjamin) Franklin

pop 4 bang, boom, come, shot, snap, soda 5 arise, blast, burst, crack 7 explode

pope 3 Leo 4 John, Paul, Pius 5 Peter, Urban 6 Adrian, Eugene, Julius, Martin, Sixtus 7 Clement, Gregory 8 Benedict, Innocent, John Paul, Nicholas 9 Alexander, Callistus
  office: 6 Papacy 7 Holy See
  elected by: 9 (College of) Cardinals
  elected in: 8 conclave
  signal that election is concluded: 10 white smoke
  resides: 4 Rome 7 Vatican
  summer residence: 8 (Castel) Gondolfo
  first pope: 5 Peter

Popeye
  cartoonist: 5 (Elzie) Segar

poplar 7 Populus

poppy 7 Papaver

drug: 5 opium 6 heroin 8 morphine

poppycock 3 rot 4 bosh, bunk, jive, tosh 5 froth, fudge, hooey, stuff, trash 6 drivel 7 baloney, blather, hogwash, rubbish 8 nonsense, wish-wash

populace, population 4 folk 6 people, public 7 society

popular 5 cheap, civic, civil, stock 6 famous, public, social 7 admired, current, in favor 8 accepted, communal, familiar, favorite, in demand

popular opinion
  Latin: 9 vox populi

populate 6 occupy, people, settle 7 inhabit

porcelain 5 china

porch 4 stoa 5 lanai, stoop 7 balcony, narthex, portico, veranda 8 solarium, verandah

pore 4 hole, read, scan 5 probe, study 6 peruse, review, search 7 dig into, examine, explore, inspect, orifice 8 consider

Porgy and Bess
   opera by: 8 (George) Gershwin
   setting: 10 Catfish Row

pornographic 4 blue, lewd **5** bawdy, dirty, gross **6** coarse, filthy, smutty, vulgar **7** obscene **8** indecent, off-color, prurient

porpoise 4 leap **6** palach, puffer, seahog **7** cowfish, dolphin **8** cetacean

porridge 4 pobs, samp **5** atole, brose, brout, gruel **6** cereal **7** oatmeal, polenta

port 4 dock, pier, quay **5** haven, wharf **6** harbor, refuge **7** dry dock, landing, mooring, seaport

port
   type: 4 wine **6** brandy
   origin: 8 Portugal

portable 5 handy, light, small **6** pocket **7** compact, movable **8** cartable

portal, portals 4 adit, arch, door, gate **5** entry **6** wicket **7** doorway, gateway, portico **8** approach, entrance

portent 4 omen, sign

5 token **6** augury, boding, threat **7** presage, warning

portentous 6 superb **7** amazing, fateful, ominous, pompous **8** alarming

porter 4 brew **5** stout **6** bearer, coolie, redcap, skycap **7** carrier

portfolio 4 case, file **5** album **6** binder, folder **7** dossier **8** envelope

portico 4 stoa **5** lanai **6** piazza **7** balcony, veranda, walkway

portion 3 cut, lot, sum **4** dole, doom, fate, luck, part **5** cut up, moira, piece, sever, share, slice, split **6** amount, divide, parcel, ration **7** deal out, fortune, measure, section, serving **8** allocate, disperse, fraction, fragment, quantity, separate

portly *see* **3** fat

portmanteau 3 bag **4** grip **5** cloak **6** mantle, valise **8** suitcase

portrait 5 cameo **6** sketch **7** drawing, picture **8** likeness, painting, vignette

Portrait of a Lady, The
  author: **5** (Henry) James
Portrait of the Artist as a Young Man
  author: **5** (James) Joyce
portray *see* **6 depict**
Portugal
  capital/largest city: **6** Lisboa, Lisbon
  highest point:
    in Azores: **4** Pico **8** Pico Alta
    on mainland: **7** (Serra da) Estrela
  river: **4** Lima, Tago, Tajo, Tejo **5** Douro, Tagus
  sea/ocean: **8** Atlantic
  island: **6** Azores **7** Madeira
  physical feature:
    peninsula: **7** Iberian
  place:
    palace: **6** Cintra
    shrine: **6** Fatima
    former colony: **3** Goa **5** Macao, Timor **6** Angola **7** Sao Tome **8** Principe, St Thomas **9** Cape Verde **10** Mozambique
  food:
    sausage: **8** linguica
    wine: **4** port **7** madeira

Portuguese Guinea *see* **12 Guinea-Bissau**
Portuguese West Africa *see* **6 Angola**
pose 3 air, set **4** cast, mien **5** order, state, style **6** line up, stance, submit **7** arrange, posture, present, show off, suggest **8** carriage
Poseidon
  origin: **5** Greek
  god of: **3** sea
  father: **6** Cronos
  mother: **4** Rhea
  brother: **4** Zeus
  wife: **10** Amphitrite
  lover: **2** Ge **6** Aethra, Medusa, Thoosa **7** Demeter
  child: **5** Arion **6** Triton **7** Antaeus, Pegasus, Theseus **8** Chrysaor
  symbol: **5** horse **7** trident
  corresponds to: **7** Neptune
posh *see* **4 rich**
position 3 fix, job, put, set **4** duty, pose, post, role, site **5** array, caste, class, place, stand, state **6** locate, office, stance, status **7** arrange, deposit, opinion, outlook, posture,

station, vantage **8** function, location, standing

positive 4 firm, good, real, sure **5** total **6** narrow, useful **7** assured, certain, gainful, helpful **8** absolute, complete, definite, salutary

possess 3 own **4** grab, have, hold **6** absorb, fixate, obsess, occupy **7** acquire, bewitch, conquer, control, enchant, overrun

possible 8 credible, feasible, workable

post 2 PX **3** fix, job, put, set **4** base, beat, camp, pale, part, pile, pole, role, seat, send, spot, work **5** brace, house, lodge, place, put up, round, shaft, stake **6** column, inform, locate, notify, office, picket, report, tack up **7** declare, install, mission, publish, quarter, routine, situate, station, support, upright **8** announce, disclose, position

postdate 6 follow **7** succeed

poster 4 bill, sign **6** notice **7** placard **8** bulletin

posterior 3 bum, can **4** back, butt, prat, rear, rump, seat, tail, tush **5** fanny, stern, tushy **6** behind, bottom **7** keister **8** backside, buttocks, derriere

posterity 5 heirs, issue, young **6** family **7** descent, history, lineage, progeny

postpone *see* **6 detain**

postscript 2 ps **5** rider **7** codicil **8** addendum

postulate 5 axiom, guess **6** assume, hazard, submit, theory **7** surmise, theorem

posture 3 air, set **4** case, mien, mood, pose, post, tone **5** phase, place **6** aspect, stance, status **7** bearing, station **8** attitude, carriage, position, standing

pot 3 pan **4** ruin **5** crock, kitty **6** vessel

potable 3 ale **5** clean, drink, water **6** liquor **8** beverage, quencher

potage 4 soup **9** thick soup

potato 16 Solanum tuberosum
   dish: 4 chip **5** baked, (French) fries, salad

6 mashed **8** au gratin **9** lyonnaise, scalloped

potent 5 solid, tough **6** mighty, strong **7** dynamic **8** forceful, forcible, powerful, vigorous

potentate 4 lord **5** chief, mogul, ruler **6** prince, satrap, sultan **7** emperor, monarch **8** overlord

potential 6 covert, hidden, latent **7** dormant, lurking, passive **8** implicit, possible

potion 4 brew, dram **5** draft, tonic **6** elixir **7** mixture, philter **8** libation

potpourri 4 hash, mess, olio, stew **6** jumble, medley, mosaic, motley **7** farrago, goulash, melange, mixture **8** mishmash, pastiche

potter's field 8 boneyard, cemetery

pottery 5 china **8** clayware, crockery

pouch 3 bag, kit, sac **4** sack **5** purse **6** pocket, wallet **7** handbag, satchel **8** carryall, ditty bag, reticule, rucksack

poultice 7 plaster **8** dressing

poultry 3 hen **4** cock, duck, fowl, swan **5** capon, geese, goose, quail **6** pigeon, turkey **7** chicken, peacock, rooster **8** pheasant

disease: 3 pip **4** roup, tick

house: 4 coop

pounce 4 jump, leap **5** fly at, swoop **6** ambush, jump at, snatch, spring **8** fall upon, surprise

pound 4 bang, beat, drub, drum, maul **5** clomp, clout, crush, grind, paste, smack, stomp, throb, thump, tramp **6** batter, bruise, cudgel, hammer, pummel, thrash, thwack, wallop **7** clobber, pulsate, trounce

abbreviation: 2 lb

pour 3 tap **4** drip, drop, flow, gush, ooze, rain, seep, slop **5** drain, flood, issue, spill, spout **6** decant, deluge, drench, effuse, squirt, stream **7** cascade

pout 4 crab, fret, fume, mope, sulk **5** brood, frown, lower, scowl **6** glower

French: 4 moue

poverty 4 lack, need, want **6** dearth, penury

7 beggary, deficit, paucity
8 scarcity, shortage

powder 4 dust, talc **5** emery
6 pollen, talcum **7**
crumble

power 4 gift, sway **5** brawn,
force, might, right, ruler,
skill, vigor **6** muscle,
status, talent **7** potency **8**
activate, aptitude,
capacity, energize,
prestige, strength, vitality
Latin: 3 vis

powwow 4 meet, talk **5**
forum **6** caucus, confer,
huddle, parley **7** consult,
convene, council, discuss,
meeting, palaver **8**
assembly, colloquy,
conclave, congress

practical 4 able **5** solid,
sound **6** expert, useful,
versed **7** skilled **8**
sensible, skillful

practical joke 4 jape **5**
caper, prank, stunt, trick

practically 6 all but,
almost, nearly **8** actually,
in effect

practice 2 do **3** use, way **4**
deed, mode, play, rule,
ruse, ways, wont **5**
apply, drill, habit, train,
usage **6** action, custom,

device, effect, follow,
manner, method, pursue,
ritual **7** conduct, process,
routine, utilize **8**
maneuver, rehearse,
tendency, training

pragmatic 5 sober **8**
sensible

Praia
capital of: 9 Cape Verde

prairie 3 bay **5** llano,
pampa, plain **6** camass,
meadow, steppe **7**
quamash **9** grassland

praise 4 laud, tout **5** cheer,
exalt, extol, honor **6**
esteem, eulogy, hurrah,
regard, revere **7** acclaim,
applaud, approve, build
up, commend, glorify,
plaudit, respect, root for,
tribute, worship **8**
accolade, applause,
approval, encomium,
eulogize, venerate

pram, praam, prahm 4 boat
5 buggy **6** vessel **7**
rowboat **8** carriage,
stroller

prance 4 jump, leap, romp,
skip **5** bound, caper,
dance, frisk, strut, vault **6**
bounce, cavort, frolic,
gambol, spring **7** swagger

prank **4** joke, lark **5** antic, caper, spoof, stunt, trick **8** escapade, mischief

prattle *see* **7 chatter**

pray **3** beg, bid, sue **4** urge **5** cry to, plead **7** beseech, entreat, implore, request, solicit **8** call upon, invocate, petition

prayer **6** litany, orison, praise **7** worship

preach **4** urge **6** advise, exhort **7** counsel, declare, expound, profess **8** advocate, homilize, proclaim

preacher **5** vicar **6** curate, parson, pastor **8** chaplain, homilist, minister, reverend, sky pilot

preachy **8** didactic, pedantic

pre-Cambrian **5** Azoic **6** Eozoic **7** primary **10** Archeozoic **11** Proterozoic

precarious **5** risky, shaky **6** chancy, unsafe **7** dubious **8** alarming, doubtful, perilous, unstable, unsteady

precaution **4** care **7** caution, defense **8** prudence, security, wariness

precede **8** antecede, antedate, go before

precedent **5** model **7** example **8** standard **9** criterion, guideline

precept **3** law **4** bull, code, rule **5** axiom, canon, edict, maxim, motto, tenet, truth, ukase **6** decree **7** dictate, mandate, statute

precious **4** dear, rare **5** fussy, sweet **6** adored, choice, dainty, valued **7** beloved, darling, lovable **8** adorable

precipice **4** crag **5** bluff, cliff, ledge **8** headland, palisade

precipitate **4** cast, hurl, rash, spur **5** drive, fling, hasty **6** abrupt, launch, propel, rushed, speedy, thrust **7** quicken, speed up **8** catapult, expedite

precipitation **4** hail, rain, rush, snow **5** haste, sleet **8** rainfall, rashness

precis **5** brief **6** apercu, digest, resume, sketch **7** epitome, outline, rundown, summary **8** abstract, synopsis

precise 4 true **5** exact, fussy, rigid **6** strict **7** careful, express **8** accurate, clear-cut, definite, explicit, specific

preclude *see* **7 prevent**

precocious 3 apt **5** quick, smart **6** bright, clever, gifted, mature **8** advanced

preconception 4 bias **6** notion

precursor 4 mark, omen, sign **5** token, usher **6** herald **7** portent, warning **8** vanguard

predate 7 precede **8** antecede, antedate, go before

predecessor 7 forbear **8** ancestor, forebear, foregoer

predetermined 5 fated **7** decided, planned **8** destined

predicament 3 fix, jam **4** bind, mess **5** pinch **6** corner, crisis, pickle **7** dilemma **8** quandary

predicate 4 base, real, rest, true **5** found, imply **6** affirm, assert **7** commend, declare **8** proclaim

predict 4 omen **5** augur **6** divine **7** betoken, foresee,

presage 8 envision, forecast, foretell, prophesy

predilection *see* **8 penchant**

predispose 4 bias, lure, sway, urge **5** tempt **6** entice, induce, prompt, seduce **7** dispose, incline, win over **8** persuade

predominant *see* **10 preeminent**

preeminent 4 best **5** famed **6** famous **7** honored, supreme **8** dominant, foremost, greatest, renowned, superior

preempt 4 take **5** seize, usurp **8** arrogate

preen 3 pin **4** perk, trim **5** adorn, dress, groom, plume, pride, primp, prink **6** brooch, smooth **wings: 4** whet

preexistent 5 prior **8** anterior, previous

preface 4 open **5** begin, proem, start **6** launch **7** prelude **8** commence, foreword, initiate, preamble, prologue

prefer 3 opt **4** file **5** adopt, elect, exalt, fancy, favor, offer **6** select, take to **7** pick out, present, proffer

prefigure 4 hint, type 6 shadow, typify 7 foresee, imagine, presage, suggest

pregnant 4 full, rich 6 fecund, filled, gravid 7 copious, fertile, fraught, replete, seminal, teeming, weighty 8 forceful, fruitful, prolific
French: 8 enceinte

prehistoric 3 old 7 ancient

prejudice *see* 4 **bias**

prelude 7 opening, preface 8 overture, preamble, prologue

premature 3 raw 5 green, hasty 6 callow, unripe 7 too soon, unready 8 abortive, ill-timed, immature, previous, too early, untimely

premeditated 7 planned, plotted, studied, willful 8 intended

premier 3 bet 4 head 5 chief, first 6 oldest 7 leading, supreme 8 earliest, foremost

premise 6 theory 8 argument

premises 4 site 8 environs, property, vicinity

premium 4 gain, gift 5 award, bonus, prize 6 bounty, return, reward 7 benefit, payment

premonition *see* 4 **omen**

preoccupy 6 absorb, arrest, obsess, take up, wrap up 7 engross, immerse

prepare 3 fix 5 adapt, prime, ready 7 arrange, be ready, provide 8 get ready

preponderant 3 key 4 main 5 chief, first, major, prime 7 highest, leading, primary, supreme 8 dominant, foremost

prepossessing 4 nice 7 winsome 8 alluring, charming, engaging, inviting, pleasant, striking

preposterous 5 inane, outre, silly 6 absurd, stupid 7 asinine, bizarre, fatuous, foolish, idiotic

prerequisite 4 need 6 demand 8 demanded, exigency, required

prerogative 3 due 5 claim, grant, right 6 choice, option 7 freedom, liberty, license, warrant

prescribe 3 fix, set 4 rule, urge 5 enact, order 6 assign, decree, direct, ordain **7** appoint, command, dictate, specify **8** proclaim

prescriptive 7 binding **8** demanded, dictated, didactic, required

presence 3 air **4** life, look, mien **5** being, curse, favor, ghost, group **6** aspect, entity, figure, manner, shadow, spirit, vision, wraith **7** phantom, specter **8** carriage, charisma, demeanor

presence of mind 6 aplomb **8** calmness, coolness

present 2 in **3** now, tip **4** alms, aver, boon, cite, gift, give, here, near, nigh, read, show, tell **5** about, award, frame, grant, offer, state, today **6** accord, assert, at hand, bestow, bounty, call up, chip in, impart, legacy, nearby, on hand, recite, relate, render, rooted, submit, summon, tender

presentable 4 chic, so-so **6** decent, modish, not bad, proper **7** stylish **8** becoming, passable, suitable

presentation 3 fee, tip

4 boon, gift, show **5** favor, grant, offer **6** bounty **7** display, exhibit **8** bestowal, exposure, offering, proposal

preservative 4 salt **5** brine, spice **8** marinade

preserve, preserves 3 can, dry, jam **4** corn, cure, park, salt, save, seal **5** guard, haven, jelly, nurse, put up, smoke, sweet **6** comfit, defend, embalm, foster, freeze, pickle, refuge, season, secure, shield **7** care for, compote, mummify, protect, reserve, shelter **8** conserve, insulate, keep safe, maintain, marinate

preside 4 boss, host, rule **5** chair, watch **6** direct, govern, manage **7** command, conduct, control, hostess, oversee **8** overlook, regulate

president, President 4 head **5** ruler **8** chairman

President of the United States
first: 16 George Washington
second: 9 John Adams
third: 15 Thomas

Jefferson
fourth: 12 James Madison
fifth: 11 James Monroe
sixth: 15 John Quincy
Adams
seventh: 13 Andrew
Jackson
eighth: 14 Martin Van
Buren
ninth: 20 William Henry
Harrison
tenth: 9 John Tyler
eleventh: 10 James K
Polk
twelfth: 13 Zachary
Taylor
thirteenth: 15 Millard
Fillmore
fourteenth: 14 Franklin
Pierce
fifteenth: 13 James
Buchanan
sixteenth: 14 Abraham
Lincoln
seventeenth: 13 Andrew
Johnson
eighteenth: 13 Ulysses S
Grant
nineteenth: 16 Rutherford
B Hayes
twentieth: 14 James A
Garfield
twenty-first: 17 Chester
Alan Arthur
twenty-second: 15 Grover

Cleveland
twenty-third: 16 Benjamin
Harrison
twenty-fourth: 15 Grover
Cleveland
twenty-fifth: 15 William
McKinley
twenty-sixth: 17 Theodore
Roosevelt
twenty-seventh: 17
William Howard Taft
twenty-eighth: 13
Woodrow Wilson
twenty-ninth: 14 Warren
G Harding
thirtieth: 14 Calvin
Coolidge
thirty-first: 13 Herbert
Hoover
thirty-second: 18 Franklin
D Roosevelt
thirty-third: 12 Harry S
Truman
thirty-fourth: 17 Dwight D
Eisenhower
thirty-fifth: 12 John F
Kennedy
thirty-sixth: 14 Lyndon B
Johnson
thirty-seventh: 13 Richard
M Nixon
thirty-eighth: 11 Gerald R
Ford
thirty-ninth: 11 (James E)
Jimmy Carter (Jr)

fortieth: 12 Ronald Reagan
forty-first: 10 George (HW) Bush
forty-second: 11 (William Jefferson) Bill Clinton
forty-third: 10 George (W) Bush
preside over 5 chair, guide **6** direct, govern, manage **7** conduct **8** dominate
Presley, Elvis Aron
  nickname: 7 The King
  born: 6 Tupelo
  wife: 9 Priscilla
  daughter: 9 Lisa Marie
  father: 6 Vernon
  mother: 6 Gladys
  twin brother: 6 Jessie (Garon)
  manager: 6 (Colonel Tom) Parker
  home: 9 Graceland
  location: 7 Memphis
press 2 TV **3** beg, bug, dun, hit, hug, jam, mob, pet, tap, tax **4** army, body, cram, duty, heap, herd, host, iron, mash, mill, pack, prod, push, rush **5** beset, clasp, force, media, set on, steam **6** bother, burden, compel, duress, reduce, smooth, strain, stress **7** flatten, implore, squeeze **8** condense, insist on, pressure, printing
press home 6 stress
pressure 4 bias, care, load, need, pull, sway, want **5** force **6** burden, demand, strain, stress, weight **7** anxiety, gravity, urgency **8** coercion
pressure measurement 6 pascal
prestige 4 fame, mark, note **5** glory, honor **6** esteem, import, regard, renown, report, repute **7** account, respect **8** eminence
presume 4 dare **5** fancy, guess, posit **6** assume, deduce, gather **7** believe, imagine, suppose, suspect **8** be so bold
pretend 4 fake, sham **5** claim, fancy, feign, mimic, put on **6** assume **7** imagine, imitate, playact **8** simulate
pretense 4 airs, fake, hoax, mask, sham, show **5** cloak, cover, guile, trick **6** deceit **8** disguise, trickery
preternatural 5 eerie, weird

6 arcane, occult **7** bizarre, strange, uncanny **8** esoteric, mystical

pretext 5 basis, bluff, feint **6** excuse, ground **8** pretense

pretty *see* **6 comely**

prevail 3 win **4** rule **5** exist, reign **6** abound, win out **7** conquer, succeed, triumph **8** overcome

prevalent 4 rife **5** usual **6** common **7** general, popular, rampant **8** abundant, everyday, familiar, frequent, habitual

prevaricate *see* **7 deceive**

prevent 3 bar, dam **4** balk, foil, halt, stop, veto **5** avert, avoid, block, deter **6** thwart **7** deflect, fend off, obviate **8** hold back, preclude, prohibit

preview 5 sneak **6** sample, survey **8** futurama

previous 5 early, prior **6** before, former **7** earlier **8** foregone

prey 3 eat **4** dupe, food, game, gull, kill **5** prize, quest **6** devour, infest, quarry, target, victim

7 cat's-paw, consume, fall guy, live off **8** feed upon

Priam
king of: 4 Troy
father: 8 Laomedon
brother: 8 Tithonus
wife: 6 Hecuba
son: 5 Paris **6** Hector **9** Polydorus
daughter: 8 Polyxena **9** Cassandra

price 3 fee **4** cost, fine, rate **5** value, worth **6** amount, assess, charge, outlay **7** expense, penalty **8** appraise, evaluate

Price Is Right, The
host: 6 (Bob) Barker **6** (Bill) Cullen

priceless 4 dear, rare **6** costly, prized, valued **8** peerless, precious, valuable

prick 5 stick **6** pierce **8** puncture

prickle 4 barb, itch **5** point, quill, smart, sting, thorn **6** tingle **7** barbule, bristle

pride 3 joy **4** airs, pomp, show **5** honor **6** egoism, parade, vanity **7** comfort, conceit, dignity, egotism, swagger **8** smugness

Pride and Prejudice
  author: 6 (Jane) Austen

priest 5 padre **6** cleric, father **8** minister, preacher

priesthood 5 cloth **6** clergy **8** ministry, the cloth

prig 5 bigot, prude **6** pedant **7** puritan **8** bluenose

prim 4 smug, tidy **5** fussy **6** prissy, proper, strict, stuffy **7** haughty, prudish **8** priggish, starched

prima donna 4 diva, lead, star **6** singer
  literally: 9 first lady

primary 3 key **4** main, star **5** basal, basic, chief, first, prime, vital **6** innate, native, oldest, primal, ruling, utmost **7** highest, initial, leading, nascent, natural **8** cardinal, dominant, earliest, primeval **9** primitive

primate 3 ape, man **5** avahi, indri, lemur, loris, potto **6** aye-aye, baboon, bishop, galago, gibbon, mammal, monkey **7** gorilla, tamarin, tarsier **8** marmoset, simpoona

prime 2 A1 **3** ace, fit **4** best, main, peak, pink **5** adapt, basal, basic, bloom, breed, brief, chief, coach, early, first, groom, raise, ready, train, tutor, vital **6** adjust, choice, fill in, flower, Grade A, height, heyday, inform, innate, native, oldest, primal, prompt, ruling, school, seemly, select, timely, utmost, zenith **7** highest, quality, supreme **8** greatest, instruct, superior

primer 3 cap **4** book **5** paint **6** manual, reader **8** hornbook, textbook

primeval 5 early **6** oldest, primal **7** ancient, archaic **8** earliest, original

primordial 5 first **6** primal **7** initial **8** original, primeval

primp 5 groom, plume, preen **6** doll up, make up **7** gussy up

primrose 7 Primula

Prince Edward Island
  abbreviation: 3 PEI
  capital: 13 Charlottetown
  gulf: 10 St Lawrence
  explored by: 7 Cartier
  province of: 6 Canada

Prince Igor
  opera by: 7 Borodin

princely 3 big **5** noble, royal **8** generous **11** magnificent

prince of darkness 5 Satan **7** Lucifer **8** the Devil **9** Beelzebub

Prince of Peace 5 Jesus **6** Christ

Prince Valiant
creator: **6** (Harold) Foster

principal 4 dean, fund, main, star **5** basic, chief, first, money, prime **6** master **7** capital, leading, primary, supreme **8** cardinal, dominant, foremost

principle *see* **5 maxim**

Pringle, John
real name of: **7** (John) Gilbert

print 3 die **4** copy, text, type **5** plate, press, stamp, write **7** compose, edition, engrave, etching, gravure, impress, picture, publish, woodcut

prior 6 former **7** earlier **8** anterior, previous

priority 7 urgency

prison 3 can, jug, pen **4** brig, gaol, jail, stir, tank **5** clink, joint **6** cooler

7 dungeon, slammer **8** bastille, big house

prissy 4 prim **5** fussy **6** proper, stuffy **7** finicky, prudish **8** overnice

pristine 4 pure **8** unmarred, virginal

private 4 dark **5** fixed, privy **6** closed, covert, hidden, lonely, remote, secret **8** confined, esoteric, hush-hush, isolated, lonesome, personal, secluded, solitary

privateer 6 pirate **7** brigand, corsair

private eye 4 dick **6** shamus **7** gumshoe

privilege 3 due **4** boon **5** allow, favor, grant, honor, power, right, title **6** patent, permit **7** benefit, liberty, license **8** pleasure

prize 3 cup, gem, pip **4** lulu **5** award, catch, crown, dandy, honey, honor, jewel, medal, peach, pearl, value **6** admire, esteem, honors, regard, reward, ribbon, trophy **7** cherish **8** accolade, hold dear, treasure

pro 3 for **5** forth **6** before,

expert, master **8** favoring
opposite: 3 con **7** amateur

probable *see* **6 likely**

probe 4 hunt, quiz, seek, test **5** query, study, trial **6** pursue, review, search, survey **7** examine, inquire, inspect **8** look into, question, research

probity 5 honor **6** virtue **7** decency, honesty **8** goodness, morality

problem 5 poser, query **6** puzzle, riddle, unruly **8** question, stubborn

proboscis 4 beak, nose **5** snoot, snout, trunk **6** siphon **7** rostrum

procedure 2 MO **3** way **4** mode **6** course, manner, method **7** process, routine **8** approach, strategy

proceed 2 go **3** act **4** come, flow, go on, grow, move, stem, work **5** arise, begin, ensue, issue, start **6** derive, follow, move on, push on, result, set out, spring **7** advance **8** continue

proceedings 4 case, suit **5** cause, trial **6** doings, events, report **7** account,

actions, affairs, lawsuit, matters

proceeds 3 net **4** gain, gate, pelf, take **5** gross, lucre, money, yield **6** assets, income, profit, reward **7** returns, revenue **8** earnings

process 3 can, dry **4** fill, flow, flux, mode, plan, ship, step, writ **5** alter, candy, smoke, treat, usage **6** change, course, freeze, handle, manner, method, motion, policy, scheme, system **7** convert, measure, passage, prepare

procession 4 file, line, rank **5** array, march, train **6** parade **7** caravan, cortege, pageant **8** progress, sequence **9** cavalcade, motorcade

proclaim 3 cry **4** tell **5** blare, state, voice **6** affirm, assert, blazon, herald, report, reveal **7** call out, declare, divulge, give out, profess, publish, release, trumpet **8** announce, disclose

proclivity 3 yen **4** bent, bias **5** taste **6** desire, liking **7** impulse, leaning **8** affinity, appetite, penchant, soft spot, tendency

procrastinate 3 lag **5** dally, defer, delay, stall, tarry **6** dawdle, linger, loiter **7** adjourn **8** hesitate, postpone

procreate 3 get **4** bear, sire **5** beget, breed, spawn **6** create **7** produce **8** conceive, engender, generate, multiply

procreation
god of: 7 Priapus

procrustean 7 drastic **8** ruthless

Procrustes
seized: 9 travelers
tied them to: 3 bed
made them fit by: 7 cutting **10** stretching
killed by: 7 Theseus

procure *see* **6 attain**

prod 3 jab, nag **4** flog, goad, lash, move, poke, push, spur, stir, urge **5** egg on, shove **6** excite, exhort, incite, needle, prompt, propel, stir up **7** provoke **8** motivate

prodigal 4 lush **5** ample **6** lavish, myriad, wanton **7** copious, profuse, replete, spender, teeming, wastrel **8** abundant, generous, numerous, reckless, swarming, wasteful

prodigy 4 whiz **6** expert, genius, marvel, master, wizard, wonder **7** whiz kid **8** rara avis

produce 4 bear, form, give, make, show **5** beget, bloom, cause, found, frame, hatch, set up, shape, yield **6** adduce, create, devise, effect, evince, evolve, flower, fruits, greens, invent, supply **7** compose, concoct, develop, fashion, provide, staples, turn out **8** generate

Producers, The
stage musical:
cast: 4 (Nathan) Lane **9** (Matthew) Broderick

production 4 film, play, show **5** drama, movie **6** cinema, circus **7** exhibit, musical, showing **8** building, carnival, creation

productive 4 busy, rich **6** active, fecund, paying, useful **7** dynamic, fertile, gainful, teeming

8 creative, fruitful, prolific, vigorous, yielding

profane 3 lay **4** evil, foul, lewd, mock, vile **5** abuse, bawdy, crude, nasty, scorn, waste **6** coarse, debase, filthy, ill-use, impure, misuse, offend, revile, ribald, sinful, unholy, vulgar, wicked **7** abusive, godless, impious, obscene, outrage, pervert, pollute

profanity 5 filth, oaths **7** cursing, cussing, impiety **8** swearing

profess 3 act, own, say **4** aver, avow, fake, sham, tell **5** admit, claim, feign, offer, put on, state, vouch **6** affirm, allege, assert, assume, depose **7** advance, certify, confess, confirm, contend, declare, embrace, purport **8** announce, maintain, proclaim

profession *see* **6 career**

professor 3 don **6** regent **7** adjoint, teacher **8** lecturer **retired: 8** emeritus

proffer 5 offer **6** extend, tender **7** advance, hold out, present

proficient 3 apt **4** able,

deft, good **5** adept, handy, quick, ready, sharp **6** adroit, clever, expert, gifted **7** capable, skilled, trained

profile 4 form, side, tale **5** shape **6** figure, sketch **7** contour, drawing, outline, picture **8** half face, portrait, side view, vignette

Profiles in Courage author: 7 (John) F Kennedy

profit 3 pay, use **4** boon, earn, gain, good, help **5** avail, favor, money, serve, value **6** income, return **7** account, benefit, revenue **8** earnings, interest, proceeds, receipts

profligate 4 evil, fast, rake, roue, wild **5** loose, satyr **6** sinner, wicked **7** corrupt, immoral **8** prodigal, reckless, wasteful

profound 4 deep, keen, sage, wise **5** acute, sober, utter **6** abject, hearty, moving, severe **7** decided, erudite, intense, serious, sincere

profuse *see* **7 copious**

progeny 3 kin, son **4** clan, heir, line, race, seed

5 blood, breed, child, heirs, issue, scion, stock, young **6** family **7** lineage **8** children, offshoot

prognosticate 7 predict, presage **8** forecast, foretell, prophesy

program 4 bill, book, card, list, plan, show **5** slate **6** agenda, design, docket, expect, intend, line up, notice, series, sketch **7** arrange, outline **8** bulletin, calendar, playbill, register, schedule, syllabus

progress 4 gain, grow, rise **5** climb, get on, mount, ripen **6** action, course, grow up, growth, mature, stride **7** advance, develop, headway, improve, proceed **8** get ahead, increase, movement

prohibit *see* **7** inhibit

project 3 aim, job **4** cast, emit, fire, goal, plan, send, task, work **5** draft, eject, expel, fling, frame, shoot, throw **6** extend, hurtle, jut out, launch, map out, propel **7** concoct, outline **8** activity, forecast, overhang, protrude, stand out, transmit

proletariat 5 plebs **6** rabble, the mob **7** populus **8** canaille, laborers

prolific 4 lush **6** fecund **7** copious, fertile, profuse **8** abundant, breeding, creative, fruitful, yielding

prolix 5 wordy **7** verbose

prologue 7 opening, preface, prelude **8** foreword, overture, preamble

prolong 5 delay **6** extend, retard **7** drag out, draw out, spin out, stretch **8** lengthen

prom 3 hop **4** ball **5** dance

promenade 3 hop **4** ball, prom, walk **5** dance **6** soiree, stroll

Prometheus
member of: 6 Titans
brother: 5 Atlas **10** Epimetheus
created mankind from: 4 clay
stole: 4 fire
punished by: 4 Zeus
chained to: 4 rock
released by: 8 Hercules

prominent 6 convex, famous **7** bulging, evident, honored, jutting, leading, notable, obvious, swollen

8 apparent, definite, extended, renowned

promiscuous 3 lax **4** fast, lewd, wild **5** loose **6** casual, impure, medley **7** immoral, jumbled, mingled, mixed-up, satyric **8** careless, immodest, unchaste

promise *see* **5 swear**

Promised Land 6 Canaan **nickname of: 10** California **6** Israel

promontory 4 cape, hill, ness, spur **5** bluff, cliff, jetty, jutty, point **6** height **8** headland, overhang

promote 3 aid **4** abet, ease, help, plug, push **5** raise **6** assist, foster **7** advance, develop, elevate, enhance, forward, support

prompt 3 cue **4** goad, keen, move, prod, push, spur, stir **5** alert, alive, cause, drive, eager, force, impel, press, quick, ready, sharp **6** active, assist, bright, excite, incite, induce, intent, lively, on time, propel, remind, thrust, timely **7** actuate, inspire, provoke **8** activate,

motivate, persuade, punctual

promulgate 6 foster **7** explain, expound, present, promote, sponsor **8** instruct, set forth

prone 3 apt **4** flat **5** level **6** liable, likely **7** subject, tending **8** disposed, face-down, inclined

prong 4 barb, hook, horn, spur, tine **5** point, spike, tooth **6** branch

pronoun 2 he, it, me, my, us, we, ye **3** all, any, few, her, his, one, she, thy, who, you **4** hers, mine, ours, some, thee, them, they, that, this, thou, what, whom **5** no one, their, these, thine, those, which, whose, yours **6** anyone, itself, myself, nobody **7** anybody, herself, himself, nothing, someone, whoever **8** somebody, whomever

pronounce 3 say **4** emit, form, rule **5** frame, judge, orate, sound, speak, state, utter, voice **6** decree **7** declare **8** vocalize

pronto 3 now **4** asap, fast,

stat **5** quick **7** quickly **8** promptly

proof 4 test **5** essay, proof, sheet, trial **6** galley, ordeal **8** scrutiny, weighing

prop 3 set **4** lean, rest, stay **5** brace, stand **6** hold up, pillar **7** bolster, shore up, support **8** buttress, mainstay, shoulder, underpin

propaganda 6 hoopla **8** ballyhoo

propagate 3 air, sow **4** bear, tell **5** beget, breed, hatch, issue, rumor, spawn, spray **6** blazon, herald, impart, notify, preach, purvey, repeat, report, spread **7** instill, scatter, trumpet **8** generate, multiply

propel *see* **5 impel**

propensity *see* **8 penchant**

proper 3 apt, fit, own **4** meet, nice, true **5** right **6** decent, marked, modest, polite, seemly **7** apropos, correct, fitting, germane **8** assigned, orthodox, suitable

property 4 hold, land, mark **5** acres, badge, funds, goods, means, point, stock, title, trait **6** aspect, assets, estate, realty **7** acreage, capital, estates, feature, grounds

prophesy 4 warn **5** augur **6** divine **7** forbode, foresee, portend, predict, presage **8** forecast, foretell, forewarn, soothsay

prophet 4 seer **5** augur, guide, sibyl **6** oracle **7** diviner, palmist, seeress **8** preacher, sorcerer

propinquity 7 kinship **8** affinity, nearness, vicinity

propitiate 4 calm **5** allay **6** pacify, soothe **7** appease, assuage, mollify, placate

proponent 6 backer, friend, patron, votary **7** booster **8** advocate, champion, defender, endorser, espouser, exponent, partisan, upholder

proportion 5 ratio **7** balance, harmony **8** evenness, symmetry

propose 3 aim, woo **4** hope, mean, plan, plot **6** aspire, design, expect, intend, scheme **7** present, suggest, venture

proprietor 5 owner **6** holder, master **7** manager **8** landlord

propriety 7 aptness, decorum, dignity, fitness **8** courtesy

propulsion 6 launch, thrust

prop up 5 brace **7** bolster, support **8** buttress

prosaic 3 dry **4** blah, dull, flat **5** prosy, stale, trite, vapid, wordy **6** common, jejune **7** humdrum, tedious

proscribe *see* **7 inhibit**

prose 3 dry **4** dull **5** novel **7** fiction, quality, tedious, writing **8** sequence

prosecute 3 sue, try **4** wage **6** direct, go with, handle, indict, manage, pursue **7** arraign, go to law, sustain **8** continue, deal with, follow up, maintain

prospect, prospects 4 hope, plan, seek, view **5** scene, vista **6** aspect, design, search, vision **7** chances, explore, go after, outlook, picture, scenery **8** panorama

prosper *see* **8 flourish**

prostitute *see* **5 whore**

prostrate 4 deck, flat **5** abase, floor, prone, spent **6** kowtow **7** bow down, flatten, laid out, worn out **8** overcome

prosy 4 dull, flat **5** banal, inane **6** stupid **7** humdrum, prosaic, tedious

protagonist 4 diva, hero, lead, star **7** heroine

protect 4 hide, keep, save, tend, veil **5** cover, guard **6** defend, harbor, shield **7** care for **8** maintain, preserve

protectorate 6 colony **7** mandate **8** province, dominion

protege 4 ward **5** pupil **6** charge **7** student, trainee

protest 3 vow **4** aver, avow, beef, deny, kick **5** gripe, march, sit-in, state **6** affirm, cry out, object, oppose, strike **7** boycott, dispute, dissent, hold out **8** complain

Proteus
   god of: 3 sea
   king of: 5 Egypt
   father: 7 Oceanus
   mother: 6 Tethys
   gift 8 prophesy

protocol 5 usage 7 customs, decorum, manners 8 good form

prototype 5 model 7 example 8 original

protozoan 4 cell 5 ameba, cilia 6 amoeba 7 euglena 8 flagella, protista

protract 6 extend, keep up 7 drag out, draw out, prolong 8 lengthen

protrude 5 belly, bulge, swell 6 jut out 7 project 8 stand out, stick out

proud 4 fine, smug, vain 5 aloof, cocky, grand, great, happy, lofty, noble 6 august, lordly, uppity 7 exalted, haughty, high-hat, pompous, revered, stuck-up, swollen 8 affected, arrogant, boastful, braggart, elevated, inflated, puffed up

prove *see* 6 **verify**

proverb 3 mot, saw 5 adage, axiom, maxim, moral, motto 6 byword, cliche, dictum, saying, truism 7 bromide, epigram, precept 8 aphorism, apothegm

provide 3 arm, fit, pay 4 give, plan 5 allow, award, cater, equip, grant, offer, state, yield 6 accord, donate, impart, render, supply, tender 7 deliver, furnish, prepare, present, produce 8 dispense

provident 4 wary 5 chary, ready 6 frugal, saving 7 careful, prudent, thrifty 8 cautious, discreet, equipped, vigilant

province 3 job 4 area, duty, part, role, zone 5 field, place, state 6 canton, charge, county, domain, office, region, sphere 7 section, station 8 business, capacity, function

provincial 4 rude 5 crude, gawky, local, rough, rural 6 clumsy, gauche, homely, oafish, rustic 7 awkward, bucolic, country 8 cloddish, down-home, homespun, regional

provisional 6 acting, pro tem 7 interim

provisions 4 feed, food, term 6 clause, fodder, forage, stores, string, viands 7 article, commons, edibles, proviso **8** supplies

proviso 5 rider **6** clause, string **8** addition

provoke 3 irk, vex **4** fire, gall, move, rile, stir **5** anger, annoy, cause, chafe, evoke, grate, impel, pique, rouse **6** arouse, elicit, enrage, excite, foment, incite, induce, madden, prompt, stir up **7** agitate, bring on, inflame, produce **8** generate, irritate, motivate

prowess 4 grit, guts **5** knack, might, nerve, power, skill, spunk, valor, vigor **6** mettle, spirit, talent **7** ability, bravery, courage, faculty, heroism, know-how, stamina **8** aptitude, boldness, strength

prowl 4 hunt, lurk, roam **5** creep, range, skulk, slink, snack, stalk, steal **6** ramble **8** scavenge

proximate 4 near **5** close **6** beside, nearby, next to **8** adjacent, imminent, next-door

proxy 3 sub **4** vote **5** agent **6** ballot, deputy **7** stand-in

prudent *see* **7 logical**

prudish 3 shy **4** prim, smug **5** timid **6** demure, modest, prissy, queasy, stuffy **7** finical, mincing, precise, stilted **8** pedantic

prune 3 cut, lop **4** clip, crop, pull, snip, thin, trim **5** shear **6** reduce **7** curtail, shorten, thin out

prurient 4 lewd, sexy **6** carnal **7** fleshy, goatish, immoral, lustful, obscene, priapic, satyric

pry 4 butt, nose, peek, peer, poke, tear, work, worm **5** break, crack, delve, force, jimmy, lever, probe, sniff, snoop **6** meddle **7** explore, inquire, intrude

psalm 3 ode **4** hymn, poem, song **5** canon, chant, verse **6** praise **7** cantata, glorify, introit **8** canticle

pseudo 4 fake, mock, sham **5** bogus, false, phony **6** forged **7** feigned **8** spurious

pseudonym 5 alias **6** anonym **7** pen name **8** cognomen, nickname

psyche 2 id **3** ego **4** mind, self, soul **5** anima

6 bowels, make up, spirit
8 superego **10** penetralia
11 personality,
unconscious **12**
subconscious

Psyche
personifies: 4 soul
loved by: 4 Eros **5** Cupid
persecutor: 5 Venus
immortalized by: 7 Jupiter

psychic 5 augur **6** medium,
mental, mystic, occult,
voyant **7** diviner, prophet,
voyante **8** cerebral

Psycho
director: 9 (Alfred)
Hitchcock
cast: 5 (John) Gavin,
(Janet) Leigh, (Vera)
Miles **6** (Martin) Balsam
7 (Anthony) Perkins

psychoanalyst 6 shrink **7**
analyst, therapist

psychology 4 head, mind **6**
makeup **7** feeling **8**
attitude
problem/illness: 6 phobia
7 obesity, smoking **8**
hysteria, neuroses,
paranoia, schizoid
term: 2 id **3** ego **6** libido
7 empathy **8** neuroses,
superego **9** catatonic,
cognition, psychoses
type: 6 social **7** Gestalt

8 abnormal, clinical **9**
cognitive

psychotic *see* **5 crazy**

Ptah
origin: 8 Egyptian
deity of: 17 universal
creation

pub 3 bar, inn **5** local **6**
bistro, saloon, lounge,
tavern **7** bar room,
ginmill, rummery, rum
shop, taproom **8** alehouse,
grogshop, pothouse

pubescent 7 teenage **8**
immature, juvenile

public 3 mob **4** folk, open
5 civic, civil, frank, overt,
plain, state, trade **6**
buyers, common, in view,
masses, nation, patent,
people, shared, social **7**
evident, exposed, general,
in sight, obvious, outward,
patrons, society **8**
apparent, communal,
divulged, everyone,
revealed

publication 4 book, news **5**
issue, paper **6** digest,
report **7** edition, gazette,
journal, tabloid **8** bulletin,
magazine, pamphlet

public disturbance 4 riot **6**
fracas, ruckus, uproar

publicity 4 hype, plug, puff **5** blurb, flack **7** build-up, puffery, write-up **8** ballyhoo, currency

publish 3 air **4** tell, vent **5** issue, print, utter **6** herald, impart, put out, spread **7** declare, diffuse, divulge, give out, placard, promote, release, trumpet **8** announce, bring out, disclose, proclaim

puce 3 red **7** dark red **13** purplish-brown

pucker 4 fold, tuck **5** pinch, pleat, purse **6** crease, gather, ruffle, rumple, shrink **7** crinkle, crumble, squeeze, wrinkle **8** compress, contract

puckish 5 elfin **6** impish **7** playful **8** annoying

pudding 5 jello **6** junket **7** custard, dessert, tapioca **8** pandowdy

pudgy, podgy *see* **3 fat**

puerile *see* **8 immature**

Puerto Rico
  name means: 8 rich port
  capital/largest city: 7 San Juan
  point: 5 Punta **7** Puntita
  sea/ocean: 8 Atlantic
  9 Caribbean
  island: 4 Mona **6** Monito **7** Culebra, Vieques **8** Palomino
  physical feature:
    rain forest: 8 El Yunque
  place:
    fortress: 7 El Morro
  feature:
    festival: 6 Casals

puff 3 bow **4** blow, draw, emit, gasp, hump, node, pant, wisp **5** bloat, smoke, swell, whiff **6** breath, dilate, exhale, expand, flurry, inhale, rising, wheeze **7** bluster, bombast, distend, inflate **8** ballyhoo, flattery

pugilist 3 pug **5** boxer **7** battler, bruiser, fighter

pugnacious 7 defiant, hostile, warlike **8** menacing, militant

puissance 5 force, might, power **6** energy **7** potency, prowess **8** strength

pulchritude 6 beauty **8** fairness

pull 2 go **3** lug, rip, tow, tug **4** drag, draw, grab, haul, jerk, lure, move, rend, rive, tear, yank **5** drive, sever **6** allure, appeal, detach, entice, sprain, strain, uproot, wrench **7** attract, draw out, extract, stretch **8** withdraw

pull one's leg 3 kid **4** fool, hoax **5** tease, trick **7** deceive

pull over, pullover 4 cite, stop **5** shirt **6** arrest, jersey, slip on, ticket, t-shirt **7** maillot, sweater

pulp 4 curd, mash, mush, pith **5** crush, flesh, paste, puree, slush, smash **6** squash, tissue **7** journal **8** magazine

pulse 4 beat **5** throb, thump **6** quiver, rhythm, stroke **7** cadence, pulsate, shudder, tremble, vibrate

pulverize 4 mash, mill **5** crumb, crush, grind, mince, pound **6** powder **7** atomize, crumble

pummel 4 beat, maul **5** pound **6** batter, thrash **7** trounce

pump 4 quiz, shoe, well **5** grill **7** inflate, slipper **8** question **9** draw water

pumpkin 5 fruit, gourd, melon **6** squash

punch 3 box, hit, jab **4** beat, blow, chop, clip, conk, cuff, pelt, plug, poke, slam, sock, swat **5** baste, clout, knock, pound, smite, thump, whack **6** pummel, strike, stroke, thrust, thwack, wallop **7** clobber **8** haymaker

punctilious 5 exact, fussy, picky, rigid **6** proper, strict **7** correct, finicky, precise **8** exacting

punctual 5 early, quick, ready **6** on time, prompt, steady, timely **7** instant, not late, regular **8** constant, on the dot

punctuate 4 lace **5** break **6** pepper **7** scatter **8** separate, sprinkle

punctuation mark 4 dash **5** colon, comma, pause, point, slash **6** accent, ending, hyphen, parens, period, quotes **7** bracket **8** ellipsis

puncture 3 cut **4** bite, hole, nick, pink **5** break, prick, stick, sting, wound

6 pierce **7** deflate, let down, opening, rupture

pundit 4 guru, sage **5** guide **6** critic, expert, mentor, savant **7** thinker

pungent 3 hot **4** acid, keen, racy, sour, tart **5** acrid, acute, nippy, salty, sharp, smart, spicy, tangy, tasty, witty **6** biting, bitter, clever, savory, snappy, strong **7** acetous, caustic, cutting, mordent, peppery, piquant, pointed **8** incisive, piercing, poignant, smarting, stinging, stirring, vinegary, wounding

punish 4 beat, fine, flog, whip **6** avenge, rebuke **7** chasten, reprove **8** admonish, chastise, imprison, penalize, sentence

punk 4 hood, lout, poor **5** bully, lousy, rowdy, tough **6** crummy, rotten **7** hoodlum, ruffian **8** hooligan

puny *see* **5 frail**

pupa 3 egg **5** larva, nymph **6** cocoon **7** wiggler

pupil 4 coed, tyro **5** tutee **6** novice **7** learner, scholar, student, trainee **8** beginner, disciple, initiate

puppet 3 toy **4** doll, dupe, pawn, tool **6** flunky, lackey **7** servant

puppy 3 dog, pet, pup **6** canine

purchase 3 buy **4** edge, hold **6** buying, pay for, pick up **7** footing, support, toehold **8** foothold, leverage

pure 4 full, mere, neat, true **5** basic, clean, fresh, moral, sheer, stark, utter, whole **6** chaste, decent, entire, higher, virgin **7** angelic, ethical, sincere, sinless, sterile, unmixed **8** innocent, sanitary, spotless, unmarred, virginal, virtuous

puree 4 bisk, pulp, soup **5** paste **6** bisque

purge *see* **5 expel**

purify 4 boil **5** clear **6** filter **7** clarify, distill **8** make pure, sanitize

Purim 4 (east of) Lots
celebrates: 11 deliverance
heroine: 6 Esther
villian: 5 Haman
month: 4 Adar

purity *see* **5** honor

purloin 3 rob **5** steal **6** pilfer

purple 4 plum, puce, racy **5** color, grape, lilac, lurid, mauve, royal **6** florid, orchid, turgid, violet **7** crimson, flowery, furious, fuchsia, magenta **8** amethyst, burgundy, imperial, lavender

purport *see* **6** allege

purpose 3 aim **4** goal, hope, mean, plan, will, wish **5** elect, point, sense **6** aspire, choose, decide, design, desire, intend, intent, motive, object, reason **7** meaning, mission, resolve **8** endeavor, function

purse 3 bag **4** fold, fund, knit **5** award, bunch, pinch, pleat, pouch, prize, stake **6** clutch, coffer, gather, pucker, wallet **7** handbag, sporran, wrinkle **8** contract, moneybag, proceeds, treasury

purser 6 bursar **7** cashier

pursue 4 seek **5** aim at, chase, track, trail **6** aim for, follow, try for **7** go after, perform

pursuit 4 hunt **5** chase **6** search **7** pastime

purveyor 4 pimp **6** seller **8** procurer, provider, supplier

purview 3 ken **4** area **5** field, range, reach, realm, savvy, scope, sweep **6** domain, extent **7** compass, horizon, outlook

push 2 go **3** dun, ram **4** butt, goad, jolt, move, plug, prod, spur, sway, urge, work, worm **5** boost, drive, egg on, force, forge, impel, nudge, press, rouse, shove **6** arouse, badger, coerce, harass, induce, inroad, jostle, prompt, thrust **7** advance, inspire, promote, provoke **8** motivate, persuade, shoulder

pushcart 5 wagon **6** barrow **8** handcart

puss 3 cat, mug, pan **4** face **6** feline, kisser, kitten

pussyfoot 5 dodge, evade, hedge, sneak **6** tiptoe, weasel **8** sidestep

put 3 fix, lay, set **4** cast, pose, rest, word **5** bring, drive, force, heave, offer, pitch, place, state, throw

6 assign, employ, impute, phrase, submit **7** deposit, propose **8** position

put a damper on 4 cool, dull **7** depress, squelch

put an end to 4 halt, stop **5** annul, quash **6** cancel, finish, repeal, revoke **7** abolish, blot out, rescind, squelch **8** abrogate, stamp out

put down 4 note, post **5** crush, enter, knock, quash, quell **6** dispel, enlist, record, subdue **7** deposit, disdain, sneer at, squelch **8** belittle, derogate, pooh-pooh

put in motion 4 move **5** begin, start **6** arouse, launch **8** activate, carry out, commence, initiate

put into effect 6 effect **7** achieve, execute, fulfill, realize **8** carry out, complete

put into words 5 voice **7** express **8** describe

put on 3 don **5** affix **6** attach **7** dress in, get into, stick on **8** fasten to

put-on 4 hoax, joke **8** pretense

put out 3 irk **5** annoy, issue **6** quench, retire **7** produce, publish **8** irritate

putrid 3 bad **4** foul, rank **5** fetid **6** rancid, rotten, spoiled **7** tainted **8** decaying, polluted, purulent, stinking

putter 4 fool, idle, laze, loaf, loll **5** dally, drift **6** dawdle, loiter, lounge, piddle, tinker **8** golf club, lallygag

put to death *see* **7 execute**

put up 3 can **4** hang **5** erect, house, lodge, raise, store **6** billet **7** shelter **8** preserve

put up with 4 bear, take **5** abide, brave, brook, stand **6** endure, suffer **7** stomach, sustain, undergo **8** submit to, tolerate

puzzle 4 foil, mull **5** brood, stump **6** baffle, enigma, outwit, ponder, riddle **7** confuse, dilemma, mystery, mystify, perplex, problem **8** bewilder, confound

Pygmalion
   author: 4 (George
   Bernard) Shaw
   basis for: 10 My Fair
   Lady
Pygmalion
   king of: 6 Cyprus
   loved: 7 Galatea
   statue changed to: 5
    woman
   wife: 7 Galatea
pygmy 3 elf, toy, wee **4**
   mite, runt, tiny **5** dwarf,

elfin, short, small **6**
bantam, midget, peewee,
shrimp **8** dwarfish,
half-pint, Tom Thumb
pyre 8 woodpile
   rite: 7 funeral
   method: 7 burning
pyrotechnics 9 fireworks
Pyrrhus
   king of: 6 Epirus
   triumphed over: 5 Romans
Pythias
   friend: 5 Damon

Q

Qatar
  capital/largest city: 4
    Doha **7** al-Dawha
  government: 7 emirate
  head of state/government:
   4 emir
  monetary unit: 5 riyal **6**
   dirham
  physical feature:
    gulf: 7 Bahrain, Persian

quack 4 fake, sham **5**
  phony **6** pseudo

quaff *see* **4 gulp**

quagmire 3 bog, fen, fix,
  jam **4** mess, mire, ooze,
  quag, sump **5** marsh,
  pinch, swamp **6** crisis,
  morass, muddle, pickle,
  plight, scrape, slough,
  sludge, strait **7** dilemma **8**
  hot water, quandary

quail *see* **5 cower**

quail
  group of: 4 bevy **5** covey

quaint 3 odd **4** rare **5** droll,
  queer **6** unique **7** antique,
  bizarre, curious, strange,
  unusual **8** charming,

fanciful, old-timey,
original, uncommon

quake 4 wave **5** quail,
  shake, spasm, throb **6**
  blanch, quaver, quiver,
  ripple, shiver, thrill,
  tremor **7** shudder, tremble

Quaker
  founder: 3 (George) Fox
  group: 7 friends

qualify 3 fit **4** ease **5** abate,
  adapt, alter, endow, equip,
  limit, ready, train **6**
  enable, modify, narrow,
  permit, reduce, soften,
  temper **7** assuage, certify,
  entitle, license, make fit,
  prepare **8** describe,
  mitigate, moderate,
  restrain, restrict, sanction

quality 4 mark, rank **5**
  blood, class, grade, merit,
  trait, value, worth **6**
  aspect, family, nature **7**
  caliber, dignity, faculty,
  feature **8** capacity,
  eminence, position,
  property, standing

qualm 4 turn **6** nausea **7** scruple, vertigo

quandary *see* **7 dilemma**

quantity *see* **6 amount**

quarantine 7 confine, isolate

quarrel 3 jar, nag, row **4** carp, feud, fuss, spat, tiff **5** argue, brawl, cavil, clash, fight, scrap **6** bicker, differ, strife **7** contend, discord, dispute, dissent, fall out, wrangle **8** argument, be at odds, conflict, squabble

quarry 3 bed, dig, pit **4** game, lode, mine, prey **5** catch, stone **6** source, victim **8** excavate

quarter, quarters 4 area, part, pity, post, side, spot, zone **5** board, house, lodge, mercy, place, put up, realm, rooms **6** billet, domain, fourth, locale, region, sphere **7** housing, lodging, shelter, station, terrain **8** locality, location, lodgings, position, precinct, province

quash 4 ruin, stop, undo, void **5** annul, crush, erase, quell, smash, wreck **6** cancel, efface, quench, recall, revoke, squash, subdue **7** blot out, destroy, expunge, repress, squelch **8** abrogate, suppress

quasi 4 near, part, semi **6** almost, ersatz **7** halfway, seeming, virtual **8** apparent, somewhat

quaver *see* **6 quiver**

quay 4 dock, mole, pier **5** basin, jetty, levee, wharf **6** marina **7** landing

queasy 5 giddy, upset **6** uneasy **7** bilious, sickish **8** nauseous, qualmish

Quebec
    cape: 5 Gaspe
    city: 6 Quebec **8** Montreal
    island: 9 Anticosti
    mineral: 4 gold, zinc **6** copper **7** iron ore **8** asbestos **9** limestone
    mountain: 10 Laurentian
    province of: 6 Canada

queen 5 ranee **7** czarina, empress **8** princess

Queen of Amazons 9 Hippolyta, Hippolyte

Queen of Heaven 4 Hera, Mary **6** Ishtar **7** Mylitta

queer 3 gay, odd **4** daft, harm, hurt, rare, ruin

5 crazy, dizzy, droll, faint, fishy, funny, giddy, shady, spoil, weird, woozy, wreck **6** absurd, exotic, quaint, qualmy, queasy, thwart, unique **7** bizarre, comical, curious, disrupt, erratic, reeling, strange, touched, unusual **8** abnormal, fanciful, freakish, peculiar, uncommon

quell *see* **4 calm**

quench *see* **7 satisfy**

Quentin Durward
   author: 5 (Sir Walter) Scott

querulous *see* **7 grouchy**

query *see* **8 question**

quest *see* **6 search**

question 3 ask, rub **4** pump, quiz, test **5** doubt, drill, grill, issue, query **6** impugn, matter, motion, oppose **7** dispute, dubiety, examine, problem, subject, suspect **8** look into, proposal, sound out

queue 3 row **4** file, line, rank **5** chain, train **6** column, string

quibble *see* **7 quarrel**

quick 3 apt **4** able, deft, fast, keen, spry **5** acute, adept, agile, alert, brief, brisk, eager, fiery, fleet, hasty, rapid, sharp, smart, swift, testy **6** abrupt, active, adroit, astute, brainy, bright, clever, expert, facile, flying, frisky, lively, nimble, prompt, shrewd, speedy, sudden **7** hurried **8** choleric

quick-tempered *see* **7 grouchy**

quick-witted *see* **5 smart**

quid pro quo 4 swap **5** trade **8** exchange

quien sabe 8 who knows

quiescence 7 latency **8** dormancy, inaction

quiet 3 low, mum **4** calm, curb, dull, ease, hush, lull, meek, mild, mute, rest, soft, stay, stop **5** abate, allay, blunt, check, fixed, inert, peace, plain, quell, still **6** at rest, deaden, docile, dozing, gentle, humble, hushed, mellow, modest, muffle, pacify, placid, repose, sedate, serene, settle, silent, simple, soften, soothe, stable, stifle, subdue

7 assuage, comfort, compose, dormant, mollify, restful, silence, unmoved **8** calmness, comatose, composed, mitigate, palliate, peaceful, reserved, reticent, serenity, sleeping, stagnant, taciturn, tranquil

Quiet Man, The
director: **4** (John) Ford
author: **9** (Liam) O'Flaherty
cast: **5** (Maureen) O'Hara, (John) Wayne **7** (Mildred) Natwick **8** (Victor) McLaglen **10** (Barry) Fitzgerald
setting: **7** Ireland

quill 3 pen **4** fold, hair, pick, seta, stem, tube **5** pluck, plume, spike, spine, spool **6** bobbin, needle **7** bristle, feather, spindle

quilt 5 cover **6** spread **7** blanket **8** coverlet

quintessence *see* **7 essence**

quip *see* **4 joke**

quirk 4 kink, turn, whim **6** fetish, foible, oddity, vagary, whimsy **7** caprice **8** crotchet, odd fancy

quisling 6 puppet **7** traitor

quit 3 end, rid **4** free, stop **5** cease, clear, forgo, leave, let go, waive, yield **6** depart, desist, disown, exempt, forego, give up, reject, resign, retire **7** abandon, disavow, drop out, forsake, take off **8** abdicate, absolved, renounce, withdraw

quite 4 very **5** fully, truly **6** highly, hugely, indeed, in fact, in toto, really, surely, vastly, verily, wholly **7** exactly, in truth, totally, utterly **8** actually, entirely

Quito
capital of: **7** Ecuador

quiver 3 tic **4** jerk, jolt, jump, pant **5** quake, shake, spasm, throb **6** quaver, shiver, totter, tremor, twitch, wobble **7** flicker, flutter, pulsate, seizure, shudder, tremble, vibrate, wriggle **8** convulse

quixotic 4 wild **6** absurd, dreamy, madcap, poetic **7** utopian **8** fanciful

quiz *see* **4 test**

quizzical *see* **3 coy**

quondam 4 erst, late, once,

past **6** bygone, former **8** formerly, sometime

quota 4 part **5** share **6** ration **7** measure, minimum, portion **8** quantity

quote 4 cite, name **6** adduce, recall, repeat, retell **7** excerpt, extract, refer to **8** instance

quotidian 5 daily **6** common **8** everyday, ordinary

Ra

also: 2 Re
origin: 5 Greek **10**
Heliopolis
god of: 3 sun
also worshipped by: 9
Egyptians

Rabat, Rabbat

capital of: 7 Morocco

rabbi 6 master, rabbin **7**
scholar, teacher

rabbit 4 cony, hare, jack,
lure **5** bunny, coney, lapin
6 novice, rodent **8**
beginner

rabble 3 mob **5** swarm **7**
the herd **8** populace,
riffraff
French: 8 canaille

rabid 4 wild **6** ardent,
crazed, raging **7** berserk,
fervent, frantic, violent,
zealous **8** deranged,
frenzied, maniacal

race 3 fly, run **4** dart, dash,
heat, rush **5** hurry **6**
hasten, hustle **7** contest,
operate **8** campaign

racism 7 bigotry **8** color
bar

rack 4 buck, gait, hurt,
neck, pace, pain, path **5**
agony, cloud, exert, frame,
raise, track, trail, worry,
wreck, wring **6** canter,
holder, strain **7** agonize,
stretch, torment

racket *see* **5 noise**

racketeer *see* **8 criminal**

raconteur 8 fabulist,
narrator, romancer

racy 4 keen **5** bawdy, crude,
heady, lurid, zesty **6**
erotic, lively, ribald,
risque, smutty, vulgar **7**
buoyant, glowing,
obscene, zestful **8** exciting,
immodest, indecent,
prurient

raddle 3 rod **4** reed, scar,
twig **5** fence, hedge,
rouge, stick, weave **6**
branch, ruddle **8** hematite,
red ocher, red ochre

radiant 5 aglow, happy,

sunny **6** bright, elated, joyous **7** beaming, glowing, shining **8** blissful, dazzling, ecstatic, luminous

radical 4 rash **5** basic, rebel **6** severe **7** drastic, extreme **8** left-wing, militant

raffish *see* **6 vulgar**

raft 3 lot **4** mass **5** barge, float **6** plenty **7** carrier, pontoon **8** flatboat, platform, quantity

rag 3 kid, rib **4** scap, song, tune, twit **5** cloth, taunt, taunt, tease **6** harass **7** torment **8** magazine

ragamuffin *see* **6 urchin**

rage 3 fad, ire **4** boil, fume, fury, mode, rant, rave, roar **5** craze, furor, mania, pique, storm, vogue, wrath **6** blow up, choler, frenzy, seethe, spleen, temper **7** explode, fashion, ferment, flare up, madness, passion, rampage, umbrage **8** paroxysm, the thing

ragout 4 hash, stew **7** borscht, goulash

raid 4 bust **5** foray, onset, sally, storm **6** attack, inroad, invade, razzia, sortie **7** assault, round-up **8** invasion

rail 3 bar **4** rage, rant **5** scold, fence, train **6** blow up, scream, take on **7** declaim, inveigh **8** banister

rail at 5 scold **6** berate **7** chew out

raillery *see* **8 repartee**

railway 4 tube **5** track, train **6** cogway, subway **7** cogroad, trolley **8** elevated, monorail

raiment *see* **7 clothes**

rain, rains 4 down, drop, mist, pour **5** spate **6** deluge, lavish, shower, squall **7** drizzle, monsoon, torrent **8** downpour, drencher, sprinkle

raincoat 3 mac **4** mack **6** poncho, ulster **7** oilskin, slicker **8** burberry

raise 3 end **4** grow, hike, lift, rear, spur, urge **5** amass, boost, breed, build, erect, nurse, pique, put up, rouse, set up, spark **6** arouse, awaken, excite, foster, hike up, jack up, kindle, obtain, stir up

7 advance, bring in, bring up, canvass, collect, develop, elevate, sharpen **8** increase

rake 4 comb, goat, roue **5** rogue, satyr, scour, sport **6** lecher, pepper, rascal **7** Don Juan, playboy, ransack, seducer, swinger **8** Casanova, Lothario, enfilade, prodigal, rakehell

rally 4 meet, rush **5** score, unite **6** caucus, gather, muster, pick up, powwow, revive **7** catch up, collect, get well, improve, recruit, reunite, revival **8** assembly, recovery

ram 3 hit, jam **4** beat, bump, butt, goat, slam **5** crash, drive, force, smash **6** batter, hammer, hurtle, strike, thrust **7** run into

ramble *see* **6 wander**

rambunctious *see* **4 wild**

ramification 3 arm **4** part, spur **5** prong **6** branch **8** division, offshoot

rampant 4 rife **5** erect **6** raging **8** epidemic, pandemic

rampart 7 barrier, bastion, bulwark, parapet

ramshackle *see* **8 decrepit**

ranch 4 farm **5** range **6** grange, spread **7** acreage, station **8** hacienda

rancid *see* **6 putrid**

rancor *see* **6 malice**

random 5 stray **6** casual, chance **7** aimless, offhand

range 3 run **4** roam, rove **5** field, gamut, limit, orbit, reach, ridge, scope **6** bounds, domain, extend, massif, plains, radius, sierra, sphere, wander **7** explore, pasture, purview, stretch, variety **8** province

rank 3 row **4** bald, file, foul, line, lush, rate, sort, tall, type, wild **5** class, crass, dense, grade, gross, level, nasty, order, sheer, stale, stand, total, utter **6** arrant, coarse, estate, filthy, jungly, lavish, rancid, status **7** echelon, glaring, profuse, rampart **8** absolute, flagrant, position, standing

rank and file 6 troops

rankle 4 gall, rile **5** chafe, gripe, pique **6** fester **8** irritate

ransack *see* **7 pillage**

ransom 3 buy **4** free, save **5** atone, price **6** redeem, rescue **7** deliver, expiate, reclaim, recover, release **8** liberate, retrieve

rant 4 fume, rage, rave, yell **5** orate, scold, spout, storm **6** bellow **7** bluster, bombast, bravado, explode **8** harangue

rap 3 jaw, pan, tap **4** bang, chat, drum, talk **5** blame, knock, roast, speak, thump **6** dump on **7** clobber **8** converse

rapacious 6 greedy **7** looting, wolfish **8** covetous, grasping, ravenous, thievish

Rape of the Lock, The author: 4 (Alexander) Pope

Raphael 9 archangel

rapid see **5 quick**

rapids 5 chute **7** current

rapport 3 tie **4** link

rapscallion 5 knave, rogue, scamp **6** rascal **7** low-life, villain **8** scalawag

rapture see **5 bliss**

rare 3 few **6** scarce, unique **7** unusual **8** uncommon

raring see **5 eager**

rascal 3 cad, imp **4** rake **5** devil, knave, rogue, scamp **7** villain **8** rakehell, scalawag

rash 5 brash, hasty **6** abrupt **7** foolish **8** careless, headlong, heedless, reckless

rasp 3 irk, nag, rub, vex **4** file **5** chafe, grate, worry **6** abrade, scrape, wheeze **7** grating, scraper, scratch **8** abrasive, irritate

rat 3 cad, cur **4** fink, heel **5** churl, knave, louse **6** betray, rascal, rotter, squeal, vermin **7** bounder, villain **8** informer

rate 3 fee **4** cost, deem, dues, levy, pace, rank, toll **5** class, count, price, speed, tempo **6** charge, figure, look on, regard, tariff **7** expense, measure **8** classify

rather 4 a bit, very **5** quite **6** fairly, kind of, pretty, sort of **8** slightly, somewhat

rathskeller 6 saloon **8** beer hall
    vessel: 4 Toby **5** stein

6 seidel **7** tankard **8** pilsener, schooner

ratify *see* **7 approve**

rating *see* **5 value**

ratio 8 equation

ration, rations 3 due **4** dole, food **5** allot **6** stores **7** measure, mete out **8** allocate

rational *see* **4 sane**

ratite 3 em(e)u, moa **4** kiwi, rhea **7** ostrich

rattan 4 cane, lash, palm, whip **5** thong **6** switch, wicker

rattle *see* **7 agitate**

ratty *see* **4 worn**

Ratzinger, Joseph 8 (Pope) Benedict XVI

raucous 4 loud **5** harsh, raspy, rough **6** hoarse, shrill **7** blaring, grating, jarring **8** grinding, jangling, piercing, strident

raunchy *see* **6 vulgar**

ravage *see* **7 pillage**

rave *see* **4 rant**

ravel 4 undo **6** unknit **7** unravel, untwine, untwist

raven 3 jet **4** crow, dark, inky, rook **5** black, ebony, sable **6** devour

Raven, The author: 3 (Edgar Allan) Poe

ravenous 6 greedy, hungry **7** piggish, starved **8** covetous, famished, grasping, ravening, starving

ravine 3 gap **4** pass, rift, wadi **5** abyss, break, chasm, cleft, crack, gorge, gulch, gully, split **6** arroyo, breach, canyon, clough, divide, valley **7** fissure **8** crevasse

ravish 4 rape **5** abuse, charm, cheer **6** defile, snatch, tickle **7** delight, enchant, gladden, outrage, overjoy, violate **8** deflower, enthrall, entrance, knock out

raw 4 bare, cold, damp, rare **5** basic, bleak, crude, frank, fresh, green, harsh, plain, rough, young **6** biting, bitter, brutal, callow, chilly, rookie, unripe **7** cutting, natural, nipping, numbing, unbaked, untried **8** blustery, immature, piercing, uncooked

rawboned 4 lean **5** gaunt, lanky, spare **7** angular

Rawlings, Marjorie Kinnan
   author of: 8 (The) Yearling

ray 3 arm **4** beam, fish, line **5** gleam, light, manta, shaft, shine, skate, trace **6** branch, streak, stream, stripe **7** radiate **8** particle, plowfish, radiance

raze *see* **7 destroy**

Razorback State
   nickname of: 8 Arkansas

reach 3 get, hit **4** find, go to, grab, make, move **5** climb, enter, get to, grasp, seize, touch **6** attain, come to, extend, secure, spread **7** contact, stretch **8** approach

react 4 work **6** answer, behave, resist, return **7** respond

read 2 go **3** say **4** note, scan, show **5** study, utter **6** adduce, peruse, recite **7** analyze, deliver, discern, explain, present **8** construe, perceive, pore over

ready 3 apt, fit, set **4** deft, keen, ripe, up to **5** acute, alert, eager, equip, handy, on tap, prone, sharp **6** adroit, all set, at hand, bright, clever, expert, facile, mature, on hand, primed, prompt **7** cunning, equal to, prepare, present, tending, willing **8** inclined, masterly, punctual

Reagan, Ronald Wilson
   nickname: 5 Dutch **6** Ronnie
   presidential rank: 8 fortieth
   party: 10 Republican
      formerly: 10 Democratic
   state represented: 2 CA
   defeated: 6 Carter (Jr) **7** Mondale **8** Anderson
   vice president: 4 Bush
   born: 2 IL **7** Tampico IL
   civilian career: 5 actor **12** sportscaster
   notable events of lifetime/ term:
      assassination attempt on: 8 Hinckley
      hostages freed in: 4 Iran
      invasion of: 7 Grenada
      marines sent to: 7 Lebanon
      scandal: 8 Irangate
   wife: 4 Jane **5** Nancy

children: 6 Ronald **7** Maureen, Michael **8** Patricia

real 4 pure, true **5** solid, valid **6** actual, honest **7** certain, factual, genuine **8** absolute, bona fide, truthful

realize 2 do **3** get, net **4** gain **5** clear, grasp **6** absorb, attain, fathom, gather, profit **7** achieve, acquire, execute, fulfill, imagine, produce **8** carry out, complete, conceive, make good, perceive

really 5 truly **6** indeed, in fact, surely, verily **8** actually

realm *see* **6 domain**

real McCoy, the 4 real **7** genuine

reap 3 get, win **4** earn, gain **5** glean, score **6** derive, gather, obtain, profit, secure, take in **7** acquire, bring in, harvest, procure

rear 3 aft, end **4** back, heel **5** after, nurse, raise, stern, train **6** dorsal, foster **7** bring up, care for, cherish, develop, educate, nurture, postern, tail end

Rear Window
director: 9 (Alfred) Hitchcock
cast: 4 (Raymond) Burr **5** (Wendell) Corey, (Grace) Kelly **6** (Thelma) Ritter **7** (James) Stewart

reason 3 wit **4** head **5** cause, logic, sense, solve **6** acumen, brains, figure, motive, sanity **7** grounds, insight **8** lucidity, occasion

reasonable *see* **4 fair**

reasoning 5 basis, logic **6** ground **7** thought **8** analysis, argument

reassure 5 cheer **6** buoy up, uplift **7** bolster, comfort **8** inspirit

rebate 6 refund **8** discount

Rebecca
author: 9 (Daphne) du Maurier

Rebecca *see* **7 Rebekah**

Rebekah
also: 7 Rebecca
husband: 5 Isaac
son: 4 Esau **5** Isaac, Jacob

rebel 3 shy **4** riot **5** avoid, quail, react, wince **6** flinch, mutiny, recoil, revolt, rise up, shrink

7 seceder, traitor, upstart **8** deserter, maverick, resister, turncoat

Rebel Without a Cause **director: 3** (Nicholas) Ray **cast: 4** (James) Dean, (Natalie) Wood **5** (Sal) Mineo **6** (Jim) Backus)

rebound 3 bob **6** bounce, recoil, re-echo **7** flounce **8** recovery, ricochet

rebuff *see* **6 refuse**

rebuke *see* **5 scold**

rebuttal 5 reply **6** answer, denial, retort **7** defense, riposte **8** disproof, negation, response

recalcitrant *see* **8 stubborn**

recall *see* **8 remember**

recant *see* **7 rescind**

recapitulate 5 recap, sum up **6** relate, repeat, reword **7** recount, restate **8** rephrase

recapture 6 retake **7** reprise

recede 3 ebb **5** abate **6** back up, go back, retire **7** regress, retreat, subside

receipts 3 pay **4** gain, gate, take **5** share, split, wages **6** income, recipe, return **7** payment, profits, returns,

revenue **8** earnings, proceeds

receive 3 get **4** meet **5** admit, greet, put up **6** accept, come by, obtain, regard, secure, suffer, take in **7** undergo, welcome **8** meet with

recent 3 new **4** late **5** fresh, novel **6** modern **8** up-to-date

receptacle 3 bag, bin, box, can, jar **4** file, tray **6** basket, bottle, hamper, holder, hopper, vessel **7** carrier **8** receiver

reception 2 do **4** fete **5** party **6** affair, soiree **7** welcome **8** greeting

receptive 8 amenable, friendly

recess 3 bay, gap **4** bend, cell, cove, fold, gulf, lull, nook, pass, rest, slot **5** break, cleft, gorge, inlet, pause **6** corner, harbor, hiatus, hollow **7** holiday, interim, respite **8** interval, vacation

recipe 2 Rx **4** cure, rule **5** axiom **6** elixir, remedy **7** formula, receipt

recipient 4 heir **5** donee,

taker **6** getter **7** legatee **8** accepter, acquirer, obtainer, receiver

reciprocate 4 feel **6** return **7** requite, respond

recite 4 tell **5** quote, speak **6** relate, repeat **7** deliver, narrate, perform, recount

reckless *see* **4 rash**

reckon 3 add **4** bank, cope, deal, deem, plan, rank, rate **5** count, fancy, guess, judge, tally, think, total **6** assess, decide, expect, figure, regard **7** bargain, compute, imagine, presume, suppose, surmise **8** consider

reclaim *see* **7 recover**

recline 4 lean, loll, rest **6** lounge, repose, sprawl **7** lie back, lie down

recluse *see* **6 hermit**

recognize 3 see **4** know, spot **5** admit, place, sight **7** discern, make out, pick out, realize, respect, yield to **8** identify, submit to

recoil *see* **7 retreat**

recollect *see* **8 remember**

recommend 4 urge **5** favor, order **6** advise **7** counsel,

endorse, propose, suggest **8** advocate, vouch for

recompense *see* **3 pay**

reconcile 5 fix up **6** adjust, make up, resign, settle, square **7** correct, patch up, rectify, reunite

reconnoiter 4 look **5** probe, scout **6** patrol, picket

reconsider 6 modify, ponder, review, revise **7** correct, rethink, sleep on **8** mull over, reassess

record 3 log **4** copy, file, list, memo, note, post, show, tape **5** admit, enter **6** annals, career, docket, enroll, report **7** account, archive, catalog, conduct, history, jot down, jotting, journal **8** document, indicate, register

recount 4 tell **6** detail, recite, relate **7** explain, narrate **8** describe

recoup *see* **6 regain**

recourse 6 choice, option, resort

recover 4 heal, mend **5** rally **6** offset, pick up, recoup, redeem, regain, retake, revive **7** balance, get back, get well, improve, reclaim, restore, win back **8** make good, retrieve, revivify

recreant *see* **6 coward**

recreation 4 play **5** hobby, sport **7** pastime

recrimination 5 blame **6** charge

recruit 4 hire **5** raise, renew **6** employ, enlist, enroll, muster, novice, recoup, revive, rookie **7** draftee, provide, recover, restore **8** beginner, newcomer

rectangle 3 box **6** oblong, square **7** polygon

rectify *see* **3 fix**

rectitude 5 honor **7** decency, probity, morality

rector *see* **6 priest**

recumbent 4 flat **5** prone **6** supine **7** leaning **8** couchant

recuperate *see* **4 heal**

recur *see* **6 repeat**

red 4 pink, rose, rosy, ruby, wine **5** aglow, coral, flame, ruddy **6** auburn, cherry, florid, maroon **7** burning, crimson, flaming, flushed, scarlet **8** blooming, blushing, cardinal, inflamed, rubicund

Red Badge of Courage, The author: 5 Stephen Crane

red-blooded *see* **6 strong**

reddish-brown 4 rust **5** henna **6** auburn, copper, russet, sienna **8** chestnut, cinnamon

redeem 4 keep, save **5** cover **6** defray, ransom, recoup, reform, regain, rescue, settle **7** buy back, convert, fulfill, reclaim, recover, satisfy **8** atone for, make good, retrieve

Redford, Robert film festival: 8 Sundance

red-letter 5 happy, lucky **6** banner

redolent *see* **8 fragrant**

redress *see* **6 remedy**

reduce 3 cut **4** bust, curb, diet, dull, ease, thin **5** abate, blunt, break, check, force, lower, slash, water **6** demote, dilute, lessen, retard, temper **7** assuage, cripple, cut down **8** diminish, discount, mark down, minimize, mitigate, modulate

redundant **5** extra **6** excess **7** surplus

reef **3** bar **4** bank, flat, spit **5** shelf, shoal **7** sandbar

reek **4** fume **5** smell, smoke, steam, stink **6** stench

reel **4** rock, roll, spin, sway **5** lurch, pitch, swirl, waver, whirl **6** rotate, teeter, totter, wobble **7** revolve, stagger, stumble

refer **2** go **4** cite, send, turn **6** advert, allude, direct, submit **7** consult, deliver, mention **8** hand over, transfer, transmit

referee *see* **6 umpire**

reference *see* **8 allusion**

refine **6** filter, purify, strain **7** cleanse, develop, improve, perfect, process

reflect **4** cast, copy, muse, show, undo **5** image, study, think, throw **6** betray, evince, expose, mirror, ponder, reason, return, reveal **7** display, exhibit, express, imitate, rebound **8** cogitate, consider, indicate, manifest, meditate, mull over, ruminate, send back

reform **4** mend **5** amend, atone, emend **6** better, remedy, repair, repent, revise **7** convert, correct, improve, rebuild, rectify, restore **8** progress

refrain *see* **6 resist**

refresh *see* **6 revive**

refreshment **4** bite, eats **5** drink, snack **6** bracer **7** potable **8** beverage, cocktail, pick-me-up, potation

refrigerate **4** cool **5** chill **6** freeze **7** congeal **8** keep cold, keep cool, put on ice

refuge **4** home **5** haven **6** asylum, harbor, resort **7** shelter **8** safehold

refugee *see* **8 fugitive**

refund **5** remit, repay **6** rebate, return **7** pay back

refurbish *see* **8 renovate**

refuse **2** no **4** deny, junk, veto **5** spurn, trash, waste **6** forbid, litter, reject **7** decline, garbage, rubbish **8** disallow, prohibit, turn down, withhold

refute **4** deny **5** rebut **6** answer **7** confute, counter **8** disprove

regain **6** recoup, redeem, retake **7** get back, reclaim, recover, win back **8** gain anew, get again, retrieve

regal *see* **5 royal**

regale *see* **5 amuse**

regard 3 eye, see **4** care, heed, hold, mind, note, rate, scan, view **5** judge, point, think, value, watch **6** admire, aspect, behold, detail, esteem, follow, gaze at, look at, matter, notice, reckon, survey, take in **7** account, concern, respect, subject, thought **8** consider, estimate, listen to, look up to, note well, relation

regarding 4 in re **5** about, anent **7** apropos

regardless 6 anyhow, anyway

regenerate *see* **7 restore**

regent 4 king **5** queen, ruler **8** governor

regime 4 rule **5** power, reign **7** command, control, dynasty **8** dominion

regimen 4 diet, rule **6** system

region 4 area, land, zone **5** field, range, realm, space, tract **6** domain **7** country,

expanse **8** district, locality, province, vicinity

register 3 log **4** dial, mark, roll, show **5** diary, gauge, meter, range, scale **6** betray, enlist, enroll, heater, ledger, record, sign up **7** betoken, check in, compass, counter, daybook, exhibit, express, logbook, set down **8** disclose, indicate, manifest, radiator, registry, take down

regress *see* **6 revert**

regret *see* **7 remorse**

regular 3 set **4** even, fine, real **5** daily, fixed, plain, usual **6** common, normal, proper, smooth, steady, trusty **7** classic, correct, genuine, habitue, natural, typical, uniform **8** accepted, constant, everyday, familiar, frequent, habitual, ordinary, orthodox, periodic, stalwart, standard, true blue

regulate *see* **6 control**

regurgitate 4 barf **5** vomit **7** throw up **8** disgorge

rehabilitate 3 fix **4** save **6** redeem, remake **7** restore, salvage **8** make over, readjust, renovate

rehash 6 repeat, retell, reword **7** restate **8** rephrase

rehearse 5 drill, ready, train **6** go over, polish, recite, relate, repeat, retell **7** narrate, prepare, recount **8** practice

reign 4 rule **6** govern, regime, regnum, tenure **7** command **8** dominion, hold sway, regnancy, tutelage

reimburse *see* **6 refund**

rein, reins 4 curb, hold **5** check **6** bridle **7** control, harness **8** hold back, restrict, suppress

reinforce 4 prop **5** steel **7** bolster, brace up, fortify, support **8** buttress

reinstate 5 renew **6** revive **7** readmit, restore

reiterate 5 resay **6** hammer, rehash, repeat, retell, reword, stress **7** iterate, reprise, restate **8** rephrase

reject *see* **4 deny**

rejoice *see* **5 exult**

rejoin 6 answer, retort **7** respond

rejuvenate *see* **6 revive**

relapse 4 fall **5** lapse **6** revert, worsen **7** decline, regress, reverse **8** fall back, sink back

relate *see* **6 convey**

relation 3 kin, tie **4** bond, link **5** tie-in **6** regard, report **7** account, bearing, concern, kinsman, recital, telling, version **8** relative

relative 3 kin **4** clan, kith **5** blood, folks, tribe **6** allied, cousin, family, people **7** cognate, germane, kinfolk, kinsman, related **8** relation, relevant

relax *see* **4 ease**

relay 3 leg **4** race, tour **5** shift **6** length **8** transfer, transmit
    race: 5 track **6** medley **8** swimming

release *see* **4 free**

relegate 3 bar **5** eject, expel **6** assign, banish, charge, commit, demote, reject **7** cast out, consign, discard, dismiss, exclude, keep out, shut out **8** delegate

relent *see* **5 yield**

relevant 3 apt, fit **6** allied, suited, tied in **7** apropos, bearing, cognate, fitting, germane, related **8** apposite, material, suitable

reliance 5 faith, trust **6** belief, credit **8** credence

relic *see* **7 memento**

relief 4 balm, cure, dole, rest **5** break, cheer **6** remedy **7** anodyne, elation, panacea, respite, welfare **8** antidote, easement, lenitive

religion 4 cult, sect **5** canon, creed, dogma, faith, piety **6** belief, church, homage **7** worship **8** devotion, theology

relinquish *see* **5 yield**

relish *see* **5 savor**

reluctant 3 shy **4** slow **5** loath **6** averse **7** laggard **8** hesitant

rely 3 bet **4** bank, lean, rest **5** count, swear, trust **6** depend **7** believe

remain 4 go on, last, stay, wait **5** abide, stand **6** be left, endure, hang on, hold up, linger **7** not move, not stir, persist, prevail, stay put, subsist, survive **8** continue, stand pat

remains 4 body **5** stiff **6** corpse, scraps **7** cadaver

remark 3 say, see **4** espy, mark, mind, note, view, word **6** behold, notice, regard, survey **7** comment, mention, pay heed

remarkable *see* **7 notable**

remedy 3 aid, fix **4** calm, cure, ease, heal, help, mend **5** amend, emend **6** relief, repair **7** assuage, correct, improve, mollify, nostrum, panacea, rectify, relieve, restore **8** medicine, mitigate, palliate, regulate

remember 3 tip **6** recall, reward

remembrance *see* **7 memento**

reminisce 4 mull, muse **6** ponder **7** reflect **8** look back, remember

remiss *see* **4 lazy**

remit 3 pay **4** free, send, ship **5** clear, let go, relax, slack **6** excuse, let out, pardon, reduce **7** absolve, forgive, forward, release, set free, slacken **8** dispatch, liberate, overlook

remnant *see* **5 shred**

remodel **4** redo **5** adapt, alter, fix up **6** change, modify **7** convert, reshape **8** overhaul, renovate

remonstrate *see* **5 scold**

remorse **3** rue **4** pang **5** grief, guilt, qualm **6** regret, sorrow **7** anguish

remote *see* **3 far**

remove **4** doff, drop, fire, move, oust, quit **5** eject, erase, expel, leave, shift **6** cancel, change, cut off, delete, depart, go away, lop off, retire, unseat, vacate **7** dismiss, extract, kick out, retreat, take off, wipe out **8** amputate, dislodge, evacuate

remove from office **4** oust **6** depose, unseat **7** impeach **9** discharge

remunerate **3** pay **5** award, grant, repay **6** reward **7** requite, satisfy

Remus
   father: **4** Mars
   twin brother: **7** Romulus
   raised by: **7** she-wolf

renaissance **7** rebirth, renewal, revival

rend **3** cut, rip **4** hurt, pain, rive, sear, tear **5** break, crack, sever, split, wound **6** cleave, divide, pierce **7** rupture, shatter **8** fracture, lacerate, splinter

render **2** do **4** cede, give, make, play **5** allot, grant, remit, yield **6** accord, donate, give up, supply, tender **7** dole out, execute, pay back, perform, present, requite **8** dispense, pay as due

rendezvous **4** date **5** focus, haunt, mecca, tryst **6** gather, muster **7** retreat **8** assemble

rendition **7** edition, reading, version

renegade *see* **8 fugitive**

renege **7** back out, fink out, pull out **8** back down, fall back, withdraw

renew *see* **6 revive**

renounce *see* **4 quit**

renovate **3** fix **4** mend **6** remake, repair, revamp **7** improve, remodel, restore **8** make over

renown **4** fame, mark, note **6** repute, status **7** acclaim **8** eminence

rent **3** fee, gap, let, rip **4** dues, gash, hire, hole, rift, slit, tear **5** break, chasm, chink, cleft, crack, lease, split **6** breach, hiatus, rental, schism, tatter, wrench **7** charter, fissure, opening, payment **8** crevasse, division, fracture

renunciation 6 denial **7** refusal **8** forgoing, spurning

repair *see* **4 mend**

reparation 6 amends, return **7** damages, redress **8** requital

repartee 6 banter, bon mot **7** riposte **8** badinage, chit chat, word play

repast 4 food, meal **5** feast, snack, table **6** spread **7** banquet **8** victuals

repay 5 match **6** refund, return, reward **7** pay back, requite

repeal *see* **6 rescind**

repeat 4 echo, redo, tell **5** mimic, quote, rerun **6** pass on, relate **7** recount, say over **8** say again

repel 4 foil, rout **5** check **6** dispel, offend, oppose, put off, rebuff, resist, revolt, sicken **7** deflect, disgust, fend off, repulse, scatter,

turn off, ward off **8** disperse, nauseate, stave off

repent 3 rue **6** bemoan, bewail, lament, regret, repine **7** deplore **8** mea culpa, weep over

repercussion 4 echo **6** effect, result **8** backlash, reaction

replace 5 spell **6** return **7** put back, restore, succeed **8** supplant

replenish 5 renew **6** refill, reload **7** refresh, reorder, replace, restock, restore

replete *see* **7 satiate**

replica 4 copy **5** model **6** double **8** likeness

reply 5 react **6** answer, rejoin, retort **7** respond **8** reaction, response

report 4 bang, boom, note, talk, tell, word **5** crack, noise, rumor, sound, state, story **6** appear, detail, expose, gossip, recite, record, relate, reveal, show up, tell on **7** account, article, divulge, hearsay, message, recount, summary **8** announce, describe, disclose, dispatch

repose *see* **4 calm**

repository 5 depot **8** magazine

reprehensible *see* **4 vile**

represent 2 be **4** mean, show **5** enact, equal, state **6** denote, depict, pose as, sketch, typify **7** betoken, express, outline, picture, portray, present, serve as **8** appear as, describe, indicate, stand for

repress *see* **7 conceal**

reprieve 4 lull, stay **5** delay, pause **6** pardon, parole **7** amnesty, respite **8** breather

reprimand *see* **5 scold**

reprisal 7 redress, revenge **8** requital

reproach *see* **5 scold**

reprobate 3 bad, low **4** base, evil, rake, roue, vile **5** scamp **6** pariah, rascal, rotter, sinner, wanton, wicked **7** corrupt, outcast **8** derelict, prodigal

reproduce 4 copy, redo, sire **5** beget, breed, match, spawn **6** mirror, repeat, re-echo **7** imitate, reflect **8** generate, multiply

reproductive system **component: 5** penis **6** testes, uterus, vagina **7** ovaries

reprove *see* **5 scold**

reptile 3 asp, eft **4** newt, teju **5** agama, anole, gecko, skink, snake, viper **6** dragon, iguana, lizard, mugger, turtle **7** crawler, creeper, serpent, tuatara **8** basilisk, dinosaur, groveler, terrapin, tortoise

republic 9 democracy

Republic **author: 5** Plato

Republican Party **also called: 3** GOP **symbol: 8** elephant

Republic of China *see* **6 Taiwan**

repudiate *see* **7 rescind**

repugnant 4 foul, vile **5** nasty **6** odious **7** adverse, counter, hateful, opposed **8** contrary, unsavory

repulse 4 shun **5** avoid, repel, spurn **6** ignore, rebuff, refuse, reject

repute 3 say **4** deem, fame, hold, view **5** judge, think **6** esteem, reckon, regard, renown **7** account, believe, suppose **8** consider, estimate, standing

request *see* **3 ask**

requiem 5 dirge **6** lament **8** threnody

require 3 bid **4** lack, miss, need, want **5** crave, imply, order **6** charge, compel, desire, direct, enjoin, entail, oblige **7** dictate

requisite 4 must, need **6** needed **8** required

rescind 4 void **5** annul, quash **6** cancel, recall, repeal, revoke **7** abolish, discard, nullify, retract, reverse **8** abrogate, dissolve, override, overrule

rescue *see* **4 save**

research 5 probe, study **7** delving, inquiry **8** analysis, scrutiny

resemble 5 favor **6** be like **8** be akin to, look like, parallel

resentful 5 angry **6** bitter **7** annoyed **8** grudging, offended, provoked

reserve 4 book, hold, keep, save **5** amass, delay, extra, hoard, lay up, spare, stock, table **6** backup, engage, retain, shelve,

unused **7** husband, nest egg, savings **8** conserve, keep back, postpone, preserve, salt away, schedule, withhold

reservoir 4 fund, pool, tank, well **5** basin, fount, hoard, stock, store **6** supply **7** backlog, cistern **8** millpond

reshape *see* **5 modify**

reside 3 lie **4** live, rest, room **5** dwell, exist, lodge **6** belong, occupy **7** inhabit, sojourn **8** domicile

residual 5 extra **7** abiding, lasting, surplus **8** enduring, leftover

residue 4 rest **5** dregs **6** scraps **7** balance, remains, remnant **8** leavings

resign *see* **4 quit**

resilient 5 hardy **6** supple **7** buoyant, elastic, rubbery, springy **8** flexible

resin 3 gum, lac, tar **5** amber, copal, elemi, epoxy, jalap, myrrh, pitch, rosin **6** balsam, guaiac, mastic **7** galipot, lacquer, shellac

resist 4 balk, foil, stem,

stop **5** fight, repel **6**
baffle, combat, oppose,
refuse, reject, thwart **7**
contest, counter, weather
8 beat back, turn down

resolute 5 stern **6** dogged,
steady **7** earnest, staunch,
zealous **8** decisive,
diligent, intrepid,
stubborn, untiring,
vigorous

resolve *see* **6 settle**

resonant 4 full, rich **7**
booming, orotund,
ringing, vibrant **8**
sonorous

resort 3 use **4** hope **5**
apply, avail **6** chance,
employ, take up **7** utilize
8 exercise, recourse

resourceful 4 able **5** ready,
sharp, smart **6** adroit,
artful, bright, shrewd **7**
capable, cunning **8**
creative, skillful, talented

resources 5 funds, means,
money **6** assets, income **7**
capital, effects, revenue

respect 5 honor, point,
sense **6** detail, esteem,
matter, notice, praise,
regard **7** bearing, feature,
viewing **8** approval,
courtesy, relation

respiratory system
component: 4 lung, nose
6 larynx **7** pharynx,
trachea **8** voice box,
windpipe **9** bronchius,
diaphragm
action: 9 breathing

respite *see* **6 recess**

resplendent *see* **7 radiant**

response 5 reply **6** answer,
retort, return **7** riposte **8**
comeback, feedback,
reaction, rebuttal

responsibility 4 duty, task
5 blame, order, trust **6**
burden, charge **8** function

rest 2 be **3** end, lay, lie,
nap, set **4** base, ease, halt,
hang, keep, laze, lean,
loaf, loll, lull, prop, rely,
stay, stop **5** break, death,
exist, hinge, let up, pause,
peace, place, quiet, relax,
sleep, stand **6** demise,
depend, holder, lounge,
others, recess, remain,
repose, reside, scraps,
siesta, snooze, trivet **7**
balance, be based, be
found, be quiet, decease,
deposit, holiday, leisure,
lie down, recline, remains,
remnant, residue, respite,
set down, slumber,

support **8** breather, platform, vacation

restaurant 5 diner **6** eatery **7** beanery, tearoom
French: 4 cafe **6** bistro

restitution 6 amends **7** redress, replevy **8** replevin, requital, restoral

restive 5 balky **6** mulish, ornery, unruly **7** fidgety, wayward, willful **8** contrary, stubborn

restless *see* **7 agitate**

restore 3 fix **4** cure, dose, heal, mend **5** rally, renew, treat **6** do over, recoup, remedy, repair, rescue, return, revive **7** get back, patch up, put back, rebuild, recover, refresh, remodel **8** energize, make over, medicate, renovate, retrieve, revivify, recreate

restrain 3 gag **4** bind, curb, hold, stop **5** check, leash, limit **6** arrest, bridle, muzzle, temper, tether **7** chasten, contain, curtail, harness, inhibit, prevent, shackle, trammel **8** hold back, restrict, withhold

restraint 4 curb **5** check **7** control

restrict 4 curb, hold **5** check, cramp, crimp, hem in, limit **6** hamper, impede, narrow, thwart **7** confine, inhibit, prevent, squelch **8** hold back, obstruct, straiten, suppress

result 4 stem **5** arise, end up, ensue, fruit, issue, owe to **6** derive, effect, happen, pan out, report, sequel, spring, upshot, wind up **7** outcome, product, verdict **8** decision, judgment, solution

resume 2 CV **3** bio **4** go on **5** brief **6** digest **7** epitome, proceed, summary **8** abstract, continue, reembark, synopsis

resurgence 6 return **7** rebirth, renewal, revival

retailer 5 store **6** dealer, seller, trader **8** merchant, provider, supplier

retain 4 hold, keep **5** grasp **6** absorb, recall **7** possess **8** hang on to, hold on to, memorize, remember

retaliate *see* **7 revenge**

retard *see* **4 slow**

reticent *see* **5 timid**

retinue 5 court, staff, suite, train **6** convoy

retire 6 depart, go away, remove, resign, resort, secede, turn in **7** drop out, retreat **8** abdicate, flake out, withdraw

retort 3 say **4** quip **5** rebut, reply **6** answer, rejoin, return **7** counter, respond

retract 4 deny **6** abjure, disown, draw in, recall, recant, recede, recoil, reel in, repeal, revoke **7** disavow, rescind, retreat, reverse **8** abnegate, abrogate, renounce, take back, withdraw

retreat 2 go **3** den **4** bolt, flee, port **5** haunt, haven, leave **6** asylum, depart, escape, flight, harbor, recoil, refuge, resort, retire, shrink **7** abscond, getaway, sanctum, shelter **8** back away, hideaway, turn tail, withdraw

retrench *see* **6 reduce**

retribution 6 amends, return, reward **7** justice, nemesis, penalty, redress, revenge **8** reprisal, requital

retrieve 4 snag **5** fetch **6** ransom, recoup, redeem, regain, rescue **7** get back, reclaim, recover, salvage

retrograde 5 worse **6** worsen **7** inverse, retreat, reverse **8** backward

return 3 net **4** earn, gain **5** gross, recur, repay, yield **6** advent, come to, go back, income, profit, render, reseat, reward **7** arrival, benefit, produce, provide, put back, requite, restore, revenue **8** come back, earnings, interest, proceeds, reappear, recovery, restoral

Return of the Native author: 5 (Thomas) Hardy

reunite 5 rewed **7** remarry

reveal *see* **6 expose**

revel 4 romp **5** caper, enjoy **6** bask in, frolic, gambol, relish **7** carouse, delight, indulge, rejoice, roister, skylark **8** wallow in

revenge 5 repay **7** pay back, requite **8** reprisal, requital

revenue *see* **6 profit**

reverberate 4 boom, echo, ring **5** carry **6** rumble **7** resound, thunder, vibrate

revere *see* **5 honor**

reverie 5 dream, fancy **6** musing **7** fantasy **8** daydream

reverse 4 back, rear, tail, undo, void **5** annul, upend, upset **6** cancel, change, defeat, invert, mishap, negate, recall, recant, repeal, revoke, unmake, upturn **7** counter, nullify, rescind, retract **8** abrogate, backward, opposite, overrule, turn over, withdraw

revert 5 lapse **6** go back, repeat, return **7** regress, relapse

review 4 show **5** study, sum up **6** notice, parade, rehash, survey **7** analyze, journal, retrace, run over **8** critique, evaluate, hash over, magazine, reassess, report on, scrutiny

revile *see* **10 defamation**

revise *see* **6 modify**

revive 5 dig up, renew **6** drag up, repeat **7** freshen, refresh, restage **8** reawaken

revoke *see* **7 rescind**

revolt 4 coup, rise **5** rebel, repel, shock **6** appall, mutiny, offend, rise up, sicken **7** dissent, horrify, repulse **8** disorder, nauseate, sedition, uprising

revolve 4 spin, turn **5** twist, wheel **6** circle, gyrate, rotate

revolver 3 gat, gun, rod **4** colt **6** pistol, weapon **7** firearm, handgun, sidearm

reward 3 due **5** bonus, prize, repay, wages **6** bounty **7** deserts, guerdon, premium, requite

rex 4 king

rhapsodic 6 elated **7** beaming, excited **8** blissful, ecstatic, thrilled

Rhea
  member of: 6 Titans
  father: 6 Uranus
  mother: 4 Gaea
  brother: 6 Cronos
  husband: 6 Cronos
  son: 4 Zeus **5** Hades **8** Poseidon
  daughter: 4 Hera **6** Hestia **7** Demeter

Rhea Silvia
  form: 12 vestal virgin
  lover: 4 Mars
  son: 5 Remus **7** Romulus

rhetoric 4 bunk, wind **5** hokum, hooey **6** bunkum, hot air **7** fustian, oratory **8** euphuism

Rhode Island
  abbreviation: 2 RI
  nickname: 5 Ocean
  capital/largest city: 10 Providence
  highest point: 12 Jerimoth Hill
  sea: 8 Atlantic
  island: 4 Goat **5** Block, Dutch, Rhode

Rhodesia *see* **8 Zimbabwe**

rhodolite
  species: 6 garnet

rhubarb 5 Rheum

rhyme 3 pun **4** poem, rune, song **5** chime, clink, meter, poesy, verse **6** jingle, poetry, rhythm **7** measure, poetize, versify **8** assonate, doggerel
  game: 6 crambo

rhythm 4 beat, lilt, time **5** meter, pulse, swing, throb **6** accent, number, stress **7** cadence, measure **8** emphasis, movement

rib *see* **5 tease**

ribald *see* **6 vulgar**

ribbon 3 bow, ray **4** band, sash **5** award, braid, prize, reins, strip **6** cordon, riband **7** binding, rosette **8** memorial, streamer

rice 5 Oryza
  liquor: 4 sake

rich 4 dark, deep, fine, lush **5** flush, heavy, loamy, sweet, vivid **6** bright, costly, fecund, lavish, mellow **7** fertile, filling, intense, moneyed, opulent, wealthy, well-off **8** abundant, affluent, prodigal, resonant, sonorous, well-to-do

rickety *see* **5 frail**

rid 4 free **5** clear, purge **6** remove **8** disabuse, liberate, unburden

riddle *see* **6 enigma**

ride 4 move **5** annoy, carry, drive, harry, hound **6** badger, handle, harass, hector, manage, needle, travel **7** control, journey, support **8** progress

rider 5 affix **6** suffix **7** adjunct, codicil **8** addendum, appendix

ridge 3 bar, rib, rim **4** bank, fret, hill, hump, rise, wale, weal, welt **5** bluff, crest, crimp, knoll, mound, spine **6** ripple **7** crinkle, hillock, wrinkle

ridicule *see* **4 mock**

rife 5 close, dense, solid, thick **6** common, packed **7** crowded, general, studded, teeming **8** epidemic, pandemic, populous, swarming

riffraff 3 mob **4** herd, scum **5** crowd, dregs, trash **6** masses, proles, rabble, vermin

rifle *see* **7 pillage**

rift *see* **8 fracture**

rig 4 gear **5** equip **6** fit out, outfit **8** carriage

right 2 OK **3** due **4** deed, fair, good, just, meet, nice, real, sane, true, well **5** amend, emend, exact, grant, honor, ideal, legal, licit, moral, power, solve, sound, valid **6** actual, decent, honest, lawful, morals, normal, proper, remedy, seemly, square, virtue **7** certain, correct, ethical, exactly, factual, fitting, genuine, perfect, precise, probity, warrant **8** accurate, clear-cut, definite, directly, morality, rational, sanction, straight, suitably, truthful, virtuous

righteous *see* **5 moral**

right hand 4 aide, ally **6** helper **7** partner **8** adjutant

rigid *see* **4 firm**

Rigoletto
  opera by: 5 Verdi

rigorous *see* **5 tough**

rig out 4 garb **5** array, dress **6** attire, clothe

rile *see* **3 vex**

rill 5 brook, cleft, creek **6** furrow, groove, runnel, stream **7** channel, rivulet

rim 3 lip **4** edge, side **5** brink, ledge, verge **6** border, margin

rime 3 ice **4** hoar **5** chink, cleft, crack, crust, frost **7** crevice, fissure

rind 4 bark, hull, husk, peel, skin **5** crust, shell **6** cortex, fringe **7** epicarp, surface **8** exterior
  pork: 9 crackling

ring 4 aura, band, bloc, buzz, call, echo, gang, hoop, loop, peal, toll, tone **5** cabal, chime, clang, knell, party, sound

6 cartel, circle, cordon, herald, jangle, jingle, strike, summon, tinkle **7** besiege, circuit, enclose, resound, seal off, vibrate **8** encircle, surround

Ring des Nibelungen, Der
also: 7 The Ring (Cycle)
opera by: 6 Wagner

ringleader 5 chief **6** master

ringlet 4 curl **6** circle

Rio de Janeiro
area: 7 Ipanema **10** Copacabana
celebration: 8 Carnival **9** Mardi Gras
former capital of: 6 Brazil
people: 8 Cariocas
replaced as capital by: 8 Brasilia
slums: 7 favelas

riot *see* **6 mutiny**

rip *see* **4 tear**

ripe 3 due, fit **4** come **5** ideal, ready **6** mature, mellow, primed, timely **7** perfect **8** complete, finished, seasoned

Rip Van Winkle
author: 6 (Washington) Irving

rise 4 bank, defy, dune, face, gain, go up, grow, hill, lift, meet, soar **5** climb, get up, knoll, march, mount, rebel, ridge, spire, stand, surge, swell, tower **6** ascend, growth, mutiny, resist, revolt, rocket, strike, thrive **7** advance, balloon, burgeon, disobey, elevate, headway, improve, prosper, stand up, succeed, upswing **8** addition, flourish, increase, progress

risible *see* **5 funny**

risk 4 dare **5** peril **6** chance, danger, gamble, hazard **7** imperil, venture **8** endanger, jeopardy

risque *see* **6 vulgar**

rite 6 ritual **7** liturgy, service **8** ceremony

rite of passage 6 ritual **7** baptism **8** ceremony, marriage

ritual 4 rite **7** service **8** ceremony

ritzy *see* **5 fancy**

rival 3 foe **5** enemy, equal, excel, fight, match, outdo, touch **6** strive **7** eclipse, surpass **8** approach, opponent, outshine

riven 4 rent, torn **5** split **7** cleaved, cracked **8** sundered

river mouth 5 delta, firth **7** estuary

rivet 3 fix, pin **6** absorb, clinch, engage, fasten **7** engross

rivulet 3 run **4** rill **5** brook, creek **6** stream

Riyadh
  capital of: 11 Saudi Arabia

road 3 via, way **4** lane, path **5** byway, route, trail **6** avenue, street **7** freeway, highway, parkway **8** turnpike

roam *see* **6 wander**

roan 5 horse **7** grayish, reddish, tannish **8** blackish, brownish

roar 3 bay, cry, din **4** bawl, boom, howl, roll, yell **5** blare, growl, grunt, noise, shout, snort **6** bellow, clamor, guffaw, outcry, racket, rumble, scream, shriek **7** bluster, resound, thunder **8** outburst

roast 3 pan **4** bake **6** berate **7** scourge **8** barbecue

rob 4 bilk, lift, loot, raid, sack, skin **5** cheat, filch, heist, rifle, seize, steal **6** burgle, fleece, forage, hold up, pilfer, thieve **7** despoil, pillage, plunder, purloin, ransack, stick up, swindle **8** embezzle

Robbins, Jerome
  choreographer of: 8 Les Noces **9** Fancy Free, Interplay
  director of: 13 West Side Story (with Robert Wise, Oscar)

robe 4 gown **5** dress, habit, smock **6** duster **7** costume, garment **8** bathrobe, vestment
  French: 8 negligee
  Japanese: 6 kimono

Robinson Crusoe
  author: 5 (Daniel) Defoe

robust *see* **5 hearty**

rock 3 bob, jar **4** crag, reef, roll, stun, sway, toss **5** cliff, flint, pitch, quake, shake, stone, swing, upset **6** gravel, marble, pebble, totter, wobble **7** agitate, bobbing, boulder, disturb

rock crystal
  species: 6 quartz

Rocky
  director: 8 (John G)

Avildsen

cast: 5 (Thayer) David, (Talia) Shire, (Burt) Young **8** (Burgess) Meredith, (Sylvester) Stallone, (Carl) Weathers

rod 4 cane, lash, mace, pale, pole, wand, whip **5** baton, birch, crook, staff, stake, stick **6** cudgel, rattan, switch **7** penalty, scepter, scourge **8** caduceus

rodent 4 cavy, vole **5** coypu, gundi, hutia, mouse **6** agouti, beaver, cururo, gerbil, gopher, jerboa, nutria **7** blesmol, cane rat, hamster, lemming, mole-rat, rock rat **8** capybara, chipmunk, dormouse, pacarana, sewellel, spiny rat, squirrel, tucu-tuco, viscacha

rodomontade *see* **7 bombast**

roe 3 doe, elk, hen **4** buck, deer, eggs, fawn, fish, hart, hind, milt **5** spawn, sperm **6** caviar **8** fish eggs

of lobster: 5 coral

Rogers, Roy

real name: 4 (Leonard) Slye

wife: 4 Dale (Evans)

sidekick: 5 Gabby (Hayes)

horse: 7 Trigger

rogue *see* **3 imp**

roil *see* **3 vex**

role 3 job **4** duty, part, pose, post, task, work **5** chore, guise **7** posture, service **8** capacity, function

Latin: 7 persona

roll 4 boom, coil, curl, echo, flip, flow, furl, knot, list, loop, reel, roar, rock, spin, sway, toss, tube, turn, wind **5** coast, sound, spool, surge, swell, swirl, twirl, twist, wheel, whirl **6** gyrate, roster, rotate, rumble, scroll, tumble **7** booming, catalog, entwine, resound, revolve, thunder **8** cylinder, drumbeat, rumbling, schedule, undulate

rollicking *see* **5 happy**

roly-poly *see* **3 fat**

roman 5 novel

Roman Catholic church

council/synod: 4 Pisa **5** Basel, Trent **6** Nicaea, Vienne, Whitby **7** Ephesus, Pistoia, Sardica

romance 4 bosh, call, pull **5** amour, idyll, novel **6** affair, allure **7** fantasy, fiction **8** illusion

Romania
  other name: 7 Rumania
  capital/largest city: 9
    Bucharest
  mountain: 7 Balkans **9**
    Moldavian **10**
    Carpathian
  highest point: 10
    Moldoveanu
  river: 4 Prut **6** Danube
  sea: 5 Black
  physical feature:
    gorge: 8 Iron Gate
    peninsula: 6 Balkan
  place:
    castle: 4 Bran **7**
      Huniady
  feature:
    game: 4 oina
    Roman province: 5
      Dacia
  food:
    pepper spice: 7 paprika
    plum brandy: 5 tuica

Roman measure 2 as **5** cubit, libra **6** pondus **7** stadium

Roman Mythology
  goddess of agriculture: 5
    Ceres

    corresponds to Greek: 7
      Demeter
  goddess of the arts: 7
    Minerva
    corresponds to Greek: 6
      Athena
  goddess of chastity: 5
    Fauna **7** Bona Dea
  goddess of heaven: 4
    Juno
    corresponds to Greek: 4
      Hera
  goddess of hunting: 5
    Diana
    corresponds to Greek: 7
      Artemis
  goddess of love: 5 Venus
    corresponds to Greek: 9
      Aphrodite
  goddess of the moon: 5
    Diana
    corresponds to Greek: 6
      Phoebe **7** Artemis
  goddess of victory: 8
    Victoria
    corresponds to Greek: 4
      Nike
  goddess of wisdom: 7
    Minerva
    corresponds to Greek: 6
      Athena
  god of commerce: 7
    Mercury
    corresponds to Greek: 6
      Hermes

god of fire/metalworking:
6 Vulcan
   corresponds to Greek:
   10 Hephaestus
god of healing: 11
  Aesculapius
   corresponds to Greek: 9
   Asclepius
god of heavens: 4 Jove **7**
  Jupiter
   corresponds to Greek: 4
   Zeus
god of love: 5 Cupid
   corresponds to Greek: 4
   Eros
god of sea: 7 Neptune
   corresponds to Greek: 8
   Poseidon
god of the sun: 3 Sol
   corresponds to Greek: 6
   Helios **8** Hyperion
god of war: 4 Mars
   corresponds to Greek: 4
   Ares
household gods: 5 lares **7**
  penates
nymphs/deities with gift of
prophecy: 7 Camenae
   correspond to Greek: 5
   Muses
protectress of women: 5
  Diana
   corresponds to Greek: 6
   Phoebe **7** Artemis
queen of heaven: 4 Juno

   corresponds to Greek: 4
  Hera
romantic 4 fond **5** mushy,
soppy **6** ardent, dreamy,
loving, tender, unreal **7**
amorous, devoted, fervent,
flighty, idyllic, utopian **8**
enamored, fanciful

Rome
  airport: 8 Ciampino **7**
  (Leonardo) da Vinci
  capital of: 5 Italy **6**
   Latium **11** Papal States,
  Roman Empire
  church: 8 St Peter's
  Italian: 4 Roma
  nickname: 11 Eternal City
  river: 5 Tiber

Romeo *see* **6 suitor**

Romeo and Juliet
  author: 11 (William)
  Shakespeare

Romeo and Juliet
  symphony by: 7 Berlioz
  opera by: 6 Gounod
  ballet by: 9 Prokofiev

romp *see* **6 frolic**

Romulus
  father: 4 Mars
  twin brother: 5 Remus
  raised by: 7 she-wolf
  first king of: 4 Rome
  founder of: 4 Rome

Roncalli, Angelo Giuseppe 4 (Pope) John XXIII

roofing 4 tile, turf **5** slate, terne **6** thatch **7** asphalt, ceiling, pantile, shingle **8** housetop

rook *see* **5 cheat**

rookie 4 tyro **6** novice **8** beginner

room 4 area **5** range, scope, space **6** chance, extent, leeway, margin **7** chamber, cubicle, expanse, lodging

Roosevelt, Franklin Delano
presidential rank: 12 thirty-second
party: 10 Democratic
state represented: 2 NY
defeated: 5 Aiken, Coxey, Dewey, Lemke **6** Babson, Colvin, Foster, Harvey, Hoover, Landon, Thomas, Upshaw, Watson **7** Browder, Willkie **8** Reynolds, Teichert
vice president: 6 Garner, Truman **7** Wallace
born: 2 NY **8** Hyde Park
died: 2 GA **11** Warm Springs
dog: 4 Fala
  notable events of

lifetime/term: 4 D-Day **7** New Deal **10** Depression, World War II
  act: 9 Lend-Lease
  attack on: 11 Pearl Harbor
  conference: 5 Cairo, Yalta **7** Teheran
wife: 7 (Anna) Eleanor

Roosevelt, Theodore
nickname: 5 Teddy
presidential rank: 11 twenty-sixth
party: 10 Republican
state represented: 2 NY
succeeded: 8 McKinley
defeated (second term): 4 Debs **6** Parker, Watson **7** Holcomb, Swallow **8** Corregan
vice president: 9 Fairbanks
born: 2 NY **11** New York City
civilian career: 6 author **7** rancher **8** lecturer
military service: 13 National Guard
  war: 16 Spanish-American
organized: 11 Rough Riders
led charge up: 11 San Juan Hill

**notable events of lifetime/
term: 10** Square Deal
  earthquake in: 12 San
  Francisco
  won: 5 Nobel **10** Peace
  Prize
wife: 5 Alice, Edith

rooster
young: 8 cockerel

root 3 fix, set **4** back, base,
bind, bulb, clap, hail, nail,
rise, stem **5** basis, boost,
cheer, fount, radix, start,
stick, tubes **6** bottom,
fasten, ground, motive,
origin, reason, second,
source, spring **7** applaud,
bolster, cheer on, radicle,
support **8** occasion

Roots
author: 9 Alex Haley
cast: 4 (John) Amos,
  (Moses) Gunn **5**
  (Edward) Asner **6**
  (LeVar) Burton, (Ben)
  Vereen **7** (Maya)
  Angelou, (Louis) Gossett

rope 3 gad, guy, tie, tow **4**
bind, cord, fast, guss,
hemp, line, lure, snag,
trap, wire, yarn **5** cable,
catch, chord, lasso, noose,
riata, shank, strap, twine
6 corral, entice, hawser,
lariat, seduce, string,
tether **7** bobstay, cordage,
halyard, lanyard, lashing,
painter **8** dragline, restrain
fiber: 5 sisal

rose 4 Rosa

Rosemary's Baby
director: 8 (Roman)
  Polanski
based on novel by: 5 (Ira)
  Levin
cast: 6 (Mia) Farrow,
  (Ruth) Gordon **8**
  (Sidney) Blackmer **10**
  (John) Cassavetes

roster *see* **6 agenda**

rostrum 4 dais **5** stage,
stand, stump **6** podium,
pulpit **7** lectern, soapbox
8 platform

rosy 4 pink **5** ruddy **6**
bright, florid **7** flushed,
glowing, hopeful, reddish
8 blooming, blushing,
cheerful, flushing,
inflamed, rubicund

rot *see* **5 decay**

rotate 4 eddy, reel, roll,
spin, turn **5** pivot, swirl,
twirl, twist, wheel, whirl **6**
change, circle, gyrate,
swivel **7** revolve

rotter *see* **6 rascal**

rotund *see* **5 round**

roue *see* **6 suitor**

rough 3 raw **4** beat, hard, rude, wild **5** bluff, blunt, bumpy, crude, cruel, draft, green, gruff, harsh, hasty, husky, quick, raspy, rocky, scaly, sharp, surly, tough, vague **6** abrupt, brutal, callow, choppy, clumsy, coarse, hoarse, jagged, ragged, roiled, rugged, savage, severe, stormy, thrash, vulgar **7** bearish, boorish, brusque, chapped, coarsen, extreme, gnarled, grating, inexact, jarring, loutish, outline, rasping, raucous, scraggy, uncouth, violent **8** churlish, rigorous, scratchy

roughneck *see* **7 hoodlum**

round 3 fat **4** full, oval **5** cycle, obese, orbed, ovate, ovoid, plump, pudgy, stout, total, tubby, whole **6** chubby, circle, curved, entire, fluent, intact, portly, rotund, series, smooth **7** flowing, globoid, perfect **8** globular, spheroid, unbroken

roundabout *see* **8 indirect**

rounds 4 beat **5** route, skirt, watch **7** circuit

roundup 6 muster, resume **7** meeting, summary **8** assembly

rouse *see* **4 spur**

roust 4 bust **5** rouse **6** arrest, hassle **7** capture, seizure

rout *see* **6 defeat**

route 3 run **4** beat, pass, path, road, ship, tack **5** remit, round, track **6** artery, course, detour, direct **7** circuit, highway, parkway, passage, roadway **8** dispatch, transmit, turnpike

routine 4 dull **5** order, usual **6** boring, custom, method, normal, system **7** formula, regular, tedious, typical **8** habitual, ordinary

rove *see* **6 wander**

row 4 file, line, rank, spat, tier, tiff **5** brawl, chain, melee, queue, range, scrap, set-to, train, words **6** column, fracas, scrape, series, string **7** echelon, quarrel, wrangle

8 argument, disorder, sequence, squabble

rowboat 3 gig **4** bark, dory **5** barge, canoe, dingy, scull, shell, skiff **6** barque, caique, dinghy, wherry
seat: 4 taft

rowdy 6 unruly **7** lawless, raffish

Rowling, J.K. (Joanne Kathleen)
author of: 17 Harry Potter and the.. **12** Goblet of Fire **14** Sorcerer's Stone **16** Chamber of Secrets, Half-Blood Prince **17** Order of the Phoenix, Prisoner of Azkaban

royal 5 grand, regal **6** august, lavish, superb **7** stately **8** imposing, majestic, splendid

rub 4 buff, swab, wipe **5** annoy, braze, catch, chafe, clean, hitch, knead, pinch, scour, scrub, smear, thing, touch, trick **6** abrade, finger, polish, secret, smooth, spread, strait, stroke **7** problem, setback, slather, trouble **8** hardship, obstacle

rubberstamp 6 affirm **7** approve, endorse

rubbish *see* **4 junk**

rubble *see* **4 junk**

rube *see* **3 oaf**

rub elbows *see* **6 mingle**

rub out 4 do in, kill, slay **5** erase **6** efface, murder **7** bump off, destroy, execute, expunge **8** massacre

ruby
species: 8 corundum
kind: 4 star
color: 3 red

ruckus *see* **9 commotion**

ruddy *see* **4 rosy**

rude 3 raw **4** wild **5** blunt, crude, fresh, green, gross, gruff, rough, saucy, sulky, surly **6** abrupt, callow, clumsy, coarse, crusty, gauche, homely, rugged, rustic, sullen, uneven, vulgar **7** boorish, brusque, brutish, ill-bred, loutish, profane, scraggy, uncivil, uncouth **8** churlish, impolite, impudent, insolent

rudimentary 5 basic **6** simple **7** initial, primary

rue *see* **5 mourn**

ruffian *see* **7 hoodlum**

ruffle 4 fold, muss, wave **5** frill, plait, pleat, ruche, upset **6** edging, excite, muss up, pucker, rimple, ripple, rumple **7** agitate, confuse, crinkle, disturb, flounce, perturb, roughen, trouble, wrinkle **8** unsettle

ruffle one's feathers *see* **3** **vex**

rugged *see* **5 rough**

ruin, ruins 3 gut, pot **4** doom, fall, fell, harm, raze, seed **5** break, crush, decay, level, quash, quell, shell, spoil, upset, wreck **6** beggar, defeat, ravage, squash **7** destroy, failure, remains, shatter **8** bankrupt, demolish, downfall, overturn, remnants, wreckage

rule 3 law, run **4** find, form, head, lead, sway **5** adage, axiom, canon, guide, judge, maxim, model, order, reign **6** custom, decide, decree, direct, empire, govern, manage, method, policy, regime, settle, system **7** adjudge, command, control, declare, formula, precept, prevail, resolve, routine **8** conclude, doctrine, dominate, practice, regnancy, regulate, standard

ruler 4 boss, czar, emir, head, khan, king, lord, shah, tsar, tzar **5** chief, judge, queen, rajah, sheik **6** dynast, leader, prince, satrap, shogun, sultan **7** arbiter, emperor, manager, measure, monarch, pharaoh, referee, viceroy **8** chairman, director, governor, suzerain

ruling *see* **8 decision**

rum
  drink: 4 Bolo, Grog **6** Mojito **7** Gauguin **8** Daiquiri, Navy Grog, Pina Fria **9** Borinquen, Hurricane **10** Pina Colada
  ingredient: 8 molasses **9** sugar cane
  origin: 10 West Indies
  type: 4 dark **5** light

rumble 4 bang, boom, clap, roar, roll **7** resound, thunder **8** drumming

ruminant 3 cow, elk, yak **4** deer, oxen **5** bison, camel, llama, moose, sheep **6** alpaca, cattle, vicuna

7 buffalo, giraffe, pensive **8** antelope

ruminate *see* **6 ponder**

rummage 4 root **5** probe **7** examine, explore, ransack

rummy 3 sot **4** lush, soak **5** drunk, souse, toper **6** barfly, boozer **7** tippler **8** card game, drunkard **9** alcoholic

    also known as: 3 gin, rum **4** rhum **5** romme **8** gin rummy

    derived from: 8 conquien

rumor *see* **6 gossip**

rump *see* **8 backside**

Rumpelstiltskin

    origin: 8 Germanic
    form: 5 dwarf
    spun: 4 flax
    made: 4 gold

rumple *see* **7 wrinkle**

rumpus *see* **9 commotion**

run 2 be, go **3** fly, get, hie, jog, pen, ply **4** bolt, boss, cost, dart, dash, defy, flee, flow, go by, head, kind, last, meet, melt, pass, pour, push, race, roll, rush, sort, tear, tour, trip, trot, type, vary **5** bleed, bound, class, court, drift, drive, genre, glide, hurry, impel, incur, issue, leave, pilot, print, speed, spell, split, stand, surge, total, while **6** course, decamp, direct, elapse, endure, escape, extend, gallop, hasten, hustle, manage, motion, move on, outing, period, pierce, propel, scurry, series, sprint, streak, stream, thrust, voyage **7** abscond, advance, bring on, compete, current, get past, journey, liquefy, operate, oversee, passage, proceed, publish, running, scamper, stretch, take off, vamoose **8** campaign, continue, dissolve, navigate, scramble, separate

    baseball: 5 score, tally

runaround *see* **5 dodge**

runaway *see* **8 fugitive**

rundown *see* **7 summary**

run-down 5 frail, seedy, tacky, tired, weary **6** ailing, beat-up, feeble, shabby, sickly **7** rickety, worn out **8** fatigued, tattered

run-in *see* **5 fight**

run off at the mouth *see* **6 babble**

run-of-the-mill *see* **8 ordinary**

runt 3 elf **4** chit **5** dwarf, pygmy **6** midget, peewee, shrimp **8** half-pint, Tom Thumb

Runyon, Damon
  author of: 12 Guys and Dolls **16** Blue Plate Special

rupture *see* **5 burst**

R U R
  author: 5 (Karel) Capek

rural 4 hick **6** rustic **7** bucolic, country **8** pastoral

ruse *see* **4 hoax**

rush *see* **5 hurry**

rush 6 Juncus
  varieties: 3 bog **4** salt, soft, wood **5** spike **6** grassy **8** scouring

Rush, Benjamin
  field: 8 medicine

Rushdie, Salman
  author of: 4 Fury **5** Shame **16** Shalimar the Clown, The Moor's Last Sigh, The Satanic Verses
  edict issued against: 5 fatwa
  issued for: 9 blasphemy
  award: 6 Booker (Prize)

Rushworth
  character in: 13 Mansfield Park
  author: 6 Austen

Russell, Jane
  discovered by: 6 (Howard) Hughes

russet 5 apple, umber **6** auburn, copper

Russia
  formerly part of: 4 USSR **11** Soviet Union
  capital/largest city: 6 Moscow
  region: 5 Volga **7** Karelia, Siberia **8** Caucasus, Chechnya
  mountain: 4 Ural **5** Altai, Urals **8** Caucasus
  highest point: 6 Elbrus
  lake: 5 Onega **6** Baikal, Ladoga
  river: 2 Ob **3** Don, Oka **4** Amur, Lena **5** Volga **6** Dniepr, Kolyma **7** Yenisei
  sea/ocean: 4 Azov **5** Black, Japan, White **6** Arctic, Baltic, Bering **7** Barents, Caspian, Pacific
  island: 5 Kuril **7** Wrangel **8** Sakhalin
  physical feature:
    gulf: 3 Obi **4** Riga

    7 Bothnia, Finland
peninsula: 4 Kola **7**
    Lapland **9** Kamchatka
place: 9 Red Square
museum: 7 Kremlin,
    Pushkin **9** Hermitage
palace: 6 Winter
feature:
  alphabet: 8 cyrillic
  collective farm: 7
    kolkhoz
  country house: 5 dacha
  dance: 5 saber **6** cossak
  dance company: 5
    Kirov **7** Bolshoi
  labor camp: 5 gulag
  musical instrument: 9
    balalaika
  secret police: 3 KGB,
    MGB **4** NKVD,
    OGPU **5** Cheka
  food:
  sour cream: 7 smetana
  drink: 4 kvas **5** kvass,
    vodka
  soup: 6 borsch **7**
    borscht
rust 3 rot **5** decay, stain **6**
auburn, blight, russet **7**
corrode, crumble, decline,
oxidize

rustic *see* **5 rural**
rustle 3 rub **4** hiss, stir **5**
swish, whish **6** riffle
rustler 5 thief **6** bandit,
outlaw **7** brigand
rut 3 cut **4** mark **5** ditch,
habit, score, tread **6**
furrow, groove, gutter,
hollow, trench, trough **7**
channel, depress, dig into,
pattern **8** monotony
Ruth, George Herman
nickname: 4 Babe **7**
    Bambino
ruthless 5 cruel, harsh **6**
brutal, deadly, savage **7**
bestial, brutish, callous,
inhuman, vicious **8** pitiless
Rwanda
capital/largest city: 6
    Kigali
highest point: 9 Karisimbi
physical feature:
  valley: 4 Western Rift
feature:
  king: 5 mwami
rye 6 Secale
type: 6 liquor **7** whiskey

S

Sabbath 8 Lord's Day

saber, sabre 3 cut **4** kill, stab **5** blade, sword, wound **6** cutlas, rapier **7** soldier **8** scimitar

sable 3 fur, jet **4** dark, inky **5** black, ebony, raven

sabotage 3 sap **6** retard **7** cripple, destroy, disable, disrupt, subvert **8** scimitar

sabra 6 native (Israel)

saccharine 5 gooey, mushy, soppy, sweet **6** sugary, syrupy **7** candied, cloying, honeyed, maudlin, mawkish, sugared

sack 3 bag, rob **4** loot, pack, raid **5** pouch, spoil, store, waste **6** duffel **7** pillage, plunder

sacrament 3 vow **4** rite **5** troth **6** pledge, plight, ritual **7** liturgy, promise, service **8** ceremony, contract, covenant

sacred 4 holy **6** church **7** blessed, revered **8** Biblical, hallowed, hieratic

sacrifice 4 cede, loss **5** forgo, waive **6** forego, give up, homage **7** cession, forfeit, offer up

sacrilege 3 sin **7** impiety, mockery, outrage

sacrosanct 4 holy **5** godly **6** divine, solemn **8** hallowed, heavenly

sad 3 low **4** blue, grim, hard, hurt **5** grave **6** dismal, solemn, trying, woeful **7** crushed, doleful, forlorn, grieved, maudlin, pitiful, unhappy **8** dejected, downcast, mournful, pathetic

sadistic 6 brutal **7** vicious **8** fiendish, perverse

Sad Sack creator: 5 (George) Baker

safe 4 firm, sure, wary **5** sound, vault, whole **6** intact, modest, secure, stable, steady, unhurt **7** certain, guarded, prudent

sag 3 bow, dip **4** drop, fail, flag, flap, flop, keel, lean, list, sink, sway, tilt, tire **5** droop, pitch, slump, weary **6** billow, plunge, settle, weaken **7** give way **8** diminish

saga 4 epic, myth, tale, yarn **6** legend **7** history, romance

sagacious *see* **6 clever**

sage 4 guru, wise **5** sound **6** astute, pundit, Salvia, savant, shrewd **7** egghead, prudent, sapient, scholar, wise man

Sagittarius
symbol: 6 archer **7** centaur
planet: 7 Jupiter
born: 8 November, December

said 5 above, quoth **6** quoted, spoken, stated **7** related, uttered **8** repeated

Saigon
capital of: 7 Vietnam
now: 9 Ho Chi Minh (City)

sail 3 fly **4** boat, scud, skim, soar **5** drift, float, glide, steam **6** course, cruise, voyage **8** navigate

sailboat 4 saic, yawl **5** craft, ketch, sloop, yacht **6** vessel **7** sunfish **8** schooner

sailor 3 gob, tar **4** salt **6** sea dog, seaman **7** mariner, voyager **8** deckhand, seafarer

saint 6 martyr
relic box: 6 chasse
remains: 5 relic
symbol: 4 halo

Saint Anthony's fire 6 herpes **8** ergotism, shingles

Saint Joan
author: 4 (George Bernard) Shaw

Saint John's wort 5 amber **6** tutsan **7** ascyrum, cammock

Saint Lucia, St Lucia
capital: 8 Castries
highest point: 5 Gimie
island group: 8 Lesser Antilles, Windward
location: 9 Caribbean

Saint Paul
born: 6 Tarsus
companion: 4 Luke

Saint Peter
  called: 4 Rock **5** Simon **6** Cephas
  brother: 6 Andrew

Saint Vincent, St Vincent
  capital: 9 Kingstown
  highest point: 9 Soufriere
  island group: 8 (Lesser) Antilles, Windward
  islands: 10 Grenadines
  location: 9 Caribbean
  volcano: 9 Soufriere

Saint Vitus' dance 6 chorea

sake 3 end **4** care, gain, good **5** cause **6** behalf, object, profit, regard **7** account, benefit, concern, purpose, respect, welfare

sake
  type: 4 wine **6** spirit
  ingredient: 4 rice

salaam 3 bow **6** homage **9** obeisance

salacious 4 lewd, sexy **7** lustful, obscene **8** indecent

salad days 5 prime, youth **6** heyday

salary *see* **6 income**

sale 3 cut **7** auction, bargain, selling, special **8** discount, exchange, markdown, transfer

salient 6 arrant, marked

7 glaring, notable, obvious **8** flagrant, manifest, palpable, striking

saline 4 salt **5** briny, salty **8** brackish

sallow 3 wan **4** gray, pale **5** ashen **6** sickly, yellow **7** bilious

sally 3 mot **4** flow, pour, quip, raid, trip **5** erupt, foray, surge **6** attack, banter, charge, outing, retort, sortie, spring, thrust **7** debouch, journey **8** badinage, repartee

salmon 4 fish, king **5** cohoe **6** silver **7** chinook, Pacific, quinnat, sockeye, spawner **8** Atlantic, humpback
  enclosure: 4 yair
  female: 4 raun **6** baggit
  genus: 12 Oncorhynchus
  hatchling: 4 pink **6** alevin
  male: 3 gib **4** buck, cock
  young: 4 parr **7** essling

Salome
  father: 5 Herod (Philip)
  mother: 8 Herodias
  husband: 7 Zebedee
  opera by: 7 (Richard) Strauss

saloon *see* **3 pub**

salt 3 wit **4** best, corn, cure, pick, save **5** brine, briny, cream, elect, humor, savor, smack, souse, spice **6** choice, flavor, pickle, saline, season, select

salubrious 7 healthy

salutary 4 good **5** tonic **6** useful **7** healing, healthy **8** curative, sanitary

salutation 3 bow **5** hello, howdy, toast **6** curtsy **7** address, welcome **8** greeting

salute 3 ave **4** hail, kiss **5** bow to, cheer, greet, honor **6** homage, praise, wave to **7** address, applaud, welcome **8** greeting

salvage 4 junk, save **5** scrap **6** debris, rescue **7** recover, remains, restore

salve 4 aloe, balm, calm, ease, hail **5** hello **6** lessen, lotion, pacify, reduce, soothe, temper **7** anodyne, assuage, mollify, relieve, unguent **8** dressing, liniment, mitigate, ointment

salvia 4 herb, mint, sage **5** shrub **8** mejorana

sambuca
 type: 7 liqueur

same 4 like, twin, very **5** alike, equal **6** on a par **7** similar, uniform **8** parallel

Samoa
 capital:
  American Samoa: 8 Pago Pago
  Western Samoa: 4 Apia
 studied by: 4 (Margaret) Mead
 highest point: 4 Fito **8** Silisili
 sea: 7 (South) Pacific
 feature:
  chief: 5 matai
  chief's daughter: 5 taupo
 food:
  drink: 3 ava

sample 3 try **4** test **5** model, taste **7** dip into, examine, example, pattern, portion, segment

Samson 11 Hebrew judge
 feature: 4 hair **8** strength
 weapon: 7 jawbone
 mistress/betrayer: 7 Delilah
 fate: 7 blinded
 brought down: 4 Gaza

Samuel 11 Hebrew judge
 anointed: 4 Saul **5** David

sanctify *see* **6 hallow**

sanction *see* **7 endorse**

sanctuary *see* **5 haven**

sand 4 grit, guts **5** pluck, spunk **6** mettle **7** bravery, courage, resolve

Sand, George
  protege: 6 Chopin

sandal 4 clog, flat, shoe, zori **5** scuff, thong **7** slipper **8** flipflop

sandbank, sandbar 4 dune, reef **5** shelf, shoal **7** shallow

sandpiper 3 ree **4** bird, ruff **5** reeve, stint, wader **6** common, oxbird, plover **7** fiddler, haybird, spotted, tipbird **8** graybird, sandpeep, shadbird

sandwich 3 BLT, sub **4** club, deli, hero **5** hogie **6** burger, hoagie, insert **7** grinder, western **8** laminate

sane 5 lucid, sober **7** logical **8** all there, balanced, credible, rational, sensible

San Francisco
  county: 5 Marin **8** San Mateo
  landmark: 8 Alcatraz **10** Golden Gate (Bridge)
  street/section: 6 Market

7 Lombard, Nob Hill **8** Presidio **9** Chinatown

sangfroid 5 poise **6** aplomb **7** balance **8** coolness

sanguine 3 red **4** rosy **5** happy, ruddy, sunny **6** bright, elated, florid **7** buoyant, crimson, flushed, glowing, scarlet **8** blooming, inflamed

sanitary *see* **5 hygienic**

San Juan
  capital of: 10 Puerto Rico

San Marino
  capital/largest city: 9 San Marino
  enclave in: 5 Italy
  mountain: 9 Apennines

sans souci 8 carefree **11** without care

Santiago
  capital of: 5 Chile

Santo Domingo
  capital of: 17 Dominican Republic

Santo Domingo *see* **5 Haiti**

Sao Tome and Principe
  capital/largest city: 7 Sao Tome
  highest point: 7 Sao Tome
  sea: 8 Atlantic

physical feature:
    gulf: 6 Guinea

sap 3 rob, tax **4** ruin, wear **5** bleed, drain **6** impair, reduce, weaken **7** afflict, cripple, deplete, destroy, disable, exhaust, subvert **8** enervate, enfeeble

sapient 4 wise **7** knowing **8** profound

sapphire 3 gem **4** blue **5** azure, jewel **6** indigo
    species: 8 corundum
    kind: 4 star

Sarah, Sarai
    former name: 5 Sarai
    husband: 7 Abraham
    son: 5 Isaac
    slave: 5 Hagar

sarcasm 3 rub **4** gibe, jeer, jest **5** irony, scorn, sneer, taunt **7** mockery **8** contempt, derision, ridicule, scoffing

sarcoma 5 tumor **6** cancer, growth **8** neoplasm

sarcophagus 4 pall **6** coffin

sardine 4 bang, cram, fish, lile, lour, pack **5** crowd **7** anchovy, herring

Sardinia
    capital: 8 Cagliari

sardonic 6 biting **7** caustic,

cynical, jeering, mocking, mordant, satiric **8** derisive, scornful, sneering, taunting

sash 3 tie **4** band, belt **5** frame, scarf, strip **6** casing, corset, girdle, ribbon, window **7** baldric **8** casement
    Japanese: 3 obi
    pulley weight: 5 mouse
    window: 5 chess

sashay 4 move, skip **5** glide

sashimi 7 raw fish

Saskatchewan 5 river **8** province
    capital: 6 Regina
    country: 6 Canada
    lake: 8 Reindeer
    mountain: 9 Porcupine
    river: 9 Churchill, Frenchman

sassy *see* **5 saucy**

Satan 5 Devil **6** Belial, Moloch **7** Lucifer, Old Nick **8** Apollyon **9** Beelzebub

satanic *see* **4 evil**

satchel 3 bag **4** case, grip, sack **5** purse **6** valise **7** handbag **8** reticule, suitcase

sate, satiate 4 cloy, fill,

glut **5** gorge, stuff **7** surfeit, content **8** saturate

satellite 4 moon **5** crony, toady **6** puppet, vassal **7** servant **8** hanger-on, parasite

satiate 4 bore, cloy, fill, glut, jade **5** slake, stuff, weary **6** overdo, quench, sicken **7** content, disgust, gratify, suffice, surfeit **8** nauseate, overfill, saturate

satiny 4 fine **5** shiny, silky **6** smooth

satire *see* **6 ironic**

satirize 4 mock **6** parody **7** lampoon

satisfy 3 pay **4** fill, meet **5** annul, clear, remit, repay, serve, slake **6** pacify, pay off, please, quench, settle **7** appease, content, delight, fulfill, gratify, mollify, requite **8** reassure

saturate 4 fill **5** cover, douse, imbue, souse **6** drench, infuse **7** immerse, pervade, suffuse **8** permeate, submerge

Saturday
   day of: 7 (Biblical) Sabbath

from: 8 Saturnus
heavenly body: 6 Saturn

Saturday Night Live
   created by: 8 (Lorne) Michaels

Saturn
   origin: 5 Roman
   god of: 11 agriculture
   corresponds to: 6 Cronos

Saturn 6 planet
   position: 5 sixth
   satellite: 4 Rhea **5** Dione, Janus, Mimas, Titan **6** Phoebe, Tethys **7** Iapetus **8** Hyperion
   characteristic: 5 rings

saturnalia, Saturnalia 4 orgy **5** revel, spree **7** carouse, debauch, revelry **8** carousal
   origin: 5 Roman
   event: 8 festival

saturnine *see* **6 morose**

satyr
   form: 4 faun **5** deity
   location: 8 woodland
   part: 3 man **4** goat
   attendant of: 7 Bacchus
   known for: 7 lechery

Satyricon
   author: 9 Petronius

sauce 3 dip **4** sass **5** booze,

gravy, salsa **6** fillip, flavor **8** dressing, pertness

saucy 4 bold, pert, rude **5** brash, fresh, smart **6** brazen, cheek **7** forward **8** flippant, impolite, impudent, insolent

Saudi Arabia
  capital/largest city: 6 Riyadh
  division: 4 Nejd **5** Hejaz
  highest point: 10 Jabal Sawda
  sea: 3 Red
  physical feature:
    desert: 3 Red **5** Dahna, Nafud **6** Dahana
    gulf: 5 Aqaba **7** Persian
    peninsula: 7 Arabian
  religion: 5 Islam
    language: 6 Arabic
  place:
    holy cities: 5 Mecca **6** Medina
    shrine: 5 Kaaba
  feature:
    laws of Islam: 6 sharia
    pilgrimage: 4 hadj, hajj

Sauk, Sac
  leader: 9 Black Hawk

Saul
  king of: 4 Edom **6** Israel
  anointed by: 6 Samuel
  successor: 5 David

Saunders, Allen
  creator: 9 Mary Worth

saunter *see* **5 mosey**

sausage 5 frank, gigot, wurst **6** hot-dog, salami, weenie, wiener **7** baloney, bologna **8** kielbasa **9** bratwurst, pepperoni
  British: 6 banger

savage 4 boor, wild **5** brute, cruel, feral **6** animal, bloody, brutal, fierce, native, rugged **7** brutish, ruffian, untamed, violent **8** barbaric, ruthless, sadistic

savanna, savannah 5 campo, plain **9** grassland

savant 6 genius **7** scholar

save 3 but **4** bank, free, help, hold, keep **5** amass, guard, hoard, lay by, lay up, put by, spare, stock, store **6** defend, except, garner, redeem, rescue, shield **7** deposit, protect, put away, reserve, salvage **8** preserve

savings 3 IRA **5** hoard **7** nest egg, reserve

savior 5 freer **7** rescuer **8** champion, defender, guardian, redeemer

Savior 5 Jesus 6 Christ 8 Redeemer

savoir-faire 4 tact 5 poise 6 aplomb, polish 7 finesse, know-how, suavity 8 presence, urbanity

savor 3 try 4 aura, gist, like, odor, soul, tang, zest 5 aroma, enjoy, scent, smack, smell, spice, taste, trait 6 flavor, nature, relish, sample, season, spirit 7 essence, quality

savvy 5 catch, get it 7 know-how

saw 3 cut 4 tool 5 adage, maxim, slash 6 saying 7 proverb 8 aphorism
type: 3 jig, rip 4 back, band, hack 5 miter 6 coping 7 keyhole 8 circular, crosscut

saxophone
type: 4 alto 5 tenor

say 2 do 4 hint, hold, read, tell, vote, word 5 bruit, claim, guess, imply, judge, mouth, rumor, speak, state, utter, voice 6 allege, convey, phrase, recite, remark, report 7 comment, contend, declare, express, mention, suggest

saying see 5 maxim

scabrous 5 dirty, rough, scaly 7 immoral, leprous 8 indecent, off-color

scalding 3 hot 5 harsh 7 boiling, caustic

scale, scales 3 key, set 4 chip, film, husk, peel, rise, rule, skin 5 crust, flake, layer, mount, order, plate, range, ratio, scour, shave, shell, weigh 6 ascend, ladder, octave, scrape 7 balance, chip off, climb up, measure 8 membrane, spectrum

scale down see 8 condense

scamp 3 imp, rip 5 cut-up, knave, rogue, tease 6 rascal, rotter 7 bounder, villain 8 blighter, scalawag

scamper 3 fly, run, zip 4 dart, dash, flit, race, romp, rush, scud 5 frisk, hurry, scoot 6 frolic, scurry, sprint

scan 4 skim 5 check, probe, scour, study, sweep 6 peruse, search, size up, survey 7 analyze, examine, explore, inspect

scandal 4 blot 5 abuse, libel, odium, shame, stain

6 expose, stigma **7** calumny, obloquy, slander **8** disgrace, ignominy

scandalmonger 6 gossip **8** busybody

Scandinavia 6 Norway, Sweden **7** Denmark, Iceland

scant *see* **6 scarce**

scapegoat 4 butt, dupe, gull **5** patsy **6** victim **7** fall guy

scar 3 cut, pit **4** dent, flaw, gash, hurt, mark, pock, seam **5** brand, wound **6** affect, bruise, damage, deface, defect, impair, mangle **7** blemish, scratch

scarce 4 rare **6** scanty, sparse **7** unusual, wanting **8** uncommon

scare 4 turn **5** alarm, daunt, panic, shake, shock, start **6** harrow, shiver **7** horrify, jitters, startle, terrify **8** frighten

scarecrow 6 effigy **8** straw man

scarf 3 boa **4** sash, veil, wrap **5** ascot, shawl, stole **6** choker, cravat, tippet **7** foulard, muffler, overlay **8** bandanna, mantilla

scarify 3 cut **6** incise, loosen **7** break up, scratch **8** lacerate **9** cultivate

scarlet 3 red **6** cherry, claret **7** carmine **8** cardinal

Scarlet Letter, The author: 9 (Nathaniel) Hawthorne

scat 3 off, out **4** away, shoo **5** be off, leave, scram **6** beat it, be gone, depart, get out, go away **7** get lost, vamoose

scathing 4 keen, tart **5** sharp **6** biting, brutal, savage **7** caustic, cutting, hostile, mordant, pointed, searing **8** incisive, stinging, virulent

scatter *see* **8 disperse**

scatterbrained *see* **7 flighty**

scattered 6 random, spotty **7** diffuse

scavenger 5 hyena **6** magpie **7** vulture **8** salvager

scenario 4 book, idea, plan **6** scheme **7** concept, outline, summary **8** abstract, game plan, synopsis, teleplay
French: 6 precis

scene 3 act **4** fuss, part, show, site, spot, to-do, view **5** place, sight, vista **6** locale, region **7** episode, picture, setting **8** backdrop, location, panorama, sequence

scent *see* **4 odor**

schedule 3 fix **4** book, list, plan, roll **5** fit in, slate, table **6** agenda **7** appoint, program, put down, set down **8** calendar

scheme 3 map, way **4** plan, plot, ruse **5** cabal, chart, frame, means, shift, study **6** course, design, device, devise, layout, method, policy, sketch, system **7** connive, drawing, network, outline, program, project **8** conspire, contrive

Schindler's List
author: 8 (Thomas) Keneally
director: 9 (Steven) Spielberg
cast: 6 (Liam) Neeson **7** (Embeth) Davidtz, (Ralph) Fiennes, (Caroline) Goodall, (Jonathan) Sagalle **8** (Ben) Kingsley

schism 5 break, split **8** division

schlepp 3 lug **4** cart, haul, tote **5** carry **6** convey

Schlesinger, Leon
creator: 9 Bugs Bunny

scholar 4 coed, sage **5** brain, grind, pupil **6** pundit, savant **7** egghead, learner, student **8** mandarin

school 3 ism **4** view **5** bunch, crowd, faith, order, style, teach, train **6** belief, lyceum, method, system, theory **7** academy, college, educate, faction **8** doctrine, instruct, seminary

schoolmaster 4 head **5** tutor **7** dominie, pedagog, scholar, teacher

Schulz, Charles
creator/artist of: 7 Peanuts

science 3 art **5** skill **6** method **7** finesse **8** aptitude, facility
god of: 7 Mercury

scintilla 3 dot, jot **4** atom, iota **5** shred, spark, speck, trace **7** glimmer

scion 3 son **4** heir, seed

5 child, issue **7** heiress, progeny **8** daughter, offshoot

scissors 5 snips **6** blades, cutter, shears **7** clipper, snipper, trimmer

scoff *see* **4 jeer**

scold 3 nag **5** chide, shrew **6** berate, carp at, nagger, rail at, rebuke, virago **7** censure, reprove, upbraid
Yiddish: 6 kvetch

sconce 7 bracket

scoop 4 bail, beat **5** clean, clear, gouge, ladle, spoon **6** burrow, dig out, dipper, hollow, shovel, trowel **7** lift out **8** excavate

scoot 3 run **4** dash, rush **6** scurry, sprint

scope *see* **7 breadth**

scorch 3 dry **4** char, sear **5** parch, singe **6** dry out, scathe, wither **7** blacken

score, scores 3 cut, mar, run, tab, win **4** bill, debt, gain, gash, goal, lots, make, mark, nick, slit **5** count, grade, hosts, judge, notch, point, slash, tally, truth **6** damage, deface, droves, masses, pile up, strike, swarms, twenty

7 account, achieve, legions, scratch, throngs

scorn *see* **4 snub**

Scorpio, Scorpius
  symbol: 8 scorpion
  planet: 4 Mars **5** Pluto
  rules: 5 death **7** passion
  born: 7 October **8** November

scotch *see* **5 quash**

scotch
  type: 6 whisky **7** whiskey
  ingredient: 5 grain

Scotland
  Roman name: 9 Caledonia
  poetic name: 6 Scotia
  capital: 9 Edinburgh
  largest city: 7 Glasgow
  mountain: 8 Grampian **9** Highlands
  highest point: Ben Nevis
  lake/loch: 4 Holy, Ness, Shin **6** Lomond
  river: 5 Clyde, Forth, Tweed
  sea: 5 Irish, North **8** Atlantic
  island: 4 Iona, Skye **6** Orkney **8** Hebrides, Shetland
  physical feature:
    firth (inlet): 3 Tay **5** Clyde, Forth, Lorne, Moray **6** Solway

place:
  castle: 8 Stirling **9** Edinburgh
  royal residence: 8 Balmoral
  street: 7 Prince's **9** Royal Mile
feature:
  clothing: 3 tam **4** kilt **6** tartan
  dance: 4 reel **5** fling
  game: 4 golf **9** caber toss
  holiday: 8 Hogmanay
  monster: 6 Nessie **8** Loch Ness
  musical instrument: 7 bagpipe
  symbol: 7 thistle
food:
  bread: 5 scone
  dish: 6 haggis

scoundrel *see* **3 cad**

scour 4 buff, comb, rake, scan **5** scrub, shine **6** abrade, polish, scrape **7** burnish, cleanse, ransack

scourge *see* **4 flog**

scout 3 spy **4** case **5** guide, pilot **6** escort, spy out, survey **7** lookout, observe **8** point man, vanguard

scowl *see* **7 grimace**

scrabble 3 paw **4** claw, rake **5** climb **6** drudge, jostle, scrape, scrawl **7** clamber, grapple, scratch **8** struggle

scram *see* **7 vamoose**

scramble 3 run, vie **4** race, rush **5** clash, fight, mix up, scrap, upset **6** battle, jostle, jumble, mess up, scurry, strive, tussle **7** scatter, shuffle **8** disorder

scrap *see* **4 iota**

scrape 3 dig **4** buff, gash, mark, rasp, save, skin **5** clean, fight, glean, gouge, grate, graze, grind, plane, run-in, scuff, stint **6** abrade, forage, gather, obtain, plight, scrimp, tussle **7** acquire, dilemma, rub hard, scratch, scuffle, straits

scratch 3 cut, mar, rub **4** claw, etch, gash, nick, omit, rasp **5** dig at, erase, grate, graze, grind, score **6** cancel, delete, incise, remove, rub out, scrape, scrawl, streak, strike **7** exclude, expunge, rule out **8** abrasion, cross out, lacerate, scribble

scrawl *see* **8 scribble**

scrawny *see* **5 frail**

scream, screech 4 howl, loud, roar, wail, yell, yelp, yowl 5 shout, whine 6 bellow, cry out, holler, outcry, shriek, squawk, squeal 7 screech

screen 3 see, web 4 cull, mask, mesh, rate, show, sift, sort, veil, view 5 class, cloak, cover, eject, films, grade, grate, group, guard, order, shade, sieve 6 buffer, cinema, defend, filter, mantle, movies, secure, shield, shroud, sifter, size up 7 conceal, curtain, lattice, preview, shutter, weed out

screw 4 bolt, join, knot, turn, warp 5 clamp, exact, force, gnarl, rivet, twist, wrest, wring 6 adjust, attach, deform, driver, extort, fasten, garble, wrench 7 contort, distort, pervert, squeeze, tighten 8 fastener, misshape

scribble 4 tear 5 squib 6 doodle, scrawl 7 scratch 8 squiggle

scribe, Scribe 3 cut 4 mark, tool 5 clerk, score 6 author, copier, penman, writer 7 teacher 8 recorder

scrimp 4 save 5 hoard, pinch, skimp, stint

scrip 5 paper 8 document

script 4 book, hand 5 lines, score 6 dialog 7 cursive 8 dialogue, libretto, longhand, scenario

Scriptures, the 5 Bible, Torah 6 oracle 7 Gospels 8 holy writ *see also* 5 **Bible**

scrub 4 swab 5 brush, scour

scrumptious 5 juicy, tasty 6 savory, tender 8 luscious, pleasant, pleasing

scruple 3 shy 4 balk, care, halt 5 demur, pause, qualm, waver 6 blench, ethics, falter 7 anxiety, concern, refrain 8 hesitate

scrutiny 5 study, watch 7 inquiry, perusal

scuffle *see* 5 **fight**

sculpture 3 cut 4 bust, cast, head, work 5 cameo, carve, erode, model, mould 6 chisel, relief, statue 7 carving, erosion, faience 8 intaglio, statuary
medium: 4 clay 5 china,

stone 6 bronze, enamel, marble **7** ceramic

scum 4 film, slag **5** crust, dregs, dross, trash **6** rabble, refuse **7** deposit, rubbish, surface **8** riffraff

scurrilous *see* **6 vulgar**

scurry *see* **7 scamper**

scurvy 3 low **4** base, mean, vile **6** shabby **7** ignoble

scuttle 4 sink **5** abort, hurry, scrap, speed, wreck **6** hasten, scurry **7** destroy, discard, scamper **8** dispatch, scramble

scuttlebutt *see* **6 gossip**

Scylla
  form: 5 nymph **7** monster
  location: 3 sea
  loved by: 8 Poseidon

sea 3 bay, ton **4** deep, gulf, host, lake, leap, lots, main, mass, slew, wave **5** bight, flock, flood, ocean, scads, spate, surge, swarm, swell, waves **6** legion, roller, scores, waters **7** breaker

Sea Around Us, The
  author: 6 (Rachel) Carson

Seagull, The
  author: 7 (Anton) Chekhov

seal 2 OK **3** dam, fix **4** cork, lock, mark, plug, shut, stop **5** brand, close, stamp **6** emblem, fasten, figure, ratify, secure, settle, signet, stop up, symbol **7** approve, certify, confirm, endorse **8** colophon, insignia, validate

seal
  young: 3 pup
  group of: 3 pod

seam 3 gap **4** line, lode, mark, scar, vein **5** break, chink, cleft, crack, joint, layer, notch **6** breach, furrow, incise, suture **7** crevice, fissure, joining, opening **8** junction

seaman 3 gob, tar **4** hand, mate, salt **5** bosun, middy **6** lubber, merman, sailor, sea dog **7** mariner

sear *see* **4 char**

search 4 comb, drag, fish, hunt, look, seek, sift **5** check, frisk, probe, quest, rifle, scour, snoop, study **7** dragnet, examine, explore, inquiry, inspect

Searchers, The
  director: 4 (John) Ford
  cast: 4 (Ward) Bond,

(Natalie) Wood **5** (Vera) Miles, (John) Wayne **6** (Jeffrey) Hunter

seashore 5 beach, coast

seasick 3 ill **5** barfy, dizzy, faint, giddy, woozy **6** queasy **8** vomitous

season 3 age, dry **4** fall, lace, tame, term **5** adapt, color, drill, inure, prime, ripen, shape, spell, spice, stage, train **6** accent, autumn, flavor, mature, period, spring, summer, winter **7** enhance, enliven, prepare, quarter, stretch **8** interval

seasoning 4 dill, herb, mace, sage, salt, zest **5** aging, basil, clove, gusto, onion, spice, thyme **6** drying, garlic, ginger, nutmeg, pepper, relish **7** oregano, paprika, parsley **8** allspice, cinnamon, marjoram, practice, ripening, rosemary, training

seat 3 box, hub **4** axis, core, home, rump, site, sofa **5** abode, bench, chair, couch, croup, divan, fanny, heart, house, locus, place **6** behind, bottom, center, locale, settle **7** address, capital, cushion, habitat, housing, nucleus, rear end, situate **8** backside

seat of justice 5 bench, court **8** tribunal

Sea Wolf, The author: 6 (Jack) London

secede *see* **8 withdraw**

seclusion 5 exile **6** asylum, hiding **7** retreat **8** cloister, hideaway, solitude

second 3 aid **4** abet, back, help, wink **5** agent, favor, flash, jiffy, other, proxy, trice **6** assist, back up, deputy, fill-in, helper, minute, moment, uphold **7** another, endorse, stand by, support **8** advocate, inferior

second childhood 6 dotage **8** senility

secondhand 4 used **8** indirect

second-rate *see* **5 cheap**

secret 3 key, mum **4** dark **6** arcane, covert, hidden, occult, unseen **7** formula, furtive, mystery, private, unknown **8** discreet, esoteric, hush-hush, secluded, stealthy

secretary 4 aide, desk **5** clerk **6** scribe **7** officer **8** recorder

secrete 4 hide, veil **5** cache, cloak, cover, stash **6** screen, shroud **7** conceal, curtain **8** disguise

sect 4 camp, cult **7** faction **8** division

section 4 area, part, side, unit, ward, zone **5** piece, range, share, slice **6** region, sample, sphere **7** portion, segment **8** division

secular 3 lay **4** laic **6** carnal **7** earthly, fleshly, mundane, profane, sensual, worldly **8** material, temporal

secure 3 get, set **4** bind, easy, safe, sure **5** fixed, tight **6** at ease, defend, ensure, fasten, immune, insure, obtain **7** certain, tie down **8** definite, in the bag, positive, surefire

securities 5 bonds, title **6** stocks

security 4 bond, keep **5** faith, trust **6** guards, pledge, police, safety, surety, troops **7** deposit **8** reliance

sedate *see* **4 calm**

sedative 6 easing, opiate **7** anodyne, calming **8** allaying, lenitive, narcotic, relaxing, soothing

sedentary 5 fixed, inert, still **6** seated **7** resting, sitting **8** inactive, unmoving

sedge 4 reed **5** grass

sediment *see* **7 residue**

sedition 6 mutiny, revolt **7** treason **8** uprising

seduce 4 lure, ruin **5** abuse, charm, tempt **6** allure, defile, entice, ravish **7** attract, win over **8** persuade

sedulous 6 dogged **8** diligent, thorough

see 3 dig, eye, spy, woo **4** date, espy, know, meet, mind, spot, view **5** court, grasp, sight, visit, watch **6** attend, behold, descry, escort, fathom, notice, regard, survey **7** consult, glimpse, observe, picture, realize, witness **8** envision, perceive

seed 3 pit, sow **4** germ

5 basis, grain, heirs, issue, ovule, plant, stone **6** embryo, origin, source **7** progeny **8** children

seedy *see* **7 run-down**

seek *see* **6 search**

seeming *see* **8 apparent**

seemly *see* **9 befitting**

seep 4 drip, leak, ooze, soak **7** diffuse, dribble, suffuse, trickle **8** permeate

seer *see* **4 sage**

seesaw 5 waver **6** teeter

seethe *see* **4 rage**

see through 3 get **6** detect, effect, finish **7** achieve, execute, perform **8** carry out, complete, conclude

segment *see* **7 portion**

segregate 6 cut off, detach, divide **7** divorce, isolate, seclude, sort out **8** disunite, insulate, separate

seine 3 net **4** drag, fish **5** trawl **7** dragnet

seism 5 quake, shock **6** tremor **8** tremblor

seize 3 bag, nab **4** grab, read **5** catch, glean, grasp, usurp **6** arrest, collar, snatch **7** capture, possess

seldom 6 rarely **8** scarcely

select 3 tap **4** A-one, pick, posh **5** elect, elite, fancy **6** choice, choose, chosen, opt for, picked, prefer **8** four-star, superior

selection 4 pick **5** range **6** choice, medley, option **7** program, variety **8** choosing, decision

Selene
  goddess of: 4 moon
  corresponds to: 5 Diana **7** Artemis

self 3 ego **6** person, psyche **8** identity

self-absorbed, –centered 4 vain 8 egoistic

self-confidence 5 nerve, pluck **6** mettle, spirit **8** boldness, gameness

self-conscious 7 awkward **8** affected

self-control 5 poise **6** aplomb **8** firmness, patience, sobriety

self-esteem 5 pride

self-evident 5 plain **6** patent **7** glaring, obvious **8** apparent, distinct, explicit, manifest, palpable

selfish 4 mean **5** tight, venal **6** greedy, stingy **7** miserly **8** covetous,

egoistic, grasping,
grudging

self-possessed 4 calm, cool
6 poised **7** assured,
courtly, refined **8**
balanced, composed,
polished, resolute

self-righteous 4 smug **5**
pious **7** pompous

sell 4 dump, hawk, vend **6**
barter, betray, deal in,
enlist, handle, market,
peddle, unload **7** deceive,
trade in, win over **8**
convince, dispense

seller 6 dealer, jobber,
monger, trader, vendor **7**
peddler **8** merchant,
retailer, salesman

sell out 6 betray

semblance 3 air **4** cast,
copy, look, show **5** image
6 aspect **7** bearing, replica
8 likeness, pretense

seminal *see* **8 original**

Seminole
   leader: 7 Osceola

Semiramis
   queen of: 7 Assyria
   husband: 5 Ninus
   founder of: 7 Babylon

send 4 cast, emit, head,
hurl, lead, show, toss

5 drive, fling, guide, refer,
relay, shoot, throw **6**
convey, direct, launch **7**
conduct, forward, project
8 dispatch, transmit

send packing *see* **4 oust**

Senegal
   capital/largest city: 5
   Dakar
   empire: 4 Mali **5** Jolof **6**
   Tekrur
   river: 6 Gambia **7** Senegal
   sea: 8 Atlantic
     leader: 7 Senghor
   feature:
     tree: 6 acacia, baobab

senile 6 doting, infirm **7**
foolish **8** decrepit

senior, Senior 4 head, over
5 above, chief, doyen,
elder, older **6** better **7**
veteran **8** superior

seniority 6 tenure

senor 2 Mr **3** don **5** title **6**
mister **8** Spaniard

senora 3 Mrs, sra **4** lady,
wife **5** madam, woman **8**
mistress

senorita 4 lass, miss

sensation 3 hit **4** stir, to-do
6 thrill, uproar **7** feeling,
scandal

sense 3 see, use **4** aura,

espy, feel, good, mind, note **5** grasp, guess, point, sight, smell, taste, touch, value, worth **6** descry, detect, divine, reason, take in **7** feeling, hearing, meaning, purpose, realize, suspect **8** judgment, perceive

Sense and Sensibility
   author: 6 (Jane) Austen

sensible *see* **7 logical**

sensitive 4 fine, keen, sore **5** acute, exact **6** tender, touchy **7** painful **8** delicate

sensual *see* **6 erotic**

sententious *see* **8 pedantic**

sentient 5 aware **7** alert to, alive to, awake to, mindful **8** sensible

sentiment, sentiments 4 idea **5** heart **6** notion **7** emotion, feeling, opinion, romance, thought **8** attitude
   Yiddish: 6 kitsch

sentinel, sentry *see* **5 guard**

Seoul
   capital of: 10 South Korea

separate 3 cut **4** cull, fork, part, sift **5** break, crack,

sever, split **6** bisect, detach, divide, ramify, remove, single, spread, sunder **7** disjoin, diverge, divorce

September
   attack: 9 terrorist (11)
   flower: 5 aster
   gem: 8 sapphire
   holiday: 8 Labor Day
   origin of name: 6 septum (Latin meaning seven)
   place in year:
      Gregorian: 5 ninth
      Roman: 7 seventh
   Zodiac sign: 5 Libra, Virgo

sepulcher 4 tomb **5** crypt, grave, vault **7** ossuary **8** cenotaph

sequel 3 end **6** finish, result, upshot **8** addendum, epilogue, follow-up, offshoot

sequence *see* **6 series**

sequester *see* **7 confine**

sequin 4 coin, disk **5** ducat **7** spangle **8** ornament

seraglio 3 oda **5** harem, serai **6** zenana

seraphic 7 angelic **8** beatific, ethereal, heavenly

647

Serbia and Montenegro
capital/largest city: 7
Beograde **8** Belgrade
division: 6 Kosovo **9**
Vojvodina
mountain: 7 Balkans
highest point: 8 Daravica
river: 4 Sava **5** Drina **6**
Danube, Morava
physical feature:
peninsula: 6 Balkan
feature:
former empire: 7
Ottoman
military governor: 7
vojvodi

sere 3 dry **4** arid **6** barren
7 parched **8** droughty,
scorched, withered

serene *see* **4 calm**

serf 6 cotter, thrall, vassal **7**
bondman, peasant, villein

Sergeant York
director: 5 (Howard)
Hawks
cast: 6 (Gary) Cooper,
(Joan) Leslie, (George)
Tobias **7** (Walter)
Brennan

serial 7 regular

series 3 set **5** chain, cycle,
group, order **6** course,
number, parade, string **8**
sequence

serious *see* **6 somber**

sermon 6 homily, rebuke,
tirade **7** lecture, reproof **8**
diatribe, harangue

serpent, Serpent 3 asp **5**
cheat, devil, rogue, Satan,
snake, viper **7** reptile,
traitor **8** deceiver
constellation of: 7
Serpens

serrate 5 notch **6** jagged,
pinked, ridged **7** dentate,
grooved, notched, toothed

servant 3 man **4** cook, girl,
help, maid **5** valet **6**
butler, flunky, helper,
lackey, menial, minion,
slavey **7** footman **8**
domestic

serve 2 do **3** act, aid **4**
help, pass, suit, tend,
work **5** avail, spend, treat
6 assist, attend, supply,
wait on **7** deliver, further,
present, satisfy, work for
8 complete, hand over,
minister

service, services 3 aid, use
4 help, mend, rite **5** avail,
labor **6** agency, bureau,
effort, profit, repair, ritual
7 benefit, support **8**
ceremony, military

Sesame Street

character: 4 Bert, Elmo **5** Ernie, Herry, Oscar **6** Cookie (Monster), Snuffy **7** Barkley, Big Bird, Muppets **8** the Count

session 4 bout, term **5** round, synod **6** course, period **7** meeting, quarter, sitting **8** assembly, conclave, semester

set 3 cut, fit, fix, gel, kit, lay, put, sic **4** club, drop, firm, line, make, plop, post, rate, sink, stud, suit **5** adapt, align, array, banal, bunch, crowd, embed, fixed, group, imbed, order, place, plunk, ready, rigid, scene, stale, stiff, stock, style, trite, usual **6** adjust, assess, assign, attach, confer, create, decree, harden, line up, locale, studio **7** congeal, decided, jellify, prepare, regular, release, routine, scenery, situate, station, thicken **8** backdrop, definite, firmness, habitual, hardened, location, position, prepared, regulate, rigidity, solidify

French: 6 clique **7** coterie

Set

also: 4 Seth
origin: 8 Egyptian
form: 6 animal
personifies: 6 desert
brother: 6 Osiris
killed: 6 Osiris

setback *see* **4 loss**

Seth

means: 12 compensation
father: 4 Adam
mother: 3 Eve
son: 4 Enos

set off *see* **8 detonate**

set out *see* **6 embark**

set store by 5 prize, value **6** esteem **7** respect **8** treasure

settee 4 seat, sofa **5** bench

settle 3 fix, pay, sag **4** calm, drop, land, sink **5** agree, allay, clear, droop, light, lodge, perch, quiet **6** decide, move to, pacify, people, soothe **7** clarify, inhabit, rectify, resolve, satisfy, sit down, situate **8** colonize, populate, take root

set-to *see* **8 argument**

setup 4 plan **6** scheme, system **8** practice

set up 3 rig **5** erect, found **7** arrange, install

Seuss, Dr
real name: **6** (Theodore) Seuss Geisel

Seven Pillars of Wisdom
author: **8** (T E) Lawrence

seven seas 6 Arctic, Indian **9** Antarctic **12** North Pacific, South Pacific **13** North Atlantic, South Atlantic

Seven Sisters colleges 5 Smith **6** Vassar **7** Barnard **8** Bryn Mawr **9** Radcliffe, Wellesley **12** Mount Holyoke

Seventeen
author: **10** (Booth) Tarkington

Seventh Heaven (7th Heaven)
network: **2** WB

sever *see* **8 separate**

several *see* **4 many**

severe 4 cold, dour, grim, wild **5** cruel, grave, harsh, plain, rough, sober, stern, stiff **6** biting, bitter, brutal, fuming, raging, savage, strict **7** drastic, extreme, intense **8** rigorous, ruthless

sew 3 hem **4** mend, seam, tack **5** unite **6** fasten, ground, stitch, suture
loosely: **5** baste

sewage 5 waste **6** efflux, refuse **8** effluent

sex 4 Eros, love, male **6** coitus, female, gender, libido **7** coition

Sex and the City
cast: **4** (Chris) Noth **5** (Kristin) Davis, (Cynthia) Nixon **6** (Sarah Jessica) Parker **8** (Kim) Cattrall

Seychelles
capital/largest city: **8** Victoria
sea: **6** Indian

shabby *see* **7 run-down**

shack 3 hut **5** cabin **6** lean-to, shanty

shackle 3 bar, tie **4** balk, bind, cuff, curb, foil, rein **5** block, bonds, chain, check, cramp, cuffs, deter, irons, limit, stall **6** hinder, impede, secure, tether **7** inhibit, manacle, prevent **8** encumber, handcuff, restrict

shade 3 bit, dim, hue, jot **4** atom, cast, hint, hood, iota, tint, tone, veil, whit

5 blind, color, drape, tinge, touch, trace **6** awning, canopy, darken, screen, shadow, shield **7** curtain, shutter

shadow, shadows 3 bit, dog **4** blot, hint, tail **5** cloud, ghost, hound, shade, smear, stain, stalk, taint, tinge, touch, trace, track, trail **6** blight, follow, pursue **7** specter

Shadrach
former name: 8 Hananiah
friend: 6 Daniel
companion: 7 Meshach **8** Abednego

shady 5 fishy **7** crooked, devious, dubious, shadowy

shaft 3 cut, pit, ray **4** barb, beam, dart, duct, flue, gibe, hilt, stem, vent, well **5** abyss, arrow, chasm, gleam, lance, patch, pylon, quill, shank, spear, spire, stalk, tower, trunk **6** cavity, column, funnel, insult, pillar, stream **7** chimney, conduit **8** monolith

shaggy 5 bushy, fuzzy, hairy, nappy **6** woolly **7** bearded, shagged, unshorn

shah *see* **4 king**

shake 3 jar, jog, mix **4** jerk, jolt, move, stir, stun, sway, wave **5** elude, quake, swing, touch **6** bounce, jiggle, jostle, quaver, quiver, rattle, shimmy, shiver, twitch, wobble **7** agitate, disturb, tremble, vibrate **8** unsettle

shakedown 6 extort, payoff, search, tryout

Shakespeare, William
also: 4 bard (of Avon)
theater: 4 Swan **5** Globe
wife: 4 Anne (Hathaway)

shallow 5 shoal **6** frothy, slight **7** surface, trivial **8** skin-deep, trifling

shalom 5 hello, peace **7** goodbye

sham *see* **5 fraud**

shame *see* **8 disgrace**

shamus 3 tec **7** gumshoe

Shane
director: 7 (George) Stevens
cast: 4 (Elisha) Cook (Jr), (Alan) Ladd **6** (Jean) Arthur, (Van) Heflin **7** (Brandon) deWilde (Jack) Palance **8** (Edgar) Buchanon

shanty 3 hut **5** cabin, hovel, shack **6** lean-to

shape 4 form, make, mold, trim **5** array, build, frame, guide, model, order **6** create, figure, health **7** contour, develop, fashion **8** physique

share 3 cut **4** dole, part **5** allot, cut up, quota, split **6** ration **7** deal out, divvy up, percent, portion

shark 3 ace **4** fish **5** cheat **6** expert, usurer, wizard **8** predator

sharp 3 sly **4** acid, curt, fine, foxy, high, keen, sour, tart, wily **5** acrid, acute, alert, angry, awake, blunt, clear, cruel, edged, harsh, nippy, piked, quick, rapid, spiny, steep **6** abrupt, artful, astute, barbed, biting, bitter, clever, crafty, fierce, keenly, pointy, severe, shrill, sudden, thorny **7** angular, bearish, brusque, caustic, cunning, cutting, drastic, prickly, raucous **8** on the dot, piercing, promptly, scathing, venomous

shatter 4 rive, ruin **5** break, burst, crack, crash, crush, smash, upset, wreck **6** topple **7** crumble, destroy, explode **8** demolish

shave *see* **5 shear**

shawl 4 wrap **5** scarf **6** mantle **7** paisley **10** fascinator
Mexican: 6 serape
Spanish: 8 mantilla

Shawnee
location: 4 Ohio **6** Kansas **8** Missouri, Oklahoma **9** Tennessee
leader: 8 Tecumseh
related to: 8 Delaware

She
author: 7 (H Rider) Haggard

shear 3 cut, lop **4** clip, crop, snip, trim **5** prune, shave **6** fleece, remove **7** deprive, relieve, scissor

sheath 3 pod **4** case, coat, skin **6** casing, jacket **7** coating, wrapper **8** covering, membrane, slipcase, wrapping

shed 3 hut **4** cast, doff, drop, emit, molt **5** exude, hovel, shack, spill, strew **6** shanty, slough **7** cast off, discard, let flow, scatter

shed tears 3 cry, sob **4** bawl, weep **6** boohoo **7** blubber

sheen *see* **5 gloss**

sheep
female: **3** ewe
family: **7** Bovidae
group of: **5** drove, flock **6** cosset
meat: **4** lamb **6** mutton
oil from: **7** lanolin
young: **4** lamb **7** lambkin **8** yearling

sheepish *see* **5 timid**

sheer *see* **5 gauzy**

sheet 3 top **4** coat, film, leaf, pane, slab **5** layer, panel, piece, plate **6** sheath, square **7** blanket, coating, overlay **8** bed sheet, covering, membrane

shelf 4 bank, prop, reef, slab **5** ledge, shoal **6** mantel, mantle **7** bedrock, bracket, stratum

shell 3 pod **4** bomb, case, hulk, hull, husk, shot **5** pound, round, shuck **6** bullet, fire on, pepper, rocket **7** grenade, missile **8** skeleton

shellfish 4 clam, crab **5** prawn **6** cockle, mussel, oyster, shrimp **7** abalone, lobster, mollusk, scallop **8** barnacle, crawfish, crayfish
spawn: **4** spat

shelter *see* **6 refuge**

shelve *see* **7 suspend**

shenanigans *see* **5 antic**

shepherd 4 herd, lead, show, tend **5** guard, guide, pilot **6** direct, escort, herder, keeper, patron, shield **7** protect, shelter **8** champion, defender, guardian, herdsman, provider

shepherds
god of: **3** Pan

sherbet 3 ade, ice **6** sorbet **7** dessert

sheriff 7 officer **9** constable

sherry
type: **4** wine **6** brandy

She Stoops to Conquer
author: **7** (Oliver) Goldsmith

shield 4 keep, star **5** aegis, badge, cover, guard **6** buffer, button, emblem, ensign, fender, harbor, screen, secure **7** buckler, defense, protect, shelter

8 insignia, keep safe, preserve

shift 2 go **4** move, slip, vary, veer **5** hitch, stint **6** change, swerve, switch **7** chemise, turning, veering **8** camisole, transfer

shifty *see* **7 devious**

shindig 3 hop **4** ball, bash, prom **5** dance, party **6** affair **7** blowout

shine 3 wax **4** beam, buff, glow **5** blink, flash, glare, gleam, gloss, light, rub up, sheen **6** dazzle, luster, polish, waxing **7** buffing, glisten, radiate, shimmer, sparkle, twinkle

ship 4 crew, send **5** craft, liner, route, tramp, yacht **6** packet, tanker, vessel **7** carrier, cruiser, forward, steamer **8** dispatch

Ship of Fools author: 6 (Katherine Anne) Porter

shipshape 4 neat, snug, taut, tidy, trip, trim **5** tight **6** spruce **7** orderly

shirk *see* **5 dodge**

shirt 3 top **4** sark **5** frock, waist **6** blouse, bodice

shirty 5 angry, irked, testy, vexed **7** annoyed

shiver *see* **5 shake**

shoal 3 bar **4** bank, flat **5** crowd, shelf **6** school **7** sand bar, shallow

shock 3 jar, mat, mop **4** blow, bush, cock, crop, daze, jolt, mane, mass, pile, rick, rock, stun, turn **5** scare, shake, sheaf, stack, start, upset **6** impact, trauma **7** astound, perturb, stagger, startle, stupefy **8** astonish, bowl over, surprise

shoddy 3 low **4** base, mean, poor **5** dirty, nasty, tacky **6** shabby, sloppy, stingy **7** low-down, miserly **8** careless, inferior, slipshod

shoemaker 7 cobbler

shoo *see* **7 vamoose**

shoot 3 bud, fly, hit **4** bolt, cast, dart, dash, drop, fell, fire, hurl, jump, kill, leap, nick, pelt, plug, race, rain, rush, stem, tear, toss, twig, wing **5** eject, fling, go off, hurry, shell, sling, speed, spray, sprig, spurt, sweep, throw **6** pepper, propel, riddle, shower, spring **7** pick off, tendril **8** detonate, open fire

shop 3 buy **4** hunt, look, mart, mill **5** plant, store, works **6** browse, market **8** emporium, purchase
French: 7 atelier **8** boutique

shopkeeper 6 dealer, monger, trader, vendor **8** merchant, purveyor, retailer

shore 4 bank, hold, land, prop **5** beach, brace, brink, coast **6** hold up, margin, strand **7** bolster, bulwark, seaside, support, sustain **8** buttress, seaboard

short 3 low **4** curt, lean, slim, thin **5** brief, cross, elfin, fleet, gruff, hasty, pygmy, quick, runty, scant, sharp, small, squat, terse, testy, tight **6** abrupt, bantam, little, meager, scanty, scarce, skimpy, slight, sparse, stubby **7** brusque, concise, stunted, summary **8** fleeting, impolite, snappish, succinct

shortcoming *see* **4 flaw**

shortening 3 fat, oil **4** lard,

oleo **6** butter, digest **7** summary **8** abstract, synopsis

shot 2 go **3** hit, try **4** dose, move, play, toss **5** balls, blast, crack, drive, essay, guess, salvo, slugs, throw **6** bowman, chance, ruined, shabby, stroke, volley **7** attempt, bullets, gunfire, shooter, surmise, worn-out

shot in the dark 5 guess **6** notion, theory

shoulder 3 rim **4** bank, bear, brow, bump, edge, push, side, take **5** brink, carry, crest, elbow, lunge, shove, skirt, verge **6** assume, border, jostle, margin, take on, thrust, uphold **7** scapula, support, sustain **8** clavicle

shout *see* **4 yell**

shove 4 bump, butt, jolt, prod, push **5** boost, crowd, drive, elbow, force, nudge **6** jostle, propel, thrust **8** shoulder

show 4 bare, bill, fair, give, lead, mark, play, pomp, pose, sham, sign **5** argue, coach, drama, endow, favor, front, grant, guide, movie, opera, prove, teach, token, tutor, usher **6** appear, attest, ballet, comedy, direct, effect, evince, expose, impart, inform, reveal, unveil **7** display, exhibit, program, uncover **8** disclose, indicate, instruct, manifest, point out

Show Boat
   author: 6 (Edna) Ferber

showcase 7 cabinet, counter, display, exhibit, vitrine

showdown *see* **6 combat**

shower 3 wet **4** fall, pour, rain, rush **5** flood, salvo, spray, surge **6** deluge, lavish, splash, stream, volley, wealth **7** barrage, bombard, drizzle, torrent **8** downpour, sprinkle

Show-me State
   nickname of: 8 Missouri

show-off *see* **4 brag**

showy 4 loud **5** gaudy, vivid **6** flashy, florid, garish, ornate **7** pompous **8** colorful, gorgeous, imposing, striking

shred 3 bit, ion, jot, rag **4** atom, band, hair, iota,

spot, whit **5** grain, piece, scrap, speck, strip, trace **6** morsel, sliver **7** snippet **8** fragment, molecule, particle

shrew *see* **3 hag**

shrewd *see* **6 clever**

shriek *see* **6 scream**

shrill 4 high, loud **6** piping **7** blaring, raucous **8** piercing, strident

shrimp 5 prawn **6** scampi **8** cocktail

shrine 5 altar **6** chapel, church, temple **7** sanctum **8** monument

shrink 3 ebb, shy **4** balk, duck, wane **5** cower, demur, dry up **6** lessen, pucker, recoil, reduce **7** curtail, decline, deflate, retreat, shrivel **8** compress, contract, decrease, diminish, withdraw

shrive 6 pardon **7** absolve, forgive

shrivel *see* **6 shrink**

shroud *see* **7 conceal**

shrubbery 4 bush **5** brush **6** bushes, shrubs

shuck 4 husk, peel, shed **5** chaff, shell, strip

shudder *see* **5 shake**

shuffle 3 mix **4** drag, gimp, limp, step **5** scuff, slide **6** clumsy, jumble, scrape **7** shamble **8** scramble

shun *see* **5 dodge**

shut 3 box **4** cage, coop, draw, fold, lock, snap **5** clasp, close, drawn, latch **6** draw to, fasten, intern, locked, lock in, secure **7** confine **8** cloister, imprison

shutter 5 blind, close, shade **6** screen **7** curtain

shy *see* **5 timid**

shyster 5 rogue **6** lawyer **8** attorney

Siam *see* **8 Thailand**

sibling 6 sister **7** brother
  problem: 7 rivalry

sibyl 4 seer **5** augur **6** oracle **7** diviner

Sicily
  capital/largest city: 7 Palermo
  highest point: 4 Etna
  sea: 6 Ionian **10** Tyrrhenian **13** Mediterranean

  physical feature:
    strait: 7 Messina
    wind: 7 sirocco
  feature:
    brigands: 5 Mafia

sick 3 ill **4** weak **5** frail, tired, weary **6** ailing, infirm, laid up, poorly, queasy, sickly, uneasy, unwell **7** crushed, grieved, invalid, unsound **8** delicate, stricken, troubled, wretched

sickness 6 malady, nausea **7** ailment, disease, illness **8** debility, disorder, vomiting

Siddhartha
  author: 5 (Hermann) Hesse
  story of: 6 Buddha

side 3 hem, rim **4** area, body, brim, edge, half, hand, part, sect, team, view **5** angle, bound, cause, facet, flank, group, house, light, limit, minor, party, phase, skirt, slant, stand, stock **6** aspect, behalf, belief, border, circle, clique, fringe, lesser **7** coterie, faction, lateral, opinion, postern, related, section, segment, surface

8 alliance, division, position, skirting

sideboard 6 buffet **8** credenza

sidekick *see* **4 chum**

sideline 5 bench, hobby **8** boundary

sidestep *see* **5 dodge**

sidewalk 4 curb **8** footpath, pavement

sideways, sideway 6 aslant **7** askance, lateral, oblique **8** crabwise, edgewise

sidle 4 cant, edge, skew, veer

Siegel, Jerry
  creator/artist of: 8 Superman

Siegfried
  origin: 8 Germanic
  father: 7 Sigmund
  same as: 6 Sigurd
  killed: 6 Fafnir

Sierra Leone
  other name: 9 Gold Coast
  capital/largest city: 8 Freetown
  sea: 8 Atlantic
  food:
    dish: 4 fufu **7** cassava
    sauce: 7 palaver

siesta 3 nap **4** rest **5** break,

sleep **6** cat nap, snooze **10** forty winks

sieve 4 sift **6** filter, riddle, screen, sorter, strain **7** tattler **8** colander, strainer

sift 4 sort **5** drift, probe, study **6** filter, review, screen, search, winnow **7** analyze, inspect, scatter, sort out **8** separate

sigh 3 sob **4** hiss, long, moan, pine, weep **5** brood, groan, mourn, whine, yearn **6** grieve, lament, sorrow

sight 3 ken, see, spy **4** bead, espy, gaze, spot, view **5** image, scene, vista **6** behold **7** display, exhibit, glimpse, scenery **8** prospect, scrutiny

Sigmund
  origin: 5 Norse **8** Germanic
  king of: 11 Netherlands
  father: 7 Volsung
  mother: 4 Liod, Ljod **5** Hliod
  wife: 7 Hiordis, Hjordis **8** Borghild **9** Sieglinde
  sister: 5 Signy
  lover: 5 Signy
  son: 6 Sigurd **9** Siegfried

sign, signal 3 cue, nod

4 sign **6** beckon, famous, motion, symbol, unique **7** command, eminent, gesture, guiding, honored, notable, warning **8** evidence, forecast, password, renowned, singular, striking

significant 4 main **5** chief, grave, great, major, prime, vital **6** cogent **7** eminent, knowing, notable, serious, telling, weighty **8** critical, distinct, eventful, symbolic

sign up 4 join **6** enlist, enroll, join up **8** register

Sigurd
  origin: 5 Norse
  mentioned in: 8 Volsunga
  father: 7 Sigmund
  wife: 6 Gudrun, Kudrun **7** Guthrun

Sikkim
  capital/largest city: 7 Gangtok
  part of: 5 India
  mountain: 9 Himalayas
  king: 7 chogyal

Silas Marner
  author: 5 (George) Eliot

silence 3 gag **4** calm, curb, halt, hush, kill, rout, stop **5** allay, check, crush, peace, quash, quell, quiet, still **6** banish, deaden, defeat, muffle, muzzle, repose, squash, stifle, subdue **7** conquer, nullify, repress, squelch **8** suppress

Silent Spring
  author: 6 (Rachel) Carson

silk
  fabric: 4 crin **5** crepe, ninon, satin, surah, tulle **6** faille, pongee, sendal, tussah **7** chiffon, foulard, organza, raw silk, taffeta **8** organzie, paduasoy
  measure: 6 denier
  watered: 5 moire

silly 3 mad **4** dumb **5** crazy, giddy, inane **6** absurd, frothy, insane, stupid, unwary, unwise **7** aimless, asinine, fatuous, foolish, idiotic, shallow, witless **8** childish, farcical

silo 3 pit **5** tower
  storage of: 6 fodder **7** missile

silver 5 coins, plate **6** argent, change **7** jewelry **8** argentum, platinum
  chemical symbol: 2 Ag

similar *see* **5 alike**

simmer *see* **4 boil**

Simon
  also known as: 5 Peter
  son: 5 Judas (Iscariot)
  disciple of: 5 Jesus

simpatico 7 likable

simper 5 smirk **6** giggle, tee-hee, titter **7** snicker, snigger

simple 4 bare, dull, dumb, easy, open, slow, soft, true **5** basic, frank, homey, naive, plain, quiet, sheer, stark **6** candid, direct, modest, rustic, stupid **7** foolish, natural **8** innocent, peaceful

simpleton *see* **5** idiot

Simpsons, The
  creator: 8 (Matt) Groening

simulate 3 act, ape **4** copy, fake, play, pose, sham **5** feign, mimic, put on **6** affect, assume, invent **7** imitate, playact, pretend

sin 3 err **4** evil, fall, slip, vice **5** crime, error, lapse, shame, stray, wrong **6** breach, do evil, offend **7** do wrong, misdeed, offense, scandal **8** iniquity, villainy

since 2 as **3** ago, for, yet **4** ergo, from **5** after, hence, later **6** whence **7** because, whereas **8** in as much

sincere *see* **7** genuine

sinew, sinews 4 grit, thew **5** fiber, nerve, power, vigor **6** muscle, tendon **7** stamina **8** ligament, strength, virility, vitality

sing 3 hum **4** lilt, pipe **5** carol, chant, chirp, croon, trill, tweet **6** intone, warble **8** melodize

Singapore
  capital/largest city: 9 Singapore
  sea: 6 Indian **10** South China
  physical feature:
    peninsula: 5 Malay
  feature:
    boat: 4 junk **6** sampan
    clothing: 4 sari

singe 4 burn, char, sear **5** brand **6** scorch

singer 4 alto, bard, bass, diva, lark **5** tenor **6** canary **7** crooner, soprano **8** baritone, minstrel, songbird, vocalist

singing group 4 trio **5** choir, nonet, octet

6 chorus, sextet 7 quartet, quintet 8 glee club

single 3 one 4 lone, sole 5 unwed 6 maiden 7 only one 8 bachelor, singular, solitary, spinster, wifeless

single-minded 4 firm 6 dogged 7 devoted, intense, staunch, zealous 8 resolved, tireless, untiring

single out *see* 6 **choose**

sinister *see* 4 **evil**

sink 3 dig, dip, ebb, lay, sag, set 4 bore, bowl, bury, drop, fall, seep, slip, soak, tilt, wane 5 basin, drill, drive, droop, drown, gouge, lower, slant, slope, slump, stoop, yield 6 engulf, go down, lessen, reduce 7 decline, descend, go under, regress, subside, succumb 8 washbowl

Sins, Seven 4 envy, lust 5 anger, pride, sloth 8 gluttony 12 covetousness

sinuous 6 curved, folded, volute, zigzag 7 bending, coiling, curving, twisted, winding 8 indirect, mazelike, rambling, tortuous, twisting

sip 3 lap, nip, sup 4 dram,

drop 5 drink, savor, taste 6 sample 7 soupcon, swallow

siphon 4 tube 5 drain 7 draw off

sire 4 king, lord 5 beget, breed 6 create, father

siren, Siren 4 horn, vamp 5 alarm, nymph, witch 6 sexpot 7 charmer, whistle 8 deceiver, sea nymph
form: 5 nymph
location: 3 sea
lured sailors by: 7 singing

sissy 6 coward 8 weakling

sister 3 nun, kin, sib 5 nurse 6 female 7 sibling 8 feminist, relation, relative
nautically: 6 secure
society: 8 sorority

Sister Carrie
author: 7 (Theodore) Dreiser

Sisyphean 4 hard 5 tough 6 uphill 7 arduous, onerous

Sisyphus
king of: 7 Corinth
rolled: 5 stone (uphill)

sit 3 lie 4 loll, meet, mind, rest, rule, stay 5 abide, chair, nurse, perch, reign, roost, squat, stand, teach, watch 6 endure, linger, remain, reside, settle **7** care for, preside **8** chaperon

site *see* **4 area**

situ 5 place

situation 3 fix, job **4** case, duty, post, role, seat, site, spot, work **5** berth, place, state **6** locale, office, plight, status **7** dilemma, posture, station **8** capacity, function, location, position

sizable 5 ample, broad, large, roomy **7** immense **8** spacious

size 3 sum **4** area, bulk, mass, sort **5** array, grade, group, scope, total **6** amount, extent, spread, volume **7** expanse, stretch **8** capacity, quantity

sizzle 3 fry **4** hiss, spit **7** crackle, frizzle, hissing, sputter **8** splutter

skate 3 nag, ray **4** skid, skim, slip **5** blade, coast, glide, horse, slide **6** rotter

skein 4 coil, hank, reel, yarn **5** twist **6** tangle, thread **9** filaments

skeleton 4 hulk **5** bones, frame, shell

purpose: 7 support **8** protects

skeptical, sceptical 6 unsure **7** cynical, dubious **8** doubtful, doubting, scoffing

sketch 3 map **4** draw, plot, skit **5** chart, draft, graph, scene **6** depict, digest, precis, satire **7** lampoon, outline, takeoff **8** abstract, synopsis, vignette

skewed *see* **5 slant**

skid 3 ski **4** drag, dray, skim, skip, sled, slip **5** coast, glide, skate, slide **6** runner, sledge **7** skitter **8** glissade, platform, sideslip

skiff 4 boat **6** dinghy **7** rowboat

skill *see* **6 acumen**

skim 3 fly **4** flip, ream, sail, scan, scud, skid, skip **5** coast, float, glide, skate, sweep **6** bounce, scrape **7** dip into **8** glissade

skimp 5 pinch, stint **6** scrimp, slight **8** withhold

skin 3 fur, pod **4** bark, case, coat, flay, hide, hull, husk, peel, pelt, rind **5** shell **6** abrade, casing, fleece, jacket, scrape,

sheath **7** lay bare
outer layer: 9 epidermis
contains: 3 fat **4** hair,
pore, root **5** gland, nerve
6 vessel
body's largest: 5 organ

skinflint *see* **5 cheap**

skinny 4 lank, lean, thin,
wiry **5** gaunt, gawky,
lanky, spare **6** slight **7**
angular, scraggy, scrawny,
slender, spindly

skip 3 bob, cut, hop **4** flee,
flit, jump, leap, miss,
omit, romp, shun, trip **5**
bound, caper, dodge,
elude, evade **6** bounce,
escape, eschew, gambol,
ignore, prance, spring **7**
abscond, neglect **8** leap
over, overlook

skirmish 4 fray, tilt **5**
brush, clash, joust, run-in,
scrap, set-to **6** action,
affray, battle, fracas,
tussle **7** scuffle **8** struggle

skirt *see* **5 dodge**

skittish 3 shy **4** wary **5**
chary, jumpy, leery, shaky,
timid **6** fitful, unsure **7**
bashful, fearful, fidgety,
flighty, guarded, jittery,
nervous, restive
8 cautious, restless,

unstable, unsteady,
volatile

**skulduggery, skullduggery
7** knavery **8** trickery

skulk 4 hide, lurk **5** cower,
creep, prowl, slink, sneak

sky blue 5 azure **8** cerulean,
pale blue

skylarking 5 sport **6** antics
7 hijinks, romping **10**
frolicking

slab 3 wad **4** hunk, slat **5**
block, board, chunk,
plank, slice, wedge

slack 3 lax **4** dull, easy,
free, lazy, limp, slow, soft
5 baggy, loose, quiet, relax
6 loosen, untied **7** flaccid
8 slothful, sluggish

slag 5 dross **6** cinder, scoria
8 clinkers

slake *see* **4 calm**

slam 3 hit **4** bang, bump,
slap **5** crash, smack,
smash, throw

slammer *see* **6 prison**

slander *see* **5 libel**

slang 4 cant, jive **5** argot,
idiom, lingo **6** jargon **7**
dialect

slant 4 bias, lean, list, rake,
tilt, view **5** angle, color,

pitch, slope **7** distort, incline, leaning **8** attitude

slap *see* **5 smack**

slash 3 cut, rip **4** drop, gash, mark, pare, rend, rent, slit, tear **5** lower, slice **6** reduce, stroke **8** decrease, lacerate

slate 4 list **6** ballot, tablet, ticket

slaughter *see* **8 massacre**

Slav 4 Pole, Serb, Sorb, Wend **5** Croat, Czech **6** Bulgar, Slovak **7** Russian, Serbian, Slovene, Sorbian **8** Bohemian, Croatian, Moravian **9** Bulgarian, Ruthenian, Slavonian, Ukrainian

slave 4 prey, serf, toil **6** addict, drudge, menial, thrall, toiler, vassal, victim **7** chattel, plodder **8** bondsman

slay *see* **4 kill**

sleazy 5 cheap, tacky **6** flimsy, shabby, shoddy, trashy, vulgar **7** schlock

sleek *see* **5 slick**

sleep 3 nap **4** doze, rest **5** death, peace **6** repose, snooze **7** slumber

god of: 6 Hypnos, Hypnus, Somnus

sleigh 4 dray, sled **6** cutter, sledge, troika **8** transport

slender *see* **4 thin**

slew 3 lot, ton **4** gang, heap, load, lots, peck, pile, raft **5** batch, did in **6** killed **8** murdered

slice 3 cut **4** pare **5** carve, piece, sever **6** cut off **7** portion, section, segment

slick 3 sly **4** coat, film, foxy, oily, scum, waxy, wily **5** sharp, shiny, sleek **6** clever, glassy, glossy, greasy, satiny, smooth, tricky **7** coating, cunning **8** slippery

slicker 8 raincoat

slide 4 fall, pass, ramp, skid, slip, veer **5** chute, coast, glide, lapse, slope **7** slither **8** sideslip

slight 3 cut **4** lean, slap, slim, snub, thin, tiny **5** frail, small, spare **6** insult, little, modest, rebuff **7** fragile, limited, slender

slim 4 lean, thin **5** faint, small **6** meager, remote, skinny, slight, svelte **7** distant, slender, willowy

slime 3 mud **4** mire, muck, ooze **6** sludge

sling 3 net **4** cast **5** fling, throw

slink 4 slip **5** creep, prowl, skulk, sneak **6** tiptoe

slip 3 put **4** dock, drop, fail, fall, leak, pass, sink, skid **5** berth, error, glide, lapse, scrap, shoot, shred, slide, sneak, sprig, steal, strip **6** escape **7** blunder, faux pas, receipt, sapling, voucher

slipper 4 mule, shoe **5** scuff **6** sandal

slipshod *see* **8 slovenly**

slip-up *see* **5 error**

slit 3 cut slash **7** crevice, fissure **8** incision

slither 5 glide, slide

sliver 5 crumb, shred, slice, snick **6** morsel **8** splinter

slivovitz
    type: 6 brandy **7** liqueur

slob 6 sloven **8** slattern

slobber 4 slop **5** drool **6** drivel, slaver **7** dribble, sputter **8** salivate, splutter

slogan 5 motto **6** byword

slop 3 mud **4** mire, muck, ooze **5** filth, slosh, slush,
spill, swash, swill, waste **6** refuse, sludge, splash **7** garbage, spatter **8** splatter

slope 3 tip **4** bank, bend, lean, tilt **5** angle, pitch, slant **7** descent, incline

slosh 3 lap **4** drop, mire, stir **5** slush, spill, swash **6** splash **8** flounder

slot 3 gap **4** slit **5** crack, niche, notch

sloth 6 phlegm, torpor **7** languor **8** idleness, laziness, lethargy

slouch 4 bend **5** droop, hunch, idler, slump, stoop **6** loafer **7** laggard, shirker, slacker **8** sluggard

Slovakia
    formerly part of: 14
      Czechoslovakia
    capital/largest city: 10
      Bratislava
    mountain: 7 Sudetes **8**
      Low Tatra **9** High Tatra
    river: 6 Danube

Slovenia
    capital/largest city: 9
      Ljubljana
    river: 4 Sava **5** Drava
    sea: 8 Adriatic

slovenly 5 dirty, dowdy, messy **6** frowzy, sloppy,

untidy **7** unclean, unkempt **8** careless, slapdash, slipshod

slow 3 dim, off **4** curb, dull, dumb, flag, late, long **5** brake, check, dense **6** hinder, hold up, impede, retard, stupid, torpid **7** laggard **8** backward, cautious, dawdling, dilatory, dragging, drawn out, hesitant, obstruct, sluggish

sludge 3 mud **4** mire, muck, ooze, slop **5** dregs, slime, slush **8** sediment

slug *see* **5 whack**

sluggish *see* **4 lazy**

slum 6 Bowery, ghetto **7** skid row
   Portuguese: 6 favela

slumber 3 nap **4** doze **5** sleep **6** snooze **8** vegetate

slump 3 dip, sag **4** drop, fall, slip **5** droop, lapse **6** plunge, slouch, tumble **7** decline, give way, reverse, setback **8** collapse

slur 3 cut, dig **4** mark, skip, spot **5** smear, stain, sully, taint **6** defame, ignore, insult, malign, mumble, mutter

slush 4 slop **6** bathos

slut *see* **5 whore**

sly *see* **4 wily**

smack 3 bit, hit, rap **4** blow, buss, clap, cuff, dash, hint, kiss, slap **5** savor, smell, smite, spank, taste, tinge, touch, trace, whack **6** buffet, flavor

small 4 mean, tiny, weak **5** faint, minor, petty, scant **6** feeble, lesser, little, meager, modest, narrow, petite, slight **7** bigoted, fragile, ignoble, trivial **8** not great, trifling

small talk *see* **8 repartee**

smart 4 ache, burn, chic, hurt, keen, neat, trim **5** brash, brisk, quick, sassy, sharp, sting, wince, witty **6** astute, blench, brainy, bright, clever, flinch, modish, shrewd, suffer **7** elegant, stylish

smash 3 hit **4** bang, bash, beat, blow **5** break, clout, crack, crash, crush **6** batter, strike, winner **7** destroy, shatter, success, triumph **8** demolish

smashed *see* **5 drunk**

smashing **5** great, super **6** superb **8** fabulous, terrific

smattering **3** bit, dab **4** dash, drop **5** scrap **7** smidgen, smidgin, snippet **8** smidgeon

smear **3** mar, rub **4** blur, coat, daub, soil **5** cover, lay on, libel, stain **6** blotch, injure, malign, smirch, smudge, spread, streak **7** blacken, blemish, degrade, slander, splotch, tarnish

smell **4** feel, nose, odor, reek **5** aroma, fetor, scent, sense, sniff, stink **6** detect, stench **7** bouquet, perfume

smidgen, smidgin, smidgeon *see* **9 scintilla**

smile **4** beam, grin **5** favor, shine, smirk **6** simper

smirk **4** grin, leer **5** sneer **6** simper **7** grimace

smite *see* **5 whack**

Smith, Al **creator:** **11** Mutt and Jeff

smithereen **3** bit **4** atom **5** crumb, shard **8** fragment, particle

smitten **8** enamored

smoke **4** draw, fume, pipe, puff, reek, suck **5** cigar, fumes **6** billow, inhale **7** light up, smolder

smoke screen **4** ruse **5** cover, dodge, front

smolder **4** burn, fume, rage **5** smoke **6** seethe

smooch *see* **4 kiss**

smooth **4** calm, ease, easy, even, flat, glib, help, mild, open, pave **5** allay, level, silky, sleek, suave **6** facile, mellow, placid, polish, refine, serene, soften, soothe, steady **7** appease, assuage, flatten, mollify, orderly, velvety

smother **4** hide, mask, wrap **5** choke, quash, snuff **6** quench **8** keep down, strangle, suppress

smudge **4** blot, mark, soil, spot **5** dirty, smear, stain

smug **8** superior, virtuous

smuggle **5** sneak

smut **4** dirt, porn, soot **5** filth, grime **6** smudge

Smythe, Reginald **creator:** **8** Andy Capp

snack **3** eat, tea **4** bite, nosh **5** munch **6** nibble, tidbit **7** take tea **8** lap lunch, munchies

snag 3 bar, rip **4** grab, stub, tear **5** block, catch, hitch, stump **7** barrier **8** obstacle

snake 5 sneak, viper **7** reptile, serpent, traitor **8** ophidian

combining form: 4 ophi **5** ophio, ophis **6** herpes **7** herpeto

genus: 7 Ophidia

shedding: 7 ecdysis **8** moulting

skin: 6 exuvia

snake killer: 8 mongoose

Snake *see* **16 Native Americans**

snap 3 nip, pop **4** bark, bite, grab, lock, yelp **5** break, catch, cinch, clasp, click, close, crack, growl, hasty, latch, quick, snarl, spell **6** breeze, period, secure, snatch

snare *see* **7 capture**

snarl 3 mat **4** bark, clog, kink, knot, mess, snap **5** chaos, growl, ravel, twist **6** hinder, impede, jumble, muddle, tangle

snatch *see* **4 grab**

sneak 3 sly **4** slip **5** creep, knave, rogue, scamp, steal **6** lurker, rascal, secret, spirit **7** bounder, furtive, skulker, slinker, smuggle **8** scalawag, surprise

sneer *see* **4 jeer**

snicker 5 snort **6** cackle, giggle, titter **7** snigger

snide 5 nasty **7** mocking **8** scoffing

sniff 4 jeer, mock, odor **5** aroma, scoff, smell, snort, snuff, whiff **6** snivel **7** disdain, sniffle, snuffle

snip 3 bit, bob, cut, lop **4** brat, clip, crop, punk, snap, trim **5** piece, prune, shear **6** sample, shrimp, swatch **8** fragment

snippy *see* **4 rude**

snivel 3 cry **5** sniff, whine **6** boohoo **8** complain

snobbish 4 vain **6** snooty, snotty **7** haughty, high-hat, stuck-up **8** arrogant, superior

snoop 3 pry **7** meddler, Paul Pry **8** busybody

snooze *see* **4 doze**

snort 4 blow, gasp, huff, jeer, pant **5** blast, grunt, scoff, sneer

snout 3 neb **4** beak, bill,

nose **5** snoot, spout **6** muzzle, nozzle

snowfall 4 firn, neve **6** flurry **8** blizzard

Snow White and the Seven Dwarfs
 dwarfs: 3 Doc **5** Dopey, Happy **6** Grumpy, Sleepy, Sneezy **7** Bashful

snowy 4 pure **5** white **7** nievous **8** pristine, spotless

snub 3 cut **5** blunt, check, scorn, short **6** ignore, rebuff, slight **7** disdain

snuff 5 scent, smell, sniff, whiff **7** sniffle, snuffle

snug *see* **4 cozy**

soak 3 wet **4** seep **5** bathe, enter, steep **6** absorb, drench, sink in, take in, take up **7** immerse **8** permeate, saturate

soar 3 fly **4** rise, wing **5** climb, float, glide, mount, tower **8** take wing

sob *see* **3 cry**

sober 3 dry, sad **4** cool, drab, dull, grim, sane **5** grave, sound, staid **6** dreary, sedate, solemn, somber, steady **7** serious, subdued **8** rational

sobriquet 7 epithet, pet name **8** nicknam

soccer players/team: 6 eleven
 position: 6 goalie, keeper **7** forward **8** fullback, halfback
 championship: 8 World Cup

sociable, social 6 social **7** affable, cordial **8** friendly, gracious, outgoing

society 4 body, club **5** elite, group **6** circle, gentry, league **7** mankind **8** humanity, nobility

sock 3 box, hit **4** belt, blow, slap **5** punch, smack, smash **6** strike, wallop **7** clobber

Socrates
 taught using: 5 irony **6** method
 disciple: 5 Plato **8** Xenophon
 wife: 9 Xanthippe
 death potion: 7 hemlock

sod 4 soil, turf **5** divot, earth, grass, sward

soda 3 pop **4** base, cola **5** tonic **6** bicarb, sodium **7** barilla, seltzer **8** beverage, root beer

sodden *see* **5 soggy**

Sodom
 destroyed with: 5 Admah **6** Zeboim **8** Gomorrah

sofa 5 couch, divan **6** canape, lounge, settee **8** love seat

soft 4 easy, kind, mild, pale, weak **5** downy, faint, furry, muted, quiet, silky, sleek **6** feeble, gentle, hushed, pliant, satiny, shaded, silken, smooth, tender **7** lenient, pliable, restful, subdued, velvety **8** delicate

soft soap 7 blarney **8** cajolery, flattery

soggy 5 heavy, mushy, pasty, soppy **6** doughy, soaked, sodden **7** sopping **8** drenched, dripping

soil 4 dirt, foul, land, loam, ruin, soot, spot **5** dirty, earth, grime, humus, muddy, smear, stain, sully **6** debase, defile, ground, region, smudge **7** blacken, country, tarnish **8** disgrace

soiree 4 ball, prom **5** dance, party

sojourn 4 stay **5** abide, pause, visit **6** stay at **7** holiday, layover **8** stay over, stopover, vacation

Sol
 origin: 5 Roman
 form: 3 god
 personifies: 3 sun
 corresponds to: 6 Helios **7** Mithras **8** Hyperion

solace *see* **7 comfort**

solder 4 fuse, join, weld **5** braze, stick

soldier 2 GI **5** GI Joe, major **6** worker, zealot **7** captain, colonel, dogface, general, private, servant, trooper, veteran, warrior **8** corporal, follower, partisan, sergeant

sole 4 lone, only **8** solitary

solemn *see* **6 somber**

solicit 3 ask **4** seek **5** plead **7** entreat, request

solid 4 firm, hard, pure, real **5** dense, massy, sober, sound, tough **6** rugged, stable, steady, strong, sturdy **7** durable, genuine, lasting, unmixed **8** concrete, reliable, sensible, unbroken

solidarity 5 union, unity **7** harmony

solitary *see* **5 alone**

solo 5 alone **8** solitary

Solomon
  father: 5 David
  mother: 9 Bathsheba
  son: 8 Rehoboam
  brother: 5 Amnon **7**
    Absalom, Chileab **8**
    Adonijah
  sister: 5 Tamar
  visitor: 5 Sheba
  built: 6 temple

Solomon Islands
  capital/largest city: 7
    Honiara
  island: 4 Buka, Gizo,
    Savo **5** Ndeni, Ulawa **6**
    Tulagi **7** Malaita,
    Rennell, Solomon,
    Vangunu **8** Choiseul,
    Sikaiana, Vanikoro
  mountain: 5 Balbi
  ocean: 7 Pacific

solution 3 key **5** blend **6**
answer, cipher **7** mixture,
solving **8** emulsion

solve 7 resolve, unravel,
work out **8** decipher,
unriddle, untangle

solvent 7 diluent, soluble

Somalia
  capital/largest city: 9
    Mogadishu
  highest point: 9 Shimbiris
  13 Shimber Berris

  sea/ocean: 6 Indian
  physical feature:
    gulf: 4 Aden
  feature:
    clothing: 4 futa, toga **6**
    sarong
    tree: 6 acacia, baobab
    7 incense **8** mangrove

somber 4 dark, drab, gray,
grim **5** grave, sober **6**
dreary, gloomy, solemn **7**
serious

sometime 4 late, once **5**
later **6** former **7** quondam
8 formerly, previous

somewhat 6 fairly, kind of,
partly, sort of **8** passably

somnolent *see* **7 docmant**

song 4 call, poem, tune **5**
ditty, lyric, verse **6** ballad,
melody, number, piping **7**
chanson

songbird 4 chat, lark, wren
5 robin, veery, vireo **6**
canary, singer, thrush **7**
warbler

sonorous 4 deep, rich **6**
florid **7** ringing, vibrant **8**
eloquent, resonant

Sons and Lovers
  author: 8 (D H) Lawrence

soon 4 anon **6** pronto **7**
betimes, by and by, early

on, ere long, quickly, shortly **8** directly

Sooner State
  nickname of: 8 Oklahoma

soot 4 dirt, smut **5** crock, grime **6** carbon, smudge, smutch **7** residue

soothe *see* **4 calm**

soothsayer 4 seer **5** sibyl **7** diviner, prophet

sop 3 dip, tip, wet **4** dunk, soak **5** bribe **6** absorb, drench, payoff, payola **8** gratuity, saturate

sophisticated 6 subtle **7** complex, studied, worldly **8** advanced, cultured, highbrow, mannered, precious, seasoned

sophomoric 6 callow **7** foolish, puerile **8** childish, immature, juvenile

soporific *see* **4 lazy**

Sopranos, The
  creator: 5 (David) Chase
  cast: 4 (Robert) Iler **5** (Edie) Falco **6** (Lorraine) Bracco, (Tony) Sirico **7** (Jamie-Lynn) DiScala **8** (Dominic) Chianese **9** (Steven) Van Zandt, (Michael) Imperioli **10** (James) Gandolfini

sorcerer 6 shaman, wizard **7** warlock **8** magician

sorceress 5 siren, witch

sorcery 8 witchery, wizardry

sordid 3 low **4** base, rank, vile **5** dirty, gross **6** filthy, putrid, rotten, vulgar, wicked **7** corrupt, ignoble, squalid, unclean **8** degraded, depraved

sore 4 hurt **5** acute, angry, great, harsh, irked, sharp, upset, wound **6** aching, pained, severe, tender **7** bruised, grieved, hurting, painful **8** smarting

sorrel 3 bay **4** herb, roan, weed **5** brown, plant, Rumex **8** chestnut

sorrow 3 woe **4** loss, weep **5** be sad, mourn, trial **6** grieve, lament **7** despair, sadness, travail, trouble

sorry 3 sad **6** woeful **7** grieved, pitiful, unhappy **8** contrite, pathetic, pitiable

sort 4 kind, list, make, sift, type **5** brand, class, grade, group, index, order **6** divide, person **7** arrange, catalog, species, variety **8** classify, organize, separate, take from

sortie 4 rush **5** onset **6** attack, charge **7** assault

so-so 4 blah, fair **5** ho-hum **6** casual, modest **7** average, humdrum **8** adequate, bearable, mediocre, middling, ordinary, passable

sought 6 hunted **7** pursued, quested

soul 5 being, force **6** person, spirit **7** essence **8** creature, vitality

sound 3 fit **4** deep, firm, good, seem, tone, wise **5** drift, hardy, noise, range, sober, solid, tenor, utter, voice **6** intact, robust, severe, signal, stable, strong, sturdy **7** durable, earshot, healthy, lasting, solvent **8** rational, sensible, thorough

Sound and the Fury, The
  author: 8 (William) Faulkner

sound measure 7 decibel

soundness of mind 6 reason, sanity

Sound of Music, The
  director: 4 (Robert) Wise
  cast: 4 (Peggy) Wood **6** (Eleanor) Parker **7** (Julie) Andrews, (Christopher) Plummer

sound out 3 ask **8** approach

soup
  clear: 5 broth **8** bouillon, consomme
  server: 6 tureen
  spoon: 5 ladle
  thick: 5 cream, gumbo **6** bisque, potage **7** chowder

soupcon *see* **4** iota

sour 3 bad **4** acid, dour, keen, tart, turn **5** nasty, sharp, spoil, surly, tangy, testy **6** crabby, cranky, curdle, rancid, sullen, turned **7** acerbic, bilious, curdled, ferment, grouchy, peevish, spoiled **8** unsavory, vinegary

source 4 font, head, root **5** basis, cause, fount **6** author, father, origin, rising, spring **8** begetter, fountain

souse 3 dip, sot **4** duck, dunk, lush, soak **5** douse, drunk, steep, toper **6** boozer, drench **7** immerse, tippler **8** drunkard, saturate, submerge

South Africa
  capital: 8 Cape Town, Pretoria **12** Bloemfontein

largest city: 6 Durban
division: 5 Natal **9** Transvaal **10** Basutoland
independent homelands: 5 Venda **6** Ciskei **8** Transkei **10** bantustans
mountain: 5 Table **11** Drakenberg
highest point: 8 Njesuthi
river: 6 Modder, Orange **7** Limpopo
sea/ocean: 6 Indian **8** Atlantic
physical feature:
    bay: 6 Walvis
    cape: 8 Good Hope
    current: 8 Benguela
    desert: 5 Namib **8** Kalahari
    peninsula: 4 Cape
feature:
    bride price: 6 lobolo
    racial segregation: 9 apartheid
    tree: 7 assagai **9** jacaranda
South America *see* **7** **America, South**
South Carolina
    abbreviation: 2 SC
    nickname: 8 Palmetto
    capital/largest city: 8 Columbia
    highest point: 9 Sassafras

river: 6 Pee Dee, Santee **8** Savannah
island: 3 Sea **10** Parris **10** Hilton Head
physical feature:
    plateau: Piedmont
place:
    beach: 6 Myrtle
    fort: 6 Sumter **8** Moultrie
    gardens: 7 Cypress
South Dakota
    abbreviation: 2 SD **4** S Dak
    capital: 6 Pierre
    largest city: 10 Sioux Falls
    highest point: 6 Harney
    river: 5 Grand, White **6** Moreau, Cheyenne, Missouri
    physical feature:
        butte: 7 Thunder
        plains: 5 Great
        Battlefield: 11 Wounded Knee
        monument: 13 Mount Rushmore
Southern Comfort
    type: 7 liqueur
Southern Cross
    constellation of: 4 Crux
Southern Rhodesia *see* **8** **Zimbabwe**

South Korea *see* **5 Korea**

South Park
   creator: 5 (Matt) Stone **6** (Trey) Parker **9** Matt Stone **10** Trey Parker

South Vietnam *see* **7 Vietnam**

South West Africa *see* **7 Namibia**

souvenir *see* **6 emblem**

sovereign *see* **5 ruler**

Soviet Union *see* **6 Russia**

sow 4 cast, seed **5** lodge, plant, set in, strew **6** inject, spread **7** implant, instill, scatter **8** disperse, sprinkle

space 3 gap, sky **4** area, part, rank, room, seat, span, spot, term, time **5** berth, blank, break, chasm, ether, field, order, place, range, reach, scope, sweep, swing, width **6** hiatus, lacuna, line up, margin, period, set out, spread **7** arrange, breadth, compass, expanse, the void **8** distance, infinity, interval, omission, separate

spacecraft 4 ship **6** rocket **7** orbiter, shuttle

space flight
   agency: 3 ESA **4** NASA
   US mission: 6 Apollo, Gemini, Skylab **7** Mercury
   US rocket: 5 Atlas, Titan **6** Saturn **8** Redstone
   US space shuttle: 8 Columbia **9** Discovery **10** Challenger
   Soviet mission: 5 Soyuz **6** Salyut, Vostok **7** Voskhod
   Soviet astronaut:
      first man in space: 11 Yuri Gagarin
      first woman in space: 19 Valentina Tereshkova
   American astronaut:
      first man on moon: 9 (Neil) Armstrong
      first US woman in space: 4 (Sally) Ride
      oldest person in space: 5 (John) Glenn

Spain
   other name: 6 Iberia
   capital/largest city: 6 Madrid
   kingdom: 4 Leon **6** Aragon **7** Castile **8** Asturias
   mountain: 8 Pyrenees
   highest point: 5 Teide

8 Mulhacen

river: 4 Ebro **5** Douro, Tagus **8** Guadiana **12** Guadalquivir

sea: 8 Atlantic **13** Mediterranean

island: 6 Canary **7** Majorca **8** Balearic, Tenerife

physical feature:
  bay: 6 Biscay
  cape: 9 Trafalgar
  peninsula: 7 Iberian
  plain: 10 Andalusian
  plateau: 6 Meseta
  strait: 9 Gibraltar

place:
  castle: 7 Alcazar
  museum: 5 Prado
  palace: 8 Alhambra, Escorial
  resort: 8 Marbella
  wall paintings/caves: 8 Altamira

feature:
  dance: 5 tango **8** fandango, flamenco
  political party: 7 Falange

food:
  custard: 4 flan
  dish: 6 paella
  drink: 6 sangria
  snacks: 5 tapas
  soup: 8 gazpacho

span *see* **7 breadth**

spangle 4 star **5** bedew **6** sequin **7** glisten, glitter, shimmer, twinkle

Spanish Guinea *see* **16 Equatorial Guinea**

Spanish Sahara *see* **13 Western Sahara**

Spanish Tragedy, The author: 3 (Thomas) Kyd

spank *see* **5 smack**

spar 4 boom, mast, pole **5** argue, fight, sprit **6** bicker **7** dispute, quarrel, wrangle

spare 3 odd **4** bony, cede, free, give, keep, lank, lean, save, thin **5** amass, extra, forgo, gaunt, grant, guard, hoard, lanky, lay up, limit, pinch, rangy, scant, stint, weedy **6** donate, excess, forego, let off, meager, pardon, shield, skimpy **7** forgive, protect, release, reserve, scraggy, scrawny **8** hold back, leftover, liberate, reprieve, withhold

spark 3 bit, jot **4** atom, beam, fire, iota, life **5** brand, ember, flash, gleam, pique, trace **6** arouse, excite, incite, spirit

7 inspire, provoke **8** vitality

sparkling 5 fizzy **6** bubbly **7** twinkly **8** dazzling, glittery

sparse *see* **6 scarce**

Spartacus
  novel: 4 (Howard) Fast
  director: 7 (Stanley) Kubrick
  cast: 4 (Nina) Foch **5** (John) Gavin **7** (Kirk) Douglas, (Lawrence) Olivier, (Jean) Simmons, (Peter) Ustinov **8** (Charles) Laughton

spartan *see* **7 austere**

spasm 3 fit, tic **4** grip, jerk, pang **5** burst, cramp, crick, flash, onset, spell, spurt, start, storm, throe **6** access, attack, frenzy, twitch **7** seizure, shudder, tempest **8** paroxysm

spat *see* **5 fight**

spatter *see* **5 spray**

spawn 4 eggs, seed, teem **5** beget, breed, brood, fruit, yield **7** lay eggs, produce, product **8** engender, generate, multiply

speak 3 air, say **4** call, chat, deal, talk, tell **5** imply, orate, refer, shout, sound, state, treat, voice **6** confer, preach, recite, remark **7** comment, declare, discuss, express, lecture **8** converse, proclaim, vocalize

spear 4 bolt, dart, gaff, gore, pike, spit, stab **5** lance, prick, shaft, spike, stick **6** impale, pierce **7** harpoon, javelin

spearhead 4 iron, lead **5** begin, found, start **6** launch, leader **7** creator, develop, founder, pioneer **8** conceive, initiate

special 4 fast, good, rare **5** close, great, novel **6** ardent, proper, select, signal, unique **7** bargain, certain, devoted, endemic, feature, unusual **8** distinct, uncommon

species 4 form, kind, make, sort, type **5** breed, class, genre, group, order **6** kidney, nature, stripe **7** variety **8** category

specify 4 cite, name **5** order **6** adduce, define, denote, detail **7** call for, focus on, itemize **8** describe, indicate, set forth

specimen **4** case, type **5** model **6** sample **7** example

specious **5** false **6** faulty, tricky, untrue **7** dubious, in valid, unsound **8** slippery, spurious

speck *see* **4 iota**

spectacle **5** scene, sight **6** marvel, parade, rarity, wonder **7** display, exhibit

spectacles **6** lenses, shades **7** glasses **8** bifocals

spectacular **4** gala, rich **5** grand, showy **6** daring **7** jeweled, opulent, stately **8** dramatic, fabulous, glorious, gorgeous, splendid, striking

spectator **3** fan **5** house **6** viewer **7** gallery, witness **8** audience, observer, onlooker

specter *see* **5 ghost**

speculate **4** muse **5** brood, dream, fancy, guess, study, think, wager **6** chance, gamble, hazard **7** imagine, suppose, surmise, venture **8** consider, ruminate, theorize

speech *see* **8 dialogue**

speed **3** aid, hie, run, zip **4** dart, dash, help, race, rate, rush, tear, zoom **5** boost, favor, gun it, haste, hurry, impel, speed, tempo **6** barrel, hasten, hurtle, hustle, propel, scurry **7** hurry up, quicken **8** alacrity, expedite, high tail, step on it, velocity

spell **2** go **3** bit, hex **4** bout, free, lull, mean, omen, snap, term, time, tour, turn, wave **5** augur, break, charm, magic, stint **6** denote, make up, period, voodoo **7** connote, portend, presage, rapture, respite, signify, sorcery, stretch **8** amount to, duration, forecast, foretell, indicate, interval

spend **3** pay, use **4** dole, fill, give, pass **5** drain, empty, use up, waste **6** devote, employ, invest, outlay, pay out **7** consume, deplete, fork out, scatter **8** allocate, shell out, squander

spent *see* **5 weary**

spew **5** eject, expel, heave, vomit **6** cast up **7** spit out

sphere **3** orb **4** area, ball **5** globe, orbit, range, realm, scope **6** domain **7** globule **8** province

Sphinx
form: **7** monster
bust of: **5** woman
body of: **4** lion
proposed: **7** riddles
location: **4** Giza **6** Thebes
answered by: **7** Oedipus

spicy **3** hot **4** keen, racy **5** acute, bawdy, fiery, nippy, pithy, salty, sharp, tangy, witty, zippy **6** clever, ribald, risque, strong **7** peppery, piquant, pungent **8** aromatic, improper, spirited

spider
class: **9** Arachnida
combining form: **6** arachn **7** arachno
famous: **9** Charlotte

spike **3** peg, pin **4** barb, nail, spur, tine **5** briar, point, prong, rivet, spine, stake, thorn **6** needle, skewer **7** bramble, bristle

spill **3** run **4** blab, drip, drop, dump, fall, flow, shed, slop, tell, toss **5** slosh, throw, waste **6** reveal, splash **7** let flow, pour out **8** disclose, overflow, overturn

spin **4** roll, tell, turn **5** swirl, twirl, wheel, whirl **6** gyrate, invent, relate, render, rotate, unfold **7** concoct, narrate, recount, revolve **8** rotation

spinach **16** Spinacia oleracea

spine **4** barb, horn, spur **5** briar, point, prong, quill, spike, thorn **6** needle **7** bramble, bristle, prickle **8** backbone

spineless *see* **5** **timid**

spinster **6** virgin **7** old maid

spiral **4** coil, curl, gyre **5** helix, screw, whirl, whorl **6** coiled, curled **7** helical, ringlet, winding **8** curlicue, twisting

spire *see* **6** **summit**

spirit *see* **5** **ghost**

spirits **3** aim, vim **4** bond, elan, fire, gist, glow, grit, guts, mood, sand, tone, vein, zeal, zest **5** ardor, drive, humor, pluck, sense, spunk, tenor, valor, verve, vigor **6** daring, effect, elixir, liquor, mettle, morale **7** alcohol, avidity, bravery, courage, essence, sparkle **8** attitude, feelings, vitality, vivacity

spiritual *see* **4 holy**

spit 3 bar, pop, rod **4** foam, hiss, reef, spew **5** atoll, drool, eject, fling, froth, shoal, throw **6** saliva, shower, shriek, skewer, slaver, sputum **7** dribble, slobber, spatter, sputter

spite *see* **3 vex**

splash 3 ado, hit **4** cast, dash, daub, soil, stir, toss, wash **5** bathe, break, fling, plash, slosh, smack, smear, stain, strew, surge, swash **6** buffet, effect, impact, paddle, plunge, shower, spread, streak, strike, uproar **7** splotch **8** besmirch, disperse, splatter

splay 4 awry **5** askew, broad **6** aslant, clumsy, extend, tilted, warped **7** awkward, crooked, fanlike

spleen 4 bile, gall **5** anger, spite **6** animus, enmity, hatred, malice, rancor **7** ill will **8** acrimony, vexation

splendor 4 fire, pomp **5** gleam, glory, light, sheen, shine **6** beauty, dazzle, luster, renown **7** burnish, glitter **8** grandeur, nobility, opulence, radiance

splenetic *see* **5 surly**

splice 3 wed **4** join, knit **5** graft, merge, plait, unite **7** connect **8** dovetail

splinter 4 chip **5** smash, split **6** needle, shiver, sliver **7** break up, crumble, explode, shatter **8** fracture

split 3 hew **4** deal, dole, dual, mete, part, rent, rift, rive, snap, tear, torn **5** allot, break, burst, cleft, crack, halve, mixed, riven, sever, share **6** bisect, breach, broken, cleave, differ, divide, ripped, schism, shiver, sunder, varied **7** diverge, divorce, fissure, rupture **8** division, fracture, splinter

splurge 5 binge, spree **6** bender **8** live it up

splutter *see* **7 stammer**

spoil 3 mar, rot **4** baby, flaw, harm, mold, ruin, sour, turn **5** addle, botch, decay, go bad, humor, taint **6** coddle, damage, deface, foul up, mess up, pamper **7** blemish, destroy, putrefy

spoils 4 haul, loot, swag, take **5** booty **6** bounty, prizes, quarry **7** plunder

spoken 4 oral, said **5** parol **6** verbal, voiced **7** uttered

spokesman 5 agent, PR man, proxy **6** backer, deputy **7** speaker **8** delegate, promoter

sponge 3 bum, dry, mop, rub **4** blot, swab, wash **5** cadge, clean, leech, mooch, towel **6** borrow, live on **7** cleanse, moisten **8** freeload, scrounge

sponsor *see* **8 advocate**

spontaneous 4 free **5** ad lib **7** offhand **8** unbidden

spoof *see* **6 parody**

spook 5 alarm, bogey, ghost, haunt, scare, shade **6** goblin, shadow, spirit **7** disturb, phantom, specter, startle, terrify, unnerve **8** disquiet, frighten, unsettle

sporadic *see* **4 rare**

sport 3 fun, toy **4** bear, butt, game, goat, jest, joke, lark, play, romp, trip **5** abuse, caper, carry, chaff, dally, frisk, hobby, mirth, revel **6** antics, cavort, frolic, gaiety,

gambol **7** buffoon, contest, exhibit, gambler, jesting, jollity, kidding, mockery **8** derision, flourish, hilarity

spot 3 dot, fix, see, spy **4** area, bind, blot, daub, espy, flaw, mark, part, seat, site, slur, soil **5** brand, fleck, grime, locus, patch, place, point, smear, space, speck, stain, sully, taint, tract **6** blotch, detect, locale, locate, sector, smudge, stigma **7** blemish, dilemma, pick out, splotch, station **8** discover, location, position

spotless *see* **8 pristine**

spouse 4 mate, wife **7** consort, husband, partner

spout 3 jet, lip **4** beak, flow, go on, gush, nose, pipe, rant, spew, tube, vent, well **5** eject, erupt, expel, exude, issue, mouth, shoot, snout, spray, spurt, surge, vomit **6** nozzle, outlet, sluice, squirt, stream, trough **7** bluster, channel, conduit, pour out **8** disgorge, harangue

sprawl 4 flop, lean, loll, wind **5** slump **6** branch, extend, lounge, slouch **7** recline **8** languish, reach out

spray 4 coat, mist, posy, twig **5** bough, burst, shoot, sprig, treat, vapor **6** dampen, nozzle, shower, splash, switch, volley **7** atomize, barrage, blossom, bouquet, drizzle, moisten, nosegay, scatter, spatter **8** disperse, moisture

spread 3 air, lay **4** area, cast, coat, open, pave, shed, span, vent **5** apply, bruit, cloak, cover, feast, field, issue, range, reach, scope, smear, spray, story, strew, sweep, table, tract, width **6** blazon, extend, extent, herald, length, notice, repeat, report, unfold, unfurl, unroll **7** advance, article, banquet, diffuse, expanse, pervade, plaster, publish, radiate, scatter, spatter, stretch, suffuse, trumpet, write-up **8** coverage, disperse

spree 4 bout, orgy, toot **5** binge, drunk, fling, revel **6** bender **7** carouse, debauch, revelry, splurge, wassail **8** carousal

sprightly *see* **6 jaunty**

spring 3 hop, jet, pop, spa **4** come, dart, flow, gush, jump, kick, leap, loom, pool, pour, rise, rush, stem, well **5** arise, baths, begin, bound, caper, ensue, fount, issue, lunge, shoot, spout, spurt, start, surge, vault **6** appear, bounce, derive, gambol, recoil, reflex, result, sprout, stream **7** burgeon, emanate, proceed, release, shoot up, stretch **8** buoyancy

sprinkle *see* **5 spray**

sprint *see* **3 run**

sprite 3 elf **5** fairy, pixie

sprout 3 bud, wax **4** grow **5** bloom, shoot, sprig **6** come up, flower, spread, thrive **7** blossom, burgeon **8** multiply, offshoot, put forth, spring up

spruce *see* **6 dapper**

spruce 5 Picea

spry *see* **6 nimble**

spunk *see* **5 pluck**

spur 3 arm, leg **4** fork, goad, prod, whet, whip, wing **5** prick **6** branch, feeder, fillip, hasten, motive, siding **7** impetus, impulse **8** stimulus

spurious *see* **8 specious**

spurn *see* **4 snub**

spurt 3 jet **4** dart, dash, emit, flow, gush, gust, rush, tear, whiz **5** burst, flash, issue, lunge, scoot, shoot, speed, spout, spray, surge **6** access, spring, sprint, squirt, stream **7** pour out **8** disgorge, fountain, outburst

spy 3 pry, see **4** find, peep, spot, view **5** scout, sight, snoop **6** behold, descry, detect, notice, shadow **7** discern, glimpse, make out, observe **8** discover, informer, Mata Hari, perceive, saboteur

Spy, The
  author: 6 (James Fenimore) Cooper

squabble *see* **7 quarrel**

squadron 5 fleet **6** armada **8** flotilla

squalid *see* **7 run-down**

squander *see* **5 waste**

square 3 box, fit **4** even, fogy, heal, hick, jerk, jibe, just, mend, park, prig **5** agree, align, blend, block,

close, equal, green, match, place, plane, plaza, prude, tally **6** accord, adjust, candid, circus, cohere, common, concur, even up, fall in, honest, pay off, settle, smooth **7** arrange, balance, clear up, compose, conform, even out, flatten, mediate, patch up, rectify, resolve **8** block out, cornball, make even, quadrate, set right, settle up, truthful

squash *see* **5 crush**

squash 9 Cucurbita

squat 5 cower, dumpy, dwell, kneel, pudgy **6** chunky, cringe, crouch, encamp, hunker, lie low, locate, move in, shrink, square, stocky, stubby, stumpy **8** thickset

squawk 5 blare, croak, gripe **6** scream, squall **7** grumble, protest, screech **8** complain

squeak *see* **6 squeal**

squeal 3 cry **4** bawl, blab, fink, peep, sing, wail, yell, yelp **5** cheep, whine **6** inform, scream, shriek, shrill, squeak **7** screech

squealer 3 pig, rat **4** fink

6 canary, piglet, snitch **7** stoolie, tattler, traitor **8** informer

squeamish *see* **7 prudish**

squeeze 3 hug, jam, pry, ram **4** butt, cram, edge, grip, hold, pack, push **5** clasp, cramp, crowd, drive, elbow, grasp, press, shove, stuff, wedge, wrest, wring **6** clutch, coerce, compel, defile, elicit, extort, jostle, thrust, wrench **7** compact, draw out, embrace, extract, passage, pull out, tear out **8** compress

squelch *see* **5 crush**

squire *see* **6 escort**

squirm 4 bend, jerk, toss, turn **5** pitch, shift, smart, sweat, twist, wince **6** blench, fidget, flinch, shrink, twitch, wiggle, writhe **7** contort, wriggle **8** flounder

squirt 3 jet **4** dash, gush, punk, runt **5** piker, shoot, spout, spray, spurt **6** shower, splash, stream **7** spatter **8** sprinkle

Sri Lanka
   other name: 6 Ceylon
   capital/largest city:

   7 Colombo
  sea/ocean: 6 Indian
  language: 5 Tamil **7** English, Sinhala **9** Sinhalese
  feature:
    animal: 5 loris
    clothing: 4 sari **5** camba **6** sarong **7** cambaya **8** sherwani

stab 2 go **3** cut, jab, try **4** ache, bite, gash, gore, hurt, pain, pang, pass, shot, spit **5** essay, gouge, knife, lance, lunge, prick, qualm, slash, spear, spike, stick, sting, trial, wound **6** cleave, dagger, effort, impale, pierce **7** attempt **8** endeavor, lacerate

stable *see* **6 steady**

stack 4 bank, flue, heap, load, lump, mass, pile, rick **5** amass, batch, bunch, clump, hoard, mound, sheaf **6** bundle, funnel, gather **7** chimney **8** assemble, mountain

stadium 4 bowl, park **5** arena, field, stade **6** circus **8** ballpark, coliseum

staff 3 bat, man, rod **4** cane, crew, help, pole, team, tend, wand, work

5 cadre, force, group, stave, stick **6** cudgel **7** retinue, scepter, service, support **8** advisors

stage 3 act **4** dais, play, spot, step **5** arena, drama, grade, level, phase, put on, sight, stump **6** period **7** perform, produce, rostrum, setting, show biz, soapbox, theater **8** location, position

Stagecoach
 director: 4 (John) Ford
 cast: 5 (Louise) Platt, (John) Wayne **6** (Andy) Devine, (Claire) Trevor **8** (George) Bancroft, (Thomas) Mitchell **9** (John) Carradine

stagger 3 jar **4** jolt, reel, stun, sway **5** amaze, lurch, shake, shock, waver **6** hobble, totter, wobble **7** astound, blunder, nonplus, stumble **8** astonish, bewilder, bowl over, confound

stagnant 4 dead, dull, foul, lazy, slow **5** close, inert, quiet, slimy, stale, still **6** filthy, leaden, putrid, static, supine, torpid **7** languid, tainted

8 lifeless, listless, polluted, sluggish

staid *see* **6 somber**

stain 3 dye, mar **4** blot, daub, flaw, foul, mark, ruin, slur, soil, spot, tint **5** color, dirty, grime, libel, shame, smear, spoil, sully, taint **6** debase, defile, impair, malign, smirch, smudge, stigma, vilify **7** blemish, slander, splotch, tarnish **8** discolor, tincture

stake 3 bar, bet, peg, pot, rod **4** ante, back, grab, haul, lash, loot, moor, pale, pawn, pile, play, pole, post, prop, risk, stay, take **5** booty, brace, hitch, kitty, prize, purse, share, spike, stand, stick, treat, wager **6** chance, hazard, hold up, marker, picket, pillar, reward, spoils **7** finance, jackpot, outline, returns, sponsor, support, trammel **8** interest, pickings, winnings

stale 4 dull, flat **5** banal, close, fusty, musty, trite, vapid **6** common **7** humdrum, insipid, prosaic, tedious, worn-out **8** not fresh, ordinary, stagnant, unvaried

stalemate 3 tie **4** draw, halt **7** dead end, impasse **8** blockage, cul-de-sac, dead heat, deadlock, standoff

stalk 4 hunt, lurk, stem **5** haunt, march, prowl, shaft, spire, stamp, steal, stomp, strut, track, tramp, trunk **6** column, menance, stride **7** pedicel, pervade, swagger **8** threaten

stall 3 box, pen **4** cell, coop, halt, shed, shop, stop **5** block, booth, check, delay, kiosk, stand **6** impede **7** confine, cubicle, disable, trammel **8** postpone

stalwart *see* **7 valiant**

stamina 4 pith **5** vigor **6** energy **8** vitality

stammer 6 falter, fumble, mumble **7** sputter, stumble, stutter **8** splutter

stamp
   block: 4 pane
   collecting: 9 philately
   first-day hand stamper: 6 cachet
   mounting paper: 5 hinge
   used mark: 8 postmark

stamp, stamp out 2 OK **3** die, tag **4** cast, kind, make, mark, mint, mold, seal, sort, type **5** brand, crush, erase, label, march, print, pound, punch, quash, smash, stalk, stomp, strut, thump, tramp **6** banish, emblem, reveal, rub out, signet, step on, stride, trudge **7** abolish, engrave, imprint, squelch, trample, variety, voucher **8** hallmark, identify, inscribe, intaglio, manifest, suppress

stampede 4 bolt, dash, flee, race, rout, rush **5** chaos, flood, panic **6** engulf **7** overrun, scatter

stanchion 4 post, prop, stay **5** brace, strut **7** support, upright

stand 2 be **3** put, set **4** draw, face, hold, last, move, rank, rear, rest, rise, stay, step, take, tent **5** abide, argue, booth, brook, erect, exist, get up, hoist, honor, kiosk, mount, place, put up, raise, shift, stall, treat **6** bear up, effort, endure, policy, stance, uphold

7 carry on, counter, defense, endorse, opinion, persist, prevail, stomach, support, sustain, undergo, weather **8** advocate, champion, position, tolerate

standard 3 leg **4** base, flag, foot, jack, post **5** basic, canon, guide, ideal, stock, usual **6** banner, column, common, ensign, normal, pillar **7** measure, pennant, regular, typical **8** accepted, ordinary

stand-in 3 sub **5** agent, proxy **6** backup, deputy, double, fill-in, second

standoff 7 impasse **8** deadlock

standoffish *see* **5 aloof**

staple 3 key **4** main **5** basic, chief, major, prime, vital **6** leader **7** feature, primary, product **8** resource, vendible

star, stars 3 god, sun, VIP **4** diva, fate, hero, idol, lead, lion, name **5** comet, excel, giant, great, omens, shine **6** big wig, do well, galaxy, meteor, nebula, planet **7** destiny, feature, fortune, goddess, heroine, notable, soloist, starlet, succeed, top draw **8** asteroid, cynosure, eminence, immortal, luminary, mainstay, Milky Way, portents, showcase, stand out, virtuoso

brightest: 6 Sirius

distance measure: 6 parsec **9** light year

double star: 6 binary

exploding star: 4 nova **9** supernova

type: 5 dwarf, giant **6** pulsar **7** cluster, neutron **8** variable **9** black hole, collapsed

starch 5 vigor **6** sizing **8** backbone, gumption

stare *see* **4 gaze**

stark *see* **4 base**

starlet 7 actress, ingenue

start 3 aid, shy **4** dawn, drop, edge, form, gush, jerk, jolt, jump, lead, leap, odds, rush, turn **5** beget, begin, birth, blink, bound, eject, erupt, evict, flush, forge, onset, spasm, spurt, wince **6** broach, chance, create, embark, emerge, flinch, ignite, kindle, launch, origin, outset, spring, take up, twitch

7 genesis, opening **8** commence, generate, get going, initiate, priority

startle *see* **8 surprise**

Star Trek
  cast: 5 (Leonard) Nimoy, (George) Takei **6** (James) Doohan, (DeForrest) Kelley **7** (William) Shatner
  ship: 10 (USS) Enterprise
  aliens: 8 Klingons, Romulans

starve 3 yen **4** burn, deny, fast, gasp, long, lust, pine **5** crave, raven, yearn **6** aspire, cut off, famish, hunger, refuse, thirst **7** deprive **8** be hungry, go hungry, languish

Star Wars
  director: 5 (George) Lucas
  cast: 4 (Harrison) Ford **6** (Carrie) Fisher, (Mark) Hamill **8** (Alec) Guinness
    voice of Darth Vader: 5 (James Earl) Jones

state 3 put **4** form, land, mind, mode, mood, pass, pomp **5** guise, offer, phase, realm, shape, stage **6** aspect, luxury, morale, nation, people, plight, recite, relate, report, ritual, status **7** country, declare, explain, express, kingdom, posture, recount **8** attitude, ceremony, dominion, monarchy, official, republic

state admittance
  first: 8 Delaware
  second: 12 Pennsylvania
  third: 9 New Jersey
  fourth: 7 Georgia
  fifth: 11 Connecticut
  sixth: 13 Massachusetts
  seventh: 8 Maryland
  eighth: 13 South Carolina
  ninth: 12 New Hampshire
  tenth: 8 Virginia
  eleventh: 7 New York
  twelfth: 13 North Carolina
  thirteenth: 11 Rhode Island
  fourteenth: 7 Vermont
  fifteenth: 8 Kentucky
  sixteenth: 9 Tennessee
  seventeenth: 4 Ohio
  eighteenth: 9 Louisiana
  nineteenth: 7 Indiana
  twentieth: 11 Mississippi
  twenty-first: 8 Illinois
  twenty-second: 7 Alabama
  twenty-third: 5 Maine
  twenty-fourth: 8 Missouri
  twenty-fifth: 8 Arkansas

twenty-sixth: 8 Michigan
twenty-seventh: 7 Florida
twenty-eighth: 5 Texas
twenty-ninth: 4 Iowa
thirtieth: 9 Wisconsin
thirty-first: 10 California
thirty-second: 9 Minnesota
thirty-third: 6 Oregon
thirty-fourth: 6 Kansas
thirty-fifth: 12 West Virginia
thirty-sixth: 6 Nevada
thirty-seventh: 8 Nebraska
thirty-eighth: 8 Colorado
thirty-ninth/fortieth: 11 North Dakota, South Dakota
forty-first: 7 Montana
forty-second: 10 Washington
forty-third: 5 Idaho
forty-fourth: 7 Wyoming
forty-fifth: 4 Utah
forty-sixth: 8 Oklahoma
forty-seventh: 9 New Mexico
forty-eighth: 7 Arizona
forty-ninth: 6 Alaska
fiftieth: 6 Hawaii

statement 3 tab **4** bill **5** check, claim, count, tally **6** avowal, charge, record, remark, report, speech **7** account, comment, invoice, mention, recital

stateroom 5 cabin **8** quarters

statesman 8 diplomat

static *see* **5 inert**

station 4 post, rank, site, spot, stop **5** caste, class, depot, grade, level, place **6** assign, degree, locate, status **7** footing, install **8** ensconce, facility, location, position, prestige, terminal

statue 8 monument

statuesque 5 regal **7** stately **8** majestic

stature, status *see* **4 rank**

staunch, stanch *see* **8 resolute**

stay 3 aim, guy, rib, rod **4** bunk, curb, foil, halt, live, pole, prop, rest, room, stem, stop **5** abide, block, brace, check, delay, dwell, lodge, quell, shore, stick, tarry, visit **6** endure, keep in, linger, rein in, remain, reside, splint, stifle, thwart **7** carry on, hold out, holiday, persist, sojourn **8** reprieve, suppress, vacation

steady 4 even, firm, sure

5 sober **6** secure, stable **7** balance, careful, devoted, regular, serious, staunch **8** constant, reliable, resolute, unending, untiring

steal 3 buy, cop **4** copy, crib, flit, flow, lift, slip, take **5** creep, drift, filch, glide, pinch, skulk, slide, slink, sneak, swipe, usurp **6** borrow, elapse, escape, extort, filter, pilfer, pocket, rip off, snatch, snitch, thieve **7** bargain, defraud, diffuse, good buy, imitate, purloin, swindle

stealthy *see* **6 covert**

steamer 4 boat, clam, ship **5** liner, trunk

steel 4 dirk, foil, gird **5** blade, brace, knife, nerve, saber, sword **6** dagger, rapier **7** bayonet, cutlass, fortify, machete **8** falchion, scimitar

steep 4 brew, bury, fill, soak **5** imbue, sharp, sheer, souse **6** abrupt, drench, engulf, infuse, plunge **7** immerse, pervade, suffuse **8** saturate, submerge

steeple 5 spire, tower **6** belfry

steer 3 aim, lay, run **4** bear, head, lead, make, sail **5** coach, guide, pilot **6** direct, govern, manage **7** conduct **8** navigate

steer clear of *see* **5 dodge**

stellar 6 astral, starry **7** leading **8** starring

stem 3 dam **4** buck, cane, come, curb, grow, halt, rise, stay, stop **5** arise, block, check, deter, ensue, issue, quell, shank, shoot, speak, spire, stalk, stall, stock, trunk **6** derive, hinder, impede, oppose, resist, thwart **7** prevent, proceed, tendril **8** obstruct, restrain, surmount

stench 4 odor, reek **5** fetor, stink **8** bad smell

step 3 act **4** clip, gait, move, pace, rank, rung, span, walk **5** notch, phase, point, riser, stage, stair, strut, track, tramp, tread **6** action, degree, hobble, period, remove, stride **7** footing, measure, process **8** maneuver

step down *see* **4 quit**

stereotype **4** type **6** cliche **7** formula **8** typecast

sterile *see* **6 barren**

sterling **4** pure, true **5** noble **6** silver, superb, worthy **7** genuine, perfect **8** flawless, superior

Steve Canyon
    creator: 6 (Milton) Caniff

stew *see* **5 worry**

steward **5** agent, proxy **6** deputy, factor, waiter **7** bailiff, manager, trustee **8** executor, overseer

stick **3** bar, bat, cue, dig, fix, jab, pin, put, rod, set **4** balk, bind, cane, club, curb, fuse, glue, hold, join, last, mire, nail, pink, poke, pole, seal, snag, stab, stop, tack, twig, wand, weld **5** abide, affix, baton, billy, check, lodge, paste, place, plant, prick, spear, spike, staff, stake, stave **6** adhere, attach, branch, cement, cudgel, detain, endure, fasten, hog-tie, impede, insert, pierce, scotch, skewer, thrust, thwart **7** crosier, inhibit, shackle **8** continue, puncture

stick up for **5** boost **6** defend **7** root for

stiff **4** body, cold, cool, firm, grim, hard, high, iron, keen, prim, sore, taut **5** aloof, awful, brave, brisk, crisp, cruel, dense, fixed, gusty, harsh, heavy, rigid, sharp, smart, solid, steep, stern, tense, thick, tight, tough, undue **6** chilly, clumsy, corpse, dogged, forced, formal, raging, steely, wooden **7** austere, awkward, cadaver, decided, intense, labored, precise, remains, settled, starchy, stately, steeled, uptight, valiant **8** grievous, mannered, pitiless, resolute, resolved, rigorous, stubborn, ungainly, unlimber, unshaken, vigorous

stifle *see* **6 muffle**

stigme *see* **5 stain**

still *see* **5 inert**

stilted **4** cold, prim **5** rigid, stiff **6** forced, formal, stuffy, wooden **7** awkward, uptight **8** mannered, priggish

stimulate 3 fan **4** spur, stir, wake **5** alert, rouse **6** arouse, awaken, excite, incite, prompt, vivify **7** animate, inspire, sharpen **8** activate

sting 3 cut, nip, rub, vex **4** ache, barb, bite, blow, burn, fire, gall, gnaw, goad, grip, hurt, itch, lash, move, pain, prod, rack, rasp, rile, sore, spur, stab, whip **5** anger, chafe, cross, egg on, grate, impel, prick, shock, smart, venom, wince, wound **6** excite, harrow, incite, insult, kindle, madden, nettle, offend, pierce **7** incense, inflame, prickle, provoke, scourge **8** irritate

Sting, The
  director: 4 (George Roy) Hill
  cast: 4 (Robert) Shaw **6** (Paul) Newman **7** (Charles) Durning, (Robert) Redford
  score: 6 (Scott) Joplin

stingy *see* **5 cheap**

stink 4 odor, reek **5** fetor **6** stench **8** bad smell

stint 3 job **4** curb, duty, part, save, task, term, turn **5** check, chore, limit, quota, shift **6** reduce, scrimp **8** hold back, restrain, restrict, withhold

stipend 5 grant, wages **6** income, salary **7** pension

stipulate 4 cite, name **5** agree, allow, grant, state **6** assure, insure **7** provide, specify, warrant **8** indicate

stir 3 act, mix **4** beat, fire, goad, jolt, move, prod, rush, spur, to-do, whip **5** blend, rouse, shake, sough, start **6** arouse, awaken, bustle, excite, flurry, hasten, hustle, kindle, mingle, rustle, tumult, uproar, vivify, work up **7** agitate, animate, inspire, provoke **8** energize

stitch 3 bit, jot, sew **4** ache, iota, kink, mend, pain, pang, seam, tack **5** baste, cramp, crick, piece, scrap, shoot, shred **6** suture, tingle, twinge, twitch **7** article, garment **8** particle

stock 4 butt, clan, form, fund, haft, herd, hold, kind, line, pull, race, root, type **5** array, basic, birth, blood, breed, broth, cache, caste, equip, goods, grasp, hoard, house, offer, shaft, store, tribe, wares **6** cattle, family, origin, source, staple, supply **7** capital, dynasty, furnish, lineage, provide, regular, reserve, routine **8** ancestry, heredity, pedigree, standard

stodgy *see* **4** dull

stoic **4** calm **8** detached, fatalist, quietist, tranquil

Stoker, Bram
    author of: **7** Dracula

stole **3** fur **4** cape, robe, took, wrap **5** crept, orary, scarf **6** swiped **7** filched, pinched, sneaked, tiptoed **8** mantilla, pilfered, snatched, vestment

stomach **3** maw, pot **4** bear, bent, bias, craw, crop, guts, mind, take **5** abide, belly, brook, fancy, humor, stand, taste, tummy **6** endure, hunger, liking, paunch, relish, retain, suffer **7** abdomen, gizzard, midriff, swallow **8** affinity, appetite, bear with, keenness, potbelly, tolerate

stone **3** gem, nut, pip, pit **4** rock, seed **5** bijou, jewel **6** kernel, pebble

stoneware **5** china **7** ceramic, pottery

stony **3** icy **4** cold **5** blank, bumpy, chill, rocky, rough, stern **6** coarse, craggy, flinty, frigid, jagged, marble, pebbly, rugged, severe, steely, stolid, uneven **7** callous, granite **8** concrete, deadened, gravelly, hardened, obdurate, ossified, pitiless, rocklike, soulless, uncaring

stool **5** bench **7** cricket, hassock, ottoman

stool pigeon *see* **8** informer

stoop **3** bow, sag **4** bend, fall, sink **5** deign, droop, porch, slump, steps, yield **6** resort, slouch, submit **7** concede, descend, succumb **8** doorstep

stop **3** ban, bar, end **4** curb, fill, halt, hold, idle, plug, quit, rest, seal, stay, stem, wait **5** abide, block, brake, break, caulk, cease, check, close, depot, deter, dwell, lapse, lodge, pause, put up, spell, stall, stand, tarry, visit **6** alight, arrest, cut off, desist, expire, hamper, hinder, repose, stanch, thwart **7** layover, prevent, station, suspend **8** abeyance, conclude, obstruct, preclude, restrain, suppress, terminal

store 3 lot **4** fund, hold, host, keep, mart, pack, pile, save, shop **5** amass, array, cache, faith, hoard, lay by, lay in, lay up, stash, stock, trust, value, wares **6** credit, esteem, gather, heap up, legion, market, plenty, regard, riches, scores, supply, volume, wealth **7** deposit, effects, husband, put away, reserve, satiety **8** emporium, lay aside, overflow, plethora, quantity, reliance, richness, salt away, sock away, stow away

storehouse 4 bank, silo **5** depot, vault **7** arsenal, granary **8** elevator, magazine, treasury

storm 3 ado, row **4** blow, fume, fuss, gale, rage, rant, rave, roar, rush, stir, tear, to-do **5** burst, furor,

snarl, stalk, stamp, stomp, tramp **6** assail, attack, charge, clamor, deluge, flurry, hubbub, pother, ruckus, squall, strike, tumult, uproar **7** assault, besiege, bluster, carry on, cyclone, rampage, tempest, tornado, torrent, turmoil, twister, typhoon **8** blizzard, brouhaha, downpour, eruption, fall upon, outbreak, outburst, upheaval

story 3 fib, lie **4** news, plot, tale, word, yarn **5** alibi, fable, piece **6** excuse, legend, report, sketch **7** account, article, parable, romance, tidings, version **8** allegory, anecdote, argument, dispatch, news item, white lie

stout *see* **6 brawny**

stow 3 jam, put, set **4** cram, load, pack, tuck **5** cache, crowd, place, stash, store, stuff, wedge **7** deposit

strafe 7 bombard **8** fire upon

straggle 4 rove **5** drift, stray **6** sprawl, wander **7** deviate, meander

straight 4 even, neat, tidy,

true **5** clear, frank, right, solid, sound **6** candid, direct, evenly, honest, square, unbent **7** aligned, orderly, upright **8** squarely, truthful

straightforward *see* **6 candid**

strain 3 air, tax, tug **4** kind, line, pull, sift, song, sort, toil, tune, type, vein **5** blood, breed, drain, force, heave, labor, press, sieve, trait, twist **6** burden, drudge, effort, extend, family, filter, genius, injure, melody, overdo, purify, refine, screen, sprain, weaken **7** descent, distend, lineage, overtax, species **8** ancestry, hardship, pressure, protract, struggle

strait 7 channel, narrows, passage

straitened 5 broke, needy **6** hard-up **7** pinched **8** bankrupt, indigent, strapped, wiped-out

straitlaced *see* **6 proper**

strand 4 bank, cord, lock, rope **5** beach, braid, coast, fiber, leave, shore, tress, twist **6** desert,

maroon, string, thread **8** filament, necklace

strange 3 new, odd **4** lost **5** alien, queer **6** uneasy, unused **7** awkward, bizarre, curious, erratic, foreign, unknown, unusual **8** aberrant, abnormal, freakish, peculiar, singular, uncommon

Strange Interlude author: 6 (Eugene) O'Neill

Stranger, The author: 5 (Albert) Camus

strangle *see* **5 choke**

strap 3 tie **4** band, beat, belt, bind, cord, flog, lash, whip **5** flail, leash, thong, truss **6** tether, thrash

strategy *see* **6 method**

stratosphere 3 sky **5** ozone **7** heavens **8** upper air

straw 3 hay **4** tube **5** chaff **7** pipette

strawberry 8 Fragaria

stray *see* **6 wander**

streak 3 bar, bed, fly **4** band, blot, blur, cast, dart, dash, daub, line, lode, race, rush, seam, tear, vein, whiz, zoom **5** layer, level, plane, smear, speed, strip, touch

6 blotch, hurtle, smirch, smudge, strain, stripe **7** portion, splotch, stratum

stream 3 jet, run **4** blow, file, flow, flux, gush, pour, race, rill, rush, teem, tide, waft, wave **5** brook, burst, creek, float, flood, issue, river, shoot, spate, spill, spout, spurt, surge **6** abound, deluge, onrush, sluice **7** current, torrent **8** fountain

street 3 way **4** lane, mews, road **5** alley, block, route **6** avenue **7** highway, roadway, terrace, thruway **8** turnpike

Streetcar Named Desire, A
author: 8 (Tennessee) Williams
director: 5 (Elia) Kazan
cast: 5 (Vivien) Leigh **6** (Marlon) Brando, (Kim) Hunter, (Karl) Malden

strega
type: 7 liqueur

strength 4 beef, grit, kick, pith, sand, size **5** brawn, force, forte, might, pluck, power, sinew, spice, vigor **6** anchor, mettle, number, purity, spirit, succor, virtue **7** bravery, muscles,

potency, stamina, support **8** solidity, tenacity

strenuous *see* **7 arduous**

stress 4 beat, mark **5** force, value, worth **6** accent, affirm, assert, burden, moment, repeat, strain, weight **7** anxiety, concern, feature, gravity, meaning, sawdust, tension, urgency **8** emphasis, pressure

stretch 4 span, term, tire **5** cover, reach, spell, stint, tract, while, widen **6** burden, deepen, expand, extend, period, sprawl, spread, spring, strain **7** distend, expanse, lie over **8** distance, duration, elongate, interval, lengthen, reach out

strew 3 sow **6** litter **7** scatter **8** disperse

stricken 3 ill **4** hurt, sick **7** injured, smitten, wounded **8** blighted, diseased

strict 4 nice **5** exact, rigid, stern **6** severe **7** austere, perfect **8** absolute, complete, exacting, rigorous, unerring

stride 4 gait, lope, pace, step **5** march, stalk

7 advance, headway **8** long step, progress

strident *see* **5 harsh**

strife *see* **8 conflict**

strike 3 bat, box, hit, run, tap **4** bang, beat, belt, bump, clap, clip, club, come, cuff, drub, find, flog, lash, make, meet, pelt, ring, slam, slap, slug, sock, toll, whip, wipe **5** chime, clout, erase, flail, knell, knock, light, pound, punch, reach, smash, smite, sound, thump, tie-up, whack, whale **6** affect, arrive, assail, attack, batter, buffet, cancel, chance, charge, cudgel, hammer, pommel, remove, seem to, thrash, wallop **7** assault, boycott, impress, protest, scourge, scratch

string 3 row **4** cord, file, line, rope **5** chain, queue, train, twine **6** parade, series, spread, strand, thread **7** stretch **8** sequence

stringent *see* **6 severe**

strip 3 rob **4** band, flay, loot, peel, raid, sack, skin, slip, tear **5** field, flake,

rifle, shave **6** denude, divest, length, ravage, remove, ribbon **7** deprive, disrobe, lay bare, plunder, pull off, ransack, uncover, undress

stripe 3 bar **4** band, line, tape **5** braid, strip, swath **7** chevron **8** insignia

stripling 3 boy, lad **5** minor, youth **8** teenager, young man

strive *see* **3 try**

stroke 3 bat, hit, pat, pet, tap **4** blow, chop, coup, deed, feat, poke, slap, sock, swat **5** brush, chime, fluke **6** caress, chance **7** ringing, seizure, tolling **8** accident, flourish

stroll 4 tour, turn, walk **5** amble, mosey **6** wander **7** meander, saunter

stroller 4 pram **5** buggy **6** ambler, walker **7** rambler **8** carriage

strong 3 hot **4** able, bold, deep, keen, tart **5** burly, clear, close, fiery, hardy, macho, nippy, sharp, solid, sound, stout, tangy, tough, vivid **6** ardent, brawny, fierce, gritty, mighty, potent, robust, severe, sinewy, sturdy **7** buoyant, fervent, healthy, intense, piquant, pungent, zealous **8** emphatic, forceful, muscular, powerful, vehement, vigorous

structure 4 form, plan **6** design, makeup **7** arrange, edifice, pattern **8** assemble, building, conceive, organize

struggle 3 vie, war **4** duel, feud, pull, push, spar, tilt **5** argue, brawl, brush, clash, fight, grind, joust, labor, match, scrap, trial **6** battle, combat, differ, effort, engage, strain, strife, strive, tussle **7** compete, contend, grapple, quarrel, scuffle **8** conflict, exertion, skirmish

strut 4 sail **6** parade, sashay **7** peacock, swagger

Stuart Little author: 5 (E B) White

stub 3 end **4** bump, butt, dock, tail **5** crush, knock, snuff, stump **7** receipt, remains, voucher

stubble 5 beard **6** stumps **8** bristles, whiskers

stubborn 6 dogged, mulish, strong, sturdy **7** willful **8** forceful, obdurate, perverse, resolute

stuck *see* **5 stick**

stuck-up *see* **4 vain**

stud 3 dot **4** beam, buck, dude, sire **5** board, rivet **6** button **8** fastener, nailhead

student 4 coed **5** pupil **6** reader **7** analyst, learner, scholar, watcher **8** disciple, examiner, observer, reviewer

study 3 den **4** cram, read **5** grind, probe **6** office, peruse, review, search, studio, survey **7** examine, inquiry, library, observe **8** analysis, research, scrutiny

stuff 3 act, bit, jam, pad, wad **4** best, bosh, bunk, cram, fill, gear, heap, load, pack, pile, sate, stow **5** cache, crowd, gorge, hokum, hooey, stash, store, thing, trash, wedge **6** fill up, matter, staple, tackle, things, thrust **7** effects, essence, hogwash, rubbish, satiate **8** material, nonsense

stumble *see* **6 falter**

stump 3 end **4** butt, foil, stub, thud **5** befog, clomp, clonk, clump, clunk, stamp, stomp, tramp **6** baffle, nubbin, stymie **7** confuse, mystify, nonplus, perplex **8** confound

stun *see* **5 amaze**

stunt 3 act **4** curb, feat **5** abort, check, cramp, dwarf, limit, stint, trick **6** impede, number, stifle **7** curtail, delimit **8** restrain, restrict, suppress

stupefy *see* **5 amaze**

stupendous *see* **8 fabulous**

stupid 4 dull, dumb **5** dense, inane, inept, silly **6** absurd, oafish, obtuse, simple, unwise **7** aimless, asinine, boorish, doltish, fatuous, foolish, idiotic, moronic, witless

stupor 4 daze **5** faint **6** apathy, torpor **7** inertia **8** blackout, lethargy

sturdy 4 able, firm **5** brave, burly, gutsy, hardy, heavy, solid, sound, stout, tough **6** heroic, mighty, robust, secure **7** defiant, doughty, durable, gallant, lasting, valiant **8** enduring, resolute, stubborn, vigorous, well-made

stygian 3 dim **4** dark **5** black, murky **6** dreary, gloomy, somber **7** hellish **8** funereal, infernal

style 3 fad **4** call, elan, kind, mode, name, pomp, rage, sort, type **5** charm, class, craze, favor, flair, grace, model, taste, trend, vogue **6** design, luxury, manner, polish **7** arrange, comfort, fashion, pattern **8** currency, elegance
French: 4 gout

stymie *see* **6 hinder**

Styx
 form: 5 river
 location: 5 Hades
 father: 7 Oceanus
 ferryman: 6 Charon

suave 6 silken, smooth, urbane **7** affable, elegant, politic **8** charming, gracious, mannerly, polished, unctuous

sub 5 below, proxy, under **6** backup, deputy, second **7** beneath, standby, stand-in

subaltern 4 aide **6** helper

subdivision 3 arm **4** wing

6 branch **7** chapter, section **8** offshoot

subdue *see* **4 calm**

subject 4 bare, case, gist, open, pith, text **5** field, issue, liege, motif, prone, study, theme, topic **6** affair, expose, liable, matter, submit, thesis, vassal **7** citizen, concern, exposed **8** follower, obedient

subjugate 4 tame **5** crush, quell **6** subdue **7** conquer, put down **8** dominate, suppress, vanquish

sublime 4 high **5** grand, great, lofty, noble **6** superb **7** exalted, stately **8** elevated, imposing, majestic, splendid, terrific

submerge, submerse 4 dive, sink **5** douse, drown, flood, souse **6** deluge, engulf, go down, plunge **7** go under, immerse **8** inundate, pour over

submissive *see* **4 meek**

submit 3 bow **4** bend, cede **5** agree, argue, claim, defer, kneel, offer, stoop, yield **6** accede, assert, commit, comply, give in, give up, resort, tender

7 present, proffer, propose, succumb, suggest **8** back down, put forth

subordinate *see* **8 inferior**

sub rosa 8 covertly, in secret, on the sly, secretly

subscribe 4 help, sign **6** assent, chip in, donate **7** consent, endorse, support **8** hold with

subsequent 4 next **7** ensuing

subservient 6 docile, menial **7** fawning, servile, slavish, subject

subside *see* **6 recede**

subsidy 3 aid **4** gift **5** award, grant **7** backing, support

substance 4 body, core, germ, gist, pith, soul **5** force, heart, means, money, sense, stuff **6** burden, import, intent, marrow, matter, riches, thrust, wealth **7** element, essence, keynote, purport, reality **8** backbone, material, property, solidity

substandard *see* **8 inferior**

substitute *see* **8 exchange**

subterfuge *see* **6 scheme**

subtle, subtile 3 sly **4** cagy, deft, fine, foxy, keen, wily **5** light, quick, sharp, slick **6** artful, astute, clever, crafty, expert, shifty, shrewd, tricky **7** cunning, devious, elusive, refined **8** delicate, skillful

subtract *see* **8 decrease**

suburbs 8 environs, vicinity

subvert *see* **7 destroy**

subway 2 El **4** tube **5** metro, train
  San Francisco: 4 BART
  overhead lines: 3 els

success 3 hit **4** fame **5** smash **7** triumph, victory **8** conquest

succession 3 run **5** chain, cycle, round, train **6** course, series **8** sequence

successor 4 heir **5** donee **7** devisee, heiress, heritor, legatee **8** follower

succinct *see* **5 short**

succor 3 aid **4** help **5** nurse **6** assist, back up, relief, shield, wait on **7** comfort, nurture, protect, relieve, support, sustain

succulent 5 juicy **6** fleshy

succumb *see* **5 yield**

sucker 3 sap **4** boob, butt, dupe, fool, goat, gull, jerk, mark **5** chump, patsy **6** pigeon, victim **7** cat's-paw, fall guy **8** easy mark, fair game, pushover

Sucre
  legal capital of: 7 Bolivia

Sudan
  capital: 8 Khartoum
  largest city: 8 Omdurman
  division: 6 Darfur
  highest point: 7 Kinyeti
  lake 4 Chad **6** Nasser
  river: 4 Nile **8** Blue Nile **9** White Nile
  sea: 3 Red
  physical feature:
    desert: 6 Libyan, Nubian
    sandstorm: 6 haboob
    swamp: 4 Sudd

sudden 4 rash **5** hasty, quick, rapid **6** abrupt, speedy **7** instant

suds 3 ale **4** beer, brew, foam **5** draft, froth, lager

sue 3 beg **4** pray **5** plead **6** appeal **7** beseech, entreat, implore **8** petition

suffer 4 ache, bear, hurt, pine **5** stand **6** endure, grieve, lament **7** agonize, despair, drop off, fall off, stomach, sustain, undergo

suffice 2 do **4** last, meet, pass **5** avail, get by, serve **6** answer, make do **7** fulfill, qualify, satisfy

suffocate 3 gag **5** choke **6** quench, stifle **7** garrote, smother **8** snuff out, strangle, throttle

suffuse *see* **8 saturate**

sugary *see* **5 sweet**

suggest *see* **5 imply**

suit 3 fit **4** duds, garb, plea, togs **5** befit, court, getup, habit, match **6** appeal, attire, become, beseem, follow, livery, oblige, outfit, please, prayer, wooing **7** apparel, clothes, content, gladden, satisfy, uniform **8** clothing, entreaty, jell with, make glad

suitcase 3 bag **4** grip **6** valise **7** satchel **8** knapsack, rucksack

suite 3 set **4** flat **5** chain, court, group, rooms, round **6** convoy, series **7** company, cortege, retinue

suitor 4 beau, love **5** flame, lover, swain, wooer

6 fellow **7** admirer, gallant **8** young man

sulk *see* **4 mope**

sullen *see* **4 glum**

sully 4 ruin, soil, spot **5** dirty, spoil, stain **6** befoul, defame, defile, smudge **7** begrime, besmear, blemish, corrupt, pollute, tarnish **8** disgrace, dishonor

sultan 4 king **5** ruler **7** emperor, monarch

sultry 3 hot **4** sexy **5** close, humid, muggy **6** erotic, stuffy, sweaty **7** sensual **8** stifling

sum 4 cash, coin, jack **5** bread, bucks, dough, funds, score, tally, whole **6** amount, moolah **7** lettuce, measure **8** currency, entirety, quantity, totality

sumac 4 Rhus

Sumerian Mythology *see* **19 Babylonian Mythology**

summarily 6 at once **7** quickly **8** directly, promptly, speedily

summary 4 curt **5** brief, hasty, rapid, short, terse, token **6** apercu, digest, precis, resume, sketch, sudden, survey **7** concise, cursory, epitome, hurried, rundown **8** abstract, succinct, synopsis

summery 3 hot **4** warm **5** balmy, close, humid, muggy, sunny **6** stuffy, sultry, torrid, vernal **8** stifling, sunshiny

summit 3 tip, top **4** acme, apex, peak **5** crest, crown **6** apogee, climax, height, vertex, zenith **8** pinnacle

summon 4 call **5** rouse **6** beckon, gather, invoke, muster, strain **7** command, send for **8** activate, subpoena

sumptuous *see* **11 extravagant**

Sun Also Rises, The
author: 9 (Ernest) Hemingway

sunbathe 3 tan **4** bask

Sunday
day of: 4 rest **7** worship **8** blue laws
observance: 7 Sabbath

Sunday best 6 finery **8** glad rags

sunder 4 rend, rive **5** crack, sever **6** cleave, divide **8** separate

sundown 4 dusk **6** sunset **7** evening **8** eventide, twilight

sundry 4 many **5** mixed **6** divers, motley, myriad, varied **7** diverse, several, various **8** assorted, manifold, numerous

sunny 4 fair, fine **5** clear, happy, jolly, merry **6** blithe, breezy, bright, cheery, genial, jovial, joyful, joyous, sunlit **7** affable, amiable, buoyant, shining, smiling **8** cheerful, sunshiny

sunrise 4 dawn **5** sunup **6** aurora **7** dawning **8** cockcrow, daybreak, daylight

sunset 4 dusk **7** sundown **8** blue hour, eventide, gloaming, twilight

Sunset Boulevard
director: 6 (Billy) Wilder
cast: 4 (Jack) Webb **5** (Fred) Clark **6** (William) Holden **7** (Gloria) Swanson **8** (Erich von) Stroheim

sunshade 3 hat **5** visor **6** awning **7** parasol, roundel **8** sombrero, umbrella

sup *see* **3 eat**

super 4 A-one, fine **5** grand, great, prime **6** grade-A, superb, tip-top **7** capital **8** peerless, terrific, top-notch

superb *see* **7 sublime**

supercilious *see* **8 haughty**

superficial *see* **7 shallow**

superfluous *see* **6 excess**

superintendent 4 boss, head **5** chief **6** warden **7** foreman, headman, manager, proctor, steward **8** director, guardian, overseer

superior *see* **6 better**

superlative *see* **4 best**

Superman
   artist: 6 (Jerry) Siegel
   creator: 7 (Joe) Shuster

supernatural 6 mystic, occult **7** psychic

supersede *see* **7 replace**

supervise 4 boss, head **5** guide **6** direct, govern, handle, manage **7** conduct, oversee **8** regulate

supplant 6 depose **7** replace **8** displace

supple *see* **6 limber**

supplement 5 add to, annex, extra, rider **6** extend, insert **7** adjunct, augment, codicil, section **8** addendum, addition

supplicate *see* **7 solicit**

supply 4 fund, give **5** cache, equip, grant, quota, stock, store, yield **6** outfit, render **7** deliver, provide

support 3 aid **4** base, bear, help, hold, keep, lift, pile, post, prop, stay **5** abide, boost, brace, brook, carry, favor, means, shore, stand **6** assist, back up, bear up, clinch, column, defend, ratify, second, succor, uphold, verify **7** backing, bolster, comfort, defense, endorse, finance, further, nurture, warrant **8** advocate, buttress, maintain, pedestal, sanction

suppose 5 fancy, guess, judge, posit **6** assume, divine, gather, reckon **7** believe, imagine, presume, suspect **8** consider

suppress *see* **8 restrain**

supreme 4 tops **5** chief, first, prime **6** ruling **7** extreme, highest, leading, perfect, topmost

8 absolute, dominant, foremost, peerless

Supreme Court
  Chief Justices: 3 Jay (John) **4** Taft (William Howard) **5** Chase (Salmon), Stone (Harlan Fiske), Taney (Roger Brooke), Waite (Morrison), White (Edward) **6** Burger (Warren), Fuller (Melville), Hughes (Charles Evans), Vinson (Frederick), Warren (Earl) **7** Roberts (John) **8** Marshall (John), Rutledge (John) **9** Ellsworth (Oliver), Rehnquist (William)

surcharge 3 tax **4** levy **6** excise, impost

surcingle 4 band, belt **5** girth **6** girdle **8** cincture

sure 4 fast, firm, true **5** solid, sound **6** stable, steady **7** assured, certain **8** accurate, fail-safe, positive, reliable, unerring

surface *see* **8 exterior**

surfeit *see* **6 excess**

surge 4 rush, wave **5** flood, swell **7** torrent

Suriname
  other name: 7 Surinam **11** Dutch Guiana
  capital/largest city: 10 Paramaribo
  highest point: 10 Julianatop
  sea/ocean: 8 Atlantic
  feature:
    canoe: 6 corial
    clothing: 4 sari **5** dhoti **6** sarong

surly 4 rude, sour **5** cross, gruff, harsh, testy **6** abrupt, crusty, grumpy, sullen, touchy **7** bearish, crabbed, grouchy, hostile, peevish, waspish **8** choleric, churlish, insolent, petulant, snarling

surmise *see* **7 suppose**

surmount *see* **6 defeat**

surpass *see* **6 exceed**

surplus *see* **6 excess**

surprise 4 stun **5** amaze, shock **6** ambush, wonder **7** astound, nonplus, set upon, startle, stupefy **8** astonish, confound, dumfound

surrender *see* **7 concede**

surreptitious *see* **6 secret**

surrogate 6 acting, deputy **7** interim, stand-in

surround 4 belt, ring **5** hedge, hem in **6** circle, enfold, engird, girdle, shut in **7** close in, compass, enclose, envelop, fence in, hedge in **8** encircle

surveillance 5 vigil, watch **8** scrutiny, trailing

survey 4 plot, poll, scan **5** gauge, graph, plumb, probe, scout, study **6** fathom, review **7** canvass, delimit, examine, inspect, measure, observe

survive *see* **6 endure**

susceptible 4 open **5** prone **7** alive to, subject **8** liable to, sensible

suspect *see* **7 suppose**

suspend 4 halt, hang, quit, stay, stop **5** cease, check, defer, delay, sling, swing, table **6** dangle, put off, shelve **7** reserve **8** postpone, withhold

suspicion 4 idea **5** guess, hunch **6** notion **7** feeling, surmise **8** mistrust

sustain 4 bear, feed, prop **5** abide, brave, brook, stand **6** bear up, endure, hold up, keep up, suffer, uphold **7** nourish, nurture, prolong, support, undergo **8** maintain, protract, tolerate, underpin

sustenance 4 food, gear **5** bread, manna, means **6** living **7** aliment, support

svelte 4 fine, lean, neat, slim, thin, trim **5** lithe, spare **7** elegant, lissome, shapely, slender, willowy **8** graceful

swab 3 dab, mop **4** daub, lout, wipe **5** clean, cloth, patch, scrub **6** cotton, sponge **7** cleanse **8** specimen
 brand name: 4 Q-tip

swagger 5 strut, sweep **6** parade, sashay **7** saunter

swain *see* **6 suitor**

swallow 3 bit, nip, sip **4** down, gulp, swig **5** drink, quaff, swill, taste **6** credit, devour, gobble, guzzle, hold in, imbibe, ingest, tipple **7** believe, fall for, repress **8** hold back, suppress, withhold

swamp *see* **8 quagmire**

swan
- **young: 6** cygnet
- **group of: 4** bevy

swanky *see* **5 fancy**

swap 5 trade **6** barter, dicker, switch **7** bargain **8** exchange

swarm *see* **5 crowd**

swarthy 4 dark **5** dusky, swart, tawny **8** brunette

swashbuckling 4 bold **7** dashing **8** boasting

swat *see* **5 smack**

sway 4 bend, grip, hold, lead, list, move, reel, rock, roll, rule, spur, vary, wave **5** alter, clout, impel, power, reign, rouse, shift, swing, waver **6** change, prompt, swerve, totter, wobble **7** command, control, dispose, mastery, stagger **8** hesitate, motivate, persuade, undulate

Swaziland
- **capital/largest city: 7** Mbabane
- **highest point: 7** Emlembe
- **river: 5** Usutu
- **physical feature:**
  - **forest: 5** Usutu

feature:
- **bride payment: 6** lobolo

swear 3 vow **4** aver, avow, cuss **5** curse, vouch **6** adjure, assert, attest, pledge **7** certify, promise, warrant

sweat 4 ooze, toil **5** exude, worry **6** effort **7** agonize **8** hard work, perspire

sweaty 3 wet **6** clammy, sticky

Sweden
- **other name: 7** Sverige
- **capital/largest city: 9** Stockholm
- **highest point: 10** Kebnekaise
- **sea: 5** North **6** Baltic **8** Atlantic
- **island: 5** Oland **7** Gotland
- **physical feature:**
  - **canal: 4** Gota
  - **circle: 6** Arctic
  - **gulf: 7** Bothnia
  - **sound: 6** Kalmar
  - **strait: 7** Oresund **8** Kattegat **9** Skagerrak
- **place:**
  - **walled city: 5** Visby
- **food: 11** smorgasbord
  - **cheese: 7** fontina

9 jarlsberg
drink: 5 glogg 7 aquavit

sweep 3 arc, fly 4 dart, dash, race, rush, scud, tear, zoom 5 hurry, spell, swing, swish, swoop, whisk 6 gather, stroke 7 stretch

sweet 4 dear, kind, nice 5 candy, fresh 6 dulcet, mellow, smooth, sugary 7 amiable, cloying, darling, dessert, lovable, nonsalt, not salt, tuneful 8 fragrant, pleasant, pleasing

sweetheart *see* 6 **suitor**

sweetmeats 5 candy 6 sweets 7 bonbons

sweet roll 3 bun 6 Danish 7 cruller 8 doughnut

sweet talk *see* 6 **praise**

swell 3 fop, wax 4 A-one, fine, good, grow, okay, puff, rise, wave 5 bloat, bulge, dandy, great, heave, mount, super, surge, throb, widen 6 billow, blow up, comber, expand, puff up 7 amplify, breaker, burgeon, distend, inflate, stretch, thicken 8 heighten, increase, terrific

sweltering 3 hot 5 humid, muggy 6 sultry, torrid 7 burning 8 sweating

swerve *see* 4 **veer**

swift *see* 4 **fast**

swill *see* 6 **guzzle**

swindle *see* 7 **deceive**

swine 3 cad, cur, rat 4 pigs 5 beast, brute 6 animal
group of: 5 drift 7 sounder

swing 4 drop, hang, loop, move, rein, rock, sway, turn 5 pivot, rally, scope, sweep, whirl 6 dangle, decide, handle, manage, rotate, seesaw, stroke, wangle 7 inveigh, liberty, license, listing, pull off, rocking, rolling, suspend, swaying

swirl 4 bowl, eddy, reel, roll, spin, swim, turn 5 churn, twirl, twist, wheel, whirl 6 gyrate, rotate

switch 3 box, rod, tan 4 cane, jerk, lash, move, whip 5 birch, lever, trade, whisk 6 button 8 exchange

Switzerland
also: 6 Suisse (French) 7 Schweiz (German)

8 Helvetia (Latin)
capital: 4 Bern **5** Berne
largest city: 6 Zurich
mountain: 4 Alps, Jura **5**
Blanc, Eiger **8** Jungfrau
10 Matterhorn
highest point: 12
Dufourspitze
lake: 6 Geneva, Lugano,
Zurich **7** Lucerne **8**
Bodensee, Maggiore **9**
Constance
river: 3 Aar **5** Rhine,
Rhone **6** Ticino
place:
   resort: 5 Arosa, Davos
   6 Gstaad **7** Zermatt
   8 St Moritz
feature:
   animal: 4 ibex **7**
   chamois **12** Saint
   Bernard
   flower: 9 edelweiss
food:
   cake: 5 torte **6** kuchen
   cheese 5 Swiss **7**
   Gruyere
   dish: 5 rosti **6** fondue
   8 raclette

swollen *see* **5 swell**

swoon 5 faint **8** collapse,
keel over

swoop *see* **4 dive**

sword 4 epee, foil **5** blade,

saber, steel **6** rapier **7**
cutlass **8** scimitar

sybaritic 4 rich **6** lavish **7**
sensual

sycophant *see* **6 flunky**

sylvan 5 bushy, leafy,
woody **6** wooded, woodsy
8 arcadian, forested,
timbered, woodland

symbol 4 mark, sign **5**
badge, token **6** emblem,
figure, signal

symmetry 4 form **5** order **7**
balance, harmony

sympathy *see* **4 pity**

symposium *see* **5 forum**

symptom 4 mark, sign **5**
token **6** signal **7** earmark,
warning **8** evidence,
giveaway

synagogue
   Yiddish: 4 shul **5** schul

syndicate 5 group, trust,
union **6** cartel, league,
merger **8** alliance

synod 4 diet

synonymous 4 like, same **5**
alike, equal **7** coequal

synopsis *see* **7 summary**

synthesize 3 mix **4** fuse **5**
blend **7** combine **8**
compound

synthetic 4 fake, sham **5** phony **6** ersatz **7** man-made

Syria
  capital/largest city: 8 Damascus
  lake: 8 Tiberias
  highest point: 6 Hermon
  river: 6 Jordan **7** Orontes **9** Euphrates
  sea: 13 Mediterranean
  physical feature:
    heights: 5 Golan
  place:
    ruins: 7 Palmyra
    clothing: 8 kafiyyah
    marketplace: 4 souk

system 4 body, unit **5** setup **6** method, scheme, theory **7** program, regimen, routine **8** organism

T

tab **3** lip **4** bill, cost, flap, loop **5** check, PC key, price, strip, tally **6** tongue

tabard *see* **4** coat

tabernacle **6** church, temple

table **4** fare, list, roll **5** board, chart, index **6** record, roster, shelve, spread **7** catalog **8** lay aside, postpone, put aside, register, schedule

tableau **4** view **5** scene **7** pageant, picture, setting

taboo, tabu **3** ban **4** no-no **6** banned **8** anathema, outlawed, verboten

tacit **7** assumed, implied **8** implicit, inferred, unspoken, unstated, wordless

taciturn *see* **5** quiet

tack **3** add, peg, pin, way **4** clap, nail, slap, veer **5** affix, sheer, shift, spike, thole **6** append, attach, change, fasten, zigzag **7** go about **8** approach

tacky **5** dowdy, gluey, gooey, gucky, gummy, messy, ratty, seedy, tatty **6** grubby, shabby, shoddy, sloppy, sticky, untidy, viscid **7** stringy, unkempt, viscous **8** adhesive, frazzled, slipshod, slovenly

tactful *see* **8** discreet

tactic *see* **6** method

Taft, William Howard
  presidential rank: 13 twenty-seventh
  party: 10 Republican
  state represented: 2 OH
  defeated: 4 Debs **5** Bryan **6** Chafin, Hisgen, Turney, Watson **8** Gillhaus
  vice president: 7 Sherman
  born: 2 OH **10** Cincinnati
  political career:
    secretary of: 3 War
    US Supreme Court: 12 Chief Justice
  wife: 5 Helen
    nickname: 6 Nellie

tag **3** add, dog, tab **4** card,

heel, mark, name, slip,
stub, tail, term **5** add on,
affix, annex, hound, label,
title, trail **6** append,
attach, fasten, marker **7**
earmark, moniker **8**
cognomen, identify,
nickname

Tahiti
artist: **7** Gauguin
author: **9** Stevenson
capital: **7** Papeete
island group: **7** Society
ocean: **7** Pacific

tail *see* **8 backside**

tailor 3 fit, sew **4** make,
redo **5** adapt, alter, build,
shape **6** change, create,
design, devise, modify **7**
convert, fashion, produce
8 clothier, costumer

taint *see* **5 stain**

Taiwan
other name: **7** Formosa
15 Republic of China
capital/largest city: **6**
Taipei
highest point: **4** Jade **6**
Yu Shan
sea: **7** Pacific **9** East
China **10** Philippine,
South China
island: **5** Matsu **6**
Quemoy, Taiwan

10 Pescadores
physical feature:
storm: **7** monsoon,
typhoon
strait: **6** Taiwan **7**
Formosa
feature:
political party: **10**
Kuomintang

Tajikistan
other name: **12**
Tadzhikistan
capital/largest city: **8**
Dushanbe
mountain: **7** Communism
(Peak)

Taj Mahal 4 tomb **9**
mausoleum
location: **4** Agra **5** India
built by: **9** Shah, Jahan
for: **4** wife

take 3 buy, get, lug, nab,
net, see, use **4** bear, bilk,
deem, draw, feel, gain,
grab, grip, haul, have,
heed, hire, hold, know,
lead, loot, mark, mind,
move, need, obey, read,
rent, sack, tote, work **5**
carry, catch, cheat, claim,
clasp, filch, grasp, guide,
lease, seize, stand, steal,
usher, usurp **6** accept,
attain, clutch, convey,

deduce, deduct, derive, endure, escort, fleece, follow, look on, obtain, pilfer, pocket, profit, regard, remove, secure, snatch, suffer **7** acquire, capture, consume, make out, pillage, plunder, purloin, receive, require, respect, stomach, suppose **8** conclude, consider, purchase, shoulder, subtract, tolerate

take after *see* **8 resemble**

take a powder *see* **8 withdraw**

take flight 3 fly **4** flee **6** escape, run off **7** abscond, fly away, run away, run free, take off

take heed 4 mind **6** beware **7** look out **8** take care, watch out

take notice of *see* **7 observe**

takeoff *see* **6 parody**

take one's breath away 4 daze, stun **5** shock **7** stupefy **8** astonish, dumfound

take out 4 date **5** court **6** delete, escort, remove **7** extract, isolate **8** abstract,

separate, take home, withdraw

take prisoner *see* **6 arrest**

take stock of *see* **6 assess**

take the cake 5 excel **7** beat all, surpass

take the edge off *see* **7 mollify**

take to heart *see* **8 consider**

take to task *see* **5 scold**

take under one's wing 6 assist, defend **7** protect **8** befriend

tale *see* **5 story**

talent 4 bent, gift, turn **5** flair, forte, knack, skill **6** genius **7** faculty **8** aptitude, capacity

Tale of Two Cities, A author: 7 (Charles) Dickens

Tales of Hoffmann, The opera by: 9 Offenbach

talisman 4 tiki **5** charm **6** amulet, fetish, grigri

talk 3 gab, jaw, rap, say **4** cant, chat, word **5** argot, idiom, lingo, noise, prate, rumor, slang, speak, state, utter **6** babble, confer, gossip, hot air, jargon, parley, patois, powwow, preach, sermon, speech, tirade **7** blather, chatter, dialect, discuss, express, lecture, oration, palaver, prattle **8** chitchat, colloquy, converse, dialogue, harangue, verbiage

talk big *see* **4 brag**

tall 3 big **4** high **5** lanky, lofty, rangy **6** absurd **7** soaring, stringy **8** elevated, towering

tallow 3 fat, tip **5** taper **6** bougie, candle, cierge

tally *see* **3 add**

talon 4 claw, nail, spur

tame *see* **6 gentle**

Taming of the Shrew, The
   author: 11 (William) Shakespeare

tamper *see* **6 meddle**

tan 4 roan **5** beige, brown, khaki, sandy, tawny **6** bronze, sorrel, suntan **7** bronzed **8** brownish, cinnamon, sunburnt

tang 3 bit **4** bite, hint, odor, reek **5** aroma, punch, savor, scent, smack, smell, sting, tinge, touch, trace **6** flavor **8** acridity, tartness

tangible 4 real **5** solid

6 actual **7** obvious **8** clear-cut, concrete, manifest, material, palpable, physical, positive

tangle *see* **6 knot**

tank 3 vat **6** boiler **7** cistern **8** aquarium, fish tank

Tannhauser
   opera by: 6 Wagner

tantalize *see* **6 entice**

tantamount 4 like **5** equal

tantrum 3 fit **5** storm **7** flare-up, rampage **8** outburst, paroxysm

Tanzania
   formed from union of: 8 Zanzibar **10** Tanganyika
   capital: 6 Dodoma **11** Dar es Salaam
   largest city: 11 Dar es Salaam
   highest point: 11 Kilimanjaro
   lake: 6 Malawi **8** Victoria **10** Tanganyika
   sea/ocean: 6 Indian
   island: 5 Pemba **8** Zanzibar
   physical feature:
      gorge: 7 Olduvai
      national park: 9 Serengeti
      valley: 9 Great Rift

feature:
animal: 6 dik-dik
fly: 6 tsetse

tap 3 pat, rap, use **4** cock, drum, peck, thud **5** spout, touch, valve **6** employ, faucet, hammer, spigot, stroke, uncork **7** exploit, utilize

taper 3 dip, wax **4** wick **5** light **6** candle, cierge, narrow **8** decrease

taper off *see* **4 wane**

tapestry 3 rug **5** arras, tapis **6** Bruges, fabric, mosaic **7** Gobelin, hanging, montage, weaving **8** Aubusson

taproom *see* **6 tavern**

Taras Bulba
author: 5 (Nikolai) Gogol

tardy *see* **4 late**

target *see* **4 goal**

tariff 3 fee, tax **4** cost, duty, fare, levy, rate, rent **5** price **6** charge, excise, impost **7** expense

tarnish *see* **5 stain**

tarot
suit: 3 cup **4** coin, wand **5** baton, money, sword **6** cudgel **8** pentacle
face card: 4 king, page **5** knave, queen, valet **6** knight

tarpaulin 4 tarp **6** canvas

Tarquin
king of: 4 Rome
origin: 8 Etruscan
wife: 8 Tanaquil

tarry *see* **6 dawdle**

tart 3 pie **4** acid, sour **5** acerb, acrid, sharp, spicy, tangy **6** acetic, barbed, biting, bitter, crusty **7** caustic, cutting **8** vinegary

tartan
fabric: 6 woolen
pattern: 5 plaid
identifies: 4 clan
in: 8 Scotland **9** Highlands
skirt: 4 kilt
trousers: 5 trews

Tartarus
form: 5 abyss
below: 5 Hades
imprisoned: 6 Titans

Tartuffe
author: 7 Moliere

Tarzan
author: 9 (Edgar Rice) Burroughs

task 3 job **4** duty, work **5** chore, labor, stint

6 charge, errand **7** mission **8** business

Tasmania
  capital: 6 Hobart
  country: 9 Australia
  formerly: 14 Van Diemen's Land
  strait: 4 Bass

taste 3 bit, nip, sip, try, yen **4** bent, bite, feel, meet, tang, test, whim **5** crumb, enjoy, fancy, savor, smack **6** desire, flavor, hunger, liking, morsel, relish, sample, thirst **7** craving, discern, forkful, leaning, longing, swallow **8** appetite, penchant, spoonful

tasteful *see* **7 elegant**

tasteless *see* **5 crass**

tasty 3 hot **5** spicy, tangy, yummy **6** savory **7** piquant, zestful **8** luscious

tattered *see* **7 run-down**

tattle 3 rat **4** blab **5** prate **6** gabble, gossip, snitch, squeal, tell on **7** blather, chatter, hearsay

taunt *see* **5 tease**

Taurus
  symbol: 4 bull
  planet: 5 Venus

  rules: 5 money **9** resources
  born: 3 May **5** April

taut 4 neat, snug, tidy, trig, trim **5** rigid, smart, tense, tight **6** spruce **7** orderly **8** not loose, not slack

tavern 3 bar, pub **4** dive **6** bistro, saloon **7** gin mill, taproom **8** alehouse, drinkery

tawdry *see* **5 cheap**

tawny 3 tan **4** fawn **5** beige, dusky, olive, sandy **6** bronze **7** swarthy **8** brownish

tax 3 sap, try **4** duty, lade, levy, load, tire, toll **5** drain, weigh **6** assess, burden, charge, custom, excise, impost, saddle, strain, tariff, weight **7** deplete, exhaust, stretch
  kind: 4 city **5** sales, state **6** county, estate, excise, income, luxury **8** property

taxicab 4 hack **6** jitney **7** droshky, hackney **8** hired car, rickshaw

taxon 5 class, genus, order **6** family, phylum **7** kingdom, species

taxonomy
  study of: 17 structure
  contrast **19** structure
  comparison

Taylor, Zachary
  presidential rank: 7
  twelfth
  party: 4 Whig
  state represented: 2 LA
  defeated: 4 Cass **8** Van
  Buren
  vice president: 8 Fillmore
  born: 2 VA **10**
  Montebello
  religion: 12 Episcopalian
  military service: 4 Army
    war: 7 Mexican **9** Black
    Hawk
  wife: 8 Margaret

tea 16 Camellia sinensis

teach *see* **7 educate**

team 3 rig, set **4** ally, band,
crew, five, gang, join,
nine, pair, side, unit, yoke
5 force, group, merge,
party, squad, staff, unify,
unite **6** circle, clique,
couple, eleven, league,
tandem **7** combine,
company, coterie, faction
8 alliance, federate

tear 3 fly, gap, hie, rip, run
4 bolt, dart, dash, grab,
hole, mist, pull, race, rend,
rent, rift, rive, rush, scud,
slit, snag, swim, whiz,
yank **5** abuse, break,
crack, fault, pluck, scoot,
seize, sever, shoot, shred,
speed, split, spurt, sweep,
whisk **6** divide, gallop,
hasten, hustle, injury,
scurry, sprint, wrench **7**
fissure, rupture, scamper,
scuttle **8** teardrop

tease 3 guy, irk, nag, rag,
vex **4** bait, gall, gibe,
goad, haze, jeer, josh,
mock, pest, rile, twit **5**
annoy, chafe, harry,
mimic, pique, scoff, sneer,
taunt **6** harass, heckle,
needle, pester **8** ridicule

technical 5 trade

technique 3 art, way **4**
form **5** craft, knack, style
6 manner, method, system
7 formula, know-how **8**
approach, facility

tedious 3 dry **4** drab, dull,
long, slow **5** vapid **6**
boring, dismal, dreary,
jejune, tiring **7** humdrum,
insipid, irksome, onerous,
prosaic **8** drawn-out,
lifeless, tiresome, wearying

teem *see* **4 gush**

teeny-weeny *see* **4 tiny**

teeter *see* **6 wobble**

teetotaler 3 dry

Tehran, Teheran
   capital of: 4 Iran

Telamon
   king of: 7 Salamis
   member of: 9 Argonauts
   brother: 6 Peleus
   wife: 6 Glauce **7** Eriboea
   son: 4 Ajax **6** Teucer
   friend: 8 Hercules

Telegonus
   father: 7 Proteus **8**
     Odysseus
   mother: 5 Circe
   wife: 2 Io **8** Penelope
   killed: 8 Odysseus
   killed by: 8 Hercules

Telemachus
   father: 8 Odysseus
   mother: 8 Penelope

telepathy 3 ESP

telephone
   type: 3 cell, pay, TDD **6**
     mobile, rotary **8** cellular,
     portable, princess,
     wireless

tell 3 ask, bid, own, say, see
   4 blab **5** bruit, count,
   order, speak, spout, state,
   utter, weigh, write **6**
   advise, babble, betray,
   blazon, depict, detail,
   direct, figure, impart,
   inform, number, recite,
   reckon, relate, report,
   reveal, sketch, unfold **7**
   apprise, command,
   confess, declare, discern,
   divulge, express, mention,
   narrate

telltale *see* **6 gossip**

temerity 4 gall **5** brass,
   cheek, nerve **8** audacity,
   boldness, chutzpah,
   rashness

temper 3 ire **4** bile, calm,
   fury, gall, mood, rage **5**
   allay, anger, humor,
   pique, quiet, still, wrath **6**
   animus, anneal, choler,
   dander, harden, pacify,
   soften, soothe, spleen **7**
   appease, balance,
   compose, passion,
   umbrage **8** mitigate,
   moderate, palliate

temperament *see* **6 temper**

tempest *see* **5 chaos**

Tempest, The
   author: 11 (William)
     Shakespeare

tempestuous 3 hot **5** fiery
   6 raging, stormy **7**
   excited, frantic, furious,
   violent **8** agitated,
   feverish, frenzied

temple 4 fane, kirk **6** chapel, church, mosque, pagoda, priory, shrine **7** convent **8** basilica, pantheon

tempo *see* **4 pace**

temporal 3 lay **5** civil **6** mortal **7** mundane, passing, profane, secular, worldly **8** day-to-day, fleeting, fugitive

temporary, temporarily 5 brief, fleet **7** interim, passing, stopgap **8** fleeting, fugitive

tempt *see* **6 entice**

tempter 5 Devil, Satan **7** enticer, seducer

tempus fugit 9 time flies

tenable *see* **6 viable**

tenacious *see* **7 adamant**

tenant 6 lessee, lodger, renter, roomer **7** boarder, denizen, dweller **8** occupant, resident

Ten Commandments
  also: 9 Decalogue
  given to: 5 Moses
  where given: 5 (Mount) Sinai
  inscribed on: 7 (stone) tablets

Ten Commandments, The
  director: 7 (Cecil B) DeMille
  cast: 6 (Anne) Baxter, (Charlton) Heston **7** (Yul) Brynner, (Yvonne) De Carlo **8** (Edward G) Robinson

tend 3 aim **4** bear, head, lead, lean, mind, move **5** be apt, guide, nurse, point, watch **6** extend, foster, manage, wait on **7** care for, nurture **8** attend to, be liable, be likely

tenderfoot *see* **6 novice**

tendon 4 cord **5** sinew
  connects: 4 bone **6** muscle

tendril 4 coil, curl **5** crook, shoot, sprig, twist **6** winder **7** climber, ringlet

tenebrous *see* **6 gloomy**

tenet *see* **5 maxim**

Tennessee
  abbreviation: 2 TN **4** Tenn
  nickname: 7 Big Bend **9** Volunteer
  capital: 9 Nashville
  largest city: 7 Memphis
  mountain: 7 Lookout, Smokies **9** Blue Ridge **10** Cumberland, Great

Smoky **11** Appalachian, highest point: **13** Clingmans Dome
river: 9 Tennessee **10** Cumberland **11** Mississippi
feature:
  fort: 5 Henry **8** Donalson, Nashboro
  national park: 6 Shiloh
  national parkway: 12 Natchez Trace

tenor 4 gist **5** drift, sense, trend **6** course, import, intent, nature, object **7** content, essence, meaning, purport, purpose **8** argument, tendency

tense 4 taut **5** brace, drawn, rigid, shaky, stiff, tight **6** braced, draw up, on edge, uneasy **7** anxious, excited, fearful, fidgety, jittery, nervous, restive, stiffen, uptight **8** agitated, make taut, restless, strained, timorous

tension *see* **6 strain**

tent 3 pup **4** care, hard **5** gauze, probe **6** bigtop, canvas, teepee, wigwam **7** shelter **8** pavilion

tentacle 3 arm **6** feeler

tentative 4 iffy **5** trial

6 acting **8** not final, proposed

tenuous *see* **7 fragile**

tenure 4 rule, term, time **5** reign **7** tenancy

tepee, teepee 4 chum, tent **5** lodge **6** wigwam **7** wickiup

tepid 4 cool, mild **7** languid, warmish **8** lukewarm, moderate

tequila
  type: 6 spirit
  made from: 5 agave **6** maguey

tergal 4 back **6** dorsal

term, terms 3 age, dub, era, tag **4** call, cite, item, name, span, time, word **5** catch, cycle, epoch, idiom, reign, spell, stage, state, style, while **6** clause, course, detail, period, phrase, status, string **7** dynasty, footing, proviso **8** duration, interval, position, standing

termagant 3 nag **4** fury **5** scold, shrew, vixen **6** ogress, virago **7** hellcat, hellion, she-wolf, tigress **8** battle-ax, fishwife, harridan, spitfire

terminal 3 end **4** last **5** depot, fatal, final, stand **6** deadly, lethal, mortal **7** station **8** terminus

termite
variety: 6 desert **7** dry wood **8** damp wood

Terms of Endearment
director: 6 (James L) Brooks
based on novel by: 8 (Larry) McMurtry
cast: 6 (Debra) Winger **8** (Shirley) MacLaine **9** (Jack) Nicholson

Terpsichore
member of: 5 Muses
personifies: 7 dancing

terrace 4 roof **5** level, patio, plane, porch **6** street **7** balcony, plateau

terra-cotta 4 clay **6** russet **8** brownish

terrain 4 area, zone **5** tract **6** ground, milieu, region **7** setting **8** district

terrapin 3 box **4** emyd, emys **6** slider, turpin, turtle **8** tortoise

terrestrial *see* **6 ground**

terrible *see* **8 dreadful**

terrific *see* **8 fabulous**

terrify *see* **7 horrify**

territory 4 area, land, pale, zone **5** clime, realm, state, tract **6** bounds, colony, domain, empire, limits, locale, nation, region, sector **7** acreage, kingdom, mandate, terrain **8** confines, district, dominion, province

terror *see* **4 fear**

Terry and the Pirates
creator: 6 (Milton) Caniff

terse *see* **6 abrupt**

test 4 exam, quiz **5** check, final, flyer, probe, proof, prove, trial **6** dry run, feeler, try out, verify **7** analyze, confirm, examine, midterm **8** analysis

testament 6 legacy **7** bequest

testify 4 show **5** prove, swear **6** affirm, attest, evince **7** declare, signify **8** indicate

testimony 5 proof **6** avowal **7** witness **8** averment, evidence

testy *see* **6 grumpy**

tete-a-tete 4 chat, talk **6** parley

tether 3 tie **4** cord, rein,

rope **5** chain, leash **6** fasten, halter, secure

Teutonic 5 Dutch **6** German, Gothic, Nordic **7** British, English **8** Germanic

Texas
  abbreviation: 2 TX **3** Tex
  nickname: 8 Lone Star
  capital: 6 Austin
  largest city: 7 Houston
  highest point: 9 Guadalupe
  river: 3 Red **5** Pecos **6** Brazos **8** Colorado **9** Rio Grande
  physical feature:
    gulf: 6 Mexico
  feature:
    fort: 5 Alamo

text 5 motif, theme, topic, verse, words **6** manual, primer, sermon, thesis **7** content, passage, subject, wording **8** sentence

textile 4 yarn **5** cloth, fiber **6** fabric **8** filament, material

texture 3 nap **4** feel, look **5** grain, touch, weave **6** makeup **7** quality, surface **8** fineness

Thailand
  other name: 4 Siam
  capital/largest city: 7 Bangkok
  highest point: 11 Doi Inthanon
  river: 6 Mekong **10** Chao Phraya
  sea/ocean: 6 Indian **7** Andaman **10** South China
  physical feature:
    gulf: 4 Siam **8** Thailand
    peninsula: 5 Malay
    strait: 7 Malacca
  feature:
    clothing: 6 panung, sarong
    houseboat: 6 sampan
    temple: 3 wat
    tree: 4 teak

thalassic 6 marine **7** aquatic, deep-sea, neritic, oceanic, pelagic

thank 5 bless

thankful 7 obliged **8** beholden, grateful

Thanksgiving
  started by: 8 Bradford, Pilgrims

thank you
  French: 5 merci
  German: 5 danke
  Italian: 6 grazie

Japanese: 4 domo
Spanish: 7 gracias

thaw 4 melt, warm **5** relax **6** soften, unbend, warm up **7** liquefy **8** dissolve

Thea
  companion of: 7 Artemis
  ravished by: 6 Aeolus
  changed into: 4 mare
    mare named: 6 Euippe

theater 4 site **5** arena, drama, house, movie, odeum, place, scene, stage **6** cinema, lyceum **7** setting **8** assembly, coliseum

theatrical *see* **5 showy**

theft 5 fraud **7** larceny, looting, robbery **8** burglary, filching, rustling, stealing, thievery
  god of: 6 Hermes **7** Mercury

theme 3 air **4** song, text, tune **5** essay, focus, motif, point, topic, tract **6** melody, report, review, strain, thesis **7** keynote, premise, subject **8** argument, critique, question, treatise

theology 5 dogma **8** divinity, doctrine, religion

theorize *see* **7 presume**

theory 3 law **4** idea, view **5** guess **6** belief, notion, thesis **7** concept, opinion, thought **8** doctrine, ideology, judgment

therapy 7 healing

thereafter 5 later

therefore 2 so **4** ergo, thus **5** hence

thereupon 4 then **6** at once **7** thereon **8** directly, suddenly, upon that

the same as 4 like **7** equal to

thesaurus 8 synonymy

Theseus
  king of: 6 Athens
  father: 6 Aegeus **8** Poseidon
  mother: 6 Aethra
  wife: 7 Phaedra
  consort: 9 Hippolyta
  lover: 7 Ariadne
  killed: 4 (Cretan) bull

thesis 5 essay, paper, tract **6** notion, theory **7** article, concept, surmise **8** argument, critique, proposal, treatise

thespian 3 ham **4** star **5** actor, extra **6** co-star, player, walk-on **7** actress, ingenue, trouper

Thetis
member of: 7 Nereids
husband: 6 Peleus
son: 8 Achilles

thick 3 big, fat **4** deep, dull, dumb, slow, wide **5** broad, bulky, close, dense, fuzzy, great, heavy, husky, piled, solid **6** chummy, heaped, hoarse, lavish, obtuse, packed, strong, stupid, viscid **7** clotted, compact, copious, crowded, intense, muffled, profuse, teeming, throaty, viscous **8** friendly

thicket 4 bush, wood **5** brake, brush, copse, grove, scrub **6** bushes, covert, forest, shrubs **7** bracken

thickheaded *see* **6 stupid**

thickset *see* **5 heavy**

thickskinned *see* **5 tough**

thick-skulled *see* **6 stupid**

thief 5 crook **6** bandit, mugger, robber **7** burglar, filcher, rustler **8** hijacker, pilferer, swindler

thigh 3 ham, leg **4** hock **5** femur, flank, ilium **6** gammon
pain: 8 meralgia

thin 4 fine, lank, lean, slim, weak **5** faint, gaunt, lanky, prune, runny, scant, sheer, spare, water **6** dilute, feeble, narrow, skinny, slight **7** fragile, scrawny, slender, spindly **8** delicate

thing, things 3 act **4** deed, feat, gear, item **5** event, gizmo, goods, point **6** action, affair, aspect, detail, entity, gadget, matter, object, person **7** article, effects, feature, thought

thingamajig 5 gizmo **6** doodad, gadget

think 4 deem, mean, plan **5** brood, fancy, guess, judge **6** design, expect, intend, ponder, reason, recall, reckon **7** believe, dwell on, imagine, presume, reflect, surmise **8** cogitate, conceive, conclude, meditate, mull over, remember, ruminate

Thin Man, The
author: 7 (Dashiell) Hammett

thin out *see* **6 dilute**

thinskinned *see* **6 grumpy**

Third Man, The
director: 4 (Carol) Reed

based on story by: 6 (Graham) Greene

cast: 5 (Alida) Valli **6** (Joseph) Cotten, (Trevor) Howard, (Orson) Welles

thirst 3 yen **4** itch, lust, pant **5** ardor, covet, crave, yearn **6** desire, fervor, hunger, relish **7** craving, passion, stomach **8** appetite, keenness, voracity, yearning

Thirty-Nine Steps, The (The 39 Steps)
author: 6 (John) Buchan
director: 9 (Alfred) Hitchcock
cast: 5 (Robert) Donat **6** (Godfrey) Tearle **7** (Madeleine) Carroll **8** (Peggy) Ashcroft, (Lucie) Mannheim

thistle 7 Cirsium
emblem of: 8 Scotland

Thomas 7 apostle
means: 4 twin
also called: 7 Didymus, Doubter **8** Doubting

thong 4 band **5** strap, strip **6** sandal **7** binding **8** swimsuit **9** underwear

Thor
origin: 5 Norse
god of: 4 rain **7** thunder

rode: 7 chariot
wielded: 6 hammer **7** Miolnir
father: 4 Odin

thorax 5 chest, trunk **6** breast, cavity **8** forebody

thorn 3 woe **4** bane, barb, care, gall, spur **5** cross, curse, spike, spine, sting **6** plague **7** prickle, scourge, torment, trouble **8** nuisance, vexation

thorough 4 full, pure **5** sheer, total, utter **6** entire **7** careful, perfect, uniform **8** absolute, complete

Thoth
origin: 8 Egyptian
god of: 5 magic **6** wisdom **8** learning
scribe of: 4 gods
corresponds to: 6 Hermes
head of: 3 dog **4** ibis

though 3 tho, yet **4** even, that **5** still **6** albeit, even if **7** granted

thought 3 aim, end **4** goal, idea, plan, view **5** credo, dogma, fancy, tenet **6** belief, intent, musing, notion **7** concept, concern, opinion, purpose, reverie, surmise **8** doctrine, judgment, kindness

thrall 4 serf **5** slave **6** chains **7** bondage, serfdom, servant, slavery

thrash *see* **4 whip**

threadbare *see* **4 worn**

threads *see* **7 clothes**

threat 4 omen, risk **5** peril **6** danger, hazard, menace **7** ill omen, portent, warning **8** jeopardy

Three Musketeers, The author: 5 (Alexandre) Dumas (pere)

Threepenny Opera, The author: 6 Brecht **composer: 5** Weill

threnody 5 dirge, elegy **6** lament **7** requiem

threshold 4 dawn, door, edge, sill **5** brink, limen, onset, start, verge **6** portal **7** doorway, gateway, opening **8** entrance

thrift 7 economy **8** prudence

thrill 4 fire, glow, kick, stir **5** flush, rouse, throb **6** arouse, excite, quiver, tickle, tingle, tremor **7** delight, impress, inspire

thrive 3 wax **4** boom **5** bloom, get on **6** fatten **7** burgeon, prosper, succeed **8** flourish, get ahead

throat 3 maw **4** craw, gula, neck **5** gorge **6** gullet **7** chamber, jugulum, passage, pharynx

throb 4 beat, jerk, pant **5** heave, pulse, shake **6** quiver, tremor, twitch **7** flutter, tremble, vibrate

throes 5 agony, chaos, pangs **6** ordeal, spasms, tumult **7** anguish, turmoil **8** disorder, paroxysm, upheaval

throng *see* **4 herd**

throttle *see* **5 choke**

through, thru 4 done, past **5** ended **6** direct **7** express **8** finished, from A to Z, to the end

throw 3 lob, pit, put, shy **4** cast, hurl, shot, toss **5** chuck, fling, floor, heave, impel, pitch, place, sling **6** hurtle, launch, let fly, propel **7** project

thrust 3 jab, jam, ram **4** butt, pass, poke, prod, push, raid, stab **5** boost, drive, foray, force, impel, lunge, press, sally, shove, swipe **6** attack, charge, pierce, plunge, propel, sortie, strike, stroke **7** assault, impetus, impulse, riposte **8** momentum

thud 4 bang **5** clunk, knock, smack, thump

thug 4 hood **6** bandit, gunman, hit man, killer, mugger, robber **7** hoodlum, mobster, ruffian **8** gangster

thumb 5 hitch **6** finger, handle

thumbnail 5 brief, short **7** compact, concise

thump *see* **5 pound**

thunder 4 boom, clap, echo, peal, roar, roll **5** crack, crash **6** rumble **7** explode, resound **8** rumbling
  god of: 4 Thor **5** Donar **7** Taranis

thunderstruck *see* **6 amaze**

Thursday
  from: 4 Thor
  heavenly body: 4 Jove **7** Jupiter

thus 2 so **4** ergo **5** hence **6** like so **8** like this

thwack *see* **5 smack**

thwart *see* **7 prevent**

Tia Maria
  type: 6 brandy **7** liqueur

tiara 4 band **5** crown, miter **6** diadem **7** coronet **8** frontlet, ornament

Tibet
  capital: 5 Lassa, Lhasa
  part of: 5 China
  mountain: 6 Kunlun **8** Himalaya **9** Karakoram
  highest point: 7 Everest
  river: 5 Hwang, Indus **6** Mekong, Yellow **7** Hwang Ho, Salween, Tsangpo, Yangtze
  feature:
    animal: 3 dzo, yak **5** panda
    dog: 9 lhasa apso
    leader: 9 dalai lama
    legend: 4 yeti
    monastery: 8 lamasery
    monk: 4 lama
  food:
    dish: 6 tsamba, tsampa
    drink: 5 chang

tic 5 spasm **6** twitch

tick 3 dot, tap **4** beat, line, list, mark, nick, note **5** blaze, check, clack, click, enter, notch, swing, throb **6** record, slight, stroke **7** scratch, vibrate

ticket 3 tag **4** card, mark,

pass, slip, stub **5** label, slate **6** ballot, coupon, marker, roster **7** voucher
type: 4 trip **7** parking, traffic **9** admission

tickle 4 itch **5** amuse, cheer, prick, sting, throb **6** divert, please, regale, stroke, thrill, tingle, twitch **7** delight, enchant, enliven, gladden, gratify, prickle, rejoice **8** enthrall, entrance

tidbit *see* **6 morsel**

tide 4 flow, neap, wave **5** drift, state **7** current **8** movement, undertow

tidings 4 news, word **6** advice, notice, report

tidy *see* **4 neat**

tie 3 rod **4** ally, band, beam, belt, bind, bond, cord, draw, duty, join, knot, lash, line, link, rope, sash, yoke **5** brace, cable, cinch, limit, marry, match, truss, unite **6** attach, bow tie, clinch, couple, cravat, fasten, girdle, ribbon, secure, string, tether **7** confine, connect, kinship **8** cincture, dead heat, make a bow, relation, restrain, restrict

tier 3 row **4** bank, file, line,

rank, step **5** layer, level, range, story **7** stratum

tiff *see* **7 quarrel**

tiger 3 cat **6** cougar, jaguar **7** fighter, wildcat
young: 5 whelp

tight 4 busy, firm, full, hard, high, snug, taut **5** blind, close, dense, drunk, exact, happy, harsh, lit up, rigid, scant, solid, stern, stiff, tense, tipsy, tough **6** juiced, scarce, secure, severe, skimpy, soused, stingy, strict **7** austere, compact, crammed, crowded, drunken, miserly, onerous

tighten one's belt *see* **8 conserve**

tightfisted *see* **5 cheap**

tight-laced *see* **4 prim**

till 3 sow **4** even, farm, plow, seed, tray, unto up to **6** before, coffer, drawer, harrow, plough **7** as far as, develop, prepare **8** moneybox, treasury
geological: 5 drift

tilt 3 row, tip **4** cant, lean, list, rake, spar, tiff **5** brawl, fence, fight, grade, joust, pitch, slant, slope

6 affray, battle, combat, oppose **7** incline, quarrel **8** argument, skirmish, squabble

timber 4 bush, logs, wood **5** copse, trees, woods **6** forest, lumber **7** thicket

timbre 4 tone **5** pitch

time, times 3 age, day, eon, era **4** beat, days, hour, term, week, year **5** clock, cycle, epoch, event, match, month, phase, spell, stage, tempo, while, years **6** moment, period, season **7** instant, measure, stretch **8** duration, incident, interval, occasion

time-honored 6 common, normal **7** regular, revered **8** accepted, standard

timeless *see* **7 eternal**

timepiece 5 clock, watch **8** horologe

timid 3 coy, shy **6** afraid, humble, modest, scared **7** bashful, fearful **8** cowardly, retiring, sheepish, timorous

Timon of Athens author: 11 (William) Shakespeare

timorous *see* **5 timid**

tin chemical symbol: 2 Sn

tincture 6 elixir **7** essence, extract, spirits **8** solution

Tin Drum, The author: 5 (Gunter) Grass

tine 3 die, tip **4** barb, lose, tyne **5** point, prong, spike **6** bodkin, branch, perish, skewer **7** destroy, forfeit

tinge *see* **3 dye**

tingle 5 sting, throb **6** thrill, tickle **7** flutter, prickle

tinkle 4 ding, peal, ping, ring **5** chime, chink, clank, clink, plink **6** jingle

tin lizzie 3 car **4** auto, heap **5** motor **6** jalopy, wheels **7** flivver, machine, vehicle

tinsel 4 sham, show **5** gloss **6** sequin **7** glitter, spangle

tint *see* **3 hue**

tintinnabulation 4 gong, peal, ring, toll **5** chime, knell **6** jingle **7** clangor, pealing, ringing **8** clanging, ding-dong, jingling, tinkling

tiny 3 wee **5** pygmy, runty, small, teeny **6** bantam, little, midget, minute, petite **8** dwarfish

tip **3** cap, pat, tap, top **4** acme, apex, barb, brow, cant, clue, head, hint, hook, lean, list, peak, rake, tilt **5** crest, crown, pitch, point, prong, slant, slope, spike, upend, upset **6** advice, reward, summit, topple, upturn, vertex, zenith **7** capsize, incline, leaning, pointer, sharpen, warning **8** gratuity, over turn, pinnacle

tip off *see* **5 alert**

tipsy *see* **5 drunk**

tip-top **4** A-one **5** elite, super **7** supreme

tirade **5** curse **6** screed **7** lecture **8** diatribe, harangue, jeremiad, scolding

tired **4** beat **5** all in, weary **6** bushed, drowsy, fagged, pooped, sleepy **7** wearied, worn out **8** fatigued, tuckered

Tiresias
   also: **9** Teiresias
   vocation: **4** seer **7** prophet
   home: **6** Thebes
   struck: **5** blind

tiresome *see* **7 arduous**

tissue
   kind: **4** bone, skin **5** nerve **6** muscle

titan **5** giant, great, mogul **7** magnate

Titan
   race of: **4** gods
   father: **6** Uranus
   mother: **2** Ge **4** Gaea

titanic *see* **8 enormous**

tit for tat **8** exchange

titillate *see* **6 seduce**

title **3** dub **4** deed, name, rank, term **5** claim, crown, grade, label, place, right **6** status, tenure **7** entitle, epithet, station **8** christen, nobility, position

Titograd **9** Podgorica
   capital of: **10** Montenegro

titter *see* **6 giggle**

tittle **3** bit, dot, jot **4** atom, iota, mite **5** speck **8** particle

Titus Andronicus
   author: **11** (William) Shakespeare

tizzy **4** snit **6** dither, swivet **7** dudgeon **8** tailspin

to **2** ad, on **3** for **4** into, near, unto, upon, with **5** about, until **6** at hand, closed, toward **7** against, forward **8** together

toad
group of: 4 knot

toady 4 fawn **6** fawner, flunky, stooge, yes-man **8** hanger-on, kowtow to, parasite, truckler

toast 3 dry **4** heat, warm **5** brown, grill, honor **6** salute, warm up

tocsin 4 bell **5** alarm **7** warning

today 3 now **7** this day, this era **8** nowadays, this time

toddler 3 tot **4** babe, baby, tyke **5** child **6** infant

to-do 3 ado **4** fuss, stir **5** furor, noise **6** bustle, flurry, hubbub, hustle, pother, racket, ruckus, rumpus, tumult, uproar **7** turmoil **8** activity

toga 3 aba **4** garb, gown, robe **6** trabea **7** garment

Togo
former name: 8 (French) Togoland
capital/largest city: 4 Lome
highest point: 7 Baumann
sea: 8 Atlantic

physical feature:
bight: 5 Benin
gulf: 6 Guinea

togs *see* **7 clothes**

toil 4 grub, moil, work **5** grind, labor, pains, slave, sweat **6** drudge, effort **7** travail **8** exertion, hardship, industry, struggle

toilet 2 WC **3** can, loo **4** john **5** privy **7** commode, latrine **8** facility, lavatory, men's room, outhouse, rest room, washroom

toilet water 5 scent **7** cologne, essence, perfume

token *see* **7 memento**

To Kill a Mockingbird
director: 8 (Robert) Mulligan
based on novel by: 3 (Harper) Lee
cast: 4 (Gregory) Peck **6** (Mary) Badham, (Phillip) Alford, (Robert) Duvall

Tokyo
airport: 6 Haneda
capital of: 5 Japan
district: 5 Ginza
former name: 3 Edo
island: 6 Honshu

tolerate 3 let **4** bear, take

5 abide, admit, allow, brook, stand **6** endure, permit **7** indulge, stomach, undergo **8** sanction

toll 3 fee, tax **4** duty, levy, loss **6** charge, tariff **7** payment, penalty, tribute **8** exaction

tom 3 cat **6** tomcat, (male) turkey

tomato
  soup: 8 gazpacho
  sauce: 6 catsup **7** ketchup

tomb 5 crypt, grave, vault **8** monument

tomboy 3 meg **4** girl, romp **5** rowdy **6** female, gamine, hoiden, hoyden, tomrig **8** strumpet

tomfoolery 4 play **6** antics **8** drollery, nonsense

Tom Jones
  author: 8 (Henry) Fielding
  director: 10 (Tony) Richardson
  cast: 4 (Susannah) York **5** (Dame Edith) Evans **6** (Albert) Finney, (Joyce) Redman **7** (Diane) Cilento **8** (Hugh) Griffith

tommyrot *see* **8 nonsense**

Tom Sawyer
  author: 5 (Mark) Twain

tone 3 hue **4** cast, lilt, mood, note, tint **5** color, pitch, shade, sound, style, tenor, tinge **6** accent, chroma, firm up, manner, soften, spirit, stress, subdue, temper **7** cadence **8** attitude, make firm, modulate

Tonga
  capital/largest city: 9 Nukualofa
  head of state: 4 king
  sea: 7 Pacific
  explorer: 4 Cook **5** Bligh **6** Tasman

tongue 3 lap **4** flap, lick, spit **5** point, shaft **6** lingua, patois, speech **7** dialect, lingula **8** language

tongue-lash *see* **5 scold**

tonic 6 bracer, pickup **7** keynote **8** pick-me-up

tonsure 3 cut **4** trim **8** bald spot

tool 4 dupe, pawn **5** agent, means **6** device, medium, puppet, stooge **7** cat's-paw, machine, utensil, vehicle **8** hireling

toot 4 blow, honk **5** binge,

blare, blast, spree **6** bender **7** trumpet

tooth 3 cog, nib **4** barb, cusp, fang, spur, tang, tine, tusk **5** molar, point, spike, thorn **6** canine, cuspid **7** grinder, incisor **8** bicuspid, sprocket

top 3 cap, lid, van **4** acme, apex, best, brow, cork, fore, head, lead, peak **5** chief, cover, crest, crown, excel, front, noted, outdo, upper **6** better, exceed, famous, summit, tiptop, vertex, zenith **7** eclipse, eminent, highest, surpass **8** foremost, greatest, outshine, pinnacle

topaz
  color: 4 blue **5** brown **6** yellow
  month: 8 November

topic 4 text **5** theme **6** thesis **7** keynote, subject

topical 5 local **6** timely **7** current, limited **9** localized, parochial

topknot 4 comb, tuft **5** crest

topnotch *see* **7 supreme**

topple *see* **crush**

topsoil 4 dirt, loam **5** earth

topsy-turvy 5 messy

6 untidy **7** chaotic **8** confused, inverted

torch 5 brand **7** cresset **8** arsonist, flambeau **9** firebrand

torment *see* **6 harass**

torn 4 rent, slit **5** split **6** ragged, ripped **8** ruptured, shredded

tornado 4 wind **5** storm **6** funnel, squall, vortex **7** cyclone, twister, typhoon **8** outburst

torpedo 4 sink **5** wreck **7** destroy, missile, scuttle

torpid *see* **4 lazy**

torrent 4 gush, rain, rush **5** burst, flood, salvo **6** deluge, rapids, stream, volley **7** barrage, cascade, Niagara **8** downpour, eruption, outburst

torrid 3 hot **4** sexy **5** fiery **6** ardent, erotic, fervid, heated, sexual, sultry **7** amorous, boiling, burning, excited, fervent, intense, lustful

torte 4 cake **7** dessert

tortilla 7 tostada **8** corncake

torture *see* **7 anguish**

tory 8 loyalist, royalist

Tosca

    opera by: 7 Puccini

toss 3 lob **4** cast, flip, hurl, jerk, rock, roll, sway **5** churn, fling, heave, pitch, shake, sling, throw **6** joggle, let fly, propel, tumble, wiggle, writhe **7** agitate, flounce, wriggle **8** flourish, undulate

total 3 add, sum **4** full **5** add up, gross, sheer, solid, sum up, utter, whole **6** entire, figure, reckon **7** add up to, compute, perfect **8** complete, sweeping, thorough

totalitarian 7 fascist **8** despotic

tote *see* **5 carry**

totter *see* **6 wobble**

touch 3 art, bit, paw, pet, rub, use **4** abut, cite, dash, feel, fire, form, gift, hand, hint, join, meet, melt, move, note, stir, sway, tint, work **5** equal, flair, match, pinch, rival, rouse, skill, smack, speck, style, taste, thumb, tinge, trace, unite **6** adjoin, affect, arouse, border, broach, caress, excite, finger, finish, fondle, handle, hint at, manner, method, pawing, polish, sadden, soften, strike, stroke, thrill **7** concern, consume, contact, finesse, impress, inspire, mention, soupcon, surface, texture, utilize

touchstone *see* **5 gauge**

touchy *see* **7 grouchy**

tough 4 cold, firm, hard, hood, lout, mean, punk, wily **5** bully, cagey, canny, cruel, hardy, rigid, rough, rowdy, solid, stern **6** brutal, crafty, dogged, knotty, mulish, rugged, savage, strict, strong, sturdy, thorny, trying **7** adamant, arduous, callous, complex, durable, irksome, onerous **8** enduring, leathery, obdurate, pitiless, puzzling, ruthless, stubborn, toilsome

toupee 3 rug, wig **6** carpet, peruke **7** periwig

tour 4 trek, trip **5** jaunt, visit **6** junket, safari, travel, voyage **7** inspect, journey **8** sightsee

tournament 4 game **5** event,

match **7** contest, rivalry, tourney

tousled 5 messy **6** mussed, untidy **7** rumpled, tangled, unkempt **8** mussed-up, uncombed

tout *see* **6 praise**

tout de suite 6 at once

tout le monde 8 everyone

tow 3 lug **4** drag, draw, haul, lift, pull **5** hoist, trail

tower 4 keep, loom, rock, soar **5** mount, outdo, spire, surge **6** ascend, belfry, castle, column, exceed, pillar, refuge, turret **7** bulwark, eclipse, shoot up, steeple, surpass **8** outshine, overhang, rise high

toxic 5 fatal **6** deadly, lethal, mortal **7** noxious **8** poisoned, venomous

toy 4 play, tiny, yoyo **5** dally, pygmy, sport **6** bantam, bauble, fiddle, gadget, gewgaw, little, midget, trifle **7** dwarfed, stunted, trinket **8** gimcrack

trace *see* **4 iota**

track 3 way **4** mark, path, rail, sign, tack **5** dirty, route, scent, spoor, trace, trail **6** course, follow

tract 3 lot **4** area, plot, zone **5** essay **6** parcel, region **7** booklet, expanse, leaflet, quarter, stretch **8** brochure, district, pamphlet, treatise

trade 3 buy **4** deal, line, shop, swap **5** craft **6** barter, buyers **7** calling, patrons, pursuit **8** business, commerce, exchange, vocation

trademark 6 emblem **7** feature **8** property

tradition 4 lore, myth, saga, tale **5** habit, usage **6** custom, legend **8** folklore, practice

traduce *see* **5 sully**

traffic 4 cars, deal **5** buses, ships, trade **6** barter, doings, planes, riders, trains, trucks **7** bootleg, contact, freight, smuggle **8** business, commerce, dealings, exchange, tourists, voyagers

tragic 3 sad **4** dire **5** awful, fatal **6** deadly, dreary, woeful **7** piteous, pitiful, ruinous, serious, unhappy

8 dramatic, dreadful, grievous, horrible, mournful, pathetic, pitiable, shocking, terrible

trail 3 dog, tow, way **4** drag, draw, fall, flow, hunt, mark, path, poke, sign, tail **5** float, hound, scent, spoor, trace, track **6** be down, course, dangle, dawdle, follow, lessen, shrink, stream **7** dwindle, pathway, subside **8** footpath, taper off

trailblazers 7 leaders **8** pioneers

train 2 el **3** aim, set **4** line **5** break, chain, drill, focus, level, point, queue, sight, teach, trail, tutor **6** column, direct, escort, school, series, subway **7** caravan, cortege, educate, prepare, retinue **8** exercise, instruct, practice, rehearse

trainee 4 boot **5** cadet **6** rookie **7** private, rookie, student

traipse *see* **5 mosey**

trait 4 mark **5** quirk **7** earmark, feature, quality **8** hallmark

traitor 3 rat **5** Judas, rebel

6 ratter **7** ratfink, serpent **8** apostate, betrayer, deceiver, deserter, mutineer, quisling, renegade, turncoat

tramp 3 bum **4** hike, hobo, roam, rove, slog, trek, walk **5** march, prowl, stamp, stomp **6** ramble, trudge, wander **7** floater, meander, traipse, trample, vagrant **8** derelict

trance *see* **4 daze**

tranquil *see* **4 calm**

transaction 4 deal **6** affair **7** bargain, dealing, venture **8** exchange

transcend 5 excel, outdo **6** exceed **7** eclipse, outrank, surpass **8** outshine, overstep, surmount

transfer 4 cede, deed, move, send **5** bring, carry, shift **6** change, convey, moving, remove **7** consign, deeding, removal, sending **8** hand over, relegate, relocate, shipment, transmit

transfix *see* **5 rivet**

transform 4 turn **5** alter **6** change, recast, remold **7** convert, remodel

transgress 3 err, sin 4 slip 5 break, cross, fault, lapse, wrong 6 exceed, impose, offend 7 digress, infract, violate 8 infringe, trespass

transient *see* 5 **brief**

transition 4 jump, leap 6 change 7 passage, passing 8 shifting

translate 4 turn 5 alter, apply 6 change, decode, recast, render, reword 7 clarify, convert, explain 8 decipher, rephrase, simplify, spell out

translucence 7 clarity 8 lucidity

transmit 4 send, ship 5 carry, issue, relay, remit 6 convey, pass on, spread 7 deliver, forward 8 dispatch, televise, transfer

transmute 5 alter 6 change 7 convert

transparent *see* 5 **clear**

transpire 5 arise, occur 6 appear, befall, chance, crop up, evolve, happen, turn up

transplant 5 graft, repot, shift 7 replant 8 displace, relocate, resettle, transfer

transport 3 bus, lug 4 bear, cart, lift, move, send, ship, take, tote 5 bring, carry, charm, fetch, train, truck 6 convey, moving, remove, thrill 7 deliver, enchant, freight, vehicle 8 airplane, delivery, dispatch, enthrall, entrance, transfer, trucking

transverse *see* 8 **traverse**

Transylvania
region of: 7 Romania
city: 4 Cluj
fictional home of: 7 Dracula

trap 3 net, pit 4 lure, ploy, ruse, seal, stop, wile 5 catch, feint, snare, trick 6 ambush, device, enmesh, entrap, lock in 7 ensnare, pitfall, springe 8 artifice, entangle, hold back, hunt down, maneuver

trappings *see* 7 **clothes**

trash 3 rot 4 bums, crap, junk, scum 5 dregs, dross, tripe, waste 6 debris, drivel, idlers, litter, refuse, rubble, tramps 7 garbage, hogwash, loafers, residue, rubbish, twaddle 8 castoffs, leavings, nonsense, riffraff

trauma 4 hurt **5** shock, wound **6** injury, stress

travail *see* **6 stress**

travel 2 go **4** be on, move, roam, rove, sail, tour, trek, wend **5** cross, drive, range, visit **6** cruise, junket, voyage, wander **7** journey, proceed **8** pass over, progress, sightsee, traverse

traverse 4 span **5** cross **6** bridge, travel **8** go across, move over, overpass

travesty *see* **8 disgrace**

Traviata, La
opera by: 5 Verdi

trawl 3 net **4** drag, fish, haul, line **5** seine, troll **6** dredge **7** dragnet

treachery 5 guile **6** deceit **7** perfidy, treason **8** apostasy, betrayal, trickery

tread 4 gait, hike, pace, roam, rove, step, walk **5** prowl, range, stamp, stomp, tramp **6** stride, stroll, trudge, walk on **7** trample **8** footfall

treason 6 mutiny, revolt **7** perfidy **8** apostasy, betrayal, sedition

treasure 3 gem **4** gold **5** hoard, jewel, prize, store, value **6** esteem, jewels, regard, revere, riches, silver **7** cherish, deposit, paragon

Treasure Island
author: 9 (Robert Louis) Stevenson

Treasure of the Sierra Madre, The
director: 6 (John) Huston
cast: 4 (Tim) Holt **6** (Humphrey) Bogart, (Walter) Huston **7** (Bruce) Bennett, (Barton) MacLane

treasury 4 bank, safe, till **5** funds, purse, vault **6** coffer **8** money box

treat 3 joy **4** blow, coat, give **5** apply, cover, favor, grant, imbue, stand **6** attend, divert, doctor, handle, manage, remedy, spring, thrill **7** comfort, delight, discuss, patch up, take out **8** consider, deal with, look upon, medicate, pleasure, relate to

treatise 4 text **5** essay, study, tract **6** manual, memoir, report, thesis **8** textbook, tractate

treaty 4 deal, pact **6** accord

7 bargain, compact, entente **8** covenant

Tree Grows in Brooklyn, A author: 5 (Betty) Smith

trek 4 hike, plod, roam, rove, sail, slog, trip **5** jaunt, march, range, tramp **6** junket, travel, trudge, voyage **7** journey, odyssey, passage **8** traverse

trellis 5 arbor, bower, cross, frame, grill, trail **6** gazebo, screen **7** lattice, network, pergola

tremble 5 quail, quake, shake, waver **6** quaver, quiver, shiver **7** flutter, pulsate, shudder

tremendous *see* **8 enormous**

tremor 3 jar **4** jolt **5** quake, shake, shock, spasm, throb, waver **6** quiver, shiver **7** flutter, shaking, shudder, tremble **8** paroxysm

trench 3 cut, rut **4** scar **5** canal, ditch, drain, fosse, slash, slice **6** dugout, furrow, gutter, trough **7** channel **8** aqueduct

trenchant 4 acid, keen, tart **5** crisp **6** bitter **7** acerbic, caustic, concise, mordant, probing **8** clear-cut, distinct, incisive, scathing

trend 4 bent, flow, mode **5** drift, style **7** fashion, impulse, leaning **8** movement, tendency

trepidation *see* **4 fear**

trespass *see* **7 intrude**

tress 4 curl, hair, lock, mane **5** braid, plait **6** strand **7** ringlet, wimpler **8** spitcurl

trestle 4 beam **5** board, brace, frame, table **6** timber

trial 2 go **3** try, woe **4** care, pain, shot, test **5** agony, essay, flyer, whirl, worry **6** burden, effort, misery, ordeal, trying, tryout **7** anguish, attempt, bad luck, hearing, testing, venture **8** distress, endeavor, hardship

tribulation *see* **6 sorrow**

tribunal 3 bar **5** bench, court, forum **6** judges

tributary 6 branch, feeder, source, stream **7** helping, subject **8** affluent

tribute 3 tax **4** duty, levy, toll **5** bribe, honor, kudos

6 esteem, eulogy, excise, impost, payoff, praise, ransom **7** payment, respect **8** accolade, encomium, memorial

trice *see* **7 instant**

trick 3 art, gag **4** bait, dupe, feat, gift, gull, have, hoax, joke, ploy, ruse, trap, wile **5** antic, blind, bluff, caper, cheat, dodge, feint, fraud, knack, prank, put-on, skill, stunt **6** deceit, number, outfox, outwit, resort, secret, take in **7** deceive, gimmick, mislead, swindle **8** hoodwink

trickle 4 drip, leak, ooze, seep **5** exude **7** dribble, seepage

trident
> **form: 5** spear
> **number of prongs: 5** three
> **scepter of: 7** Neptune **8** Poseidon

trifle *see* **4 iota**

trigger 5 shoot **6** set off **7** fire off **8** activate, detonate, touch off

trim 3 cut, fit, lop **4** clip, crop, deck, form, lean, pare, slim, thin **5** adorn, array, lithe, prune, shape, shave, shear, shift, sleek, state **6** adjust, bedeck, border, change, fettle, svelte **7** compact, cutting, fitness, furbish, garnish, lissome, slender, willowy **8** athletic, decorate, ornament

Trinidad and Tobago
> **capital/largest city: 11** Port of Spain
> **highest point: 5** Aripo
> **sea: 8** Atlantic **9** Caribbean
> **explorer: 8** Columbus
> **place:**
>> **asphalt lake: 5** Pitch (Lake)
> **feature:**
>> **bird: 7** oilbird **8** cocorico
>> **clothing: 4** sari **5** dhoti
>> **music: 7** calypso, goombay

trinket 3 toy **5** bijou, charm, jewel **6** bauble, gewgaw, notion, trifle **8** gimcrack, ornament

trip 3 bob, err **4** flip, flub, fool, muff, pull, skip, slip, tour, trek, undo **5** caper, catch, dance, fluff, foray, jaunt, outdo, throw, upset **6** bungle, cruise, frolic, gambol, junket, outing, safari, set off, slip up, voyage **7** blunder, commute, confuse, journey, misstep, stumble **8** activate, fall over, flounder

Triple Crown 5 (Kentucky) Derby **7** Belmont **9** Preakness

Tripoli
  capital of: 5 Libya

Tristan and Isolde
  opera by: 6 Wagner

tristesse 6 sorrow **7** sadness

Tristram Shandy
  author: 6 (Laurence) Sterne

trite *see* **8 ordinary**

Triton
  god of: 3 sea
  father: 8 Poseidon
  mother: 10 Amphitrite
  shape: 6 merman
  trumpet: 5 conch (shell)

triumph 3 hit, win **4** best, coup **5** smash **6** subdue **7** conquer, mastery, prevail, succeed, success, surpass, victory **8** conquest, overcome

trivial *see* **5 petty**

troglodyte 5 brute **6** hermit

Troilus
  father: 5 Priam
  mother: 6 Hecuba

Troilus and Cressida
  author: 11 (William) Shakespeare

Trojan Horse
  made of: 4 wood
  contained: 8 Odysseus, warriors

Trojans, The
  opera by: 7 Berlioz

Trojan War
  length: 6 decade
  combatants: 6 Greeks **7** Trojans
  cause: 5 Helen, Paris

troll 3 imp **4** ogre **5** dwarf, gnome **6** goblin
  origin: 5 Norse

trollop *see* **5 whore**

troop, troops 4 army, band, file, gang, herd, step, unit **5** bunch, crowd, crush, drove, flock, horde, march, press, swarm, tramp **6** parade, stride, throng, trudge **7** cavalry, company, militia **8** infantry, soldiers, soldiery

trop 3 too **7** too many, too much

trophy 4 palm **5** award, booty, honor, kudos, medal, prize, relic, spoil **6** wreath **7** laurels, memento **8** citation, souvenir

tropical 5 muggy **6** sultry, torrid **8** stifling

trot 3 jog

trouble 3 fix, row, vex, woe **4** blow, care, fuss, heed, mess, pain, pass, snag, work **5** agony, annoy, grief, harry, labor, pains, pinch, think, trial, upset, worry **6** badger, bother, burden, crisis, defect, dismay, effort, grieve, harass, misery, ordeal, pester, pickle, plague, pother, put out, scrape, sorrow, strain, strait, stress, strife, unrest **7** afflict, agitate, concern, depress, dilemma, discord, disturb, ferment, perturb, setback, torment **8** distress, hardship, hot water, quandary, struggle, nsettle

trough *see* **6 trench**

trounce 4 beat, drub, lick, trim, whip **5** cream, skunk **6** humble **7** clobber

troupe 4 band, cast **5** group, troop **6** actors **7** company, players

trousers 5 jeans, pants **6** chinos, slacks **7** drawers **8** breeches, britches, jodhpurs, knickers

Trovatore, II
opera by: 5 Verdi

Troy
abducted queen: 5 Helen
defender: 5 Eneas **6** Aeneas
Greek name: 5 Ilion
hero: 6 Hector
king: 5 Priam
Latin name: 5 Ilium
mountain: 3 Ida
story: 5 Iliad **7** Odyssey

truant 4 gone **5** idler **6** absent, dodger, evader, loafer, no show **7** drifter, goof-off, missing, not here, shirker, slacker, vagrant **8** absentee, deserter, layabout

truce 4 halt, lull, rest, stay, stop **5** break, pause **7** respite

Trucial Oman, Trucial States *see* **18 United Arab Emirates**

truck 3 rig, van
type: 5 panel **6** pickup **7** trailer **8** delivery

truckle 3 bow **4** fawn **5** court, defer, yield **6** grovel, pander, submit **7** flatter **8** bootlick, butter up, suck up to

truculent *see* **4 rude**

Trudeau, Garry
  creator of: 10 Doonesbury

trudge 4 drag, limp, plod **5** clump, march, tramp **6** hobble, lumber **7** shamble

true 4 even, firm, full, just, pure, real **5** exact, legal, loyal, right, usual, valid **6** actual, lawful, normal, proper, steady, strict, trusty **7** correct, devoted, factual, genuine, literal, precise, regular, staunch, typical **8** absolute, accurate, bona fide, positive, reliable, rightful

Truman, Harry S
  presidential rank: 11 thirty-third
  party: 10 Democratic
  state represented: 2 MO
  succeeded upon death of: 9 Roosevelt
  defeated: 5 Dewey, Dobbs **6** Thomas, Watson **7** Wallace **8** Teichert, Thurmond

  vice president: 7 Barkley
  born: 2 MO **5** Lamar
  military service: 5 major **9** World War I
  notable events of lifetime/ term: 4 NATO **5** V-E Day, V-J Day **8** Fair Deal **9** Korean War
    airlift to: 6 Berlin
    dropping of first: 5 A-bomb **8** atom bomb
    plan: 8 Marshall
  wife: 9 Elizabeth
    nickname: 4 Bess
  children: 8 (Mary) Margaret

trumpet 4 honk, horn **5** blare, bugle **6** cornet **7** clarion **8** proclaim

Trumpet of the Swan, The
  author: 5 (E B) White

trump up 4 fake **6** invent, make up **7** concoct, falsify

truncate 3 bob, lop, nip **4** clip, crop, dock, snub, trim **7** abridge, shorten **8** amputate

truncheon 3 bat **4** club **5** baton, billy, stick **6** cudgel **8** bludgeon

truss *see* **3 tie**

trust 4 care, duty, hope **5** faith, hands **6** accept, assume, belief, charge, credit, expect, look to, rely on **7** believe, count on, custody, keeping, presume, swear by **8** reliance, sureness

truth 3 law **4** fact **5** facts **6** verity **7** reality **8** accuracy, fidelity, veracity

try 2 go **3** aim, use **4** risk, seek, shot, test, turn **5** crack, essay, fling, prove, trial, whack **6** effort, sample, strain, strive, tackle **7** adjudge, attempt, venture **8** endeavor

tryout 4 test **5** trial **7** hearing **8** audition

tryst 4 date **7** meeting, vis-a-vis

tub 3 keg, kit, pot, tun, vat **4** bath, boat, butt, cask, ship, tank, tram, wash **5** barge, bathe, fatso, fatty, keeve, tramp **6** barrel, bucket, firkin, ore car, vessel **7** cistern, tankard **8** cauldron, slow boat

tube 4 duct, hose, pipe **7** conduit **8** cylinder

tuber 3 anu, yam **4** beet, bulb, corm, eddo, root, taro **5** jalop, shoot **6** potato, turnip **8** rutabaga

tuck *see* **7 conceal**

tuckered out 5 all in, tired, weary **6** bushed, done in, pooped **8** fatigued

Tuesday
 from: 3 Tiw
 heavenly body: 4 Mars
 French: 5 mardi
 German: 8 dienstag
 Italian: 7 martedi
 Spanish: 6 martes

tuft 4 wisp **5** batch, brush, bunch, clump, crest, plume, sheaf **6** bundle, tassel **7** cluster, topknot

tug 3 lug, tow **4** drag, draw, haul, jerk, pull, yank **6** wrench **7** wrestle

tulip 6 Tulipa

tumble 3 mix **4** dive, drop, fall, flip, roll, toss **5** whirl **6** bounce, jumble, plunge, stir up, topple **7** descend, shuffle, stumble

tumbler 3 cog, dog **5** drier, glass, lever **6** goblet, vessel **7** acrobat, athlete, gymnast, juggler

tumbrel 4 cart **5** wagon **7** tipcart **8** dumpcart

tumid *see* **6 turgid**

tummy 3 gut **5** belly

6 paunch **7** abdomen, midriff, stomach

tumor 3 wen **4** cyst, lump, wart **5** pride **6** cancer, growth **7** bombast, sarcoma **8** hematoma, neoplasm, tubercle

tumult *see* **6** clamor

tun 3 keg, tub, vat **4** butt, cast, drum **6** barrel

tune 3 air **4** aria, line, song, step **5** adjust, ditty, motif, pitch, theme **6** accord, adjust, melody, number, strain, unison **7** concert, concord, harmony

tunic 4 robe **5** cloak **6** jacket, mantle, poncho, tabard **7** garment, surcoat

Tunisia
  capital/largest city: 5 Tunis
  empire: 8 Carthage
  mountain: 5 Atlas
  highest point: 6 Chambi
  sea: 13 Mediterranean
  physical feature:
    desert: 6 Sahara
    plains: 5 Sahel
    wind: 7 sirocco
  place:
    ruins: 8 Carthage
  feature:
    market: 4 souk

food:
  dish: 7 mesfouf **8** couscous

turbulent 5 rowdy **6** fierce, raging, stormy, unruly **7** chaotic, furious, riotous, violent **8** agitated, restless

tureen 4 bowl, dish

turf 3 sod **4** area, peat, plot, soil **5** divot, grass, haunt, sward, track **7** verdure

turgid 5 puffy, showy **6** florid, ornate **7** flowery, pompous, swollen **8** inflated, puffed up

Turkey
  capital: 6 Ankara
  largest city: 8 Istanbul
    previous names: 9 Byzantium **14** Constantinople
  highest point: 6 Ararat
  lake: 3 Van
  river: 6 Tigris **9** Euphrates
  sea: 4 Aral **5** Black **6** Aegean **7** Marmara **13** Mediterranean
  physical feature:
    inlet: 10 Golden Horn
    peninsula: 9 Anatolian, Gallipoli
    plateau: 9 Anatolian
    strait: 9 Bosphorus

11 Dardanelles
place:
>   **bridge: 6** Galata
>   **mosque: 4** Blue **11**
>   Hagia Sophia
>   **museum: 7** Topkapi
>   **ruins: 4** Troy **7** Ephesus
>   **8** Pergamum
feature:
>   **cap: 3** fez
>   **clothing: 6** caftan
>   **goat hair: 6** mohair
>   **harem: 5** serai **8**
>   seraglio
food:
>   **dish: 5** halva, kebab,
>   pilaf
>   **pastry: 7** baklava
>   **raisin: 7** sultana

Turkmenistan
capital/largest city: 9
>   Ashkhabad
river: 8 Amu Darya
sea: 7 Caspian
physical feature: 7 Kara
>   Kum (Desert)

turmoil *see* **5 chaos**

turn 2 do, go **3** act, arc, lie,
put **4** bend, coil, come,
deed, flex, hang, look,
loop, make, rest, ride, roll,
send, shot, sour, spin,
time, veer, walk, wing **5**
alter, crack, curve, drive,
eject, pivot, round, scare,
shift, shock, spell, spoil,
swing, twist, whirl **6**
become, chance, change,
curdle, effort, fright,
gyrate, invert, period,
reside, rotate, sprain,
swerve, swivel, wrench,
zigzag **7** acidify, attempt,
convert, execute, ferment,
reverse, revolve, service,
winding **8** gyration,
rotation, surprise

turncoat *see* **7 traitor**

turn one's stomach 6
revolt, sicken **7** disgust **8**
nauseate

turnout 5 crowd **6** output,
throng **8** assembly,
audience

turn tail 4 flee **7** retreat,
run away **8** back away

turn turtle 5 upset **7**
capsize, tip over **8** flip
over, overturn

turn up *see* **6 appear**

turpitude *see* **4 evil**

turquoise 4 aqua **5** stone **7**
mineral, sky-blue

turret 5 tower **6** belfry,
cupola, garret, gazebo,
louver, terret **7** minaret,
rotator, steeple

8 gunhouse, gunmount
tool: 5 lathe

turtle 7 reptile **8** terrapin, tortoise
dorsal shell: 8 carapace
order: 8 Chelonia
ventral shell: 8 plastron
young: 7 turtlet

tussle *see* **5 fight**

tussock 4 hair, tuft **5** brush, bunch, clump, grass, sedge **7** bulrush, cluster, thicket **8** feathers

tutelage 8 coaching, guidance, teaching, training, tutoring

tutti
music: 3 all

Tuvalu
other name: 6 Ellice (Islands), Lagoon (Islands)
capital: 8 Funafuti
highest point: 5 Nuwak
sea: 7 Pacific

twaddle *see* **5 trash**

Twain, Mark
real name: 7 (Samuel) Clemens

tweet 4 peep **5** cheep, chirp **7** chirrup, chitter, twitter

Twelfth Night
author: 11 (William) Shakespeare

Twenty-Four (24)
cast: 7 (Carlos) Bernard **8** (Elisha) Cuthbert, (Dennis) Haysbert **10** (Kiefer) Sutherland

Twenty Thousand Leagues Under the Sea
author: 5 (Jules) Verne
submarine: 8 Nautilus

twilight 3 ebb, eve **4** dusk **6** sunset **7** decline, evening, sundown **8** even-tide, moonrise

Twilight of the Gods 8 Ragnorak

Twilight Zone, The
host: 7 (Rod) Serling

twin 4 dual, like **5** alike **6** double, paired **7** matched, twofold

twine 4 coil, cord, rope, wind **5** braid, cable, plait, twist, weave **6** string, thread **7** binding, entwine

twinge 4 pain, pang, stab **5** cramp, spasm, throb **6** stitch, tingle, twitch

twinkle *see* **4 glow**

Twins
constellation of: 6 Gemini

twirl *see* **4 spin**

twist 3 arc, way **4** bend, coil, curl, idea, kink, knot, pull, roll, spin, turn, veer, wind, wrap, yank **5** curve, pivot, ravel, slant, snake, swing, twine, whirl, wrest **6** rotate, spiral, sprain, swerve, swivel, system, tangle, wrench, zigzag **7** contort, entwine, meander **8** surprise

twitch *see* **5 spasm**

twitter 4 fuss, peep, stew **5** cheep, chirp, tizzy, tweet, whirl **6** bustle, flurry, pother, uproar, warble **7** chatter, fluster

two-faced 5 false **7** devious **8** slippery

twofold 4 dual **6** double **7** two-part

Two Gentlemen of Verona, The
author: 11 (William) Shakespeare

two of a kind 4 pair **5** twins **6** couple **7** doublet

2001: A Space Odyssey
author: 6 (Arthur C) Clarke
director: 7 (Stanley) Kubrick
computer: 3 HAL
cast: 6 (Keir) Dullea **8** (Gary) Lockwood **9** (William) Sylvester

two-timing 5 false **6** tricky **7** perfidy **8** bad faith, betrayal, disloyal, trickery

Two Years Before the Mast
author: 4 (Richard Henry) Dana (Jr)

tycoon *see* **5 mogul**

tyke 3 kid, tad, tot **5** child **6** shaver, squirt, wee one

Tyler, John
presidential rank: 5 tenth
party: 4 Whig **20** Democratic-Republican
state represented: 2 VA
succeeded upon death of: 8 Harrison
born: 2 VA **8** Greenway
notable events of lifetime/ term:
annexation of: 5 Texas
wife: 5 Julia **7** Letitia

type 4 font, kind, race, sort **5** brand, class, genus, group, model, order, print **6** design, family, phylum, sample **7** species, variety **8** category, specimen

typhoon 4 gale, gust, wind **5** storm **7** cyclone, tempest, tornado, twister

Typhoon
  author: 6 (Joseph) Conrad

typical *see* **6 normal**

typify 5 sum up **6** embody
  7 betoken, connote, pass
  for **8** instance, stand for

tyranny 7 cruelty, fascism
8 coercion, iron fist,
iron hand, iron rule,
severity

tyro *see* **6 novice**

tzimmes 4 fuss **6** uproar
  literally: 4 stew

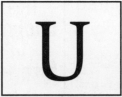

ubiquitous 7 allover

Uganda
  capital/largest city: 7 Kampala
  mountain: 9 Ruwenzori (also, Mountains of the Moon)
  highest point: 7 Stanley **10** Margherita
  lake: 6 Albert **8** Victoria
  river: 9 White Nile **10** Albert Nile
  physical feature:
    falls: 4 Owen **8** Kabalega **9** Murchison
    valley: 9 Great Rift
  place:
    airport: 7 Entebbe
  feature:
    king: 6 kabaka

ugly 4 foul, mean, vile **5** nasty **6** homely, horrid, odious **7** hideous, hostile, ominous **8** dreadful, horrible, unseemly

Ugly Duckling, The
  author: 8 (Hans Christian) Andersen

ukase *see* **5 order**

Ukraine
  capital/largest city: 4 Kiev
  mountain: 7 Crimean **10** Carpathian
  river: 3 Bug **6** Donets **7** Dnieper
  sea: 5 Black

Ulan Bator
  capital of: 8 Mongolia

ulcer 4 sore **6** canker

ulna
  bone of: 8 lower arm
  neighbor: 6 radius

ulterior *see* **6 covert**

ultimate 3 end **4** acme, apex, last, peak **5** final **6** height, utmost **7** extreme, maximum, supreme **8** crowning, eventual, greatest, terminal

ultra 7 extreme

ululate 4 hoot, howl, wail **6** lament

Ulysses
  author: 5 (James) Joyce

umber 5 brown 7 pigment

umbilicus 5 navel

umbrage 5 pique, shade 6 leaves, shadow 7 foliage, offense, outrage

umbrella 6 brolly 7 parasol

umpire 5 judge 7 arbiter, mediate, referee 8 mediator, moderate

umpteen 4 many, slew 5 loads (of)

unaccountable *see* 5 **weird**

unalloyed 4 pure 7 unmixed

unanimous 6 allied, united

unbalanced *see* 5 **crazy**

unbecoming *see* 4 **ugly**

unbelievable *see* 6 **absurd**

unblemished *see* 7 **perfect**

unborn 5 fetal, later 6 coming, future, to come 7 in utero

uncanny 5 eerie, weird 6 spooky 7 curious, strange

uncertain *see* 8 **variable**

unchain 4 free 7 release, set free 8 liberate, unfetter

uncharacteristic 8 atypical

unchecked 4 free 5 loose 6 unruly 7 liberal, rampant 8 reinless, unreined

uncial 6 script

form: 5 large, round
used in: 5 Greek, Latin

uncivilized 4 rude 6 savage, vulgar 7 boorish, brutish, ill-bred, uncouth, untamed 8 barbaric, churlish

Uncle Remus
author: 6 (Joel Chandler) Harris

Uncle Sam
personification of: 7 America

Uncle Tom's Cabin
author: 5 (Harriet Beecher) Stowe

uncomfortable 4 edgy 5 tense, upset 6 on edge, uneasy 7 awkward, keyed up, nervous, painful 8 confused, strained

uncommon *see* 4 **rare**

uncompromising 4 firm 5 rigid, stiff 6 strict 8 exacting, hardline, obdurate

unconcerned 4 cold 5 aloof 6 serene 7 distant, unaware, unmoved 8 composed, uncaring

unconditional 5 utter 6 entire 8 absolute, complete, outright

unconscious 3 out 6 latent

7 in a coma, out cold **8** comatose, in a faint

unconstitutional 7 illegal **8** unlawful

unconventional *see* **7 strange**

uncouth 4 rude **5** crass, crude, gross, rough **6** callow, coarse **7** boorish, brutish, ill-bred, loutish, uncivil **8** barbaric, churlish, impolite

uncover 4 bare, undo **5** dig up, strip **6** denude, dig out, expose, reveal, unmask, unveil, unwrap **7** disrobe, lay bare, uncloak, undrape, undress, unearth **8** disclose, unclothe

unctuous 4 oily, smug **6** smarmy **7** fawning, honeyed, servile **8** slippery, too suave

uncultivated 3 raw **4** wild **7** uncouth **8** unfarmed, unplowed, untilled

under 3 sub **5** below, lower, neath, short **7** beneath, sedated **8** inferior, less than

undercover 3 sly **6** covert, hidden, secret **7** furtive,

sub rosa **8** hush-hush, stealthy

undercurrent 4 aura, hint, mood **5** sense, tinge, vibes **7** quality, riptide **8** undertow

underestimate 7 dismiss, put down **8** belittle, minimize, misjudge

undergarment *see* **9 underwear**

undergo 5 brave, stand **6** endure, suffer **7** sustain, weather **8** submit to

undergraduate 4 coed, soph **5** frosh, plebe **6** junior, senior **7** scholar, student **8** freshman

underground 6 buried, covert, secret **7** sub-rosa

underhand, underhanded *see* **6 covert**

underline 6 accent, stress **7** dwell on, point up

underling 4 serf **6** flunky, lackey, menial, minion, thrall, vassal **7** servant, subject **8** employee, hireling, inferior

underlying 5 basic **6** covert **7** beneath, radical **8** implicit

undermine 4 foil, ruin **5** erode **6** injure, riddle, scotch, thwart, weaken **7** cripple, destroy, subvert, torpedo **8** sabotage

underneath 5 below, lower **6** bottom, hidden

underprivileged *see* **4 poor**

underscore 4 mark **6** accent, deepen, play up, stress **7** feature, point up **8** heighten

understand 3 dig, get, see **4** hear, know, read, take **5** grasp, learn **6** absorb, accept, assume, can see, fathom, gather, take it **7** be aware, discern, make out, presume, realize **8** conclude, perceive

understudy 3 sub **6** backup, double, fill-in, relief **7** stand-by, stand-in

undertake 3 try **5** begin, essay, start **6** assume, strive, tackle, take on **7** attempt **8** commence, embark on, endeavor, set about, shoulder

under the influence 5 drunk **6** sodden, soused, wasted, zapped, zonked **7** smashed **8** besotted

under the weather 3 bad, ill **4** sick **6** ailing, sickly

undertone 4 aura, hint,

mood **5** scent, sense, tinge, trace **6** flavor, mumble, murmur, nuance **7** feeling, inkling, quality **8** coloring

underwear 3 bra **4** BVDs, slip **5** pants, teddy, thong **6** boxers, briefs, corset, girdle, shorts **7** chemise, panties **8** bloomers, camisole, knickers, lingerie, skivvies

underweight 4 bony, lank **5** gaunt, lanky **6** skinny **7** scrawny, spindly **8** skeletal, underfed

underworld 4 Hell **5** Hades, limbo **6** the mob **8** mobsters, the Mafia

underwrite *see* **7 endorse**

undiluted 4 neat, pure **5** sheer **7** unmixed **8** straight

undo 3 end **4** free, open, ruin, void **5** annul, erase, loose, quash, untie **6** cancel, defeat, loosen, offset, repair, unbind, unfold, unhook, unknot, unlace, unlock, unwrap **7** destroy, nullify, rectify, reverse, subvert, unchain, unravel, wipe out

8 demolish, overturn, unbutton, unfasten

undoing *see* **8 downfall**

undone 6 ruined

undoubtedly 6 surely **7** no doubt

undress 5 strip **6** nudity **7** disrobe, uncover, undrape **8** disarray, unclothe

undue 6 unmeet **8** impolite, improper, needless, overmuch, too great, unseemly, unworthy

undulate 4 coil **5** slink, weave

undying *see* **7 eternal**

unearth *see* **7 uncover**

uneasy *see* **7 anxious**

unenlightened 8 ignorant

unequal 6 biased, uneven, unfair, unjust, unlike **7** bigoted, partial

unequivocal 5 clear, final **7** certain **8** absolute, clear-cut, decisive, definite, emphatic

unerring 4 sure **7** certain, precise **8** constant, faithful, reliable

unethical 5 dirty, shady, wrong **6** shoddy, unfair **7** devious **8** unworthy

uneven 4 awry, bent **5** bumpy, lumpy, rough **6** angled, coarse, craggy, curved, jagged, tilted, unfair, unjust, unlike **7** crooked, not flat, slanted, sloping, unequal **8** lopsided, not level, not plumb, one-sided, unsmooth

uneventful 4 dull **5** quiet, usual **6** boring **7** average, humdrum, prosaic, routine, tedious **8** ordinary, standard

unexpected 6 sudden

unfaded 5 fresh **6** bright **8** undimmed

unfailing 4 true **5** loyal **6** steady **7** endless **8** constant, enduring, faithful, reliable

unfair 4 foul **5** dirty **6** biased, unjust **7** corrupt, crooked, partial, unequal **8** not right, onesided, partisan

unfamiliar 3 new **5** novel **6** exotic, unique **7** curious, foreign, strange, unknown, unusual

unfathomable 4 deep, vast **6** arcane, remote, subtle **7** complex, extreme, obscure

8 abstract, abstruse, esoteric, profound

unfavorable 3 bad **4** poor **7** adverse, unhappy **8** unsuited, untimely

unfeeling 4 cold **5** cruel

unfinished 5 crude, rough **6** undone **7** lacking, sketchy, wanting **8** immature

unfit 4 sick, weak **5** frail **6** infirm, not fit, sickly **7** not up to, unequal, unready, unsound, useless **8** delicate, disabled, unsuited

unflagging 4 firm **5** fixed **6** steady **7** staunch **8** constant, enduring, resolute, tireless, unshaken, untiring

unflappable 4 calm, cool **6** placid, serene **8** composed

unflinching *see* **6 steady**

unfold *see* **6 expose**

unforeseen 6 abrupt, sudden **8** surprise

Unforgiven, The
  director: 8 (Clint) Eastwood
  cast: 6 (Richard) Harris **7** (Morgan) Freeman, (Gene) Hackman **8** (Clint) Eastwood

unfounded 4 idle **5** false **6** untrue **8** baseless, spurious

unfulfilled 8 thwarted

unfurl 4 open **6** expand, spread, unfold, unroll **7** develop, roll out

ungainly 5 stiff **6** clumsy, klutzy **7** awkward

ungodly 4 base, vile **5** awful **6** rotten, sinful, wicked **7** corrupt, ghastly, godless, heinous, immoral, impious **8** dreadful, terrible

unguent 4 balm **5** cream, salve **6** lotion **8** ointment

ungulate 2 ox **3** cow, gnu, hog, pig, yak **4** boar, calf, deer, goat, ibex **5** camel, daman, horse, llama, tapir **6** hoofed, vicuna **7** buffalo, caribou, giraffe, peccary **8** antelope, elephant, hooflike, ruminant

unhappy *see* **3 sad**

unhealthy *see* **4 sick**

unheard-of 3 odd **4** rare **6** unique **7** amazing, curious, unknown, unusual **8** freakish, original, singular, uncommon

unhinge 6 detach **7** disrupt
8 separate, unsettle

unicorn
form: 5 horse
feature: 4 horn
symbolizes: 6 purity **8**
    chastity

unification 5 union, unity **6**
fusion, merger **7** uniting **8**
alliance, junction

uniform 4 even, garb **5**
alike, array, at one, dress,
equal, habit **6** attire, in
line, in step, livery **7**
apparel, costume, regalia,
regular, similar, the same
8 agreeing, constant, in
accord, of a piece,
unvaried, vestment

unify 3 wed **4** ally, fuse,
join **5** blend, merge, unite
6 couple, link up **7**
combine **8** federate

union 5 blend, guild, unity
6 fusion, league, merger **7**
amalgam, joining, mixture,
oneness, uniting, wedding
8 alliance, marriage,
unifying
    type: 5 craft, labor,
        trade

unique 8 by itself, peerless,
singular

unit 4 part **5** group, whole

6 entity, member **7**
element, measure,
package, section, segment
8 category, division

unite *see* **5** unify

United Arab Emirates
other name: 11 Pirate
Coast, Trucial Oman **13**
Trucial States
capital/largest city: 8 Abu
Dhabi
components: 5 Ajman,
Dubai **7** Sharjah **8** Abu
Dhabi, Fujairah **11** Ras
al Khaima, Umm al
Qaiwan
war: 4 Gulf

United Arab Republic 3
UAR
onetime union of: 5
Egypt, Syria

United Kingdom
union of: 7 (Great)
Britain, (Northern)
Ireland

United States
capital: 2 DC **10**
Washington
largest city: 11 New York
City
mountain ranges: 5 Rocky
6 Brooks **7** Cascade **8**
Aleutian **9** Allegheny **10**
Adirondack, Grand

Teton, Great Smoky **12** Sierra Nevada
highest point: 6 Denali **8** McKinley
lake: 4 Erie **5** Great, Huron **7** Ontario **8** Michigan, Superior **9** Champlain, Great Salt **10** Okeechobee
river: 3 Red **4** Ohio **5** Snake, White, Yukon **6** Hudson, Platte **7** Potomac **8** Cheyenne, Missouri **9** Tennessee **10** St Lawrence **11** Connecticut, Mississippi, Susquehanna
sea: 6 Arctic, Bering **7** Pacific **8** Atlantic, Beaufort
island: 4 Guam, Long, Maui, Oahu **5** Block, Ellis, Kauai, Samoa **6** Hawaii, St John, Staten, Virgin **8** Aleutian, Catalina, St Thomas **9** Manhattan, Nantucket
physical feature:
  bay: 5 Tampa **7** Prudhoe **8** Biscayne, Monterey **10** Chesapeake
  desert: 4 Gila **6** Mojave **11** Death Valley
falls: 7 Niagara
gulf: 6 Alaska, Mexico **10** California
plains: 5 Great
strait: 6 Bering **7** Florida
feature:
  national symbol: 9 bald eagle
  tree: 7 redwood, sequoia

unity *see* **5** peace

universal 7 general

universality 8 currency

university 6 campus, school **7** academy, college **11** institution
  session: 4 term **7** seminar **8** semester

unjust 6 biased, unfair, warped **7** partial **8** one-sided, partisan, wrongful

unkempt 5 messy **6** sloppy, untidy **7** rumpled, tousled **8** mussed-up, slovenly, uncombed

unlawful 7 illegal, illegit, illicit, lawless **8** criminal

unleash 4 free **5** let go **7** release, set free **8** let loose, liberate

unlettered 8 ignorant, untaught

unlimited 4 huge, vast **5** total **7** endless, immense **8** absolute, complete, infinite

unload 4 dump **7** off-load **8** get rid of, unburden

unmanly 5 timid **6** yellow **8** cowardly, sissyish, womanish

unmarked 5 clean, clear

unmarried girl
　French: 10 jeune fille
　German: 8 fraulein
　Spanish: 8 senorita

unmask 4 bare, show **6** betray, expose, reveal, unveil **7** lay open, uncover **8** disclose, discover

unmatched 6 unlike **7** diverse, supreme, unequal **8** peerless, variable

unmerciful 4 cold, evil **5** cruel, harsh **6** brutal, severe, unkind **7** brutish, extreme, inhuman **8** inhumane, pitiless, ruthless

unmindful 3 lax **6** remiss **7** unaware **8** careless, derelict, heedless

unmistakable 5 clear, plain **6** patent **7** evident, glaring, obvious

8 apparent, distinct, manifest, palpable

unmitigated 6 arrant **8** absolute, unabated, unbroken

unnerve 5 daunt, scare, upset **7** agitate, unhinge **8** frighten, unsettle

unobtrusive 3 shy **6** humble, modest **7** bashful **8** reserved, reticent, retiring

unofficial 8 informal

unorthodox 7 erratic

unpalatable 5 nasty **8** inedible, unsavory

unparalleled 4 best, rare **5** alone, crack, elect **6** unique **8** gilt-edge, peerless, singular

unpolished 3 raw **5** gawky, inept, rough **6** cloudy, clumsy **7** amateur, awkward, unwaxed **8** inexpert, unbuffed, unglazed, unshined

unprecedented 5 novel **6** unique

unquestionable 4 sure **5** clear, plain **6** proven **7** certain, evident, obvious, perfect **8** definite, flawless

unravel 4 undo **5** feaze,

solve **6** unfold, unfurl, unknit **7** clear up, resolve **8** decipher, separate, untangle

unreal 4 airy **5** dream **6** dreamy **7** ghostly, not real, phantom, shadowy **8** ethereal, illusive, illusory, imagined, spectral

unreasonable 5 undue **6** absurd, biased, mulish, unfair **7** bigoted **8** obdurate, stubborn

unrefined 3 raw **5** crude, rough **6** coarse, vulgar **7** boorish, low-bred

unremarkable 5 usual **6** common **7** average **8** everyday, mediocre, ordinary

unrest 5 chaos **6** tumult **7** anarchy, discord, ferment, protest, turmoil **8** disorder, disquiet, upheaval

unrivaled 8 superior, topnotch

unruffled 4 calm, cool, even, mild **5** quiet, still **6** placid, serene, smooth **8** composed, tranquil

unruly 4 wild **5** rowdy **7** restive, wayward, willful **8** contrary, perverse

unsatisfactory 4 poor **5** inept, unfit **8** below par, inferior, unworthy

unsavory 3 bad **4** flat, foul **5** nasty **7** insipid, tainted

unscrupulous 5 sharp **6** amoral **7** crooked, devious, immoral

unseasonable 6 too hot **7** too cold, too warm **8** abnormal, untimely

unseemly 4 rude **5** crude, gross **6** coarse, vulgar **7** boorish, loutish **8** churlish, improper, indecent, unworthy

unsettle 5 upset **6** bother, rattle, ruffle **7** agitate, confuse, disturb, fluster, perturb, trouble, unhinge **8** bewilder, confound

unshackle 4 free **7** release, set free, unchain **8** liberate, unfetter

unsheathe 4 bare **6** expose **7** pull out **8** withdraw

unsightly 4 ugly **6** horrid, odious **7** hideous

unskilled 5 green, inept **7** untried

unsoiled 4 pure **5** clean,

fresh, white **6** chaste **8** innocent, pristine, spotless

unsolicited 4 free **8** unforced, unsought, unwanted

unsound 3 mad, off **4** weak **5** risky, shaky, unfit, wrong **6** absurd, ailing, faulty, feeble, flawed, infirm, insane, marred, sickly, unsafe **7** foolish, invalid, rickety, tottery **8** confused, crippled, decrepit, deranged, diseased, drooping, impaired, insecure, not solid, not valid, perilous, specious, spurious, unstable, unsteady

unsparing 4 full **6** giving, lavish **7** copious, liberal, profuse **8** abundant, generous

unspeakable 4 huge, vast **5** awful, great **6** odious **7** fearful, immense **8** enormous, shocking

unspoken 5 tacit **6** silent **7** implied **8** implicit

unstable *see* **4 weak**

unsteady *see* **4 weak**

unstudied 4 glib **6** casual **7** artless, natural

8 informal, unforced, unversed

unsuitable 5 inapt, unfit **7** unhappy, useless **8** improper, unseemly

unsullied 5 clean **8** spotless, unsoiled

unsure 3 shy **5** timid **7** bashful **8** hesitant, insecure, reserved

unsurpassed 4 best **7** highest, supreme **8** greatest, peerless, superior

unsuspecting 5 naive **7** unaware **8** gullible, off guard, trusting

unswerving *see* **6 steady**

untamed 4 wild **5** feral **6** savage

untangle 5 solve **7** clear up, unravel, unsnarl, untwist

untenable 4 weak **6** faulty, flawed **7** invalid, unsound **8** baseless, specious, spurious

untie 4 free, undo **5** loose **6** loosen, unbind, unlace **7** unchain, unstrap **8** make free, unfasten

untilled 6 fallow **8** unplowed

until we meet again
French: 5 adieu **8** au revoir
German: 14 auf Wiedersehen
Hawaiian: 5 aloha
Italian: 4 ciao **5** addio
Japanese: 8 sayonara
Spanish: 5 adios

untimely 5 inapt **7** unhappy **8** ill-timed, mistimed, unseemly

untiring *see* **8 constant**

untold 6 myriad, secret, unsaid **7** endless, private, unknown **8** hushed up, infinite, numerous, unspoken, withheld

untouched *see* **3 new**

untutored 5 naive **6** native, unread **8** ignorant, untaught

unusual 4 rare **5** novel **6** unique **7** curious, offbeat, strange **8** atypical, peculiar, singular, uncommon

unvarnished 3 raw **4** bald, bare **5** blunt, crude, frank, naked, plain, stark **6** candid, direct, honest, simple **7** sincere **8** straight

unveil *see* **8 disclose**

unwarranted 7 illegal **8** culpable, unlawful

unwavering 4 firm **6** steady, strong **7** staunch **8** faithful, resolute, unshaken, untiring

unwelcome 7 outcast **8** excluded, rejected, unwanted

unwieldy 5 bulky, heavy **6** clumsy **7** awkward, weighty **8** not handy

unwilling 5 loath **6** averse **7** against, opposed

unwitting 7 unaware, unmeant

unwrap 4 open **6** loosen, unbind **7** uncover

unwritten 4 oral **5** tacit, vocal **7** assumed, implied **8** implicit, inferred, unstated

unyielding *see* **8 resolute**

up 4 atop, lift, over, rear **5** about, above, aloft, along, aside, astir, at bat, built, close, equal, erect, raise **6** apiece, ascend, higher, lifted **7** abreast, batting, forward, promote, skyward, through **8** advanced, cheerful, increase, out of bed, overhead, standing, together, windward

upbraid **5** scold **6** berate, rebuke, revile **7** bawl out, censure, chew out, reprove **8** admonish, chastise, denounce, reproach

upbringing **7** rearing **8** breeding, training

upcoming **6** coming, nearby **7** looming, nearing, pending **8** imminent

update **5** amend, emend, renew **6** recast, revamp, revise, rework **7** restore, touch up, upgrade **8** overhaul, renovate

up for grabs **4** open

upgrade **5** raise, slope **6** ascent, better **7** advance, elevate, incline, inflate, promote **8** gradient

upheaval **5** flood, quake **6** blowup, tumult **7** turmoil **8** disorder, upthrust

uphill **4** hard **5** tough **6** rising, taxing, tiring **7** arduous, onerous **8** toilsome, wearying

uphold **4** bear, prop **5** brace, carry, raise, shore **6** defend, hold up, prop up **7** approve, bolster,

confirm, elevate, endorse, protect, shore up, support, sustain **8** advocate, buttress, champion, maintain, preserve

upkeep **4** keep **6** living **7** support **8** expenses, overhead

upland **4** high, rise **5** ridge **6** height **7** plateau **8** eminence, highland

uplift **5** edify, raise **6** better, refine **7** advance, bracing, elevate, improve, inspire, lifting, shoring, support, upgrade **8** propping

upon **2** at, on **4** atop **5** about **6** toward **7** against, thereon

upper **3** top **4** high **5** major **6** higher **7** eminent, greater, topmost **8** elevated, northern, superior

upper class **5** elite **6** gentry, uptown **7** (high) society **8** highborn, highbred, wellborn

upper crust **5** elite **6** gentry **7** (high) society

upper hand **4** edge, sway **5** power **7** command, control, mastery

Upper Volta *see* **11 Burkina Faso**

uprightness 5 honor **7** dignity, honesty **8** morality

uprising 4 riot **6** mutiny, revolt **8** outbreak

uproar 3 ado **4** stir, to-do **5** furor **6** clamor, tumult **7** turmoil

uproarious 4 loud, wild **5** noisy **6** raging, stormy **7** furious, intense, riotous

uproot 6 banish **7** abolish, cast out, destroy, root out, wipe out **8** dislodge, displace, force out

upset 3 ire, irk, mad, vex **4** beat **5** anger, annoy, crush, irked, messy, mix up, pique, quash, smash, upend, vexed, worry **6** bother, change, defeat, enrage, grieve, jumble, mussed, rattle **7** agitate, annoyed, confuse, conquer, disturb, enraged, fluster, furious, grieved, jumbled, perturb, tip over, trouble, worried **8** agitated, bothered, disorder, distress, overcome, overturn, unnerved

upshot 3 end **6** effect, payoff, result, sequel **7** outcome **8** offshoot

upside down 7 chaotic **8** reversed

upstanding *see* **6 honest**

upstart 4 snip, snob, snub **6** nobody **7** bounder, parvenu **8** mushroom

upswing 4 rise **6** pickup **7** upsurge

uptight *see* **7 anxious**

up-to-date 2 in **3** new **5** today **6** modern, modish, timely, trendy, with-it **7** current, stylish

upward 4 high, more **5** above, aloft **7** skyward

Uranus
mother: 4 Gaea
wife: 4 Gaea
father of: 6 Giants, Titans **8** Cyclopes
castrated by: 6 Cronos

Uranus
position: 6 planet **7** seventh
characteristic: 5 rings

urban 4 city, town **5** civic **8** citified

urbane 5 civil, suave **6** polite, smooth **7** courtly, elegant, gallant, genteel, politic, refined, tactful **8** debonair, gracious, mannerly, polished, well-bred

urchin 3 boy, imp, lad **4** brat, waif **5** gamin, stray, whelp, youth **6** gamine, laddie **8** young pup

urge 3 yen **4** back, coax, goad, itch, poke, prod, push, spur, sway, wish **5** drive, egg on, fancy, force, press, prick, speed **6** desire, exhort, hunger, reason, thirst **7** beseech, counsel, craving, dictate, entreat, implore, impulse, longing, passion, quicken, request, solicit, suggest **8** advocate, champion, convince, persuade, petition, yearning

urgent *see* **7 crucial**

urinary system
component: 6 kidney, ureter **7** bladder, urethra
rids body of: 5 salts, waste, water **8** minerals

urn 3 jar, pig **4** ewer, kist, tomb, vase **5** grave, steen **6** teapot **7** samovar

Uruguay
capital/largest city: 10 Montevideo

highest point: 8 Catedral
lake: 5 Merin, Mirim, Negra, Negro, Rocha **11** Salto Grande **15** Rincon del Bonete
river: 5 Plata **6** Parana **7** La Plata
sea: 8 Atlantic
feature:
cattle ranch: 8 estancia
cowboy: 6 gaucho
dance: 5 tango **7** milonga
food:
drink: 4 mate

use 3 aid, ply, sap **4** good, help, work **5** apply, avail, drain, exert, spend, treat, usage, value, waste, wield, worth **6** devour, employ, expend, handle, profit **7** benefit, consume, deplete, exhaust, exploit, operate, service, utilize **8** function, squander

useful 5 handy, utile **7** helpful **8** valuable

useless 4 vain **6** futile **7** of no use **8** bootless

usher 4 lead, show **5** guide, steer **6** attend, convoy, direct, escort, herald, launch, leader, porter, ring in, squire **7** conduct, precede **8** announce, director, proclaim

USSR *see* **6 Russia**

usual 5 stock, trite **6** common, normal, wonted **7** popular, regular, routine, typical **8** expected, familiar, habitual, ordinary, orthodox, standard

usurp 4 grab **5** steal **7** preempt **8** arrogate

Utah
    abbreviation: 2 UT
    nickname: 6 Mormon **7** Beehive
    capital/largest city: 12 Salt Lake City
    highest point: 9 Kings Peak
    lake: 4 Mead, Utah **6** Powell **9** Great Salt
    river: 8 Colorado
    physical feature:
        basin: 5 Great
        salt flats: 10 Bonneville
    feature:
        dam: 6 Hoover

utensils 4 gear **5** tools **6** outfit, silver, tackle **8** flatware

utilitarian 5 handy **6** usable, useful **8** sensible, valuable, workable

utility 3 aid, gas, use **4** help **5** avail, extra **6** backup **7** benefit, reserve, service **8** function

utilize *see* **3 use**

utmost, uttermost *see* **8 ultimate**

utopia 4 Eden **6** heaven **7** Erewhon **8** paradise

utter *see* **3 say**

uxorious
    doting on: 8 one's wife
    from Latin: 4 uxor, wife

Uzbekistan
    capital/largest city: 8 Tashkent
    river: 8 Amu Darya, Syr Darya
    sea: 4 Aral

vacant 4 dull, free, idle, open **5** aloof, blank, blase, clear, empty, vapid **6** unused, wooden **7** deadpan, for rent, leisure, vacuous **8** forsaken, unfilled

vacation 4 rest **5** leave, R and R **6** recess **7** holiday **8** furlough, holidays

vaccine 5 serum **8** antitoxin

vacillate *see* **6 falter**

vacuous *see* **6 vacant**

vagabond 4 hobo **5** gypsy, nomad, rover, tramp **6** roamer, roving **7** drifter, floater, migrant, nomadic, rambler, roaming, vagrant **8** bohemian, carefree, homeless, rambling, wanderer, wayfarer

vagary 4 kink, whim **5** fancy, humor, quirk **6** notion, oddity, whimsy **7** caprice, fantasy, impulse **8** crotchet, daydream

vagrant 3 bum **4** hobo **5** nomad, rover, tramp **6** beggar, loafer, roamer, roving **7** floater, migrant, nomadic, roaming **8** homeless, rambling, vagabond, wanderer

vague 4 hazy **5** fuzzy, loose **6** casual, random, unsure **7** general, unclear **8** confused, nebulous

vain, vainglorious *see* **7 haughty**

valedictory 4 last **5** final **7** parting **8** farewell, terminal, ultimate

Valhalla
  origin: 8 Teutonic
  hall of: 4 Odin **5** Othin

valiant 4 bold **5** brave, noble **6** daring, heroic **7** gallant **8** fearless, intrepid, knightly, stalwart, unafraid, valorous

valid 4 good **5** legal, licit, sound **6** lawful, proper, strong **7** fitting, genuine, logical, weighty **8** accurate, decisive, forceful,

validate

official, powerful, suitable, truthful

validate 5 enact, prove, stamp **6** ratify, verify **7** certify, confirm, sustain, warrant, witness **8** legalize, sanction

valise 3 bag **4** grip **7** handbag, luggage, satchel **8** suitcase

Valkyrie
origin: 8 Teutonic
home: 8 Valhalla
attendant of: 4 Odin **5** Othin
queen: 8 Brunhild

valley 3 cut, dip, gap **4** dale, dell, glen, vale **5** basin, chasm, glade, gorge, gulch, gully **6** bottom, canyon, divide, hollow, ravine **8** water gap

valor _see_ **7 courage**

valse 5 waltz

valuable 4 dear, good **6** costly, prized, useful, valued **7** admired, helpful **8** esteemed, precious

value, values 3 use **4** cost, help, rate **5** assay, count, judge, merit, price, prize, rules, weigh, worth **6** admire, amount, assess,

charge, esteem, ideals, profit, reckon, revere, size up **7** beliefs, benefit, cherish, compute, customs, respect, service, utility **8** appraise, evaluate, prestige, treasure

vamoose 3 out **4** away, scat, shoo **5** be off, leave, scram **6** beat it, begone, depart, get out, go away **7** get lost

vamp 5 siren

van 4 cart, dray, head **5** lorry, scout, truck, wagon **6** camper, picket **7** trailer **8** sentinel, vanguard

Van Buren, Martin
nickname: 6 Red Fox
presidential rank: 6 eighth
party: 10 Democratic
state represented: 2 NY
defeated: 5 White **6** Mangum **7** Webster **8** Harrison
vice president: 7 Johnson
born/died/buried: 2 NY **10** Kinderhook
wife: 6 Hannah

vandalize 3 mar **5** trash, wreck **6** damage, deface **7** despoil, destroy

vanguard 3 van **7** leaders **8** forerank

vanish 3 die, end **5** cease **6** die out, expire, perish **7** die away **8** dissolve, fade away, melt away

vanity *see* **5 pride**

vanquish *see* **6 defeat**

Vanuatu
  other name: 11 New Hebrides
  capital/largest city: 8 Port Vila
  highest point: 11 Tabwemasana
  sea: 7 Pacific
  explorer: 4 Cook **7** Queiros
  feature:
    cult: 5 cargo

vapid *see* **4 dull**

vapor 3 dew, fog **4** haze, mist, smog **5** fumes, smoke, steam **6** miasma **8** moisture

variable 6 fickle, fitful, uneven, unlike **7** diverse, mutable **8** changing, shifting, unstable, wavering

variegated 4 pied **6** motley **7** checked, dappled, mottled, piebald

variety 4 hash, kind, race, sort, type **5** brand, breed, class, genre, genus, group, stock, tribe **6** change, family, jumble, medley, motley, strain **7** melange, mixture, species **8** category, division, pastiche

various 3 few **4** many, some **5** other **6** divers, myriad, sundry, varied **7** diverse, several **8** assorted, manifold, numerous

varlet 3 cur **6** rascal, wretch **7** villain

varnish 4 gilt **5** adorn, cover, gloss, stain **6** excuse, soften **7** conceal, lacquer **8** disguise, mitigate

vary *see* **6 change**

vase 3 jar, jug, pot, urn **5** crock, diota **8** canister

vassal 4 serf **5** helot, liege, slave **6** tenant, thrall **7** bondman, servant, subject, villein **8** retainer

vast *see* **7 immense**

Vatican City 10 papal state
  enclave in: 4 Rome
  includes: 7 Sistine (Chapel), Vatican **8** St. Peter's (Basilica)

vault 4 arch, dome, jump, leap, safe, tomb **5** bound,

clear, crypt **6** arcade,
cupola, hurdle, spring **7**
ossuary **8** catacomb, jump
over, leapfrog, leap over,
wall safe

vaunt 5 strut **6** brag of,
flaunt **7** exult in, show
off, swagger

veer 3 yaw **4** jibe, tack,
turn **5** curve, dodge, drift,
shift, wheel **6** swerve,
zigzag **7** go about

vegetable 3 pea **4** bean,
beet, corn **6** carrot,
greens, legume, squash,
turnip **7** cabbage, lettuce,
parsnip, produce, spinach
8 broccoli, eggplant, lima
bean, rutabaga, zucchini

vegetarian 5 vegan **8**
meatless

vegetation 5 flora, grass,
sloth, weeds **6** leaves,
plants, torpor **7** foliage,
herbage, languor, loafing,
verdure **8** dormancy,
idleness, lethargy

vehement *see* **7 intense**

vehicle 3 bus, car **4** tool **5**
agent, means, organ,
plane, train, truck **6**
agency, device, medium **7**
bicycle

veil *see* **4 hide**

vein 3 rib, web **4** bent, hint,
line, lode, mark, mood,
seam, tone **5** fleck, layer,
stria, style, touch **6**
furrow, manner, marble,
nature, strain, streak,
stripe, temper, thread **7**
stratum **8** tendency

velocity *see* **5 speed**

venal *see* **7 corrupt**

vendor, vender 6 dealer,
hawker, monger, seller,
trader **7** peddler **8**
huckster, merchant,
purveyor, retailer,
salesman, supplier

veneer 4 coat, mask, show
5 front, layer **6** casing,
facade, facing, jacket,
sheath **7** coating, overlay,
wrapper **8** covering,
envelope, pretense

venerate *see* **5 honor**

venereal 6 carnal, sexual **7**
genital

Venezuela
capital/largest city: 7
Caracas
highest point: 7 Bolivar
lake: 8 Valencia **9**
Maracaibo
river: 3 Oro **6** Amazon

sea/ocean: 8 Atlantic **9** Caribbean

physical feature:
  falls: 5 Angel
  plains: 6 Ilanos **7** Orinoco

feature:
  cowboy: 7 llanero
  musical instrument: 7 maracas

vengeance 7 revenge **8** avenging, reprisal, requital

Venice
  Italian: 7 Venezia
  resort: 4 Lido (Beach)
  sea: 8 Adriatic
  small canal: 3 rii
  traveler: 4 (Marco) Polo

venom 3 ire **4** gall, hate **5** anger, spite, toxin, virus **6** choler, enmity, grudge, hatred, malice, poison, rancor, spleen **7** ill will **8** acrimony, savagery

vent 3 air, tap **4** bare, drip, emit, flue, gush, hole, ooze, pipe **5** exude, spout, utter, voice **6** effuse, escape, faucet, let out, outlet, reveal, spigot **7** air hole, chimney, debouch, declare, divulge, express, opening, orifice, release

8 aperture, disclose, exposure, venthole

ventilate 3 air, sow **5** voice **6** aerate, air out, report, review, spread **7** analyze, declare, discuss, dissent, divulge, examine, express

venture *see* **7 attempt**

Venus
  origin: 5 Roman **7** Italian
  goddess of: 4 love **6** beauty, spring **7** gardens
  son: 6 Aeneas
  see **9 Aphrodite**

Venus (planet)
  position: 6 second
  closest to: 5 Earth
  named after: 7 goddess
  characteristics: 6 clouds
  space probes: 6 Venera **7** Galileo, Pioneer **8** Magellan

veracity 5 truth **6** candor, verity **7** honesty, probity **8** accuracy, openness

verbal 4 oral, said **5** vocal **6** spoken, voiced **7** in words, of words, uttered

verbatim *see* **5 exact**

verbose 5 gabby, wordy **6** prolix **7** voluble **8** effusive

verdant 4 lush **5** green, leafy, shady, turfy

6 grassy **7** meadowy **8** blooming, thriving

verdict 6 answer, decree, ruling **7** finding **8** decision, judgment, sentence

verge *see* **4 edge**

verify 5 prove **7** certify, confirm, support, sustain, witness **8** accredit, attest to, document, validate, vouch for

verily 4 amen **5** truly **6** really

veritable *see* **4 true**

vermilion 3 red **7** scarlet **8** cinnabar

vermin 4 ants, lice, mice, owls, rats **5** crows, fleas, foxes, pests **6** snakes, wolves **7** bed bugs, coyotes, roaches, spiders, weasels **8** termites

Vermont
abbreviation: 2 VT
capital: 10 Montpelier
largest city: 10 Burlington
mountain: 5 Green
highest point: 9 Mansfield
lake: 9 Champlain
river: 5 Black, Johns **8** Winooski **11** Connecticut

feature:
  ski resort: 4 Pico **5** Okemo, Stowe **7** Bromley **8** Stratton **9** Mount Snow, Sugarbush **10** Killington

vermouth
  type: 4 wine **6** brandy **8** aperitif
  varieties: 3 dry **5** sweet

vernacular *see* **6 jargon**

vernal 3 new **5** fresh, green **6** spring **8** youthful

versatile 3 apt **4** able **5** handy **6** adroit, clever, expert, gifted **7** protean **8** talented

verse 4 poem **5** meter, rhyme, stave **6** jingle, poetry, stanza **7** measure, strophe

versed *see* **4 able**

version 4 side **5** story **6** report **7** account

vertex *see* **6 summit**

vertical 5 plumb, sheer **7** upright

vertiginous 5 dizzy, giddy, shaky **6** whirly **7** reeling

vertigo 7 reeling **8** fainting

verve *see* **5 vigor**

very 4 bare, mere, most, much, pure **5** exact, extra, plain, quite, sheer, truly **6** deeply, highly, hugely, mighty, really, simple, vastly **7** awfully, exactly, fitting, greatly, notably, perfect, precise, totally **8** markedly, suitable, terribly

vessel 3 cup, jar, jug, keg, mug, pot, tub, vat **4** boat, bowl, butt, cask, dish, duct, scow, ship, tube, vase, vein **5** barge, craft, crock, flask, glass, liner, plate, yacht **6** artery, barrel, beaker, carafe, flagon, goblet, packet, tanker, whaler **7** caldron, collier, cruiser, platter, tankard, trawler, tugboat, tumbler, utensil **8** decanter, sailboat

vest 3 rig **4** garb, robe **5** array, drape, dress **6** attire, clothe, enwrap, fit out, jacket, jerkin **7** apparel, deck out, doublet, envelop **8** accouter

Vesta
   origin: 5 Roman
   goddess of: 6 hearth
vestal *see* **4 pure**
vestibule 4 hall **5** entry,

foyer, lobby **6** lounge **7** hallway, passage **8** anteroom, corridor

vestige *see* **7 memento**

vestment *see* **7 clothes**

vesture 4 robe **5** robes **7** apparel, clothes, garment, raiment **8** clothing

veteran 3 vet **6** expert, master **7** old hand **8** old-timer, seasoned

veto 4 deny, void **6** denial, enjoin, forbid, negate, reject **7** nullify, prevent, refusal **8** disallow, prohibit, turn down

vex 3 bug, irk **4** fret, gall, miff, pain, rile **5** anger, annoy, chafe, harry, pique, upset, worry **6** badger, bother, grieve, harass, hassle, nettle, pester, plague, ruffle **7** chagrin, disturb, provoke, torment, trouble **8** distress, irritate

viable 6 usable **8** feasible, workable

viaduct 4 ramp, span **8** overpass

vial 5 ampul, flask, phial **7** ampoule

viands *see* **4 food**

vibrant *see* **7 radiant**

vibrate *see* **5 shake**

vicar 6 cleric, parson, pastor **8** preacher

vice 4 flaw **5** fault **6** defect **7** blemish, failing, frailty **8** iniquity, weakness

vice president
resigned: 5 (Spiro) Agnew **7** (John C) Calhoun
accused of treason: 4 (Aaron) Burr **12** (John C) Breckinridge
youngest elected: 12 (John C) Breckinridge
elected by Senate: 7 (Richard) Johnson
elected but did not serve: 4 (William) King
rejected nomination: 6 (Frank) Lowden, (Silas) Wright
lived longest: 6 (John Nance) Garner
succeeded to presidency: 4 (Gerald) Ford **5** (John) Tyler **6** (Chester A) Arthur, (Harry S) Truman **7** (Andrew) Johnson, (Lyndon B) Johnson **8** (Calvin) Coolidge, (Millard) Fillmore **9** (Theodore) Roosevelt

vicinity 4 area **6** region **8** environs, locality, vicinage

vicious *see* **4 evil**

vicissitude 6 change **8** mutation

victim 4 butt, dead, dupe, gull, mark, pawn, prey, tool **5** patsy **6** pigeon, quarry, sucker, target **7** injured, wounded **8** casualty, fatality, innocent

Victoria, Queen
House of: 7 Hanover
Prince Consort: 6 Albert
son; successor: 6 Edward (VII)

Victoria
origin: 5 Roman
goddess of: 7 victory
corresponds to: 4 Nike

Victorian 4 prim, smug **6** narrow, proper, stuffy **7** insular, prudish **8** priggish

victory 7 laurels, success, the palm, triumph **8** conquest, the prize

victuals *see* **4 food**

vie 4 life **5** fight **6** strive **7** compete, contend, contest **8** be a rival, struggle

Vienna
capital of: 7 Austria
early name: 4 Wena

9 Vindobono
German: 4 Wien
river: 6 Danube
ruler: 8 Hapsburg
Vietnam
other name: 5 Annam **9**
Indochina
former colony of: 6
France
capital: 5 Hanoi
largest city: 6 Saigon **13**
Ho Chi Minh City
highest point: 8 Fansipan
lake: 4 Ba Be, West **5**
Ho-Tay **8** Hoan Kiem **9**
Dam Van Tri
river: 3 Red **6** Mekong,
Saigon
sea: 10 South China
island: 4 Co To **6** Can
Gio, Con Son **7** Phu
Quoc **9** Halong Bay
physical feature:
delta: 6 Mekong **8** Red
River
gulf: 4 Siam **6** Tonkin
8 Thailand
peninsula: 11
Indochinese
feature:
clothing: 5 ao dai
new year: 3 Tet
view 3 eye, ken, see **4** gaze,
look, note, peek, peep,
scan **5** judge, scene, sight,

study, vista, watch **6**
behold, belief, gaze at,
glance, look at, notion,
regard, survey, take in,
theory, vision **7** examine,
feeling, glimpse, observe,
opinion, outlook, scenery,
witness **8** attitude,
panorama, perceive
vigilant 4 wary **5** alert,
chary **7** careful, guarded,
heedful, on guard, prudent
8 cautious, watchful
vigor 3 pep, vim, zip **4**
dash, elan, fire, zeal **5**
ardor, drive, force, might,
power, verve **6** energy,
fervor, spirit **7** passion,
stamina **8** haleness,
strength, vitality, vivacity
Viking, viking 4 Dane **6**
pirate **7** mariner **8**
Norseman, Northman,
searover
legend: 4 Edda, saga
origin: 6 Norway, Sweden
7 Denmark, Finland
warrior: 7 beserk **9**
berserker
writing: 4 rune
vile 3 bad, low **4** base, evil,
foul, lewd, mean, ugly **5**
awful, gross, nasty **6**
coarse, filthy, odious,

sinful, smutty, sordid, vulgar, wicked **7** beastly, hateful, heinous, ignoble, immoral, obscene, vicious **8** depraved, shameful, shocking, wretched

vilify *see* **5 libel**

villa, Villa 5 aldea, dacha **6** castle, Pancho **7** chateau, mansion

village 4 burg **6** hamlet, suburb **8** hick town

villain 3 cad, cur, rat **5** knave, louse, rogue **6** rascal, varlet **7** caitiff **8** evil doer, scalawag

villein 4 carl, esne, serf **5** ceorl, churl, slave **6** drudge **7** bondman, peasant

vim *see* **5 vigor**

vin, vino 4 wine

vindicate *see* **6 acquit**

vindictive 6 bitter, malign **8** avenging, punitive, spiteful, vengeful

vintage *see* **7 antique**

violate 4 rape **5** abuse, break **6** defile, invade, ravish **7** disobey, outrage, profane **8** dishonor, infringe, trespass

violent *see* **6 savage**

violet 5 Viola

violin family
  instruments: 3 kit **5** cello, rebec, viola **7** baryton **8** bass viol, lyra viol, violetta

viper 3 asp, boa **5** adder, krait

virago 3 nag **4** fury **5** harpy, scold, shrew, vixen **6** dragon, gorgon **7** she-wolf **8** battle-ax, fishwife, harridan

virgin 4 girl, lass, maid, Mary, pure **6** chaste, damsel, maiden, unused **7** unmixed **8** pristine

Virginia
  abbreviation: 2 VA
  nickname: 11 Old Dominion
  capital: 8 Richmond
  largest city: 13 Virginia Beach
  highest point: 6 Rogers
  river: 5 James **7** Potomac, Rapidan, Roanoke
  sea/ocean: 8 Atlantic
  physical feature:
    bay: 10 Chesapeake
    caverns: 5 Luray
    valley: 10 Shenandoah

Virgo
  symbol: 6 virgin
  planet: 7 Mercury
  rules: 7 service
  zodiac: 5 sixth
  born: 6 August **9** September

virile *see* **7 valiant**

virtual 5 tacit **7** implied **8** implicit, indirect

virtue *see* **5 honor**

virtuoso *see* **6 genius**

virulent *see* **5 toxic**

virus 3 bug **4** germ **7** microbe

visage 3 air **4** face, look, mien **5** image **6** aspect **7** profile **8** demeanor, features

vis-a-vis 8 eye to eye, together

viscera 4 guts **6** bowels **7** innards, insides **8** entrails

viscous 5 gluey, gooey, gummy, slimy, tacky, thick **6** sticky, syrupy, viscid

Vishnu
  in trinity of: 4 Siva **5** Shiva **6** Brahma
  religion: 8 Hinduism

visible 4 open **5** clear, plain **6** in view, marked, patent **7** blatant, evident, glaring, in focus, obvious **8** apparent, distinct, manifest, palpable, revealed

vision 4 idea **5** dream, fancy, ghost, sight **6** notion **7** concept, phantom, specter **8** daydream, eyesight, illusion

visit 4 call, stay **5** haunt, smite **6** affect, assail, attack, befall, call on, punish **7** afflict, assault, go to see, sojourn **8** drop in on, frequent, stay with

vista *see* **4 view**

visual *see* **7 visible**

vita 3 bio **6** resume

vital 4 life, live **5** alive, basic, chief, quick **6** lively, living, urgent, viable **7** animate, crucial, dynamic, primary, serious, vibrant **8** animated, cardinal, critical, existing, forceful, foremost, material, pressing, spirited, vigorous

vitiate *see* **4 void**

vitriolic 4 acid **5** acerb, nasty, sharp **6** biting

7 abusive, acerbic, caustic, cutting **8** sardonic

vituperation *see* **6 insult**

vivacious *see* **6 lively**

viva voce 5 aloud **6** orally

vivid 3 gay **4** deep, loud, rich **5** clear, shiny, showy **6** bright, florid, garish, lively, moving, strong **7** glowing, graphic, in tense, radiant, shining **8** colorful, definite, distinct, dramatic, emphatic, luminous, lustrous, powerful, stirring, striking

vixen 4 fury **5** scold, shrew, witch **6** virago **8** fishwife, harridan, spitfire

vocabulary *see* **7 lexicon**

vocal 4 open, oral, sung **5** blunt, frank, lyric **6** candid, choral, direct, spoken, voiced **7** uttered, voluble **8** operatic

vocation *see* **3 job**

vociferous *see* **4 loud**

vodka
  origin: 6 Poland, Russia

vogue *see* **5 trend**

voice 3 air, say **4** alto, bass, part, role, tone, vent, vote, will, wish **5** speak, state, tenor, utter **6** choice, desire, option, reveal, singer, speech **7** declare, divulge, express, opinion, singers, soprano **8** announce, baritone, delivery, disclose, proclaim, vocalize

voice of the people
  Latin: 9 vox populi

void 4 bare, emit, free, null, pass **5** annul, blank, clear, drain, eject, empty, purge **6** barren, cancel, devoid, recant, repeal, revoke, vacant, vacuum **7** abolish, drained, emptied, exhaust, invalid, lacking, nullify, pour out, rescind, reverse, vacuity, wanting **8** depleted, evacuate, nugatory, renounce, throw out

volatile *see* **7 erratic**

volition *see* **6 choice**

volley 5 burst, salvo **6** shower **7** barrage **8** outbreak, outburst

Volsung
  origin: 5 Norse
  mentioned in: 8 Volsunga
  grandfather: 4 Odin **5** Othin

son: 7 Sigmund
daughter: 5 Signy

Volsunga
origin: 5 Norse **9**
Icelandic
form: 4 saga
subject: 8 Volsungs

voluble 4 glib **5** wordy **6**
chatty, fluent **7** twining **8**
effusive, flippant, rotating

volume 4 book, bulk, heap,
mass, size, tome **5** folio,
sound, tract **6** amount,
extent, quarto **7** measure
8 capacity, loudness,
quantity, treatise, vastness

voluminous *see* **5 large**

volunteer 5 offer **6** extend,
tender, unpaid **7** advance,
present, proffer **8** enlistee

Volunteer State
nickname of: 9 Tennessee

voluptuous 4 soft **6** carnal,
erotic, sexual, smooth,
wanton **7** fleshly, lustful,
sensual **8** sensuous

vomit 4 barf, emit, puke **5**
eject, expel, heave, retch **7**
bring up, throw up,
upchuck **8** disgorge

voracious 6 greedy **7**
hoggish **8** edacious,
ravenous

vortex 4 eddy **7** cyclone,
twister

votary *see* **3 fan**

vote 3 say **4** poll **5** voice **6**
ballot, choice, option,
ticket **8** approval,
decision, election,
judgment, suffrage

vouch *see* **6 affirm**

voucher 4 chip, chit **5**
check, proof **6** surety,
ticket **7** receipt, warrant **8**
warranty

vow *see* **4 oath**

voyage 4 sail **6** cruise **7**
passage **8** crossing,
navigate

Vulcan
origin: 5 Roman
god of: 4 fire
corresponds to: 10
Hephaestus

vulgar 3 low **4** base, rude **5**
crude, dirty, gross, rough
6 coarse, common, filthy,
ribald, risque, smutty **7**
boorish, ill-bred, lowbrow,
obscene, uncouth **8**
impolite, off-color,
ordinary, plebeian

vulnerable 4 weak **7**
exposed **8** helpless,
insecure

wacky, whacky *see* **5 crazy**

wad 3 bat, pad **4** cram, head, heap, lump, mass, tuft **5** money, stuff **6** bundle, riches, stop up **7** fortune **8** bankroll

waddle 3 wag **4** sway **6** hobble, toddle, totter, wobble

wade 4 ford, plod, plow, toil, trek **5** labor **6** drudge, trudge

wafer 4 chip **5** candy, flake **6** cookie **7** cracker **15** unleavened bread

waft 4 blow, puff **5** drift, float

wag 3 bob, wit **4** card, move, stir, wave **5** clown, droll, flick, joker, shake **6** jester, jiggle, switch, twitch, waggle, wiggle, wigwag **7** buffoon, farceur, flicker, flutter **8** comedian, humorist

wage *see* **6 income**

wager 3 bet, pot **4** ante, pool, risk **5** fancy, guess, stake **6** assume, gamble, hazard **7** imagine, jackpot, presume, suppose, surmise, venture **8** make a bet, theorize

waggish 5 droll, funny **7** comical, puckish **8** humorous

waggle 4 wave **5** wield **8** brandish

wagon 3 car, van **4** cart, dray, tram, wain **5** coach, lorry, tonga, truck **7** caisson

waif 5 gamin, stray **6** gamine, urchin **7** mudlark

wail 3 cry **4** bawl, howl, keen, moan, roar, weep, yell **5** groan, shout, whine **6** bellow, bemoan, bewail, cry out, lament, outcry, plaint **7** keening, moaning, wailing

waist 3 top **5** shirt **6** blouse, bodice, middle **7** midriff

waistband 4 belt, sash **5** cinch **6** girdle

waistcoat 4 vest **5** benjy **6** jacket, jerkin, veskit, vestee, weskit **7** singlet

wait *see* **8 withhold**

wait on 5 serve **6** assist, attend

waive 4 stay **5** defer, forgo, let go, table, yield **6** give up, not use, put off, shelve **7** forbear, lay over **8** disclaim, forswear, postpone, renounce

wake 4 fire, path, stir, wash **5** rally, rouse, trail, train, vigil **6** arouse, course, excite, kindle, revive **7** enliven, provoke

Walden, or Life in the Woods
   author: 7 (Henry David) Thoreau

Wales
   other name: 5 Cymru **7** Cambria
   capital/largest city: 7 Cardiff
   highest point: 7 Snowdon
   river: 3 Dee, Usk, Wye **6**, Severn
   sea: 5 Irish **8** Atlantic
   island: 4 Mona **8** Anglesey, Holyhead

   physical feature:
      channel: 7 Bristol **9** St George's
      hills: 7 Malvern
   feature:
      emblem: 4 leek

wander 5 amble, stray **6** ramble, stroll **7** meander, saunter

wane 3 ebb **4** fade, sink **5** abate, droop, waste **6** ebbing, fading, lessen, weaken, wither **7** abating, decline, dwindle, subside **8** decrease, diminish

want 4 hunt, lack, need, seek, wish **5** covet, crave, fancy **6** dearth, demand, desire, hunger, penury **7** be needy, paucity, poverty, require, wish for **8** scarcity, shortage, yearning

wanton *see* **4 lewd**

wapiti 3 elk **4** deer

war 5 clash, fight **6** attack, battle, combat, invade **7** contend **8** conflict, fighting, struggle

War and Peace
   author: 7 (Leo) Tolstoy

warble 4 lump, purl, sing **5** carol, larva, trill, tumor, yodel **6** growth, quaver, ripple **7** twitter, vibrate

war cry 6 slogan **8** Geronimo

ward *see* **7 prevent**

wardrobe *see* **7 clothes**

wares 4 line **5** stock **7** staples **8** supplies

warm 3 hot **4** cook, heat, kind, melt, thaw **5** cheer, happy, sunny, tepid, vivid **6** bright, heated, heat up, joyful, joyous, kindly, lively, loving, simmer, tender **7** affable, cordial, earnest, fervent, glowing, intense **8** cheerful, friendly, gracious, outgoing, pleasant

warn 5 alert **6** advise, inform, notify, signal **7** apprise, caution, counsel **8** admonish

War of the Worlds, The author: 5 (H G) Wells

warp 4 bend, bent, bias **5** quirk, twist **6** debase, deform, infect **7** contort, corrupt, distort, leaning, mislead, pervert **8** misguide, misshape, tendency

warrant 3 vow **4** aver, avow

5 swear **6** affirm, assert, assure, attest, permit, pledge **7** certify, declare, justify, license, promise

Warsaw
capital of: 6 Poland

warship 5 Maine, U-boat **6** corvet **7** Alabama, cruiser, frigate, gunboat, Monitor **8** Bismarck, corvette, Graf Spee, ironclad, man-of-war
fleet: 6 armada

wary 5 alert **7** careful, guarded, heedful, mindful, prudent, wakeful **8** cautious

wash 3 mop, rub, wet **4** bath, lave, soak, swab, wipe **5** bathe, clean, float, flood, rinse, scour, scrub **6** drench, shower, sponge **7** cleanse, immerse, launder, moisten, shampoo **8** ablution, irrigate

washed out 4 drab, dull, pale **5** dingy, faded, white **6** dreary, grayed **8** bleached

washed up 4 lost, shot **6** bathed, broken, ruined, undone **7** done for, through **8** bankrupt, done with, finished, scrubbed

Washington (state)
abbreviation: 2 WA **4** Wash

nickname: 7 Chinook **9** Evergreen

capital: 7 Olympia

largest city: 7 Seattle

highest point: 7 Rainier

river: 5 Snake, White **7** Spokane **8** Columbia

sea: 7 Pacific

island: 5 Puget **6** Mercer **7** San Juan, Whidbey

physical feature:
   sound: 5 Puget **7** Rosario
   strait: 10 Juan de Fuca

Washington, George
presidential rank: 5 first

party: 10 Federalist

state represented: 2 VA

vice president: 5 Adams

born: 2 VA **9** Wakefield

died/buried: 11 Mount Vernon

civilian career: 6 farmer **8** surveyor

notable events of lifetime/ term: 18 American Revolution
   rebellion: 7 Whiskey
   winter at: 11 Valley Forge

wife: 6 Martha

stepchildren: 4 John **6** Martha

Washington DC
baseball team: 9 Nationals

basketball team: 7 Mystics, Wizards

capital of: 12 United States

designed by: 7 L'Enfant

football team: 8 Redskins

hockey team: 8 Capitals

river: 7 Potomac **9** Rock Creek

wash one's hands of *see* **4 quit**

washout *see* **4 fail**

wasp 5 vespa **6** vespid

waspish *see* **7 grouchy**

wassail *see* **6 liquor**

waste 3 die, ebb, rob **4** fade, loot, melt, rape, raze, ruin, sack, sink, void, wane **5** abate, crush, decay, drain, dregs, droop, empty, offal, smash, spoil, strip, trash, wreck **6** barren, burn up, debris, devour, litter, misuse, ravage, razing, refuse, scraps, steppe, tundra, weaken, wither **7** deplete, despoil, destroy, dwindle, exhaust, garbage, pillage, plunder, rubbish, shatter, subside **8** demolish, diminish, misapply, misspend, needless, prey upon, remnants, squander

Waste Land, The author: 5 (T S) Eliot

watch 3 eye, see **4** heed, look, mark, mind, note, ogle, save, tend **5** alert, guard, scout, stare **6** attend, be wary, gaze at, guards, look at, look on, notice, patrol, peep at, peer at, picket, regard, sentry, survey, tend to **7** care for, examine, lookout, observe, oversee, protect, stare at **8** preserve, sentinel

watchtower 6 beacon, pharos, signal **7** seamark **8** landmark

watchword 5 motto **6** byword, slogan

water 3 cut, dip, sea, wet **4** damp, lake, pond, pool, soak, tear, thin **5** douse, flood, H two O, ocean, river, souse **6** dampen, deluge, dilute, drench, lagoon, splash, stream **7** immerse, moisten

8 inundate, irrigate, sprinkle, submerge

watercourse, waterway 5 canal, river **6** strait **7** channel, conduit, narrows, passage **8** aqueduct

water down 3 cut **6** censor, dilute, weaken **7** thin out

waterfall 7 cascade, Niagara **8** cataract

waterfront 4 dock, mole, pier, quay **5** basin, jetty, levee, wharf **6** marina

water of life Latin: 9 aqua vitae

wave 4 coil, curl, file, flap, line, rank, rise, roll, rush, sway, tier **5** curve, flood, pulse, shake, surge, swell, swing, train, twirl, wield **6** billow, deluge, motion, quiver, ripple, roller, signal, spiral, string **7** breaker, flutter, gesture, pulsate, vibrate **8** flourish, undulate, whitecap

waver *see* **6 falter**

wax *see* **4 grow**

way 3 far, off **4** area, form, lane, pass, path, road, room, wont **5** habit, means, route, space, trail, usage **6** course, custom, far off, manner, method, nature, region, system **7** conduct, passage, pathway, process **8** behavior, distance, practice, remotely, vicinity

waylay *see* **9 intercept**

Way of All Flesh, The author: 6 (Samuel) Butler

wayward *see* **8 stubborn**

weak 4 lame, poor, puny, soft, thin **5** faint, frail, shaky, spent **6** feeble, flimsy, unsafe, wasted, watery **7** brittle, diluted, exposed, fragile, insipid, lacking, unmanly **8** cowardly, delicate, helpless, timorous, unsteady, wide open

wealth 4 fund, mine **5** goods, means, money, store **6** assets, bounty, estate, luxury, mammon, riches **7** capital, fortune **8** opulence, property

weapon 3 arm **5** guard, means **6** attack, resort **7** bulwark, defense, measure, offense **8** armament, resource, security

wear 3 don, tax, use **4** duds, fray, last, tire, togs, wrap **5** drain, erode, put on, shred, weary **6** abrade, attire, damage, endure, injury, shroud, slip on, swathe **7** apparel, corrode, dress in, eat away, exhaust, fatigue, rub away, service, swaddle, utility **8** overwork, wash away

wearisome *see* **7 tedious**

weary 3 fag **4** beat, dull, tire **5** all in, blase, bored, fed up, jaded, spent, tired **6** boring, bushed, done in, drowsy, pooped, sleepy, tiring, tucker **7** annoyed, drained, exhaust, fatigue, humdrum, overtax, play out, routine, tedious, tire out, worn-out **8** dog tired, fatigued, overwork, tiresome

weather 3 dry, tan **4** face, rust **5** brave, clime, stand **6** bleach, season **7** climate, oxidize, toughen **8** confront, windward
  god of: 4 Jove **7** Jupiter

weather line 6 isobar

weave 4 fuse, join, knit, lace, link, loom, meld, wind **5** blend, braid, curve, plait, snake, twist, unify, unite **6** mingle,

writhe, zigzag **7** combine,
entwine, meander, texture

web 3 net **4** maze, mesh,
trap **5** snare **6** screen,
tangle, tissue **7** network **8**
gossamer

wed 3 tie **4** bind, fuse, link,
mate, meld **5** blend, hitch,
marry, merge, unify, unite,
weave **6** attach, commit,
couple, devote, pledge,
splice **7** combine, espouse,
make one, win over **8**
dedicate

wedding, wedlock 8
marriage, nuptials

wedding anniversaries
  first: 5 clock, paper
  second: 5 china **6** cotton
  third: 5 glass **7** crystal,
   leather
  fourth: 4 silk **5** linen
  fifth: 4 wood **10**
   silverware
  sixth: 4 iron, wood
  seventh: 4 wool **6** copper
  8 desk sets
  eighth: 4 lace **6** bronze,
   linens
  ninth: 5 china **7** leather,
   pottery
  tenth: 3 tin **8** aluminum
  eleventh: 5 steel
  twelfth: 4 silk **6** pearls

  thirteenth: 4 furs, lace **8**
   textiles
  fourteenth: 5 ivory
  fifteenth: 7 crystal,
   watches
  twentieth: 5 china **8**
   platinum
  twenty-fifth: 6 silver
  thirtieth: 5 pearl **7**
   diamond
  thirty-fifth: 4 jade **5** coral
  fortieth: 4 ruby
  forty-fifth: 8 sapphire
  fiftieth: 4 gold
  fifty-fifth: 7 emerald
  sixtieth: 7 diamond

weddings
  god of: 8 Talassio

wedge *see* **3 jam**

Wednesday
  French: 8 mercredi
  German: 8 mittwoch
  heavenly body: 7 Mercury
  Italian: 9 mercoledi
  name comes from: 4 Odin
  5 Woden
  Spanish: 9 miercoles

wee *see* **4 tiny**

weed 3 bur, hoe, nag, pot **4**
burr, butt, cull, dock,
hemp, rake **5** cigar, joint,
vetch **6** darnel, harrow,
pull up, root up, uproot

7 tobacco **8** nuisance, plantain, purslane

weed out 6 banish **7** abolish, discard **8** get rid of, throw out

weeny *see* **4 tiny**

weep *see* **3 cry**

weigh 4 lift **5** count, hoist, raise, scale **6** burden, charge, ponder, regard **7** balance, compare, measure **8** consider, encumber, evaluate, ruminate

weigh anchor 4 sail **7** cast off, set sail, ship out

weird 3 odd **4** wild **5** crazy, eerie, kooky, nutty, queer **6** far-out, mystic, spooky **7** bizarre, curious, ghostly, magical, strange, unusual **8** abnormal, freakish, peculiar

welcome 4 meet **5** admit, greet **6** at home, salute, wanted **7** embrace, receive, usher in, winning **8** accepted, admitted, charming, engaging, enticing, greeting, inviting, pleasant, pleasing

welfare 4 good **6** health, profit, relief **7** benefit, success, the dole

well 3 jet, run **4** flow, fund, good, gush, hale, mine, ooze, pool, pour, rise **5** amply, fount, fully, issue, lucky, right, shaft, sound, spout, spurt, store, surge **6** easily, fairly, hearty, justly, kindly, nicely, proper, robust, source, spring, stream, strong, warmly **7** chipper, fitting, healthy, readily, rightly **8** fountain, properly, suitably, very much

well-being *see* **7 welfare**

well-bred 5 civil, suave **6** polite, urbane **7** elegant, gallant, genteel, refined **8** cultured, ladylike, mannerly, polished

well-favored 4 fair **5** bonny **6** comely, pretty **7** sightly, winsome **8** fetching, handsome

well-heeled *see* **4 rich**

Wellington
  capital of: 10 New Zealand

wellspring 4 font **6** origin, source

well-to-do *see* **4 rich**

well up 4 boil, rise **6** bubble **7** surface

well-versed **7** knowing

well-wisher **6** friend **8** advocate, champion

welt **4** bump, lump, mark, wale, weal **6** bruise, streak, stripe **8** swelling

wench *see* **5 whore**

went **3** ran **4** flew, left **5** faded, got on **6** flew by, lapsed, passed **7** elapsed, sallied **8** departed, filed off, passed by, vanished

Western Sahara
former name: **7** Spanish (Sahara)
claimed/occupied by: **7** Morocco
capital: **6** Al Aiun **7** El Aaiun
sea: **8** Atlantic
physical feature:
  desert: **6** Sahara
  wind: **5** leste

Western Samoa
capital/largest city: **4** Apia
sea: **7** Pacific
feature:
  chief: **5** matai
  clothing: **5** pareu **8** lavalava, puletasi
  dance: **4** siva
food:
  drink: **3** ava

West Indies **11** archipelago
bird: **4** tody **6** mucaro
channel: **7** Jamaica **9** Old Bahama
component: **4** Cuba **5** Haiti **6** Tobago **7** Bahamas, Curacao, Grenada, Jamaica, St Lucia **8** Anguilla, Barbados, Dominica, Trinidad **10** Guadeloupe, Montserrat, Saint Lucia, Saint Barts, Hispaniola, Puerto Rico **11** Saint Martin **12** St Kitts-Nevis **13** Cayman Islands, Virgin Islands **14** Leeward Islands, Lesser Antilles, Turks and Caicos **15** Greater Antilles, Windward Islands **17** Antigua and Barbuda, Dominican Republic

West Side Story
director: **4** (Robert) Wise **7** (Jerome) Robbins
cast: **4** (Natalie) Wood **6** (Richard) Beymer, (Rita) Moreno **7** (Russ) Tamblyn **8** (George) Chakiris

West Virginia
abbreviation: **2** WV **3** W Va

nickname: 8 Mountain **9** Panhandle

capital/largest city: 10 Charleston

others: 8 Wheeling

mountain: 9 Allegheny, Blue Ridge **11** Appalachian

highest point: 10 Spruce Knob

river: 4 Ohio **7** Potomac **10** Shenandoah **11** Monongahela

feature:

　historical site: 12 Harper's Ferry

　national road: 10 Cumberland

wet 3 dip **4** damp, dank, rain, soak **5** humid, moist, rainy, soggy, steep, storm, water **6** clammy, dampen, drench, liquid, shower, soaked, sodden, splash, stormy, watery **7** immerse, moisten, showery, soaking, sopping, squishy, wetness **8** drenched, dripping, irrigate, moisture, sprinkle, submerge

wet blanket 4 drag **6** damper

whack 2 go **3** box, hit, rap, try **4** bang, belt, blow, cuff, slam, slap, slug, sock, stab, turn **5** baste, clout, crack, knock, pound, punch, smack, smite, thump, trial **6** strike, wallop **7** attempt, venture **8** endeavor

whale 4 beat, cane, drub, flog, orca, whip **6** baleen, thrash **9** bastinado

constellation of: 5 Cetus

group of: 3 gam, pod

swallowed: 5 Jonah

whammy 3 hex **4** jinx **5** curse **7** evil eye

wharf 3 key **4** dock, pier, quai, quay, slip **5** jetty **6** marina **7** landing

What's My Line?

　host: 4 (John) Daly

wheat 8 Triticum

wheedle *see* **4 coax**

wheel 4 disk, drum, hoop, ring, roll, spin **5** pivot, round, swirl, twirl, whirl **6** caster, circle, gilgal, gyrate, roller, rotate, swivel **7** revolve

Wheel of Fortune

　host: 5 (Pat) Sajak

　assistant: 5 (Vanna) White

wheeze 4 gasp, hiss, pant, puff **7** panting, whistle

whelp 3 boy, cub, kid, lad, pup **4** brat **5** child, puppy, youth **6** urchin

wherefore 2 so **3** why **7** because

wherewithal *see* **4 cash**

whet *see* **6 excite**

whiff *see* **5 smell**

while 2 as **3** yet **4** idle, till, time, when **5** until **6** during, effort, whilst **7** filling, interim, whereas **8** although, occasion

whim 4 urge **5** fancy, quirk **6** notion, vagary **7** caprice, conceit, impulse **8** crotchet

whimper 3 sob **4** pule **5** whine **6** snivel **7** blubber, sniffle, sobbing

whimsical 5 droll **6** fickle, fitful, quaint **7** amusing, erratic, waggish **8** fanciful, notional, quixotic

whine *see* **3 cry**

whip 3 rod **4** beat, cane, drub, flap, flog, jerk, jolt, lash, lick, maul, rout **5** birch, flick, spank, strap, thong, whisk **6** rattan, snatch, switch **7** cowhide, rawhide, scourge, trounce **8** birch rod, vanquish

whir 3 hum **4** buzz, purr **5** drone **7** whisper

whirl *see* **4 spin**

whirlpool 4 eddy **5** swirl, whirl **6** vortex

whirlwind 4 rash **5** hasty, quick, rapid, short, swift **7** cyclone, tornado, twister **8** headlong

whisk 3 fly, zip **4** beat, bolt, dart, dash, race, rush, tear, whip, whiz **5** bound, brush, flick, hurry, scoot, shoot, speed, spurt, sweep **6** hasten, scurry, sprint

type: 4 wire **6** French **8** omelette

whiskers 3 awn **5** beard **7** stubble **8** bristles

whiskey, whisky 3 gin, rum, rye **4** corn, shot **5** booze, hooch, Irish, juice, vodka **6** liquor, red eye, rotgut, Scotch **7** alcohol, aquavit, blended, bourbon, spirits **8** eau-de-vie

whisper 3 hum **4** blab, buzz, hint, purr, sigh, tell **5** blurt, bruit, drone, rumor **6** gossip, murmur, mutter, reveal, rustle **7** breathe, confide, divulge, inkling **8** disclose, innuendo, intimate

whist
derived from: 8 triomphe
descendant: 6 bridge

whistle-stop 5 stump **8** campaign

whit *see* **4 iota**

white 3 wan **4** ashy, fair, gray, pale, pure **5** ashen, blond, clean, filmy, hoary, ivory, milky, pasty, pearl, smoky, snowy **6** benign, chalky, chaste, cloudy, frosty, leaden, pallid, pearly, sallow, silver **7** ghostly, silvery **8** bleached, innocent, spotless, virtuous

White Company, The
author: 5 (Sir Arthur Conan) Doyle

whittle *see* **5 carve**

whiz 3 fly, hum, zip **4** bolt, buzz, dart, dash, hiss, race, rush, scud, tear, whir, zoom **5** adept, drone, scoot, shark, shoot, speed, spurt, sweep, swish, whine, whisk **6** expert, genius, hasten, master,

scurry, sizzle, sprint, wizard **7** prodigy

whole 4 body, bulk, full, hale, unit, well **5** sound, total, uncut **6** entire, intact, robust, system **7** essence, perfect **8** complete, entirety, totality, unbroken, unharmed

wholesome *see* **5 moral**

whoop *see* **4 yell**

whopper 3 fib, lie **6** big one

whore 3 pro **4** bawd, doxy, jade, slut, tart **5** hussy, tramp **6** chippy, harlot, hooker, prosty, wanton **7** demirep, hustler, trollop **8** call girl, mistress, strumpet

whorl 4 coil, curl, roll **5** helix **6** circle, spiral

Who's Afraid of Virginia Woolf?
author: 5 (Edward) Albee
director: 7 (Mike) Nichols
cast: 5 (George) Segal **6** (Richard) Burton, (Sandy) Dennis, (Elizabeth) Taylor

Who's on First?
comedy routine by: 6 Abbott **8** Costello

wicked *see* **4 evil**

wide 4 vast **5** ample, broad,

fully, great, large, roomy **7** dilated, immense **8** expanded, extended, spacious

wield 3 ply, use **4** wave **5** apply, exert, swing **6** employ, handle, manage **7** display, utilize **8** brandish, exercise, flourish

wife 3 rib **4** mate **5** bride, squaw, woman **6** missus, spouse **7** consort, old lady **8** helpmate, helpmeet

wig 3 rug **4** fall **6** carpet, peruke, switch, topper, toupee, wiglet **7** periwig

wiggle 3 wag **4** jerk **5** shake, twist **6** quiver, squirm, twitch **7** flutter

wigwam, Wigwam 3 hut **4** tent, tipi **5** hogan, lodge, tepee **6** teepee **7** weekwam, wickiup

wild, wilds, the wild 3 mad **4** bush, rash **5** bleak, feral, giddy, madly, nutty, rabid, rough, waste **6** choppy, crazed, fierce, insane, madcap, raging, raving, rugged, savage, unruly, wooded **7** berserk, bizarre, flighty, frantic, furious, howling, lawless, natural, untamed, violent

8 barbaric, blustery, demented, desolate, fanciful, forested, frenzied, insanely, maniacal, reckless, unhinged

wild animal 5 beast, brute

wildcat 3 cat **4** lynx **6** ocelot

wilderness 4 bush **5** waste **6** barren, desert, forest, plains, tundra **7** barrens **8** badlands, wasteland

Wild Kingdom host/narrator: 5 (Stan) Brock **6** (Jim) Fowler **7** (Marlin) Perkins

wile, wiles *see* **6 seduce**

will 4 want, wish **5** endow **6** bestow, confer, desire **7** craving, feeling, longing, resolve, wish for **8** attitude, bequeath, pleasure, yearning

Willard, Frank creator of: 11 Moon Mullins

willful *see* **8 stubborn**

William Tell opera by: 7 Rossini

willing 4 game **5** ready **7** content **8** amenable

willow 5 Salix

willowy 5 lithe **6** limber, pliant, supple, svelte **7** lissome **8** flexible

Wilson, (Thomas) Woodrow
nickname: 5 Tommy
presidential rank: 12 twenty-eighth
party: 10 Democratic
state represented: 2 NJ
defeated: 4 Debs, Taft **5** Handy **6** Benson, Chafin, Hughes, Reimer **9** Roosevelt
vice president: 8 Marshall
born: 2 VA **8** Staunton
civilian career:
   president of: 9 Princeton
notable events of lifetime/
term: 11 Prohibition **14** Fourteen Points **15** League of Nations
   Act: 8 Sedition **9** Espionage
   conference: 3 ABC **10** Paris Peace:
   sinking of: 9 Lusitania
   Treaty: 10 Versailles
   won Nobel Prize for: 5 Peace
   wife: 5 Edith, Ellen

wilt *see* **4 fade**

wily 3 sly **4** foxy **5** alert, sharp **6** artful, crafty, shifty, shrewd, tricky **7** crooked, cunning, devious **8** guileful, scheming

win 3 bag, get, net **4** earn, gain, sway **6** attain, induce, master, obtain, pick up, secure **7** achieve, acquire, collect, conquer, convert, prevail, procure, realize, receive, success, triumph, victory **8** conquest

wince *see* **6 cringe**

wind 3 air, lap **4** bend, blow, clue, coil, curl, fold, gale, gust, hint, loop, news, puff, roll **5** blast, bluff, curve, draft, scent, smell, snake, twine, twirl, twist, whiff **6** breath, breeze, zephyr, zigzag **7** bluster, bombast, cyclone, entwine, inkling, meander, sinuate, tempest, tidings, tornado, twaddle, twister, typhoon

windfall 7 bonanza

Windhoek
   capital of: 7 Namibia

window 3 bay **5** oriel **6** dormer **7** opening, orifice, transom **8** aperture, casement, porthole

windstorm 4 gale **6** squall

7 cyclone, tempest, tornado, twister, typhoon

windswept 4 bare **5** bleak **6** barren **8** desolate

windup 3 end **5** close **6** ending, finish

wine
French: 3 vin
Italian: 4 vino
god of: 7 Bacchus
goddess of: 6 Libera

wine-colored 6 claret **8** burgundy, cardinal

wing 3 ala, fly, set **4** band, clip, flap, knot, nick, soar, zoom **5** annex, graze, group **6** circle, clique, pennon, pinion **7** adjunct, aileron, coterie, faction, section, segment **8** addition, coulisse

Winged Horse
constellation of: 7 Pegasus

wink at 6 ignore **7** condone, let pass **8** overlook

winner 5 champ **6** master, victor **8** champion

Winnie-the-Pooh
author: 5 (A A) Milne

winsome *see* **6 genial**

Winter's Tale, The
author: 11 (William) Shakespeare

wintry 3 icy, raw **4** cold **5** bleak, chilly, harsh, polar, snowy, stark **6** arctic, chilly, dreary, frigid, frosty, frozen, stormy **7** glacial **8** Siberian

wipe 3 dry, mop, rub **4** swab **5** apply, brush, clean, erase, rub on, scour, scrub, swipe, towel **6** banish, remove, rub off, sponge, stroke

wire 5 cable **8** filament, telegram

wiry *see* **6 nimble**

Wisconsin
abbreviation: 2 WI **3** Wis
nickname: 6 Badger
capital: 7 Madison
largest city: 9 Milwaukee
highest point: 9 Timms Hill
lake: 8 Michigan, Superior **9** Winnebago
river: 5 Black **7** St Croix **9** Wisconsin **11** Mississippi
physical feature:
rock formation: 8 The Dells

wise 3 way **4** sage

6 manner **7** knowing, respect, sapient **8** profound

wiseacre 4 fool, sage **5** idiot **7** tomfool

wisecrack see **4 joke**

Wise men see **4 Magi**

wish 3 yen **4** hope, long, love, pine, want, whim, will **5** crave, yearn **6** aspire, desire, hunger, thirst **7** command, craving, leaning, longing, request **8** ambition, appetite, penchant

wishy-washy see **6 jejune**

wisp 4 lock, tuft **5** bunch, shred, torch, twist **8** fragment

wistful 3 sad **6** musing, pining **7** craving, forlorn, longing **8** desirous, mournful, yearning

wit see **5 humor**

witch 3 hag **4** fury **5** crone, scold, shrew, vixen **6** beldam, ogress, virago **7** seeress **8** harridan

witchcraft 5 obeah **6** hoodoo, voodoo **7** sorcery **8** black art, witchery

withdraw 2 go **5** leave, split **6** depart, go away, recall, recant, remove, retire **7** extract, rescind, retract, retreat, take off, vamoose

withered 3 dry **4** arid, sere **5** dried, faded **6** shrunk, wilted **7** decayed, dried up, drooped

withhold 4 hide, keep **6** hush up, retain **7** conceal, cover up **8** suppress

within 2 on **4** into **5** inner **6** during, inside **7** indoors

with-it 7 current **8** up-to-date

without 4 save **5** minus **6** beyond, except, unless **7** lacking, nowhere, outside, wanting **8** outdoors

withstand see **6 endure**

witness 3 see **4** mark, note, sign, view **5** proof **6** attend, behold, look on, notice, verify **7** bear out, certify, confirm, endorse, initial, observe **8** attester, deponent, document, evidence, onlooker, perceive, validate

witticism 4 jest, joke, quip **5** sally **7** epigram **French: 6** bon mot

wizard 4 sage, seer, whiz **5** adept, shark **6** expert, genius, oracle **7** diviner, prodigy, wise man **8** conjurer, magician, sorcerer, virtuoso

Wizard of Id, The
creator: 4 (Johnny) Hart **6** (Brant) Parker

Wizard of Oz, The
director: 7 (Victor) Fleming
author: 4 (L Frank) Baum
cast: 4 (Burt) Lahr **5** (Jack) Haley **6** (Ray) Bolger **7** (Judy) Garland **8** (Margaret) Hamilton
Dorothy's dog: 4 Toto
Dorothy wore: 8 red shoes

wizened *see* **3 dry**

wobble 4 reel, sway **5** quake, shake, waver **6** shimmy, teeter, totter **7** quaking, shaking, stagger, swaying **8** wavering

Woden
origin: 10 Anglo-Saxon
chief of: 4 gods

woe *see* **6 sorrow**

Wojtyla, Karol
real name of: 8 (Pope) John Paul (II)

wolf 4 bolt, gulp **5** scarf **6** devour, gobble **7** consume

Wolverine State
nickname of: 8 Michigan

woman 4 girl, lady, maid, wife **5** flame, lover **6** damsel, maiden, matron **7** beloved, darling, dowager, females, fiancee, sweetie **8** ladylove, mistress
French: 5 femme

Women, The
director: 5 (George) Cukor
based on play by: 4 (Clare Boothe) Luce
cast: 7 (Paulette) Goddard, (Rosalind) Russell, (Norma) Shearer **8** (Joan) Crawford, (Joan) Fontaine

Women in Love
director: 7 (Ken) Russell
based on novel by: 8 (DH) Lawrence
cast: 4 (Eleanor) Bron, (Oliver) Reed **5** (Alan) Bates **6** (Jennie) Linden **7** (Glenda) Jackson

wonder 3 awe **4** gape **5** sight, stare **6** marvel, ponder, rarity **7** miracle **8** cogitate, question

wonderful *see* **5 great**

wont *see* **5 habit**

woo *see* **5 court**

wood 3 log **4** bush **5** brake, brush, copse, grove **6** boards, forest, lumber, planks, siding, timber **7** thicket **8** kindling

wooden 4 dull **5** frame, rigid, stiff **6** clumsy, vacant **7** awkward, deadpan

woodwind instrument 4 oboe **5** flute **7** bassoon, piccolo **8** clarinet

wool-gather 8 daydream, muse idly

woolly, wooly 5 downy, furry, fuzzy, hairy, sheep, vague **6** fleecy, lanate, lanose **7** blurred, muddled, unclear **8** confused

woozy *see* **5 dizzy**

word, words 3 vow **4** chat, dirt, news, poop, term **5** edict, order, rumor, set-to, voice **6** advice, avowal, decree, gossip, letter, notice, phrase, pledge, remark, report, ruling, signal **7** comment, dictate, dispute, explain, express, hearsay, mandate, message, promise, quarrel, tidings **8** argument, chitchat, colloquy, describe, dialogue, locution, telegram

word of honor 3 vow **4** oath **6** pledge

word play 6 banter **7** jesting, kidding
French: 8 badinage, repartee

wordy *see* **7 verbose**

work, works 2 do, go **3** act, job, run, win **4** book, deed, duty, feat, form, gain, line, make, mill, mold, move, shop, song, task, toil, yard **5** beget, cause, chore, craft, enact, labor, opera, piece, plant, shape, slave, solve, sweat, trade **6** drudge, effect, effort, office, output **7** achieve, calling, execute, factory, foundry, operate, perform, produce, succeed **8** business, concerto, creation, drudgery, endeavor, exertion, function, industry, maneuver, painting, progress, symphony, vocation

working-class 5 labor **8** plebian

workmanlike 5 adept **8** skillful **9** efficient

work out 5 solve, train **6** figure, reckon **7** compute, resolve **8** exercise, practice

work up 4 goad, urge **5** upset **6** excite **7** agitate, ferment, provoke

world 3 age, era, orb **4** gobs, lots, star **5** class, Earth, epoch, globe, group, heaps, realm, times **6** domain, nature, planet, sphere, system **7** mankind, society **8** everyone, humanity, universe

worldly *see* **6 astute**

world-weary 5 blase, bored, jaded

worm 4 edge, inch **5** crawl, creep, steal **7** wriggle
  kinds: 4 inch, tape **5** angle, earth

worn 4 weak **5** dingy, drawn, faded, seedy, spent, tired, weary **6** frayed, shabby, wasted **7** abraded, haggard, rickety **8** battered, decrepit, dog-tired, fatigued

worry 3 vex, woe **4** care, fret, stew **5** agony, beset, dread, grief, harry, upset **6** badger, bother, dismay, harass, hector, misery, pester, plague **7** agitate,

agonize, anguish, anxiety, bugaboo, concern, despair, disturb, perturb, problem, torment, trouble **8** distress, vexation

worship *see* **6 praise**

worst 3 bad **4** beat, best, rout **5** floor, outdo **6** defeat, lowest, outwit **7** conquer, poorest, triumph **8** inferior, overcome

worth 3 use **4** cost, good **5** merit, price, value **6** assets, estate, wealth **7** benefit, effects, utility **8** holdings

worthy 3 fit, VIP **4** good, name **5** moral, noble **6** bigwig, decent, honest, leader, proper **7** big shot, ethical, fitting, notable, upright **8** suitable

Wotan
  origin: 8 Germanic
  chief of: 4 gods
  corresponds to: 4 Odin **5** Othin

wound 3 cut **4** gash, harm, hurt, pain, slit, tear **5** slash, sting **6** bruise, damage, grieve, injure, injury, lesion, offend, pierce, trauma **7** anguish, mortify, torment **8** distress, lacerate, vexation

wrack 4 kelp, ruin **5** ruins, trash **6** clouds, refuse **7** destroy, seaweed **8** downfall, eelgrass

wraith *see* **5 ghost**

wrangle *see* **7 quarrel**

wrap 4 bind, cape, coat, fold, gird, hide, mask, veil, wind **5** cloak, cover, scarf, shawl, stole **6** bundle, clothe, encase, enfold, girdle, jacket, mantle, shroud, swathe **7** conceal, enclose, envelop

wrap up *see* **3 end**

wrath *see* **4 fury**

wreak 4 vent, work **5** visit **7** execute, indulge, inflict, unleash

wreath 5 crown **6** diadem, laurel **7** chaplet, coronet, festoon, garland
Hawaiian: 3 lei

wreathe 4 bend, coil, wind **5** curve, twist **7** entwine, envelop **8** encircle

wreck *see* **4 ruin**

wrench 3 rip **4** jerk, pull, tear, warp **5** force, twist, wrest, wring **6** sprain, strain **7** distort, pervert

type: 6 monkey, socket **7** spanner

wrest 3 get, rip **4** earn, gain, grab, jerk, make, pull, take, tear **5** force, glean, twist, wring **6** attain, obtain, secure, wrench **7** achieve, extract

wrestle 4 toil **5** labor **6** battle, strive **7** contend, grapple **8** struggle

wretched *see* **8 pathetic**

wriggle 5 twist **6** squirm, wangle, writhe **7** meander

wring 4 hurt, pain, rend, stab **5** choke, force, press, twist, wrest **6** coerce, grieve, pierce, sadden, wrench **7** agonize, extract, squeeze, torture **8** compress, distress

wrinkle 4 fold, idea **5** crimp, fancy, pleat, slant, trick **6** crease, device, furrow, gather, notion, pucker, rimple, rumple **7** crumple, gimmick

write 3 pen **4** copy, show **5** draft **6** author, draw up, record, scrawl **7** compose, dash off, jot down, produce, turn out **8** inscribe, scribble

writhe *see* **6 squirm**

writing 4 book, play, poem, tome, work **5** diary, essay, novel, print, story **6** column, letter, report, script, volume **7** article, journal, penning **8** critique, document, libretto, longhand

written agreement 6 treaty **7** compact **8** contract

wrong 3 bad, sin **4** awry, bilk, evil, harm, hurt, ruin, vice **5** abuse, amiss, cheat, crime, false, inapt, kaput, unfit **6** faulty, fleece, injure, injury, ruined, sinful, unfair, unjust, untrue, wicked **7** crooked, defraud, illegal, illicit, immoral, inexact, misdeed, offense, swindle, unsound **8** criminal, dishonor, evil deed, ill-treat, improper, iniquity, mistaken, mistreat, trespass, unlawful, unseemly, villain

wrought 4 made **6** beaten, formed, worked **7** crafted **8** hammered

wrought-up 7 excited **8** agitated

Wyoming
  abbreviation: 2 Wy **3** Wyo
  nickname: 8 Equality capital/largest city: Cheyenne
  highest point: 7 Gannett
  river: 5 Green, Snake **6** Platte, Powder **8** Cheyenne **11** North Platte, Yellowstone
  physical feature:
    plains: 5 Great
  feature:
    fort: 7 Laramie

XYZ

Xanthippe, Xantippe 3 hag
4 fury **5** scold, shrew,
vixen **6** dragon, virago **7**
scolder **8** spitfire
husband: 8 Socrates

Xanthus and Balius
horses of: 8 Achilles
trait: 8 immortal

xeno- 6 prefix **7** foreign,
strange

Xenoclea
form: 9 priestess

xenon
chemical symbol: 2 Xe

xenophobia
fear of: 9 strangers

Xerox 4 copy

yacht 4 boat, race, sail,
ship, yawl **5** ketch, sloop
6 cruise, cutter **7** catboat
8 schooner

yahoo 4 lout **5** brute, yokel
7 lowbrow

Yahweh 3 God **4** Lord **5**
Jahve, Jahwe, Yahve **6**
Author, I am I am,
Jahveh **7** Creator, Eternal,

Jehovah **8** Absolute,
Almighty, Infinite
component: 2 he **3** yod,
vav

yam 9 Dioscorea
varieties: 4 wild **5** Negro,
water, white **6** Attoto,
potato, yellow **7** Chinese

yammer *see* **8 complain**

Yangon
capital of: 5 Burma **7**
Myanmar
former name: 5 Dagon **7**
Rangoon

yank *see* **4 pull**

Yankee, Yank 2 GI **5** teddy
6 gringo **8** American,
doughboy
Spanish: 6 yanqui

Yaounde
capital of: 8 Cameroon

yap *see* **4 talk**

yard 4 lawn **5** close, court **6**
garden **7** confine,
grounds, pasture **8**
compound
abbreviation: 2 yd

yardbird 3 con **5** felon **7** convict **8** prisoner

yard goods 5 cloth **6** fabric **8** material, textiles

yardstick 4 rule **7** measure **8** standard

yarn 4 tale **5** story **7** account **8** anecdote

Yastrzemski, Carl
  nickname: 3 Yaz
  sport: 8 baseball
  team: 6 (Boston) Red Sox

yawn 3 gap **4** bore, gape **5** chasm **8** open wide

year, years 3 age, era **4** time **5** cycle, epoch **6** period
  abbreviation: 2 yr

Yearling, The
  author: 8 (Marjorie Kinnan) Rawlings

yearn 4 ache, long, pine, sigh, want, wish **5** crave **6** hanker, hunger, thirst **8** languish

yell 3 boo, cry **4** bawl, hoot, howl, roar, yowl **5** cheer, hollo, shout, whoop **6** bellow, clamor, cry out, holler, hurrah, huzzah, outcry, scream, shriek, squall, squeal **7** screech

yellow 4 gold **5** blond, lemon, ocher **6** afraid, canary, craven, flaxen **7** chicken, fearful, saffron **8** cowardly, timorous

Yellowhammer State
  nickname of: 7 Alabama

Yellow Kid, The
  creator: 8 (R F) Outcault
  trademark: 10 nightshirt
  first: 10 comic strip

yelp *see* **4** yell

Yemen
  other name: 4 Sana
  capital/largest city: 4 Sana **5** Sanaa
  island: 5 Perim, Zugar **6** Hanish **7** Kamaran, Socotra
  highest point: 6 Shuayb
  sea: 3 Red **6** Indian **7** Arabian
  physical feature:
    gulf: 4 Aden
    peninsula: 7 Arabian
    strait: 11 Bab el Mandeb
  language: 6 Arabic
  religion: 5 Islam
  feature:
    animal: 4 ibex, oryx
    dagger: 7 jambiya
    kingdom: 4 Saba **5** Sheba **11** Arabia Felix
    tree: 3 fig **5** carob,

mango, myrrh

food:

   coffee: 5 mocha

yen *see* **4 want**

yenta 3 hen **6** gossip **8** busybody

yeoman 4 chap, exon **5** churl, clerk, swain **6** farmer, fellow **7** granger, plowman, servant **8** graycoat, retainer **9** beefeater **10** freeholder **12** petty officer

yes 3 aye, yea **4** amen, okay, true **5** truly **6** assent, indeed, it is so, just so, really, so be it, surely, verily **7** consent, exactly, granted, no doubt **8** approval, of course, to be sure

   French: 3 oui

   German: 2 ja

   Spanish: 2 si

yesterday 7 the past **10** bygone days, days of yore, olden times, time gone by **11** former times

yet 3 but **4** also, even, then, up to **5** again, still, while, until **6** no less, though **7** besides, earlier, even now, further, however, thus far

8 although, hitherto, moreover

yew 5 Taxus

Yggdrasil

   also: 9 Iggdrasil

   origin: 12 Scandinavian

   kind of tree: 12 evergreen ash

   roots: 5 three

   binds: 6 Asgard **7** Midgard **8** Niflheim **10** Mithgarthr

yield 3 pay, sag **4** bear, crop, earn, gain, give **5** beget, break, burst, defer, droop, forgo, grant, spawn, split, waive **6** accede, cave in, give in, give up, kowtow, render, return, submit, supply **7** concede, harvest, payment, premium, produce, revenue, succumb **8** earnings, generate, interest, proceeds

Ymir

   origin: 5 Norse

   progenitor of: 6 giants

   earth made from: 5 flesh

   water made from: 5 blood

   heavens made from: 5 skull

yoga, yogi 5 Hindu **6** mystic **7** ascetic

yoke 3 tax **4** bond, join, link, load, pair, span, team **5** brace, clasp, hitch, trial, unite **6** at tach, burden, collar, couple, fasten, strain, weight **7** bondage, coupler, harness, serfdom, slavery **8** distress, pressure, troubles

yokel *see* **7 peasant**

yolk 6 yellow

yonder 3 yon **5** there **6** far-off **7** faraway, farther, thither

You Bet Your Life
   host: 4 (Groucho) Marx

You Can't Go Home Again
   author: 5 (Thomas) Wolfe

You Can't Take It With You
   author: 4 (Moss) Hart **7** (George S) Kaufman
   director: 5 (Frank) Capra
   cast: 4 (Mischa) Auer **6** (Edward) Arnold, (Jean) Arthur **7** (James) Stewart **9** (Lionel) Barrymore

young 3 cub, pup **4** baby, kids **5** child, issue, minor, whelp **6** boyish, callow, junior, kitten, youths **7** budding, girlish, growing, progeny, puerile, teenage **8** childish, children, immature, juvenile, underage, youthful

Young, Chic
   creator of: 7 Blondie

young Turks 6 rebels **8** radicals, upstarts

youth 3 boy, kid, lad **4** kids **5** bloom, child, minor, prime, teens **6** heyday **7** boyhood **8** children, girlhood, juvenile, minority, teenager

yowl *see* **3 cry**

yucca 5 agave

Yugoslavia *see* **19 Serbia and Montenegro**

Yukon Territory
   capital: 10 Whitehorse
   country: 6 Canada
   event: 8 gold rush (1897)
   lake: 9 Great Bear
   mineral: 4 gold **6** silver
   mountain: 3 Joy **5** Logan **6** Harper **7** Kennedy **8** Campbell
   region: 8 Klondike
   river: 5 Pelly **9** Porcupine
   sea: 8 Beaufort

yule 4 Noel **9** Christmas

Zachariah
   wife: 9 Elizabeth
   son: 3 Abi **4** John (the Baptist)

succeeded: 8 Jeroboam
visitor: 7 Gabriel

zaftig 5 buxom, plump **6** bosomy

Zaire *see* **26 Congo, Democratic Republic of**

Zambia
  other name: 16 Northern Rhodesia
  capital/largest city: 6 Lusaka
  highest point: 12 Mafinga Hills
  river: 5 Congo, Lunga **7** Luapula, Zambezi
  physical feature:
    falls: 8 Victoria
    gorge: 6 Kariba
    swamp: 7 Lukanga **9** Bangweulu
    valley: 9 Great Rift
  feature:
    king: 7 litunga
    king's aide: 5 sungu, twite **8** inabanza
    taxi: 6 zamcab

zany *see* **5 crazy**

zeal *see* **5 vigor**

zealot *see* **7 fanatic**

Zebedee
  wife: 6 Salome
  son: 4 John **5** James

zenith *see* **6 summit**

zero 2 no **3** nil, zip **5** aught, nadir, zilch **6** cipher, naught **7** nothing **8** goose egg

zest *see* **5 vigor**

Zeus
  brother: 5 Hades **8** Poseidon
  corresponds to: 4 Amen, Amon, Jove **5** Ammon **6** Amen Ra, Amon Ra **7** Jupiter
  daughter: 4 Hebe **6** Athene **10** Eileithyia, Persephone
  father: 6 Cronus
  form: 5 deity
  god of: 7 heavens
  lover: 4 Leto **7** Demeter
  mother: 4 Rhea
  sister: 4 Hera **6** Hestia **7** Demeter
  son: 4 Ares **6** Apollo, Hermes
  wife: 4 Hera **5** Metis

zigzag 4 awry, tack **6** angles, forked, jagged **7** chevron, crankle, crooked, notched, sinuous, stagger **8** crotched, serrated, sideling, traverse

Zimbabwe
  other name: 8 Rhodesia

capital/largest city: 6
 Harare
highest point: 9 Inyangani
lake: 4 Kyle **6** Kariba
river: 7 Limpopo,
 Umniati, Zambezi
physical feature:
  falls: 8 Victoria
  grassland: 4 veld
place:
  dam: 6 Kariba
feature:
  cattle pen: 5 kraal
zinc
  chemical symbol: 2 Zn
zing *see* **5 vigor**
zingara, zingaro 5 gypsy
Zion 6 utopia
  hill in: 6 Israel **9**
   Jerusalem
  built on the hill: 6 Temple
zip 3 fly, nil, pep, run, vim
 4 buzz, dart, dash, hiss,
 life, nada, rush, zero, zest
 5 aught, close, drive,
 force, gusto, hurry, power,
 punch, speed, verve, vigor,
 whine, zilch **6** cipher,
 energy, impact, naught,
 spirit, streak **7** nothing,
 whistle **8** goose egg,
 strength, vitality, vivacity

zodiac 4 belt, zone **5** stars
 7 circuit
fire sign: 3 Leo **5** Aries
 11 Sagittarius
earth sign: 5 Virgo **6**
 Taurus **9** Capricorn
air sign: 5 Libra **6**
 Gemini **8** Aquarius
water: 6 Cancer, Pisces **7**
 Scorpio
division: 4 sign **5** decan **6**
 trigon
number of houses: 6
 twelve
falling between two signs:
 4 cusp
zone *see* **4 area**
zoo 8 vivarium
zoom 3 fly, zip **4** buzz, race,
 rise, soar **5** climb, flash,
 shoot, speed **6** ascend,
 rocket, streak
zoophobia
 fear of: 7 animals
Zorba the Greek
 director: 10 (Michael)
  Cacoyannis
 cast: 5 (Alan) Bates,
  (Anthony) Quinn **6**
  (Irene) Pappas **7** (Lila)
  Kedrova
zucchini 5 gourd **6** squash

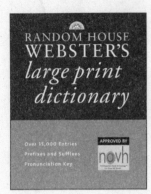